Not By Bread Alone

An Outlined Guide to Bible Doctrine

But He answered and said, "It is written,
man shall not live by bread alone, but on every word
that proceeds out of the mouth of God".
Matt. 4:4

Dr. Steven Waterhouse
Th. M., D. Min.

Westcliff Press
P.O. Box 1521, Amarillo TX 79105

Other Titles By Steven Waterhouse

Strength For His People, A Ministry
For the Families of the Mentally Ill

The Sanctity of Life

Blessed Assurance: A Defense of the Doctrine of Eternal Security

What Must I Do To Be Saved?
The Bible's Definition of Saving Faith

Demons and Pastoral Care

Depression: Biblical Causes and Counsel

For additional unpublished research see www.webtheology.com

Revised Edition 2003

Copyright 2000 by Steven W. Waterhouse

Westcliff Press
P.O. Box 1521
Amarillo TX 79105
1-806-359-6362
www.webtheology.com

ISBN: 0-9702418-2-8
Library of Congress Catalog Card Number 00-134710

Printed in the United States of America

About The Author

Dr. Steven W. Waterhouse has served as the Pastor of Westcliff Bible Church in Amarillo, Texas, since 1985. He has degrees from Dallas Theological Seminary (D. Min.); Capital Bible Seminary, Lanham, MD (Th. M., Hebrew and Greek); Spring Arbor University, Michigan (B.A., Social Science) and Cornerstone University in Grand Rapids, MI.

Dr. Waterhouse and his wife, Marilyn, have three children; Carlton, Nathan, and Rachel.

Information about this book and others written by Dr. Waterhouse can be accessed at his web site at:
http://www.webtheology.com

Suggested Cataloging Data

Waterhouse, Steven W.
    Not By Bread Alone: An Outlined Guide to Bible Doctrine/Steven
W. Waterhouse
    573 p. 24cm
    Includes Biblical references, Bibliology, Topical and Biblical Indexes,
Illustrations
    ISBN 0-9702418-2-8
    1. Bible – Theology. Theology -Doctrinal. Bible – Research.
    Suggested Library of Congress Number: BS543
    Suggested Dewey Number: 230.041

Foreword

Only God can write a perfect book. I was taught that Luther believed we could understand only the basics of God's truth, the theology of the cross, while Calvin tried to write a complete systematic theology. Both of them were right. A perfect theology may be impossible, but the Word of God deserves the most exhaustive effort toward accurate doctrine.

Despite our best efforts, "we see in a mirror darkly" (1 Cor. 13:12). None of us with a fallen mind and finite strength and lifespan can understand and then classify all the teaching of Scripture. The Proverbs warns only a fool would always feel right in his own eyes (Prov. 12:15). Since print cannot convey emotional tone, let it be clearly said that the author knows this doctrine book has flaws. Also, the reader must not think he or she would have to have the same conclusions in every respect in order to be regarded as a fellow Christian. In fact, deep research into the Scriptures produces sympathy for other believers who also search for the truth and charity to those who can not agree on the details. Discovering God's truth is far too imposing a task not to appreciate others who give it their best. If we only trust in Jesus Christ, God the Son, Who died for our sins and rose from the dead, that is sufficient agreement in doctrine to acknowledge salvation and fellowship.

Still, God reminds us to seek Him with all our heart (Jer. 29:13). He commands us to meditate on His Word day and night (Josh. 1:8). Paul told Timothy to give himself totally to the Scriptures (1 Tim. 4:13, 15-16). The Word of God is our bread of life (Matt. 4:4). If we really believe the Scriptures are the Word of God, then the smallest of details matter and ought to be of intense interest. We might not understand the Bible with perfection, but we must become approved workmen "handling accurately the Word of truth" (2 Tim. 2:15). We must give the Bible our full attention and apply our full strength to its study. Most Christians refuse to obey the command for exhaustive study of the Word. Most Christians are primarily driven by their emotions and experiences. The Church had better be warned that emotions have value but only as they are a response to the truth of God's Word. All believers, especially Christian workers, are accountable before God to "examine the Scriptures daily to see whether those things were so" (Acts 17:11). I dare not claim to have the final answers on every detail. I will humbly claim that this flawed research has been my personal sacrifice to give the Bible the strength of my best years.

We are accountable before God should we neglect His Word. We are rewarded and blessed if it becomes our bread of life. Christian leaders must have a message before they have a ministry. It is awesome to claim to speak for God. In the book of Job, God was livid with those who gave only guesswork and human opinion in efforts to teach and counsel (Job 38:2). God warns us about having our facts straight (James 3:1).

I hope these studies help and bless you and that you will give the Word of God the diligence, attention, and respect it deserves.

Dr. Steven Waterhouse

Acknowledgments

Many faithful servants of God labored
on this project. My own strength
would have failed without you.

Hugh Akin
Daphne Barry Cox
Dan Bentley
Mary Daily
Dwight Davis
Janet Kampschroeder
Gabriel Trevizo
Alan N.Good, Editor

Dedication

To the congregation of Westcliff Bible Church, Amarillo, Texas. God has recorded your faithful commitment to teaching ministry. Your love for God's Word has enabled years of labor to be devoted to Bible study instead of being sidetracked to secondary pursuits. Even more than the financial support, it was this loyalty to the Scriptures that made this research possible. I would also like to acknowledge the fine Christian example of my father-in-law, Russell D. Aseltine, (1937-1990). Pastor Aseltine's Bible appears on the cover.

Steven Waterhouse

ABBREVIATIONS
Old Testament

Genesis	Gen.	Ecclesiastes	Eccl.
Exodus	Ex.	Song of Solomon	Song
Leviticus	Lev.	Isaiah	Isa.
Numbers	Num.	Jeremiah	Jer.
Deuteronomy	Deut.	Lamentations	Lam.
Joshua	Josh.	Ezekiel	Ezek.
Judges	Judg.	Daniel	Dan.
Ruth	Ruth	Hosea	Hosea
1 Samuel	1 Sam.	Joel	Joel
2 Samuel	2 Sam.	Amos	Amos
1 Kings	1 Kings	Obadiah	Obad.
2 Kings	2 Kings	Jonah	Jonah
1 Chronicles	1 Chron.	Micah	Micah
2 Chronicles	2 Chron.	Nahum	Nahum
Ezra	Ezra	Habakkuk	Hab.
Nehemiah	Neh.	Zephaniah	Zeph.
Esther	Esth.	Haggai	Hag.
Job	Job	Zechariah	Zech.
Psalms	Psa.	Malachi	Mal.
Proverbs	Prov.		

New Testament

Matthew	Matt.	2 Thessalonians	2 Thess.
Mark	Mark	1 Timothy	1 Tim.
Luke	Luke	2 Timothy	2 Tim.
John	John	Titus	Titus
The Acts	Acts	Philemon	Philem.
Romans	Rom.	Hebrews	Heb.
1 Corinthians	1 Cor.	James	James
2 Corinthians	2 Cor.	1 Peter	1 Pet.
Galatians	Gal.	2 Peter	2 Pet.
Ephesians	Eph.	1 John	1 John
Philippians	Phil.	2 John	2 John
Colossians	Col.	3 John	3 John
1 Thessalonians	1 Thess.	Jude	Jude
		Revelation	Rev.

Miscellaneous Abbreviations

Macc.	Maccabees
LXX	Septuagint, early Greek translation of the Old Testament
KJV	Authorized King James Version
NIV	New International Version
ff.	Two or more verses following Scripture Reference
v.	Verse
Cf.	Compare (confer)

vv.	Verses
i.e.,	For example

Table Of Contents

Not by Bread Alone

Chapter 1

BIBLIOLOGY

The Doctrine of the Bible

1

BIBLIOLOGY: THE DOCTRINE OF THE BIBLE

I. Introduction

A Distinction between Bibliology and Christian Evidences

It is important to understand the distinction between bibliology and apologetics. The Scriptures can be demonstrated to be trustworthy and reliable by objective facts from various fields of study. This is the purpose of the studies called apologetics or Christian evidences. By contrast, bibliology begins where apologetics ends. The student begins with the conclusion that the Bible is trustworthy. He then proceeds to research the Scriptural teachings about the origin and nature of Scripture. The purpose of bibliology is not to confirm or validate Scripture but rather to develop the Scriptural teachings on the Scripture. Those who would charge circular reasoning to this material because Scripture is used to validate Scripture do not understand the full methodology of a conservative theologian. Here is a brief explanation of the classical method of establishing the infallibility of the Bible.

B. Classical Method of Establishing the Infallibility of the Bible

1. The Bible is a basically reliable and trustworthy document in all areas where it can be tested. (This is the domain of apologetics.)

2. On the basis of this reliable document we should trust what Jesus Christ and His approved leaders teach about the Bible as well as what they teach about all other theological areas.

Most theological points must be accepted by faith in Christ's authority since they are not subject to verification. (This is the basis for all theology.)

3. Christ, the apostles, and the prophets teach that the Scripture is of divine origin and without error. (This is the domain of bibliology.)

II. Revelation

A. Definition

Revelation is the communication of truth by God to man.

B. Distinction between Revelation and Inspiration

Revelation is not the same as inspiration. Revelation occurred when God imparted truth to man, especially to the prophets and apostles. Inspiration occurred when He insured the accurate recording of the revelation so that others might benefit.

C. Kinds of Revelation

1. Natural or general revelation is truth given to all peoples at all times by means of creation or conscience (Job 12:7-9; Psa. 19:1-3; John 1:4; Acts 14:15-17; 17:24-28; Rom. 1:19-20; 2:14-15; 2 Pet. 3:5).

> The heavens are telling of the glory of God; and their expanse is declaring the work of His hands. Day to day pours forth speech, and night to night reveals knowledge. There is no speech, nor are there words; their voice is not heard [Psa. 19:1-3].

> [B]ecause that which is known about God is evident within them; for God made it evident to them. For since the creation of the world His invisible attributes, His eternal power and divine nature, have been clearly seen, being understood through what has been made, so that they are without excuse [Rom. 1:19-20].

> For when Gentiles who do not have the Law do instinctively the things of the Law, these, not having the Law, are a law to themselves, in that they show the work of the Law written in

2

their hearts, their conscience bearing witness, and their thoughts alternately accusing or else defending them [Rom. 2:14-15].

2. Special revelation occurred when God gave a specific message to an individual or a limited group. The following are forms of special revelation:

a. Theophanies (appearances of God on earth, such as the Angel of The Lord)

b. Audible speech

c. Visible miracles, signs, wonders

d. Angelic messengers

e. Casting lots

f. Urim & Thummin (objects by which high priests could detect God's will)

g. Dreams

h. Visions

i. Israel's history

j. Life and oral teachings of the Lord Jesus Christ

k. Old Testament and the New Testament

D. Written Revelation (Scripture)

Written revelation is a sub-category of special revelation.

1. Written revelation was progressive. God gave His truth in small portions and over a lengthy period (e.g., Dan. 12:8-9, 13; Matt. 13:17; John 16:12-13; 1 Pet. 1:10-12).

2. Written revelation is not exhaustive (Deut. 29:29; Isa. 40:13-14; Rom. 11:33).

3. Written revelation has been simplified so we can understand some of the truths about God (Isa. 55:8-9; 1 Cor. 13:12).

4. The Bible claims to be a special revelation from God to man. (See "Inspiration," sections III. C. and D. of this chapter, pp. 4 and 5, on the Old Testament prophets and on the New Testament's claim to being a revelation equal to the Old Testament.)

III. Inspiration

A. Definition

Inspiration is God's superintending the pro-duction of the Scriptures so that they were produced without error in the original manuscripts. Inspiration means the Bible is "God-breathed," i.e., it is a work of God, a creation of God, a divine product. Inerrancy means that, being a work of the God of truth, the Bible is without factual error. Infallibility overlaps inerrancy, but the emphasis is not just on factual truth, but also on practical dependability. Not only are the facts of the Bible true, but its promises are completely dependable. They are not going to fail us.

B. Views on Inspiration

In order to have a complete and accurate understanding of Scripture, it is imperative that incorrect views of inspiration be recognized and avoided and that the correct view of inspiration be understood.

1. The following are incorrect views of inspiration.

a. The dictation view states that God dictated every word of the Bible to men who simply wrote the words down.

b. The conceptual view says that God gave the ideas to men who were left to their own abilities to record them.

c. The partial inspiration view declares that the Bible is inspired in religious areas but can make mistakes on secular subjects.

d. The natural inspiration view holds that Scripture was written as a result of natural excitement or genius such as any good musician or poet might experience.

2. The correct (dual-authorship) view is that Scripture is a combination of human and divine authorship. God revealed the subject matter and supervised its writing so that it was free from error. Yet, God allowed the human author latitude in his own diction, idioms, and logic. The result of dual-authorship is that, while each human author wrote in a unique style, the end product said what God wanted communicated and did so without error. Many verses assert that both

3

God and the human author wrote a particular section (Matt. 1:22; 2:15; 12:17; 19:4-5; 22:43; Mark 12:36; Acts 1:16; 2:16; 3:18; 4:25; 28:25; 1 Cor. 14:37; 1 Tim. 4:1; Heb. 1:5-13; 2:12-13; 3:7; 4:7; 10:15).

"...which the **Holy Spirit** foretold **by the mouth of David**..." [Acts 1:16].

"...this is what was **spoken of through the prophet** Joel" [Acts 2:16].

"...**God** announced beforehand **by the mouth of all the prophets**..." [Acts 3:18].

"...**through the mouth of our father David** Thy servant, didst say..." [Acts 4:25].

..."**The Holy Spirit rightly spoke through Isaiah** the prophet to your fathers" [Acts 28:25].

C. Old Testament Doctrine of the Scripture

1. The key phrases "Thus saith the Lord" and "The Word of the Lord came unto" are used literally thousands of times.

2. Statements from the Law and the Prophets assert not only that the Old Testament is a divine revelation, but, more specifically, that the words were at times dictated by God and at all times guided by God. This is verbal inspiration.

"I will raise up a prophet from among their countrymen like you, and **I will put My words in his mouth,** and he shall speak to them all that I command him" [Deut. 18:18].

Since then no prophet has risen in Israel like Moses, whom the LORD knew face to face [Deut. 34:10].

Now these are the last words of David. "David the son of Jesse declares, and the man who was raised on high declares, the anointed of the God of Jacob, and the sweet psalmist

of Israel, '**The Spirit of the LORD spoke by me, And His word was on my tongue**' " [2 Sam. 23:1-2].

For thus **the LORD spoke to me** with mighty power and instructed me not to walk in the way of this people... [Isa. 8:11].

To the law and to the testimony! If they do not speak according to this word, it is because they have no dawn [Isa. 8:20].

"And as for Me, this is My covenant with them," says the LORD: "**My Spirit which is upon you, and My words which I have put in your mouth,** shall not depart from your mouth, nor from the mouth of your offspring, nor from the mouth of your offspring's offspring," says the LORD, "from now and forever" [Isa. 59: 21].

Then the LORD stretched out His hand and touched my mouth, and the LORD said to me, "Behold, I have put **My words in your mouth**" [Jer. 1:9].

Thy words were found and I ate them, and **Thy words** became for me a joy and the delight of my heart; For I have been called by Thy name, O LORD God of hosts [Jer. 15:16].

"Thus says the LORD, the God of Israel, 'Write all **the words which I have spoken** to you in a book' " [Jer. 30:2].

Then He said to me, "Son of man, eat what you find; eat this scroll, and go, speak to the house of Israel." So I opened my mouth, and He fed me this scroll. And He said to me, "Son of man, feed your stomach, and fill your body with this scroll which I am giving you." Then I ate it, and it was sweet as honey in my mouth. Then

He said to me, "Son of man, go to the house of Israel and **speak with my words** to them" [Ezek. 3:1-4].

3. Statements from the poetic books also make it clear that Scripture is perfect, pure, and true (Psa. 12:6; 18:30; 19:7-8; 119:140, 142, 151, 160; Prov. 30:5).

The **law of the LORD is perfect**, restoring the soul; the testimony of the LORD is sure, making wise the simple. The precepts of the LORD are right, rejoicing the heart; the commandment of the LORD is pure, enlightening the eyes [Psa. 19:7-8].

...Thy law is **truth** [Psa. 119:142].

...**all Thy commandments are truth** [Psa. 119:151].

The sum of **Thy word is truth**, and **every one** of Thy righteous ordinances is everlasting [Psa. 119:160].

D. New Testament Claim to Equality with the Old Testament

Christ pre-authenticated the New Testament by teaching His apostles that the Holy Spirit would come and guide them into all truth (John 14:16). Thus, the New Testament is just as much Scripture as the Old Testament.

1. The New Testament authors assumed the same experiences as the Old Testament authors relative to receiving revelations and guidance by the Holy Spirit, and they claimed equal authority with the Old Testament (John 14:26; 15:26-27; 16:12-14; Rom. 16:25-26; 1 Cor. 2:10, 13; 4:1; 11:23; 14:37; 2 Cor. 12:7; Gal. 1:11-12; Eph. 3:2-5; Col. 1:25-26; 1 Thess. 2:13; 2 Thess. 2:15; 3:6, 14; 1 Tim. 4:1; 2 Pet. 3:1-2; 1 John 4:6; Rev. 1:1).

2. The New Testament calls itself Scripture. Therefore, the main passages that teach about the Scriptures refer to both testaments.

a. 2 Pet. 3:15-16 calls Paul's epistles "Scripture."

b. 1 Tim. 5:18 quotes Luke 10:7 and calls it "Scripture."

E. The New Testament Doctrine of the Scripture

1. The Lord's view should be the most determinative in developing a theology of the Scripture. Christ recognized the Old Testament as infallible and He pre-authenticated the writing of the New Testament (See Page 10).

"Do not think that I came to abolish the Law or the Prophets; I did not come to abolish, but to fulfill. For truly I say to you, until heaven and earth pass away, not the **smallest letter or stroke** shall pass away from the Law, until all is accomplished" [Matt. 5:17-18].

Matt. 5:17-18 teaches that man has no authority to change even the smallest detail of Scripture. This does not directly teach inerrancy, but it inescapably implies it. Consider the following line of reasoning:

a. God does not want even the smallest detail of written Scripture to be changed. He is not interested in retracting, restating, reteaching, modifying, or "correcting" anything in the Old Testament.

b. God is a God of truth with a great concern for the truth (e.g., Num. 23:19; John 17:17; Titus 1:2; Heb. 6:18).

c. Therefore, even the minute details of Scripture must be true, because God could not be satisfied with imperfections. Furthermore, there can be no doubt that Matt. 5:17-18 intentionally implies the inerrancy of Scripture because its parallel passage in Luke 16:17 demonstrates that Christ was teaching the infallibility of the Bible by the same words in Matthew.

"But it is easier for heaven and earth to pass away than for one **stroke of a letter** of the Law to **fail**" [Luke 16:17].

This text is perhaps the best verse in the Bible on the subject of inerrancy. It shows that Matt. 5:17-18 is teaching the inerrancy of Scripture since Luke 16:17 is a parallel passage. Furthermore, Luke 16:17 does not merely imply infallibility; rather, it directly states it. The Lord is teaching that it is impossible for the smallest detail of the Bible to fail. This means that the Bible had to have been composed without error, for, if a portion of it is error, then it does fail in the most basic sense: it fails to tell the truth. Yet, Christ says it is not possible for even a minute portion of the Scripture to fail. Also, the Greek word translated *fail* means *fall*. The verse is an assertion of infallibility. One can depend upon every detail of Scripture to be trustworthy.

> "...(and the Scripture cannot be broken)" [John 10:35].

Jews were constantly speaking about "breaking the Law" or "breaking the Sabbath." To break the Law is to disregard or ignore the Law. Likewise, when the Lord Jesus Christ says, "the Scripture cannot be broken," He means no one can disregard what it says. A person must accept a Scriptural statement as binding, final, and the end of all argument. There can be no disagreement once the Scripture speaks. In the context the Lord is arguing with His opponents; but, after quoting Scripture, He considers the argument to be ended. Since the Lord would not allow disagreement with the Scripture, then Jesus must have understood the Bible to be without error. If there were errors in Scripture, then there could be legitimate disagreements with its statements. However, the Lord will not allow any disregard for what the Scripture affirms to be true.

> And He said to them, "O foolish men and slow of heart to believe in **all** that the prophets have spoken!" [Luke 24:25].

The Lord calls a person who fails to believe all that the prophets have spoken a "fool." It is unthinkable to Christ that anything in the Old Testament should be denied. If there are errors in the Old Testament, then Christ's statement would be ridiculous. He would be saying people are foolish not to believe in mistakes.

> "...Thy word is truth" [John 17:17].

What can be clearer than the Lord's statement that the Word of God is true? If it is true, it is by definition without error.

> **"David himself said in the Holy Spirit,** 'The LORD said to my LORD, "Sit at my right hand, until I put thine enemies beneath thy feet" ' " [Mark 12:36].

(See also Matt. 22:43-44.)

By this statement Christ is teaching that when David wrote he was being guided by the Holy Spirit.

> And He answered and said, "Have you not read, that **He who created** them from the beginning made them male and female, and **said,** 'For this cause a man shall leave his father and mother, and shall cleave to his wife; and the two shall become one flesh'?" [Matt. 19:4-5].

Christ said God created "male and female, and **[God]** said, 'For this cause a man shall leave father and mother....' " He is quoting Gen. 2:24; however, in the Genesis context there is no direct indication that God is the one speaking. The reader would presume that Moses alone wrote Gen. 2:24. The implication of this verse is that Christ felt at liberty to select any Old Testament passage and assert that God is the one who wrote it.

In the argument with the Sadducees found in Matt. 22:29-33, the Lord builds His case upon the tense of a single verb. He argues for the resurrection and the immortality of the souls of Abraham, Isaac, and Jacob by God's statement in Moses' day, "**I am** the God of Abraham, Isaac, and Jacob." Had these Patriarchs no after-life whatsoever, God would have said to Moses, "**I was** the God of Abraham, Isaac, and Jacob." The Lord regarded every small detail of Scripture as both significant and true.

Christ often used phrases which indicated the authoritative nature of the written Scriptures: "It is written...," " Have you not read...," "You do err not knowing the Scriptures."

2. The Apostolic View of Scripture

> For to us God revealed them through the Spirit; for the Spirit searches all things, even the depths of God....which things we also speak, not in words taught by human wisdom, but in those taught by the Spirit, combining spiritual *thoughts* with spiritual *words* [1 Cor. 2:10, 13].

The pronouns *we* and *us* in the opening chapters of 1 Corinthians seem to refer to the apostles (e.g., 1 Cor. 4:9). Paul is saying his message was not from human philosophy but by divine revelation. Technically, this is emphasizing an oral message and cannot be limited to Scriptures (cf. v. 13, *speak*). However, the text also implies that same guidance by the Holy Spirit down to the very words of a written message.

> ...they [the Jews] were entrusted with the **oracles of God** [Rom. 3:2].

> For though by this time you ought to be teachers, you have need again for some one to teach you the elementary principles of the **oracles of God**, and you have come to need milk and not solid food [Heb. 5:12].

> You, however, continue in the things you have learned and become convinced of, knowing from whom you have learned them; and that from childhood you have known the sacred writings which are able to give you the wisdom that leads to salvation

through faith which is in Christ Jesus. **All Scripture is inspired by God** and profitable for teaching, for reproof, for correction, for training in righteousness; that the man of God may be adequate, equipped for every good work [2 Tim. 3:14-17].

The key to this text is the Greek phrase *pasa graphe theopneustos*.

Pasa is a form of *pan*. It means "all" as in panacea, pandemonium, Pan-American, panorama, etc. In this grammatical structure, the word usually means "every." To say "every" Scripture is inspired is to assert "all" of it is inspired. However, the idea of "every" concentrates upon every small detail. Every detail of the Bible is inspired. A good sense would be "any Scripture you choose to consider is inspired." Paul is saying "the whole of Scripture in all of its parts is inspired."

Graphe is the Greek word for Scripture. The context emphasizes the Old Testament Scripture, as the Old Testament would be Timothy's reading material in childhood. However, it is certain Paul also considered the New Testament to be Scripture as is evidenced by his calling Luke 10:7 "Scripture" in 1 Tim. 5:18. Therefore, both the Old Testament and New Testament are within the scope of this statement about inspiration.

Theopneustos is the Greek word. The English "inspiration" comes from the Latin Vulgate "inspire" which means to inflate. This may give the impression that God breathed into some existing Scriptures to enhance their quality. This is not the best translation (although it is too well established to eliminate). The Greek term means "breathed out by God," "exhaled by God": Theos - God; pneuma - breath, as in pneumonia. It is not that God breathed into some pre-existing books to "inflate" their quality. Rather, God breathed out the Scripture in the first place. They have their origin in God. The Scriptures are a creation, a work, a product of

God. In other parts of the Bible, the act of God breathing out something is associated with His creative power (e.g., Gen. 2:7; Psa. 33:6; Ezek. 37:5ff.; John 3:8). **The whole of Scripture in all of its parts is a creation of God.**

Arguments for inerrancy springing from 2 Tim. 3:16 follow. This passage teaches that every detail of the Bible is a work of God. It does not directly teach inerrancy. However, no other conclusion is possible.

Major premise: Every detail of Scripture is a work of God.

Minor premise: God's Word is truth (John 17:17).

Conclusion: Every detail of the Scripture is true (inerrant).

The premise that the Bible contains errors makes absurd consequences arising from 2 Tim. 3:16.

Major premise: Every detail of Scripture is a work of God.

Minor premise: There are mistakes in the Scriptures.

Conclusion: God makes mistakes when He writes.

(See, also, "Inspiration," pp. 3-4 above, for information concerning dual-authorship verses and claims to divine revelation.)

> But know this first of all, that no prophecy of Scripture is a matter of one's own interpretation, for no prophecy was ever made by an act of human will, but men moved by the Holy Spirit spoke from God [2 Pet. 1:20-21].

This passage teaches at least three important truths about the Scriptures. They are not derived from human origin alone, the men who wrote Scriptures were speaking from God, and they were being moved by the Holy Spirit.

The word *moved* means to lift up and carry. The same word is used of the wind driving a ship in Acts 27:15, 17. Peter is saying that God the Holy Spirit pushed the authors of Scripture in the direction He wanted them to go relative to the composition of the Bible. Thus, 2 Pet. 1:20-21 confirms 2 Tim. 3:16 on the point that the Scriptures are of divine origin and planning. The truth of their inerrancy necessarily follows. Given that the Bible is a product of the Holy Spirit's control and guidance, it must be without imperfections. We should also keep in mind that 2 Pet. 3:15-16 shows Peter regarded the New Testament writings to be Scripture.

IV. Illumination

Illumination is distinct from either revelation or inspiration. Illumination refers to the teaching ministry of the Holy Spirit when He takes His own Word and reveals to a believer its true significance, its beauty, and its relevance (Psa. 119:18; John 14:26 by application; John 16:12-13 by application; 1 John 2:20, 27; and 1 Cor. 2:15).

V. Canonicity

From the Greek word *canon* we derive the word *cane*. By the term *canon of Scripture* one refers to the books by which Christians are supposed to rule or measure their lives. Canonicity takes up the issue of which books belong in the Bible.

A. Old Testament Canon

The Roman Catholic Church recognizes eleven more books and the Eastern Orthodox Church four more books in the Old Testament canon than do Protestants or Jews. Protestants and Jews recognize the same material as belonging to the Old Testament although they count and order the books differently. The important issue for Christians ought to be which books did the Lord Jesus Christ recognize. It is clear that He adhered to the Jewish (and hence the Protestant) canon of the Old Testament.

"You worship that which you do not know; we worship that which we know, for salvation is from the Jews" [John 4:22].

The Samaritans in the Lord's day rejected all of the Old Testament except the Law of Moses. By saying, "Salvation is of the Jews," Jesus sides with the Jews in the debate against the Samaritans. Part of that debate was over which books belonged in the Old Testament.

"[F]rom the blood of Abel to the blood of Zechariah, who perished between the altar and the house of God; yes, I tell you, it shall be charged against this generation" [Luke 11:51].

(See parallel passage Matt. 23:35.)

To appreciate this verse we will have to know that the Hebrew canon begins with Genesis and closes with 2 Chronicles. Abel's death is recorded in Gen. 4:8. Zechariah's death is recorded in 2 Chron. 24:21. Abel was the first man of God to be slain. Zechariah, in the order of the Hebrew Old Testament, was the last man of God to be slain. Jesus is saying, "From Genesis to Chronicles you are guilty of killing the prophets." Therefore, Jesus delineates and implicitly endorses the limits of the Jewish Old Testament canon.

...."These are My words which I spoke to you while I was still with you, that all things which are written about Me in the Law of Moses and the Prophets and Psalms must be fulfilled" [Luke 24:44].

There is some evidence that the modern three-fold division of the Hebrew canon predated Christ. If we remember that Psalms was the largest and probably the first of the section called "The Writings," then Jesus is perhaps referring to the three Jewish sections of the canon: the Law, the Prophets, and the Writings. In the modern Hebrew Bible, the Kethubim, "The Writings," begins with Psalms.

Jesus answered them, "Has it not been written in your Law, 'I said, you are gods'? If he called them gods, to whom the word of God came (and the Scripture cannot be broken...' "[John 10:34-35].

In these verses Jesus refers to "your law," meaning the official law of the Jews. He also calls this law "the Scripture." At no time did Jesus debate with the Jews over the books in the Old Testament. He accepted and used the Jews' authoritative books. So do modern evangelicals.

B. New Testament Canon

Roman Catholics, Eastern Orthodox and Protestants all agree that there ought to be twenty-seven books in the New Testament canon. Christ founded His church upon the New Testament apostles (Eph. 2:20). The issue of whether a book belongs in the New Testament is its apostolic origin. Was it either written by an apostle or under the supervision of an apostle? The evidence for twenty of the twenty-seven books is conclusive. No objective person doubts their apostolic origin. Seven of the New Testament books were disputed (Hebrews, James, 2 Peter, 2 John and 3 John, Jude and Revelation). However, there is enough evidence that these are of apostolic origin to persuade most to accept them. The doctrines presented by conservative Christianity would not be altered if proof-texts from these seven books were deleted. However, the preponderance of factual evidence shows there is good reason to accept them as genuine. Also, one with faith in the sovereignty of God tends to accept that the universal agreement on twenty-seven New Testament books is not coincidental but providential.

VI. Texts of the Bible

Textual criticism does overlap with bibliology on at least one point. Critics object that the doctrine of inerrancy is worthless since the originals no longer exist. However, this thinking fails to consider that our existing texts are extremely close to the originals and that the dependability of the original statements is a matter of paramount importance.

Relative to the Old Testament, we possess copies that predate the time of Christ. Hence, we use virtually the same Old Testament Scriptures as He did. If He found them acceptable, then we know they have been preserved to an acceptable degree for us.

Relative to the New Testament, it is the best-preserved book of the ancient world both in terms of number of manuscripts (5,000 Greek, 25,000 total) and in closeness to time of composition (earliest manuscript is A.D. 125). Bible scholars estimate that we know the original wording at somewhere between 98% and 99.5% purity. The differences between ancient Greek manuscripts are no greater than differences between the New International Version, the New American Standard Bible, and the King James Version. The doctrinal positions in this study would be the same regardless of which variants in manuscripts are followed.

VII. Bibliology and Continuing Revelation .

Should the student of the Bible be open to the possibility that God might give new Scriptures in modern times? Are there any new authors obtaining direct revelation? Can any new writings be "God-breathed?"

A. The Basis of Authority for the Church

A Christian looks to Christ Jesus for authority. In the closing days of His ministry the Lord Jesus Christ told the apostles that the Holy Spirit would come to be their Teacher. He would guide them into all truth. He would cause them to remember and understand teachings and events from the Lord's earthly ministry. He would show them "things to come." These instructions from John 14-16 are a pre-authentication that the

apostles would receive divine revelation and provide authority for the church. Although such statements, as in John 14:26; 15:26, 27; and 16:12-14, might be applied to the illuminating ministry of the Holy Spirit to every believer, they are technically restricted to the apostles. Consider these textual statements that show the Lord was speaking to the apostles:

> "These things have I spoken to you, while abiding with you" [John 14:25].
>
> "...and bring to your remembrance all that I said to you" [John 14:26].
>
> "[A]nd you will bear witness also, because you have been with Me from the beginning" [John 15:27].
>
> "I have many more things to say to you, but you cannot bear them now" [John 16:12].

The Upper Room Discourse, given on the evening before the crucifixion, was spoken to the apostles alone. They are designated by Christ to be recipients of divine revelation from the Holy Spirit. Eph. 2:20 teaches that the apostles are the foundation of the church. 2 Pet. 3:2 teaches that the commandments of our Lord and Savior were spoken by the apostles. 1 Cor. 12:28 says "first apostles." Matt. 16:18 is capable of diverse interpretations; however, as long as one does not give Peter precedence over the other apostles, it is possible Christ was saying He would build the church upon Peter along with the rest of the apostles. There was a good basis for the early church's concern that a book be proven to be apostolic before it was accepted into the canon. The Apostles are the bases for all authoritative teaching that is universally binding on the church. (Compare how Paul asserted authority by claiming apostleship.)

B. Contemporary Authority for the Church

Acts 1:21-22 and 1 Cor. 9:1 indicate that to be an apostle one had to be a witness of the resurrected Lord. There is no one living to-day who saw the Lord in His post-resurrection ministry. Likewise, it is absurd to think we are in the founding period of the church (cf. Eph. 2:20). Christ pre-authenticated the apostles to obtain divine revelation by the Holy Spirit. He did not give the same authority to any others. There-fore, since there are no apostles today, no one can claim to have revelations that are binding upon the universal church. It is not possible for anyone to add more Scripture to the Bible.

C. Other Considerations

There are several verses that teach that **the faith** (i.e., the body of doctrine for the church) would be given once and would be unchangeable. Although the statement at the close of Revelation technically refers only to the book of Revelation, it is probably more than coincidence it occurs at the close of the Bible.

> Beloved, while I was making every effort to write you about our common salvation, I felt the necessity to write to you appealing that you contend earnestly for **the faith** which was **once for all** delivered to the saints [Jude 3].

> But even though we, or an angel from heaven, should preach to you a gos-pel contrary to that which we have preached to you, let him be accursed [Gal. 1:8].

> I testify to everyone who hears the words of the prophecy of this book: if anyone adds to them, God shall add to him the plagues which are written in this book; and if anyone takes away from the words of the book of this prophecy, God shall take away his part from the tree of life and from the holy city, which are written in this book [Rev. 22:18-19].

VIII. Bibliology and Church History

The doctrine of the infallibility of the Bible was the basis for every major denomination.

Those who have denied the inspiration of Scripture are usually espousing doctrine that would be considered heresy by the founders of their own group. The liberal assertion that the inerrancy position is a modern develop-ment is either based on ignorance or is a deliberate misinterpretation.

> For it seems to me that most disas-trous consequences must follow upon our believing that anything false is found in the sacred books; that is to say, that the men by whom the Scrip-ture has been given to us, and com-mitted to writing, did put down in these books anything false. . . . [1]

Augustine (Catholic-pre-Reformation)

Luther quoted from Augustine's letter to Jerome in which he wrote, "This I have learned to do: to hold only those books which are called the Holy Scriptures in such honor that I finally believe that not one of the holy writ-ers ever erred." Luther endorsed this view of Augustine and himself stated, "The Scriptures cannot err. It is cer-tain that Scripture cannot disagree with itself. It is impossible that Scrip-ture should contradict itself, only that it so appears to the senseless and ob-stinate hypocrites."[2]

> Therefore, we either believe roundly and wholly and utterly, or we believe nothing: the Holy Ghost doth not let Himself be severed or parted, that He should let one part be taught or be-lieved truly and the other part falsely... For it is the fashion of all heretics that they begin first with a

---

[1] Harold Lindsell, *God's Incomparable Word* (Wheaton, Illinois: Victor Books, 1977) 55.

[2] Ibid., 58.

single article, but they must then all be denied altogether, like a ring which is of no further value when it has a break or cut...[3]

> Martin Luther (founder of the Lutherans)

The sure and infallible record
The unerring standard
The pure Word of God
The infallible rule of His Holy truth
The unerring certainty
The certain and unerring rule
Unerring light
Infallible Word of God
Has nothing belonging to man mixed with it
Inviolable
Infallible oracles [4]

> John Calvin (leader of the Presbyterian and Reformed traditions)

"Whatever is found in Holy Scripture," affirms Archbishop Cranmer, "must be taken for a most sure ground and infallible truth; and whatsoever cannot be grounded upon the same, touching our faith, is man's device, changeable and uncertain."[5]

Let us stay, quiet, and certify our consciences with the most infallible certainty, truth, and perpetual assurance of them [the Scriptures]. [6]

> Thomas Cramner (Among the founders of the Anglican Church: in America this is the Episcopalian Church.)

Nay, if there be any mistakes in the Bible there may as well be a thousand. If there be one falsehood in that book it did not come from the God of truth. [7]

> John Wesley (founder of Methodism)

Then, since God wrote it, mark its truthfulness. If I had written it, there would be worms of critics who would at once swarm on it, and would cover it with their evil spawn; had I written it, there would be men who would pull it to pieces at once, and perhaps quite right too. But this is the Word of God. Come, search, ye critics, and find an error. This is a vein of pure gold, unalloyed by quartz or any earthly substance. This is a star without a speck; a sun without a blot; a light without darkness; a moon without paleness; a glory without a dimness. O Bible! it cannot be said of any other book, that it is perfect and pure; but of thee we can declare all wisdom is gathered up in thee, without a particle of folly. This is the judge that ends the strife where wit and reason fail. This is the book un-

---

[3] John Gerstner, "The Church's Doctrine of Biblical Inspiration," *The Foundation of Biblical Authority*, ed. James Montgomery Boice, (Grand Rapids: Zondervan Publishing Co. 1978) 35.

[4] John Gerstner, "The View of the Bible Held by the Church: Calvin and the Westminster Divines", *Summit Papers International Council of Biblical Inerrancy*, ed. Norman Geisler, (Oakland, California: ICBI, 1978), paper 14, p. 8.

[5] Philip E. Hughes, *The Theology of the English Reformers* (Grand Rapids: Eerdmans Publishing Co., 1965) 20.

[6] Ibid., 22.

[7] Lindsell, 77.

tainted by any error, but is pure, unalloyed, perfect truth. Why? Because God wrote it. Ah! charge God with error if you please; tell Him that His book is not what it ought to be. Blessed Bible, thou art all truth.[8]

Charles Haddon Spurgeon
(Prominent Baptist)

---

[8] Ibid., 72-73.

Chapter 2

THEOLOGY PROPER

The Doctrine of God

OUTLINE

7. God Is Omnipotent
8. God Is United
B. God's Moral Attributes
1. God Is Holy
2. God Is True
   a. Factually True
   b Ethically True
   c. Metaphysically True
3. God Is Good
   a. God Is Merciful
   b. God Is Longsuffering
   c. God Is Gracious
   d. God Is Love
4. God Is Righteous, or God Is Just
5. God Is Wise
6. God Is Blessed
7. God Is Glorious

THEOLOGY PROPER: THE DOCTRINE OF GOD

I. Definitions of Views about God

A. Atheism

Atheism denies that there is a God. Atheism is compatible with humanism and with strict materialism. Humanism believes that man is autonomous and the glory of man is the highest good. Strict materialism makes the physical universe to be the only reality.

B. Agnosticism

Agnosticism denies that man can ever know about God's existence. Agnosticism is also compatible with both humanism and materialism. A humanist might concede that it is possible God exists. Yet, since we cannot know about God, He is irrelevant to life. Likewise, a materialist might live without any consideration of God although he may theoretically concede God could possibly exist.

C. Theism

Theism refers to a belief in any God.

1. Deists assert that God does exist; however, God is neither interested in being involved with the world nor does God communicate with man.

2. Polytheism describes the belief in many gods.

3. Pantheists believe that the universe itself is God. This school of thought is close to atheistic materialism. Both pantheists and true materialists believe the physical universe is the only reality. However, the former views the physical universe as "god."

4. Monotheists believe there is only one God. Jews, Moslems, Christians, and various cults are monotheists.

II. The Existence of God

Full material concerning the existence of God is within the domain of Christian Evidences rather than in Theology Proper. The greatest proof for God's existence is the supernatural character of Scripture and the Person of the Lord Jesus Christ. The goal of Theology Proper is to develop what the Scriptures teach about God, not to argue for His existence. The Scriptures everywhere assume God's existence and label those who deny Him as "fools" (see Psa. 14:1; 53:1). The student who wishes to consider the topic of God's existence should study Christian Evidences. However, theologians usually do include basic philosophical arguments for God's existence under Theology Proper. We will include them to be thorough; however, the best argument for God's existence remains "Christological," the life of Christ.

A. The Cosmological Argument

The cosmological argument contends every effect must have a sufficient cause. The universe is an effect. Therefore, its uncaused first cause must be God.

B. The Teleological Argument

The teleological argument contends that design implies a sufficient designer. The universe gives abundant evidence of design. There must be a designer who is God.

C. The Moral Argument

The moral argument contends that an inborn sense of moral law points to a lawgiver. People do have a sense of moral standards. This is especially active in the moral outrage that occurs when they have been a victim of wrong. Since there is a sense of law, there must be a lawgiver who is God.

D. The Ontological Argument

The ontological argument contends that a sense of need implies a supply for that need. The child who is hungry innately knows that food exists. Since most people are theists, there must be a God.

III. The Definition of God

Nowhere is God totally defined in the Scriptures. He is described as "spirit" in John 4:24, as "light" in 1 John 1:5, as "love" in 1 John 4:16, and as a "consuming fire" in Heb. 12:29. By the commonly given definition of personhood, God is a person, possessing intellect, emotion, and a will. God is said to be "the living God" (see 1 Sam. 17:26; Matt. 16:16; 1 Thess. 1:9). Theologians struggle in trying to give any kind of a concise definition for God. The following suggested definitions appear to be worthy attempts to define the Supreme Being.

"God is the infinite and perfect Spirit in whom all things have their source, support, and end."[1]

"God is the one infinite, eternal Being, Creator, Preserver, and Ruler of the universe who is Spirit, Love, and Light, and in whom all things have their source and end."[2] As long as we understand God is not the direct cause but only the permissive cause of fallen beings and their evil, the following might also be acceptable: God is the invisible and personal Spirit who is the self-existent cause of all else and who is infinite and good.

IV. The Unity and Trinity of the Godhead

The Scriptural teaching about God is that there is one God who exists in three equal persons: Father, Son, and Holy Spirit. It is not true that there are three gods, nor that there is one god who manifests himself at various times in three different forms. It is not that God consists of three parts, for God cannot be divided. Some aspects of the Godhead are capable of being understood; others are inscrutable. An unknown author has concluded: "The received doctrine of the Christian church may be fairly stated to be that we are taught by the Scriptures to believe that there is but one God and yet three equal subjects in the Godhead, who are described as Persons, but that we are unable to determine in what sense these three are separate and in what sense they are one."

A. The Unity of God

The Scriptures teach monotheism. There are three persons who are united into one God (Deut. 4:35; 6:4; 1 Kings 8:60; 2 Kings 19:15; Isa. 43:10; 44:6, 8; Zech. 14:9; 1 Cor. 8:6; Gal. 3:20; 1 Tim. 2:5; James 2:19).

> Hear O Israel! The LORD is our God, the LORD is **one**! [Deut. 6:4].
>
> [Y]et for us there is but **one** God [1 Cor. 8:6].
>
> ...whereas God is only **one** [Gal. 3:20].

[1] Augustus H. Strong, *Systematic Theology*, 3 vols. in 1, reprint edition (Old Tappan, N.J: Fleming H. Revell Co., 1976) 52.

[2] John Miles, "Doctrine," Unpublished class notes, Grand Rapids School of The Bible and Music, 1974) 16.

For there is **one** God...[1 Tim. 2:5].

You believe that God is **one**. You do well...[James 2:19].

B. The Triune Nature of God

Although the Trinity cannot be completely understood, it should be accepted as being a clearly taught and repeated Bible doctrine.

1. The Trinity in the Old Testament

The doctrine of the Trinity is most fully developed in the New Testament; however, it is interesting that Trinitarian doctrine is also present in the Old Testament in an indirect way (See also Isa. 9:6, Psa. 110:1, Jer. 23:5-6).

a. The Hebrew word for God is plural (*Elohim*). The fact that the Hebrew word for God is plural **would not by itself** prove the Trinity. It could be what grammarians call "the plural of majesty." The Hebrew words for face, water, and heaven are also plural. However, the plural grammatical form of *God* does make room for a Trinitarian concept. Also, when supported by other clearer evidences for the Trinity, one satisfactory explanation for the plural form is that it was intended to be a veiled hint to the triune nature of God.

b. In a number of texts of the Old Testament, pronouns that are best taken to refer to God are plural. Again, by themselves, they would not establish the Trinity for other explanations are possible. Yet, in the light of other clearer texts these do support the doctrine of the Trinity as secondary evidences.

...Let **Us** make man in **Our** image...[Gen. 1:26].

Then the LORD God said, "Behold, the man has become like one of **Us**..." [Gen. 3:22].

And the LORD said,..."Come, let **Us** go down and there confuse their language...[Gen. 11:6, 7].

Then I heard the voice of the Lord, saying, "Whom shall I send, and who will go for **Us**?"...[Isa. 6:8].

John 12:41-42 indicates **Christ** was the one on the throne speaking in Isaiah 6. Acts 28:25ff. says the **Holy Spirit** said these things. In the Isaiah context one would assume **God the Father** was speaking. A combination of these texts supports the Trinity.

c. God seems to be distinguished from God although there is only one God.

...And the LORD said to him..."But I will have compassion on the house of Judah and deliver them by the LORD their God..." [Hosea 1:6-7].

d. Even the Old Testament indicates that God has a Son (See also Isa. 9:6).

I will surely tell of the decree of the LORD: He said to Me, "Thou art My Son, today I have begotten Thee." [Psa. 2:7].

Do homage to the Son, lest He become angry, and you perish in the way...[Psa. 2:12a].

...Who has established all the ends of the earth? What is His name or His son's name?...[Prov. 30:4].

e. The Angel of the LORD appears to be separate from God and yet is God.

(1) The Angel of the LORD is separate from God.

Then the angel of the LORD answered and said, "O LORD of hosts... [Zech. 1:12].

(2) The Angel of the LORD is recognized as God

- By Hagar - "Thou art **a** God who sees" [Gen. 16:13].

- By Moses as the author of Genesis - "...the **LORD** who spoke to her" [Gen.16: 13].

- By the author of Judges - "And the **LORD** looked at him and said..." [Judg. 6:14] and "But the **LORD** said to him..." [Judg. 6:16].

- By Gideon - "O **LORD**, how shall I deliver Israel?" [Judg. 6:15].

- By Samson's parents - "...we have seen **God**" [Judg. 13:22].

(3) The Angel of the LORD claims to be God (see Gen. 22:11-12).

> I am the **God** of Bethel... [Gen. 31:13].

> ...I am the **God** of your Father... [Ex. 3:6].

> Now the angel of the LORD came up from Gilgal to Bochim. And he said, "I brought you up out of Egypt and led you into the land which I have sworn to your fathers; and I said, 'I will never break My covenant with you' " [Judg. 2:1].

(4) Conclusions

The Angel of the LORD is God, yet, He is separate from God. There can be two possible conclusions: either there are two gods (which Scripture will not allow), or the Old Testament hints that there is more than one person in the Godhead.

f. The Messiah is sent by God, however, He is God (Psa. 110:1; Jer. 23:5-6; Isa. 7:14; 9:6).

(1) Messiah is separate from God: He is God's servant.

> Behold, My Servant, whom I uphold; My chosen one in whom My soul delights. I have put My Spirit upon Him; He will bring forth justice to the nations [Isa. 42:1].

(2) Messiah is God.

> For a child will be born to us, a son will be given to us; and the government will rest on His shoulders; and His name will be called Wonderful Counselor, **Mighty God**, Eternal Father, Prince of Peace [Isa. 9:6].

g. There are a number of plurals used in reference to God (e.g., verbs in Gen. 20:13 and 35:7 and nouns in Eccl. 12:1 and Isa. 54:5). These would not by themselves prove the Trinity. They could be dismissed as grammatical oddities by anyone wishing to object to the Trinitarian doctrine. Since the Trinity can be established by other texts, it is possible by hindsight to view these plurals as intentional hints to the Trinity.[3]

> Remember also your Creator [Hebrew: "Creators"] in the days of your youth [Eccl. 12:1].

> For your husband is your Maker [Hebrew: "Makers"][Isa. 54:5].

2. The Trinity in the New Testament

a. Each person of the Trinity is called God or claims deity.

(1) The Father (Rom 1:7; Gal. 1:3; Eph. 1:2; Phil. 1:2, etc.)

(2) The Son (John 1:1, 18; 5:18; 8:58; 10:30; 14:9; 20:28; Acts 20:28; Rom. 9:5; Phil. 2:6; Col. 1:15-16; 2:9; Titus 2:13; Heb. 1:8; 2 Pet. 1:1; 1 John 5:20. (For a more complete study of the deity of Christ see "Christology," Chapter 8.)

> In the beginning was the Word, and the Word was with God, and the **Word was God** [John 1:1].

> Thomas answered and said to Him, "My Lord and my **God**!" [John 20:28].

---

[3] (F. H. W. Gesenius, *Gesenuis Hebrew Grammar*, ed. and trans. F. Kautzch, rev. A. F. Cowley, 2nd ed. (Oxford: Clarendon Press, 1910) 273, 399.

For in Him **all the fullness of Deity** dwells in bodily form [Col. 2:9].

Looking for the blessed hope and the appearing of the glory of our **great God and Savior, Christ Jesus** [Titus 2:13].

But of the Son He says, "Thy throne, **O God**, is forever and ever, and the righteous scepter is the scepter of His kingdom" [Heb. 1:8].

(3) The Holy Spirit

But Peter said, "Ananias, why has Satan filled your heart to lie to the **Holy Spirit**, and to keep back some of the price of the land? While it remained unsold, did it not remain your own? And after it was sold, was it not under your control? Why is it that you have conceived this deed in your heart? You have not lied to men, but to **God**" [Acts 5:3-4].

Now the **Lord is the Spirit**; and where the Spirit of the Lord is, there is liberty" [2 Cor. 3:17].

b. Two persons are associated in the Godhead

..."This is My beloved Son..." [Matt. 17:5].

I and my Father are one [John 10:30].

"...He who has seen me has seen the father..." [John 14:9].

c. Three persons may be associated together as God. There are a number of passages that make reference to all three persons of the Trinity (see Matt. 3:16-17; 28:19; John 14:16-17; 15:26; 16:7-15; Rom. 8:14-17; Gal. 4:4-6; Eph. 1:3-14; 4:4-6; 1 Cor. 12:4-6; 2 Cor. 1:21-22; 13:14; Heb. 9:14; 1 Pet. 1:2).

And after being baptized, Jesus went up immediately from the water; and behold, the heavens were opened, and he saw the **Spirit of God** descending as a dove, and coming upon Him, and behold, a **voice** [the Father] out of the heavens, saying, "This is My beloved **Son**, in whom I am well-pleased" [Matt. 3:16-17].

...baptizing them in the name [note the singular] of the **Father** and the **Son** and the **Holy Spirit** [Matt. 28:19].

And I [God the Son] will ask the **Father**, and He will give you another Helper,...that is the **Spirit of Truth** [John 14:16-17].

But when the fullness of the time came, **God** sent forth His **Son**, born of a woman, born under the Law...And because you are sons, God has sent forth the **Spirit** of His **Son** into our hearts, crying, "Abba! **Father!**" [Gal. 4:4, 6].

The grace of the **Lord Jesus Christ**, and the love of **God**, and the fellowship of the **Holy Spirit**, be with you all [2 Cor. 13:14].

...according to the foreknowledge of **God the Father**, by the sanctifying work of the **Spirit**, that you may obey **Jesus Christ** and be sprinkled with His blood; may grace and peace be yours in fullest measure [1 Pet. 1:2].

V. Names for God.

Often the Bible describes a person by a name. A name is not always a certain indication of a personality. Yet, the principle is most valid with God. We can learn about Him by studying His Names.

A. *Elohim*

Elohim occurs approximately 2,570 times in the Old Testament. The corresponding Greek word is *Theos*. Technically, this is not a name. It rather gives a classification just as we might call a man "pastor" when his actual name is Richard. *Elohim* is plural in form (cf.

seraphim, cherubim). This by itself does not prove the Trinity, but it may be a clue of God's triune nature. *Elohim* may emphasize God in His role as Creator (Gen. 1:1; Isa. 45:18; Jonah 1:9), as God of all the earth rather than of Israel alone (Gen. 24:7; Isa. 37:16; 54:5; Jer. 32:27), and as Judge of all the earth (Psa. 50:6; 58:11; 75:7). *Elohim* may also emphasize God as personal Savior (Gen. 17:8; Ex. 3:6; Jer. 23:23).[4]

Elohim seems to picture God as Creator, Sovereign, and Savior of all the earth.

1. *El Shaddai* or *Shaddai* (Gen. 17:1; Ex. 6:3) occurs forty-eight times in the Old Testament (thirty-one times in Job). The Greek equivalent is *Pantokrator* (Rev. 1:8; 19:6). The term means "Almighty." The Hebrew derivation is hard to trace. *Shaddad* is Hebrew for destroyer. *Shad* means breast. *Shadu* is Akkadian for mountain. Any of these suggestions is plausible. The basic meaning of Almighty could be derived from His power to destroy the wicked, His complete sufficiency as a nourisher, or being strong as a mountain.[5] It is best to follow the LXX (Septuagint) and give *El Shaddai* a basic meaning of "Almighty" regardless of its exact derivation. As *El Shaddai*, God is omnipotent and sufficient to take care of man.

> Now when Abram was ninety-nine years old, the LORD appeared to Abram and said to him, I am **God Almighty**; walk before Me, and be blameless [Gen. 17:1].

> And I appeared to Abraham, Isaac, and Jacob, as **God Almighty**, but by My name, LORD, I did not make Myself known to them [Ex. 6:3].

2. *El Elyon* (Gen. 14:18) means Most High God. In the Scriptures it is nearly always used by gentiles or in reference to gentiles. Therefore, this title emphasizes God in His rule over all the earth. Melchizedek calls *El Elyon* "the possessor of heaven and earth" (Gen. 14:19). Daniel teaches that "the **Most High** is ruler over the realm of mankind and bestows it on whom He wishes" (Dan. 4:17). The evil King of Babylon and the wicked spirit behind him wanted to be as the Most High (Isa. 14:14). As *El Elyon,* God is the owner of all people and all things.

> And Melchizedek king of Salem brought out bread and wine; now he was a priest of **God Most High**. And he blessed him and said, "Blessed be Abram of **God Most High,** possessor of heaven and earth; and blessed be **God Most High**, Who has delivered your enemies into your hand." And he gave him a tenth of all [Gen. 14:18-20].

3. *El Olam* (Gen. 21:33) in English, "Eternal God, Everlasting God." He is the Being who always existed in the past and will always exist in the future.

> ...he called on the name of the LORD, the Everlasting God [Gen. 21:33].

4. *El Gibbor* (Isa. 9:6) occurs in reference to the Messiah. He is Mighty God. This phrase is used of brave fighting men in the vast majority of references. Messiah is courageous and valiant in battle.

B. *Yahweh*

Yahweh is the most common title for deity. It is used 5,321 times in the Old Testament and is translated by LORD (note all capitals) except seven times in the King James Version where it is translated Jehovah.[6] The Greek word is *kurios.* While *Elohim* (God) describes Him, God's real name is *YHWH.*

---

[4] (See, Harris, Archer, Waltke, ed. *Theological Wordbook of the Old Testament,* 2 vols. Chicago: Moody Press, 1980), 1:44-45.

[5] Ibid., 2:907.

[6] Ibid., 1:210-11.

1. Out of reverence, the ancient Jews would not pronounce God's name. Consequently, the vowel sounds have been lost. By tradition the vowels of Adonai have been inserted between the consonants *YHWH* to form *Ya-HoWai*. Germans pronounce *J* as *Y* as in Johann Sebastian Bach. They also pronounce *W*'s as *V*. Thus, a German would tend to spell the above hybrid with a *J* and give the *W* a *V* sound (JaHoVeh). English speaking peoples should have pronounced the *J* as *Y* (e.g., hallelujah), but we added a corrupt *J* sound to the already corrupted *V* sound of German. Thus, the combination of *YHWH* with the vowels of *Adonai* passed through German with the *W* sound as *V* and *Y* written as *J*, and through English with the *J* pronounced as *J*. The resulting "mutant" from Hebrew, German and English is "Jehovah." Hebrew does not even have a *J* in it! In reality we do not know for certain how to pronounce God's name. *Yahweh* is a good guess as the *Yah* sound is prominent in names and words (e.g., Isaiah, Jeremiah, Jehosaphat, Johnathan, Hallelujah, etc.).

2. Conservative theologians do not agree on the derivation of God's name. Maybe there is none. Some argue for a derivation from an archaic form of the Hebrew word *to be (HWH)* which in the Qal imperfect or Hiphil imperfect would become *YHWH*. There is some plausibility to this. When Moses spoke God's name, He replies, "I AM WHO I AM" (Ex. 3:14-15). Also, Christ claims deity by asserting, "I AM" (see John 8:58; also, Rev. 1:8). It is possible that God's name (*YHWH*) speaks of His self-existence or His being the source for the existence of everything else.

3. By observing its usage, some contend *YHWH* refers to the God of covenants. He is a God who enters into special relationships with specific people instead of being just the God of the universe as a whole. If the above derivation is correct, the name *YHWH* also speaks of a self-existent being. No one caused His existence. He is not dependent upon anybody or anything for sustenance.

4. There are several secondary names derived from *YHWH*.

a. *Yahweh-Sabaoth* (1 Sam. 17:45; Psa. 24:10; James 5:4). *Yahweh-Sabaoth* in English means "LORD of Hosts" or "LORD of Armies." The Greek is *Kurios Sabaoth*. It is interesting that God is never called "LORD of Hosts" in the Law of Moses, yet, this title is extremely popular with the prophets. It is used approximately 285 times including 62 times in Isaiah, 77 in Jeremiah, 53 in Zechariah, and 24 in Malachi.[7] The title "LORD of Hosts" teaches that God is a warrior and captain of both angelic and human forces. In His war with the evil one, He will not suffer loss.

> Then David said to the Philistine, "You come to me with a sword, a spear, and a javelin, but I come to you in the name of the **LORD of hosts**, the God of the armies of Israel, whom you have taunted" [1 Sam. 17:45].

> Who is the King of glory? **The LORD of hosts**, He is the King of glory [Psa. 24:10].

b. *Yahweh-Yireh* (Gen. 22:13-14) in English is Jehovah-Jireh. It means, "the LORD will provide." He is the caretaker for and sustainer of His people.

> And Abraham called the name of that place The **LORD Will Provide**...[Gen. 22:14a].

c. *Yahweh-Rapha* (Ex. 15:26) in English means "Jehovah-Rapha" meaning "the LORD that heals." He is the source for both spiritual and physical healing.

> For I, **the LORD, am your healer** [Ex. 15:26].

d. *Yahweh-Nissi* (Ex. 17:15) in English is Jehovah-Nissi and means "the LORD is my banner." This name has a similar idea to

---

[7] Ibid., 2:750.

"LORD of Hosts." The LORD protects, defends, and fights for His people.

> And Moses built an altar, and named it **The LORD is My Banner** [Ex. 17:15].

e. *Yahweh-Shalom* (Judg. 6:24) in English is Jehovah-Shalom and means "the LORD is our peace." The LORD sends peace into our lives. In salvation He gives peace with Himself (Rom. 5:1). In growth He gives His peace in our hearts (Phil. 4:7).

> Then Gideon built an altar there to the LORD and named it **The LORD is Peace** [Judg. 6:24].

f. *Yahweh-Rohi* (Psa. 23:1) is Jehovah-Rohi in English and means "The LORD is my shepherd." The LORD is our guide, our protector, and our provider.

> The LORD is my shepherd...[Psa. 23:1].

g. *Yawheh-Tsidkenu* (Jer. 23:6) is Jehovah-Tsidkenu in English and means "the LORD Our Righteousness." God the Son is our righteousness when we trust in Him (2 Cor. 5:21).

> ...and this is His name by which He will be called, **"The LORD our righteousness"** [Jer. 23:6].

C. *Adonai*

In the Old Testament the word *LORD* translates *(YHWH)*. The word *Lord* (lower case *ord*) translates Adonai. Adonai is technically not a name. It is a form of address and means "Master." The word can be used of either human masters or the divine Master. It is used approximately three hundred times of God and teaches us that God is our absolute authority in life.

VI. The Attributes of God

The attributes of God are those qualities which are the essential, permanent, and distinguishing features of His person. One sat-

isfying way to classify God's attributes is to divide His non-moral attributes from His moral attributes. Another possible strategy would be to list all attributes under either "infinity" or "goodness." A third would be to classify attributes under incommunicable (attributes humans can never share) or communicable (attributes that saved humans can share in glory).

A. God's Non-moral Attributes

1. God is Spirit.

Although God may assume bodily form either temporarily as in the Angel of the Lord or permanently as in Christ, God is not a physical being. God neither needs a body nor can His fullest essence be contained in a body alone. God's spiritual character also relates to His invisibility.

> God is **spirit**...[John 4:24].

> And He is the image of the **invisible** God [Col. 1:15].

> Now unto the King, eternal, immortal, **invisible**, the only God, be honor and glory forever and ever...[1 Tim. 1:17].

> ...and whom no man has seen or can see...[1 Tim. 6:16].

2. God is Eternal.

God is infinite in relation to time. He is without beginning and without ending. Eternality means not only that God dwells in unending duration from eternity past to eternity future, it also means He dwells in another dimension outside of time. To God all history appears past. The Lamb was slain before the foundation of the world (Rev. 13:8 NIV). The justified are as good as already glorified (See past tenses in Rom. 8:30). All history is also present (Ex. 3:14; John 8:58). We view the parade of time from the street corner. God above sees the whole parade past, present and future at once. Eternality seems to be an "infinite" attribute that is at least partially communicable to believers. (See Gen. 21:33; Ex. 3:14; Deut. 32:40; Job 36:26; Psa. 90:2; 93:2; 102:27; Isa. 9:6; 40:28; 41:4; 57:15; Micah 5:2; John 1:1; 8:58; Rom. 16:26; 1 Tim. 1:17; 6:16; Heb. 1:10-12; 2 Pet. 3:8; Rev. 1:4, 8; 10:6; 15:7).

...even from **everlasting to everlasting**, Thou art God [Psa. 90:2].

Do you not know? Have you not heard? **The Everlasting God**, the LORD, the creator of the ends of the earth does not become weary or tired...[Isa. 40:28].

For thus says the high and exalted **One who lives forever**...[Isa. 57:15].

Now to the King **eternal**...[1 Tim. 1:17].

...But Thou art the same, and **Thy years will not come to an end** [Heb. 1:12].

"I am the Alpha and the Omega," says the Lord God, "**Who is and who was and who is to come**, the Almighty" [Rev. 1:8].

3. God is Omnipresent.

God is not only infinite relative to time, He is also infinite relative to space. God is above being subject to time, and He is above being subject to space. He is ever present both in time and in space, and He is greater than either time or space. Nevertheless, the Bible teaches there is a special presence of God in certain places: heaven (Matt. 6:9; Col. 3:1; Heb. 1:3; 12:2), the tabernacle (Ex. 25:8; 40:34-35), the temple (Matt. 23:21), between the cherubim (Psa. 80:1), in Jerusalem (Matt. 5:35), inside believers (John 14:16-17, 23; Rom. 8:9-10; 1 Cor. 6:19-20), and with the humble (James 4:6-8; Isa. 57:15). The Bible also teaches there is a special removal of God's presence from the wicked and proud (Isa. 59:1-2; Hab. 1:13; 2 Thess. 1:8-9; 1 Pet. 3:12). Thus, difficult as it may be to grasp,

we must distinguish between a general presence of God in all places and a special presence of God in certain localities. Here are proof-texts for omnipresence: 1 Kings 8:27; 2 Chron. 2:6; 6:18; Psa. 139:7ff.; Prov. 15:3; Isa. 66:1; Jer. 23:24; Matt. 18:20; 28:20; Acts 17:27; Heb. 4:13; 13:5.

But will God indeed dwell on the earth? Behold, **heaven and the highest heaven cannot contain Thee**, how much less this house which I have built! [1 Kings 8:27].

Where can I go from Thy Spirit? **Or where can I flee from Thy presence**? If I ascend to heaven, Thou art there. If I make my bed in Sheol, behold, Thou art there [Psa. 139:7-8].

The eyes of the LORD are **in every place**, watching the evil and the good [Prov. 15:3].

"Can a man hide himself in hiding places, so I do not see him?" declares the LORD. "**Do I not fill the heavens and the earth**?" declares the LORD [Jer. 23:24].

4. God is Immutable.

Although God can and does vary His works, He never changes in His attributes. He is infinite in perfection. He cannot change for the better because He is already perfect. He cannot change for the worse, because He would no longer be perfect. This attribute relates to the dependability of God's promises and predictability in His standards (Mal. 3:6; James 1:17; Heb. 1:12, 13:8).

For I, the LORD, **do not change**; therefore you, O sons of Jacob, are not consumed [Mal. 3:6].

...but Thou art the **same**...[Heb. 1:12].

Jesus Christ is the **same yesterday and today, yes and forever** [Heb. 13:8].

Every good thing bestowed and every perfect gift is from above, coming down from the Father of lights, **with whom there is no variation**, or shifting shadow [James 1:17].

5. God is Omniscient.

God is infinite in knowledge. He knows about inanimate creation (Psa. 147:4), animals (Matt. 10:29), Sheol (Job 26:6; Psa. 139:8; Prov. 15:11), the days in a man's life (Job 14:5; Psa. 139:16), and hairs on a head (Matt. 10:30). God knows about the future (Isa. 41:22; 42:9; 44:7; 46:10; Acts 2:23) and about our needs before we discover them (Matt. 6:8, 32). Not only does God know all things actually in the future, He knows all things potentially in the future (1 Sam. 23:11-12; 2 Sam. 12:8; 2 Kings 13:19; Psa. 81:14-15; Jer. 1:5; 38:17-20; Ezek. 3:5-7; Matt. 11:21-24). God knows the most secret thoughts (1 Sam. 16:7; 1 Kings 8:39; 2 Chron. 16:9; Job 34:22; Psa. 44:21; 139:1, 4, 23-24; Prov. 16:2; Jer. 11:20; 17:9-10; 20:12; Ezek. 11:5; Luke 16:15; Rom. 8:27; 1 Cor. 3:20). God's omniscience is supported by many texts (Psa. 147:5; Isa. 40:13-14, 28; John 2:24; 16:30; 21:17; Rom. 11:33-34; 1 John 3:20).

Great is our Lord, and abundant in strength; **His understanding is infinite** [Psa. 147:5].

...His **understanding is inscrutable** [Isa. 40:28].

...Lord, You know all things... John 21:17].

Oh, the depth of the riches both of the **wisdom and knowledge of God!** How **unsearchable** are His judgments and **unfathomable** His ways! [Rom. 11:33].

...for **God** is greater than our heart, and **knows all things** [1 John 3:20].

6. God is Self-Existent.

Some call this "aseity." God is self-sufficient. He never has depended upon another for existence. He is the uncaused first cause, infinite in self-sufficiency.

For just as the Father has **life in Himself** ...[John 5:26].

...**I AM** WHO I AM...[Ex. 3:14 (see also John 8:58)].

For from Him and through Him and to Him are all things...[Rom. 11:36].

...the **first-born of all creation.** For [because] by Him all things were created... [Col. 1:15-16].

7. God is Omnipotent.

God is infinite in power. This assumes He will not do anything contrary to His own nature. He cannot deny Himself (2 Tim. 2:13), lie (Num. 23:19; 1 Sam. 15:29; Titus 1:2; Heb. 6:18), be tempted with evil (James 1:13), change (James 1:17), or tolerate sin (Hab. 1:13). This raises some interesting questions. Can God fit inside a shoebox? Can God make a rock so big that He cannot lift it? Some additional proof-texts for God's omnipotence can be found under a study of His names (see Gen. 17:1; 18:14; Ex. 6:3; Job 42:2; Psa. 62:11; Isa. 9:6; 26:4; Jer. 32:17, 27; Matt. 19:26; 28:18; Luke 1:37; 18:27; Eph. 3:20; Rev. 1:8; 4:8, 11; 16:14; 17:14; 19:6, 15-16).

Is anything too difficult for the LORD?...[Gen. 18:14].

Ah Lord God! Behold, Thou hast made the heavens and the earth by Thy great power and by thine outstretched arm! **Nothing is too difficult for Thee** [Jer. 32:17].

Behold, I am the LORD, the God of all flesh; **is anything too difficult for Me**? [Jer. 32:27].

..."With men this is impossible, but **with God all things are possible"** [Matt. 19:26].

For nothing will be impossible with God [Luke 1:37].

Now to Him who is **able to do** exceeding abundantly **beyond all that we ask or think**, according to the power that works within us... [Eph. 3:20].

They do not cease to say, "Holy, holy, holy is the LORD God, **the Almighty**, who was and who is and who is to come." [Rev. 4:8].

"Hallelujah! For the Lord our God, the **Almighty**, reigns" [Rev. 19:6].

...God the **Almighty**. And on His robe and on His thigh He has a name written, "**KING OF KINGS, AND LORD OF LORDS**" [Rev. 19:15, 16].

8. God is United

(See "The Unity and Trinity of the Godhead," section IV, p.17 of this chapter.)

B. God's Moral Attributes

1. God is Holy.

Holiness means God is separate and distinct from all His creatures, exalted above them, transcendent. Holiness also means that God is totally separate from all sin and impurity. Some theologians distinguish "majestic holiness" from "ethical holiness." Majestic holiness means God is separate, transcendent above His creatures. Ethical holiness means He is separate from any sin. Holy is used approximately 699 times in the Old Testament with 111 of these references referring to an attribute of God. The New Testament contains 230 references to holiness. (Approximately 94 of these attribute holiness to the Holy Spirit, 6 to God the Father, and 3 to God the Son.) The last 4 references in this list concerning God's holiness do not contain the word *holy* but assert that God the Son is "without sin" (Ex. 15:11; Lev. 11:44; 19:2; 20:26; 21:8; Josh. 24:19; 1 Sam. 2:2; 6:20;

Job 6:10; Psa. 22:3; 30:4; 47:8; 60:6; 89:35; 92:15; 97:12; 99:3, 5, 9; 145:17; Isa. 5:16; 6:3; 43:14; 47:4; 49:7; 57:15; Ezek. 39:7; Hos. 11:9; Hab. 1:12-13; Luke 1:49; John 17:11; Heb. 12:10; 1 Pet. 1:15-16; Rev. 4:8; 15:4; Mark 1:24; Luke 4:34; John 6:69; 8:46; 2 Cor. 5:21; Heb. 4:15; 1 Pet. 2:22).

...who is like Thee, **majestic in holiness...**? [Ex. 15:11].

...and be holy; **for I am holy**... [Lev. 11:44].

And one called out to another and said, "**Holy, Holy, Holy, is the LORD of hosts**, the whole earth is full of His glory" [Isa. 6:3].

For thus says the high and exalted One Who lives forever, **whose name is Holy** [Isa. 57:15].

"Art Thou not from everlasting, O LORD, my God, **my Holy One**? ...Thine eyes are **too pure to approve evil**." [Hab. 1:12-13].

...saying, "What do we have to do with You, Jesus of Nazareth? Have You come to destroy us? I know who You are **the Holy One** of God!" [Mark 1:24].

...**Holy Father**, keep them in Thy name... [John 17:11].

...who **committed no sin**, nor was any deceit found in his mouth [1 Pet. 2:22].

2. God is True.

To say that God is true involves at least three distinguishing concepts. First, God gives factual truth. Secondly, He is true in the sense of being reliable and dependable as in the phrase "a true friend." Thirdly, to say God is true means He is the real or genuine God as opposed to false or counterfeit gods. One could say that God is true in the sense of being factually true, ethically true, and metaphysically true. The proof-texts for God being factually and ethically true overlap.

a. God is factually true (Ex. 34:6; John 14:6, 17; 15:26; 16:13; 17:17; 1 John 4:6). These verses contain the following phrases: "**I am** the way, and **the Truth**," "the **Spirit of truth**," and "**Thy Word is truth**." God does not make factual error. He is always correct.

b. God is ethically true. God is trustworthy and reliable. His ethical truth is a synonym for His faithfulness. God would never lie to us or mislead us. He is not only factually correct, but He is faithful to His promises (Num. 23:19; Deut. 32:4; 1 Sam. 15:29; 2 Sam. 7:28; Psa. 19:9; 25:10; 31:5; 33:4; 36:5; 57:3; 89:14; 111:7; 119:86, 142, 151; 138:2; Isa. 25:1; Jer. 5:3; Lam. 3:23; Rom. 1:25; 3:4; 1 Cor 1:9; 2 Cor. 1:20; 1 Thess. 5:24; Titus 1:2; Heb. 6:18).

> God is **not a man, that He should lie**, nor a son of man, that He should repent; has He said, and will He not do it? Or has He spoken, and will He not make it good? [Num. 23:19].

> And also **the Glory of Israel will not lie** or change His mind; for He is not a man that He should change His mind [1 Sam 15:29].

> Thy lovingkindness, O LORD, extends to the heavens, **thy faithfulness reaches to the skies** [Psa. 36:5].

> They are new every morning; **Great is Thy faithfulness** [Lam. 3:23].

> ...let **God be found true**, though every man be found a liar...[Rom. 3:4].

> God is **faithful**...[1 Cor. 1:9].

> **Faithful** is He who calls you, and He also will bring it to pass [1 Thess. 5:24].

> ...God who **cannot lie**...[Titus 1:2].

> ...it is **impossible for God to lie**...[Heb. 6:18].

c. God is metaphysically true. God is real and genuine. All other claims to deity are false.

> But the LORD is the **true God**...[Jer. 10:10].

> And this is eternal life that they may know Thee, **the only true God**...[John 17:3].

> ...and how you turned to God from idols to serve a living and **true God** [1 Thess. 1: 9].

> ...This is the **true God** and eternal Life [1 John 5:20].

3. God is Good.

The idea that God is good encompasses a massive amount of truth and numerous characteristics (mercy, longsuffering, grace, love, kindness, gentleness, and possibly even ethical holiness which equals sinlessness and ethical truth which equals faithfulness). While some would classify each of the above as a separate attribute, it is perhaps more logical to view them all as extensions of God's goodness.

> **For the LORD is good**; His lovingkindness is everlasting, and His faithfulness to all generations [Psa. 100:5].

> The **LORD is good** to all and His mercies are over all His works [Psa. 145:9].

> And Jesus said to him, "Why do you call Me good? **No one is good except God** alone" [Mark 10:18].

> **Every good thing** bestowed and every perfect gift is from above, coming down **from the Father** of lights...[James 1:17].

a. God is merciful. God's mercy is an expression of His goodness toward those who are in misery or distress. It is similar to pity or compassion (Psa. 103:13; 116:5; Isa. 55:7; Lam. 3:22; Matt. 9:13, 36; Luke 1:50; Rom. 11:32; 12:1; 15:9; 2 Cor. 1:3-4; Eph. 2:4; Phil. 1:8; Titus 3:5; Heb. 2:17; 4:16; James 5:11; 1 Pet. 1:3).

Just as a father has compassion on his children, so the LORD **has compassion** on those who fear Him [Psa. 103:13].

[T]he LORD'S **lovingkindnesses** indeed never cease, for His compassions never fail [Lam. 3:22].

And seeing the multitudes, He felt **compassion** for them...[Matt. 9:36].

...that He might show **mercy to all** [Rom. 11:32].

But God, being **rich in mercy**...[Eph. 2:4].

He saved us, not on the basis of deeds which we have done in righteousness, but according to His **mercy**...[Titus 3:5].

Let us therefore draw near with confidence to the throne of grace, that we may receive **mercy** and may find grace to help in time of need [Heb. 4:16].

...who according to His great **mercy** has caused us to be born again [1 Pet. 1:3].

b. God is longsuffering. Longsuffering is an expression of God's goodness towards those who deserve punishment. He is patient with those who deserve immediate punishment (Ex. 34:6; Num. 14:18; Neh. 9:17; Psa. 86:15; 103:8; 145:8; Joel 2:13; Jonah 4:2; Nah. 1:3; Rom. 2:4; 3:25; 9:22; 1 Tim. 1:16; 2:4; 2 Pet. 3:9,15).

..."The LORD, the LORD God, compassionate and gracious, **slow to anger**..." [Ex. 34:6].

The LORD is compassionate and gracious, **slow to anger** and abounding in lovingkindness [Psa. 103:8].

The Lord is **slow to anger**...[Nahum 1:3].

Or do you think lightly of the riches of His kindness and **forbearance** and **patience**...? [Rom. 2:4].

And yet for this reason I found mercy, in order that in me as the foremost, Jesus Christ might demonstrate His **perfect patience**...[1 Tim. 1:16].

The Lord is not slow about His promise, as some count slowness, but is **patient** toward you, not wishing for any to perish but for all to come to repentance [2 Pet. 3:9].

c. God is gracious. God's grace is also an expression of His goodness to those deserving punishment. However, there is a distinction between being longsuffering and being gracious. In being longsuffering, God withholds punishment to those who deserve punishment. On the other hand, being gracious is not just negatively withholding punishment, it is positively showing kindness and favor to those who deserve wrath and punishment. God's grace is undeserved favor, unmerited kindness (Ex. 34:6; John 1:14,17; Rom. 3:24; 5:20; Eph. 2:7-9; Titus 2:11; 1 Pet. 5:10).

..."The LORD, the LORD God, compassionate and **gracious**..." [Ex. 34:6].

...and we beheld His glory, glory as of the only begotten from the Father, **full of grace** and truth....For the law was given through Moses; **grace** and truth were realized through Jesus Christ [John 1:14, 17].

...the surpassing **riches of His grace**...[Eph. 2:7].

...the **God of all grace**...[1 Pet. 5:10].

d. God is love. God's love is an expression of His goodness. It is a commitment to do what is best for the objects of His love regardless of the pain or cost. God's love is eternal, sacrificial and unconditional. One could classify kindness and gentleness under love (John 3:16; 15:13; Rom. 5:8; Gal. 2:20; 1 John 3:1; 4:8-10).

> For God so **loved** the world...[John 3:16].

> Greater **love** has no one than this, that one lay down his life for his friends [John 15:13].

> But God demonstrates His own **love** toward us, in that while we were yet sinners, Christ died for us [Rom. 5:8].

> ...**who** loved me, and delivered Himself up for me [Gal. 2:20].

> ...**God is love** [1 John 4:8].

4. God is Righteous or Just.

Some would combine the attributes of righteousness and holiness, especially ethical holiness. However, in both Hebrew and Greek the words for righteousness differ from the words for holiness. Unlike holiness, righteousness conveys action. To say God is holy means He is separate from sin. He is holy because of what He does not do. To say God is righteous means He acts in righteousness and must demand that all other creatures do so as well. Holiness is more intransitive and pertains to His transcendence. It is what God is. Righteousness has been called God's "transitive holiness." It involves what a Holy God does and insists others do. It pertains more to His immanence.[8] By the righteous-

ness and justice of God we mean that phase of the holiness of God which is seen in His treatment of creatures. God is called righteous or just approximately 112 times in the Old Testament and 44 times in the New Testament (see Deut. 10:17; 32:4; Job 37:23; Psa. 19:9; 33:5; 89:14; 92:15; 96:13; 103:6; 111:7; Jer. 9:23-24; John 17:25; Acts 3:14; 17:31; Rom. 3:26; 2 Thess. 1:5-9; and 1 John 2:1).

> **For all His ways are just**; a God of faithfulness and **without injustice**, righteous and upright is He [Deut. 32:4].

> He loves **righteousness** and **justice**...[Psa. 33:5].

> **Righteousness and justice** are the foundation of thy throne...[Psa. 89:14].

> ...there is **no unrighteousness** in Him [Psa. 92:15].

> ...I am the LORD who exercises lovingkindness, justice, and **righteousness** on earth...[Jer. 9:24].

> O **righteous** Father...[John 17:25].

> But you disowned the Holy and **Righteous** One...[Acts 3:14].

> ...an advocate with the Father, Jesus Christ the **righteous** [1 John 2:1].

5. God is Wise.

To say that God is wise can be different than saying He is omniscient. God is more than an "infinite computer." He knows all, but He also can choose the best means for the best end.

He is wisdom in that He applies His omniscience to the best possible control of the universe (Psa. 19:7; Prov. 1:7; 8:22, 27; Rom. 16:27; 1 Cor. 1:24, 30).

---

[8] The author is indebted to George Pardington for these thoughts. (George Pardington, *Outline Studies in Christian Doctrine* (Harrisburg, PA: Christian Publications, Inc., 1926) 80.

The LORD possessed me [wisdom] at the beginning of His way....When He established the heavens, I [wisdom] was there...[Prov. 8:22, 27].

...Christ Jesus, who became to us **wisdom**...[1 Cor. 1:30].

6. God is Blessed.

In references to God's inner character, *blessed* means God is completely and eternally satisfied with Himself. He is joyful and content with His own perfection. It is best not to view this as an attribute. Rather God is inwardly blessed because of His perfections from His attributes. Human happiness is grounded in this aspect of God's person. Our God, perfect in Person and works, is the source of our satisfaction in life. The sum of His attributes equals perfection. This perfection makes Him inwardly "blessed."

...the glorious gospel of the **blessed** God...[1 Tim. 1:11].

...He who is the **blessed** and only Sovereign, the King of kings and Lord of lords [1 Tim. 6:15].

7. God is Glorious.

The sum of God's perfection results in His internal blessedness and also His external glory. Again, glory is not an attribute in the truest sense. God is glorious in all of His attributes. Humans should recognize God's glory and glorify Him (Psa. 24:7-10; 96:3; 138:5; Isa. 6:3; 42:8; Matt. 25:31; John 1:14; 17:5; Rom. 3:23; Eph. 1:17; Heb. 1:3; James 2:1).

I am the LORD, that is My name; I will not give **My glory** to another...[Isa. 42:8].

And the Word became flesh, and dwelt among us, and we beheld His **glory**, glory as of the only begotten from the Father, full of grace and truth [John 1:14].

...that the God of our Lord Jesus Christ, the **Father of glory**... [Eph. 1:17].

And He [the Son] is the radiance of His [the Father's] **glory**...[Heb. 1:3].

My brethren, do not hold your faith in our **glorious** Lord Jesus Christ with an attitude of personal favoritism [James 2:1].

Chapter 3
ANGELOLOGY
The Doctrine of Angels

ANGELOLOGY:
THE DOCTRINE OF ANGELS

I. The Existence of Angels

Angels are not the main characters of Scripture. Yet, if they were removed from the Bible, many of the Bible's greatest texts would be greatly altered (e.g., Christ's birth, temptation, agony in the garden, resurrection, and ascension). There are references to angels and cherubim in thirty-four of the sixty-six books (seventeen in each Testament). The Hebrew word for angel, *Malak*, is related to Malachi, "my messenger." Chafer counted at least 108 references to angels in the Old Testament.[1] The Greek word for angel is *aggelos* from which evangelism is partially derived. Angels occur approximately 165 times in the New Testament.[2] The Lord Jesus Christ taught the existence of angels clearly. The Sadducees neither believed in the resurrection nor in angels. In one line Christ criticized them on both counts by saying that in the resurrection people would be like angels in respect to marriage (Matt. 22:30). The Lord said angels would come with Him at His Second Coming (Matt. 24:31; 25:31). He said He could call more than twelve legions of

---

[1] Lewis Sperry Chafer, *Systematic Theology*, vol. 2 (Dallas: Dallas Seminary Press, 1947) 3. His statistics appear generally accurate, but there are many more if references to cherubim and seraphim are included.
[2] Ibid.

angels to prevent His crucifixion (Matt. 26:53). People who respect Jesus Christ are going to accept the existence of angels.

II. The Origin of Angels

A. All Things Created by God

God created all things, for He alone has immortality. By deduction, all beings must be created, including angels.

> All things came into being by Him... [John 1:3].

> For by Him **all things were created**, both **in the heavens** and on the earth, visible and invisible, whether thrones or dominions or rulers or authorities - all things have been created by Him and for Him [Col. 1:16].

> [W]ho alone possesses immortality... [1 Tim. 6:16].

B. Angels Mentioned in God's Creative Work

> Praise Him, all His **angels**; Praise Him, all His hosts!...Let them praise the name of the LORD, for He commanded and **they were created** [Psa. 148:2, 5].

C. Time of Angelic Creation

In chapters one and two of Job, the term *sons of God* is used of spirit beings including Satan. Also, it seems that often stars and angels are grouped together as in the phrase *heavenly hosts*.[3] These two facts lead one to believe Job 38:4-7 is teaching that angels were created **before the earth**.

> "Where were you when I laid the foundation of the earth! Tell Me, if you have understanding....When the morning **stars** sang together, and all the **sons of God** shouted for joy?" [Job 38:4, 7].

If the *sons of God* in Job 38 are not angels,

[3] In Deut. 4:19 and Zeph. 1:5 *hosts* means *stars*, but in 1 Kings 22:19 and Luke 2:13 *hosts* means *angels*. See also Rev. 12:1-4.

then who are they? They cannot be humans as they exist before the earth. Psa. 148:2ff. associates the creation of angels with the creation of the rest of the physical universe. Ex. 20:11 teaches that "in six days The LORD made the **heavens** and the earth, the sea, and **all** that is in them...." It is preferable, therefore, to view the creation of angels as taking place on the first creative day, perhaps after the heavens but before the earth.

D. Angels Created as Angels

Some naively assume that angels are exalted or glorified humans. The Bible teaches that angels were created as angels without any transformation from something else. Heb. 12:22-23 gives a list of heaven's inhabitants and lists "myriads of angels" separate from "spirits of just men made perfect." In the description of heaven found in Rev. 21-22 angels and humans are distinct. Humans will not become angels in the future, rather believing humans will judge the angels (1 Cor. 6:3).

E. Population of Angels

At creation the number of angels was fixed for all eternity. They never die. They never reproduce (Matt. 22:30; Mark: 12:25; Luke 20:35-36). Since chapter two of Genesis indicates that God is no longer involved with creative work, the number of angels must remain constant.

> "[B]ut those who are considered worthy to attain to that age and the resurrection from the dead, neither marry, nor are given in marriage; for neither can they die anymore, for they are like angels, and are sons of God, being sons of the resurrection" [Luke 20:35-36].

The exact number of angels is a mystery, but there are many indications that it is an extremely large number.

1. Since "host of heaven" can refer to either stars or angels, the inference may be drawn

that the number of angels is just as impossible to count as the stars.

2. Heb. 12:22 mentions "myriads of angels." Thus, they can be grouped by lots of 10,000. This is also true in Psa. 68:17; Dan. 7:10; and Rev. 5:11. 2 Kings 6:17 and Luke 2:13 use general terms speaking of "multitudes" of angels.

> The chariots of God are myriads, thousands upon thousands [Psa. 68:17].

> "...thousands upon thousands were attending Him, and myriads upon myriads were standing before Him..." [Dan. 7:10].

> And I looked, and I heard the voice of many angels around the throne and the living creatures and the elders; and the number of them was myriads of myriads, and thousands of thousands [Rev. 5:11].

3. Christ indicated He had more than twelve legions of angels at His disposal (Matt. 26:53).

F. Purpose of Angelic Creation

Angels were created to be God's servants. This could be deduced from statements about creation in general (Rom. 11:36; Col. 1:16; Rev. 4:11). However, the Bible gives specifics as to angelic creation.

> And of the angels He says, "Who makes His **angels** winds, and His ministers a flame of fire"....Are they not all ministering spirits, sent out to **render service for the sake of those who will inherit salvation**? [Heb. 1:7, 14].

G. Angels and Sin

Since God can neither be tempted with evil (James 1:13) nor can He stand the presence of sin (Hab. 1:12-13), it is certain that He did not create angels with sin; they were all created holy.

H. Limitations of Angels

The following references will establish that angels have superhuman abilities. They are, however, still creatures. They cannot be in more than one place at a time. Gabriel needed time to travel (Dan. 9:21-23). An unnamed angel was delayed on his journey. Thus, angels have limits to their strength (Dan. 10:13). Rev. 12:7 mentions struggles between holy and unholy angels. Finally, angels have limitations in knowledge. They do not know the time of the Second Coming (Matt. 24:36). They learn by watching the Church (Eph. 3:10; 1 Tim. 3:16; 5:21; 1 Pet. 1:12; possibly also 1 Cor. 11:10). In summary, angels are creatures and are not omnipresent, omnipotent, or omniscient.

III. The Nature of Angels

A. Angels and Personhood

The standard definition for personhood is a self-conscious being who has intellect, emotions, and will. By this definition, angels would be classified as persons. They must have intelligence to learn (Eph. 3:10; 1 Pet. 1:12), emotions to praise and worship (Job 38:7; Isa. 6:3; Rev. 5:11-12) and to appreciate God's joy (Luke 15:10), and a will to obey His commands (Matt. 24:31; Heb. 1:6).

B. Angels and Holiness

Consistency dictates that a holy God created the angels holy. Since angels are called *the sons of God* (Job 1:6; 2:1; 38:7), they were undoubtedly created in God's image. The Bible teaches that some angels are still holy and will be holy at Christ's Second Coming (Mark 8:38; Luke 9:26; Acts 10:22; Rev. 14:10). The fact that some angels are called *His chosen angels* (1 Tim. 5:21) and that they will still be sinless at the Second Coming causes most Bible teachers to conclude that holy angels have been confirmed in holiness. It is no longer possible for these angels to sin or rebel against God. The good angels are, in all probability, incapable of sinning.

C. Angels and Power

1. Relative to Man

The Bible teaches directly and by example that angels have superhuman powers. Heb. 2:7 and 9 describe humanity as being lower than the angels for "a little" (probably a little time). Angels destroyed Sodom (Genesis 19). An angel killed 185,000 of the Assyrian army (Isaiah 37), and Scripture implies that an angel killed 70,000 Hebrews (2 Samuel 24). One angel could have destroyed Jerusalem (2 Samuel 24). Elisha prayed and his servant saw that the Syrian army would be no match for God's hosts (2 Kings 6). Angels are mentioned in Revelation more than any other book. Their powers during the end time will be truly incredible. They seem to have power over winds, power over fire, and power over the sun (Rev. 7:1; 14:18-19; 16:8-9) and will assist in destroying Antichrist at Armageddon (Rev. 14:18). In the future, exalted humans are going to be superior to angels (Heb. 2:5ff.; Rom. 8:17).[4]

> Bless the LORD, you His angels, **mighty in strength**, who perform His word, obeying the voice of His word! [Psa. 103:20].

> [W]hereas angels who are **greater in might and power**…[2 Pet. 2:11].

2. Relative to God

While angels are superhuman in power, they have limitations and are subject to God's authority (2 Sam. 24:16; Rev. 7:1-4). Angelic conflicts reveal limitations in power (Dan. 10:13, 20; Jude 9; Rev. 12:7-9). The main point of Heb. 1:4ff. is that Christ is superior to angels.

> …**Christ**…**far above** all rule and authority and power and dominion…[Eph. 1:20-21].

> [W]ho is at the right hand of God, having gone into heaven, after **angels** and authorities and powers had been **subjected to Him** [1 Pet. 3:22].

D. Angels and Physical Material

Although angels may appear in physical form, they are by nature spirit beings (Psa. 104:4; Heb. 1:7,14; also, in reference to fallen angels, Eph. 6:12). By assuming that demons are fallen angels, we could infer that a legion of holy angels could also occupy the same space (Mark 5:9, 13; Luke 8:30). Thus, they are not physical beings limited by space. To say angels are spirit beings does not mean they are omnipresent. It took one angel three weeks to travel, and another was subject to delay (Dan. 10:12ff., see also Dan. 9:21-23).

> And of the angels He says, "Who makes his **angels winds**, and his ministers a **flame of fire**."…Are they not all ministering **spirits**, sent out to render service for the sake of those who will inherit salvation? [Heb. 1:7, 14].

E. Angelic Immortality and Gender

Angels are immortal (Luke 20:35-36). Although they appear as men and masculine pronouns are used of them (Genesis 19), it is also possible that they are in reality without gender. Masculine pronouns are also used of the Holy Spirit, and He is not a man. The inability of angels to reproduce can also be explained by thinking they are sexless as opposed to thinking they are all males. With spirit beings, a distinction must be made between appearance and essence.[5]

---

[4] Because the Hebrew is the same for "The Angel of the LORD" and "an angel of the LORD," it is sometimes difficult to tell whether a destroying action occurs from God the Son as "The Angel of the LORD" or an ordinary angel. Even if some of these examples of major destruction were God the Son and not an ordinary angel, there is still ample proof that angels are superior to men in power.

---

[5] Angels are spirits (Heb. 1:14). By definition a spirit does not inherently possess flesh and blood (see Christ's remarks in Luke 24:39). Angels seem

IV. Appearance of Angels

Angels are spirit beings and are normally invisible. However, if God wills for them to appear, they can become visible to man.

A. On Earth

When angels are seen in an earthly setting, they usually look like humans and are always male (unless Zech. 5:9ff. is interpreted to be the only exception). When some angels came to visit Abraham and Sarah, they sat, walked, ate, and spoke as ordinary humans (Genesis 18). The author of Hebrews probably has this incident in mind when he says, "some have entertained angels without knowing it" (Heb. 13:2). The angels looked so human that the perverted Sodomites wanted to abuse them sexually (Gen. 19:1, 5). Other occasions when angels appeared as men include Mark 16:5; Luke 24:4; and Acts 1:10. Often while angels appeared as "men", they appeared as superhuman men in the sense of having a dazzling and terrifying radiance both from their person and their apparel (Dan. 10:5ff.; Matt. 28:3; Luke 24:4).

B. In Non-earthly Settings

When angels appear on earth, they appear basically human; but when they appear in other settings, they appear as unusual creatures.

1. The Seraphim in Isaiah 6 have six wings.

2. The Cherubim in Chapters one and ten of Ezekiel have the following features:

- Four faces on one head (man, lion, ox, eagle)
- Four wings

to always appear as men in earthly surroundings. However, when they appear in heavenly surroundings they do not look like men. Their essence seems to be without gender. Also, it is more reasonable to suppose God created the angels sexless (and thereby incapable of reproduction) than to suppose He created countless male angels but no corresponding female angels.

- Full of eyes
- Lacking knee joints
- Hoofed feet
- A wheel below them so that they never turn (a gyroscope mechanism?)
- Human hands under wings

3. The Living Creatures in Rev. 4:6-8 have the following:

- many eyes,
- six wings
- faces of a man, lion, calf, eagle

4. An angel in Rev. 10:1-3 is

- clothed with a cloud
- has a rainbow for a crown

V. The Names and Classifications of Angels

A. General Names

- *Angels* = messengers
- *Ministering spirits* (Heb. 1:14) = servants
- *Heavenly hosts* (Luke 2:13) = God's armies
- *Watchers* (Dan. 4:13-17) = observers and supervisors of civil governments
- *Sons of God* (Job 1:6; 2:1; 38:7) = original character in God's image
- *Stars* (cf. Rev. 12:3-4, 9) = those who dwell in heaven

B. Specific Names and Classifications

1. There is a surprising number of references to cherubim (singular, *cherub*) in the Old Testament (over ninety). The first angels in the Bible are cherubim that guarded Eden lest man return (Gen. 3:24). Cherubim were embroidered on tapestries for the tabernacle, and golden cherubim were built into the ark (Ex. 25:17-22; 26:1, 31). The appearance of cherubim is described in Ezek. 10:1ff. and probably also Ezek. 1:4-28. God's presence is often indicated by the phrase *enthroned above the cherubim* or *sits above the cherubim* (see 1 Sam. 4:4; 2 Sam. 6:2; 2 Kings 19:15; 1 Chron. 13:6; Psa. 80:1; 99:1; see also Psa. 18:9-10). An inference from Gen. 3:24 is that cherubim guard the holiness of God. They are also indicators of His presence. The symbolism of the tabernacle has a correspondence in heaven.

Just as the cherubim surrounded the presence of God above the ark, so they must surround His presence on the heavenly throne.

2. *Seraphim* is only used twice in reference to angelic beings (Isa. 6:2, 6). It seems to be derived from the Hebrew word *to burn*. They are flashy fiery creatures. Their purpose seems to be to direct worship to God.

3. Michael is one of only two angels who are named in Scripture. The name means "who is like God?" and is given five times (Dan. 10:13, 21; 12:1; Jude 9; Rev. 12:7).

Angels seem to be ranked as in a military organization (Rom. 8:38; Eph. 1:21; 3:10; 6:12; Col. 1:16; 2:10, 15). Michael is said to be one among the chief princes in Dan. 10:13. Yet, he is the only angel that is called *the archangel* (Jude 9), and he will lead angelic armies against Satan in the Tribulation (Rev. 12:7ff.). Perhaps there are other angels comparable to him, but he is the archangel by virtue of being in charge of protecting Israel (Dan. 10:21; 12:1). Michael will probably be instrumental in announcing the Rapture (1 Thess. 4:16).

4. The angel Gabriel, "Mighty one of God," is mentioned four times in Scripture (Dan. 8:16; 9:21; Luke 1:19, 26). Gabriel is not called an archangel. He seems to be a special messenger. He interpreted visions for Daniel and announced the births of John the Baptist and Christ.

VI. The Abode of Angels

Although angels may visit earth and probably either live in or visit the stellar heavens (as stars and angels are paired together), the Bible presents their main habitation as being heaven. Luke 1:19 says, "I am Gabriel, who stands in the presence of God…" (see also Luke 15:10). Other pertinent phrases are "angels in heaven" (Matt. 22:30) and "an angel from heaven" (Gal. 1:8).

VII. The Duties of Angels

A. Past Works

The past works of angels are too numerous to give all the details. They witnessed creation (Job 38:7). They helped bring plagues on Egypt and were present at the giving of the law (Psa. 78:43, 49; Gal. 3:19; Heb. 2:2). They announced the births of John the Baptist and Christ (Luke 1:11-13, 26-37). They strengthened Christ at His temptation and in Gethsemane (Matt. 4:11; Luke 22:43). They announced the resurrection (Matt. 28:1-2, 6) and observed the ascension (Acts 1:10).

B. Present Works

1. Angels protect believers. There is reason to believe in such things as guardian angels. Whether they are present all the time and whether a specific angel is assigned to each believer is unknown. We do know that one angelic duty is to protect and assist believers when dangers arise.

> The angel of the LORD **encamps around those who fear Him**, and rescues them [Psa. 34:7].

> For He will give His angels charge concerning you, **to guard you in all your ways**, they will bear you up in their hands, lest you strike your foot against a stone [Psa. 91:11-12].

> "See that you do not despise one of these little ones, for I say to you, that **their angels in heaven** continually behold the face of My Father who is in heaven" [Matt. 18: 10].

> Are they not all ministering spirits, sent out to render **service for the sake of those who will inherit salvation?** [Heb. 1:14].

2. Angels probably assist in working out God's answers to prayer. The evidence for this is an example from Daniel's life. A being sent in response to Daniel's prayer mentions Michael as a colleague in Dan. 10:13; therefore, he seems to be angelic. There is every reason to assume that God works by similar methods today.

"**At the beginning of your supplications the command was issued, and I have come** to tell you, for you are highly esteemed..." [Dan. 9:23].

Then he said to me, "Do not be afraid, Daniel, for from the first day that you set your heart on understanding this and on humbling yourself before your God, **your words were heard, and I have come in response to your words**" [Dan. 10:12].

3. One of the duties of angels is to take souls to heaven. The story of the rich man and Lazarus implies that angels transport the souls of other believers to paradise.

"Now it came about that the poor man died and he was **carried away by the angels** to Abraham's bosom..." [Luke 16:22].

4. Another duty of angels is to be involved with civil government. It seems that both elect and evil angels have members assigned to influence in the kingdoms of the world. Dan. 10:13 and 20 mention the wicked "prince of Persia" and "prince of Greece". Michael is the holy angel assigned to Israel (Dan. 10:21; 12:1).

C. Future Works

Angels will be involved in the Rapture (1 Thess. 4:16). They will be judged by humans (1 Cor. 6:3). They will be involved in meting out God's judgment in the Tribulation (Rev. 8:2ff.; 16:1ff.). The angelic hosts will assist in the battle of Armageddon (Rev. 14:18-19), will return with Christ, and will assist in bringing the peoples of the world for judgment (Matt. 24:31; 25:31). Near the end of the Bible, John writes of an angel binding Satan in the abyss (Rev. 20:1-2).

Chapter 4

SATANOLOGY
The Doctrine of Satan

SATANOLOGY: THE DOCTRINE OF SATAN

I. The Existence of Satan

Satan is not emphasized in the Old Testament although there is enough material to confirm his existence. There is no Hebrew word that corresponds to *devil*. Satan is a term used of God's evil opponent sixteen times in three Old Testament passages (1 Chron. 21:1; Job 1-2; Zech. 3). The serpent in Genesis 3 is not called Satan in the Old Testament, but it is clear from Rev. 12:9 that the serpent in Genesis is Satan. The New Testament more strongly emphasizes Satan's existence. Every New Testament author refers to either "Satan" or "Devil." Nineteen of twenty-seven books mention the devil by some name. Twenty-three out of twenty-seven mention either the devil or demons by some name. Christ speaks of Satan twenty-five times.[1] For those who respect the authority of the Bible and of Christ, the existence of Satan is a settled issue.

II. The Personality of Satan

Some think that "Satan" is a force or influence rather than a personal being. Often it is implied that Satan is just another term for evil or temptation. The Scripture teaches that Satan is a personal being.

A. The Elements of Personhood

Satan has intellect. He is full of wisdom (Ezek. 28:12,17). He schemes and deceives (Gen. 3:1ff.; 2 Cor. 11:3; Rev. 12:9). Satan has emotions. He will have "great wrath" when his time is short (Rev. 12:12). Satan has a will. Being the tempter, he tries to influence choices (e.g., Luke 4:3, 9). He will be very persistent and stubborn in opposing God even when he knows it is hopeless (Rev. 20: 7-9).

B. Personal Pronouns

The Bible uses personal pronouns to refer to Satan (Matt. 4:10; John 8:44; 2 Cor. 11:14-15).

C. Moral Accountability

Inanimate objects do not have moral accountability, but Satan is going to be punished (Matt. 25:41; John 12:31; 16:11).

III. Names and Titles for Satan

A. Lucifer (Isa. 14:12-14)

This is the King James Version translation of the Hebrew *Helel* which means "shining one," "son of dawn," or "morning star." Isaiah 14 may have some reference to Satan (although the link is debatable). If Isaiah 14 is a reference to Satan, the name "shining one" speaks of Satan's original glory and majesty. If Isaiah 14 does not include Satan as the power behind the king of Babylon, Paul still teaches the devil is a "shining one" in 2 Cor. 11:14.

> "How art thou fallen from heaven, O **Lucifer**, son of the morning!..." [Isa. 14:12 (KJV)].

B. Satan

Satan is a Hebrew word that means "to resist, to be an adversary, to impede progress." The word is used a total of twenty-five times in the Old Testament (sixteen of them referring to Satan) and thirty-six times in the New Testament.[2] Passages which use the word *Satan* in its original sense of "resist" give insight into Satan's character.

> But God was angry because he [Balaam] was going, and the angel of the LORD took his stand in the way as **an adversary** [Hebrew *Satan*] against him... [Num. 22:22; see also 32].

> "...lest in the battle he [David] become an **adversary** [Hebrew *Satan*] to us..." [1 Sam. 29:4].

> ...Satan standing at his right hand **to resist** [Hebrew *Satan*] him [Zech. 3:1 (KJV)].

---

[1] C. Fred Dickason, *Angels Elect and Evil* (Chicago: Moody Press, 1975) 116.

[2] One could add Psa. 109:6.

C. Devil

The term *devil* is not in the Old Testament. *Devil* is strictly a New Testament word occurring thirty-eight times with thirty-five occurrences speaking of the person. Rev. 12:9 clearly equates Satan with devil, as do Matt. 4:1-11 and Mark 4:15 taken with its parallel passage, Luke 8:12. The Greek term is *diabolos* from which is derived "diabolical." The word *devil* means "slanderer" or "accuser." In Rev. 12:10 the devil is called "the accuser of our brethren." The original meaning of *diabolos* gives insight into Satan's character.

1. Uses of *Diabolos*

   ...not **malicious gossips** (Greek *diabolos*)... [1 Tim. 3:11].

   ...in the last days difficult times will come. For men will be...**malicious gossips** (Greek *diabolos*)...[2 Tim. 3:1-3].

   Older women likewise are to be reverent in their behavior, not **malicious gossips** (Greek *diabolos*)...[Titus 2:3].

2. Etymology of *diabolos*

Dia means "through," as in "diameter," the line through a circle's center. *Bolos* is related to *ballo*, to throw or cast. A *diabolos,* then, was originally a person who cast a verbal spear or made a wedge between others. The devil accuses by lies (or even the truth) to separate. He wishes believers to accuse self to God, brother to brother, and self to self.

D. Old Serpent (Rev. 12:9; 20:2)

By calling the devil *the serpent of old* in Rev. 12:9 and 20:2, John links him to the fall in Gen. 3:1ff. and reminds us of a primary character trait. Satan is subtle, deceptive, crafty, and tricky. He is not above twisting the truth to an evil end (Gen. 3:1; 2 Cor. 11:3; 1 Tim. 2:14). He can even quote or misquote God (Gen. 3:1; Matt. 4:6).

And he laid hold of the dragon, the serpent of old, who is the devil and Satan, and bound him for a thousand years [Rev. 20:2].

E. The Destroyer

John uses both Hebrew and Greek in Rev. 9:11 to give two names for Satan.

The Hebrew is *Abaddon*. The Greek is *Apollyon.* Both mean destroyer. Satan desires to destroy God and His kingdom. Yet, he is in reality pursuing a path of self-destruction for himself and all that follow him. That these names refer to the devil is deduced from the fact that the king of those in the abyss is under discussion.

They have as king over them, the angel of the abyss; his name in Hebrew is **Abaddon**, and in the Greek he has the name **Apollyon** [Rev. 9:11].

F. Great Dragon (Rev. 12: 3, 7, 9)

To say that Satan is a dragon also pictures him as a destroyer. He is fierce, reckless, and beastly in character. He is a murderer.

And the **great dragon** was thrown down, the serpent of old who is called the devil and Satan, who deceives the whole world; he was thrown down to the earth, and his angels were thrown down with him [Rev. 12:9].

G. The Evil One (John 17:15; 1 John 5:18-19)

The evil one is equated with Satan by the parable of the sower (cf. Matt. 13:19, 38-39 with Mark 4:15 and Luke 8:12). Satan is not just content with being evil; he desires to actively promote evil and to influence others to join his wickedness. He is a corrupter.

We know that we are of God, and the whole world lies in the power of the **evil one** [1 John. 5:19].

H. Belial (2 Cor. 6:15)

The Hebrew term *Belial* means "without value or worth." By New Testament times it came to be a name for Satan. This name tells us what God thinks of Satan's character. He is "the worthless one."

> Or what harmony has Christ with **Belial**... [2 Cor. 6:15].

I. The Anointed Cherub Who Guards (Ezek. 28:14, 16)

As the anointed cherub Satan was among the highest or was perhaps the highest of angelic beings. As a cherub he served to identify and guard the very presence of God. Most interpreters view Satan as the topic of Ezek. 28:11-19. Satan was the power beneath the King of Tyre. Otherwise there can be no clue to the identity of the anointed cherub.

> "You were the **anointed cherub** who covers ..." [Ezek. 28:14].

J. The Prince of the World (John 12:31; 14:30; and 16:11)

Satan is the head of an evil system that includes fallen angels and unsaved humans. Although he is restrained within the confines that God allows (see Job 1-2; 2 Thess. 2:6), Satan, in a sense, does rule the world. He is the father of the unsaved (John. 8:44). The entire world is in his control (1 John. 5:19). God has ultimate control over world kingdoms (Dan. 4:17; Rom. 13:1-4), yet Satan has some control over them as well (Matt. 4:8-9; Dan. 10:13ff.). Christ came to destroy the devil (1 John. 3:8; Heb. 2:14-15). Thus, he must be the one in mind in John 12:31.

> "Now judgment is upon this world; now the **ruler of this world** shall be cast out" [John 12:31].

K. Prince of the Power of the Air (Eph. 2:2)

Satan is the best choice for identifying this spirit. In addition to limited control over the earth, Satan seems to have some control over the atmosphere and even the stellar heavens. It is a scene of angelic conflict (Daniel 10).

> ...in which you formerly walked according to the course of this world, according to the **prince of the power of the air**... [Eph. 2:2].

L. The God of this Age or World (2 Cor. 4:4)

We use such terms as *space age* and *atomic age* to denote an important idea that occupied human thought and effort in a particular time. Satan fits the description as the *god of this age* for he desires worship (Matt. 4:9), blinds to the gospel (Mark 4:15) and controls the world (1 John 5:19). God characterizes the present time as the **Satanic age**. All non-Biblical systems of thought either directly or indirectly promote Satan or the worship of Satan.

> [I]n whose case **the god of this world** [Greek, *eon*] has blinded the minds of the unbelieving... [2 Cor. 4:4].

M. Beelzebul, Prince of Demons (Matt. 12:24; Luke 11:15)

The ancient Hebrews called a Philistine god "Baal-zebub" (2 Kings 1:2). This means "Lord of the flies" and was probably a Hebrew modification of the god's actual name intended as an insult. The better text in the New Testament reads "Beelzebul." Some would say this is another way of saying "Lord of the flies." However, Beelzebul seems to mean "Lord of the house." It is better to think that the false god's original name was Beelzebul from which Beelzebub was derived as a ridicule. Matt. 10:25 suggests the meaning "Lord of the house," and, in both Matthew 12 and Luke 11, Christ speaks of a "house divided" just after the reference to Beelzebul. Beelzebul is said to be the "ruler of demons." Also, after being called Beelzebul, the Lord responds by speaking of Satan. For these two reasons, Beelzebul is usually considered to be a name for Satan. Apparently the ancient Jews had transferred the original name for a false god to the being behind all false gods, Satan.

> But some of them said, "He casts out demons by **Beelzebul, the ruler of the demons**" [Luke 11:15].

N. The Tempter (Matt. 4:3; 1 Thess. 3:5)

This title names Satan for one of his most basic activities. His tempting is a solicitation to evil and an attempt to reveal a failure.

> And the **tempter** came and said to Him, "If You are the Son of God, command that these stones become bread" [Matt. 4:3].

O. Accuser of the Brethren (Rev. 12:10)

This title relates to Satan's character as the *diabolos.* It might also relate to his efforts "to sift as wheat" (Luke 22:31). The devil loves to display the chaff and impurities in believer's lives. By such accusations he can both discredit and discourage.

> And I heard a loud voice in heaven, saying, "Now the salvation, and the power, and the kingdom of our God and the authority of His Christ have come, for the **accuser of our brethren** has been thrown down, who accuses them before our God day and night" [Rev. 12:10].

IV. Origin, Original State, and First Sin of Satan

A. Satan's Original State

> Again the word of the LORD came to me saying, "Son of man, take up a lamentation over the king of Tyre, and say to him, 'Thus says the Lord God, "You had the seal of perfection, full of wisdom and perfect in beauty. You were in Eden, the garden of God; every precious stone was your covering; the ruby, the topaz, and the diamond; the beryl, the onyx, and the jasper; the lapis lazuli, the turquoise, and the emerald; and the gold, the workmanship of your settings and sockets, was in you. On the day that you were created they were prepared. You were the anointed cherub who covers, and I placed you there. You were on the holy mountain of God; you walked in the midst of the stones of fire. You were

> blameless in your ways from the day you were created, until unrighteousness was found in you. By the abundance of your trade you were internally filled with violence, and you sinned; therefore I have cast you as profane from the mountain of God. And I have destroyed you, O covering cherub, from the midst of the stones of fire. Your heart was lifted up because of your beauty; you corrupted your wisdom by reason of your splendor. I cast you to the ground; I put you before kings, that they may see you. By the multitude of your iniquities, in the unrighteousness of your trade, you profaned your sanctuaries. Therefore I have brought fire from the midst of you; it has consumed you, and I have consumed you, and I have turned you to ashes on the earth in the eyes of all who see you. All who know you among the peoples are appalled at you; you have become terrified, and you will be no more" ' " [Ezek. 28:11-19].

Logic dictates that Satan is a creature and that he was created without sin. The Bible teaches that God created all beings (John 1:3; Col. 1:16-17) including angels (Psa. 148:2-5). Logic also dictates that God created all beings without sin. Thus, the creation and sin of Satan could be deduced without any special Scripture.

However, Ezekiel 28 does seem to speak specifically of Satan's origin. If Ezek. 28:11-19 does not refer to Satan, then the passage is inexplicable. Twice he is called a cherub (vv. 14 and 16), and Ezek. 28:15 speaks of **blamelessness** "from the day you were **created.**" Satan is also linked with angels in other texts (e.g., Matt. 25:41; Rev. 12:7, 9). Like them he is a created being.

Being an angel, Satan initially shared in the characteristics of all angels, as developed in the preceding chapter. (He has, of course, lost his holiness; but he retains much of the strictly natural, as opposed to moral, characteristics of angels). He was created a sinless spirit being with superhuman intelligence and power. Even now Satan is beautiful (2 Cor. 11:14-15) and powerful (Jude 9).

Not only is Satan described as an angel, he seems to be in a special class of angels (anointed cherub) and perhaps was the greatest of angels. Ezekiel 28 teaches that he was a guarding cherub (vv. 14 and 16), that he was perfect in wisdom and beauty (v. 12), that he lived in paradise (v. 13), and that he was created sinless (v. 15). Although Michael wins his battle with the devil (Rev. 12:7ff.), he seems to respect the devil as his equal or even his superior in power (Jude 9). Satan was and probably still is the most intelligent and powerful of created beings.

B. Nature of Satan's First Sin

Even if there were no direct Scripture on Satan's first sin, we would still have to assume by logic such a sin. However, Ezekiel 28 probably gives some specific information. It is the only text in the Bible that clearly details Satan's first sin.[3] Ezek. 28:17 teaches that the

first sin was basically pride (see also 1 Tim. 3:6).

> "**Your heart was lifted up** because of your beauty; you corrupted your wisdom by reason of your splendor..." [Ezek. 28:17].

C. Consequences of Satan's First Sin

Ezek. 28:16-17 teaches that Satan was cast "from the mountain of God" and cast "to the ground." His pride caused him to be removed from his duties as a cherub that guards God's presence. In this sense Satan "fell" from heaven. However, Satan still has some limited access to heaven, not for service but for purposes of communication (Job 1:6, 2:1; Zech. 3:1; Rev. 12:10). He will make a war in heaven during the Tribulation (Rev. 12:7ff.) and will fall from heaven in the fullest

---

[3] In Ezek 28:2 the prince of Tyre is being addressed. In Ezek. 28:12 the king of Tyre is being addressed. Some interpreters do not see any reference to Satan in the entire chapter. The first ten verses do seem to refer exclusively to an earthly ruler (See vv. 2 and 9). However, beginning in v. 11, the chapter seems to speak not just of the earthly ruler but the supernatural being who energizes the earthly ruler. The only known candidate for such a role is Satan. Otherwise, the passage is incapable of being understood. In vv. 14 and 16, the king is said to have been a cherub; in v. 12 perfection in wisdom and beauty is ascribed to him; in v. 13 he is said to have lived in Eden, and vv. 14 and 16 say he lived in the mountain of God. In v. 15, the being is said to be without sin at his creation. These descriptions almost force the interpreter to conclude Ezek. 28:11ff. refers not just to the human king of Tyre, but also to an evil supernatural being behind him. Thus, Ezekiel 28 probably teaches about Satan's original state and first sin. This study presumes that it does. Yet, the basic conclusions would be unaffected if Ezekiel 28 does not speak of Satan.

Isa. 14:4 is addressed to the "king of Babylon." If Isaiah 14 refers exclusively to a past king of Babylon, then it probably doesn't refer to Satan at all. Unlike Ezekiel 28 there is nothing in the context that forces the reader to conclude that Isaiah has gone beyond a condemnation of an earthly ruler to the spirit being energizing that ruler.

It is possible to view Isaiah 14 as being a double reference. Then it would not only be speaking of a past ruler of Babylon but also a future one. There are some indications in both Isaiah 13 and 14 that a future end-time judgment is also within the scope of Isaiah's statements, and Revelation 17-18 does emphasize a future judgment for Babylon. (See Isa. 13:4, 6, 9, 10, 11, 13, 20; 14:2, 3, 7, 15, 17 for indications of end-time destruction.) If Isaiah also has reference to the end-time destruction of Babylon, then Satan may be viewed as being the superhuman force behind the king of Babylon. (Yet, it seems that the satanic beast hates Babylon in Rev. 17:16.) However, even if these speculations are valid, Isaiah 14 would be referring to a **future** fall of Satan from heaven rather than a **past** one. (See Rev. 12:7ff., which speaks of such a future fall.) Thus, in this study, Isaiah 14 will not be used to form teachings about Satan's original state.

sense of that phrase at that time. Satan definitely has fallen in a moral sense. Yet, because the term *fall* may indicate a future total exclusion from heaven, the phrase, *the fall of Satan,* has been avoided in reference to his original sin.

D. Satan's First Sin and Consequences for Angels

We know for certain that Satan is the leader of other wicked angels (Matt. 25:41; Rev. 12:7-9). Rev. 12:4 hints that one third of the angels followed Satan. There is little direct information on the subject. We know other angels have sinned. We know that Satan is now their leader. Based upon the assumption that angels would not have sinned after they saw the consequences of Satan's first sin, it is best to infer that other angels participated with Satan in his first sin because of his enticement.

E. Time of Satan's First Sin

If angels were created along with material creation, as Ex. 20:11 and Psa. 148:2-5 imply, then Satan was created on the first creative day before the earth was made (Job 38:7). His first sin must have occurred before the serpent tempted Eve in Gen. 3:1. Thus, Satan sinned sometime between the first creative day and man's temptation. Throughout the creative week God called His creation good; and, at the close of the sixth day He, evaluated creation as "very good" (Gen. 1:31). It is harder to view creation as being "very good" if it was already marred by a cosmic conflict of great proportions. The best time to place Satan's first sin is after the creative week but before the temptation of Eve. We do not know the duration between the creation of man and the fall.[4] (The gap theory should be respectfully

---

[4] Ezek. 28:13 says Satan walked in Eden. However, *Eden* means "paradise." It could be a reference to the presence of God and not the Garden of Eden. Ezekiel teaches that Satan was cast from the "mountain of God" and that he walked among the "stones of fire." Thus, *Eden* could equal God's presence in Ezekiel 28. Satan's presence in Eden, therefore, would not by itself prove that the earth

declined as being neither good Hebrew nor good science.)

V. Satan's Works

There is much Scriptural information about Satan's works. This study will emphasize his known present activities while briefly listing his past and future works.

A. Satan's Past Works

1. Satan lied to Adam and Eve causing death (Gen. 3:1ff.; John. 8:44; 1 John. 3:8).

2. Perhaps Satan tried to corrupt the human race so that Messiah could not be born (Gen. 6:1-4).

3. Satan accused Job and was permitted to afflict him. He had power to cause a windstorm, bring fire from heaven, and cause disease (Job 1-2).

4. Satan fought with Michael for Moses' body (Jude 9).

5. He withstood Israel by tempting David to take a census (1 Chron. 21:1).

6. He accused Joshua the high priest (Zech. 3:1-3).

7. The devil tempted Christ (Matt. 4:1-11; Mark 1:12-13; Luke 4:1-13).

8. He tested Peter and possessed Judas (Matt. 16:22-23; Mark 8:33; Luke 22:31-32).

9. Satan hindered Paul and afflicted him physically (1 Thess. 2:18; 2 Cor. 12:7).

10. He influenced Ananias and Sapphira to lie (Acts 5:3-4, 8).

Relative to Satan's past, we must also include the fact that his destruction was rendered certain by Christ's defeat of sin on the cross. Prior to the Lord's death God's holiness would have necessitated the destruction of all humans along with Satan. By the cross Christ made a way to deliver humans from Satan. Thus, the

---

was created before Satan's first sin.

Devil's inevitable judgment began at Calvary. When the program of salvation is over, then God will destroy Satan (John 12:31; 16:11; Col. 2:14-15; Heb. 2:14-15; 1 John 3:8).

B. Satan's Present Works

The doctrine of Satan must be balanced. He is powerful. Yet, he is restricted and faces a certain doom. Satan is still a murderer, liar, and sinner as he has been since the beginning (John 8:44; 1 John 3:8). He still opposes God and His people (1 Pet. 5:8). Although he is the prince of this world (John 12:31; 16:11; 1 John 5:19), the God of this age, (2 Cor. 4:4), the ruler of fallen angels (Matt. 25:41; Rev. 12:9) and prince of demons (Matt. 12:24; Luke 11:15), he is restrained (2 Thess. 2:6) and must operate within the confines of God's authority (Job 1:12; 2:6; John 17:15; 1 John 4:4; 5:18).

Although Satan has a restricted dominion, his range of activity is still very great.

1. Satan blinds the lost (Matt. 13:19; Mark 4:15; Luke 8:12; 2 Cor. 4:4).

"And these are the ones who are beside the road where the word is sown; and when they hear, immediately Satan comes and takes away the word which has been sown in them" [Mark 4:15].

[I]n whose case the god of this world has blinded the minds of the unbelieving, that they might not see the light of the gospel of the glory of Christ, who is the image of God [2 Cor. 4:4].

a. Satan blinds through counterfeit religions that mimic genuine Christianity.

(1) By false doctrines (1 Tim. 4:1)

But the Spirit explicitly says that in later times some will fall away from the faith, paying attention to deceitful spirits and **doctrines of demons**... [1 Tim. 4:1].

(2) By false ministers (Matt. 7:15, 21-23; 2 Cor. 11:13-15)

And no wonder, for even Satan disguises himself as an angel of light. Therefore it is not surprising if **his servants** also **disguise** themselves as **servants of righteousness**; whose end shall be according to their deeds [2 Cor. 11:14-15].

(3) By false Christs (Matt. 24:23-24; 1 John 2:18, 22; 4:3)

Children, it is the last hour; and just as you heard that antichrist is coming, even now **many antichrists have arisen**; from this we know that it is the last hour [1 John 2:18].

Beloved, do not believe every spirit, but test the spirits to see whether they are from God; because **many false prophets** have gone out into the world [1 John 4:1].

[A]nd every spirit that does not confess Jesus is not from God; and **this is the spirit of the antichrist**, of which you have heard that it is coming and now it is already in the world [1 John 4:3].

(4) By false followers (Matt. 13:25, 36-39)

"...and the **tares are the sons of the evil one**; and the enemy who sowed them is the devil..." [Matt: 13:38-39].

(5) By a false, complicated, and perverted gospel (2 Cor. 11:3-4; Gal. 1:8)

But I am afraid, lest as the serpent deceived Eve by his craftiness, your minds should be led astray from the simplicity and purity of devotion to Christ. For if one comes and preaches another Jesus whom we have not preached, or you receive a different spirit which you have not received, or a different gospel which you have not accepted, you bear this beautifully [2 Cor. 11:3-4].

(6) By false powers

It is possible that Satan allows "miracle" workers to manipulate evil spirits so that they have the appearance of supernatural power (Matt. 12:27; 2 Tim. 3:8; Rev. 2:9).

> "And if I by Beelzebul cast out demons, by whom do your sons cast them out? Consequently they shall be your judges" [Matt. 12:27].

> "I know your tribulation and your poverty (but you are rich), and the blasphemy by those who say they are Jews and are not, but are a **synagogue of Satan**" [Rev. 2:9].

b. Satan blinds through religions and philosophies that are openly anti-Christian.

(1) By materialism, the lust of the eyes

If the "love of money is a root of all kinds of evil" as stated in 1 Tim. 6:10, then it is logical to trace a promotion of materialism back to the evil one. The love of this world, including materialism that God condemns in 1 John 2:15ff., is a love of a Satan-dominated world spoken of in 1 John 5:19. Also, if idolatry is demon worship and if covetousness is idolatry (Col. 3:5), then materialism is a tool to prevent worship going to God. The most outstanding example of Satan promoting materialism is Judas Iscariot.

> And during supper, the **devil having already put into the heart of Judas Iscariot**, the son of Simon, to betray Him... [John 13:2].

> And after the morsel, Satan then entered into him...[John 13:27].

(2) By hedonism, the lust of the flesh (Eph. 2:1-3; John 3:19-20)

> And you were dead in your trespasses and sins, in which you formerly walked according to the course of this world, according to the prince of the power of the air, of the **spirit that is now working in the sons of disobedience**. Among them we too all formerly **lived**

in the lusts of our flesh, indulging the desires of the flesh and of the mind, and were by nature children of wrath, even as the rest [Eph. 2:1-3].

(3) By spiritism (The occult is covered in Chapter 5, "Demonology.")

(a) Direct devil worship (Lev. 19:31; 20:6, 27; Deut. 18:9-12)

(b) Idolatry

Idolatry is nothing more than demon worship (Deut. 32:16-17; Psa. 106:36-37). **All false religions are idolatry.** Indeed anything that hinders devotion to God is an idol.

(c) Self-worship, humanism, the pride of life

Samuel equates rebellious pride to witchcraft (1 Sam. 15:23). Worship of self is a form of idolatry, and all idolatry is indirect Satan worship. Furthermore, Satan is the ultimate master of the unsaved human race (1 John 5:19; Eph. 2:2). Thus, the worship of self or humanity in general is also homage to the prince of this world system. Finally, the human spirit is just that, a spirit. The worship of humanity (humanism) is a form of spiritism whether it is acknowledged as such or not.

2. Satan Opposes God's People (Matt. 16:23; 2 Cor. 2:11; Eph. 6:11-12)

> [I]n order that no **advantage be taken of us by Satan**; for we are not ignorant of his schemes [2 Cor. 2:11].

> Put on the full armor of God, that you may be able to stand firm against the schemes of the devil. For **our struggle is not against flesh and blood**, but against the rulers, against the powers, against the world forces of this darkness, against the **spiritual forces of wickedness** in the heavenly places [Eph. 6:11-12].

a. Satan opposes believers through temptation (Matt. 4:1; 1 Thess. 3:5).

(1) Temptation to materialism (Matt. 6:24; 1

John 2:15-17)

Although the Lord likens mammon to a master, in the final analysis Satan is the master who uses the love of money to control men. He is head of the world that believers are told not to love (1 John 2:15-17; 5:19), and he is the foundation of all idol worship including materialism (Col. 3:5).

> "No one can serve two masters; for either he will hate the one and love the other, or he will hold to one and despise the other. You cannot serve God and mammon" [Matt. 6:24].

(2) Temptation to immorality

> Stop depriving one another, except by agreement for a time that you may devote yourselves to prayer, and come together again lest **Satan tempt** you because of your **lack of self-control** [1 Cor. 7:5].

(3) Temptation to pride and self-sufficiency

This is the approach Satan used to tempt David to number Israel (1 Chron. 21:1ff.).

> ...and not a new convert, lest he become **conceited and fall** into the condemnation incurred **by the devil** [1 Tim. 3:6].

(4) Temptation to lie

He is the father of lies (John 8:44ff.).

> But Peter said, "Ananias, why has **Satan filled your heart to lie...?**" [Acts 5:3].

(5) Temptation to doubt

The devil not only wanted Adam and Eve to doubt the truth of God's word, he implied they should doubt the fairness of God's commands. The impressions were given that maybe God did not say something, maybe God was wrong in what He said, or maybe God was being restrictive because He did not want man to enjoy the pleasures of sin.

Now the serpent was more crafty than any beast of the field which the LORD God had made. And he said to the woman, "Indeed, **has God said**, 'You shall not eat from any tree of the garden'?" And the woman said to the serpent, "From the fruit of the trees of the garden we may eat; but from the fruit of the tree which is in the middle of the garden, God has said, 'You shall not eat from it or touch it, lest you die.' " And the serpent said to the woman, "**You surely shall not die! For God knows** that in the day you eat from it your eyes will be opened, and you will be like God, knowing good and evil" [Gen. 3:1-5].

b. Satan opposes believers through the creation of divisions. He loves to use anger and bitterness.

> Be angry, and yet do not sin; do not let the sun go down on your **anger**, and **do not give the devil an opportunity** [Eph. 4:26-27].

> But if you have bitter jealousy and selfish ambition in your heart, do not be arrogant and so lie against the truth. This wisdom is not that which comes down from above, but is earthly, natural, **demonic**. For where jealousy and selfish ambition exist, there is disorder and every evil thing [James 3:14-16].

c. Satan opposes believers by accusing them and thereby discouraging them. "To sift as wheat" may indicate Satan tries to emphasize our "chaff" (i.e., worthless aspects of life) so that we feel discouraged (Luke 22:31). Christ is our helper and our defense (1 John. 2:1-2). There is a reason that 1 Pet. 5:7, which tells us to cast our care upon Him, is followed by 1 Pet. 5:8, which teaches that the devil is trying to destroy believers. *Diabolos is* a slanderer, a liar, an accuser who wants us to be continually discouraged and continually worrying (see Rev. 12:10).

"Simon, Simon, behold, Satan has de-
manded permission to **sift you like
wheat**; but I have prayed for you, that
your faith may not fail; and you, when
once you have turned again, strengthen
your brothers" [Luke 22:31-32].

d. Satan opposes believers by trying to destroy Christian leaders (1 Chron. 21:1, and
implied in 1 Tim. 3:7).

Then **Satan stood up against Israel**
and **moved David** to number Israel [1
Chron. 21:1].

e. Satan opposes believers by mixing unbelievers in the church (Matt. 13:25, 36-39; Acts
20:29).

"Beware of the false prophets, who
come to you in sheep's clothing, but
inwardly are ravenous wolves" [Matt.
7:15].

"I know that after my departure savage
wolves will come in among you, not
sparing the flock!" [Acts 20:29].

f. Satan can oppose believers by causing
physical problems (Job 1-2; Luke 13:11, 16; 2
Cor. 12:7).

Then **Satan** went out from the presence
of the LORD, and **smote Job with sore
boils** from the sole of his foot to the
crown of his head [Job 2:7].

...there was given me **a thorn in the
flesh, a messenger of Satan** to buffet
me—to keep me from exalting myself!
[2 Cor. 12:7].

g. Satan can oppose believers through civil
governments and persecution (Dan. 10:10ff.;
Rev. 2:10).

"Do not fear what you are about to suffer. Behold, **the devil** is about to **cast
some of you into prison**, that you may
be tested, and you will have tribulation
ten days. Be faithful until death, and I
will give you the crown of life" [Rev.
2:10].

h. Satan opposes believers by such general
methods as lies (John 8:44), false miracles (2
Thess. 2:9) and other unspecified hindrances
(1 Thess. 2:18).

(The limitations on Satan's "work" to destroy
believers is covered in Chapter 5, "Demonology.")

C. Satan's Future Works

A complete list of Satan's future works would
overextend this study. (See Chapter 12, "Eschatology," for this information.) After the
close of the church age, Satan will be able to
dominate the world by a government imposed
by the Antichrist (2 Thess 2:3-10; Rev 13:3-
4). He will persecute believers (Rev. 13:7-8)
and will oppose Christ's Second Coming in
the battle of Armageddon (Rev. 17:14; 19:11-
20:3). After the Tribulation, Satan will be
bound in the abyss for 1,000 years, the entire
Millennium (Rev. 20:1-3). He will try one
more rebellion after the Millennium, and then
be cast into the eternal Lake of Fire (Rev.
20:7-10).

Chapter 5

DEMONOLOGY
The Doctrine of Demons

DEMONOLOGY: THE DOCTRINE OF DEMONS

I. The Existence of Demons

Demons are not as prominent in the Old Testament as the New Testament, but they are mentioned (Deut. 32:17; Psa. 106:37). Demons are mentioned in the New Testament over one hundred times: *demon*, approximately sixty-three times; *to demonize*, thirteen times; and some type of unclean or evil spirit about forty-three times. All the New Testament authors, except the writer of Hebrews, refer to demons.

Adherents to Christ's authority will believe in the existence of demons. He conversed with demons (Matt. 8:29), He gave his disciples power over them (Matt. 10:1ff.), and the Lord refers to the devil as "the Prince of demons" (Matt. 12:24-30).

II. The Origin of Demons

The Bible never directly teaches about the origin of demons. There is a difference of opinion as to their origin, although the view that demons are fallen angels is acceptable to most Bible students.

A. Spirits of Pre-Adamic Men

Some who accept a gap in time between Gen. 1:1 and 1:2 have concluded demons are the spirits of a pre-Adamic race that lived before the creation of mankind. God judged that world; and the dead, disembodied spirits from it now seek to possess human bodies. By this view fallen angels and demons are different.

The gap theory is weak enough, but this view of demons adds speculation to improbability.

B. Spirits of Monstrous Offspring that Resulted from Union of Fallen Angels and Women

In Genesis 6 there is some reason to believe that fallen angels assumed human form or possessed men's bodies and intermarried with women to produce a hybrid offspring.[1] Some take this idea one step further and say that when this mixed race drowned in the flood, their spirits became demons. Assertion is not evidence. Regardless of the interpretation of Genesis 6, this view is pure assertion with no evidence as an explanation for the origin of demons. Notice that fallen angels would be related to but not identical to demons by this view.

C. Sinful Angels

When the Scriptures do not directly teach on an issue, the next best recourse is to lean upon inferences from the Scripture. The Bible does not directly say that demons are fallen angels, but this is the most probable interpretation of what Scriptural evidence there is on the subject. Satan is said to be the leader of demons (Matt. 12:24ff.) and of wicked angels (Matt. 25:41; Rev. 12:7-9). Both demons (Matt. 8:16; Luke 10:17-20) and angels are called spirit beings (Heb. 1:14). The sinful angel, Satan, can enter and control men (Luke 22:3; John 13:27) and demons seek to enter and control men (Matt. 12:22ff.; Luke 11:14-15). Although demons and wicked angels are not absolutely equated, these similarities cause most to conclude demons are fallen angels.

Assuming that demons are wicked angels, they became demons when they first sinned. Little information is provided, but it is logical to assume that these angels (perhaps one-third of all angels, cf. Rev. 12:4) sinned along with Satan. He is their leader, and it is unlikely they would have rebelled against God after they saw the consequences of sin in the devil's experience.

There are two classes of wicked angels: some are free to roam about the earth doing Satan's work as illustrated by demon activity in the gospels, while others are confined in the abyss (2 Pet. 2:4; Jude 6; Rev. 9:2ff.) which is the intermediate place of judgment for angels as they await the final punishment in the lake of fire (Luke 8:31). It is possible that sinful angels intermarried with women to produce a mixed race and that these are the fallen angels chained in the abyss.

III. The Personhood of Demons

Some would think that *demon* refers to an influence to wickedness or that it is a name used by the ignorant ancients to describe mental

---

[1] Holy angels do not reproduce (See Luke 20:35-36 and Chapter 3, pp. 34-35). We can either assume angels are all males (with no females) or that they are neuter in essence. They only **appear** as men in earthly settings. However, the actions of holy angels might not preclude reproduction among fallen angels. Perhaps when angels appear in earthly forms they could hypothetically reproduce, or perhaps fallen angels can possess men's bodies and cause genetic alterations. The view that Genesis 6 involves the mixture of fallen angels and women cannot be excluded on the basis that holy angels do not reproduce. However, this is a poor explanation for the origin of demons.

illness.[2] Yet, the Bible teaches demons are persons in the sense of having intellect, emotions, and will. They have intelligence and are aware of prominent Christians (Mark 1:24, 34; Luke 4:34; 8:28; Acts 19:15). They know theology (James 2:19). Demons have emotions. The Bible emphasizes fear (Luke 8:28; James 2:19). Demons also have a will. They made a choice of entering swine as opposed to going into the abyss (Luke 8:32). Their wills are subject to Christ's authority (Matt. 8:16; 10:1; Mark 1:27). Another evidence that demons are persons is that personal pronouns are used of them.

> [S]aying, "What do **we** have to do with You, Jesus of Nazareth? Have you come to destroy **us**? I know who You are—the Holy One of God!" [Mark 1:24].

IV. Properties of Demons

A. Demons are Spirit Beings

Demons are called spirits approximately forty-three times in the New Testament (e.g., Matt. 8:16; Luke 10:17-20). They are contrasted with flesh and blood (Eph. 6:12). Being spirit they are normally invisible, and they are not subject to spatial limitations. It seems that over two thousand demons can reside in the space of one human body (see Mark 5:9ff.).

B. Demons are Morally Perverted

Not only are demons called spirits, they are called unclean spirits (Matt. 10:1; Mark 1:23; Luke 11:24), evil spirits (Luke 7:21), and rulers of darkness in spiritual wickedness (Eph. 6:12). Some are more wicked than others (Matt. 12:45).

C. Demons are Invisible but Capable of Manifestation

---

[2] See Steven Waterhouse, *Strength For His People: A Ministry To Families of the Mentally Ill* (Amarillo, TX: Westcliff Press, 2002) 91-101 for the distinction between mental illness and demon possession.

In their essence demons are spirit beings and are, therefore, invisible. They can appear as angels of light (2 Cor. 11:14 by implication). Yet, when demons appear in prophetic events, they are portrayed as ugly and hideous (Rev. 9:7-10, 17; 16:13-16).

V. Powers of Demons

A. Demons are Superhuman but Limited in Strength

Demon-possessed people have superhuman strength. They can snap chains (Mark 5:3-4; Luke 8:29). Demons easily overpowered the exorcists in Acts 19:16. When the demonic hordes rise from the abyss in the Tribulation, God will not allow them to kill. Yet, their torment will be so unbearable that people will prefer death (Rev. 9:1-11). Demons also have superhuman but limited abilities to do miracles. (Sorcerers in Exodus 7-8; Matt. 7:21-23; 24:24; Acts 8:9ff.; 16:16; 2 Thess. 2:9; 2 Tim. 3:8; Rev. 13:13; 16:13-14).

> And I saw coming out of the mouth of the dragon and out of the mouth of the beast and out of the mouth of the false prophet, three unclean spirits like frogs; for they are spirits of demons, performing signs, which go out to the kings of the whole world, to gather them together for the war of the great day of God, the Almighty [Rev. 16:13-14].

B. Demons Have Superhuman but Limited Intelligence

Since demons have existed from Creation, they have had a much greater opportunity to learn than have had humans. Since angels are greater in intelligence than humans, so are demons (2 Sam. 14:20).

C. Demons are Superhuman in Relationship to Space

Since two thousand plus demons can reside in the same place, demons are not limited by space (Mark 5:9ff.). Also, the act of possessing a body shows that demons can pass through physical barriers. They are not, however, omnipresent, as angels are not omnipresent.

VI. Works of Demons

A. General Works

1. Demons extend Satan's power by being subject to him (Matt. 12:24; 25:41; Rev. 12:7) and by working in union with him and with each other (Matt. 12:26, 45; Eph. 6:11-12; 1 Tim. 4:1). Idleness may be "the devil's workshop" as Franklin said, but the devil himself is never idle. Job 1:7 says Satan goes up and down the earth. 1 Pet. 5:8 pictures him as a prowling lion. By his demons the devil can make his influence felt in many places and with a much greater force than he could otherwise do without their assistance.

2. Demons influence the philosophy and activity of world leaders. Daniel 10 mentions both the demonic Prince of Persia (v. 13) and the demonic Prince of Greece (v. 20). Both Persian and Greek societies were heavily involved in the occult. It is likely that the "god of this world" still has demonic agents to influence world governments.

3. Demons promote false religions. Deut. 32:17; Psa. 106:36-38 and 1 Cor. 10:20 teach that the reality behind the heathen religions of Bible days was a worship of demons. There is every reason to believe that demons are still behind false religions today.

4. Demons promote immorality. Eph. 2:1-3 teaches that Satan promotes immorality. It is logical to infer that demons are also involved.

5. Demons can afflict the human mind and body. Paul writes of a messenger of Satan afflicting him physically (2 Cor. 12:7). Also, Luke 13:11 mentions a sickness caused by a spirit that Satan had sent (v. 16). The Bible definitely does **not** attribute all sickness to demons. Yet, it links some blindness, deafness, muteness, deformity and seizures to a demonic origin (Matt. 12:22; Mark 9:20-29; Luke 13:11). In addition to afflicting the body, demon influence can also harm people emo-

tionally. Subjects of demon possession in the gospels were withdrawn, unclean (nudity, living in cemeteries) and suicidal (Mark 5:3, 5; Mark 9:22; Luke 8:27; 9:39).

> ...and he had his **dwelling among the tombs**. And no one was able to bind him anymore, even with a chain...And constantly night and day, among the tombs and in the mountains, he was crying out and **gashing himself** with stones [Mark 5:3, 5].

> "And it has often **thrown him** both **into the fire** and **into the water to destroy him.** But if You can do any thing, take pity on us and help us!" [Mark 9:22].

B. Demons and the Occult

Occult is a Latin term meaning hidden, secret, mysterious. By the occult Satan uses demons to sidetrack people away from God's truth.

1. Divination or fortune telling is predicting the future. There are many ways by which those in the occult claim to make predictions: astrology, rods and pendulums, Ouija boards, palmistry, crystals, signs and omens, augural divinations, tea-leaves, dreams and visions, etc. The Scriptures condemn divination in general and astrology in particular. God is opposed to fortune telling.

a. Scriptures about fortune telling or divination include the following:

> "...Causing the omens of boasters to fail, making **fools** out of **diviners**..." [Isa. 44:25].

> "For thus says the LORD of hosts, the God of Israel, 'Do not let your prophets who are in your midst and your **diviners** deceive you, and do not listen to the dreams which they dream. For they prophesy falsely to you in My name; **I have not sent them,**' declares the LORD" [Jer. 29:8-9].

For the teraphim speak iniquity, and the **diviners** see **lying** visions, and tell **false** dreams; they comfort in vain. Therefore, the people wander like sheep, they are afflicted, because there is no shepherd [Zech. 10:2].

And it happened that as we were going to the place of prayer, a certain slave-girl having a spirit of divination met us, who was bringing her masters much profit by fortune telling [Acts 16:16].

(See also Ezek. 21:21ff.)

b. Scriptures about astrology include the following:

If there is found in your midst, in any of your towns, which the LORD your God is giving you, a man or a woman who does what is evil in the sight of the LORD your God, by transgressing His covenant, and has gone and served other gods and **worshipped** them, or **the sun or the moon** or any of the heavenly host, which I have not commanded...then you shall bring out that man or that woman who has done this evil deed, to your gates, that is, the man or the woman, and you shall **stone them to death** [Deut.17:2, 3, 5].

"...Let now the **astrologers**, those who **prophesy by the stars**, those who predict by the new moons, stand up and save you from what will come upon you. Behold, they have become like stubble, **fire burns them**; they cannot deliver themselves from the power of the flame; there will be no coal to warm by, nor a fire to sit before" [Isa. 47:13-14].

Thus says the LORD, "Do not learn the way of the nations, and **do not be terrified by the signs of the heavens** although the nations are terrified by them" [Jer. 10:2].

So I will stretch out My hand against Judah and against all the inhabitants of Jerusalem. And I will cut off the remnant of Baal from this place, and the names of the idolatrous priests along with the priests. And those who **bow down** on the housetops **to the host of heaven**, and those who bow down and swear to the LORD and yet swear by Milcom [Zeph. 1:4-5].

(See also 2 Kings 23:1ff.; Amos 5:26; Acts 7:41-43.)

c. Conclusion

In both Testaments the Bible warns believers about false prophets. It says there are many of them and that sometimes their predictions will be true. However, Satan does not know the future with complete accuracy. Therefore, his predictions are not always accurate. Old Testament saints could test a false prophet by whether his message conformed to Scripture and whether his predictions were always correct (Deut. 13:1-5; 18:20-22; Isa. 8:19-20). Under the church system we should reject all claims to being a prophet because the apostles and prophets were part of the founding of the church (Eph. 2:20). Often those who claim to prophesy by divine revelation today do not know Christ (Matt. 7:15; 24:24). (It does not even matter that some predictions might come true! The Old Testament takes for granted that false prophets could sometimes make accurate predictions.) Demons use human false prophets to give their lying messages. In situations where no claims to being a prophet are made, the message must still be evaluated as to whether it is Scriptural (1 John 4:1ff.).

2. Spiritism

Spiritism refers to attempts to contact the dead. People who try to contact the dead are called mediums, necromancers, and wizards. It is crucial to understand that the human dead are not contacted at all. The story of the rich man and Lazarus teaches that there is no communication from the departed spirits to earth (Luke 16:24ff.; see also Psa. 88:10; Heb. 9:27).[3] Whatever communication does occur is with demons. Demons have lived since creation, and they have much information about the lives of humans who have lived in the past and demons could possibly even imitate their voices. By spiritism, demons keep human minds more interested in the power of the occult than in the saving power of the cross. Since we are not under the Law of Moses, the death penalty need not pertain to spiritism. However, passages from the Law do give God's attitude toward such occult activity. (See also 1 Sam. 28:7ff.; 1 Chron. 10:13-14; 2 Kings 23:24.)

> "Do not turn to **mediums** or **spiritists; do not seek them out** to be defiled by them. I am the LORD your God" [Lev. 19:31].

> "As for the person who turns to **mediums** and to **spiritists**, to play the harlot after them, **I will also set My face against that person** and will cut him off from among his people" [Lev. 20:6].

> "Now a man or a woman who is a **medium** or a **spiritist** shall **surely be put to death.** They shall be stoned with stones; their blood guiltiness is upon them" [Lev. 20:27].

And when they say to you, "Consult the **mediums** and the **spiritists** who whisper and mutter," should not a people consult their God? Should they consult the dead on behalf of the living? To the law and to the testimony! If they do not speak according to this word, it is because they have no dawn [Isa. 8:19-20].

3. Magic

When used in a context dealing with the occult, magic does not refer to optical illusions, but rather to calling upon demonic powers to perform some feat beyond the normal ability of man. The Bible calls people involved in such magic practices "magicians," "sorcerers," or "witches." Areas of occultic magic include voodoo, spells, fertility charms and drugs, amulets, love potions, and hypnotism. The Scripture fully recognizes the power of Satan and demons to do miracles. (See section V. of this chapter on the powers of demons. See also 2 Kings 21:6; 2 Chron. 33:6.)

> "You shall not allow a **sorceress** to live" [Ex. 22:18].

> "If a prophet or a dreamer of dreams arises among you and gives you a **sign** or a **wonder,** and the sign or the wonder comes true, concerning which he spoke to you, saying, 'Let us go after other gods (whom you have not known) and let us serve them,' you shall not listen to the words of that prophet or that dreamer of dreams; for the LORD your God is testing you to find out if you love the LORD your God with all your heart and with all your soul. You shall follow the LORD your God and fear Him; and you shall keep His commandments, listen to His voice, serve Him, and cling to Him" [Deut. 13:1-4].

> "**There shall not be found among you** anyone who makes his son or his daughter pass through the fire, one who uses divination, one who practices **witchcraft,** or one who interprets omens, or a sorcerer, or one who **casts a spell,** or a medium, or a spiritist, or one who calls up the dead" [Deut. 18:10-11].

---

[3] Communication with the prophet Samuel in 1 Sam. 28 was a special exception allowed by God. Notice the witch was surprised to see Samuel (1 Sam. 28:12).

4. Illicit Use of Drugs

The Scriptures associate occult activity with illicit use of drugs. This is easier to grasp if we consider the practice of a "medicine man" or "witch doctor." By the use of drugs, demons more easily influence and control human minds. It is not coincidental that drug abuse and occult activities have simultaneously increased in recent generations. The relationship between illicit drug use and the occult is easiest to see in the Greek word *pharmakia*, from which is derived *pharmacy*. The very word for sorcerer contains within it a reminder of the role that illicit drug use plays in the occult. (See also Rev. 9:21; 18:23.)

> Now the deeds of the flesh are evident which are... idolatry, **sorcery**... (*pharmakia*) [Gal. 5:19-20].

> But for the cowardly and unbelieving and abominable and murderers and immoral persons and sorcerers (*pharmakoi*) and idolaters and all liars, their part will be in the lake that burns with fire and brimstone, which is the second death [Rev. 21:8].

> Outside (the heavenly city) are the dogs and the **sorcerers** (*pharmakoi*) and the immoral persons and the murderers and the idolaters, and everyone who loves and practices lying [Rev. 22:15].

VII. Demon Possession

A. Definition and Cause

Demon possession is a condition in which one or more demons inhabit the body of a human being and take control of the victim. The Scriptures do not give a specific cause for demon possession although most believe that a victim is responsible for showing initial interest in occult activity or voluntarily yielding control of his mind to supernatural forces. In the case of minor children, it is perhaps parental involvement in the occult that leads to possession (Mark 9:21).

B. Characteristics of Demon Possession

The human heart is more than wicked enough to be involved in gross and habitual sin without any demonic influence whatsoever (Jer. 17:9; Matt. 15:19ff.). The diagnosis of demon possession must be made with great caution. A person can be greatly damaged by naive Christians who are quick to attribute problems to the direct involvement of demons. The description of demon-possessed people in the gospels presents rather distinct characteristics.

1. Scriptural characteristics of demon possession are given in accounts in Matt. 8:28ff.; Mark 5:1ff.; 9:17ff.; and Luke 8:26ff. The following characteristics describe a demon-possessed individual.

a. Unusual physical strength (could not be bound by chains)

b. Withdrawn from society (living in tombs)

c. Fits of rage (crying out)

d. Split personality (running to Jesus to worship but at the same time opposing Jesus)

e. Resistance to Spiritual things (desires the Lord to leave him alone)

f. Supernatural insight (knows the identity of the Christ and His powers to condemn)

g. Alterations in voice (demons speaking through body)

h. Seizures and foaming at the mouth (Mark 9:18ff.)

i. Uncleanness (nudity, living in cemetery)

j. Suicidal tendencies (cutting with stones, runs into fire or water)

2. Characteristics of demon possession have been suggested by counselors and missionaries. The following is a list of characteristics which have been observed in people thought to be demon-possessed:

- Projection of a new personality
- Superhuman knowledge including the ability to speak in unlearned languages

57

- Superhuman strength
- Moral depravity
- Deep depression
- Ecstatic or ferocious behavior
- Spells of unconsciousness
- Foaming at the mouth
- Resistance to prayer or Scripture
- Reaction to the name of Jesus
- Fear
- Feelings of pain unrelated to sickness or injury[4]

C. Demon Possession and Christians

Conservative Bible teachers do not agree on whether Christians can be possessed by demons. Usually, the fact that the Holy Spirit indwells a believer is presented as evidence that Christians cannot be possessed. However, the same point could be used to argue that sin cannot indwell a believer. Since the Holy Spirit obviously does reside in the presence of sin, the fact of His presence may not be enough to teach confidently demon possession is impossible for believers. It certainly is safe to conclude that even if Christians could be possessed by a demon, it would have to be a temporary control that does not cause the loss of salvation and that any possession would have to be initiated by the voluntary cooperation of the believer.

1. The Bible teaches that the cross has defeated Satan – and demons.

> "Now judgment is upon this world; now the **ruler of this world** shall be **cast out**" [John 12:31].

> ...and concerning judgment because the **ruler of this world** has been **judged** [John 16:11].

> When He had disarmed the rulers and authorities, He made a public display of them, **having triumphed over them** through Him [Col. 2:15].

Since then the children share in flesh and blood, He Himself likewise also partook of the same, that through death He might **render powerless** him who had the power of death, that is, **the devil** [Heb. 2:14].

The Son of God appeared for this purpose, that **He might destroy** the works of **the devil** [1 John 3:8].

2. The devil's defeat by the cross made a just basis for God to deliver people from the devil's control. Prior to the payment for human sin, Satan had a legitimate claim upon fallen humanity. The cross made possible a just basis for deliverance because Christ fully paid the penalty for sin and thereby destroyed any control Satan might claim over a human. While demons are still active, the cross has already inevitably destroyed their power.

The believer has been delivered from the inevitable and involuntary dominion of Satan and his angels. At the very least this means there can be no such thing as an involuntary seizure or control by demons. **The unwilling and uncooperative believer cannot be demon-possessed.** If there is such a thing as demon-possession for the believer, it can only occur in the life of a receptive, willing, voluntary, cooperative Christian.

Also, Christians can never again revert to having a position in the kingdom of darkness or having the devil as a master. Regardless of practice, the believer's position is that of being in the kingdom of Christ Jesus and being His servant. There is no such thing as a Christian in the devil's kingdom or a believer who is the devil's slave. Thus, if demon possession is possible for a believer, it must be viewed as only a **temporary condition that does not alter a Christian's position in Christ**. Assuming that the Bible might not rule out all demon possession for a Christian, such possession could at its worst be only a voluntary and temporary control but never an involuntary and permanent control.

---

[4] See C. Fred Dickason, *Angels: Elect and Evil* (Chicago: Moody Press, 1975) 185-86.

"[A]nd you shall know the truth, and the truth shall **make you free**."..."If therefore the Son shall **make you free**, you shall be **free indeed**" [John 8:32, 36].

"I do not ask Thee to take them out of the world, but to **keep** them **from the evil one**" [John 17:15].

But thanks be to God that though you were slaves of sin, you became obedient from the heart to that form of teaching to which you were committed, and **having been freed** from sin, you became slaves of righteousness...For when you were slaves of sin, you were free in regard to righteousness [Rom. 6:17-18, 20].

For I am convinced that neither death, nor life, **nor angels, nor principalities**, nor things present, nor things to come, nor powers, nor height, nor depth, nor **any other created thing, shall be able to separate us from the love of God,** which is in Christ Jesus our Lord [Rom. 8:38-39].

[F]or you were **formerly darkness**, but now you are light in the Lord: walk as children of light [Eph. 5:8].

For He **delivered us** from the domain of darkness, and transferred us to the kingdom of His beloved Son [Col. 1:13].

Submit therefore to God. **Resist the devil** and **he will flee** from you [James 4:7].

...and might **deliver** those who through fear of death were subject to slavery all their lives [Heb. 2:15].

Be of sober spirit, be on the alert. Your adversary, **the devil**, prowls about like a roaring lion, seeking someone to devour. But **resist him** firm in your faith... [1 Pet. 5:8-9].

...because **greater is He who is in you** than he who is in the world [1 John 4:4].

...but He who was born of God **keeps** him and the **evil one does not touch him** [1 John. 5:18b].

3. Conclusion

Regardless of ones view of the Christian and demon possession, all agree that believers can be influenced by the devil through demons (2 Cor. 11:13-15; Eph. 4:27; James 3:15). A faithful believer will avoid all dabbling in the occult. Then the issue of demon possession for a believer will revert to a moot point of the theoretical and never become a practical problem.

Chapter 6
ANTHROPOLOGY
The Doctrine of Man

ANTHROPOLOGY: THE DOCTRINE OF MAN

I. The Origin of Man

A study of the scientific flaws in the theory of evolution belongs more in the domain of apologetics than in Biblical theology. Those who want scientific truth in support of creationism should request a catalog of publications from organizations that promote creation science or intelligent design. As students of Biblical theology, our immediate concern is the teaching of the Scriptures on the origin of man. The Bible affirms the direct and instantaneous creation of man by God without evolutionary mechanism.

A. The Fact of Creation

The creation of man is so clearly and repeatedly taught in the Scriptures that a denial of this doctrine cannot be accommodated to a belief in the Bible. Furthermore, the authority of the Lord Jesus Christ is at stake, for He both believed and taught in the literal creation of the first man, Adam (see Job 38; Psalms 8 and 148; Mark 10:6; Heb. 2:7).

> Then God said, "**Let Us make man** in Our image, according to Our likeness..." [Gen. 1:26].

> Then the LORD **God formed man** of dust from the ground, and breathed into his nostrils the breath of life; and man became a living being [Gen. 2:7].

> "For in six days **the LORD made the heavens and the earth, the sea and all** that is in them..." [Ex. 20:11].

> "Thou alone art the LORD. Thou hast

61

made the heavens, the heaven of heavens with all their host, the earth and all that is on it, the seas and all that is in them. **Thou dost give life to all** of them and the heavenly host bows down before Thee" [Neh. 9:6].

By the word of the LORD the heavens were made, and by the breath of His mouth all their host...**For He spoke, and it was done**; He commanded, and it stood fast [Psa. 33:6, 9].

And He answered and said, "Have you not read, that **He who created** them from the beginning **made them male and female...**?" [Matt. 19:4].

Therefore, just as through **one man** sin entered into the world, and death through sin, and so death spread to all men, because all sinned...death reigned from **Adam** until Moses [Rom. 5:12, 14a].

For as in **Adam** all die, so also in Christ all shall be made alive...So also it is written, **"The first man, Adam, became a living soul"** [1 Cor. 15:22, 45].

"Worthy art Thou, our Lord and our God, to receive glory and honor and power; for **Thou didst create all things**, and because of thy will they existed, and were created" [Rev. 4:11].

B. The Time of Creation

The Hebrew idea of *begat* means "to become the ancestor of." Likewise, the *son* of a man means his "descendants" (consider the phrase "Father Abraham" or "Son of David"). There are known gaps in the Biblical genealogies (e.g., Uzziah is given as the son of Jehoram in Matt. 1:8 even though he was technically his great-great-grandson).[1] Apparently, the author

wished to list only the prominent people in the family line and not every generation.

It is not necessary to believe that man was created in 4004 B.C. as Bishop Ussher concluded by studying the genealogies of Genesis 5 and 11. However, the practice of listing only the prominent in a family line will not allow the staggering amount of time some give to the human race. To make humanity one million years old would envision an average gap of 50,000 years between each of the names from Adam to Abraham. This clearly would be a ridiculous extension of the possible gaps in genealogies and make such genealogies a comic waste. At most, unknown gaps could allow man to be a few thousand years older than 4004 B.C. with the exact date being a mystery. Even with a few gaps taken into consideration, the human race is relatively young.

II. Man's Original Condition

A. Created in God's Image

Both the Hebrew and Greek words for *soul* are used of animals (e.g., Gen. 1:20-21, 24, 30; Rev: 8.9; 16:3), and animals are also said to have the "breath of life" in them (Gen. 6:17; 7:15, 22).[2] Therefore, the real distinguishing factor between men and animals is that, unlike the animals, humans were created in the image of God.

The fact that God specially breathed into the dust to create man shows that man is more important than animals, which, although possessing the breath of life, are never said to be the special objects of His life-giving breath (Gen. 2:7). However, the main outstanding and unique feature of man is that he is made in the image of God (Gen. 1:26). The definition of being made in God's image is most clearly

---

[1] See J. Dwight Pentecost, *The Words and Works of Jesus Christ* (Grand Rapids, Zondervan Publishing,

1981) 33-39 for an excellent treatment of genealogies.
[2] This is in no way to be construed to teach that animals have the same kind of souls as humans, but it does help establish that the primary superiority of man over animals lies in his creation in the image of God.

understood in the verses that deal with the loss and/or retention of that image by the Fall.

> Then God said, "**Let Us make man in Our image, according to Our likeness**" [Gen. 1:26].

B. Man's Current Status Relative to the Image of God

Gen. 9:6; 1 Cor. 11:7 and James 3:9 teach that even after the Fall man retained some elements of God's image. Therefore, cursing and murder are unacceptable to God, for even an unsaved man still retains part of God's image. To the degree that society rebels against this doctrine, it will also lose respect for human life. Man's value is rooted in his creation in God's image. To the degree the doctrine of creation is undervalued, the same lack of worth will be directed to the creature, that is man.

> "Whoever sheds man's blood, by man his blood shall be shed, for in the **image of God** He made man" [Gen. 9:6].

> For a man ought not to have his head covered, since **he is the image** and glory **of God** [1 Cor. 11:7].

> With it [the tongue] we bless our Lord and Father; and with it we curse men, who have been **made in the likeness of God** [James 3:9].

Although the above verses teach that fallen (even unsaved) man has retained some elements of God's image, Eph. 4:24 and Col. 3:10 also teach that a believer has positionally regained a part of God's original image and, practically, is constantly coming closer to God's image. These two texts also link the **parts of God's image** that men **lost by sin** to the areas of **truth** and **holiness**.

> [A]nd that **you be renewed** in the spirit of your mind, and put on the new self, which in the **likeness of God** has been created **in righteousness and holiness** of the truth [Eph. 4:23-24].

> [A]nd have put on the new self who is **being renewed to a true knowledge according to the image of the One who created** him [Col. 3:10].

All of the relevant passages taken together make it desirable to distinguish between aspects of God's image that men lost by the Fall and aspects that are retained. These two categories are best described as **God's moral image** and **God's personal image**. Fallen man lost the former and can regain it in Christ. He never lost the latter. Therefore, all people are still valuable.

1. Man in God's Moral Image

The **moral image of God was lost** in the Fall. Man lost true knowledge of God and His truth (including right and wrong) according to Col. 3:10. Man lost holiness and righteousness according to Eph. 4:24. As to his original condition, the image of God means that man was created with a tremendous amount of knowledge about God and of God's creation. He was created like God in the sense of holiness and righteousness. When he sinned, man became very much unlike God's image in the areas of spiritual knowledge, holiness, and righteousness.

2. Man in God's Personal Image

We are taught that even **fallen man retains some of God's personal image**. No specifics are given. Yet, logical deductions that arise from comparing God to man yields promising ideas. God is a person (intellect, emotion, and will). Man is a person (intellect, emotion, and will). God is a spirit being. Man is fundamentally a spirit being. God is immortal. Man's soul is immortal. God is the ruler of all. Man is like God in that he has dominion.

It is possible that as God uses speech and is a social being so the image of God includes man as a social being who uses speech. Even as fallen, man is an eternal spirit being and retains some elements of God's personal image. Therefore, every human, saved or unsaved, is precious and valuable.[3]

III. The Fall of Man

A. The Fact of the Fall

The doctrine of man is so intertwined within the doctrine of sin that a total separation is impossible. The fact of man's fall will simply be reviewed at this point with more extensive texts following under the sub-section of universal depravity.

> Now the serpent was more crafty than any beast of the field which the LORD God had made. And he said to the woman, "Indeed, has God said, 'You shall not eat from any tree of the garden'?" And the woman said to the serpent, "from the fruit of the trees of the garden we may eat; but from the fruit of the tree which is in the middle of the garden, God has said, "You shall not eat from it or touch it, lest you die.' " And the serpent said to the woman, "You surely shall not die! For God knows that in the day you eat from it your eyes will be opened and you will be like God, knowing good and evil." When the woman saw that the tree was good for food, and that it was a delight to the eyes, and that the tree was desirable to make one wise, she took from its fruit and ate; and she gave also to her husband with her, and he ate [Gen. 3:1-6].

B. The Consequences of the Fall

Under this section, the tragic results of the Fall will be listed. The more difficult issue of how Adam's sin is imputed to all his offspring will be addressed in Chapter 7, "Hamartiology: The Doctrine of Sin", (pp. 78-79).

1. Separation

The original couple was separated from the garden, from the tree of life, and from God (Gen. 3:22-24).

2. Physical Death

Physical death is separation of the spirit from the body (James 2:26). God told Adam that one of the consequences of his sin was that he would return to dust (Gen. 3:19; see also Gen. 5:5). Paul teaches that Adam's sin brought physical death upon all of humanity (Rom. 5:12-14; 1 Cor. 15:21-22).

> Therefore, just as through one man sin entered into **the world**, and death through sin, and **so death spread to all men**, because all sinned.... Nevertheless **death reigned** from Adam until Moses, even over those who had not sinned in the likeness of the offense of Adam, who is a type of Him who was to come [Rom. 5:12, 14].
>
> **For since by a man came death**, by a man also came the resurrection of the dead. For as **in Adam all die**... [1 Cor. 15:21-22].

Other verses teach that sin causes death, but, instead of directly teaching that Adam's sin caused physical death, they blame death on sin in general, whether imputed from Adam's sin, the indwelling sin principle, or the individual's acts of sin. Individual sin was not imputed before the law (Rom. 5:13). Yet, pre-law people still died **because of Adam's sin**. Since the imposition of the Law, it is likely that physical death can be a result of **any or all** of the following: the imputation of Adam's sin, the sin "nature" in each person, and personal sins. [4]

---

[3] Some suggest that as God is a tripartite being composed of three persons, so also man is tripartite composed of body, soul, and spirit. The comparison does not seem to be an exact parallel. Each man is not one being composed of three persons who communicate and interact with each other.

[4] Likely, the sin "nature" and acts of sin are a factor in the cause of physical death for the unsaved. Believers are forgiven of sin. Yet, they die physically. The main cause of a spiritual person's physical death is probably imputed sin, not so much personal sins. Death for the believer is usually not so

"Our father died in the wilderness, yet he was not among the company of those who gathered themselves together against the LORD in the company of Korah; **but he died in his own sin,** and he had no sons" [Num. 27:3].

"I said therefore to you, that **you shall die in your sins**; for unless you believe that I am He, **you shall die in your sins**" [John 8:24].

...**the body is dead because of sin**...[Rom. 8:10].

The sting of death is sin... [1 Cor. 15:56].

3. Spiritual Death

God warned the couple that the day they disobeyed Him would be a day of death (Gen. 2:17). Adam and Eve died spiritually when they sinned, and the consequences of spiritual death affect all that are born into the human race. A human being is born spiritually dead, which means he is separated from God. Luke 15:24 and 32 give evidence that death equals separation. A study on the basis for eternal death does not directly fit the outline of this point, but careful theologians will consider the material below. [5]

---

much viewed as a penalty but a blessing (Phil. 1:23; Rev. 14:13). It is more a natural consequence of sin than a penalty. God does not reverse the natural consequences of sin. Instead, He transfers it into a means to glory. There is, however, still the possibility that unconfessed and persistent personal sins are a factor in the physical death of a believer (1 Cor. 11:30; 1 John 5:16).

Although the author unreservedly believes in the doctrine of eternal punishment, he cannot in good conscience classify eternal death as a consequence of the Fall. Many would consider eternal punishment in hell to be one of the results of the sin of Adam and/or personal acts of sin. The author believes that the Biblical basis for eternal death is solely a rejection of Christ (either a direct rejection or an indirect rejection based upon God's foreknowledge that the person never will believe and has no potential for faith). A person's eternal destiny is self-determined and is not based upon what Adam did or did not do. Rom. 5:12-20 contains some of the most difficult of Bible mysteries and humbles all theologians. Fortunately, the main point remains obvious in spite of all theological speculation: only One can bring life. Material about Adam is illustrative of the point that one life can alter all of humanity. Paul is not primarily giving a lecture on Adam. Adam's example proves one life can affect the whole world to show readers it is not surprising that one Savior can give life to the world. Paul does not continue his secondary comparison to answer all complexities about inherited guilt. All interpreters end up with unanswered questions arising from material on Adam in Romans 5. How is the human soul transmitted from one generation to the next? What ramification does the answer have for birth control or abortion? What does inherited guilt mean for infant salvation upon death? The precise legal charge that actually brings eternal damnation may be one of the questions not enrtirely answered in Romans 5. Romans 5 teaches that one man's sin brought death to humanity. It is sufficient to carry Paul's argument if we were to define death here as physical and spiritual death and not include eternal death. Just as Adam brought physical and spiritual death to the world, Christ is the source of life for the entire human race. In fact, Paul's further explanation in verse 14 *may not* include eternal death. With the unique exception of Enoch, those from Adam to Moses all died physically and were all born spiritually dead (separated from God). However, eternal death did not universally reign over everyone from this period. Heb. 11:1-22 gives prominent names to the contrary. If death in verse 14 only refers to physical and spiritual death, it may also refer to only these kinds of death in verse 12.

Romans 5 teaches that without Christ transmitted guilt from Adam causes universal spiritual death (separation from God) as well as a present condemnation before God our Judge (vv. 16 and 18). The *natural* condition of every human is that he or she is dead and unjustified. These truths definitely relate to eternal death. Paul expects us to understand that our natural condition inherited from Adam makes us vulnerable to everlasting death and that eternal death will be the outcome without life by the One, the Lord Jesus Christ. Our natural status is that all we need to do to end in eternal death is nothing. Indeed, it is possible to understand from Romans 5 that inherited sin is the legal charge that leads to eternal damnation. However, it is also sufficient to Paul's argument to conclude our inherited condition places us at risk of eternal death if we do nothing, and Paul does not go into the details here in Romans 5 as to the specific cause of damnation in God's courtroom. To understand that we risk eternal death in the natural course of events and that Christ is the only hope of escape would be an adequate alternative interpretation. Given the specific information discussed below (see also pp. 112-113, 117) the author prefers to take Romans 5 as a warning of the danger of eternal death arising from our natural condition but thinks other texts give a clearer basis for eternal damnation. The *main points* are simply that all are born spiritually dead and unjustified (condemned) because of Adam and that only One can give life. Those who refuse justification by faith (Rom. 5:1) and will not "receive the abundance of grace and the gift of righteousness" (Rom. 5:17) will end up under the wrath of God (Rom. 5:9) because they will not "be saved by **His** life" (Rom. 5:10). If eternal condemnation does in fact occur, what will be the exact legal charge under God's system of justice? Adam did expose the entire human race to eternal disaster. If our natural risk becomes reality, will not damnation occur because an individual has accountability for his or her eternal destiny by not having a relationship to the only One who brings life? This failure may come by direct rejection, indifference, or even God's foreknowledge that he or she would never accept Christ. Adam put everyone on the path to hell, but whose fault will it really be if an individual remains on this natural course? The specific legal charge at the Great White Throne is more likely to be "name not in the Lamb's book of life" rather than "the natural condition of humanity." Verses that link past sins to death may be understood in a similar fashion. In the unbeliever, personal sins cause a physical death from which there will not be a glorified resurrection. In addition, the stress in Rom. 6:16, 21, 23, and James 1:15 may be that personal sin causes spiritual death in the present life (the separation of the soul from God) and places us in a direction leading to eternal death (the eternal separation of the soul from God in hell). Readers are to understand that personal sin leaves us in a hopeless and dangerous condition that needs to be changed by faith in Christ. Otherwise, our sinful life will transition to eternal death even if personal sins are not the precise charges that cause eternal death. Even if these texts do in-

tend to teach that personal sin causes eternal death, then is still may be that **rejection** (or foreknown rejection) **is the** primary or perhaps exclusive **personal sin that brings eventual eternal death**. Personal sins are a factor in the degree of punishment in hell and do bring God's temporal wrath (chastisement) in this life. It would be just for God to damn us for inherited or personal sins. However, when all teachings about the basis of eternal condemnation are taken into consideration, one can question whether He actually does so. Believing He does not has no bearing on the doctrine of how one is saved or the fact of eternal punishment. However, the issue does affect one's understanding of God's justice and grace and one's view of the full power of the cross over sin. The Bible assumes that if Christ had not come, then man could have been eternally condemned for his personal sins and/or our mysterious participation in the sin of Adam (see Chapter 7, "Hamartiology: The Doctrine of Sin"). However, the Bible falls short of saying that God ever does condemn man in the eternal sense for his acts of sin or for Adam's sin. A person goes to hell for rejecting Christ, not for individual acts of sin. It is almost as though God condemns man for the greater infraction, i.e., rejection of Christ, and then does not even bother to prosecute in the relatively minor infraction of personal sins or inherited guilt from Adam. John 3:18 and 2 Thess. 1:8-9 teach that the basis for eternal death is a rejection of Christ (probably also John 3:36, see *A Greek-English Lexicon of the New Testament* by Bauer, Arndt, and Gingrich, p. 82, on *apeitheo*, Section 3). "...whoever does not believe stands condemned already **because he has not believed**..." [John 3:18, NIV]. John 16:9 shows that the one sin the Holy Spirit convicts the world of is a failure to believe in Christ. This is the sin that is of greatest concern to God. One major reason that personal sin should not be viewed as a basis for eternal wrath is that 1 John 2:2 says that God has been **propitiated for the sins of all** mankind. Therefore, the interpreter may see that man is guilty of personal acts of sin and worthy of eternal punishment because of them, but our theology must be adjusted so that we do not see God as being angry in the eternal sense because of man's personal sins. **God is not imputing the trespasses of the world to them** (2 Cor. 5:19), and there is a sense in which Jesus took away the sins of the world, John 1:29. When God is said to be angry over sins or men are said to be punished for personal acts of sin (Rom.

a. Adam as the Originator of Spiritual Death

Therefore, just as through one man sin entered into the world, and death through sin, and so death spread to all men, because all sinned [Rom. 5:12].[6]

b. All Are Born Spiritually Dead

Since sin is universal and begins at conception and is the basis for spiritual death, it must be that all are born spiritually dead.

And you were **dead** in your trespasses and **sins** [Eph. 2:1].

We know that we have **passed out of death into life**... [1 John 3:14].

(See also Psa. 51:5; 58:3; Job 14:4; 15:14 and section III.B.4., pp. 67-69).

c. Personal Sin's Association with Spiritual Death

Rom. 6:23 and James 1:15 do not distinguish

1:18; Eph. 5:6; Col. 3:6), the teachings of 1 John 2:2; 2 Cor. 5:19 and John 1:29 demand that we understand that the wrath be defined as temporal wrath, i.e., punishment in this life. God's anger over a person's sins probably also influences an unbeliever's **degree** of punishment in hell without being the primary basis for a person going to hell (perhaps Col. 3:6; Eph. 5:6). In some cases (e.g., Romans 2) the author may be talking about eternal wrath but, in a hypothetical sense, showing what would have happened had Christ not come to make an alternative destiny possible for man. (Consider this view's consequences for infant salvation and those who are mentally handicapped). See Lewis Sperry Chafer, *True Evangelism*, reprint ed. (Grand Rapids: Zondervan, 1973) 33-34, 64 for a similar conclusion on the basis of eternal condemnation.

[6] That spiritual death should be traced back to Adam could be deduced from the fact that sin (the cause of death) is universal, begins at conception, and entered the world by Adam. Also, Rom. 5: 12, 14 is probably teaching that both physical death and spiritual death originated in Adam. In vv. 18 and 21, the subject is eternal life. Therefore, a fitting contrast to eternal life is spiritual death in v. 17 and further back in the context, i.e., vv. 12 and 14.

between Adam's sin imputed to all people or personal sins. They emphasize the individual's sin "nature" and acts of sin. Both types of sin are factors in spiritual death.

Therefore what benefit were you then deriving from the things of which you are now ashamed? For the **outcome of those things** [i.e., personal sins] **is death** [Rom. 6:21].

For the **wages of sin is death**... [Rom. 6:23].

Then when lust has conceived, it gives birth to **sin**; and when sin is accomplished, it **brings forth death** [James 1:15].

d. Other Texts on Spiritual Death

"Truly, truly, I say to you, he who hears My word, and believes Him who sent Me, has eternal life, and does not come into judgment, but has passed **out of death into life**. Truly, truly, I say to you, an hour is coming and now is, when the dead shall hear the voice of the Son of God; and those who hear shall live" [John 5:24-25].

[B]eing darkened in their understanding, **excluded from the life of God**, because of the ignorance that is in them, because of the hardness of their heart [Eph. 4:18].

(See also Matt. 8:22; John 8:51; 11:26.)

4. Universal and Total Depravity

Adam and Eve's sin resulted in death, but also in a universal and total depravity. *Universal* refers to the scope and *total* to man's entirely hopeless condition without the Lord Jesus Christ. Man has a propensity to sin. He is biased in sin's favor and is inclined to it. He is an incorrigible rebel that cannot please God by any merit of his own. That this propensity to sin should be traced back to Adam could be inferred from the Scriptural teaching that it is universal. All men are born with it (see

III.B.3.b., p. 67). However, Rom. 5:12 directly teaches that all sin entered the world by Adam. The singular *sin* stresses that sin as a principle (i.e., the sin "nature" within each person) had its origin in the Edenic Fall. All particular acts of sin arise out of the universal depravity of the race as a result of Adam's original sin. [7]

a. A Heart Problem

The following verses teach that man's individual acts of sin arise out of a heart that is by inclination sinful. In other words, they stress not just that man sins, but rather that he is by nature an incorrigible sinner enslaved to sin's dominion. Although most verses do not bother to mention Adam, this condition of universal depravity arose from him. (See also Gen. 8:21; Psa. 51:5; 58:3; Matt. 12:33-35; Luke 6:43-45; Rom. 7:5, 14-24; Eph. 2:3; Col. 3:5-7; Titus 3:3; 1 Pet. 4:4.)

> Then the LORD saw that the **wickedness** of man was **great** on the earth, and that **every intent of the thoughts of his heart was only evil continually** [Gen. 6:5].

> "The heart is more deceitful than all else and is **desperately sick**; who can understand it?" [Jer. 17:9].

> "But the things that proceed out of the mouth come **from the heart**, and those **defile the man**. For out of the **heart** come evil thoughts, murders, adulteries, fornications, thefts, false witness, slanders" [Matt. 15:18-19].

> "If you then, **being evil**, know how to give good gifts to your children, how much more shall your heavenly Father give..." [Luke 11:13].

> Jesus answered them, "Truly, Truly, I say to you, **everyone who commits sin is the slave of sin**" [John 8:34].

> But thanks be to God that though you were **slaves of sin...** [Rom. 6:17].

> For when you were **slaves of sin...** [Rom. 6:20].

b. A Universal Problem

The following verses emphasize the **universal** scope of man's depraved heart. Depravity does not mean that every man is as extremely gross and wicked as he can be. There is such a thing as relative human good (e.g., Cornelius in Acts 10:1-2 where he is called devout though unsaved, and Rom. 2:14-15). Depravity means that every unsaved person is a rebel, and therefore, even his good displeases God for it is done with a rebellious heart (Prov. 15:8; 21:4; 21:27). Even human good is filthy before God (Isa. 64:6). Depravity, rather than meaning every man is as vile as possible, means each is a rebel who is enslaved to a heart that strays from God. None tries to please God in God's way. None can earn salvation. The vain materialist who believes in a works salvation and attends a liberal church is not considered wicked by human standards, but he is just as unacceptable to God as a child molester, and he is pursuing a path that is just as opposed to God (though perhaps without the more base sins). [8]

> "When they sin against Thee (for **there is no man who does not sin**)..." [1 Kings 8:46].

> The LORD has looked down from heaven upon the sons of men, to see if there are any who understand, who seek after God. They have all turned aside; together they have become corrupt; **there is no one who does good,**

---

[7] Man's depravity has led to a darkness of mind so that man is blind to spiritual things (1 Cor. 1:18; 2:14; 2 Cor. 4:4; Eph. 4:18).

[8] Verses which speak of universal condemnation outside of Christ would also by deduction prove universal depravity (John 3:18,36; Rom. 11:32; Gal. 3:22; 1 John 5:12). This view of the universality of depravity is essential to sound decisions in law and government. An unscriptural view of man leads to all sorts of unwise decisions in governing men.

not even one [Psa. 14:2-3].

Every one of them has turned aside; together they have become corrupt; there is **no one who does good, not even one** [Psa. 53:3].

If Thou, LORD, shouldst mark iniquities, O Lord, who could stand? [Psa. 130:3].

And do not enter into judgment with Thy servant, for in Thy sight **no man living is righteous** [Psa. 143:2].

Who can say, "I have cleansed my heart, I am pure from my sin"? [Prov: 20:9].

Indeed, there is **not a righteous man on earth** who continually does good and who never sins [Eccl. 7:20].

All of us like sheep **have gone astray**, each of us has turned to his own way; but the LORD has caused the iniquity of us all to fall on Him [Isa. 53:6].

What then? Are we better than they? Not at all; for we have already charged that both Jews and Greeks are **all under sin**; as it is written, "There **is none righteous, not even one**" [Rom. 3:9-10].

Now we know that whatever the Law says, it speaks to those who are under the Law, that every mouth may be closed, and **all the world may become accountable** to God [Rom. 3:19].

[F]or **all have sinned** and fall short of the glory of God...[Rom. 3:23].

But the Scripture has shut up **all men under sin**...[Gal. 3:22].

For **we all stumble** in many ways... [James 3:2].

If we say that we have no sin, we are **deceiving ourselves**, and the truth is not in us....If we say that we have not sinned, we make Him a liar, and His word is not in us [1 John 1:8,10].

5. Consequences of the Fall for Woman

The woman would have pain in childbirth and continued subjection to her husband, which would now be complicated by a propensity to sin.

> To the woman He said, "I will greatly multiply your **pain in childbirth**, in pain you shall bring forth children; yet your desire shall be for your husband, and he shall rule over you" [Gen. 3:16].

6. Consequences of the Fall for Man

The man would now find labor distasteful and a matter of survival.

> Then to Adam He said, "Because you have listened to the voice of your wife, and have eaten from the tree about which I commanded you, saying, 'You shall not eat from it'; cursed is the ground because of you; in **toil you shall eat of it all the days of your life**. Both thorns and thistles it shall grow for you and you shall eat the plants of the field; **by the sweat of your face you shall eat bread**, till you return to the ground, because from it you were taken; for you are dust, and to dust you shall return" [Gen. 3:17-19].

7. Consequences of the Fall for the Rest of Creation

The Fall resulted in a curse upon the ground and in pain and death for all animal life. The curse will be partly removed in the millennial Kingdom (see Isa. 11:6ff.; 65:25 and verses concerning agricultural fertility in the kingdom).

> "...**Cursed** is the **ground** because of you..." [Gen. 3:17].

For we know that the **whole creation** groans and **suffers** the pains of childbirth together until now [Rom. 8:22].

IV. The Origin of the Soul

The origin of the immaterial side to man's composition is a proper subject for either Anthropology or Hamartiology. Does God create a new soul each time a child is conceived or born? Is there some process by which the parents procreate a new human soul, as well as, an infant's body? The subject of the soul's origin is discussed in Chapter 7, "Harmartiology: The Doctrine of Sin," in covering the origin of man's sinful condition, (pp. 76-78).

V. The Composition of Man's Immaterial Nature

There are two views among conservative Christians as to the composition of man's immaterial nature. Some believe man is composed of only **two parts, body and soul**, with the terms *spirit* and *soul* totally interchangeable. This view is called **dichotomy**. Others maintain that man is a **tripartite** being composed of *body, soul* and *spirit*. This view is called **trichotomy**.

A. Evidences for the Dichotomist View of Man

1. Terms *Soul* and *Spirit* Are Often Interchangeable (compare Gen. 41:8 with Psa. 42:6)

> Now it came about in the morning that his **spirit** was troubled, so he sent and called for all the magicians of Egypt, and all its wise men. And Pharaoh told them his dreams, but there was no one who could interpret them to Pharaoh [Gen. 41:8].

> O my God, my **soul** is in despair within me... [Psa. 42:6].

Compare John 12:27 with 13:21.

> "Now My **soul** has became troubled..."[John 12:27].

> When Jesus had said this, He became troubled in **spirit**... [John 13:21].

Compare Matt. 20:28 with Matt. 27:50.

> "[J]ust as the Son of Man did not come to be served, but to serve, and to give His life [Greek *soul*] a ransom for many" [Matt. 20:28].

> And Jesus cried out again with a loud voice, and yielded up His **spirit** [Matt. 27:50].

Compare Rev. 6:9 with Heb. 12:23.

> And when He broke the fifth seal, I saw underneath the altar the **souls** of those who had been slain because of the word of God, and because of the testimony which they had maintained [Rev. 6:9].

> [T]o the general assembly and church of the firstborn who are enrolled in heaven, and to God, the Judge of all, and to the **spirits** of righteous men made perfect [Heb. 12:23].

2. Sometimes "Body and Soul," or "Body and Spirit," Said to Constitute the Whole Man

> "And do not fear those who kill the **body**, but are unable to kill the **soul**; but rather fear Him who is able to destroy both soul and body in hell" [Matt. 10:28].

> For I, on my part, though absent in **body** but present in **spirit**, have already judged him who has so committed this, as though I were present [1 Cor. 5:3].

> Beloved, I pray that in all respects you may prosper and be in **good health** [body], just as your **soul** prospers [3 John 2].

3. Rebuttal of Trichotomist View

Trichotomists usually teach that the spirit of a man is the religious part of his immaterial nature while the soul contains the intellect, the emotions, and the will. However, the dichotomists note that even animals are said to have a "spirit" in Eccl. 3:21 and that the highest exercises of religion are attributed to the soul

(Mark 12:30; Luke 1:46; Heb. 6:18-19; and James 1:21). God is a spiritual being, but He is said to have a soul (Amos 6:8 in Hebrew). The disembodied dead in heaven are said to be souls (Rev. 6:9; 20:4). Therefore, there is no tight separation in the Scripture where *spirit* refers strictly to man's relationship to God, and *soul* refers strictly to his relationship with fellow man. The soul is also clearly a part of man that relates to spiritual interests.

To the dichotomist, 1 Thess. 5:23 does not prove that soul and spirit are separate. In the phrase "body, soul, and spirit" the last two words are viewed as synonymous just as in the pattern of Mark 12:30 which gives a list of synonymous items ("love the Lord your God with all your heart, and with all your soul, and with all your mind"). Likewise, to the dichotomist, Heb. 4:12 speaks of soul and spirit in synonymous terms. To say the Word of God divides the soul and spirit may not be the same as saying it divides soul from the spirit. It simply asserts the Word of God cuts into man's immaterial nature (soul and spirit being synonymous). The Word of God cuts or divides into man's hidden being which may be called either soul or spirit.

B. Evidence for Trichotomist View

Several times *spirit* and *soul* are divided, and several times they are distinguished.

> Now may the God of peace Himself sanctify you entirely; and may your **spirit and soul** and body be preserved complete, without blame at the coming of our Lord...[1Thess. 5:23].

> For the word of God is living and active and sharper than any two-edged sword, and piercing as far as the **division of soul and spirit**, of both joints and marrow, and able to judge the thoughts and intentions of the heart [Heb. 4:12].

> But a **natural** (Greek *soulish*) man....But he who is **spiritual**...[1 Cor. 2:14-15].

> [I]t is sown a **natural** (Greek *soulish*) body, it is raised a **spiritual** body...[1 Cor. 15:44].

Paul considers man tripartite in 1 Thess. 5:23. Likewise, the author of Hebrews divides soul from spirit in Heb. 4:12. In 1 Corinthians 2 and 1 Corinthians 15, there is a clue given to the difference between the soul and the spirit. The soul refers to man in non-heavenly, natural relationships. The spirit refers to man in heavenly relationships. A trichotomist contends soul is the part of man's immaterial nature that relates to other humans, to self, and to the created world. Spirit refers to the part of man's immaterial nature that has a capacity for a religious relationship.[9]

C. Thoughts on the Issue

There is merit in both positions. Trouble arises out of a failure to see a difference in dividing something into two parts and distinguishing different functions. One cannot fully divide chocolate from vanilla in chocolate ripple ice cream, but one can distinguish the differences easily.

The truth in the dichotomist position is that man's immaterial nature is not severed into soul and spirit. The immaterial nature of man is a single united entity. Thus, when speaking in general terms about man's immaterial nature, it is perfectly correct to use the words *soul* and *spirit* interchangeably with no difference in meaning. Biblical authors usually do this.

However, it also seems *soul* and *spirit* can be distinguished if one wants to use precise language. In certain contexts, the Biblical author

---

[9] It is the author's belief that even an unsaved person can be said to have a spirit. He has one, but it is not functioning properly. There is a difference between having a car and having one that works. Unsaved people still have a spiritual side to their being though they may worship falsely. (Consider the idea of an evil spirit and also 1 Cor. 2:11; 2 Cor. 7:1; Heb. 12:9; James 4:5 for the idea that "spirit" can be evil).

wants to be technical and exact. Therefore, he makes a difference between *soul* and *spirit*. In such contexts, it is best to view the *soul* as referring to man's immaterial composition (intellect, emotion, and will) as it interacts with things of this world, with self, and with other humans. *Spirit* refers to man's immaterial composition (intellect, emotion, and will) as it interacts with non-earthly, i.e., supernatural realities. The truth in trichotomy is that the functions of man's immaterial nature can be distinguished even if man's immaterial nature is not strictly severed into two antithetical parts.

VI. Man's Physical Being

Unlike a dualistic philosophy where material is considered wicked and spirit good, the Bible does not condemn the body just because it is physical. Certainly, the body can be controlled by sin (Rom. 6:12-13), but Christians should not view the body as inherently evil. The key factor is how a person uses the body. It is supposed to be a "holy sacrifice" to God (Rom. 12:1-2), and for believers the body is the temple where the Holy Spirit resides (1 Cor. 6:19-20).[10]

---

[10] For related topics on the value of the unborn and infant salvation, please consult Westcliff Bible Church tapes titled *God's View of the Unborn* (March 10, 1985) and also 2 Sam. 12:15-31 (June 17, 1987).

Chapter 7

HAMARTIOLOGY
The Doctrine of Sin

OUTLINE

HAMARTIOLOGY: THE DOCTRINE OF SIN

I. The Definition of Sin

A. Biblical Descriptions of Sin

The Bible does not give one all-inclusive definition for sin, but it does give several descriptions of sin.

1. Lawlessness

...sin is lawlessness [1 John 3:4].

2. Unrighteousness

All unrighteousness is sin... [1 John 5:17].

3. Not from Faith

...whatever is not from faith is sin [Rom 14:23].

4. Haughty Eyes, Proud Heart

Haughty eyes and a proud heart, the lamp of the wicked, is sin [Prov. 21:4].

5. Knows Right, Does Not Do

Therefore, to one who knows the right thing to do, and does not do it, to him it is sin [James 4:17].

6. Injures Self

"But he who sins against me injures himself" (Prov. 8:36a).

B. Word Studies of Selected Biblical words for Sin

1. Instructive Hebrew Words for Sin

a. *Hata* - pronounced kata (Sin)

This is the most common word for sin in the Old Testament. It occurs approximately 580 times. In secular contexts, it refers to missing a mark or a way. Judg. 20:16 speaks of left-handed slingers who could hit a target and not miss (literally not sin!). Prov. 19:2 speaks of the hasty (absent-minded) man who sins with his feet, i.e., he misses the right path as he travels. The word in moral contexts speaks of "failure to live up to expectations," "failure to respect the rights and interests of others," and "strong personal opposition."[1]

b. *Pasha* (Transgression)

This word occurs approximately 93 times as a noun and 41 times in verbal form. In political contexts it means to rebel or revolt against authority (1 Kings 12:19; 2 Kings 3:7; 8:20). In contexts pertaining to God, it means "to reject God's authority," "to renounce allegiance to God." The most common English translation is "transgression."

c. *Awon* (Iniquity)

This noun occurs 231 times and the verb 17.[2] The main English translation is "iniquity." The basic meaning is "to bend, to twist, to distort." Psa. 38:6 says, "I am **bent over** and greatly bowed down...." Lam. 3:9 says relative to God's chastisement, "He has blocked my ways with hewn stone, He has **made my paths crooked**." In contexts of moral behavior, the word came to mean "crooked behavior, perversions, infractions, iniquity." It is very interesting that in the Hebrew mind there is a strong and inevitable connection between the wicked deed and its punishment. This word *iniquity* has a range of meaning which includes the ideas of both **deed** and **punishment**, e.g., Isa. 53:6 KJV: "And the LORD hath laid on him the iniquity [punishment for the iniquity] of us all."[3] Iniquity is a collective word that often gives the sum of man's misdeeds rather than isolating a single act of sin.

d. *Ra* (Wicked)

This word is used approximately 444 times.[4] It is contrasted with the Hebrew word for *good* (*tov* - Gen. 3:5; Prov. 14:22). In non-theological usages it means "ruin," "injury" or "distress." *Ra* describes sickly or weak cattle (Gen. 41:21, 27), poison water or stew (2 Kings 2:19; 4:41), calamity (Isa. 45:7), "good-for-nothing" merchandise (Prov. 20:14), or a bad messenger (Prov. 13:17). From this word we see that sin causes injury and ruin to self and others. Thus *ra* is unacceptable to God (Mal. 2:17). Both God and His people should hate it and the damage it causes (Psa. 97:10; Prov. 8:13).

e. Summary of Old Testament Words

The Old Testament terms for sin refer to a diversion from a standard. *Sin* is missing the standard. "Transgression" is to rebel or deviate from the standard. "Iniquity" is to alter the standard, choosing a perverted way of

---

[1] Harris, Archer & Waltke, editors, *Theological Word Book of the Old Testament*, 2 vols, (Moody Press, 1980) 1:277-79.

[2] Ibid., 2:650-51.

[3] The word for sin, *hata,* also has a range of meanings to include the idea of punishment. Num. 32:23 says, "...your sin will find you out." This includes the idea of your sin's punishment will find you. It is significant that punishment and sin are so clearly intertwined that words for sin take on the definition of punishment.

[4] Charles C. Ryrie, *Basic Theology* (Wheaton, IL: Victor Books, 1986) 209.

living.

2. Instructive Greek Words for Sin

a. *Hamartia and Harmartano* (Sin)

The *harmartia* family is the most common New Testament word for sin. The verb occurs approximately 43 times and the noun 174 times. In the Septuagint, *harmartia* often translates the Hebrew word *hata* (about 238 times).[5] This indicates a basic meaning of "to miss the mark."

Ancient Greek usage of the word in secular literature confirms this definition. Homer used the word over 100 times of a warrior who hurled his spear but failed to hit his target. Thucydides used the word to describe the inability of a poet to do justice to a particular theme. Plato and Xenophon use the word as an ethical failure.[6]

Both the Hebrew and classical Greek background indicate a basic definition of "to miss the mark." Rom. 3:23 is the clearest example of this definition for sin.

> [F]or all have sinned and **fall short** of the glory of God [Rom. 3:23].

b. Words Other than *Hamartia*

(1) *Adikeo, Adikia* (Unrighteousness)

The verb is used 26 times and the noun is used 26 times. This word means "unrighteousness" or "wrongdoing." It can also imply the idea of hurting others. It is the opposite of God's righteousness, character, or standards. The alpha (*a*) signifies negation.

(2) *Paraptoma* (Trespass, Offence)

This word is used 21 times in the New Testament. It comes from an original word which means to "fall down beside" (*parapipto*). It is hardly used in the Greek classics but is sometimes used of literary mistakes. Polybius used the noun as meaning "mistake, blunder, or error."[7]

The New Testament word might be used of sins that are not of the greatest severity (Gal. 6:1), but this is not always the case (Eph. 2:1). English translators usually render this term "trespass" or "offence." Apparently "falling down beside" is close enough in meaning to "missing the mark" so that the two words are synonyms. Trespass means "to trip" or "to fall".

(3) *Anomia* (Lawlessness, Iniquity)

This word is used 15 times. It means to act contrary to law or to be without law.

(4) *Parabasis* (Transgression)

Parabasis, unlike sin, can only occur when there is a law to violate.[8] Rom. 4:15 KJV teaches, "for where no law is, there is no transgression" (*parabasis*). Thus, the term *transgression* clarifies that human sin should not be viewed as just an honest mistake, a natural human flaw. It is also a deliberate willful violation of a known law. In classical Greek, the term was used of the breaking of an agreement, e.g., a surrender or peace treaty. The original meanings of the words translated "transgression" were to "step beyond" or to "step over."[9] *Parabasis* is usually translated "transgression." It is found

---

[7] Ibid. 246.

[8] Rom. 5:13 teaches that sin occurred in the absence of the Law. However, God was gracious and did not impute personal sins in the absence of the Mosiac Law. People still died from **Adam's sin,** not personal sins, before the Law. Though sin can occur in absence of Law, transgression implies a moral boundary (Law) has been established.

[9] G. Kittel and G. Freidrich, editors, *The Theological Dictionary of the New Testament* 10 vols. (Grand Rapids: Wm. B. Eerdmans Publishing Co., 1967), 5:736ff.

---

[5] G. Kittel and G. Freidrich, eds., *The Theological Dictionary of the New Testament*, 10 vols., (Grand Rapids: Wm. B. Eerdmans Publishing Co., 1967) 1:268.

[6] Ibid., 1:293; see also Richard C. Trench, *Synonyms of the New Testament,* reprint ed. (Grand Rapids: Wm. B Eerdmans Publishing Co., 1976) 241.

seven times while a similar term, *parabatis,* is used five times.

(5) *Asebia* (Ungodliness)

This refers to a failure to render God what is due to Him both in terms of attitude and action. The word is used six times.

(6) *Kakos* (Bad)

The beggar Lazarus experienced "bad" things in his life while the rich but unsaved man experienced good things (Luke 16:25). Also, *kakos* can refer to "bad" health (Mark 1:32). In a moral sense, this word reminds us that sin causes damage, injury, harm to self and others. When sinful people insist upon their freedom to sin, they really desire a freedom to destroy themselves and others. The love of money can lead to all sorts of injury (1 Tim. 6:10).

(7) *Poneros* (Evil)

This Greek word for "evil" has much in common with the immediately preceding term. However, there often is the additional idea of actively involving others in sin so that corruption can spread. The "evil" creature is not content to sin in isolation. He wants to promote evil and include others in it. One of Satan's names is "the evil one" (Matt. 13:19, 38; 1 John 2:13-14; 5:18).

3. Summary

There have been several definitions for sin offered by theologians. The following does a good job of bringing much of the truth about sin into one sentence: "Sin is the transgression of or lack of conformity to the holy character of God."

II. The Origin of Sin

A. The Origin of Sin in the Universe

At the creation of man, the sons of God (angels) sang for joy (Job 38:7). Thus, there does not seem to have been any sin at that point. Since God declared everything that He had made to be "very good" even on the sixth day (Gen. 1:31), it is probable that there was not any sin in the universe even at that point in time. The devil is said to be the Father of lies and the first murderer (John 8:44). He is the first being in the Bible that is depicted as having sin (Gen. 3:1, cf. Rev. 12:9). In point of time, the first sin probably occurred after creation of man but definitely before the temptation in the garden. There may be some doubt as to the exact point in time that sin originated in the universe, but there is no doubt as to the originator. The devil was created perfect, but iniquity was found in him (Ezek. 28:12ff.). Specifically, Ezek. 28:17 says of him, "Your heart was lifted up because of your beauty; you corrupted your wisdom by reason of your splendor...."

B. The Origin of Sin in the Human Race

Sin originated in the human race through Adam. This has been covered under chapter 6, "Anthropology: The Doctrine of Man", pp. 64-69 (see also, Genesis 3; Rom. 5:12ff.; 1 Cor. 15:21ff.; 1 Tim. 2:14).

C. The Origin of Sin in the Individual Soul

The origin of sin in the individual involves two distinct questions. First, how is the sin principle (nature) transmitted to each individual born into the world? Secondly, how can it be that Adam's sin in the garden has been imputed to people alive today?

1. The Transmission of Sin to Each Generation

In order to understand what the Bible says about the transmission of sin, it will be necessary to delve into the broader subject of the origin (transmission) of the human soul. There are two basic views as to the soul's origin.

a. The Creationist Position

The creationist position maintains that a mother and father make the body of a human being according to the natural laws of procreation. However, the creationist maintains that God performs a special act of creating the soul when a baby is conceived and infuses this soul into the developing body. Verses which are used to support this idea often refer to God as the "Father of Spirits" (Num. 16:22; Eccl. 12:7; Isa. 57:16; Zech. 12:1; Heb. 12:9).[10]

There are some major weaknesses to the creationist view as to the origin of the soul. The above verses could just be saying that God created the human soul in an indirect sense through natural reproduction. This is what happens in the physical development of the unborn. The parents by natural processes make the bodies of their children, but it is also Scripturally true that God is the ultimate creator of the physical side of a child (Psa. 139:13-16). In addition, Gen. 2:1ff. and Heb. 4:4ff. teach that God is resting from His creative work. This makes it difficult to believe that God creates thousands of new human souls each day. Finally, the strongest objection to the creationist view is that it means God must be the one who either creates the sin principle or causes it to reside in each person.

b. The Traducian View

The Traducian view is that the parents are the primary agents in the origin of a new soul. This position has the advantage of deriving sin from the parents and not from a special act of God. It also allows God to have ceased from His creative activity.

Traducianism states that the parents (by an unknown process) generate both the material and immaterial elements in man. There are several verses that support (but admittedly do not prove) Traducianism). The literal translation of Gen. 2:7 teaches that "God breathed into Adam the breath of lives" (plural). The plural may imply that Adam had somehow within him the potential to gener-

ate the immaterial natures of all that have descended from him. Gen. 5:3 teaches that Adam produced a son after his own likeness. This seems to refer to more than physical characteristics. Adam produced a son after his own likeness in terms of a sinful condition. Many verses teach that people are conceived and born in sin (Psa. 51:5; 58:3; Job 14:1, 4; 15:14; Eph. 2:1). This sin is never said to be placed in the soul by God when He creates the soul. On the contrary, the reader is left with the impression that the unborn infant inherits sin from its parents. Heb. 7:9-10 show that God can view the souls of unborn children as somehow being within their parents. (God views Levi as paying tithes to Melchizedek through Abraham, Levi's great grandfather.) This supports the idea that the souls of children are somehow produced by parents as opposed to a direct creation of God. The key text to hamartiology is Rom. 5:12.[11]

> Therefore, just as through one man sin entered into the world, and death through sin, and so death spread to all men, **because all sinned**— [Rom. 5:12].

The closing phrase "because all sinned" favors some kind of actual, as opposed to representative, participation in Adam's sin. This fits nicely with the Traducian view that parents somehow produce the souls of children.[12]

Since the Traducian view best explains the transmission of the human soul, it also is the best explanation for the origin of sin within the individual. The indwelling propensity to sin is passed on from parents to child just as are all the basic components of man's immaterial nature and just as the body originates in its parents. The only exception was Jesus Christ because He was conceived by the

---

[10] Those in the Calvinist tradition tend to be creationists. It fits well with the federal headship idea of sin's imputation and with covenant theology.

[11] Rom. 5:12 could be explained along creationist lines if the federal theory of imputation is accepted.

[12] Lutheran theology tends to Traducianism.

Holy Spirit, and the Holy Spirit overshadowed Mary so that Christ was born without sin. For all others, an individual's sin originates from his parents and is present at conception.[13]

2. The Imputation of Adam's Sin to Us

Thiessen teaches that the Traducian theory of the soul's origin is sufficient to answer how Adam's sin became imputed to us.[14] There is much truth in this. If parents produce a child's soul just as they do the body, then we were all in some mysterious way present in Adam when he sinned. Although the full details are a mystery, it was our presence with father Adam that somehow contributed the imputation of sin to us. Down through the centuries several views as to the imputation of sin have been espoused. It will be helpful to treat this important but difficult subject in more detail.

a. The Pelagian View

The Pelagian view is that Adam's sin affected himself only. His only relationship to us is that he is a bad example to us. Those who are Pelagianists believe that every soul is created innocent with no tendencies to sin. Only personal and conscious sin could ever bring condemnation upon a person. This view is wholly unscriptural (see Chapter 6, pp. 64-69, "Anthropology: The Doctrine of Man" on man's universal depravity).

b. The Semi-Pelagian View

Semi-Pelagianists feel that every human is born with an evil tendency but that there is no guilt or punishment unless it is based upon personal and conscious acts of sin. Adam's sin, while causing a tendency to sin, did not bring any guilt or condemnation to his descendants.

The thrust of Rom. 5:14 is that all people prior to the Law of Moses experienced physical death because of Adam's sin. Even when there was no Law and people were not being held accountable for personal sins (see Rom. 4:15; 5:13), people still died physically because of Adam's sin. Therefore, Adam's sin not only caused a moral tendency to evil in the human race, it is also said to be the primary factor in guilt, condemnation, and death, both physical and spiritual. The Semi-Pelagian view is based more in rationalizing than in exegesis.[15]

c. The Federal Headship View

Those who propound this view believe that Adam's sin is the cause of humanity's ruin. It caused the sin nature, physical death, and spiritual death. We are the recipients of both guilt and condemnation due to the fall in the garden.

The federal theory of imputation maintains that Adam was the **representative** for the human race. This position holds that God made a covenant with Adam that he would be the representative for all mankind. Thus, Adam "voted" for us much the same way our congressman votes on laws for us. We do not have a personal voice in making the law, but what our representative decides affects us. When Adam sinned, he made a choice for us. Thereafter, God considered all humans to be guilty sinners and created each soul with an inborn sin nature. It is because of our representative's decision that we inherit guilt, condemnation, a sin nature, and death. Since the federal headship view does usually not consider us to have been present in Adam at the time of the fall, the federal view is often merged with a creationist view

---

[13] The author believes that the mother transmits the sin nature as much as the father does. Apparently, it was the "overshadowing of the Holy Spirit" that restricted Mary from passing sin to her Son. Perhaps future science will enable the production of children without participation of males. Such offspring will still have sin natures.

[14] Henry Thiessen, *Lectures in Systematic Theology*, (Grand Rapids: Wm. B. Eerdmans, 1949), 260.

---

[15] Semi-Pelagian ideas are held by many Methodists.

on the origin of the soul (though Traducianism and a federal headship view of imputation may not be mutually exclusive).

The federal headship theory of imputation is certainly orthodox and likely has an element of truth in it. Perhaps Adam was a representative. Yet, there are several weaknesses. There is no mention in Scripture of a covenant between God and Adam that Adam would be a representative of the whole human race. Also, the federal view usually has the tension of making God directly responsible for creating each soul with its sin nature rather than seeing the sin nature as originating directly from the parents traced back ultimately to Adam in a direct sense.

Finally, Rom. 5:12 does not say all were regarded as or treated as sinners because Adam was our representative. It says: "...so death spread to all men, because **all** <u>sinned</u>." There seems to be some level of personal participation of the part of "all" when Adam sinned. Admittedly, this is hard to explain under any theory of the imputation of sin; but the next view comes closer than the federal view.

d. The Augustinian, Natural, or Seminal View

This view teaches that, because of the unity of the human race, all of us were present in a latent sense in Adam when he sinned. We actually participated in his sin. Therefore, we inherit a sin nature, guilt, and death, because of Adam's sin (see pp. 65-67).

This view has the advantage of not having to resort to the creationist view on the origin of the soul. It also sees us as having at least some kind of participation in the first human sin. It is admittedly very difficult to understand how we could be held accountable for being present in germ form within our first father when he sinned. However, the Augustinian view does allow for at least some kind of participation in the Fall, and therefore, accords better with a sense of justice and the

actual participation implied in Rom. 5:12. The principle of the seminal view is established in Heb. 7:9-10. The Augustinian or Seminal view best meshes with the Traducian view on the origin of the soul and transmission of the sin nature.

e. Conclusions about the Imputation of Adam's Sin to Us

Whatever view is adopted to explain how Adam's sin was or could be imputed to us, it is a Scriptural fact that Adam is the immediate ground and cause for inborn depravity, guilt, and physical/spiritual death of the human race. Any theory which tries to explain this fact must wrestle with the difficulty of how we can be held accountable for Adam's transgression. If he was our representative, we did not choose him to be our representative. If we were present in some mysterious way when Adam sinned, we were not present in a conscious manner participating in the decision Adam made. The Bible student who bears in mind that man's inborn sin may **not** be the basis of eternal condemnation will go a long way toward solving any problems with God's justice in imputing Adam's sin to us.[16]

III. The Extent of Sin

For this topic consult Chapter 6, "Anthropology: The Doctrine of Man", pp. 67-69.

IV. The Two Natures of a Believer

A. Precision in the Term *Nature*

Before using the terms *old nature* and *new nature*, it is helpful to define what is meant by the word *nature*. If by *nature* we refer to a portion of man's immaterial being, then the term *nature* is poorly used with this topic. It is not the case that, when a person is converted, God creates a new portion of "soul" and adds it on to previous parts of the soul. Likewise, at death or glorification, it is not the case that a part of our immaterial being

---

[16] See Chapter six, footnote 5, pp. 65-67.

(the old sin nature) is lopped off to remain behind either on earth or in hell. Since God is finished with His creative work, we should not see Him as creating a new portion of the human soul (the new nature) at conversion and merging it with the old soul. Neither should Christians view themselves as only partially saved, i.e., the new nature (portion of soul) is saved and heaven-bound, while our old nature (portion of soul) is neither. If the term *nature* is not carefully defined, then many such misconceptions could arise.

What is really meant by the phrase *old sin nature* is a behavioral process or behavioral mechanism that alone was functioning in the life prior to salvation. This was the only behavioral process before faith in Christ. The phrase *new nature* denotes a new behavioral process or new behavioral mechanism that can also function in the life of a believer. The saved person is able to overcome the inevitable domination of sin and not live after the pattern of the old behavioral process. Several terms could be used to describe the behavioral processes that do not so easily give rise to misunderstandings that one is discussing concrete portions of the human soul:

Old Behavioral Mechanism	New Behavioral Mechanism
Old Sin Condition	New Condition
Old Function	New Function
Old Process	New Process

The terms *old nature* and *new nature* will be retained in this study because they are in common usage. Yet, they should be taken to refer to behavioral mechanisms or processes rather than to concrete parts of the human soul.

B. The Old Nature

Previous material demonstrated that every person is born with a propensity to do evil. In unsaved people the principle of sin (the sin nature) inevitably dominates. The Lord Jesus calls the unsaved "slaves to sin" (John 8:34-36) as does Paul (Rom. 6:14, 16-18, 20-22; 7:15, 25).[17] Rom. 7:5 teaches: "For while we were in the flesh [i.e., unsaved, see Rom. 8:9a], the sinful passions, which were aroused by the Law, were at work in the members of our body to bear fruit for death." Rom. 6:14 implies that before salvation people are under the absolute dominion of the sin mechanism.

Does this *old nature*, this old behavioral process, continue in the life of a believer? The answer is a qualified "yes." The old behavioral mechanism that functions inevitably in the life of an unregenerate person still exists in a Christian in the sense that there is the possibility and the option for it to function. It would not be correct to view the sin mechanism to function exactly as it did before salvation. The situation is much different for a Christian because he now has a new alternative mechanism for behavior. Before salvation the dominion of sin was inevitable; after salvation the control of sin is possible but not inevitable, and sin's control always occurs with the consent of the believer.

Perhaps an illustration of the change in the believer's position can help. Before the American Civil War slaves were legally bound to serve their masters. They had no option whatsoever. They were inevitably under their master's dominion.

However, after the Emancipation Proclamation, the legal status of the slave changed. He was no longer obligated to serve the old master who in reality was no longer his master at all in the legal or positional sense. However, even after freedom had been given and the victory won, many slaves stayed on to continue to serve their old masters. Legally, they did not have to do so, but in a practical sense they consented to and allowed their old master's dominion to continue even after they were no longer slaves.

---

[17] Rom. 7:25 is capable of a different classification, but it arguably also refers to Paul's slavery to sin before his conversion.

In spiritual realms there are several parallels. Christians are no longer under the positional dominion of sin. They do not have to allow the old behavioral mechanism to operate. Unlike the unsaved, there is the alternative of a new behavioral mechanism. However, Christians still have the option to choose to serve an old master who in reality is not a master in a legal or positional sense. The old behavioral mechanism, the old conditions, the old nature still exist in believers except its inevitable power and positional right to authority has been destroyed. Texts which show that the possibility for sinning still exist in the believer include: Rom. 6:12-13; Gal. 5:13, 16-17; Phil. 3:12-15; James 3:2a; 1 John 1:8, 10. All the New Testament commandments against sinning, and all teachings about the need for the Holy Spirit's power imply that believers still sin.

C. The New Nature

When people trust in Christ, they are regenerated or born again (John 3:3-7; Titus 3:5; James 1:18; 1 Pet. 1:3, 23; Rom. 6:4) and become children of God (John 1:12; 1 John 5:1, 4; adoption imagery in Rom. 8:15, 16 and Gal. 4:5-7). New birth means that a believer is caused to have a share in God's life by partaking of Christ's resurrection life (see Rom. 6:1ff.). Since a new convert shares in Christ's life and also is indwelt by and baptized with the Holy Spirit, there is a new behavioral mechanism available for him through which he may operate and live by totally different means than in the past. He can actively yield himself to God and depend upon the Holy Spirit to give sufficient ability to live out the life of Christ (Rom. 6:11-13; Gal. 5:22-25).

This new behavioral mechanism is what is commonly referred to as the *new nature* (see Rom. 6:4-6; Eph. 4:24; Col. 3:10). A Christian possesses two natures in the sense that he has the option or alternative to operate by the old behavioral mechanism which dominated him before conversion, or he can operate his conduct by a new way under the power of the living Christ and Holy Spirit within him. He is certainly **able to sin**, but **he is able not to sin** (John 8:36; Rom. 6:14; 1 Cor. 10:13). Within broad limitations the believer can decide whichever process he wishes to control his body and soul.[18] A Christian is free not in the sense that he has no master. He is free in the sense that he can now choose to obey his new master and is no longer enslaved to the old one.

---

[18] God will chastise a believer if his behavior is too wicked. However, within limitations, God gives a believer the freedom to choose sin over righteousness.

Chapter 8
CHRISTOLOGY
The Doctrine of Christ

OUTLINE

I. The Preexistence and Eternality of Christ
  A. Direct Statements Concerning Christ's Preexistence
  B. Indirect Evidence For Christ's Pre-existence

II. The Incarnation and Virgin Birth
  A. The Incarnation
  B. The Virgin Birth
    1. Proof of the Virgin Birth
    2. Importance of Virgin Birth

III. The Deity of Christ
  A. Christ Directly Called "God" in Texts
  B. Old Testament God Equated with New Testament Christ
    1. Isa. 40:3/Luke 1:76
    2. Psa. 102:24-28/Heb. 1:8a, 10-12
    3. Zech. 12:10/Rev. 1:7
    4. Psa. 68:17-18/Eph. 4:7-8
    5. Isa. 8:13-14/1 Pet. 2:7-8
    6. Isa. 6:1, 3/John 12:41-42
    7. Joel 3:1-2/Matt. 25:31-32
    8. Isa. 44:6/Rev. 22:13
  C. Old Testament Angel of the LORD Was God and Was Christ
  D. Christ as Lord of the Sabbath
  E. Christ Performs Works of God
    1. Christ Creator of All Things
    2. Christ Preserver of All Things
    3. Christ the Author of Life
    4. Christ Judge of All the Earth
    5. Christ Forgives Sin
  F. Christ Possesses Attributes of God
    1. Christ Both Eternal and Self-existent
    2. Christ Is Immutable
    3. Christ Is Omnipresent
    4. Christ Is Omniscient
    5. Christ Is Omnipotent
  G. Christ Accepted Worship Yet Taught Only God Should be Worshipped
  H. Trinitarian Formulas Support Christ's Deity

IV. Humanity of Christ
  A. Statements about Christ's Humanity
  B. Evidence of Christ's Humanity
    1. Grew from Infancy to Manhood
    2. Experienced Human Hunger, Ate Food
    3. Grew Tired
    4. Wept
    5. Appeared as an Ordinary Man
    6. Had a Body
    7. Suffering, Bleeding, Dying Established His Humanity
  C. Meaning of *The Kenosis*
  D. Perpetuity of Christ's Humanity
    1. His Post-resurrection Appearances
    2. His Ascension and in Visions Afterward
    3. Still Human because He is High Priest
    4. Will Return as Son of David and Son of Man
    5. Believers Will Be Like Christ at Rapture, therefore, He Is Still Human

V. Christ's Temptation

VI. Major Names
  A. Lord
  B. Jesus
  C. Christ
  D. Son of God
  E. Son of Man
  F. The Word, or Word of God
  G. Savior
  H. Lamb of God
  I. Master

VII. Christ's Major Works and Offices
  A. He Is Prophet
  B. He Is Priest

C. He Is King
D. Other Offices, Works, Titles
E. Christ as Lawkeeper
F. Works of Christ's Death
G. The Resurrection
  1. Scriptural Facts on Resurrection
  2. Significant Facts of Resurrection
    a. Demonstrated Deity of Christ
    b. Proved that God was Satisfied
    c. Forms a Basis for Believers' Bodies to be Raised
    d. Means Christ is Alive
    e. Means Believers Can Never Die in Ultimate Sense
    f. Means Christ Will Come Again
  3. Nature of Christ's Resurrection Body
H. Christ's Ascension, Exaltation, Present Ministry
  1. Christ Head of the Church
  2. High Priest and Intercessor
  3. Our Advocate
  4. Gift Giver through Holy Spirit
I. Christ's Work at Second Coming

CHRISTOLOGY: THE DOCTRINE OF CHRIST

I. The Pre-existence and Eternality of Christ

A. Direct Statements Concerning Christ's Pre-existence

Scripture is conclusive that Christ did not begin His existence as a baby in Bethlehem. The Lord Jesus Christ pre-existed in eternity past. Many times Christ Himself asserted that He had pre-existed and had come to earth from God in heaven (John 3:13; 6:38, 41, 42, 50, 51, 58; 7:29; 8:23, 42). In the book of Revelation, Christ is said to be the "**first** and the last, the **beginning** and the end" (Rev. 1:8, 17; 2:8; 21:6; 22:13).

For a child will be born to us, a **son**

will be given to us; and the government will rest on His shoulders; and His name will be called Wonderful Counselor, Mighty God, **Eternal Father**, Prince of Peace [Isa. 9:6].

"But as for you, Bethlehem Ephrathah, too little to be among the clans of Judah, from you One will go forth for Me to be ruler in Israel. **His goings forth are from long ago, from the days of eternity**" [Micah 5:2].

In the beginning was the Word, and the Word was with God, and the Word was God. **He was in the beginning with God**. All things came into being by Him, and apart from Him nothing came into being that has come into being [John 1:1-3].

Jesus said to them, "Truly, truly, I say to you, before Abraham was born, **I am**"[John 8:58].

For by Him [Christ] all things were created, both in the heavens and on earth, visible and invisible, whether thrones or dominions or rulers or authorities—all things have been created by Him and for Him. **And He is before all things**, and in Him all things hold together [Col. 1:16-17].

[W]ho, although He **existed** in the form of God...[Phil. 2:6].

But of the **Son** He says...."Thou, Lord, in the **beginning** didst lay the foundation of the earth, and the heavens are the works of Thy hands" [Heb. 1:8, 10].

B. Indirect Evidence for Christ's Preexistence

The Angel of the LORD in the Old Testament is said to be God.[1] Yet, John 1:18 teaches

---

[1] See Gen. 16:13, 22:11-12; Ex. 3:2,6; Judges 2:1, 6:11-16, 13:21-22.

that no one had ever seen God the Father and that God the Son is the revealer of the Father.[2] Therefore, the Angel of the LORD in the Old Testament is the preexistent Christ (see Chapter 2, "Theology Proper: The Doctrine of God").

II. The Incarnation and Virgin Birth

The preexistent Son of God became human flesh by being born of a virgin. Furthermore, this incarnation is permanent so that Christ is still human.

He will possess a human nature and glorified body through eternity (Zech. 12:10; Acts 1:11).

A. The Incarnation

The passages that teach that Christ became human are too numerous to list here; however, a partial list would include: Gen. 3:15; Isa. 9:6-7; Matt. 1:23; Luke 2:11; John 1:14; Rom. 8:3; Gal. 4:4; Phil. 2:6ff.; Col. 1:22; 2:9; 1 Tim. 3:16; Heb. 2:14; 10:5.

> And the Word **became flesh**, and dwelt among us, and we beheld His glory, glory as of the only begotten from the Father, full of grace and truth [John 1:14].

> But when the fullness of the time came, God sent forth His Son, **born of a woman**, born under the Law [Gal. 4:4].

> Since then the children share in **flesh and blood**, He Himself likewise also **partook of the same**, that through death He might render powerless him who had the power of death, that is, the devil [Heb. 2:14].

B. The Virgin Birth

1. Proof of the Virgin Birth

The classic passage in Isa. 7:14 clearly predicts a virgin birth. The Hebrew word *almah* has a range of meaning that includes virgin. In Gen. 24:16, Rebekah is called a *bethulah,* a term that all agree means virgin. Then in verse 43 she is said to be an *almah.* Therefore, the Hebrew word *almah* can mean virgin.[3] The translators of the Septuagint rendered the *almah* of Isa. 7:14 as *parthenos,* i.e., virgin. They understood that the context of Isaiah demands an unusual sign. It demands something comparable to "deep as sheol or high as heaven" (Isa. 7:11). A young woman conceiving and giving birth is not unusual; rather, Isaiah predicts the **virgin** birth.

The New Testament uses the word *parthenos* (virgin) of Mary three times: Matt. 1:23 and twice in Luke 1:27. In addition, there are descriptive phrases that leave the objective reader with no doubt as to what is meant by *parthenos.* They are hard to miss:

> ...before they came together ... [Matt. 1:18].

> But he had no union with her...[Matt. 1:25 NIV].

> "How shall this be, seeing I know not a man?" [Luke 1:34 KJV].

A denial of the virgin birth cannot be classified as an honest interpretive mistake. It denies a repeated and clear doctrine.

2. The Importance of the Virgin Birth

Perhaps some in naivete might classify the virgin birth as a secondary doctrine. The truth is that the virgin birth is inseparable from the main doctrines of Christology. If the virgin birth is denied, then so must

---

[2] See also 1 Tim. 1:17, 6:16; John 6:46; 1 John 4:12 on the point that no one has seen God the Father. A comparison of John 8:58 with Exodus 3:14 also shows the pre-incarnate existence of Christ.

[3] The Ugartic Word, "*almah*" also can refer to a virgin. See Cyrus H. Gordon, *Ugartic Handbook*, (Rome: Pontifical Bible Institute, 1965) 183.

Christ's deity, for He would then be as any other human. Without the virgin birth, without its "overshadowing" conception by the Holy Spirit, it becomes impossible to maintain the sinlessness of Christ. Both these points in turn affect the doctrine of Christ's atonement. If He were not God, he would not have the capacity to die for all of mankind or to bear the equivalent of eternal punishment in a few hours. If he were not sinless, He would not have been qualified to be the Savior. The virgin birth is rightly classified as one of the fundamentals of the faith.

III. The Deity of Christ

The main distinguishing mark of a cult is that it denies the deity of Christ. This is incredible considering the massive Scriptural evidence that supports Christ's deity.

A. Christ Directly Called "God" in Texts

Christ is directly called God, or some term indicating deity, in many texts (see Isa. 7:14; Psa. 110:1; Jer. 23:5-6; Matt. 1:23; John 5:18; 8:58; 10:30; 14:9; Acts 16:31-34; Rom. 9:5; 2 Cor. 4:4; Phil. 2:5-8; Col. 1:15a; Heb. 3:4 understood in context; 2 Pet. 1:1; 2:20).

> For a child will be born to us, a son will be given to us; and the government will rest on His shoulders; and His name will be called Wonderful Counselor, **Mighty God**, Eternal Father, Prince of Peace [Isa. 9:6].

> In the beginning was the Word, and the Word was with God, and the **Word was God** [John 1:1].

> No man has seen God at any time; **the only begotten God**, who is in the bosom of the Father, He has explained Him [John 1:18].

> Thomas answered and said to Him, "My Lord and my **God!**" [John 20:28].

> "Be on guard for yourselves and for all the flock, among which the Holy Spirit has made you overseers, to shepherd **the church of God which He purchased with His own blood**" [Acts 20:28].

> For in Him **all the fullness of Deity dwells in bodily form** [Col. 2: 9].

> [L]ooking for the blessed hope and the appearing of the glory of our great **God and Savior, Christ Jesus** [Titus 2:13].

> And He is the radiance of His glory and the exact representation [Greek, *character*, as in a typewriter character that produces an exact image] of His nature...[Heb. 1:3].

> But of the **Son** He says, "Thy throne, **O God**, is forever and ever, and the righteous scepter is the scepter of His kingdom" [Heb. 1:8].

> And we know that the Son of God has come, and has given us understanding, in order that we might know Him who is true, and we are in Him who is true, in **His Son Jesus Christ.** This is **the true God** and eternal life [1 John 5:20].

B. Old Testament God Equated with New Testament Christ

In several cases the God of the Old Testament is equated with Jesus Christ of the New Testament.[4]

1. Isa. 40:3/Luke 1:76

> A voice is calling, "Clear the way for the **Lord** in the wilderness; make smooth in the desert a highway for our **God.**"

---

[4] There is another possible parallel between Jer. 23:1-6, Jer. 33:15-16 and 1 Cor. 1:30 where both the LORD of the Old Testament and Christ of the New Testament are called "righteousness".

"And you, child, will be called the prophet of the Most High; for you will go on before **the Lord to prepare His** ways."

When John the Baptist prepared hearts for Jesus, he was announcing the coming of God.

2. Psa. 102:24-28/Heb. 1:8a, 10-12

I say, "O my **God,** do not take me away in the midst of my days, Thy years are throughout all generations. Of old Thou didst found the earth; and the heavens are the work of Thy hands. Even they will perish, but Thou dost endure; and all of them will wear out like a garment; like clothing Thou wilt change them, and they will be changed. But thou art the same, and Thy years will not come to an end. The children of Thy servants will continue, and their descendants will be established before Thee."

But of the **Son** He says...."Thou, **Lord,** in the beginning didst lay the foundation of the earth, and the heavens are the works of thy hands; they will perish, but Thou remainest; and they all will become old as a garment, and as a mantle Thou wilt roll them up; as a garment they will also be changed. But Thou art the same, and Thy years will not come to an end."

3. Zech. 12:10/ Rev. 1:7

"And I will pour out on the house of David and on the inhabitants of Jerusalem, the Spirit of grace and of supplication, so that they **will look on Me whom they have pierced;** [i.e., Yahweh]; and they will mourn for Him, as one mourns for an only son, and they will weep bitterly over Him, like the bitter weeping over a firstborn."

Behold, He is coming with the clouds, and every eye will see **Him,** even those who **pierced Him**; and all the tribes of the earth will mourn over **Him** [Jesus Christ]. Even so. Amen.

4. Psa. 68:17-18/Eph. 4:7-8

The chariots of **God** are myriads, thousands upon thousands; the Lord is among them as at Sinai, in holiness. Thou hast ascended on high, Thou hast led captive Thy captives; Thou hast received gifts among men, even among the rebellious also, that the **Lord God** may dwell there.

But to each one of us grace was given according to the measure of **Christ's** gift. Therefore it says, "When **He** ascended on high, He led captive a host of captives, and He gave gifts to men."

5. Isa. 8:13-14/1 Pet. 2:7-8

"It is the **Lord of hosts** whom you should regard as Holy. And He shall be your fear, and He shall be your dread. Then He shall become a sanctuary; but to both the houses of Israel, a **stone** to strike and a **rock to stumble over**...

In Isaiah, the stone is the Lord of hosts.

This precious value, then, is for you who believe. But for those who disbelieve, "The stone which the builders rejected, this became the very corner stone," and, "A **stone of stumbling** and a rock of offense...."

In 1 Peter, the stone is Christ.

6. Isa. 6:1, 3/John 12:41-42

In the year of King Uzziah's death, I saw the Lord sitting on a throne, lofty and exalted, with the train of His robe filling the temple....And one called out to another and said, "Holy, Holy, Holy, is the LORD of hosts, the whole earth is full of His glory."

These things **Isaiah** said, because he saw His glory, and he **spoke of Him** [i.e., Isaiah saw the Lord Jesus]. Nevertheless many even of the rulers believed in Him, but because of the Pharisees they were **not confessing Him,** lest they should be put out of the synagogue....

7. Joel 3:1-2/Matt. 25:31-32

"For behold, in those days....**I** [God] **will gather all the nations...**"

"But when the **Son of Man comes in His glory,** and all the angels with Him, then He will sit on His glorious throne. **And all the nations will be gathered before Him;** and He will separate them from one another, as the shepherd separates the sheep from the goats.

8. Isa. 44:6/Rev. 22:13

"...I am the **first** and I am the **last**, and there is no God besides Me."

(See also Isa. 41:4 and 48:12.)

"I am the **Alpha** and the **Omega**, the **first** and the **last**, the beginning and the end."

(See also Rev. 1:8, 17.)

C. The Old Testament Angel of the LORD Was God and Was Christ

Christ assumed that no man had ever seen God the Father (John 1:18, 6:46).[5] Yet, there are many Old Testament theophanies, appearances of God (Gen. 16:13; 18:1; 31:13; 32:30; Ex. 3:6; Judg. 2:1; 6:14-16; 13:22).[6] It must be that all Old Testament theophanies (including the Angel of the LORD) were manifestations of Christ. This fact indirectly

establishes that Christ is God.

D. Christ as Lord of the Sabbath

Given the prominent place that the Sabbath had under the Old Testament system, the title "Lord of the Sabbath" is a most impressive title. The claim to have authority over the Sabbath is a claim to having the very authority of God Himself (see also Matt. 12:8; Luke 6:5).

Consequently, the Son of Man is Lord even of the Sabbath [Mark 2:28].

E. Christ Performs the Works of God

1. Christ Creator of All Things

Then God said, "Let **Us** make man in Our image, according to **Our** likeness..." [Gen. 1:26].

All things came into being by Him, and apart from Him nothing came into being that has come into being [John 1:3].

For by Him all things were created, both in the heavens and on earth, visible and invisible, whether thrones or dominions or rulers or authorities—all things have been created by Him and for Him [Col. 1:16].

But of the **Son** He says...."Thou Lord in the beginning **didst lay the foundation** of the earth, and the heavens are the works of Thy hands" [Heb. 1:8a, 10].

2. Christ Preserver of All Things

And He is before all things, and in **Him all things hold together** [Col. 1:17].

And He is the radiance of His glory and the exact representation of His nature, and **upholds all things** by the word of His power...[Heb. 1:3].

3. Christ Author of life

---

[5] See also verses under footnote 2
[6] See also verses under footnote 1. Some Old Testament theophanies do not use the name *Angel of the LORD*. This accounts for some additional verses being listed here (e.g., Gen. 18:1).

In Him was life, and the life was the light of men [John 1:4].

"For just as the Father has life in Himself, even so He gave to the **Son** also **to have life in Himself**" [John 5:26].

Jesus said to her, "I am the resurrection and the **life**; he who believes in Me shall live even if he dies" [John 11:25].

Jesus said to him, "I am the way, and the truth, and the **life**; no one comes to the Father, but through Me" [John 14:6].

...but put to death the **Prince of life** [Author of life], the one whom God raised from the dead, a fact to which we are witnesses [Acts 3:15].

For as in Adam all die, so also **in Christ all** shall be made **alive** [1 Cor. 15:22].

4.   Christ Judge of All the Earth

Note that **God** is the Judge in Gen. 18:25 and Psa. 9:7-8, but all judgment is given to the Son. Therefore, the **Son** must be God.

"But when the **Son of Man** comes in His glory, and all the angels with Him, then He will sit on His glorious throne. And all the nations will be gathered before Him..."[Matt. 25:31-32].

"For not even the Father judges anyone, but He has given **all judgment to the Son**" [John 5:22].

"[B]ecause He has fixed a day in which **He will judge** the world in righteousness **through a Man** whom He has appointed, having furnished proof to all men by **raising Him** from the dead" [Acts 17:31].

[A]nd to give relief to you who are afflicted and to us as well when the **Lord Jesus** shall be revealed from heaven with His mighty angels in flaming fire, **dealing out retribution** to those who do not know God and to those who do not obey the gospel of our Lord Jesus [2 Thess.1:7-8].

5.   Christ Forgives Sin

And seeing their faith, He said, "Friend, **your sins are forgiven you.**" And the scribes and the Pharisees began to reason, saying, "Who is this man who speaks blasphemies? **Who can forgive sins, but God alone**?" But Jesus, aware of their reasoning, answered and said to them, "Why are you reasoning in your hearts? Which is easier, to say, 'Your sins have been forgiven you,' or to say, 'Rise and walk'? But in order that you may know that the **Son of Man has authority** on earth **to forgive** sins..."[Luke 5:20-24].

And turning toward the woman, He said to Simon, "Do you see this woman? I entered your house; you gave Me no water for My feet, but she has wet My feet with her tears, and wiped them with her hair. You gave Me no kiss; but she, since the time I came in, has not ceased to kiss My feet. You did not anoint My head with oil, but she anointed My feet with perfume. For this reason I say to you, her sins, which are many, have been forgiven, for she loved much; but he who is forgiven little loves little." And He said to her, "**Your sins have been forgiven.**" And those who were reclining at the table with Him began to say to themselves, "**Who is this man who even forgives sins?**" [Luke 7:44-49].

(See also Matt. 9:1-6; Mark 2:5ff..)

F.   Christ Possesses the Attributes of God

1. Christ Is Both Eternal and Self-existent

"But as for you, Bethlehem Eph-rathah, too little to be among the clans of Judah, from you One will go forth for Me to be ruler in Israel. His goings forth are from long ago, **from the days of eternity**" [Micah 5:2].

In the beginning was the Word, and the Word was with God, and the Word was God [John 1:1].

Jesus said to them, "Truly, truly, I say to you, before Abraham was born, **I am**" [John 8:58].

"I am the Alpha and the Omega, the **first** and the **last**, the **beginning** and the **end**" [Rev. 22:13].

(See also Isa. 9:6; John 5:26.)

2. Christ Is Immutable

But of the **Son** He says..."**But Thou art the same**, and Thy years will not come to an end" [Heb. 1:8a, 12b].

Jesus Christ is the same yesterday and today, yes and forever [Heb. 13:8].

3. Christ Is Omnipresent

"For where two or three have gath-ered together in My name, **there I am** in their midst" [Matt. 18:20].

"[T]eaching them to observe all that I commanded you; and lo, **I am with you always**, even to the end of the age" [Matt. 28:20].

Jesus answered and said to him, "If anyone loves Me, he will keep My word; and My Father will love him, and We will come to him, and make Our abode with him" [John 14:23].

...Him who fills all in all [Eph. 1:23].

(See Heb.13:5b.)

4. Christ Is Omniscient

But Jesus, on His part, was not en-trusting Himself to them, for **He knew all men** [John 2:24].

"Now we know that You **know all** things..." [John 16:30].

...And he said to Him, "**Lord, You know all things**..." [John 21:17].

(See Matt. 12:25; Mark 2:8; 9:34; Luke 5:22; 6:8; 7:39ff.; 9:47; 11:17; John 1:47-48; 4:17-19 for Christ's mind reading abili-ties.)

5. Christ Is Omnipotent

And Jesus came up and spoke to them, saying, "**All authority** has been given to Me in heaven and on earth" [Matt. 28:18].

"[E]ven as Thou gavest Him **author-ity over all mankind,** that to all whom Thou hast given Him, He may give eternal life" [John 17:2].

[F]ar **above all rule and authority** and power and dominion, and every name that is named, not only in this age, but also in the one to come [Eph. 1:21].

[W]ho will transform the body of our humble state into conformity with the body of His glory, by the exertion of the power that He has even to **sub-ject all things** to Himself [Phil. 3:21].

[A]nd in Him you have been made complete, and **He is the head over all** rule and authority [Col. 2:10].

And He is the radiance of His glory and the exact representation of His nature, and **upholds all things by the word of His power**...[Heb. 1:3].

"I am the Alpha and the Omega", says the Lord God, "who is and who was and who is to come, **the Al-mighty**" [Rev. 1:8; see also Rev.

1:17 and 22:13 to establish that Jesus is the subject in Rev. 1:8].

G. Christ Accepted Worship Yet Taught Only God Should Be Worshiped

Then Jesus said to him, "Be gone, Satan! For it is written, 'You shall **worship** the Lord your God, and **serve Him only**'" [Matt. 4:10].

And those who were in the boat **worshiped Him**, saying, "You are certainly God's Son!" [Matt. 14:33].

Jesus heard that they had put him out; and finding him, He said, "Do you believe in the Son of Man?" He answered and said, "And who is He, Lord, that I may believe in Him?" Jesus said to him, "You have both seen Him, and He is the one who is talking with you." And he said, Lord, "I believe." And he **worshiped** Him [John 9:35-38].

Thomas answered and said to Him, "My Lord and my God!" [John 20:28].

(See also Ex. 34:14; Isa. 42:8.)

H. Trinitarian formulas that link Christ with the Triune God support Christ's deity. (These are listed in Chapter Two, "Theology Proper: The Doctrine of God", p. 20.)[7]

---

[7] Certain cults misuse the terms "first-born" (Rom. 8:29; Col. 1:15, 18; Heb. 1:6; Rev. 1:5) and "only begotten" (John 1:14, 18; 3:16, 18; 1 John 4:9) to teach that Christ was the first of created beings.

There is no argument that the word "first-born" can refer to birth. It does so in Matt. 1:25 (some manuscripts) and Luke 2:7. However, in some contexts the word has little or nothing to do with birth or origin. It comes to mean, "supreme, chief, honored one." The Hebrew word for first-born is used in Job 18:13, "the first-born of death," and Isa. 14:30, "the first-born of the poor," (see NASB marginal note). In each case the idea of time of birth has been lost to the idea of supremacy because in Hebrew thinking "first-born" gives the idea of supremacy in matters of inheritance. In Job 18:13, "the first-born of death" means the "deadliest of diseases" and, in Isa. 14:30, "the first-born of the poor" means the very poorest. In the LXX *prototokos* (which is the same word used of Christ in the New Testament) at times emphasizes position with little or nothing to do with origin. Israel is the "first-born" of the nations even though it was not the first nation in terms of time or origin. The term means Israel is supreme over the other nations (Ex. 4:22; Jer. 31:9; 38:9 in the LXX). Deut 21:16 speaks of the theoretical possibility of making a son who is born second in time to become the "first-born" in terms of rank. Also, Psa. 89:27 (88:27 in LXX) teaches that God will make David (and his offspring) His first-born. This refers to David's supreme rank and has nothing to do with time of birth or origin. Some translations of the LXX use the title first-born in the phrase "the chief of the thirty" speaking of David's mighty men (1 Chron. 11:11).

Non-Scriptural usage of the word also throws light on its range of meanings. In 4 Esdras 6:58, Israel is called "my first-born, only one, elect and beloved." Again, the word *prototokos* speaks of rank, position, supremacy. Rabbi Bechai wrote, "God is the firstborn of the world" (see J. B. Lightfoot, *Saint Paul's Epistles to the Colossians and to Philemon.* rev. ed. (Grand Rapids: Zondervan, 1977) 146-47. This means that God is supreme and not that God is born. The early church fathers called the heretic Marcion "the first-born of Satan." This means a chief of Satanic workers and has nothing to do with birth. (Polycarp, quoted by Irenaeus, *Against Heresies*, 3:3:4). Finally, even adopted children could be called first-born. *The Theological Dictionary of the New Testament* quotes an early deed of adoption as saying "in order to be your genuine son and first-born as having been begotten from your own blood." (See Wilhelm Michaelis, *Theological Dictionary of the New Testament*, edited by Gerhard Kittel and Gerhard Friedrich, trans. by Geoffrey Bromiley, (Grand Rapids: Wm. B. Eerdmans Publishing Co., 1968), VI 872. (Translation from the Greek original is my own). All these references establish that "first-born" has a range of meaning to include the ideas of being **supreme** with **no thought of birth** at all.

In the Col. 1:15 context, v. 16 is giving the reason for the statement of v. 15. Verse sixteen

IV. The Humanity of Christ

A. Statements about Christ's Humanity

(See sections II.A. and B., pp. 85-86, this chapter on the incarnation and virgin birth.)

B. Evidence of Christ's Humanity

1. He grew from infancy to adulthood (Luke 2:40, 52).

2. He experienced human hunger and ate food (Matt. 4:2; Mark 11:12; Luke 22:19ff.;

---

reads, "For by Him were all things created." Christ is the first-born because He created all things. In such a context the meaning of supreme fits nicely. However, the idea of His being the first created being is excluded by the idea of His being the creator of all things. Col. 1:15 teaches that Christ is supreme over all creation. It is not teaching He had an origin in time. Likewise, the description of "only-begotten" should not be taken to teach that Christ had an origin in time. This term (*monogenees*) need not refer to birth or origin. Just as with "first-born" the term came to refer to an exalted position. In Heb. 11:17 Isaac is called Abraham's only begotten son. However, Abraham also fathered Ishmael (Gen. 16:16) and at least six other sons (Gen. 25:1-2). Therefore, Isaac was an "only-begotten" not in the sense of the only one born but in the sense of unique position and priority. Christ is the only begotten of the Father not in the sense that He has a birth or an origin in time. He is rather the Father's special son.

There is even some question as to whether *monogenees* should be derived from *mono* (only) and *gennao* (to be born). It might be better understood as *mono* (only) and *gen* (the second aorist stem of *ginomai* "to be"). Notice there are two *n*'s in *gennao* but only one *n* in both the stem *gen* and the word *monogenees*. The resulting translation would be "the "unique," "the only son of His kind," and so forth. The NIV seems to favor this alternative derivation (see John 1:14, 18; 3:16, 18; 1 John 4:9). John wanted us to know that Christ is the Son of God in a unique sense different than the meaning intended when calling a believer a son of God (John 1:12; 1 John 5:1). Paul's way of making the same distinction is to liken believers to adopted sons (Rom. 8:15; Gal. 4:5-6).

24:30; John 21:12ff.).

3. Christ grew tired (Matt. 8:24; Mark 4:38; John 4:6).

4. He wept (Matt. 23:37; John 11:35).

5. He appeared as an ordinary man (Isa. 53:2ff.; John 4:9; Phil. 2:7-8).

6. He had a body (John 1:14), soul (Matt. 26:38), and spirit (Luke 23:46).

7. His suffering, bleeding and death establish His humanity (Matt.26:26-29).

C. The Meaning of *The Kenosis*

The term *kenosis* comes from the verb *kenao* in Phil. 2:7. It means to empty. Some argue that in becoming human Christ emptied Himself of His deity. Neither the context nor other statements about Christ's nature will allow such a heretical interpretation.

It is an attribute of God to be immutable (Mal. 3:6; James 1:17). As God, Jesus Christ can not vary in His attributes (Heb. 1:8-12; 13:8). Therefore, it is quite impossible that Phil. 2:7 could be teaching that Christ emptied Himself of divine attributes.

In its context, the most simple interpretation of Phil. 2:7 is that Christ laid aside legitimate self-interests in order to become human. Many texts teach of Christ's humility (Matt. 11:29; John 13:3ff.). Other possible interpretations are that Christ laid aside His visible glory and/or the independent use of His divine attributes. Given the attribute of being immutable, it must be that Christ became human without ceasing to be God.

D. Perpetuity of Christ's Humanity

It is not true that Christ stopped being human when He ascended to heaven. All Scriptural lines of evidence point to the conclusion that Christ is and will be eternally human.

1. In His post-resurrection appearances Christ was human (Matt. 28:9; Luke 24:39; John 20:14-15).

2. At His ascension and in visions thereafter, Christ appears as human. He will come in "like manner" as He departed (Acts 1:11; note phrases *Son of Man* in Acts 7:56 and *like a Son of Man* in Rev. 1:13).

3. It must be that Christ is still human for He is our high priest (Rom. 8:34; Heb. 3:1; 4:14-16; 7:23ff.; 9:24ff.).

4. Christ will return as the "Son of David" and the "Son of Man." All eyes will look upon the one who was pierced (2 Sam. 7:12-16; Psa. 89:2-4; 132:11; Isa. 9:6-7; Jer. 23:5-6; Dan. 7:13-14; Zech. 12:10; Matt. 24:30; 25:31, 26:64; and Rev. 1:7).

5. Believers will be like Christ at the Rapture. Therefore, He is still human (Rom. 8:29; 1 Cor. 15:49; Phil. 3:21; 1 John 3:2).

V. Christ's Temptation

There is full agreement among Bible believers that Christ was tempted (Matt.4:1ff.; Mark 1:12ff.; Luke 4:1ff.; Heb. 2:18; 4:15) and that He overcame all temptation in His sinless perfection (2 Cor. 5:21; Heb. 4:15; 1 Pet. 2:22). Temptation must have been directed against His human nature alone as God cannot be tempted with evil (James 1:13). Christ was conceived by the Holy Spirit and did not possess a sin nature as a part of His humanity. Therefore, the issue arises over whether the Lord could have sinned. Was He peccable or impeccable?[8] Was His temptation a real temptation?

Unless we separate Christ's two natures (the human and divine), it seems that His deity demands that we view His overall person as impeccable.[9] God can neither sin nor be tempted to sin.

The possibility, however, for genuine temptation lies in that His human nature, were it totally unsustained by the divine nature, may indeed have been susceptible to sin. Therefore, He had a peccable nature (the human nature) which made the temptation real, but He was impeccable in His overall person. That an impeccable person could face temptation is no more strange than the fact that an invincible army can be assaulted. An isolated stick may be liable to bend or break. Yet, when tied in a bundle, no one can break it. A piece of paper can be torn, but when connected to hundreds in a metropolitan phone book, it can not be torn. Likewise, the human nature of Christ was capable of being tempted, but his two natures joined in one person were incapable of sinning.

> For since He Himself was tempted in that which He has suffered, He is able to come to the aid of those who are tempted [Heb. 2:18].

> For we do not have a high priest who cannot sympathize with our weaknesses, but one who has been tempted in all things as we are, yet without sin [Heb. 4:15].

VI. Major Names

A complete study on Christ's names would over-extend this study. However, the Lord's major names should be defined.

A. Lord

The title *Lord* is from the Greek *(kurios)*. It has a range of meaning from "sir" (John 4:11ff.; 20:15) to a reference to deity (Matt. 4:10; Rev. 1:8). There are enough times that Jesus of the New Testament is linked with the LORD of the Old Testament (see III.B. this chapter) to ensure that *Lord* should be understood to ascribe **deity** when used as a name for Christ.

B. Jesus

The name Jesus has both human and divine implications. The Greek name *(Iasous)* is a form of the Hebrew *Yeshua (Joshua)*. The

---

[8] Peccable means capable of sin. Impeccable means incapable of sin.

[9] Christ the mediator between God and man (1 Tim. 2:5) is the God-man. The theological term for the union of His two natures into a person is the "hypostatic-union".

original meaning is "*Yahweh* saves" or "salvation is of *Yahweh*." In an indirect way, this speaks of Christ being the God who saves. Yet, fundamentally Jesus is Christ's **human** name.

C. Christ

Christos is Greek for the Hebrew term Messiah and means "anointed one." In the Old Testament, the title *Messiah* was often used of anointed priests and kings (e.g., Lev. 4:3, 5, 16; 1 Sam. 16:6; 2 Sam. 23:1). The references to **the Messiah** in Dan. 9:25-26 and Psa. 2:2 caused the title to become more restricted to God's primary annointed One. By New Testament times, *Christos*, "anointed one," was the title for the **anointed deliverer** promised so clearly in the Old Testament.

D. Son of God

This title does not mean God married a wife and fathered a son. The Israelites commonly used the idiom *son of* something to ascribe the characteristics of that something. Both the Old Testament and New Testament are replete with examples:

- Deut. 25:2 – "Sons of beating" meaning a criminal worthy of beatings

- 2 Sam. 13:28 – "Sons of valor" meaning courage

- Job 41:34 – "Sons of pride" meaning proud people

- Jer. 48:45 – "Sons of tumult" meaning people involved in revelry

- Mark 3:17 – "Sons of thunder" meaning angry dispositions

- Acts 4:36 – "a Son of encouragement" meaning an encourager.

When Christ is called the *Son of God*, it is an assertion that He has the **characteristics of God.** The Jewish authorities understood fully the implications of the title "Son of God."

For this cause therefore the Jews were seeking all the more to kill Him, because He not only was breaking the Sabbath, but also was **calling God His own Father**, making Himself **equal with God** [John 5:18].

E. Son of Man

This is Christ's favorite title for Himself. Though the name does assert His humanity, the emphasis of the phrase lies elsewhere. The "Son of Man" in Dan. 7:13-14 is the **coming ruler** who has both a universal and everlasting kingdom. This meaning is Christ's primary intention by using the title "Son of Man" (see Matt. 24:30; 25:31; 26:64; John 1:51).

"I kept looking in the night visions, and behold, with the clouds of heaven One like a **Son of Man** was coming, and He came up to the Ancient of Days and was presented before Him. And **to Him was given dominion**, glory and a kingdom, that **all the peoples**, nations, and men of every language **might serve Him**. His **dominion is an everlasting dominion** which will not pass away; and His kingdom is one which will not be destroyed" [Dan. 7:13-14].

F. The Word, or Word of God (John 1:1, 14; Rev. 19:13)

There are many possible sources to John's usage of this title. Regardless of the exact derivation, John intends to teach that Jesus Christ is the outward expression and **revelation of the inner mind and thinking of God**.

G. Savior (Titus 2:13; Phil. 3:20)

The word *salvation* is treated separately in Chapter 9, "Soteriology." To call Christ *Savior* means He is the **deliverer** from sin's penalty and power. Eventually, He will save believers from sin's very presence.

H. The Lamb of God (John 1:29; 1 Pet.

1:18-19; Rev. 5:6ff.)

Building upon the Old Testament practice of blood **sacrifice to atone for sin**, the New Testament calls Christ "the Lamb."

I. Master (John 13:13)

The English reader might miss the meaning of this title. The underlying meaning of this Greek word is "teacher."

VII. Christ's Major Works and Offices

A. He Is Prophet

Christ is the fulfillment of the Old Testament prediction of a Great Prophet (Deut. 18:15; John 1:21, 45; 6:14; Acts 3:22; 7:37). Jesus was the ultimate prophet who explained God to man (John 1:18; Heb. 1:1-2; Rev. l:l, 19:10). He prophesied while on earth (e.g., Matthew, Chapters 13, 24, and 25) and continued His prophetic work through the Holy Spirit after His ascension (John 16:13).

> "The LORD your God will raise up for you a **prophet** like me from among you, from your countrymen, you shall listen to him" [Deut. 18:15].

> **God**, after He spoke long ago to the fathers in the prophets in many portions and in many ways, in these last days **has spoken to us in His Son**, whom He appointed heir of all things, through whom also He made the world [Heb. 1:1-2].

B. He Is Priest

Psalm 110:4 predicted that the greater Son of David would be a priest not from the tribe or order of Levi but from Melchizedek. As our High Priest, He was both the sacrifice and the sacrificer who offered a final sacrifice that did not need to be repeated (1 Cor. 15:3-4; Heb. 1:3; 7:27; 9:12, 28; 10:10-14, 18; 1 Pet. 3:18). Also, related to His work as high priest are the functions of intercessor (Rom. 8:34; Heb. 7:25) and mediator (1 Tim. 2:5). Christ's intercessory ministry was

in operation even before the cross (Luke 22:32; John 17). Christ is high priest forever (Psa. 110:4; Heb. 5:6, 9-10; 7:16-17, 23-25).[10]

All believers in Christ are also priests (1 Pet. 2:5, 9; Rev. 1:6; 5:10; 20:6). Therefore, we have sacrifices to offer: our bodies (Rom. 12:1-2), praise (Heb. 13:15), and material wealth (Phil. 4:18). As priests we also have a priestly access to God in prayer without having to go through a human mediator (John 14:13, 14; 16:24; Eph. 2:18; Heb. 4:16; 10:19-22).

> The LORD has sworn and will not change His mind, "Thou art a **priest forever** according to the order of Melchizedek" [Psa. 110:4].

> ...He became to all those who obey Him the source of eternal salvation, being designated by God as a **high priest** according to the order of Melchizedek [Heb. 5:9-10].

C. He Is King

Christ is the head of a spiritual kingdom in the world today, i.e., the church (Rom. 14:17; 1 Cor. 4:20; Col. 1:13; 4:11). However, He will be the monarch of a worldwide political Kingdom when He comes again to assume authority upon the throne of David in Jerusalem (2 Sam. 7:12-16; Psalms 2, 45, 72, 89; Isa. 9:6-7; 33:22; Jer. 23:5, 6; 33:22; Dan. 7:13-14; Micah 5:2; Zech. 9:9; 14:9; Matt. 2:2; Luke 1:32-33; John 1:49; Rom.11:26; 1 Cor. 15:25; Rev. 1:5-6; 17:14; 19:16).

> For the LORD is our judge, the LORD is our lawgiver, the LORD is our **king**; He will save us— [Isa. 33:22].

> "He will be great, and will be called

---

[10] The eternality of Christ's role as priest shows the perpetuity of His humanity. It also relates to the doctrine of eternal security. Since He ever is our priest, He ever intercedes and His blood ever atones (see Heb. 7:25).

the Son of the Most High; and the Lord God will give Him the **throne** of His father David; and He will **reign** over the house of Jacob forever; and His **kingdom** will have no end" [Luke 1:32-33].

D. Other Offices, Works, and Titles

- The Last Adam (1 Cor. 15:21ff.)

- The head of a new creation (2 Cor. 5:17)

- The head of the body (1 Cor. 12:12ff.; Eph. 4:15-16)

- The Great Shepherd of the Sheep (John 10:11ff.; Heb. 13:20; 1 Pet. 5:4)

- The Vine to the Branches (John 15)

- The Cornerstone to the building (Matt. 21:42; 1 Cor. 3:11; Eph. 2:20; 1 Pet. 2:5ff.)

- The Bridegroom to the bride (Eph. 5:22ff.)

E. Christ as Lawkeeper

Christ came to fulfill the Law (Matt. 5:17). He kept the Law fully (2 Cor. 5:21; Heb. 4:15; 1 Pet. 2:22). His perfect righteousness is credited to the account of those who believe in Him (2 Cor. 5:21). Thus, Christ's role as lawkeeper is not a task that is irrelevant to believers. Rom. 5:10 teaches, "we shall be saved by his life." Because Christ is totally and eternally righteous and because we are saved by His righteousness and not our own, believers have an eternal and complete salvation.

F. The Works of Christ's Death

The Atonement receives major consideration in Chapter 9, "Soteriology: The Doctrine of Salvation."

G. The Resurrection

1. Scriptural Facts on the Resurrection

The Gospels clearly teach the bodily resurrection of Jesus Christ (Matt. 28:5ff.; Mark 16:6ff.; Luke 24:1ff.; John 20-21). There were post-resurrection appearances to Mary, to other women returning from the tomb, to Peter, to the disciples on the Emmaus road, to the disciples without Thomas present, to the disciples with Thomas present, to the seven by the Sea of Galilee, to James, and to over 500 at one time (see 1 Cor. 15:1-8).[11]

---

[11] Historical evidence for the resurrection is more pertinent to the topic of Christian Evidences than doctrine. In brief, consider that Christ's tomb had to have been empty on the first Easter or His enemies would have turned it into an exhibit to squelch the claims of a resurrection. If they could have produced the dead body of Jesus, they would have certainly done so. How did the tomb get empty? Logic rules out all options except the resurrection. If the disciples had gone to the wrong tomb or if they were having hallucinations, then the body was still in the correct tomb and could have been produced. The claim that the disciples stole the body was such a clear fabrication that Pilate never arrested anyone for grave robbing due to lack of evidence. First, guards in those times did not sleep on duty. It was the death penalty for Roman soldiers. Jewish guards who slept had their clothes set on fire (Rev. 16:15). Next, sleeping people obviously cannot witness anything and cannot make charges they saw grave robbing. Also, no one could have removed the massive stone and body without making noise that would have awakened the guards. Evidently even Pilate did not believe the guards' story.

Another objection to the resurrection is the "swoon" theory. This maintains the Lord Jesus did not die on the cross, that He later regained strength and claimed to rise again. However, Pilate's soldiers certified His death (Mark 15:43-45; John 19:34). See also Edwards et al, "On the Physical Death of Jesus Christ," *Journal of the American Medical Association*, March 21, 1986, Vol. 255, No. 11; 1463: "...interpretations based on the assumption that Jesus did not die on the cross appear to be at odds with modern medical knowledge."

The best explanation for the empty tomb is the resurrection. The disciples were ethical men who went to their deaths claiming that Jesus arose. One could not ask for more credible witnesses or more evidence to confirm an event from

"He is not here, for He has risen, just as He said. Come, see the place where He was lying" [Matt. 28:6].

2. The Significance of the Resurrection

The resurrection is a cardinal tenet of Christianity (1 Cor. 15:14ff.). It was a main component in the message of the early church. An examination of the word *witness* in the book of Acts will show that the early church was mainly witnessing to the fact of the resurrection (see Acts 2:32; 3:15; 5:30-32, etc.).

a. The resurrection demonstrated the Deity of Christ (Rom. 1:4).

[W]ho was **declared the Son of God** with power **by the resurrection** from the dead... [Rom. 1:4].

b. The resurrection proved that God was satisfied that a way of justification had been secured (Rom. 4:25).

He who was delivered up because of our transgressions, and was **raised because of our justification** [Rom. 4:25].

c. The resurrection forms a basis for believer's bodies being raised (John 14:19; 1 Cor. 15:20).

...but you will behold Me; **because I live, you shall live** also [John 14:19].

But now **Christ has been raised** from the dead, **the first fruits** of those who are asleep [1 Cor. 15:20].

d. The resurrection means Christ Jesus is live to be our high priest and intercessor (Heb. 7:25).

Hence, also, He is able to save forever those who draw near to God through Him, since He **always lives to make intercession** for them [Heb. 7:25].

history.

e. The resurrection means that believers can never die in the ultimate sense. We share His life and His "life will never end" (John 11:25-26; Rom. 6:9-10).

[K]nowing that Christ, having been raised from the dead, is never to die again; death no longer is master over Him [Rom. 6:9].

f. The resurrection means Christ will come again (Acts 1:11) and will rule as the Son of Man over the entire human world (Isa. 9:6-7; Dan. 7:13-14; Luke 1:32-33).

[A]nd they also said, "Men of Galilee, why do you stand looking into the sky? This Jesus, who has been taken up from you into heaven, will come in just the same way as you have watched Him go into heaven" [Acts 1:11].

3. The Nature of Christ's Resurrection Body

Since believers will have a glorified body in the likeness of Jesus Christ (1 Cor. 15:49; 1 John 3:2), it is of interest to consider the nature of His resurrection body. It was composed of flesh and bones (Luke 24:39). Yet, He could move rapidly and physical barriers could not deter Him (John 20:19, 26). His resurrection body enjoyed food (Luke 24:30; John 21:12-13) and is glorious (Phil. 3:21).

H. Christ's Ascension, Exaltation, and Present Ministry

The Ascension of Christ to heaven is recorded in Acts 1:11 ff. Before His crucifixion Christ prayed that His previous glory would be restored (John 17:1, 5). The Bible teaches that Christ is now at the right hand of God in glory (Acts 7:56; Col. 3:1; Heb. 1:3; 8:1; 12:2). He is not in the least inactive.

1. Christ is the head of the church (Eph. 1:20-23; Col. 2:10).

[W]hich He brought about in Christ,

when He raised Him from the dead, and seated Him at His right hand in the heavenly places, far above all rule and authority and power and dominion, and every name that is named, not only in this age, but also in the one to come. And He put all things in subjection under His feet, and gave Him as **head over all things to the church**, which is His body, the fullness of Him who fills all in all [Eph. 1:20-23].

2. He is our high priest and intercessor (Rom. 8:34; Heb. 7:25).

[W]ho is the one who condemns? **Christ Jesus** is He who died, yes, rather who was raised, who is at the right hand of God, who also **intercedes for us** [Rom. 8:34].

3. He is our advocate, i.e., helper and defense against Satan's accusations (1 John 2:1).

My little children, I am writing these things to you that you may not sin. And if anyone sins, we have an **advocate with the Father, Jesus Christ** the righteous [1 John 2:1].

4. He is a gift giver through the Holy Spirit (Eph. 4:7).

But to each one of us grace was given according to the measure of Christ's gift [Eph. 4:7].

I. Christ's Work at His Second Coming

Christ's work in the future is discussed in detail in Chapter 12, "Eschatology."

Chapter 9
SOTERIOLOGY
The Doctrine of Salvation

PART 1:
SALVATION PROVIDED

OUTLINE

I. *Salvation* Word Study
  A. Usage of *Salvation*
    1. *To Save*
    2. *Salvation*
    3. *Savior*
    4. *Salvation*
  B. The Meaning of *Salvation*
    1. Non-theological Contexts
      a. Deliverance from Sickness
      b. Deliverance from Demons
      c. Rescue from Enemies
      d. Deliverance from Death
      e. Rescue from Danger
    2. Theological Contexts
      a. Saved from Sin
      b. Saved from Wrath, Judgment, Condemnation
      c. Saved from Perverse Genera-tion
      d. Saved from Being Lost
      e. Saved from Death
      f. Saved from Perishing
  C. The Time of Salvation
    1. In the Past, Believers Saved from the Penalty of Sin
    2. In the Present, Believers Saved from Power of Sin
    3. In the Future, Believers Saved from the Presence of Sin and from All Wrath
  D. Summary
II. Substitutionary (Vicarious) Atonement
  A. Accidental Theory of Atonement
  B. Example Theory of Atonement
  C. Moral Influence Theory of Atonement
  D. Governmental Theory of Atonement

E. Substitutionary Theory of Atonement Defended
    1. The Word *Anti*
    2. The Word *Huper*
    3. Substitutionary View Established on Grounds Other than *Anti* and *Huper*
    4. Conclusion on Substitutionary Atonement
III. Redemption: The Sinward Aspect of Atonement
  A. *Agorazo*
    1. Secular Usage
    2. Biblical Usage
    3. Conclusion
  B. *Exagorazo*
    1. Secular Usage
    2. Biblical Usage
  C. *Lutrao*
    1. Secular Usage
    2. Biblical Usage
  D. *Lutron*
    1. Secular Usage
    2. Biblical Usage
  E. *Lutrosis*
  F. *Apolutrosis*
    1. Secular Usage
    2. Biblical Usage
  G. Summary and Conclusions about Re-demption
    1. To Whom Redemption Price Paid
    2. Redemption Sinward Aspect of Atonement
    3. Subtle Differences of Word Groups
      a. *Agorazo* group
      b. *Lutrao* group
IV. Reconciliation: The Manward Aspect of the Atonement
  A. Backgroud to the Idea of Reconciliation
  B. Meaning of Words Translated *Reconciliation*
    1. Usage in Ancient Secular World

2. Biblical Usage
   a. Non-salvation Contexts
   b. Salvation Contexts
C. Details on the Doctrine of
   Reconciliation
   1. Two Phases of Reconciliation
      Observed
   2. Two Phases of Reconciliation
      Explained
      a. Universal Reconciliation at the
         Cross
      b. Individual Reconciliation at
         Time of Salvation
   3. God as Initiator in Reconciliation
   4. Summary
V. Propitiation: The Godward Aspect of the
   Atonement
   A. Definition of *Propitiation*
      1. Ancient Secular Usage of the
         Propitiation Word Group
      2. Biblical Usage of the *Propitiation*
         Word Group
         a. God Angry about Sin
         b. Propitiation in the Septuagint
         c. Propitiation in the New
            Testament
   B. Three Applications or Phases of
      Propitiation
      1. Propitiation for Whole World at
         Time of the Cross
      2. Propitiation that Occurs at Time of
         Faith in Christ
      3. Propitiation that Occurs When
         Believer Confesses Sin
   C. Greater Implications to Doctrine
      of Propitiation
VI. The Role of Christ's Blood in the
    Atonement
    A. Observations about Blood in the
       Bible
    B. Conclusions about Role of Christ's
       Blood in the Atonement
       1. Blood is More than a Symbol
       2. Other Factors in Providing Salva-
          tion
VII. Meaning and Extent of The Atonement
     A. The Old Testament Term *atonement*
        1. To Cover Sin

2. To Divert Wrath
3. To Give Payment to Secure Favor
4. To Reconcile
5. Summary
B. Atonement as a Theological Term
C. The Extent of the Atonement
D. The Finality of the Atonement

PART 1:
SALVATION PROVIDED

I. *Salvation* Word Study

A. Usage

1. *To save (sozo)* is used approximately 106-108 times in the New Testament depending on which manuscripts are counted.

2. *Salvation (soteria)* is used approximately 45 or 46 times in the New Testament depending on which manuscripts are counted.

3. *Savior (soter)* is used approximately 24 times in the New Testament.

4. *Salvation (soterion)* is used four times.

The total for all four terms is about 180 times whether one follows either the critical or majority texts.

B. The Meaning of Salvation

1. In non-theological contexts *salvation* is used in a variety of ways that do not refer to deliverance from sin's penalty. These help to establish that the word means basically "to rescue, to deliver."

a. It is common for the New Testament, especially the gospels, to call the "deliverance from sickness" *salvation*. *Salvation* can refer to restoration to health. A person's well being has returned. (See Matt. 9:21, 22; Mark 3:4; 5:23, 28, 34; 6:56; 10:52; Luke 6:9; 7:50; 17:19; 18:42; John 11:12; Acts 4:9; 14:9; 27:34; 2 Cor. 1:6; James 5:15.)

...for she was saying to herself, "If I only touch His garment, I shall get well" (Greek: saved). But Jesus turning and seeing her said, "Daughter, take courage; your faith has made you well" (Greek: saved). And at once the woman was made well (Greek: saved) [Matt. 9:21-22].

...and the prayer offered in faith will restore (Greek: save) the one who is sick [James 5:15a].

b. *Salvation* may be used of deliverance from demons (Luke 8:36).

c. Salvation may be used of rescue or deliverance from enemies (Luke 1:71; Acts 7:25).

"Salvation from our enemies..." [Luke 1:71a].

d. Jesus Christ asked to be saved. This helps to show that the word means "deliverance."

"Now My soul has become troubled; and what shall I say, 'Father, **save** Me from this hour'? But for this purpose I came to this hour" [John 12:27].

In the days of His flesh, He offered up both prayers and supplications with loud crying and tears to the One able to **save** Him from death, and He was heard because of His piety [Heb. 5:7].

e. The word *salvation* is used of rescue from danger in a variety of situations: storms on the sea (Matt. 8:25; 14:30; Acts 27:20, 31); deliverance at the end of the tribulation period (Matt. 10:22; 24:13, 22; Mark 13:13, 20); rescue from the cross (Matt. 27:40, 42, 49; Mark 15:30, 31; Luke 23:35, 37, 39); from trouble (1 Tim. 4:16); from prison (Phil. 1:19); from slavery in Egypt (Jude 5); from the flood (Heb. 11: 7).

Before the Christian authors of the New Testament used the word *save*, it was used of common dangers to man. *Salvation* means "deliverance, rescue, preservation, help, assistance, aid, escaping trouble."

2. Biblical authors took a normal word that means "deliverance" and used it in a theological sense. Believers are "saved" from a number of troubles.

a. Believers are saved from sin (Matt. 1:21; Luke 1:77, 7:50; 1 Tim. 1:15).

"And she will bear a Son; and you shall call His name Jesus, for it is He who will **save His people from their sins**" [Matt. 1:21].

It is a trustworthy statement, deserving full acceptance, that **Christ Jesus came** into the world **to save sinners**, among whom I am foremost of all [1 Tim. 1:15].

b. Believers are saved from wrath, judgment, and condemnation (John 3:17; Rom. 1:16 in context, see v. 18; 5:9; 1 Thess. 5:9; 1 Pet. 4:17-18).

Much more then, having now been justified by His blood, we shall be **saved from the wrath of God** through Him [Rom. 5:9].

c. Believers are saved from a perverse generation, a wicked world (Acts 2:40).

...Be **saved from this perverse generation**! [Acts 2:40].

d. Believers are saved from being lost (Luke 19:10).

"For the Son of Man has come to seek and to **save that which was lost**" [Luke 19:10].

e. Believers are saved from death (Matt. 16:25; Mark 8:35; Luke 9:24.) See, also, the following verses which speak of deliverance from death but do not use the word salvation: John 5:24; Rom. 6:23; Eph. 2:1.

"For whoever wishes to save his life shall lose it, but whoever **loses his life** for My sake, he is the one who will **save** it" [Luke 9:24].

f. Believers are saved from perishing (1 Cor. 1:18; 2 Cor. 2:15-16) and from destruction (James 4:12).

> For we are a fragrance of Christ to God among those who are being **saved** and among those who are **perishing** [2 Cor. 2:15].

> There is only one Lawgiver and Judge, the One who is able to **save** and to **destroy**; but who are you who judge your neighbor? [James 4:12].

C. The Time of Salvation

A Bible student needs to catch the fact that sometimes the Bible speaks of salvation as past, sometimes present, and sometimes future.

1. **In the past,** believers in Christ **were saved from the penalty of sin** (Rom 8:24; Eph. 2:5, 8; 2 Tim. 1:9; Titus 3:5).

> For by grace you **have been saved** [past tense] through faith; and that not of yourselves, it is the gift of God... [Eph. 2:8].

> He **saved** [past tense] us, not on the basis of deeds which we have done in righteousness, but according to His mercy, by the washing of regeneration and renewing by the Holy Spirit [Titus 3:5].

2. In the **present,** believers **are being saved from the power of sin** (Phil.2:12; 1 Pet. 2:2).

> So then, my beloved, just as you have always obeyed, not as in my presence only, but now much more in my absence, **work out your salvation** with fear and trembling [Phil. 2:12].

3. In the **future, we will be saved from the presence of sin** and from all wrath (Rom. 5:10; 13:11; 1 Thess. 5:9; 2 Tim. 4:18; Heb. 1:14; 9:28; 1 Pet. 1:5; 4:18).

> ...we **shall be saved** [future tense] by His life [Rom. 5:10].

D. Summary

To save means to deliver, to rescue, to help, to aid, etc. This is shown in non-theological contexts (rescue from sickness, demons, enemies, storms, slavery, and so forth). In theological contexts the meaning is the same. Christians are delivered from sin, wrath, judgment, condemnation, a wicked world, being lost, death, and destruction. Believers **have been** saved from sin's penalty, **are being** saved from its power, and **will be saved** from its presence.

II. Substitutionary (Vicarious) Atonement

Atonement, as a theological term, refers to all that Christ did on the cross. A complete study of atonement immediately follows in sections III through VII of this chapter. This section is, however, more limited. It concerns the following questions: What was the purpose of Christ's death? What was He trying to accomplish on the cross? Several theories have been advocated which are either inadequate or wrong.

A. Accidental Theory of Atonement

The accidental theory of atonement is basically a liberal view. Its adherents maintain that Christ was a great moral teacher but fate tragically ended His life. As with Lincoln, Kennedy, King, or Ghandi, His death was senseless and without purpose. This view is totally inadequate to the Scriptures.

B. Example Theory of Atonement

If the example view of the atonement is true, then Christ died as a martyr to give us the supreme example of devotion to truth and duty. Those who hold this view usually maintain that He purposefully (as opposed to accidentally) became a martyr to show to us that we must be willing to die for our principles and to arouse great devotion to the cause of the Christian faith.

It is true that Christ is our example. However, it is hardly sufficient to view a planned martyrdom as His sole or main purpose for dying.

This turns Christ into a religious fanatic who seeks death to enter the glories of martyrdom.

C. Moral Influence Theory of Atonement

The moral influence theory is similar to the example theory. According to this theory, Jesus died in the process of helping us much the same way a doctor might die helping in an epidemic or a coastguard seaman might die in a rescue attempt. This theory maintains that the purpose of His death was, not to become a martyr for a cause, but rather, to demonstrate His great love. The purpose of His death was to soften our hearts by the influence of His love. Thus, He hoped His death would cause us to change our evil ways and work to earn salvation by holiness.

Christ's death was a demonstration of His love, and it should change our lives. However, this view deletes God's anger over sin and Christ's payment for sin. It makes the demonstration of love to be the only purpose for Christ's death and, therefore, does not do justice to the Scriptures.

D. Governmental Theory of Atonement

The governmental theory of atonement is also popular in circles that tend to believe in salvation by works. According to this theory, God has a government with laws. If Christ had not died to show respect and honor for these laws, then the human race would have grown in disrespect for God and His laws. However, in reality, it is the lack of enforcement of laws that leads to violation of them. This view takes the position, not that Christ had to die to satisfy an offended God, but that His death would be useful in alerting others to the seriousness of working toward salvation by keeping laws. Some could have been saved without Christ's death, but more would pursue salvation with Christ's death. Therefore, Christ's death was designed to promote respect for God's law by showing the serious nature of infractions against that law. As a result of Christ's death, people would work harder at keeping God's laws in order to earn salvation.

This view sounds orthodox to some, but it is quite deficient. Christ did not die just so that God's government could continue in smooth operation by increased respect for law. While His death does relate to offended laws and should promote respect for God's laws, there was no intention that this increased respect for law would lead people to work for salvation. This view makes Christ's death an optional, but wise, tool to maintain order in God's government, and it promotes salvation by works. It fails to see that Christ's death was an absolutely necessary factor in salvation and that the offense was not just against law but against the character of God. His death was not just useful in promoting salvation by works; it was necessary to provide salvation that could never be gained by works. Christ died, not just to pay respect for God's laws, but to pay the penalty of their violation.

E. Substitutionary (Vicarious) Theory of Atonement Defended

Other views of the atonement contain partial truths. Christ was our example. He did demonstrate duty to a cause. He did demonstrate love. Christ's death did show the importance of law and should promote respect for it. Yet, none of these ideas is primary and none is complete.

The Biblical view of the atonement is that Christ died as our **substitute**. He died in our place taking our punishment and paying our penalty; and, thereby, He satisfied an angry God. Other purposes for His death are secondary.

To establish the doctrine of substitutionary atonement, it is essential to prove that *for* can mean substitution (in place of) in such phrases as "Christ died *for* us." One with a liberal view or with a works orientation would take the phrase "Christ died for us" to mean simply, "Christ died to benefit us." How does one know that substitutionary atonement is intended in Bible texts that teach "Christ died **for** us"?

1. One Greek word that definitely refers to substitution is the word *anti.* The Antichrist will be a substitute Christ. There is ample precedent for *anti* meaning "instead of." Consider the following examples:

> "... 'an eye **for** (meaning instead of, or in exchange for) an eye, a tooth **for** a tooth' " [Matt. 5:38].

> "...will he **for** (instead of) a fish give him a serpent?" [Luke 11:11 KJV].

> "...evil **for** (in return, in place of) evil..." [Rom. 12:17].

> ...evil **for** evil... [1 Thess. 5:15].

> ...evil **for** evil, or insult **for** insult...[1 Pet. 3:9].

> ...**for** (instead of, in exchange for) one morsel of meat (Esau) sold his birthright [Heb. 12:16 KJV].

Matt. 20:28 and Mark 10:45 are key texts in the doctrine of substitutionary atonement. Since *anti* means substitution, the phrase "a ransom **for** many" means that Christ gave His life as a **substitute** for the many.[1] He died **in the place** of sinners. His life was given **in exchange** for our lives that should have been forfeited.

> "...just as the Son of Man did not come to be served, but to serve, and to give His life a ransom **for** (in place of) many" [Matt. 20:28].

> "For even the Son of Man did not come to be served, but to serve, and to give His life a ransom **for** many" [Mark 10:45].

> For there is one God, and one mediator also between God and men, the man Christ Jesus, who gave Himself as a ransom **for** (anti) all...[1 Tim. 2:5-6].

2. Another word translated "for" is *huper.* This word can mean "for the benefit of," but it can also mean "in place of." Philem. 13 and 2 Cor. 5:14-15 are two important texts that establish that *huper* can refer to substitution. When Paul says "whom I would have retained with me, that **in thy stead** *(huper)* he might have ministered unto me in the bonds of the gospel" [Philem. 13 KJV], he is saying that he would have liked to retain Onesimus to minister **in the place of** the absent Philemon.

The following passage in 2 Corinthians is perhaps more important. It proves that *huper* can refer to substitution in contexts dealing with Christ's death.

> For the love of Christ controls us, having concluded this, that one died for *(huper)* all, therefore all died; and He died for *(huper)* all, that they who live should no longer live for themselves, but for Him who died and rose again on their behalf [2 Cor. 5:14-15].

In this context Paul reasons that all died with Christ because He died **for** all. This means that Christ died **in place of all.** Therefore, all died with Him. Furthermore, Paul asserts that since Christ gave His life for ours, those who live owe their lives to Him. This evidently means that Christ gave His life in exchange for ours, so believers owe Him their lives in return.

Matt. 20:28 and Mark 10:45 clearly teach substitutionary atonement as do forthcoming texts in sub-section 3 below. Philem. 13 and 2 Cor. 5:14-15 show that texts that use the word *huper* can be taken to teach substitutionary atonement. Many passages use *huper* in reference to the atonement. Without the evidence from the above key texts, it would be difficult to know whether these passages mean that Christ died in our place or merely that Christ died on our behalf. However, because of Philem. 13 and 2 Cor.5:14-15, the author believes that many other less clear verses should be understood to include the idea of substitutionary atonement. Perhaps most of them **also**

---

[1] *Many* in these passages could be restricted to the elect. Other verses argue that Christ died for the whole world. Our main point here is that the Lord's death was as a substitute.

mean **Christ died "in our behalf"** but the main and biblically emphasized view of atonement should be that **Christ died in our place as our substitute.** This must be included as a part of the meaning in all the following texts:

> "For this is my blood of the new testament which is shed **for** many..." [Matt. 26:28 KJV].

> "...This is my blood of the new testament, which is shed **for** many" [Mark 14:24 KJV].

> "...This cup is the new testament in my blood, which is shed **for** you" [Luke 22:20 KJV].

> "...my flesh which I will give **for** (in exchange and for the benefit of) the life of the world" [John 6:51 KJV].

> "...the good shepherd lays down his life **for** the sheep" [John 10:11] .

> "Greater love has no one than this, that a one lay down his life **for** his friends" [John 15:13].

> ...Christ died **for** the ungodly [Rom. 5:6].

> ...while we were yet sinners, Christ died **for** us [Rom. 5:8].

> He who did not spare His own Son, but delivered Him up **for** us all...[Rom. 8:32].

> ...Christ died **for** our sins according to the Scriptures.[2] [1 Cor. 15:3 KJV].

> He made Him who knew no sin to be sin **for** (substitution seems prominent in this usage of *huper)* us... [2 Cor. 5:21].

---

[2] Perhaps this could mean Christ died "to benefit" us relative to sin, but it does not mean Christ died to benefit **sin.** However, the statement is more clear if it means Christ died "in exchange for our guilt," i.e., as a substitute, He took our guilt. (See also Gal. 1:4.)

> Who gave Himself **for** our sins...[Gal. 1:4].

> I have been crucified with Christ... who loved me, and delivered Himself up **for** me [Gal. 2:20].

> Christ hath redeemed us from the curse of the law, having become a curse **for** us... [Gal. 3:13].

> Who gave Himself **for** us...[Titus 2:14].

> ...by the grace of God He might taste death **for** every one [Heb. 2:9].

> For Christ also died for sins, once for all, the just **for** the unjust...[1 Pet. 3:18]

3. The substitutionary view can be established on grounds other than the prepositions *anti* and *huper.* The concept of Christ as the Lamb of God who bore our sins also supports the concept of His substitutionary death. Also, Paul in Romans 6 teaches that believers died when Christ died on the cross. This fact is closely linked to the idea that He was dying in our place.

> Surely our griefs He Himself **bore**, and our sorrows He carried... [Isa. 53:4].

> All of us like sheep have gone astray, each of us has turned to his own way; But the LORD has caused **the iniquity of us all to fall on Him** [Isa. 53:6].

> ...For **the transgression of my people** to whom the stroke was due? [Isa. 53:8b].

> But the LORD was pleased to crush Him, putting Him to grief; if He would render Himself as a **guilt offering**... [Isa. 53:10a].

> And He Himself **bore our sins in His body** on the cross... [1 Pet. 2:24a].

> So Christ also, having been offered once **to bear the sins of** many... [Heb. 9:28].

For if we have become **united with Him in the likeness of His death,** certainly we shall be also in the likeness of His resurrection, knowing this, that **our old self was crucified with Him,** that our body of sin might be done away with, that we should no longer be slaves to sin [Rom. 6:5-6].

4. Conclusion: While other theories of the atonement have partial truth, the Bible is clear that the main purpose of Christ's death was to die in our place. Substitutionary atonement has been regarded as one of the fundamentals of the faith.

III. Redemption: The Sinward Aspect of Atonement

Although **redemption** pertains to God and man, it can be said to be primarily the sinward aspect of atonement. Christ paid the redemption price for sin and ransomed man from slavery to sin. To say that Christ redeemed us from sin means that He bought us. More specifically, it means that He ransomed us from sin (and the law's curse) by the payment of a price just as one would ransom a hostage, a slave, or a prisoner of war. Redemption included both the payment of a price and, in the fullest sense, the release of the hostage.

There are many Greek forms for the two word families behind the English word redemption. Because *redemption* uses words that were in common usage in the ancient world, it will be helpful to study both its secular and sacred usage. The New Testament authors took a word that was used secularly and gave it a theological meaning.

A. *Agorazo* (verb) - To buy, to purchase, to redeem

1. Secular usage - *Agorazo* is related to *Agora,* "the market place" (Acts 17:17). It was a common word in deeds of sale.[3] There are

examples of it being used of the purchase of slaves, wheat, and houses. Although *agorazo* can be used of buying slaves, it was a basic word used of purchasing in general.[4]

2. Biblical usage - In the Septuagint *agorazo* is used of purchasing anything in general (e.g. Chapters 41-44 of Genesis when Joseph's brothers redeemed grain from him). The New Testament uses *agorazo* 30-31 times depending on the manuscripts used. It means to buy or to purchase, and usually there is a non-theological usage (e.g., buying a field or a pearl - Matt. 13:44, 46; 27:7; food - Matt. 14:15; things for Jesus' burial - Mark 15:46; 16:1; buying and selling in the temple - Mark 11:15; land and oxen - Luke 14:18-19).

Several times the New Testament authors use *agorazo* in contexts pertaining to the salvation of believers (1 Cor. 6:20; 7:23; Rev. 5:9; 14:3, 4). All of these references speak of redemption as past. Once *agorazo is* used of the unsaved (2 Pet. 2:1).

> For you have been **bought** with a price... [1 Cor. 6:20].

> And they sang a new song, saying "Worthy art Thou to take the book, and to break its seals; for Thou wast slain and didst **purchase** for God with Thy blood men from every tribe and tongue and people and nation" [Rev. 5:9].

> But false prophets also arose among the people, just as there will also be false teachers among you, who will secretly introduce destructive heresies, even denying the Master who **bought** them, bringing swift destruction upon themselves [2 Pet. 2:1].

3. Conclusion: *Agorazo* is a general word meaning "to buy something". It may be used

---

[3] James Hope Moulton and George Milligan, *The Vocabulary of the Greek Testament* (1930; Glas-

gow, Scotland: Hodder and Stroughton Limited, 1972) 6.

[4] Leon Morris, *The Apostolic Preaching of the Cross,* 3rd ed. (1965; Grand Rapids: Wm. B. Eerdman Publishing Co., 1980) 53-55.

of buying people, but it was commonly used of purchasing any property. *Agorazo* stresses the payment of a price (Christ's broken body and shed blood) and the resulting transfer of ownership. It does not, however, stress a release from captivity, as do some of the following words for redemption. Therefore, this word is appropriately used of the "redemption" of unsaved people. Christ has paid the price. He bought and owns them. Yet, they have not been released.

B. *Exagorazo* (verb) - This word is simply *agorazo* compounded with the prefix *Ex* (out). It also means "to buy, to purchase, to redeem."

1. In some contexts in secular usage, this word may mean to buy back something that was lost. Theologians are quick to make the point that Christ bought back people that already belonged to Him but had been made slaves to sin. [5]

2. *Exagorazo* is only used four times in the New Testament. Twice it means to pay a price to retain ownership of time (redeeming the time - Eph. 5:16; Col. 4: 5).

The remaining two usages have significance for the doctrine of salvation. They teach that Christ redeemed believers from the curse of the Law (Gal. 3:13; 4:5). This is similar to speaking of redemption from sin because sin is what causes the Law's curse. In both verses the redemption has already occurred for believers. Christ paid the redemption price, and therefore, believers have been freed from the Law's curse (and indeed the Law itself).

> Christ **redeemed** us from the curse of the Law, having become a curse for us... [Gal. 3:13a].

> In order that He might **redeem** those who were under the Law... [Gal. 4:5a].

Unlike *agorazo*, *exagorazo* is only used of **believers** and it does speak of a **complete release**. It is hard to determine whether the additional thought of release comes only from the context and subject matter or whether it lies in the prefix *ex* as in exit, **with *exagorazo* meaning to purchase and take out.**

C. *Lutrao* (verb) - This word more clearly gives the idea of paying a ransom price in order to set free. It means "to ransom, to redeem."

1. In secular usage *lutrao* often means to buy back something that was previously owned. Examples include the following: "the cloak has not yet been redeemed from pawn," "redeem my clothes," and "please redeem my property."[6] Not only is there more stress on buying back, but *lutrao* also emphasizes the price paid to **free** slaves. Morris teaches that when someone in the first century heard this word, he would naturally think of the price paid to free slaves from bondage.[7] The following quote from Josephus illustrates the idea of paying a ransom price to secure the release of a hostage: "...for not knowing what was become of his [Herod the Great's] brother, he was in haste to redeem (*lutrao*) him out of the hand of his enemies, as willing to give three hundred talents for the price of his redemption."[8]

The secular usage of *lutrao* emphasizes the payment of a price to secure freedom for a slave, a prisoner, or a hostage. This secular meaning prevails in the New Testament with a ransom price nearly always stated in a context containing the *lutrao* word family. [9]

---

[5] Moulton and Milligan 220; and Walter Baur, *The Greek-English Lexicon of the New Testament and Other Early Christian Literature*, trans. Wm. F. Arndt and F. Wilbur Gingrich (Chicago: University of Chicago Press, 1957) 271.

[6] Moulton and Milligan 383.
[7] Morris 14.
[8] Josephus, *The Works of Josephus*, trans. William Whiston, (Peabody, Massachusetts: Hendrickson Publishers, 1985) 308.
[9] The price is not stated in Luke 1:68, 2:38 and 24:21. However, these verses are primarily speaking of the national salvation of Israel.

2. The New Testament uses *lutrao* in three places (Luke 24:21; Titus 2:14; and 1 Peter 1:18-19).

> Who gave Himself for us, that He might **redeem** us from every lawless deed and purify for Himself a people for His own possession, zealous for good deeds [Titus 2:14].

> Knowing that you were not **redeemed** with perishable things like silver or gold from your futile way of life inherited from your forefathers, but with precious blood, as of a lamb unblemished and spotless, the blood of Christ [1 Pet. 1:18-19].

Notice that in both of the references from the epistles, the price of the redemption is stated. Titus 2:14 says Christ gave **Himself** to redeem us. 1 Pet. 1:18 bases redemption upon the price of the "**precious blood.**" Liberals tend to think of redemption as just meaning deliverance. It does relate to deliverance, but the **cost** to secure freedom is also a New Testament emphasis. In both Titus 2 and 1 Peter 1, redemption seems to be a past occurrence for the believer, although this is definitely more clear in the 1 Pet. 1:18-19 reference. (Titus 2 conceivably refers to a present deliverance from sin's power.)

The Bible portrays the lost as slaves to sin (John 8:34; Rom. 6:6, 14, 17, 20; 7:14ff.) and in bondage to the fear of death (Heb. 2:14-15). Because the secular word family of *lutrao* was commonly used of deliverance for slaves, because the Bible teaches man is a slave to sin, and because both Titus 2 and 1 Pet.1 mention release from former slavery to wickedness,[10] the imagery of ransoming a prisoner or slave seems foremost in the mind of the Biblical writers when they use this word for redemp-

tion. Christ paid the price to buy slaves from sin and to secure their release.

Agorazo stresses the purchase price and transfer of ownership but not release. That is why it can be used of the unsaved. *Lutrao* stresses both **price and release**. Thus, it is never used of unsaved people.

D. *Lutron* (noun) - This word means "ransom," the "price paid to secure release."

1. In secular usage, this was the word that the ancients used for the purchase money to free slaves.[11] Many passages could be given from Josephus where *lutron* means "the price of release or ransom."[12]

2. *Lutron* is used only twice in the New Testament, but both texts are very significant for the doctrine of salvation. They are the two that most clearly teach substitutionary atonement.

> "Just as the Son of Man did not come to be served, but to serve, and to give His life a **ransom** for many" [Matt. 20:28].

> "For even the Son of Man did not come to be served, but to serve, and to give His life a **ransom** for many" [Mark 10:45].

Christ taught that the ransom price to be paid would be His life. If one keeps in mind that *anti* means "in place of, in exchange, as a substitute," the idea of price is reinforced. Christ gave His life as a ransom in exchange for us, i.e., both in our place and in order to buy us.

E. *Lutrosis* (noun)

This word for redemption is used only three times in the New Testament (Luke 1:68; 2:38; Heb. 9:12). It can be studied in conjunction with the next word, the compound form *apolu-*

---

[10] Titus 2:14 mentions redemption from "every lawless deed," and 1 Pet. 1:18 speaks of redemption from a "futile way of life inherited from your forefathers."

[11] Moulton and Milligan 382-383; Baur, Arndt, and Gingrich 483-84.

[12] Gerhard Kittel, ed., *Theological Dictionary of the New Testament*, vol. 4, trans. Geoffrey W. Bromiley (Grand Rapids: Wm. B. Eerdmans Publishing Co., 1967) 340.

trosis. It is significant that Heb. 9:12 speaks of "eternal redemption." Once Christ has redeemed from slavery to sin, there can be no more slavery to sin in a positional sense. A believer might practice service to sin, but he or she is never in the position of being a servant to sin. The work on the cross provides a total and permanent release. *Lutrosis* is translated "redemption" meaning "a release secured by a payment of a price."

F.   *Apolutrosis* (noun*)*

This word means a release secured by payment of a price.

1. In the ancient secular world, *apolutrosis* was used infrequently, but it clearly spoke of a release for slaves/hostages secured by the payment of a ransom.[13]   Plutarch speaks of ransoming captive cities.[14]   Philo speaks of a slave who committed suicide because he felt no one would pay for his redemption.[15]   The Epistle of Aristeas uses the word in connection with ransoming prisoners of war at a cost of "twenty drachmae per head."[16]   Josephus has a section where the cost of redeeming captives was "more than four hundred talents."[17]   In such contexts, there is often the thought of buying back. There can be little doubt that when the original readers of the New Testament saw the word *apolutrosis,* they thought of a hostage or slave situation. A person was free because someone else paid a price.

2. The word *apolutrosis* occurs ten times in the New Testament. Often the price to secure release is specifically mentioned (blood - Rom. 3:24-25; Eph. 1:7; Col. 1:14[18]; death and blood - Heb. 9:12, 15; also Eph. 1:14, by context).

---

[13] Baur, Arndt, and Gingrich 95; Morris 16.
[14] Ibid. 16.
[15] Ibid. 16-17.
[16] Ibid.
[17] Ibid.
[18] If *blood* is not mentioned in the original text, blood would still be the purchase price by virtue of the parallel text in Eph. 1:7.

...being justified as a gift by His grace through the **redemption** which is in Christ Jesus; whom God displayed publicly as a propitiation in His **blood** through faith... [Rom. 3:24-25].

In Him we have **redemption** through His **blood**... [Eph. 1:7].

And for this reason He is the mediator of a new covenant, in order that since a death has taken place for the **redemption** of the transgressions that were committed under the first covenant, those who have been called may receive the promise of the eternal inheritance [Heb. 9:15].

Given the ancient common usage of the word to speak of a ransom, given the general Biblical teachings about a price being paid, and given these verses that stress price, it is best to conclude that redemption in theological terms approximates the secular idea of redemption. Christ paid the price to purchase those in slavery to sin and then to set them free. The price was His life given in death, His broken body, and His shed blood.

Although the New Testament usually views redemption as being a past event, *apolutrosis* is used of a future redemption three times (Rom. 8:23; Eph. 1:14; Eph. 4:30). There is a future aspect of redemption because the complete deliverance (freedom) of our bodies from sin and its affects is future. Viewed from this angle, believers are still awaiting a future and complete redemption.

And not only this, but also we ourselves, having the first fruits of the Spirit, even we ourselves groan within ourselves, **waiting** eagerly for our adoption as sons, the **redemption** of our body [Rom. 8:23].

...who is given as a pledge of our inheritance, **with a view to the redemption** of God's own possession, to the praise of His glory [Eph. 1:14].

And do not grieve the Holy Spirit of God, by whom you were sealed for the day of **redemption** [Eph. 4:30].

This future aspect of redemption should be anticipated. Yet, it will be based upon a more fundamental past payment on the cross and a past deliverance at conversion that the believer already has experienced. It is more common for the New Testament to refer to redemption as already being past with the result that it is a present possession (e.g., Eph. 1:7, "we have redemption"; 1 Cor 1:30). Believers already have been redeemed from the law's curse, from sin's penalty, and from sin's dominion. This is the basis for any future redemption from sin's presence.[19]

In all contexts *apolutrosis* speaks of a **complete** deliverance. Therefore, unlike *agorazo,* it is **never used of unbelievers**. Some think that the idea of release is intensified by the prefix *apo* (which means away from as in apostasy).[20] Others maintain this is merely a stylistic variation and complete release comes from the context and not the prefix *apo*.[21] Regardless of this difference, *apolutrosis* means **release** secured by the payment of a price or ransom.

G. Summary and Conclusions about Redemption

1. The Bible does not say to whom the redemption price was paid. Some believe God the Son paid the price to God the Father. Others think Christ paid a price to Satan to secure human release from bondage to Satan. This issue cannot be settled. However, it is fair to conclude that the Bible emphasizes the idea of price. Redemption is not just deliverance, freedom, rescue. It is release obtained by the payment of a price (Christ's death, His blood).

2. Redemption is the sinward aspect of the atonement. We are redeemed from sin (Rom. 3:23-24, Col. 1:14), from trespasses (Eph. 1:7), from lawless deeds (Titus 2:14), from transgressions (Heb. 9:12, 15), and from our former futile way of life (1 Pet. 1:18-19). Teaching that believers are redeemed from the law's curse is not so different from teaching that we are redeemed from sin (Gal. 3:13, 4:5). It was sin that caused the law to curse man and obligated man to the law's penalty.[22]

3. Although the word groups *agorazo* and *lutrao* are very similar, a knowledge of their subtle differences deepens our understanding of redemption.

a. Although the *agorazo* word family can be used of the purchase of slaves or buying back something, it is a generic word for purchasing anything. It speaks of a price and the transfer of ownership, but it may or may not refer to release. Thus, it would be proper to speak of the whole world being redeemed (2 Pet. 2:1). Christ paid the price to purchase the whole human race. The stress is on the price paid and the transfer of ownership.

b. The *lutrao* family can be used of buying objects, but it is more specific than *agorazo* and often refers to the purchase or ransom of humans such as slaves, hostages, or prisoners of war. It more clearly refers to buying back something that was originally owned. The common ancient imagery of a release of slaves and prisoners by a ransom fits well with the New Testament teachings that people are in slavery to sin and death.[23] Unlike agorazo,

---

[19] The two remaining usages of *apolutrosis* are Luke 21:28 and Heb. 11:35. It is difficult to know whether Luke 21 refers to future redemption of individuals or a national deliverance of Israel from her enemies. The Hebrews 11 reference is to apostasy as the price of release from torture.

[20] Richard Chenevix Trench, *Synonyms of the New Testament* (1880; Grand Rapids: Wm. B. Eerdmans Publishing Co., 1976) 290.

[21] Morris, 16.

[22] The context of both Galatians 3-4 and Hebrews 9 show that believers have been redeemed not only from the curse of the Law but from the Law itself.

[23] See John 5:24, 8:34; Rom. 6:6, 14, 18, 22; 7:14, 23; 8:2; 1 Cor. 15:24-26; 2 Tim. 1:10, Heb. 2:14-15; 1 John. 3:14. Heb. 2:14-15 gives the concept of redemption from death but does not use the precise word *redemption*.

which need not speak of release, the *lutrao* group (as used in the New Testament) always speaks of a release, deliverance, and freedom from sin. Therefore, this word is never used of the unsaved. Its stress is on freedom, release, deliverance secured at a price which Christ paid.

IV. Reconciliation - The Manward Aspect of the Atonement

A. Background to the Idea of Reconciliation

The truth of reconciliation presupposes that man was/is God's enemy. The enmity of man toward God is taught not only in contexts concerning reconciliation (Rom. 5:10; Col. 1:21-22), but also in many other verses (Luke 19:27; Rom. 8:7 KJV, "carnal" referring to unsaved; 1 Cor. 15:25; Phil. 3:18).

> ...because the mind set on the flesh (unsaved) is **hostile toward God**; for it does not subject itself to the law of God, for it is not even able to do so[24] [Rom. 8:7].

> For many walk, of whom I often told you, and now tell you even weeping, that they are **enemies of the cross** of Christ [Phil. 3:18].

It is also evident from experience that the unsaved are antagonistic toward God. To complete the picture we must add that God loves his enemies (John 3:16; Rom. 5:8, etc). The estrangement was man's fault. It was man who had caused the alienation. Man turned his back on God and wandered from Him. God is blameless. However, God reacted to man's hostility with righteous and holy indignation. Therefore, it would be true to say that the hostility was mutual. Man viewed God as an en-

emy, but God also viewed man as His enemy. The difference was that man was being sinful in his hostility toward God, while God was fully justified in His hostility toward man. The doctrine of reconciliation considers how the work of the cross affected the strained and hostile relationship between God and Man.

B. The meaning of words translated *reconciliation*.

1. In the ancient secular world, *reconciliation* seems to have begun as a financial term. It was used of exchanging one set of coins for another (either making change or exchanging foreign monies). In time the word came to refer to a change in relationships between people, specifically a change from a relationship of hostility to one of peace.[25] In some ways the secular usage for the term has not changed. Reconciliation still refers to finances (e.g., reconciling accounts) and relationships (e.g., a couple with marital trouble reconciles).

2. In Scripture, *reconciliation* is used in both non-salvation and salvation contexts.

a. In non-salvation contexts, the idea of changing a relationship for the better prevails. There is a change from hostility to peace and friendship. The word *diallasso* is used:

> "...and wherewith will he (David) be reconciled (*diallasso*) to His master (Saul)? Will it not be with the heads of those men?" [1 Sam. 29:4 (LXX)].

> "...first be reconciled (*diallasso*) to your brother, and then come and present your offering" [Matt. 5:24].

> ...but if she does leave, let her remain unmarried or else be reconciled (*katallasso*) to her husband... [1 Cor. 7:11].

b. Notice that the idea of hostility is nearly always present when the word *reconciled* is used. This fact, plus the general teaching about man's enmity with God, validates that there is no change in meaning when recon-

---

[24] Rom. 8:9 defines those in the flesh as not possessing the Holy Spirit and not belonging to Christ. Thus, by Paul's own definition "in the flesh" in this context refers to unsaved people who lack the Holy Spirit. That is the reason verse 7 quoted here classifies them as enemies who are hostile to God (lacking reconciliation).

[25] Morris, 215.

ciliation is used in salvation contexts. It speaks of a change in relationship from hostility to peace.

> For if while we were **enemies**, we were **reconciled** to God through the death of His Son, much more, having been reconciled, we shall be saved by His life [Rom. 5:10].

> And although you were formerly **alienated** and **hostile** in mind, engaged in evil deeds, yet He has now **reconciled** you... [Col. 1:21-22].

> For He Himself is our **peace**, who made both groups into one, and broke down the barrier of the dividing wall, by abolishing in His flesh the **enmity**, which is the Law of commandments contained in ordinances, that in Himself He might make the two into one new man, thus establishing peace, and might **reconcile** them both in one body to God through the cross, by it having put to death the enmity[26] [Eph. 2:14-16].

Scriptures use *reconciliation* in the ordinary sense to change a relationship for the better. The relationship is altered from enmity and hostility to friendship and peace.

C. Details on the doctrine of reconciliation

1. The Bible gives two aspects, or phases, for reconciliation. In an **objective sense** reconciliation occurred **in the past** on the cross. The **whole world** was reconciled whether believing or unbelieving. However, in a **subjective sense** the **individual** becomes reconciled to God at the **time of conversion**. These two phases to reconciliation can be observed in the main Biblical texts on the subject. Bold print sections indicate universal reconciliation on the cross. Italicized words indicate individual reconciliation at the time of trusting in Christ for salvation.

---

[26] Eph. 2:14-16 includes reconciliation of people to each other (Jew and gentile) and also reconciliation to God.

> For if **while we were enemies, we were reconciled** to God through the death of His Son, much more, *having been reconciled*, we shall be saved by His life. And not only this, but we also exult in God through our Lord Jesus Christ, through whom *we have now received the reconciliation* [Rom. 5:10-11].

Paul tells his readers that, in one sense, they were reconciled to God **in the past** at the time of Christ's death; but in another sense they have been **now,** at the time of salvation, reconciled to God.

> Now all these things are from God, who reconciled us to Himself through Christ, and gave us the ministry of reconciliation, namely, that God was in Christ **reconciling the world** to Himself, not counting their trespasses against them, and He has committed to us the word of reconciliation. Therefore, we are ambassadors for Christ, as though God were entreating through us; we beg you on behalf of Christ, *be reconciled* to God [2 Cor. 5:18-20].

Even though God through Christ reconciled the whole world to Himself, Paul claimed that he (Paul) was still appealing to individuals to be reconciled to God. The "ministry of reconciliation" is the work of offering reconciliation to individuals who, in a more universal sense, have already been reconciled by the cross.

> ...and **through Him to reconcile all things to Himself**, having made peace **through the blood of His cross**; through Him, I say, whether things on earth or things in heaven. And although you were formerly alienated and hostile in mind, engaged in evil deeds, yet *He has now reconciled you* in His fleshly body through death, in order to present you before Him holy and blameless and beyond reproach [Col. 1:20-22].

Verse twenty speaks of a universal reconciliation that occurred through the cross. Verse twenty-two refers to an individual reconciliation that occurs for believers at the time of salvation.

2. The two phases of reconciliation are universal reconciliation and individual reconciliation.

a. Universal reconciliation occurred at the cross. What does the Bible mean when it teaches that all the world has been reconciled to God? It certainly does not mean that all have been saved or that all have ceased to be God's enemies. In what sense did the cross restore man's relationship to God and cause it to be changed for the better?

The author believes the key lies in 2 Cor. 5:19 where it is written, "God was in Christ reconciling the world unto Himself, **not counting their trespasses against them.**" Before the fall, sin was not a factor in threatening man with eternal hell; after the fall sin entered the world and became a potential basis for the eternal condemnation of man. Relative to sin being the basis for eternal death, the cross reconciled all men back to their original relationship with God. The cross so defeated sin that the basis for eternal death is now not sin but only the rejection of Christ.[27] Sin is no longer the relevant issue in determining a person's eternal destiny. God is only interested in what a person does with His Son, Jesus Christ. On this restricted but major point, the whole world has been restored to its original condition. The unsaved are still guilty, and God could have justly damned the human race for sin; but God, through the cross, is just and gracious in not exercising this option. No one will suffer punishment in the eternal sense either for Adam's sin or his own individual sins. If they enter hell, it will be because of indifference to Christ. Relative to eternal damnation caused by sin alone, the entire

world is reconciled to God. The world is back to its original relationship to God relative to sin being a basis for eternal condemnation.

b. Individual reconciliation occurs at the time of salvation. The whole world was reconciled at the cross in the limited sense of sin not being a basis for eternal condemnation. However, unsaved people are still guilty of sin. They are still hostile to God, are alienated from God, and are still His enemies. Therefore, an individual reconciliation must occur to eliminate completely all areas in which God and man are at odds - a reconciliation without restrictions.

Every believer is reconciled to God on an individual basis at the time of salvation. This could be called the second phase of reconciliation, subjective reconciliation, or individual reconciliation. Hostility and antagonism cease and are replaced by fellowship, friendship and peace (cf. the words *peace* and *reconciliation* in the same context, e.g., Rom. 5:1, 10-11; Eph. 2:14-16; Col. 1:20).

3. **The Bible always speaks** of God as taking the initiative in reconciliation and **of man as being the one who is reconciled**. God reconciled man to Himself. Man is reconciled. God brings it about. Man is pictured as rebellious and not interested in friendship with God. God is pictured as reaching out to man, making every effort to reconcile us. It is understandable that man is always said to be the one who needs reconciliation. He is the one who brought about the strained relationship in the first place.

Though the Bible does not use any phraseology where God is reconciled to man, theologians ponder whether or not it is proper to think in such terms. Man definitely needed to be reconciled to God. He was the one who created the enmity, and he is the one who needed "change for the better." However, man's rebellion did change the way God works with and views man. Thus, the author believes it is proper to say that God was also reconciled to man by the cross (though the Bible always

---

[27] See discussion in footnote number 5 under the "Doctrine of Man," Chapter 6, pp. 65-67.

phrases the change in relationship as man being reconciled to God). The cross changed man's relationship to God but also changed God's relationship to man.

4. Summary: To reconcile means to change a relationship. Specifically, from one of hostility and enmity to one of peace and friendship. The whole world was reconciled to God on the cross in the sense that inherited sin and acts of sin are no longer the threatened basis for condemnation. Rejection of the Savior brings eternal damnation. Thus, there is still a need to appeal to individuals to trust in Christ as Savior and receive an individual and personal reconciliation that eliminates all areas where man and God are enemies and brings man to fellowship and peace with God.

V. Propitiation: The Godward Aspect of the Atonement

To say Christ propitiated God means He removed the offense of sin and thereby turned God's wrath away. Other synonymous ways of explaining the concept include the following: the cross **pacified** God's anger, **appeased** God's anger, and **placated** God's anger. Christ's death **satisfied** the righteous **wrath of God** so that His wrath was turned away (diverted) from us. Thus, just as redemption is the sinward aspect of the atonement and reconciliation the manward aspect of atonement, so propitiation is the Godward aspect of atonement.

Redemption pictures man as a slave held as a hostage in sin. Reconciliation pictures man as an enemy who is estranged from God. Propitiation pictures man as a guilty criminal whose offense has rightly angered the Judge.[28]

There has been a tendency in modern times to do away with the translation of *propitiation*. Great care must be given that conservatives do not follow liberal thinking on this word. Because liberals are hesitant to emphasize God's wrath, they think in terms of Christ's death being a satisfactory or expiatory death. In an unspecified way that death was satisfactory to God and expiated (or covered) our sins. It removed our guilt and obligation due to sin. These are true concepts, but the Bible is more specific. Christ's death was satisfactory because it diverted God's wrath. In order to propitiate God, Christ did have to expiate (or cover) sin, but unless the turning away of wrath is included, one is giving an inadequate definition for propitiation. It is best to retain the term of propitiation and explain it accurately so that people are accustomed to it.[29] Because there has been a movement to redefine propitiation, the next section presents the case for a traditional definition.

A. Definition of Propitiation

1. In non-biblical Greek there are abundant ancient examples where the *propitiation* word-group is used of pacifying anger, particularly the wrath of gods. Homer contains these lines: "So the whole day they sought to **appease** the gods with a song," "that first of all the gods I may **propitiate** Athene."[30] Josephus writes of the Old Testament incident in 1 Samuel 14 where Saul had made a curse against anyone who ate on the day of a battle. Jonathan, being unaware of his father's curse, had eaten some honey. Saul wanted to slay Jonathan and thereby pacify God's wrath.

> Aye and I swear by God Himself that verily, be it my own son Jonathan who

---

[28] By His death Christ paid the redemption price for sin. He propitiated God's wrath, and He reconciled man to God. There is no chronological order as all were accomplished at once. However, the logical order would be first, Christ paid the redemption for sin; secondly, He propitiated God's wrath because the redemption price had been paid; and thirdly, He reconciled man to God because the

redemption price had been paid and God's wrath was satisfied.

[29] The New International Version drops the translation *propitiation* in 1 John 2:2 and uses *atoning sacrifice.*

[30] Homer, *The Odyssey,* Vol. 1 *(Loeb Classical Library)* 99; and Homer, *The Iliad,* Vol. 1 *(Loeb Classical Library)* 39.

hath committed this sin, I will **slay him** and thus **propitiate God** even as though it were from a stranger without kinship with me that I was taking revenge on His behalf.[31]

Philo lived at the time of the apostles. He also uses the idea of placating God's wrath. In the following quotation the word "master" refers to God.

For I accept both him who wishes to enjoy my (God's) beneficial power and thus partake of blessings, and him who **propitiates** the dominance and authority of the master (God) **to avoid chastisement.**[32]

Even after the time of the New Testament, the *propitiation* word-group continued to refer to the satisfaction of wrath. *The Pastor of Hermas*, written approximately A.D. 160, has a section which reads as follows: "If this sin is assigned to me, how can I be saved, or how shall I propitiate God...?"[33] All of these examples show that the ancient world regarded *propitiation* as meaning the satisfaction of the wrath of the gods (or God).

When the Bible student turns to the Scriptures, he should demand strong evidence before giving a redefinition to the *propitiation* word group. Without such evidence, the definition of "placating or appeasing God's wrath" must be retained.

2. The *propitiation* word group is used in Scripture to mean the diversion of God's wrath and is found in the Septuagint and in the New Testament.

a. It is evident even to the casual Bible reader that the Bible can picture God being angry

about sin. This is so common that a complete listing is not necessary (John 3:36; Rom. 1:18, 12:19; Eph. 5:6; Col. 3:6; 2 Thess. 1:7-8; Heb. 10:31, 12:29; Rev. 6:16; 19:15, 20:11-15). The background of the non-biblical usage of the *propitiation* word-group coupled with the general teaching that God can be angry would cause the interpreters to expect that *propitiation* means the diversion or satisfaction of wrath. If the Biblical contexts in which propitiation is found also contain a mention of God's wrath, then there should be no doubt as to the intended meaning of the term.

b. The Hebrew Old Testament was translated into Greek in approximately 200 B.C. Because the New Testament authors were familiar with this Greek Old Testament (called the Septuagint), definitions of words in the Septuagint tended to influence their thinking. In certain contexts of the Septuagint, words for the *propitiation* word-group clearly mean to divert wrath. In Exodus 32 Moses discovers that the children of Israel have just worshiped the golden calf. Moses is trying to persuade God to not "consume them from off the face of the earth" in His holy anger. Then in Ex. 32:14 the Septuagint reads, "and the Lord was propitiated to preserve His people." By his intercession Moses diverted God's anger away from the idolatrous nation. Another Old Testament example where words from the *propitiation* word-group refer to appeasing anger is Psa. 130:3-4 (LXX, Psa. 129). Verse three teaches that all men are guilty of sin and that none could stand before God's wrath if God were not gracious: "If Thou, O Lord, shouldest mark iniquities, O Lord, who shall stand?" Then verse four uses a member of the *propitiation* word group to explain that God's wrath need not bring destruction: "For with thee is propitiation." The word in this context means the satisfaction or diversion of wrath. Given ancient secular usage, the doctrine of God's righteous anger, and the background of the Greek Old Testament, if God's wrath is mentioned in New Testament contexts containing

---

[31] Josephus, *Jewish Antiquities*, Vol. 5 (*Loeb Classical Library)* 229.

[32] Philo, Vol. 6 *(Loeb Classical Library)* 67.

[33]Alexander Roberts and James Donaldson, ed., *The Ante-Nicene Fathers*, vol. 2 (Grand Rapids: Wm. B. Eerdmans) 10. (See also 1 Clement 7:17.)

propitiation, then its definition should be understood as the pacification of wrath.[34]

c. Propitiation in the New Testament

The words of the *propitiation* family (Greek: *ilasmos*) occur only a handful of times in the New Testament. The verb (*to propitiate*) appears in Luke 18:13 and Heb. 2:17, and two Greek noun forms (both translated *propitiation*) appear in Rom. 3:25; Heb. 9:5; 1 John 2:2 and 4:10. Finally, the adjective (*propitious*) occurs in Heb. 8:12 and Matt. 16:22.

Rom. 3:25 is a key text both in the book of Romans and in the doctrine of propitiation: "whom God displayed publicly as a propitiation in His blood through faith." Is the idea of God's wrath in the context? Beginning in Rom. 1:18, Paul's goal in the first section of Romans has been to establish that all are guilty sinners threatened by God's holy wrath. He states, "For the **wrath** of God is revealed from heaven against all ungodliness and unrighteousness on men" (Rom. 1:18). The apostle goes on to say in Rom. 2:6-8 "who will render to every man according to his deeds...to those who are selfishly ambitious and do not obey the truth, but obey unrighteousness, **wrath** and indignation." Before this wrathful God, all are sinners (Rom. 3:10, 23) and all are guilty (Rom. 3:19). It is within such a context that Rom. 3:25 asserts Christ Jesus is a propitiation. There is every reason to believe that the concept intended is that of diverting wrath. Remember Paul is writing to gentiles. It would have been senseless for him to have chosen a word that universally means the satisfaction of wrath among pagan authors and expect his readers to understand it as meaning something else.

Luke 18:13 also seems to involve the idea of diverting wrath. One can cover or expiate sin (an act or action) but one propitiates God (a person). The plea, "God, be propitious to me, the sinner," is not asking to be covered by God. Since the subject involved is God and not sin, the plea almost has to involve a diversion of wrath.

Although the words wrath and anger do not appear in the context of 1 John 2:1-2, it seems most logical to infer John had God's potential indignation in mind. In verse one he tells his readers not to sin, but he also wants them to have comfort and assurance should they sin. They can have peace because, as verse two asserts, Christ is the propitiation for our sin.

It seems that the main concern sinners must have would be over God's wrath. If the believer sins, will God the Judge inflict a penalty? The answer is, "No!" Christ is our advocate and He is our propitiation.

If someone thinks the idea of covering sins is sufficient to the context, then the follow up question is, "Why should it be of such concern to a believing sinner that Christ has covered over our sins?" We are relieved that He has covered our sins because without this blessing we might be liable to God's eternal wrath. The need for assurance for the believer who sins is likely caused from a fear of God's potential wrath. Thus, although the word *wrath* does not appear, the most logical interpretation to 1 John 2:1-2 is that John is comforting wayward believers by teaching that Christ has satisfied God's wrath.

In the remaining theological texts involving propitiation (Heb. 2:17, 8:12; 1 John 4:10), the concept of diverting wrath can neither be conclusively excluded nor definitely proven. The verses could refer to covering sin or diverting wrath. However, unless there is strong evidence to the contrary, the word must be given its customary meaning. An expiation of sin is indeed needed to effect a propitiation of God, but to emphasize the former concept and neglect the latter is to stop short of a Scriptural view of the atonement. Christ on the cross both satisfied God's wrath with reference to our sin and turned away God's wrath. This is the meaning of *propitiation*.

---

[34] See also 2 Macc. 7:32-38; 4 Macc. 6:28, 9:24, 12:18.

B. Three applications or phases of propitiation

It has been established that *to propitiate* is to placate and divert God's wrath. The New Testament seems to give three different aspects of propitiation.

1. A propitiation for the whole world occurred at the time of the cross. 1 John 2:2 teaches that Christ propitiated God in reference to the sins of the whole world. **In some sense God's wrath was satisfied for the sins of the whole world by Christ's death on the cross.** The idea is usually not taken into consideration in the formulation of theology. It seems that God's wrath has been diverted in the sense that He does not inflict eternal damnation based upon inherited or personal sins. God's wrath for the world's sins has been satisfied relative to damnation on the basis of sin. It is still true that the unsaved are guilty of sin. Yet, eternal anger is now based upon the primary sin of not obeying the gospel (2 Thess. 1:8; John 3:18). Other texts which speak of God's wrath over sin are speaking of temporal wrath (e.g., Rom. 1:18 where the punishment is not hell but the devastation caused by a reprobate lifestyle), or of what would have happened if Christ had not come to provide a solution (e.g., Rom. 2:6-8). While individual sins will play a role in determining the degree of punishment (Luke 12:48), it is rejection of Christ rather than sin, inherited or personal, that will be the basis for eternal condemnation. Relative to God's eternal wrath, God has been propitiated for the sin of the whole world (1 John 2:2; cf. 2 Cor. 5:19).

[A]nd He Himself is the propitiation for our sins; and not for ours only, but also for those of **the whole world** [1 John 2:2].

1 John 2:2 is the only verse that clearly makes propitiation at the time of the cross to be universal in scope. However, two other texts refer to propitiation at the time of the cross with benefits for an entire class of people: God's people or the elect (see Heb. 2:17 and 1 John 4:10).

2. Propitiation for the individual occurs at the time of faith in Christ. If John teaches in 1 John 2:2 that God's eternal wrath over sin has been satisfied, he still teaches in John 3:36 and 16:9 that God is eternally angry with those who reject His Son (see also 2 Thess. 1:8-9). Thus, while propitiation for sins in general did take place on the cross, propitiation for the main sin of unbelief does not occur until a person trusts in Christ for salvation. Rom. 3:25 is broad enough to cover both aspects of propitiation. This verse teaches that Christ at the time of His death became propitiation. This probably allows the idea of His death being the satisfaction of God's eternal wrath for personal and inherited sins. However, the phrase "through faith" stresses that a full removal of God's wrath awaits the time of faith. Regardless of the idea that personal sins alone do not eternally condemn, the unbeliever is still the subject of God's wrath for the sin of unbelief. A full propitiation of God in His eternal wrath does not take place until faith is placed in Christ as the propitiation. Though it is true to base this complete removal of God's eternal wrath upon what was done on the cross, the anger remains until the time of faith.

[W]hom God displayed publicly as a propitiation in His blood through faith.... [Rom. 3:25a].

3. Propitiation of God's anger occurs when a believer confesses sin. Before salvation a person is mainly related to God in His role as Judge. After salvation God views Himself in a new role as Father. In His role as Judge, God has been propitiated for all sins of the believer. God can not be angry with the believer in an eternal sense (John 5:24; Rom. 5:9, 8:1; 1 Thess 5:9). However, in His role as Father, God can be grieved when a believer sins, and He can become angry. John wants his readers to know that God is propitiated towards His children's sins (1 John 2:1-2). Because Christ is our propitiation there are two resulting

truths. First, it is impossible for the child of God to be the object of God's eternal wrath. This provides assurance for a believer who sins. Secondly, God is propitious, i.e., inclined to or predisposed to stop His paternal anger over our sin. Because of Christ's propitiation for the believer's sins, God easily diverts His temporal wrath and forgives. This also is a comforting truth to believers "if anyone should sin" (1 John 2:1). Since the cross, God is always propitious. Propitiation of God's fatherly anger over a believer's sins occurs when we confess them (1 John 1:9).[35]

C. Greater Implications to the Doctrine of Propitiation

Christ's satisfying of God's wrath over personal and inherited sin has an impact upon both the doctrine of infant salvation and the basis for eternal condemnation. Since God condemns a soul to hell not for personal sin, but rather for rejecting Christ or because God knows that a soul has no potential for faith, we can have assurance He is most gracious to those lacking volition such as infants. Also, condemnation in the eternal sense rests upon the basis of a person's response, or lack of it, to Jesus Christ. This point has already been developed in Chapter 6, pp. 65-67.

VI. The Role of Christ's Blood in the Atonement

The exact role of Christ's blood has been no small source of controversy within Christian circles. Some have contended that the blood is a symbol for Christ's suffering and death and that the literal physical blood played a comparatively insignificant role. Christ's death, it is contended, provided salvation, not so much His physical blood. Several questions must be considered. Is blood symbolic for Christ's suffering and death, or does it refer to literal blood? Was the actual physical blood of Christ necessary to provide salvation? If so, did it constitute all that was necessary, or are there other aspects to His sacrifice?

A. Observations about Blood in the Bible

The word *blood* occurs approximately ninety-nine times in the New Testament depending upon the manuscripts that are counted.[36] There are approximately thirty-eight references to Christ's blood. The rest refer to human or animal blood. Here are texts that teach about Christ's blood in providing salvation.

> And when He had taken a cup and given thanks, He gave it to them, saying, "Drink from it, all of you; for this is My **blood** of the covenant, which is poured out for many for forgiveness of sins" [Matt. 26:27-28].

(See also Mark 14:24; Luke 22:20)

> Jesus therefore said to them, "Truly, truly, I say to you, unless you eat the flesh of the Son of Man and drink His **blood**, you have no life in yourselves" [John 6:53].

(See also John 6:55-56.)

> "...to shepherd the church of God which He purchased with His own **blood**" [Acts 20:28].

> [W]hom God displayed publicly as a propitiation in His **blood** through faith... [Rom. 3:25].

> Much more then, having now been justified by His **blood**... [Rom. 5:9].

> Is not the cup of blessing which we bless a sharing in the **blood** of Christ? [1 Cor 10:16a].

---

[35] Some have thought the prayer of Luke 18:13 is irrelevant after the cross. Since the Lord's death, one need not pray for God to be propitiated. He already has been propitiated for the sins of the whole world. However, because He is still angry over the sin of not believing (2 Thess. 1:8-9), the sinner's prayer in Luke 18 still seems appropriate at the time of faith in Christ.

[36] Col. 1:14 has variants concerning the word *blood*.

In the same way He took the cup also, after supper, saying, "This cup is the new covenant in My **blood**; do this, as often as you drink it, in remembrance of Me. For as often as you eat this bread and drink the cup, you proclaim the Lord's death until He comes. Therefore whoever eats the bread or drinks the cup of the Lord in an unworthy manner, shall be guilty of the body and the **blood** of the Lord" [1 Cor. 11:25-27].

In Him we have redemption through His **blood,** the forgiveness of our trespasses, according to the riches of His grace [Eph. 1:7].

But now in Christ Jesus you who formerly were far off have been brought near by the **blood** of Christ [Eph. 2:13].

[A]nd through Him to reconcile all things to Himself, having made peace through the **blood** of His cross [Col. 1:20].

(See Col. 1:14 in some versions.)

[A]nd not through the blood of goats and calves, but through His own **blood**, He entered the holy place once for all, having obtained eternal redemption [Heb. 9:12].

Since therefore, brethren, we have confidence to enter the holy place by the **blood** of Jesus [Heb. 10:19].

How much severer punishment do you think he will deserve who has trampled under foot the Son of God, and has regarded as unclean the **blood** of the covenant by which he was sanctified...? [Heb. 10:29].

You have not yet resisted to the point of shedding **blood** in your striving against sin [Heb. 12:4].

[A]nd to Jesus, the mediator of a new covenant, and to the sprinkled **blood** [Heb. 12:24a].

Therefore Jesus also, that He might sanctify the people through His own **blood**... [Heb. 13:12].

Now the God of peace, who brought up from the dead the great Shepherd of the sheep through the **blood** of the eternal covenant, even Jesus our Lord, equip you in every good thing to do His will... [Heb. 13:20-21].

[A]ccording to the foreknowledge of God the Father, by the sanctifying work of the Spirit, that you may obey Jesus Christ and be sprinkled with His **blood**... [1 Pet. 1:2].

[K]nowing that you were not redeemed with perishable things like silver or gold from your futile way of life inherited from your forefathers, but with precious **blood**, as of a lamb unblemished and spotless, the **blood** of Christ [1 Pet. 1:18-19].

[B]ut if we walk in the light as He Himself is in the light, we have fellowship with one another, and the **blood** of Jesus His Son cleanses us from all sin [1 John 1:7].

This is the one who came by water and **blood**, Jesus Christ; not with the water only, but with the water and with the **blood**...For there are three that bear witness, the Spirit and the water and the **blood**; and the three are in agreement [1 John 5:6, 8].

To Him who loves us, and released us from our sins by His **blood** [Rev. 1:5b].

... Worthy art Thou to take the book, and to break its seals; for Thou wast slain, and didst purchase for God with Thy **blood** men from every tribe and tongue and people and nation [Rev. 5:9].

...These are the ones who come out of the great tribulation, and they have washed their robes and made them white in the **blood** of the Lamb [Rev. 7:14].

And they overcame him because of the **blood** of the Lamb... [Rev. 12:11].

B. Conclusions about the Role of Christ's Blood in the Atonement

1. The blood is more than a symbol. It is understandable to conclude that there was more to Christ's agony than bleeding. Nevertheless, this truth should not relegate the literal blood to an insignificant factor in making salvation possible. The shedding of blood may not have been the only sacrifice/cost to the Savior. Yet, it was one necessary aspect to Christ's sacrifice. Salvation could not have been offered without the shed blood. The New Testament clearly stresses the blood of Christ and relates it to all major aspects of the atonement (e.g., forgiveness of sins - Matt. 26:28, Eph. 1:7; justification - Rom. 5:9; redemption - Eph. 1:7, Heb. 9:12, 1 Pet. 1:19, Rev. 5:9; reconciliation - Col. 1:20; and propitiation - Rom. 3:25).

One of the penalties for sin is physical death. Without the shedding of physical blood, an essential requirement for man's salvation, there would have been no forgiveness, redemption, propitiation, reconciliation, and justification for mankind. The "blood" of Christ should not be viewed as just a symbol or as a minor component in providing salvation. However, this is not the same as denying that Christ made additional sacrifices and endured additional pains that were equally vital. Also, it is probable that when the New Testament authors used the word *blood,* they meant both literal blood and also all other aspects of his suffering and death. *Blood* means blood, but it also has a deeper meaning: it speaks of a greater death, agony, and sacrifice.

2. Factors other than Christ's blood are at work in providing salvation. The cross will never be totally understood. We can be sure that there are other factors than the blood at work on the cross. Being a human physically, Jesus bled at His circumcision and when His baby teeth fell out. He perhaps bled in the carpenter's shop or from traveling on rough roads. He bled when Pilate's men whipped Him and when the thorns pierced His head. Yet, these drops of blood were, alone, not sufficient for the atonement.

We should first consider that the statement "the wages of sin is death" refers primarily to **spiritual** death. Christ paid the penalty of physical death. It was both literal and absolutely necessary. However, He must have also paid the pain of spiritual death and eternal death. He endured spiritual death, i.e., the separation from God the Father (Matt. 27:46), and eternal death in the lake of fire. He must have endured not the identical punishment in eternal hell but rather an equivalent punishment. Somehow Christ felt the agony of eternal hell multiplied by billions to pay for the sin of billions, and He did so during those short hours on the cross. Bleeding was necessary, but the difference between Christ bleeding at His circumcision and Christ bleeding as He hung on the cross is that Christ was the sin-bearer at the time He hung on the cross. The flow of blood was necessary, but it had to be the flow of blood at the precise **time He was the sin-bearer** or else the blood in and of itself would not have accomplished God's goal. It was the blood of Christ at the time He was the sin-bearer that was so necessary to salvation, and the importance of bearing sin opens the mind to depths of additional agonies Christ suffered. The blood of Christ was literal and necessary, but there are additional sufferings of which we are ignorant. We would not understand them any better than we understand heaven or hell. Thus, the Bible presents the blood as the most emphasized aspect to Christ's suffering. The blood was necessary and was the factor we can understand best, but salvation was more complicated and even more painful than bleeding.

> Yet it pleased the LORD to bruise him; he hath put him to grief: when thou shalt make his **Soul** an offering for sin... [Isa. 53:10 (KJV)].

> "...My God, My God, why hast Thou forsaken Me?" [Matt. 27:46].

VII. The Meaning and Extent of the Atonement

A. The Old Testament Term *Atonement*

As a Biblical word, *atonement* is strictly an Old Testament term concerning animal sacrifice. The verb *kapar* (cf. Yom Kippur, Day of Atonement) occurs approximately 102 times, and 3 various noun forms have a total of about 52 uses. Atonement seems to be a complex idea with many aspects.

1. One aspect of atonement is the covering of sin or the expiation of sin (i.e., to remove or wipe out sin's guilt and obligation). Both the verb and noun forms occur in Gen. 6:14 when God tells Noah "**cover** it" (the ark) inside and out with pitch. Gen. 6:14 could be giving the original meaning, to cover, to the words used for atonement. The priests covered the mercy seat (Hebrew: atonement seat) with blood. Rom. 3:25 and Heb. 9-10 seems to teach that sins were temporarily covered under the Old Testament system but were not permanently removed. Christ's sacrifice definitely expiated sin. It is probably wise to view Old Testament atonement as the covering of sins, the temporary removal of sin's obligation, until Christ could come.

2. A second aspect of atonement is propitiation or the diversion of wrath. If a Bible student had to choose one New Testament concept that is most closely related to the Old Testament term *atonement*, it would have to be propitiation. The most common translation used in the Septuagint for the Hebrew *kapar* is the Greek term for propitiation. Furthermore, Heb. 2:17 is a key text that relates the work of

a priest (in the context Christ) to making propitiation by sacrifice.

> Therefore, He had to be made like His brethren in all things, that He might become a merciful and faithful high priest in things pertaining to God, to make **propitiation** for the sins of the people [Heb. 2:17].

There are several Old Testament examples when a word from the *atonement* family is used of offering a price or gift in order to divert wrath. When Jacob is about to be reunited with his alienated brother Esau, he sends gifts of livestock to divert Esau's wrath.

> For he said, "I will appease (Hebrew- atone) him with the present that goes before me. Then afterward I will see his face; perhaps he will accept me" [Gen. 32:20].

Proverbs 16:14 refers to a wise man who seeks to atone (i.e., appease or pacify) the wrath of a king. The idea of propitiate needs to be included in the definition of atonement.

3. A third aspect of atonement is to give a payment to secure favor; redemption. The Hebrew noun form in the atonement group is often translated *ransom*. The payment of the price by the innocent for the guilty is not hard to see in Old Testament sacrificial ritual. Several Old Testament texts using the noun form for atonement are referring to paying a price. Often the price is paid to secure favor. In Ex. 32:30 Moses tells the children of Israel that he will try to make atonement for the sin of worshiping the golden calf. He then proceeds to offer God his life as a payment in exchange for preserving Israel. Num. 35:31 instructs civil authorities not to take atonement for the life of a murderer. This means that they should not take a ransom price to secure the favor of the judges. 1 Sam. 12:3 gives a similar meaning for atonement. Samuel is about to reconfirm Israel's king, but first he defends his own integrity.

"...Whom have I oppressed, or from whose hand have I taken a bribe (atonement money) to blind my eyes with it?..." [1 Sam. 12:3].

In this verse the word related to atonement refers to a price paid to secure favor, a bribe, a ransom. Moses, in Deut. 32:43, promises that God will avenge the blood of the Hebrews by destroying their enemies. He will thereby "atone for His land and His people." God would cause Israel's enemies to pay a price in order to satisfy the land and the people. These usages suggest that paying a price to secure favor is another aspect to atonement. Atonement involves redemption in the sense of paying a price to straighten out a relationship.[37] In Psa. 49:7 redemption and atonement are given as parallels.

4. A fourth aspect of atonement is reconciliation. It is evident that the purpose of the Old Testament sacrifices was to bring man to a relationship with God; i.e., to effect reconciliation. The King James translators thought atonement meant reconciliation in seven verses (e.g., Lev. 8:15; Ezek. 45:15, 17, etc.).

5. Summary: Atonement is a word that the Old Testament uses to describe the significance of animal sacrifices. The concept involves several factors. The animal blood covered sins as a temporary measure until the true Lamb of God would be sacrificed. There was a temporary removal of the guilt and obligation of sin (i.e., expiation) pending the final removal by the cross.

When the Old Testament person expressed faith in God by offering the sacrifices (as opposed to offering in self-righteous pride as an effort to earn salvation), he was saved.[38]

Pending the death of Christ, those animal sacrifices that were offered as an expression of faith in God caused atonement. They covered sin (expiation) tentatively removing its obligation and guilt. They paid a price (redemption) to secure God's favor by appeasing His anger (propitiation). The outcome of the faith expressed by sacrifices was a relationship with God (reconciliation). Atonement is a word that stands for **all** that was accomplished by the animal sacrifices (expiation, redemption, propitiation, and reconciliation).

B. Atonement as a Theological Term

Atonement is not a New Testament word. (It occurs in the King James Version in Rom. 5:11 but is a mistranslation.) However, the New Testament, especially the book of Hebrews, teaches that Old Testament sacrifices pictured the sacrifice of Christ. Therefore, it is common for theologians to use the word *atonement* as a catch-all term for the work of the cross. Atonement refers to **all** that Christ's death accomplished in order to provide salvation. When one wishes to be inclusive and not emphasize only one aspect of the cross's work (such as redemption, reconciliation, propitiation), the term atonement is appropriate.

---

[37] Other verses include the idea of paying a price: Ex. 30:12; Num. 31:50; Deut. 21:1-9; Isa 43:3. The Old Testament seems to have a general idea of redemption. A price had to be paid to secure standing with God. The New Testament more specifically links redemption with the purchase and liberation of a slave.

[38] Animal sacrifices alone could not bring salvation (Psa. 40:6; 51:16-17; Isa 1:11ff.; Amos 5:22; Micah 6:6-8). Old Testament saints were saved by faith (Gen. 15:6; Rom. 4; Heb. 11:2ff.). God wanted Old Testament saints to express their faith by giving animal sacrifices. Without knowing the precise role of animal blood, they knew animal blood was not sufficient. Without knowing the precise role of animal blood, they simply met God's requirement and trusted Him to take care of the details of salvation in His time and in His way. In essence God told the Old Testament people, "sacrifice alone can not fully save you, but show Me that you trust Me by offering them. Trust Me to work out all the additional provisions for salvation that will be needed." Those who sacrificed without faith thinking their works of righteousness would save them missed the point of animal sacrifices.

C. The Extent of the Atonement

"Five-point" Calvinists assert Christ died for only the elect. While acknowledging that many fine Christians believe in this "limited atonement," the Bible teaches an unlimited atonement. There is a sense in which redemption (2 Pet. 2:1), reconciliation (2 Cor. 5:19; Col. 1:20), and propitiation (1 John 2:2) occur for the whole world. Texts that teach unlimited atonement include the following:

"...Behold, the Lamb of God who takes away the sin of the **world**!" [John 1:29].

"For God so loved the **world**..." [John 3:16].

"...this One is indeed the Savior of the **world**" [John 4:42].

"...and the bread also which I shall give for the life of the **world**..." [John 6:51].

"And I, if I be lifted up from the earth, will draw **all** men to Myself" [John 12:32].

"...I did not come to judge the world, but to save the **world**" [John 12:47].

"...God is now declaring to men that **all everywhere** should repent" [Acts 17:30].

...God was in Christ reconciling the **world** to Himself, not counting their trespasses against them [2 Cor. 5:19].

[W]ho desires **all** men to be saved and to come to the knowledge of the truth [1 Tim. 2:4].

[W]ho gave Himself as a ransom for **all**... [1 Tim. 2:6].

[W]ho is the Savior of **all** men, especially of believers [1 Tim. 4:10].

For the grace of God has appeared, bringing salvation to **all** men [Titus 2:11].

[B]y the grace of God He might taste death for **every one** [Heb. 2:9].

But false prophets also arose among the people, just as there will also be false teachers among you, who will secretly introduce destructive heresies, even denying the Master who **bought** (redeemed) **them**, bringing swift destruction upon themselves [2 Pet. 2:1].

[A]nd He Himself is the propitiation for our sins; and not for ours only, but also for those of the **whole world** [1 John 2:2].

D. The Finality of the Atonement

The Reformers found the Roman Catholic view of communion particularly offensive because it implies that Christ is sacrificed over and over as the actual body and blood of the Lord is offered in each mass. The Scriptures teach that the atonement on the cross was sufficient and final. There will never be any need for additional work or additional sacrifice. Often the word *once* is used in reference to the cross. Also, the idea of Christ "sitting down" conveys a completed work as opposed to the Levitical priests who had to stand making continual animal sacrifices. (See Rom. 6:10; Heb. 7:27; 9:12; 9:26, 28; 10:10; 10:14; 1 Pet. 3:18; references to Christ sitting after a completed work - Col. 3:1; Heb. 1:3, 8:1, 10:12, 12:1-2).

[A]nd not through the blood of goats and calves, but through His own blood, He entered the holy place **once for all**, having obtained eternal redemption [Heb. 9:12].

Otherwise, He would have needed to suffer often since the foundation of the world; **but now once** at the consummation of the ages He has been manifested to put away sin by the sacrifice of Himself [Heb. 9:26].

By this will we have been sanctified through the offering of the body of Jesus Christ **once** for all [Heb.10:10].

[B]ut He, having offered **one sacrifice** for sins for **all time, sat down** at the right hand of God [Heb. 10:12].

For by **one offering** He has **perfected for all time** those who are sanctified [Heb. 10:14].

…"**It is finished!**"… [John 19:30].

SOTERIOLOGY

The Doctrine of Salvation

Part 2
Salvation Applied

I. Salvation Applied by God in Eternity Past

God does have a predetermined plan for the ages (Isa. 46:10; Acts 4:28). Christ's death on the cross did not catch God by surprise for it had been planned in the eternal counsels of God (Acts 2:23; Heb. 13:20; 1 Pet. 1:20; Rev. 13:8). God determines all events either in the direct sense that He causes something to happen or in the indirect sense that He allows something to happen by foreknowing it but not intervening to change it. In the day-to-day course of life, we do things and make decisions that seem from our perspective to be based upon our own choices. However, God controls all. Sometimes God has narrowed our course of action so that we never really had a choice at all. Other times we are genuinely operating on our own initiative by God's permission. The most important soteriological aspects to God's sovereign control are the subjects of predestination and election. In what sense does God choose and predestine a person be saved?

A. Factors Influencing One's view of Election

The proper method of interpreting Scripture is to interpret difficult truths (such as election and predestination) in the light of clearer truths. There can be no doubt that God's compassion and plan of salvation is universal in scope.

1. God Loves the Whole World

> "For God so loved the **world,** that He gave His only begotten Son, that whoever believes in Him should not perish but have eternal life" [John 3:16].

2. Christ Died for the Whole World

(See verses on unlimited atonement in Chapter 9, Part 1, VII.C., p. 123.)

The work of the cross was for the whole world (redemption, 2 Pet. 2:1; reconciliation, 2 Cor. 5:19; propitiation, 1 John 2:2).

> "Behold, the Lamb of God who takes away the sin of the **world!**" [John 1:29].

> "...and the bread also which I shall give for the life of the **world** is My flesh" [John 6:51].

> "...God is now declaring to men that **all** everywhere should repent" [Acts 17:30].

> ...that by the grace of God He might taste death for **everyone** [Heb. 2:9].

3. The Gospel Message of Salvation is Directed to All People

> "Go therefore and make disciples of **all the nations,** baptizing them in the name of the Father and the Son and the Holy Spirit" [Matt. 28:19]

> "[A]nd that repentance for forgiveness of sins should be proclaimed in His

name to **all the nations…**" [Luke 24:47].

"…you shall be My witnesses both in Jerusalem, and in all Judea and Samaria, and even to the **remotest part of the earth**" [Acts 1:8].

4. God Says He Desires **All** to be Saved

"Thus it is **not the will** of your Father who is in heaven that one of these little ones **perish**" [Matt.18:14].

…who desires **all men to be saved** [1 Tim. 2:4].

The Lord is not slow about His promise, as some count slowness, but is patient toward you, **not wishing for any to perish** but for **all to come to repentance** [2 Pet. 3:9].

…And **whosoever will**, let him take the water of life freely [Rev. 22:17 (KJV)].

5. Basis for Eternal Condemnation is Failure to Accept Christ

(For details see Chapter 6, Footnote 5.)

Each person is accountable and must be responsible for his own eternal destiny.

"He who believes in Him is not judged; he who does not believe has been judged already, **because he has not believed** in the name of the only begotten Son of God" [John 3:18].

…when the Lord Jesus shall be revealed from heaven with His mighty angels in flaming fire, dealing out retribution to those who do not know God and to those **who do not obey the gospel** of our Lord Jesus [2 Thess. 1: 7-8].

6. Conclusion

These simple Bible facts must be incorporated into any specific views on election and predestination. Since God wants "all to be saved and to come to the knowledge of the truth," it is

difficult to maintain He has decreed only some to salvation. Since God has commanded "all men everywhere to repent," it is difficult to believe He has devised a system in which the major responsibility for repentance or unrepentance lies with Himself rather than with man. Since the primary basis for eternal condemnation is not inherited or personal sin, but rather failure to accept Christ, it is difficult to adopt a position in which the majority have no real responsibility for whether or not they accept Christ. Indeed, if Calvinism is true, most people simply are unable to accept Christ because **God** has not chosen them. The result is that there is no remaining basis for eternal condemnation. God does not condemn in the eternal sense for sin. How could He condemn a soul for unbelief if God Himself is primarily responsible for belief or for unbelief?

Some are willing to accept all of these contradictions in their theology. To them the doctrines of election and predestination are conundrums, mysterious doctrines that must be accepted even if not understood. It is true that a doctrine can be true without being well understood. However, it is better not to give up prematurely in an effort to understand the Bible. Perhaps it is possible to view election and predestination in a way so that they are compatible with the simple facts about God's universal compassion and worldwide plan for salvation.

B. The Reason for God's Program of Election

Satan blinds all unsaved people to the gospel. Unless there is conviction by the Holy Spirit, the natural man cannot see the importance of revealed truth. He may intellectually know of a cross and a death, but blindness prevents receptivity or an appreciation for the truth. There is no welcoming of the truth. There is no impression that the gospel is important, precious, relevant, significant. If God did nothing to dispel this blindness, there would be no salvation at all. Unless God had intervened, no one would have ever understood the gospel.

The blindness of unsaved humanity is a primary factor that makes a system of election absolutely imperative. God must take the initiative to dispel darkness and blindness in a lost person's heart. The Holy Spirit penetrates that darkness so that the gospel is fully understood. Then, and only then, is it possible for the person to exercise his or her **own** faith in Christ. There will be more evidence for the Holy Spirit's role in election on the following pages. God does not give the faith, but He makes it possible for faith to be expressed. These verses establish that man is blinded to the truth. Therefore, a program of election was necessary if salvation were to ever be applied.

"No one can come to Me, **unless the Father** who sent Me **draws him**; and I will raise him up on the last day" [John 6:44].

And a certain woman named Lydia, from the city of Thyatira, a seller of purple fabrics, a worshiper of God, was listening; and **the Lord opened her heart to respond** to the things spoken by Paul [Acts 16:14].

"...**to open their eyes** so that they may turn from darkness to light and from the dominion of Satan to God" [Acts 26:18].

For the word of the cross is **to those who are perishing foolishness**...[1 Cor. 1:18].

But **a natural man does not accept** the things of the Spirit of God; for they are foolishness to him, and he cannot understand them, because they are spiritually appraised [1 Cor. 2:14].

...in whose case the god of this world has **blinded the minds of the unbelieving**, that they might not see the light of the gospel...[2 Cor. 4:4].

C. The Basis of God's Program of Election

Scripture makes a direct connection between election/predestination and foreknowledge.

God does not arbitrarily and unconditionally choose one soul for heaven and shut the other out to inevitable hell. God knows all the people who will ever believe, if given enlightenment. Yet, even those with a latent potential for faith will never respond unless their blindness is penetrated and dispelled by God Himself so their faith can be exercised. Therefore, God has a program of election to reach all of those whom He foreknows will believe if the blindness is dissipated. His election is **conditional**. It is conditioned upon a foreknowledge of potential faith. God does not irresistibly cause the faith, but He causes understanding of the gospel so that the expression of the person's faith can take place. God also knows those who have no potential for faith. They would never believe regardless of the amount of God's gracious efforts. Apparently, many of these still receive conviction (John 16:8-11); yet, regardless of whether these "non-elect" are recipients of a convicting work of the Holy Spirit, God knows they will never believe. He holds them accountable for not having any latent potential for faith, and He certainly did not actively decree their unbelief (though He does not force belief and thus indirectly decrees unbelief). **No one who would have ever believed will be in hell.**[39] Just as it is a mistake to fail to incorporate God's universal love into views of His sovereignty, it is also a serious mistake to fail to note the connection between election, predestination, and foreknowledge. God's election and predestination means that anyone foreknown to have a potential for faith will have an opportunity to have blindness removed by the Holy Spirit so that he can understand the gospel and so that the result will be faith and salvation.

---

[39] The author does not view man's will as totally free. Still, God can righteously hold a person accountable for his or her eternal destiny. Either a person rejects the truth after direct enlightenment, or God foreknows that he would eternally do so even if given enlightenment. God knows there would not be faith in Christ regardless of the frequency or strength of His merciful efforts.

For whom He **foreknew,** He also pre-destined to become conformed to the image of His Son, that He might be the first-born among many brethren [Rom. 8:29].

...who are **chosen according to the foreknowledge** of God the Father, by the sanctifying work of the Spirit, that you may obey Jesus Christ and be sprinkled with His blood...[1 Pet. 1:1-2].

Because unsaved man is blind (1 Cor. 1:18; 2:14; 2 Cor. 4:4) and God's work is necessary to penetrate the darkness (John 6:44; 16:8-11; Acts 16:14; 26:18), one would expect the Scriptures to associate election with the con-victing ministry of the Holy Spirit. A person is not so much chosen to salvation: in reality God chooses those with a latent potential for faith to be recipients of the Holy Spirit's min-istry to cause enlightenment to the gospel. Then the individual's latent faith can become an expressed faith. The connection between the Holy Spirit and election is found in 2 Thess. 2:13 and 1 Pet. 1:2. Keep in mind that sanctification means "setting apart". The elect are chosen to be set apart to a special work of grace and influence of the Holy Spirit. The Spirit penetrates and dispels blindness, and then faith can occur.

...God has chosen you from the begin-ning for salvation **through sanctifica-tion by the Spirit and faith** in the truth [2 Thess. 2:13].

...who are chosen according to the foreknowledge of God the Father, **by the sanctifying work of the Spirit that you may obey Jesus Christ** and be sprinkled with His blood...[1 Pet. 1:1-2].

D. The Ultimate Goal for God's Program of Election

It is common for the doctrines of predestina-tion and election to cause a focus upon the time of conversion. They do pertain to the time of salvation. However, the teachings of predestination and election have implications far beyond the time of enlightenment and re-ception of Christ as Savior. Eph. 1:5 says, "He predestined us to adoption as sons...." While the term *adoption* gives rise to the thought of time of entering a family, Biblical authors give the term the more general meaning of *son-placing*, and they commonly associate adop-tion with inheritance and a level of maturity.

In Gal. 4:5-7 adoption does refer to the time of entering God's family and becoming an "heir apparent" (one who is named as an heir but does not yet possess all the inheritance). The believer in Christ is placed as a mature son as compared to a lesser degree of maturity that the "children" of God had under the Law Sys-tem. He is presently an heir but doesn't have full possession of the inheritance.

However, in Rom. 8:23 the term *adoption* has a future thrust. It refers to the "redemption of our body," i.e., the "son-placing" in which we become like the Lord Jesus Christ as a glori-fied human (1 John 3:2). Believers will be-come mature sons at this future point, and then they will obtain full inheritance as opposed to being just named as heirs. This progression is also implied in the context of Rom. 8:15 and following. Those with the Spirit of adoption (v. 15) are heirs (v. 17). Yet, they are awaiting their full glory and full inheritance (vv. 17-18). The first fruits or partial inheritance is a reality (v. 23), but a more complete "son-placing" is a future event when our bodies become like mature sons of God after the pat-tern of Christ (v. 23; see also 1 John 3:2). It is significant for the doctrine of predestination and election that, further in the context, Paul links the outcome of predestination to being conformed to the image of Christ (v. 29) and full glorification (v. 30). **Adoption,** while re-ferring to the **entrance into God's family** at salvation, **also refers to a future "son-placing"** when believers are mature sons after the image of a glorified Christ. Paul teaches in Romans 8 that Christians are predestined to this future adoption, "son-placing."

When the context of Eph. 1 is considered, it seems best to view the term *adoption* as also giving a future orientation as in Rom. 8:23 (rather than a more present orientation as in Gal. 4:5 and Rom. 8:15). The phrase itself, "He predestined us to adoption as sons," is capable of meaning, "He predestined us to enter God's family at salvation" or "He predestined us to obtain glorification, a full inheritance, and a full son-placing when we are mature sons like Christ." In the Ephesians 1 context, Paul goes on to speak on the topic of inheritance. Believers have a down payment, or "pledge," of their inheritance but the full inheritance is future (v. 14). Verse 14 is also dealing with the redemption of believer's bodies and is in ideology and phraseology reminiscent of Romans 8. Both Eph. 1:5 and Rom. 8:15ff. teach that believers are going to receive full inheritance and redemption of their bodies. Romans 8 specifically includes the idea that a future adoption (son placing) is predestined. **In fact the final goal of predestination is not conversion but glorification**. Because of the parallels between Romans 8 and Ephesians 1, it is difficult to exclude future aspects when Paul speaks of predestination to son placing in Eph. 1:5. Both books are by the same author.

When Paul teaches about predestination and the "adoption of sons" in Eph. 1:5, he probably does have the "son-placing" (which initially brings us into God's family) in mind as in Gal. 4:5ff. and Rom. 8:15. However, to stop with this is incomplete. It actually misses the main goal of God's predestination. Paul is also teaching that believers have been predestined to obtain their full "son-placing," i.e., the glorification of their bodies after the image of a mature Son, Jesus Christ. Believers are predestined to the possession of their inheritance. Election and predestination must be given a future thrust. They are teachings that make the doctrine of Eternal Security unquestionable. **The elect are predestined to eternal glory.**

In summary, God foreknows all those with a latent potential for faith. Not one will miss salvation. He chooses them to be special recipients of the Holy Spirit's enlightenment. Blindness is removed so that the individual's faith responds. This leads to a "son-placing" or adoption. Yet, election and predestination do not end at conversion. Regardless of whether election is viewed as conditional or unconditional, all should agree a proper view of God's sovereignty needs to include a future orientation. These doctrines are controversial, but they are a blessing. Believers are inevitably predestined to a future "son-placing" with its future inheritance and future glory being conformed to the image of His Son (Rom. 8:29-30). Nothing and no one can stop this destiny for it is an immutable decree by a sovereign God.

II. Salvation Applied in This Life to Those Who Comply With God's Condition for Salvation

A. Introduction

If one browses a typical tract rack in a Bible-believing church, he may be surprised at the number of terms and phrases that are given as conditions for salvation. Gospel appeals come across variously as "believe," "repent," "confess," "deny self," "yield," "surrender," "receive," "accept," "make Jesus Lord," "ask Jesus into the heart," "forsake all," etc. Sometimes the terms are combined to give three, four, or five steps to salvation (e.g., first repent, then believe, then confess, and so forth). Do all of these terms mean the same thing? Is there one, or is there more than one, condition for salvation? Before a Christian is ready to witness, and certainly before an evangelist is equipped to speak in public, the question, "What must they do to be saved?" must be answered with precision.

B. Believe, Trust, and Exercise Faith

Many scriptural texts present **the only condition for salvation as being belief** (synonyms: trust and faith). In fact, there are over 150 New Testament passages where salvation is conditioned upon believing alone. If any other requirement is added, it will cause these verses to be incomplete and misleading. Therefore, **all terms that express a condition genuinely necessary for salvation** (such as repentance) **must be interpreted as to be compatible with a salvation based upon faith alone.** Terms that cannot be made compatible with faith alone as a condition for salvation are used improperly and dangerously at best and, at worst, are sheer heresy. All Protestant theologians began with that basic tenet of the Reformation, *sola fide,* **faith alone.** Here are some of the key texts where the Bible declares faith alone brings salvation:

"For God so loved the world, that He gave His only begotten Son, that **whoever believes in Him** should not perish, but have eternal life" [John 3:16].

"**He who believes** in Him is not judged; he who does not believe has been judged already, **because he has not believed** in the name of the only begotten Son of God" [John 3:18].

"Truly, truly, I say to you, he who hears My word, and **believes Him who sent me,** has eternal life, and does not come into judgment, but has passed out of death into life" [John 5:24].

"For this is the will of My Father, that everyone who beholds the Son **and believes in Him**, may have eternal life; and I Myself will raise him up on the last day" [John 6:40].

"Truly, truly, I say to you, **he who believes** has eternal life" [John 6:47].

Jesus said to her, "I am the resurrection and the life; **he who believes in Me shall live** even if he dies, and **everyone who lives and believes in Me shall never die.** Do you believe this?" [John 11:25-26].

Many other signs therefore Jesus also performed in the presence of the disciples, which are not written in this book;

but these have been written that you may believe that Jesus is the Christ, the Son of God; **and that believing you may have life in His name** [John 20:30-31].

"[A]nd through Him everyone **who believes** is freed from all things..." [Acts 13:39].

"Sirs, what must I do to be saved?" And they said, "**Believe in the Lord Jesus**, and you shall be saved, you and your household" [Acts 16:30-31].

For I am not ashamed of the gospel, for it is the power of God **for salvation to everyone who believes**... [Rom. 1:16].

...even the righteousness of God through **faith in Jesus Christ** for **all those who believe**...[Rom. 3:22].

...whom God displayed publicly as a propitiation in His blood **through faith** [Rom. 3:25].

For we maintain that a man is **justified by faith** apart from works of the Law [Rom. 3:28].

...since indeed God who will justify the circumcised **by faith** and the uncircumcised **through faith** is one [Rom. 3:30].

But to the one who does not work, but **believes** in Him who justifies the ungodly, **his faith** is reckoned as righteousness...[Rom. 4:5].

Therefore, having been **justified by faith**, we have peace with God through our Lord Jesus Christ [Rom. 5:1].

For the Scripture says, "**Whoever believes** in Him will not be disappointed"....So **faith** comes from hearing, and hearing by the word of Christ [Rom. 10:11, 17].

"[N]evertheless knowing that a man is not justified by the works of the Law but **through faith in Christ Jesus,** even we have **believed in Christ Jesus,** that we may be **justified by faith** in Christ, and not by the works of the Law; since by the works of the Law shall no flesh be justified." [Gal. 2:16]

Even so Abraham **believed God,** and it was reckoned to him as righteousness. Therefore, be sure that it is those who are of **faith** who are sons of Abraham [Gal. 3:6-7].

Now that no one is justified by the Law before God is evident; for, "the righteous man **shall live by faith**" [Gal. 3:11].

But the Scripture has shut up all men under sin, that the promise **by faith** in Jesus Christ might be given to **those who believe** [Gal. 3:22].

Therefore the Law has become our tutor to lead us to Christ, that we may be **justified by faith** [Gal. 3:24].

For you are **all sons of God through faith** in Christ Jesus [Gal. 3:26].

For by grace you have been **saved through faith;** and that not of yourselves, it is the gift of God; not as a result of works, that no one should boast [Eph. 2:8-9].

It is possible to accept the Scriptural fact that faith alone saves but give a wrong definition to faith. It is imperative that saving faith be accurately defined by Scriptural contexts.

1. The Hebrew Background for the Meaning of Faith

With the exception of Dr. Luke, all the New Testament authors were Jews, and all the authors were conversant with the Old Testament. Their understanding of faith would be based upon the meaning of faith in the Old Testament.

The Hebrew word for "to believe" is *aman,* which relates to our word *Amen.* In some ver-

bal stems (*qal/niphal*), the word means "to be firm, to support, to be secure, to be faithful." B.B. Warfield, that great theologian from Princeton, said *aman* describes "whatever holds, is steady, or can be depended upon."[40] This definition is based upon observation of how *aman* is used in the Old Testament.

Aman (in the *qal* stem) is used of people who are caretakers for children who support and sustain them (support by literally carrying them or by financial support). The word means "foster father" or "nurse" in Num. 11:12, Ruth 4:16, 2 Sam. 4:4, 2 Kings 10:1,5; Esth. 2:7; Isa. 49:23; Lam. 4:5. A guardian, nurse, nanny, foster father is someone on whom the infant utterly depends. He or she is reliable, trustworthy, dependable, firm, and supportive. *Aman* is used (in the *qal* stem) of door posts and pillars which are supportive, secure, firm, in 2 Kings 18:16 and with a negative in Jer. 15:18 to describe an unreliable stream.

Another grammatical form of *aman* (the *niphal*) yields the same meaning. The word refers to something that is firm, supportive, and dependable. Isaiah uses the word of a wall that can securely hold a nail in Isa. 22:23, 25 and of supporting children in Isa. 60:4. There are references to a stream that can be relied upon to provide water and not go dry in Isa. 33:16 and a kingdom that will be stable in 2 Sam. 7:16. When this form of *aman* is used of personal beings, the meaning is that God can be depended upon to keep a promise (e.g., Deut. 7:9; Psa. 89:28) and that a treasurer can be relied upon in handling money (Neh. 13:13). These examples prove that the Hebrew word *aman* refers to firmness, dependability, faithfulness, trustworthiness, and reliability.

From these usages one would expect that the causative form of *aman* (the *hiphil*) means not so much to be firm, dependable and so forth,

---

[40] Benjamin B. Warfield, *Biblical and Theological Studies,* ed. Samuel G. Craig, reprint ed. (Philadelphia: The Presbyterian and Reformed Publishing Co., 1968) 429.

but to "**consider someone** or **something to be** firm, dependable, faithful, trustworthy, reliable." The change is from being a faithful one to **considering another** to be a faithful one. When we consider another to have these characteristics we are trusting them, depending upon them, relying upon them. This is a basic meaning to Hebrew ideas of faith. The specific meanings might range from intellectually accepting a fact to trusting upon a person.

Hab. 1:5 uses believe in the sense of to intellectually believe the truth of a message. Verses that seem to contain the idea of trust often use the phrase *to believe in*. The idea of trust seems to be included in these Old Testament references using *aman* (*hiphil* stem) Gen. 15:6; Ex. 14:31; Num. 14:11; Deut. 1:32; 9:23; 28:66; 2 Kings 17:14; 2 Chron. 20:20; Job 24:22; Psa. 27:13; 78:22; 106:24; Isa. 28:16; 43:10. Sometimes both the ideas of intellectually believing a fact and trusting a person are combined. In Num. 14:11, Deut. 1:32, and 9:23, belief is the opposite of the Israelite failure to invade Canaan from Kadesh-Barnea. In other words, they should have both intellectually believed the message that God would give them the land, but also they should have trusted Him enough to begin the conquest. In Ex. 4:31 the people believed intellectually Moses' message that God was going to lead them out of Egypt, but they also believed in the sense of trust. In Isa. 7:9 Isaiah wants King Ahaz to believe intellectually in the prediction of deliverance from enemies, but he also wants the king to have confidence and assurance in God's gracious promise.

Contrasts and parallels help define a word. In Psa. 27:13-14 *aman* is parallel to hope and in Psa. 78:22 it is parallel to another Hebrew word that means trust. 2 Kings 17:14 and Deut. 9:23 show that faith is the opposite of rebellion, i.e., allegiance.[41] In Hab. 2:4, "the

just shall live by faith," is contrasted with the pride exhibited by the insolent and self-assertive Babylonians. Thus, faith is humble dependence.

New Testament authors carry over these concepts of the meaning of faith into their teachings. Therefore, we would anticipate that to them faith in God would mean to consider God to be secure, firm, dependable and trustworthy. **Viewed from man's perspective this is called trust, confidence, dependence, and reliance.**

2. Saving Faith: What It Is Not

The New Testament is clear that saving faith is more than intellectual faith in certain facts about Jesus or orthodox doctrines (James 2:19; John 2:23-24; 3:2). Nicodemus believed in the existence of God and that Jesus was sent by Him as a miracle worker, but the Lord told him that he still needed salvation (John 3:3ff.). James reminds us that even demons intellectually believe in correct doctrine (James 2:19; see also Matt. 4:3; 8:29; Mark 1:34; 3:11; 5:7; Luke 8:28; Acts 16:17; 19:15).[42] Saving faith does indeed include a belief in certain key facts about Christ. Yet, saving faith is more than intellectual faith.

> You believe that God is one. You do well; the demons also believe, and shudder [James 2:19].

If intellectual assent to doctrine is not saving faith, neither is the attitude that could be called emotional or temporal faith. Emotional faith is the kind of faith that the crowds expressed when they proclaimed Christ as their king on Palm Sunday (Matt. 21:1-11; Mark 11:1-11; Luke 19:28-40; John 12:12-19). In these accounts one reads of great emotional assertions about Christ. The crowd cried, "Blessed is the king of Israel!" "Blessed is He that comes in the name of the Lord" and "Hosanna to the Son of David." Nevertheless, one week later the same crowd shouted, "Let Him

---

[41] This study argues that saving faith can exist in a heart that is less than totally yielded to Christ's authority. However, this does not mean saving faith can exist with total rebellion.

[42] In Matt. 4:3 *if* means "since." Satan concedes that Jesus is the Son of God.

be crucified," "His blood be upon us and our children" (Matt. 27:22 and 25), and "We have no king but Caesar" (John 19:15). Why was there such a change?

The Jewish people on Palm Sunday were expressing an emotional or temporal faith. They wished to accept Jesus solely as a political deliverer from their present distresses, mainly the Romans. Earlier in His ministry the people were desirous of making Jesus king by force (John 6:15). They wanted Jesus to save them from their temporal problems, but that is all they really wanted from Him (John 6:26). They did not care about a spiritual Savior from sin. Christ resisted such an emotional and temporal faith. The crowds got all excited and were willing to believe He could deliver from temporal political problems, but there was no real spiritual interest in being saved from sin. This type of emotional faith is described as "seed on rocky places" in the parable of the sower. The message is received with emotional joy, but, since there is no depth, the results are temporary (Matt. 13:20-21; Mark 4:16-17; Luke 8:13). They wanted a political savior, or a medical savior, or an economic savior, but not a Savior from sin.

Today a person may desire Jesus to save them from sickness, a broken relationship, combat, financial burdens, etc., and may genuinely believe He can help in such temporal problems. They may even be excited about it. Of course, it is neither wrong nor unwise to want help from Christ for these trials, but this type of faith by itself is not saving faith. If all a person wants from Jesus Christ is that He will take away a given temporal trouble, yet he could care less about being saved from his sins, this is not saving faith. Believing that Jesus can help in taking away a problem is not the same as believing in Jesus as Savior from one's sin and guilt. Many people respond to high-pressure gospel invitations out of emotional turmoil or confusion. They walk aisles with hearts full of problems. They may even believe Christ can solve these problems and may beg Him to do so. Yet, if there is not also

trust in Jesus Christ **to save from sin**; then all that results is an emotional religious experience that makes one temporarily feel better about life's problems. Such an emotional or temporal faith in Jesus to make life better is not saving faith and does not endure.

> "And those on the rocky soil are those who, when they hear, receive the word with joy; and these have no firm root; they believe for a while, and in time of temptation fall away" [Luke 8:13].

3. Saving Faith: What It Is

There are approximately 480 references to the verb *believe* and the noun *faith* in the New Testament. (*Faith* and *belief* are the same word in Greek.) An examination of each of these is impossible in such a limited study. However, they may be categorized into groups and discussed in a logical fashion.

Saving faith is more than intellectual adherence to certain facts and is more than an emotional attraction to Jesus believing He can be of assistance in temporal trials. Yet having said this, it must be stressed that genuine saving faith involves activity on the part of all three main components of the human soul: intellect, emotions, and will.

With the mind, a person must intellectually believe certain basic truths about the person and work of Christ. This is the **content** of saving faith. However, though a person believes the gospel is factually true with his mind, it is with his emotions that a person develops a conviction about the facts. He views them not only as true but also as an important need in his or her life. With emotions he gives assent to the value of the gospel and believes in it in a personal (as opposed to a strictly theological) way. The facts are not only deemed true but also personally needful and relevant.

The faith expressed by the mind and emotions is incomplete without the faith expressed by the will. With the will a sinner chooses to place **confidence** (trust, faith, reliance, dependence) in Christ and His shed blood, believing in Jesus Christ and the cross for salvation. It is the nature of saving faith that it also involves a choice to **commit** the soul's eternal destiny to Jesus Christ and His perfect work upon the cross. The mind, the emotions, and the will, all play a role in genuine saving faith (though the process often takes place simultaneously). The definition of saving faith can best be studied under the three words indicated above (content, confidence, and commitment).

a. Saving Faith: Its Content

This section might be called the "**believe thats**" of the gospel. A person who believes that Jesus Christ was a guru or that He was merely a great religious teacher does not have saving faith because he is not believing in the "Biblical Christ." There have been, there are, and there will be many people who claim to be Christ. There are also many more that have great misconceptions about Jesus of Nazareth. While saving faith is more than an intellectual faith, the Scriptures are clear that saving faith does have its intellectual aspects. There is a content to saving faith. While a sinner does not need to know a complex doctrinal system, he must accept certain basic truths about Jesus Christ and the cross so that he believes in the Christ of the Bible and not a Christ of his own imagination or man's fabrication. The intellectual content of saving faith can be traced by following the phrase "believe that." Twenty times the Greek word for *believe* (*pistuo*) is followed by *that (hoti)*. This construction reveals the facts that must be believed intellectually in order to trust Christ.

A sinner must believe "that Christ died for our sins according to the Scriptures, that He was buried, and that He was raised on the third day according to the Scriptures" (1 Cor. 15:3-4; cf. Rom. 10:9-10; 1 Thess. 4:14). A sinner must believe "that Jesus is the Christ, the Son of God" (John 20:30-31; cf. John 8:24; 11:27). This involves accepting Him as Lord **in the sense of acknowledging His deity** (Rom. 10:9). A sinner must believe that Jesus Christ

was sent from God (John 11:42; 16:27; 17:8,21; 1 John 2:22) and that Jesus Christ is the Son of God who took upon Himself human flesh (1 John 4:2-3). Of course, the belief that one is a sinner and in need of help is implied in coming to Christ to find salvation.

These doctrines are the intellectual content of saving faith. To have saving faith one must believe in the Christ of the Bible. To have saving faith one must believe intellectually that Jesus Christ is the Son of God (deity), Lord, and Messiah who was sent from God. He must believe that God the Son took upon Himself flesh, died for our sins, and is now the risen Savior. If one claims to believe in God or be a Christian and yet denies the deity of Christ or the resurrection, he is either lying or is badly deceived.

Notice that saving faith does acknowledge that Jesus is God, and therefore, is also Master. **This is not the same as making a commitment to live for Him**, but there is the acknowledgement that Jesus, being the Master, does have a right to command.

b. Saving Faith: Its Confidence and Commitment

Saving faith has its intellectual content. However, when witnessing to others, a Christian is not just asking an unbeliever to believe Jesus was telling the truth or to cognitively accept certain facts about Jesus. The unbeliever is being urged to believe in, on, or upon Jesus Christ, meaning that he should place his **confidence**, trust, and reliance in Jesus Christ and His cross. Saving faith has its factual content, but it also places **confidence** in a person and His work: Jesus Christ.

In earthly matters one may place confidence in another person without committing his soul to that person. However, it is the nature of saving faith that its confidence in Christ must be expressed by and is inseparable from **a commitment of the soul's eternal destiny to Christ**. Although a person may recite and believe every fact in the apostle's creed, there is no salvation without a personal confidence in Christ and entrusting of the soul's safekeeping to Him.

How does one know that intellectual or emotional faith alone is not saving faith? How does one know that the type of faith that saves refers to confidence and commitment? The following points establish that the Greek word for belief has the range of meaning to specifically mean confidence, trust, reliance, and they also show that this specific meaning is what the New Testament authors intended by saving faith.

(1) The New Testament word for *Faith* or *Belief* (*pistuo*, verb; *pistis*, noun) can specifically mean confidence, trust.

Previous material on the Hebrew word for *faith (aman)* proved that it could refer to trust, confidence, and reliance. When the New Testament verb for *to believe* is used in the Septuagint, it is always (except Prov. 26:25) a translation for *aman*. One can, therefore, safely assume that the New Testament authors felt that one of the specific nuances for the *pistuo* family is trust.

One hint from the New Testament itself that saving faith involves a commitment of the soul's destiny is that the Greek word *to believe* (*pistuo*) is translated "commit" (KJV) in John 2:24; Luke 16:11 (active forms) and Rom. 3:2; 1 Cor. 9:17; Gal. 2:7; 1 Tim. 1:11 and Titus 1:3 (passive forms). It means the same in 1 Thess. 2:4 where it is translated "put in trust." *To believe* in such contexts is to **entrust**.

Thus, both the Old Testament background and New Testament usage of *pistuo* (*to believe*) establish that one of the primary meanings of the term is to trust, to entrust, i.e., to have confidence, to commit something to someone because they are trusted. The following sections continue to establish that the specific meaning of **confidence** is not only a possible meaning for the term *believe*, it is the specific meaning the authors intended in connection with salvation.

(2) The command is not to believe Jesus Christ but to believe **in** Jesus Christ. This refers to confidence, trust.

The Greek verb *to believe (pistuo)* often appears with prepositions. B. B. Warfield says of these prepositions, "When we advance to the constructions with prepositions, we enter a region in which the deeper sense of the word' that of **firm trustful reliance**, comes to its full rights."[43]

The truth of Warfield's conclusion may be realized by pondering that the gospel invitation is not just to believe Jesus Christ is telling the truth but rather to **believe in, on, or upon Jesus Christ** to be saved. The statement, "I believe the politician," means, "I believe he is telling the truth," i.e., not lying. However, the statement, "I believe **in** the politician," means not only that he is telling the truth, but also, "I have a personal confidence in his leadership and ideas." There is a great difference between believing Jesus and believing **in** Jesus. The later phrase expresses confidence and trust. It is striking that *believe in (pistuo* with *eis)* **is virtually unknown in secular Greek** but *believe* is followed by *eis,* the Greek preposition, indicating the goal or object of faith, **forty-nine** times in the New Testament. The New Testament authors must intend the contrast. They are purposely calling for a belief **in** Jesus Christ, not just a belief in facts about Him.

Among the forty-nine times where **believe** is followed by **in** (*i.e., pistuo* with *eis)* are these: John 1:12; 3:16, 18, 36; 6:29, 40; 11:25-26; 14:1, 12; 16:9; 17:20; Rom. 10:14; Gal. 2:16; 1 Pet. 1:8; 1 John 5:13. Twelve times *believe* is followed by *upon* (*pistuo* with *epi* followed by the dative case five times and an accusative case seven times) as in Rom. 4:5, 24; Acts 9:42; 11:1; 16:31; 22:19. *Belief* is followed by

---

[43]Benjamin B. Warfield, *Biblical and Theological Studies*, ed. Samuel G. Craig, reprint ed. (Philadelphia: The Presbyterian and Reformed Publishing Co., 1968) 437.

another Greek word for *in (pistuo* with *en)* between one and three times depending on the manuscripts that are counted. The use of *pistuo* with these various prepositions reveals that the New Testament authors are urging **trust, confidence,** i.e., **and belief in** Jesus Christ in order to be saved. (Usage with the above prepositions totals between sixty-three and sixty-five references. There are twenty times where *belief* is followed by *that,* (*pistuo* with *hoti),* and forty-five times where *belief* is followed by a dative. (*Pistuo* is used absolutely ninety-three times).

(3) Saving faith must mean confidence (Trust) by a process of elimination.

One obvious way to establish that saving faith is confidence (which is expressed by a commitment of the soul to Jesus) is by elimination. It has already been shown that the New Testament clearly teaches that neither intellectual nor emotional faith is sufficient to save. Since the nuances of intellectual and emotional faith have been ruled out, the New Testament writers are stressing something more when they write of saving faith. They must have the specific meaning of **trust or confidence** in mind when they use the *pistuo* family in connection with obtaining salvation.

(4) Parallel phrases show that saving faith is the equivalent of confidence (Trust)

Another method to show that the Bible means confidence (trust) when it refers to saving faith involves an examination of phrases that are parallel with and mean the same thing as believing in Jesus. Such expressions suggest confidence and commitment, not just an intellectual faith (which is merely the opposite of atheism). Believing in Christ for salvation is synonymous with having "committed (*one's soul* is implied) unto Him against that day" in 2 Tim.1:12 (KJV), fleeing to Him as a refuge for protection in Heb. 6:18, coming unto God in Heb. 11:6, receiving or welcoming Jesus in John 1:12, looking unto Jesus for deliverance as the children of Israel looked to the bronze serpent in John 3:14, eating and drinking of

Him both in John 4 and 6. These phrases speak of much more that intellectual adherence to a creed. They speak of a personal appropriation of the work of the cross, especially eating and drinking, and also of a personal relationship of confidence, entrusting oneself to Jesus Christ for deliverance and protection (flee to, look to, come to). Therefore, the meaning of saving faith must involve a **personal confidence in Christ** expressed by entrusting (committing) the destiny of one's soul to Him.

(5) Believing in the Name refers to confidence (Trust) in the Person of Christ

A final reason that *belief* refers to confidence (trust) when used of saving faith lies in the appeal to "believe in His name" (John 1:12; 3:18; 1 John 3:23; 5:13). Are these verses teaching that salvation is granted to all who believe intellectually that there was a man named Jesus? That would be a nonsensical interpretation. In such contexts, *belief* must refer to having confidence, to trusting the person of Christ, rather than just believing the fact that there was a person named Jesus Christ.

4. Summary on Believe, Trust, Exercise Faith

Saving faith involves the mind, emotions and will. With the mind the sinner must **believe that** Jesus Christ is the Son of God and Lord (i.e., God) who took upon Himself human flesh and was sent by God into the world as the Messiah to die for our sins and rise again. Saving faith entails these facts as its content. However, saving faith is more than believing intellectually certain basic facts about Christ. There is also an emotional assent in which a soul believes that these facts are not only true but also desirable, relevant, and personally needed.

Although intellectual belief in a content of facts about Jesus and emotional faith that these facts are personally needed are necessary to full saving faith, they are not sufficient. The gospel appeal is not just to believe facts about

Jesus or to believe that He can help us, but to **believe in Christ**, i.e., to personally trust Him.

Saving faith exists when the will of a person commits the soul's eternal destiny to Christ and the cross, i.e., by an act of the will a person chooses to place his confidence in the Lord Jesus Christ and the finished work of the cross.

A deathly ill person may intellectually believe that a certain pill can save. He may emotionally believe that the pill is relevant to his own troubles. However, it is only when he chooses to depend upon the pill personally and expresses confidence in it by personal appropriation that a cure takes place. Salvation takes place when a person believes in the sense of personally appropriating the benefits of Christ's death by trust (i.e., confidence, reliance, dependence, and faith).

The sole condition for salvation is to trust in the Biblical Christ as Savior. All legitimate ways of communicating this one condition for salvation are either synonyms for faith or involve a specialized aspect of faith. All terms and phrases that are not compatible with faith alone as the condition for salvation are error.

C. Repentance as a Condition for Salvation

1. The Meaning of *Repentance*

The verb *repent* (*metanoeo*) is used thirty-five times in the New Testament and the noun (*metanoya*) occurs twenty-two times. Usage is frequent in Luke, Acts, and Revelation. Probably most people think of "feeling sorry" or "feeling guilty" when they hear the term *repentance*. However, several considerations show that being sorry is not a synonym for repenting.

First, the word is a compound derived from *meta* meaning "to change" (as in metamorphosis) and *noeo* which refers to the mind (i.e., notion). Etymology indicates a meaning of "changing the mind." Biblical examples confirm this definition. While sorrow often accompanies repentance and even promotes re-

pentance, 2 Cor. 7:9-10 and Heb. 12:17 show that sorrow is not the same as repentance. Since 2 Cor. 7:9-10 teaches that sorrow can often lead to repentance, one must conclude sorrow is not exactly the same thing as repentance. Heb. 12:17 is even more clear. Esau is portrayed as being very sorry, to the point of tears, about selling his birthright. Nevertheless, he was unable to repent concerning the sale of his birthright for a bowl of lentil soup (Gen. 25:34). Repentance in Esau's case did not just mean feeling sorry (which he did), but rather it meant changing his mind about the sale (which he could not do). Repentance does not mean "feeling sorry" or "feeling guilty." It means "to change the mind."

Several times the Bible associates repentance with repudiation and departure from a former position. Acts 3:19 says, "repent therefore and return." Acts 26:20 contains the phrase "repent and turn to God" (see also Heb. 6:1 and Acts 8:22). Therefore, repentance involves turning away from something to something else. This must involve a change of mind because one may sorrow or feel guilty without ever repudiating a former idea or belief. When one repents of a belief and/or behavior, he must not only feel sorry but also change his mind about that issue. Therefore, repentance emphasizes a change of mind involving a turning away from something to something else.

To this point repentance has been defined. The next issue is whether or not the Bible teaches repentance is essential to salvation.

2. Repentance as a Necessity for Salvation

As long as it is properly defined to be compatible with *sola fide* (faith alone), repentance is a legitimate term to express the condition for salvation. This is evident from texts like the following: Luke 15:7, 10; Acts 2:38; 3:19; 17:30; 26:20 (verb repent) and Luke 15:7; 24:47; Acts 11:18; 20:21; 26:20; Rom. 2:4; and 2 Pet. 3:9 (noun, repentance).[44]

---

[44] Verses that contain John the Baptist's call to repentance are not included in this section. His call

"Therefore having over looked the times of ignorance, God is now declaring to men that **all everywhere should repent**" [Acts 17:30].

[A]nd He said to them, "Thus is it written, that the Christ should suffer and rise again from the dead the third day; and that **repentance** for forgiveness of sins should be proclaimed in His Name to all the nations, beginning from Jerusalem" [Luke 24:46-47].

[T]he Lord is not slow about His promise, as some count slowness, but is patient toward you, not wishing for any to perish but for **all to come to repentance** [2 Peter 3:9].

The role of repentance in salvation gives rise to many questions. Since repentance involves a change of mind and turning away from a former position, what are the things from which an unsaved person must turn away in order to be saved? What are the truths about which a person must change his mind to be saved?

The object from which a person must repent is not the same in every passage. In Acts 2:38 and 3:19 Peter seems to be asking the Jews to change their minds about what they did to Christ by executing Him, i.e., to change their minds about who He is. Not everyone in the world was directly involved in the guilt of sending Christ to die in the same sense as these first century Jews. Therefore, this specific object of repentance, changing the mind about participation in Christ's crucifixion would not be applicable to everyone. Heb. 6:1 mentions a changing of the mind about dead works. This object of repentance is applicable to all the unsaved in religions that teach that works are a means to salvation. However, the typical ex-atheist never believed in "dead

works" in the first place because he never believed in the existence of a heaven for which man could work. Therefore, there is no need for the atheist to change his mind about dead works. People in different false religions and false philosophies with different backgrounds and ideas need to change their minds, i.e., repent, about different misconceptions. Acts 20:21 and 1 Thess. 1:9 mention that people must change their mind about God. Repentance about God is probably involved in every conversion. Yet, the specific ideas about which a sinner repents would be quite diverse. An idolater definitely needs to change his mind about God to be saved. He must repent of idols (1 Thess. 1:9). Yet, a change of mind about God would involve a different idea for a Satan worshipper or an atheist or an orthodox Jew. All must believe in Christ to be saved, but the misconceptions and hindrances that must be changed in order to believe are extremely diverse. In several places where repentance is linked with salvation, the object of repentance is **totally unspecified**: Acts 11:18; 17:30; 26:20; Luke 24:47; 2 Pet. 3:9.

Both logic and examples of Scripture indicate that, while some degree of repentance is involved in every conversion, the specific ideas or action about which a person must change his mind varies from person to person. An unsaved **person has to change the mind (repent) about anything that stands in the way of his coming to faith in Christ**. For some this will be a change about a philosophy, e.g., idol worship. For others this is a change of mind about sin, e.g., refusing to trust in Christ because they know He will command them to break off an immoral affair. The object of repentance is probably not the same in any two individuals. **A person must repent about whatever it is that keeps him or her from faith in Christ.**

3. Repentance and Evangelism

The fact that an evangelist does not know the precise falsehood of which a potential convert must repent should not be upsetting or confus-

---

to repentance seems to have involved a preparation for the future salvation that the Christ would offer. For more information on John the Baptist's call to repent and be baptized see pp. 149-51.

ing. Since the only condition for salvation is faith, it stands to reason that if faith is placed in Christ, then repentance has already occurred. When a person honestly and seriously entrusts his or her soul's eternal destiny to Christ, then that person has also changed his mind about whatever it was that had been a barrier to coming to Christ. Faith and repentance are not two separate conditions for salvation. Repentance is a particular aspect of saving faith. By trusting in Christ, the person has changed his mind, i.e., repented, about whatever kept him from accepting the Savior. The act of faith contains within it all the repenting that needs to be done to secure salvation. Faith in Christ includes both the specific objects that needed to be repented of and also the degree of repentance that needed to take place. By turning in faith to Jesus Christ, the soul has already fulfilled all the "change in thinking" and "turning away from" that is required for salvation. It is true that repentance is required of everyone for salvation, but the specific type of repentance varies with individuals and is ultimately unknown to the evangelist. The responsibility of the evangelist is to teach that the person must trust in Christ (and obviously this implies he or she must change their mind about anything that hinders faith in Christ). It is not the business of the evangelist to determine the specific ideas or sins that pose the barrier or for him to make a list of items from which a person must turn. If there is a "turning to" Christ, then the specific "turning away from" will take care of itself. (See Acts 3:19; 20:21; 26:20; 1 Thess. 1:9.)

4. "Repentance" vs. "Forsaking Sin" as a Prerequisite for Salvation

There must be caution or the term *repentance* will be misused to create a salvation based upon works. We dare not tell a potential convert that there must be a turning away from sins A, B, and C before there can be salvation. Salvation is based upon faith alone. **If a person can believe, then he has already repented of whatever hindered faith and that is all the repentance he needs for salvation.**

No man has any authority to add more as a basis for salvation.

The Bible does not make the cessation of sin in general or of a specific sin, such as alcoholism, a prerequisite for salvation. This would not only be a works method for salvation, but it would be an impossible method for salvation. Asking a potential convert to overcome an addictive sin before conversion is asking him to obtain victory when he has absolutely no power to overcome sin. The command "to repent" is not the same as a command "to cease" all sin or any given sin before there can be salvation. Furthermore, the Bible never requires a person to promise to cease a particular sin in order to find salvation. Repentance should not be confused with a vow to stop or a promise to cease a particular sin that especially tempts an individual. Asking for a commitment to cease from a sin is asking for a commitment that cannot be made at a pre-conversion stage. There is no power in the life to make such an unrealistic promise. In fact the appeal for a vow to stop sinning encourages the unsaved to have confidence in their own abilities, and that is the opposite of saving faith. A potential convert should be made to see that he has absolutely no ability to overcome sin and that he cannot in good faith even promise to forsake it. He is hopelessly dominated by sin. That is why he must believe in Christ. Salvation is based upon an empty hand that takes God's blessing as a free gift: "nothing in my hand I bring, simply to Thy cross I cling". Salvation is not based on a full hand that makes offers to God in order to have eternal life.

5. Repentance and Lordship Salvation

The concept of "Lordship Salvation" will be covered separately. It is enough to say here that there is nothing in the term *repentance* that involves what is commonly called "Lordship Salvation". Telling a person that he must cease from sinning or promise to cease from sinning before he can have salvation is putting an impossible obstacle in front of him and adding to the one condition for salvation. An unsaved person who has tried repeatedly and unsuccessfully to break a sinful addiction does not have, nor does he understand, the power of Christ which comes after salvation. He might have enough faith to trust in Christ for salvation but lack the faith in self to promise to forsake a given dominating sin. There may be enough faith to trust in Christ, but the person feels that he cannot honestly make any promise to forsake sin because he has never been able to overcome it in his pre-conversion life. To people such as this, asking that they promise to forsake sin is useless and hypocritical. By misunderstanding repentance, some Christians make such hopeless people feel they cannot meet God's condition for salvation. Although they might believe in Christ, they know they are unable to promise a cessation from sin. The misunderstanding of repentance as the demand for a pre-conversion cessation from sin, or for a vow to cease sinning, creates an additional and heretical condition for salvation. In fact, it is best if an unbeliever feels utterly hopeless about overcoming slavery to sin. It is best if he realizes that he himself cannot forsake sin or promise to forsake sin and that he needs divine help. **All God requires from a sinner is that he wants deliverance from sin badly enough to trust in Christ for it.**

It is logical that every convert wants deliverance from sin in at least some unknown degree. It is also logical, since salvation involves believing Christ is God, that every convert acknowledges that Christ does have a right to direct the individual's life by virtue of being God. Therefore, it is true that saving faith cannot co-exist with a total rebellion against Christ's rule as Master or with an absolute lack of desire for deliverance from sin. However, this is not at all the same as concluding there must be efforts to obey Christ as Master or commitments which promise a cessation from sin and a yielding to Christ's authority before salvation. The sinner indeed acknowledges Christ's authority by virtue of believing

in the deity of Christ. However, he is not required to follow that authority or promise to follow it before he can be saved. God does not require so much of sinners to be saved. Neither should we. **If a potential convert can trust in Christ, he has recognized Christ's authority to a sufficient degree. He has made all the commitments he needs to make, he has desired all the deliverance from sin he needs to desire, and he has done all the repenting that needs to be done in order to have salvation.**

We dare not incorrectly define repentance so that it adds any requirement to *faith alone* for salvation. Repentance means, "to change the mind." If a person can arrive at the point of trusting Christ, he has already repented (i.e., changed his mind about/turned away from) of whatever ideas or behavior that prevented faith in Christ. This is all God requires both as to the type of repentance and degree of repentance.

6. Summary on Repentance as a Condition for Salvation

When it is properly defined, repentance is a genuine condition for salvation. It is not only compatible with the term faith; it is a part of faith. **In turning to Christ, there must be a turning away from all that hindered faith.** Repentance is distinguishable but not separable from saving faith. The founder of Dallas Seminary wrote this about repentance:

"It is true that repentance can very well be required as a condition of salvation, but then only because the change of mind which it is has been involved when turning from every other confidence to the one needful trust in Christ. Such turning about, of course, cannot be achieved without a change of mind. This vital newness of mind is a part of believing, after all, and therefore it may be and is used as **a synonym for believing at times**...."[45]

---

[45] Lewis Sperry Chafer, *Chafer Systematic Theology*, vol. 7 (Dallas, Dallas Seminary Press, 1948) 7:265.

D. Conversion as a Condition for Salvation

Though *be converted* is not used as frequently as other terms, it does express a legitimate condition for salvation as long as it is properly defined. The Greek word for *to convert* is used between thirty-six and thirty-nine times depending on the manuscripts that are counted. From its usage in non-salvation passages, one can tell it means "to turn toward" or "to turn back" (e.g., Matt. 12:44; 24:18; Mark 5:30; 8:33; 13:16; Luke 8:55; 17:31; John 21:20; Acts 9:40; 15:36; 16:18; Gal. 4:9; 2 Peter 2:22; Rev. 1:12). When a person trusts in Jesus Christ for salvation, he is turning to Him for salvation. Thus, saving faith equals conversion in the sense of turning to Christ in faith for salvation and, also, turning back to God from whom all have strayed (Isa. 53:6).

Usually, the Bible does not use the command "be converted" in evangelistic appeals as a condition for salvation as it does in Acts 3:19. It is far more common that a Biblical author refers **back** to the time of salvation and calls it conversion or refers to a **third party's** conversion or lack of conversion (Matt. 13:15; Mark 4:12; John 12:40; Acts 9:35; 11:21; 15:19; 26:18, 20; 28:27; 2 Cor. 3:16; 1 Thess. 1:9 and 1 Pet. 2:25). In other words, it is more common for the Bible to use the word *conversion* to teach saved people what has happened when they believed than it is for the Bible to appeal to the unsaved to have a conversion. *Conversion* must be defined as "turning to Christ in saving faith" and must not be misunderstood to mean to add anything to faith alone as the one condition to salvation. *Conversion* simply means saving faith. It does not mean a person must totally change his lifestyle before salvation is granted. Conversion is turning to Christ in faith for salvation.

E. Receive or Accept Jesus as Savior

This term is not prominent as a Biblical condition for salvation, but it does occur in John 1:12.

> But as many as **received** Him, to them

He gave the right to become children of God, even to those who **believe** in His name [John 1:12].

John 1:12 is quite clear that receiving Jesus Christ is the same as believing in His name. The meanings are the same. *Believe* gives more emphasis upon the active nature of saving faith. We must choose to trust Christ. *Receive* emphasizes more the passive aspect of saving faith. We must, by believing, be willing to receive a free salvation from Jesus Christ. *Believe* and *receive* are the same condition for salvation viewed with a slightly different emphasis. If by receiving or accepting Jesus Christ as Savior, we mean to trust in Him and His work on the cross, then it is proper to use the appeal to "receive (meaning *welcome*) or accept Christ as Savior."

F. Believe and Work to Earn Salvation

There are few errors that are more widespread and dangerous than the misconception that either works or religious rituals (or both) are conditions for salvation. On the positive side, this study has already demonstrated that over 150 Biblical texts condition salvation upon faith alone! If one adds works or rituals to faith, these passages would all be rendered contradictory and those who gave them liars (including the Lord Jesus Christ). Paul responded to the Galatian tendency toward a works salvation in some of the harshest language in the entire Bible. The position that salvation can be earned by works is an "arch-heresy." It can not be opposed too strongly!

> But even though we, or an angel from heaven, should preach to you **a gospel contrary** to that which we have preached to you, let him **be accursed.** As we have said before, so I say again now, if any man is preaching to you **a gospel contrary** to that which you received, let him be **accursed** [Gal. 1:8-9].
>
> **For all of us have become like one who is unclean, and all our righteous**

deeds are like a filthy garment [Isa. 64:6].

They said therefore to Him, "What shall we do, that we may work the works of God?" Jesus answered and said to them, **"This is the work of God, that you believe in Him whom He has sent"** [John 6:28-29].

[A]nd through Him everyone who believes is freed from all things, from which **you could not be freed through the Law of Moses** [Acts 13:39].

[B]ecause **by the works of the Law no flesh will be justified** in His sight; for through the Law comes the knowledge of sin [Rom. 3:20].

For we maintain that a man is justified by faith **apart from works** of the Law [Rom. 3:28].

But to the **one who does not work,** but believes in Him who justifies the ungodly, his faith is reckoned as righteousness [Rom. 4:5].

[B]ut Israel, pursuing a law of righteousness, did not arrive at that law. Why? Because they did not pursue it by faith, but **as though it were by works. They stumbled** over the stumbling stone [Rom. 9:31-32].

But if it is by grace, **it is no longer on the basis of works**, otherwise grace is no longer grace [Rom. 11:6].

"[N]evertheless, knowing that a man **is not justified by the works** of the Law but through faith in Christ Jesus, even we have believed in Christ Jesus, that we may be justified by faith in Christ, and **not by the works of the Law;** since **by the works of the Law shall no flesh be justified"** [Gal. 2:16].

Now that **no one is justified by the Law** before God is evident; for, "the

righteous man shall live by faith" [Gal. 3:11].

For by grace you have been saved through faith; and that not of yourselves, it is the gift of God; **not as a result of works**, that no one should boast [Eph. 2:8-9].

[W]ho has saved us, and called us with a holy calling, **not according to our works**, but according to His own purpose and grace which was granted us in Christ Jesus from all eternity [2 Tim. 1:9].

He saved us, **not on the basis of deeds** which we have done in righteousness, but according to His mercy, by the washing of regeneration and renewing by the Holy Spirit [Titus 3:5].

[H]ow much more will the blood of Christ, who through the eternal Spirit offered Himself without blemish to God, **cleanse your conscience from dead works** to serve the living God? [Heb. 9:14].

There are texts in the Scriptures that can be misinterpreted so as to establish that salvation is conditioned upon good works. However, the interpreter still must face the facts that over 150 verses condition salvation upon faith alone and that the New Testament is adamant about the truth that works do not lead to salvation. The solution, in those texts that seem to indicate that salvation comes by merit, is simply to find another equally valid interpretation that is compatible with faith alone as a condition for salvation. In fact it will nearly always be the case that the interpretation that makes the text compatible with the rest of Scripture will also be the one that better fits the context and the author's own ideas elsewhere.

As an example, consider James 2:26: "...faith without works is dead." Of course, this passage can be stubbornly interpreted as being contradictory to the verses that are quoted above in this section. Yet, it can and should be interpreted to be consistent with them. In the context, James had defined faith as intellectual faith in certain orthodox facts about God, specifically monotheism: "You believe that God is one. You do well, the demons also believe and shudder" [James 2:19]. Verse 26 simply means that an intellectual faith in certain facts about God is not enough for salvation. The type of faith that is genuine saving faith is the type that results in good works. A valid paraphrase would be "The type of faith that is just a belief in facts about God and never results in works is dead."

The resulting theology is not in contradiction to the *faith alone* doctrine emphasized by Paul and developed under the definition of saving faith in this book. James had previously asked in v. 14, "Can that [type of] faith save him?" James answers, "No," and Paul would have also agreed. Intellectual faith alone does not save. Paul would have also agreed that genuine saving faith results in good works (Eph. 2:8-10). When the term *faith* means intellectual acceptance of correct doctrine, as in James 2, then faith alone does not save. When the term *faith* means trust, reliance, confidence, as in Paul's writings, then such faith saves and also results in good works. The interpreter must notice that James and Paul use the term *faith* with different shades of meanings.

James 2 teaches that intellectual faith does not save. However, it does not and should not be used to disprove that faith alone (defined in the sense of trust) is insufficient to obtain salvation. When careful attention is given to the precise definition each author employs, these statements in James are not contradicting that faith (in the sense of confidence) saves. Every text that seems to be teaching a works salvation is better interpreted in ways that make it compatible with salvation by faith alone.

G. Believe and be Baptized to Obtain Salvation

If the reader is beginning to read at this point, it would be beneficial to go back and study

pp. 130-138 which establishes that God's only condition for salvation is faith. Also, it is pertinent to consider the preceding section that established that works and/or religious rituals do not save.

If some verses are studied in isolation from the rest of Scripture, they could be taken to prove that baptism is essential to salvation. However, it is just as true that these same texts can also be interpreted to be compatible with faith alone as a condition for salvation. Obviously, the correct interpretation is that which harmonizes all Scriptures rather than the one that causes contradictions between Scriptures. Since over 150 verses give faith alone as the condition for salvation, baptism cannot be viewed as a requirement for salvation (though baptism is a requirement for complete obedience to God.)

It is common to bring the examples of Jesus (John 4:2) and Paul (1 Cor. 1:17) into a discussion of baptism and salvation. Neither was personally involved in baptizing others to a great degree. Paul stated that his God-given task was to preach the gospel (the Greek word means "evangelize") rather than emphasizing baptism. Also, the thief on the cross is an example of one who obtained salvation without baptism (Luke 23:43), and Cornelius was clearly saved before he was baptized (Acts 10:47).[46] These points are legitimate. However, they are secondary to the main fact that baptismal regeneration would make the Scriptures a massive contradiction. If salvation is by faith alone, nothing can be added to it. If the troubling texts can be interpreted in any way that is compatible with faith alone as a condition for salvation, then that would be the correct interpretation. The rest of this section will show that texts commonly used to prove

---

[46] The thief on the cross technically died before Christian baptism had been initiated. However, he did live during the period in which John the Baptist's baptism was being commanded. Therefore, his example still gives a parallel that one can be saved without baptism.

baptism is essential to salvation are really quite compatible with the view that faith alone saves.

1. Mark 16:15-16

> And He said to them, "Go into all the world and preach the gospel to all creation. He who has believed and has been baptized shall be saved; but he who has disbelieved shall be condemned."

There is a real probability that this portion of Mark was not in the original New Testament. Most modern translations and commentaries will mention the point that Mark 16:9ff. are not found in the oldest existing manuscripts.

However, even if we assume these statements to be genuine, they can be interpreted to be compatible with faith alone. The last part of verse 16 shows that disbelief (rather than lack of baptism) is the sole condition that brings about eternal condemnation. Thus, it is belief that brings salvation. Verse 16a is true and correctly lists both belief and baptism as responses that God requires. It is teaching that God wants both belief and baptism, and that those who comply are saved. Yet, it is still possible to view that, of these two genuine requirements, belief is the sole element that brings about salvation. The interpreter's options are either to take Mark 16:16 in this manner or cause it to be a contradiction to many clearer passages of Scripture.

2. John 3:5

> Jesus answered, "Truly, truly, I say to you, unless one is born of water and the Spirit, he cannot enter into the kingdom of God."

Many views can be adopted of John 3:5 that would make it compatible with faith alone as a condition for salvation. For the purpose of this study, it is not important which is the best. As long as the verse can be taken legitimately in ways other than requiring baptismal regeneration, the result is the same, i.e., there is no proof that baptism regenerates.

Some take water to refer to physical birth (i.e., the water sack around an infant) because verse 6 contrasts physical birth with spiritual birth. Another grammatical possibility is to view the construction as a "hendiadys." This would make the translation read, "unless one is born of water, even the Spirit." Thus, water would be a symbol for the Holy Spirit. Precedent for associating the Holy Spirit with water is in Ezek. 36:25-27; Isa. 44:3; John 7:38-39; Titus 3:5. A third view would see water as a symbol for the Word of God. It is true that the Holy Spirit uses the Word to bring about the new birth (James 1:18; 1 Pet. 1:23) and that water is associated with God's Word in other Scriptures (John 15:3; Eph. 5:26).

Finally, it is even possible to take water as referring to John's baptism and still not read baptismal regeneration into the statement. John the Baptist's baptism is different than Christ's baptism. It is not even being practiced today.[47] However, it was at the time of John 3, and Nicodemus observed that John and Jesus were requiring people to be baptized. Perhaps John 3:5 is Christ's way of teaching that baptism alone is not sufficient. A paraphrase might be as follows: "Nicodemus it is true that I require my followers to be baptized. Yet, if that is all they have, they will not enter the kingdom of God. I require John's baptism, but the requirement to enter the kingdom of God is being born of the Spirit." If this interpretation is correct, then Christ is teaching that while John's baptism was God's will, it is the new birth by the Spirit that brings salvation. Nicodemus should not think that the ritual alone (though it was required) had any saving merit. Salvation is a work of the Spirit giving new life on the basis of faith (see John 3:16 in context). Thus, water could be understood as

---

[47] John was baptizing people as a preparation to accept the Messiah's earthly ministry and kingship. As a nation, Israel rejected the Lord's earthly rule at His first coming. Thus, John's preparatory baptism has ceased. Christian baptism, based upon the Lord's death, burial, and resurrection, is different than John's baptism.

being baptism in John 3:5 without making the text teach baptismal regeneration. In fact, Jesus would be saying the opposite. Though He approves of John's baptism, he wants clear understanding that baptismal water does not save. Nicodemus was taught that only life from the Spirit though faith causes salvation.

The main truth must not be lost in details. John 3:5 can be interpreted to not teach that baptism is a requirement for salvation. Regardless of which view is preferred, all of them make John 3:5 compatible with clear texts that teach salvation is by faith alone.

3. Acts 2:38

> And Peter said to them, "Repent, and let each of you be baptized in the name of Jesus Christ for the forgiveness of your sins; and you shall receive the gift of the Holy Spirit."

This verse is a favorite of those who think baptism is a condition for salvation. However, it can also be interpreted to fit nicely with the *sola fide* (faith alone) position. The word *for* has many usages. One of its meanings is "because of." In the sentence, "The police arrested him for shoplifting," it is evident that *for* means "because of." The police arrested him because of shoplifting. The Greek word *eis,* which is translated "for" in Acts 2:38, also has a wide range of meanings. Like the English word *for,* *eis* can mean "because of." Matt. 12:41 speaks of the men of Ninevah and says: "they repented (*eis*) the preaching of Jonah." (The people repented **because** of the preaching of Jonah.) The same meaning prevails in Luke 11:32. It is also possible that *eis* means "because" in Matt. 3:11, which reads: "I baptize you in water for (eis) repentance." A good understanding of John's statement would be, "I baptize you with water **because of** your repentance." (See also Rom. 4:20; 11:32; and Titus 3:14 for other possible causal uses of *eis).* The solution to reconciling Acts 2:38 with the rest of Scripture lies in seeing that *for,* both in Greek and English, can mean "because of." Peter is saying, "Repent! Then

be baptized **because** your sins have been forgiven!" Rather than telling them to be baptized so that they could obtain forgiveness he is telling them to be baptized because of a forgiveness that comes about through repentance.

Interpreters have a choice with Acts 2:38. They can either understand the verse in isolation and contradiction to the rest of Scripture, or they can adopt another legitimate (but admittedly more rare) meaning for the word *for.* The latter choice is obviously preferable since it best harmonizes Scripture keeping intact the principle of faith alone.[48] Yet, if one insists *eis* gives purpose *or* result, then the verse can still be made compatible with salvation by faith alone. One should understand "repent" to be the essential element in leading to "remission of sins." In the Acts 2 context, repentance would be a change of mind about killing Jesus as a false messiah and acceptance of Him as the Christ, the Savior (see Acts 2:23, 36). Such repentance qualifies for baptism and brings about salvation. Notice the precise question being answered is "what shall we do?", not just "what shall we do to be saved?" Peter's answer gives both repentance and baptism as actions which those directly guilty of killing Jesus could do to please God. However, his answer includes more than meeting the minimal condition for salvation. God wanted the listeners to both change their minds about the person and work of Christ, and God wanted them to be baptized. However, if one insists *eis* gives purpose or result in Acts 2:38, then repentance (which qualifies for baptism) should be viewed as the saving factor. Otherwise, Acts 2:38 contradicts hundreds of verses that teach faith alone saves. Most of these do not even mention baptism.

---

[48] There are yet other explanations of Acts 2:38 that would not involve baptismal regeneration, Baptism might be a symbol for faith as no unbeliever would ever be baptized in New Testament conditions of persecution, nor would there ever be an unbaptized believer. (See parallel logic in footnote 49, especially the bold portion, or the explanation on John 3:5, above).

4. Rom. 6:3-4

> Or do you not know that all of us who have been baptized into Christ Jesus have been baptized into His death? Therefore, we have been buried with Him through baptism into death, in order that as Christ was raised from the dead through the glory of the Father, so we too might walk in newness of life.

Confusion over this text can arise if one is ignorant of the doctrine of Spirit baptism. John the Baptist kept predicting that Christ would baptize with the Spirit as opposed to baptizing with water (Matt. 3:11; Mark 1:8; Luke 3:16; John 1:33). As the book of Acts begins, Christ tells His followers to wait for this Spirit baptism (Acts 1:5), and it is from Peter's statements in Acts 11:15-16 that one knows the first such baptism of the Spirit took place on Pentecost (Acts 2). Paul explains that the placing of a person into Christ takes place by a Spirit baptism (1 Cor. 12:13). Since he uses the word *all* and since Spirit baptism occurs at the time of union with Christ, it is evident that every believer is baptized with the Holy Spirit at the time of salvation, i.e., at the time of **faith** in Christ as Savior. This Spirit baptism causes a union with Christ and all the benefits of Christ's death and resurrection. It also causes a union with all other believers who are also "in Christ." When Paul says in Eph. 4:5 there is "one baptism," he probably refers to the reality of "Spirit baptism" which makes a person a Christian, as opposed to the symbol, i.e., "water baptism." It is unquestionable that Scripture places more importance upon Spirit baptism than water baptism. Spirit baptism occurs on the basis of faith (see Chapter 10). It is sufficient at this point to note that the Scripture knows of more than just water baptism and that Spirit baptism is the more important of the two. Spirit baptism is the reality of which water baptism is the symbol.

There are several choices for dealing with Romans 6:3-4. First, one can interpret the text as requiring baptism for salvation. This inter-pretation makes the Scriptures inconsistent with each other. The second option is to take baptism as referring to Spirit baptism. Spirit baptism comes through faith in Christ as Savior uniting a believer with the benefits of the Lord's death and resurrection life. This not only harmonizes Scripture, it also meshes with what is known of Spirit baptism. Paul taught in 1 Cor. 12:13 that Spirit baptism unites a believer with Christ. Probably, Rom. 6:3-4 is teaching about a type of baptism that unites a believer with Christ's death and resurrection life. Rom. 6:3-4 should probably be linked with Spirit baptism rather than with water baptism.[49]

5. Col. 2:11-12

> And in Him you were also circumcised

---

[49] Though the author prefers to take baptism in Rom. 6:3-4 as Spirit baptism, one could understand Paul to mean water baptism without the inference that water baptism is a requirement for salvation. Baptism is to a believer what a wedding ring is to a married man or woman. It is the symbol of a relationship. It is possible to wear a ring and not be married (just as one could be baptized but not be a believer). It is also possible to be married without wearing a ring (just as one could be saved without ever being baptized). However, wedding rings for practical purposes do indicate marriage. The Apostle Paul probably could not imagine anyone in his day being baptized without faith. Since being a Christian might result in persecution, only those with genuine faith wanted water baptism. Neither could Paul imagine a believer rejecting water baptism. (There is seldom any valid reason for a believer refusing baptism today either.) To Paul there was no such thing as a baptized unbeliever or an unbaptized believer. Therefore, baptism was actually even a surer sign of **faith** than a wedding ring is of a marriage. If Rom. 6:3-4 is not taken as a reference to Spirit baptism, Paul could be understood to mean that **water baptism, as practiced in the New Testament Church during conditions of persecution, was a certain evidence of faith**. It is the faith symbolized by baptism that saves. Romans 6 would be teaching the faith that inevitably results in baptism (faith evidenced by baptism) causes a sharing in the benefit of Christ's death, burial, and resurrection.

with a circumcision made without hands, in the removal of the body of the flesh by the circumcision of Christ; having been buried with Him in baptism, in which you were also raised up with Him through faith in the working of God, who raised Him from the dead.

This is the text used by those who believe that water baptism for infants has some redemptive merit. Failing to appreciate the radical newness of the church system, they believe water baptism for infants has replaced the Old Testament circumcision of infants. Since infant baptism is unscriptural, the only "proof" that one can offer for it is that infant baptism must be God's replacement for circumcision. Thus, in coming to Col. 2:11-12 there is a blind spot that causes them to think of only water baptism when reading the word circumcision.

However, the Bible speaks of a spiritual circumcision just as it does Spirit baptism. (See Deut. 10:16; 30:6; Jer. 4:4; 9:25-26; Ezek. 44:7-9; Rom. 2:26-29; and Phil. 3:3). "Spiritual circumcision" is a figure of speech that refers to the removal of the flesh's inevitable control over a believer's life. Rom. 6:3-4 teaches that the believer shares in Christ's resurrection life by Spirit baptism. Then it goes on to discuss the removal of the flesh's inevitable control over the believer. Death means separation. Since we died with Christ by Spirit baptism, there has been a separation of "the body of sin's" inevitable control (Rom. 6:6ff.).

It is evident that Paul is referring to spiritual circumcision, not literal circumcision, in Col. 2:11. How much clearer could he make it than to say, "a circumcision made without hands"? Furthermore, it is also evident that the teachings of Romans 6 and Colossians 2 are parallel. Believers have been united with Christ and have died with Him. Death means separation, not the cessation of existence. Therefore, believers are dead to "the body of flesh" not in the sense of sin ceasing to exist, but in the sense of its dominion being removed, separated from us. This is spiritual circumcision. Finally, it ought to be evident that the union with Christ and benefits coming from it are based in Spirit baptism rather than water baptism. Colossians 2 is teaching the same thing as Romans 6 (although with varying terminology). Those who have been united with Christ by Spirit baptism have undergone what Paul calls a spiritual "circumcision" in Colossians 2 and "death to sin" in Romans 6. Both images refer to a removal or separation of sin's control.

The only explanation that can be given for taking Col. 2:11-12 to teach that baptism saves is theological bias. If one wants to maintain a system, he interprets texts in support of it (even if the result contradicts the rest of the Bible). Clearly one superior view of Col. 2:11-12 is that it refers to Spirit baptism instead of water baptism. With this view there is harmony with the rest of Scriptures teaching salvation by *faith alone*, there is a clear parallel with Romans 6, and there is not any basis for infant baptism or baptismal regeneration. Spirit baptism is an immediate result of faith in Christ and causes a sharing in the benefits of Christ's death and resurrection life. It also brings a spiritual circumcision, the cutting off of the inevitable power of sin. An acceptable alternative would be to take baptism in Col. 2:12 to mean water baptism without thinking that baptism is a requirement for salvation. Paul would be assuming that water baptism is the certain token of faith. Faith as symbolized by baptism would be the real basis for sharing in the benefits of Christ's death and resurrection. Faith as displayed by baptism would be the basis for the separation of filth's control over the life, i.e., spiritual circumcision. (See footnote 49 for a parallel interpretation of Romans 6.)

6. 1 Pet. 3:21

Which [water] even you as a figure now saves, i.e., baptism (not of the flesh putting away of filth but for a good conscience an appeal unto God) through the resurrection of Jesus Christ.

This literal translation of the verse in approximate Greek word order shows that it is a difficult, obscure statement. Doctrine must be built upon clear and repeated texts. Furthermore, easy statements must help in the interpretation of difficult ones. To insist that 1 Pet. 3:21 can overturn the teaching of over 150 clear verses is quite obstinate.

First, notice that in the context, Peter is comparing the waters of baptism to the waters of Noah's flood. Water did not save Noah. The ark did. The ark saved Noah, and Noah went through the floodwaters. The waters of the flood remind Peter of the waters of baptism. To the early church there was no such thing as an unbaptized believer. Baptism inevitably and properly followed genuine faith in Christ. Peter's comparison seems to be something like this, "Just as Noah was saved by the ark and passed through the waters, you have been saved by Christ and have passed through the waters." A comparison can be drawn involving the salvation of Noah through floodwaters and the salvation of believers through baptismal waters without resorting to making 1 Pet. 3:21 imply baptismal regeneration.

Next it must be emphasized that Peter does not have to be interpreted as saying that baptism saves. It is equally valid to take Peter as saying baptism saves in a **figurative sense**. If the parentheses are dropped, the figurative sense in which baptism saves is associated with Christ's resurrection. Baptism symbolizes a union with Christ in His death and resurrection. Coming up from the water symbolizes a sharing in Christ's new life, the resurrection. The reality behind this figure does indeed save. By Spirit baptism a believer is united to share in the benefits of Christ's death and to share in His resurrection life. Water baptism symbolizes this sharing of Christ's resurrection life. Thus, Peter can say baptism saves in a figure.

Finally, notice Peter adds parenthetical mate-

rial so that his readers will not think he is teaching baptismal regeneration. He qualifies what he means by saying baptism saves. It is not the literal washing of the body's filth that causes salvation. It is rather the appeal to God for the cleansing of the heart that has both brought salvation and rendered the sinner a qualified candidate for water baptism. The cleansing of the flesh by a ritual is utterly worthless to save. However, the candidate's appeal unto God to be cleansed from sin through the blood of Christ is the basis both for salvation and legitimate water baptism.

1 Pet. 3:21 teaches that water baptism saves only in the figurative sense of symbolizing a sharing in Christ's life that came about by faith. Also, the only element pertaining to water baptism that actually saves is the appeal to God for cleansing (by faith in Christ) that makes a person qualified to be baptized. There is absolutely no warrant in taking 1 Pet. 3:21 to deny salvation by faith alone and teach baptismal regeneration.

7. The Baptism of John and Salvation

Most Bible teachers correctly make a distinction between John's baptism and Christian baptism. John the Baptist's baptism was preparatory and future looking. Its goal was for people to prepare to welcome the King. Christian baptism is oriented to the past. It symbolizes identification with Christ's death, burial, and resurrection (Rom. 6:3-4 by application). Christ instituted Christian baptism when He gave the great commission (Matt. 28:18-20). Obviously, a ritual that symbolizes Christ's death and resurrection would not be instituted before the crucifixion and resurrection. John's baptism must be different than Christian baptism.

Since the rejection of the King, John the Baptist's baptism is no longer being practiced. Even many who believe that baptism is essential for salvation would not look to texts concerning John the Baptist to establish their error. However, because such texts could bring confusion they will be studied in this section.

"As for me, I baptize you with water for repentance..." [Matt. 3:11].

John the Baptist appeared in the wilderness preaching a baptism of repentance for the forgiveness of sins [Mark 1:4].

And he came into all the district around the Jordan, preaching a baptism of repentance for the forgiveness of sins [Luke 3:3].

The call to "prepare ye the way of the Lord" teaches that John's work was basically preparatory. He himself was not technically bringing or offering forgiveness of sins. He was directly attesting to One who could and would offer such forgiveness upon His arrival. He was calling people "to repent," i.e., to change their minds. The people of Judea especially needed to change their minds about the Messiah and His soon coming. They needed to be mentally changed and prepared to accept the King. The line "baptism of repentance for the forgiveness of sins" need not be taken to mean the people automatically were saved on the basis of John's baptism. The word *for* can mean "with a view to." (Mark is working for a graduation next year, i.e., with a view to graduation next year). John the Baptist was telling people to repent (change their thinking about the Messiah's coming) and be baptized with a view to obtaining forgiveness of sins that the Messiah would bring upon His arrival. The above verses do not conclusively teach that all who submitted to John's work were saved at the time of baptism. If one professed to be mentally prepared and willing to accept the king and was baptized by John upon this basis, he still had to accept the King after his arrival in order to have salvation and forgiveness. John's message and baptism prepared a person to accept the King with a view to a forgiveness of sins, which the King would provide when He arrived. The promised forgiveness of sins did not happen unless the King was indeed accepted when He did come to Israel. Likely, some that John baptized later

rejected Jesus' messianic claim, and, the fact that they had been baptized would not, in itself, save them. (See previous comments of John 3:5.) The above texts can be paraphrased as follows:

"I baptize you with water because of repentance" (i.e., because of a change on thinking that is prepared to accept the coming King) [Matt 3:11].[50]

John the Baptist appeared in the wilderness preaching a baptism based upon repentance with a view to a forgiveness of sins that the King would bring [Mark 1:4].

And he came into all the district of Jordan, preaching a baptism based upon repentance (i.e., a changed mind about the coming Messiah) with a view to a forgiveness of sins that the King would bring [Luke 3:3].

It is best to view John's work as totally preparatory. He himself was not offering forgiveness of sins to the people. He called for people to be mentally and morally changed and prepared to accept One who would grant such forgiveness when He came. John's baptism symbolized a readiness to accept the future King and His future forgiveness. John's baptism related to salvation by preparing people to accept the Savior. However, the promised forgiveness of sin had to await the King's arrival. John prepared for salvation by baptism. Christ provided salvation by **faith alone**.

If one should still insist that John's ministry actually provided forgiveness, as opposed to preparing for a future forgiveness that Christ

---

[50] Matt. 3:11 might also be translated: "I baptize you in water with a view to repentance." It would have to be understood that repentance was a prior condition to John's baptism but, also, that baptism was intended to produce still more repentance. Such a translation would make a nice parallel to 1 Cor. 12:13: (John baptized in water with a view to repentance; Christ baptizes in the Holy Spirit with a view to union in one body).

would offer, then one could contend that such a forgiveness must have been based upon repentance not baptism.

If John actually offered forgiveness of sins, it was based upon repentance not baptism. Yet, there is every reason to believe John was not himself offering forgiveness. His baptism symbolized a preparation to receive a future forgiveness of sins that the Messiah would bring. Finally, John's baptism is not even being practiced since the rejection of the King. Therefore, there is no basis for using texts relative to John the Baptist's baptism as evidence that baptism is a condition for salvation.

H. Confess Jesus Before Men to be Saved.

The practice of giving an invitation to walk an aisle in order to trust in Christ is neither Scriptural nor unscriptural. It is neither commanded nor forbidden. Churches will vary in opinions as to the wisdom of this evangelistic method. However, there is a danger of creating a major error in order to pressure people into "coming forward."

The Scriptures base salvation upon faith alone. If one adds "a public confession of Jesus" to the sole condition of faith, he is preaching "another gospel". The addition of "public confession of Jesus" as a requirement for salvation is often done with an "end-justifies-the-means" attitude. It can also arise out of sheer ignorance, sloppy habits, the desire to count numbers of conversions, or the uncritical acceptance of tradition without consideration of its Scriptural foundation. By telling people they must publicly confess to be saved, speakers create pressure to get "decisions." However, consider the poor timid soul who has no trouble deciding he should trust in Christ but not enough courage to decide to step forward in a crowded church. For such, the speaker has given a man-made and erroneous condition for salvation. It is an artificial barrier to salvation that is contrary to God's Word and should not be accepted by the church. Isn't it possible to believe in Christ in settings where public confession is not possible such as a motel room

with a Gideon Bible or a quiet bedroom with mother? Would it not also be possible to make a public profession without having real faith? The most commonly abused text used to show that public confession is required for salvation is Rom. 10:9-10a.[51]

1. Rom. 10:9-10

> ...that if you confess with your mouth Jesus as Lord, and believe in your heart that God raised Him from the dead, you shall be saved; for with the heart man believes, resulting in righteousness, and with the mouth he confesses, resulting in salvation.

In Rom. 10:9-10 Paul is giving an example of his method for Jewish evangelism. (See Rom. 10:1.) He says that the method he uses involves confessing with the mouth the Lord Jesus and believing in the heart that God raised Him from the dead. As a good Bible expositor, Paul proves that his evangelistic method is valid by supporting it with Scripture. The context following v. 10 proves from the Old Testament that Paul is correct to ask for belief and confession. Verse 11 proves that his appeal to believe in the resurrection is valid: "For [because] the Scriptures say [in Isa. 28:16] whoever believes in Him will not be disappointed." Then in v. 13 Paul gives Scriptural proof for his appeal to confess that Jesus is Lord (i.e. God, Messiah, Master). Quoting Joel 2:32, v. 13 says, "For [because] whoever will call on the name of the Lord will be saved." In condensed version Paul's argument runs like this: "I ask the Jews to believe in the resurrected Lord because Isa. 28:16 asks for belief, and I ask for confession because Joel 2:32 gives the invitation to call upon the

---

[51] Obviously, none of the contexts of the verses under consideration refer to the modern practice of a public altar call. Furthermore, few people would want to take this view to its logical outcome and base salvation upon witnessing. This would end in a works based system parallel to the Jehovah's Witnesses' concept that salvation comes through working at witnessing.

Lord for salvation." Notice carefully that v. 13 defines the type of confession Paul wanted. He urged people to "confess" in the sense of "calling upon the Name of the Lord." **The confession Paul wanted is made in a prayer to God. He is not thinking of a confession made before humans**. Confess in Romans 10:9 equals calling upon God in prayer and acknowledging to Him that Jesus is the Lord in Rom. 10:13. The argument of this text makes it clear the confession of which v. 9 speaks is expressed by calling upon the name of the Lord (as in vv. 12-13). **Paul is not asking his fellow Jews to give a confession of faith before men in order to obtain salvation. He is asking them to confess that Jesus Christ is their Lord (Messiah) in a prayer to God.** Acknowledging that Jesus Christ is the Son of God is an essential part of saving faith. One good Scripturally-approved method of expressing this acknowledgment is through a prayer to God. However, Rom. 10:9-10 has nothing to do with a confession made to other people either in public or private.

2. Matt. 10:32-33 and Luke 12:8-9

> "Everyone therefore who shall confess Me before men, I will also confess him before My Father, who is in heaven. But whosoever shall deny Me before men, I will also deny him before My Father who is in heaven" [Matt. 10:32-33].

> "And I say to you, everyone who confesses Me before men, the Son of Man shall confess him also before the angels of God; but he who denies Me before men shall be denied before the angels of God" [Luke 12:8-9].

Matt. 10:32ff. and Luke 12:8ff. are also texts that have been used to establish that public confession of Jesus is a requirement to salvation. When viewed in isolation from the rest of Scripture, these texts could be so interpreted. However, the result would be a contradiction with over 150 texts that condition salvation upon faith alone.

If the Lord's statements can also be viewed in a way that harmonizes them with the rest of Scripture, then not only will the *faith alone* position be maintained but so will Biblical infallibility. It is not of ultimate importance which of the following views of Matt. 10:32 and Luke 12:8 is the correct one. The important concern is that there are interpretations that do harmonize all the Scriptures and preserve both Biblical infallibility and *sola fide* (faith alone). **Any** of these interpretations are preferable to taking these two texts to make a contradiction in Scripture. The possibilities will now be discussed.

a. Apostolic View

One way of reconciling Matt. 10:32 and Luke 12:8-9 with the 150 plus verses that teach *faith alone* is to interpret and apply them strictly to the persons to whom the words were spoken. They are parallel texts given **primarily to the apostles** (Matt. 10:1-2; Luke 12:1 "to His disciples first...") who were announcing the Kingdom (Matt. 10:7) to Israel only (Matt. 10:6). If the warning is restricted to the twelve, then the emphasis upon acknowledging Christ by confessing or denying Him may have been for the benefit of Judas Iscariot. Perhaps it is true of the twelve that those who confessed Christ will be honored in heaven, but those who denied (Judas) will be denied by Christ before the Father in heaven. By restricting these statements to the specific persons being addressed, they can be handled in a way that does not contradict *sola fide*.[52]

b. Tribulation View

There is also precedent for Christ viewing the apostles as representatives of tribulation saints. Apparently, Christ considered the tribulation saints as extensions of the apostolic work, and He could view the connection rather

---

[52] The context of Matthew 10 would give stronger support to restricting these comments to the apostles than does the context of Luke 12. The Lord speaks to "His disciples first" though the multitude listened (Luke 12:1).

directly without the intervening church system. This occurs in Luke 21 where Christ's discourse about Jerusalem's destruction in apostolic times ends up merging with the conflicts in the end times. The Lord speaks to His apostles as though they were the ones who would experience tribulation anguish in the end times. In the Matt. 10:32-33 context this same process occurs. In Matt. 10:6 Christ tells the apostles to go **only to Israel**, but, before the lecture is over, Christ seems to view the apostles as representatives of the tribulation saints. He says they will be dragged before rulers and **gentiles** to give witness (Matt. 10:18). In language paralleling the Tribulation account of Matt. 24:9 and 13, Christ tells them they will be hated by all (Matt. 10:22) and will be delivered from this time of trouble by endurance to the end (Matt. 10:22). Matt. 10:23 is the most explicitly tribulational. It says the persecuted witnesses would not get to all the cities in Israel "until the **Son of Man comes**."

It is possible to view Christ's words in Matt. 10:32-33 as also having a dual reference to both the apostles and tribulation saints. This allows for interesting possibilities in the reconciliation of the texts with the *faith alone* doctrine taught elsewhere in Scripture. During the Tribulation believers will be forced to either identify with Christ or against Him by the acceptance or rejection of the mark of the beast, i.e., Antichrist (see Rev. 13:16-17). The only God-imposed condition for salvation is faith. Yet, conditions will be such in the tribulation time that a Satanic engendered requirement to being a believer will be a public confession of Christ by refusal of the mark (Rev. 20:4). All who do not believe in Christ will deny Him by the same mark. God requires only faith to be saved, but the devil's system will require a refusal of the mark to be a believer. Thus, the result is that **all believers in the Tribulation will publicly confess Christ and all unbelievers in the Tribulation will deny Him.**

If the interpreter restricts the words of Matt. 10:32-33 and Luke 12:8-9 strictly to the apostles and the Tribulation generation, the resulting interpretation harmonizes with *sola fide.* God's only condition for salvation is faith. Yet, with the twelve and with the religious in the Tribulation (viewed as an extension of apostolic work), conditions on earth will be such as to force these groups to either confess or deny Christ in a **definitive and irrevocable way**. While applications may be drawn for other groups of God's people (including those, in our time, under pressure to deny Christ), no other groups will face the same absolute pressure to confess or deny Christ in such an irrevocable sense. These verses teach us by application that a believer, in the present time, should never deny Christ. However, present embarrassment about being a Christian is not the same as publicly betraying the Messiah to death (Judas) or selling one's soul to the Antichrist. If the statements of Matt. 10:32-33 and Luke 12:8-9 are restricted to the special conditions facing the apostles and the tribulation generation, then they can be harmonized with the truth that faith in Christ is God's only requirement for salvation. Those with a dispensational view of Scripture (discussed in Chapter 11, "Ecclesiology") will more readily adopt this possible means of reconciling Matt.10:32-33 and Luke 12:8-9 with the *faith alone* position. There is nothing unusual about a truth referring to the apostles or to tribulation saints but not directly referring to the church. However, it is possible to understand Matt. 10:32-33 and Luke 12: 8-9 in additional ways that leave it both unrestricted and yet compatible with the *faith alone* doctrine.[53]

---

[53] One problem with the apostolic view is that Peter did deny the Lord in a limited sense while Judas confessed Jesus for a number of years. If we restrict Matthew 10 and Luke 12 to the apostles, then Jesus must be talking about apostolic descriptions which accurately reveal beliefs. In Peter's case, he customarily confessed Jesus when viewed as a trend over a lifetime (though he had occasional lapses). In Judas' case, he confessed Jesus for a while but denied Him to a degree that proved he lacked faith. All interpretations of Matthew 10 and Luke 12 must include the fact that words do not

c. Rewards View

Perhaps Jesus speaks of future rewards rather than of salvation. Jesus might mean those who confess Him as a worthy Savior would be confessed as being worthy of rewards at the Judgment Seat. Those who deny the Lord as unworthy of acknowledgment here will not be acknowledged as worthy of full reward in heaven. Though Matt. 10:28 and Luke 12:5 refer to the soul's eternal destiny, it is preferable to view the overall text as referring to the rewards of a believer rather than to contradict salvation by faith alone. This view does have the advantage of being simple.

d. The "Either Extreme" View

Perhaps Jesus presupposes the words of confession or denial truly reveal a person's faith or lack of faith. We could limit the passage only to definitions of confession and denial which are strictly consistent with salvation by faith. Confession would become virtually a synonym for believing. Denial means refusal to believe.

In the **extreme**, one who **always denies Christ** shows he is an unbeliever. On the other hand, a **believer** will confess Christ to others (at least to other believers) at some point in life. He or she **will not deny at all times** (like a typical unbeliever).

Thus, the interpreter might take for granted that the Lord speaks only of a type of confession to others based in faith or a type of denial to others based in unbelief though the text has not given such explicit restriction. The Lord's teaching could be paraphrased to read: "Unbelievers display their rejection by constantly denying Me all their lives. **Those who deny** and reject Me at **all times** prove they are **unsaved**. A believer will at some time in life confess to others, at least to other trustworthy

Christians, that he knows Me. A **believer** might deny occasionally but he **will not deny always**. At some time and to someone he will admit he has faith."

One who always denies is an unbeliever. One who is a believer will acknowledge Christ sometime.[54] The direct application to the original listeners would be to confess Christ in settings involving pressure rather than just in calm, unpressured settings involving trustworthy friends. Believers will confess Jesus at least some of the time. They should be consistent during persecution and not act like typical unbelievers who always deny Christ. The context clearly warns of persecution, (Matt. 10:28, 34-39) but perhaps the confession or denial under view need not only take place in a setting of persecution. [55]

e. "Here" vs. "Hereafter" or the "Confession to God View"

The words of Matthew 10 and Luke 12 seem to contrast the "here" and the "hereafter", earth and heaven, now and eternity. Suppose we do not take the phrase *before men* to refer to a confession (or denial) made in the presence of others but rather understand it to mean something like "during your time among men." The Lord would be contrasting the present life among or before men on this earth with a future in heaven. Furthermore, if the **confession** under consideration **is made to the Father** (as in Rom. 10:9-10), then Jesus' teachings have been reconciled with the truth

---

[54] To use a sports analogy, a believer may not bat 1,000, but, unlike a person who constantly denies Christ, a true believer will not bat .000 either.

[55] Perhaps the reader can tell why the author calls this the "Either Extreme View." A person who denies Christ at all times over a lifespan reveals he has no faith. A believer will confess Jesus at least minimally. He will confess to some people in some settings, (maybe a private conversation or in the hospital room with a pastor) that he believes. Because the unbeliever's denial would have to be total while a believer's confession could be timid, occasional, and minimal, the intensity of behavior would go in the opposite direction.

---

always reveal the heart and that unbelievers have occasionally confessed while believers can occasionally deny. Even if we restrict the Lord's direct words to the apostles, we end up with a view similar to sub-section "f", p.155.

of salvation by faith alone. The resulting meaning would be this: "If you confess Me **to the Father** during your life before men, I will confess you **to the Father** in eternity before the angels. If you deny Me as Savior during your life before men, I will deny you to the Father in eternity before the angels." The contrasting destinies would be confession to the Father now in this life before men, or Christ's denial to the Father at a future time before angels.[56] If we understand the confession to be made to God and take the phrase *before men* to mean life on earth, there is no conflict with salvation by *faith alone*. Any of the above views is preferable to making public confession a condition for salvation. The final option might stand on its own or overlap with a and b (see footnote 53).

f. General Description View

Believers usually (but not always) admit they know the Lord. Unbelievers usually (but not always) deny the Lord. If the preceding ways to reconcile Matthew 10 and Luke 12 with the doctrine of salvation by faith alone are unacceptable, the final attempt at explanation may satisfy because it is quite simple.

The Lord's words do **not** give a **condition of salvation** but rather a **general description** of most believers most of the time.[57] Most believers typically confess and admit they know Jesus as an **overall trend during their life-spans.** This is especially true if we include all types of situations rather than just those involving intimidation or pressure (e.g., believers nearly always confess faith to other believers). Most unbelievers typically deny and will not acknowledge Jesus as an overall trend during their life span. Again, this is especially true in non-pressure situations involving other non-Christians. The Lord would neither be teaching that salvation is based upon confession or witnessing nor that salvation is lost by denials. **His point would be that His disciples should be consistent to the typical and general behavior they will frequently exhibit throughout their lives.** In time of threat or persecution they should not change from the normal behavior of most believers most of the time.

As a **general and loose description**, believers admit they believe. Unbelievers deny they believe. There may be individuals who are exceptions to the general rule. Furthermore, almost anyone is capable of occasional words inconsistent with their usual pattern. Still, as a basic tendency believers acknowledge Christ, unbelievers do not. The Lord wants us to be consistent to the overall trend and general description of a Christian in situations when it would be easy to speak like an unbeliever. The general **description** view is another way to reconcile Matthew 10 and Luke 12 with a salvation **conditioned** upon faith alone. [58]

---

[56] The context refers to persecution. Persecution gives the opportunity to confess Christ to others or the temptation to deny Christ to others. Still Jesus might be thinking of a confession of faith **made to the Father** in Matt. 10:32-33 and Luke 12:8-9. He would be building upon a confession made to the Father as an example of how a believer should consistently confess Jesus in times of persecution. We should confess Jesus to others just as we have confessed Him to the Father.

[57] Jesus employs a similar thought pattern in Matt. 25:31-46. The sheep who feed, clothe, and visit the Lord's brethren (technically the Jews in the tribulation period) do not earn salvation by these good works. Feeding, clothing and visiting are **not conditions** for salvation but rather **descriptions** that reveal the person has faith. Only those with faith will minister to the Jews against the objection of the Antichrist. Salvation comes through faith, but those saved can be described as those who do good works. Faith is demonstrated by behavior. Likewise, in Matthew 10 and Luke 12 confession is not a condition for salvation but a description of the way a believer should and usually does act. Denial is the description of the way an unbeliever usually acts. A Christian who denies is not acting out the normal description of a believer but instead hypocritically acts like an unbeliever.

[58] Viewing the Lord's words as a loose and general description of believers (rather than a condition for salvation) has the advantage of taking other Scrip-

3. Summary

Rom. 10:9-10 is not discussing a public confession, but rather the confession associated with salvation is a private confession made to God. Rom. 10:9 should be equated with Rom. 10:12-13. **Confession equals a calling on the name of the Lord to be saved.**

Likewise, Matt. 10:32-33 and Luke 12:8-9 do not have to be interpreted as contradicting the 150 plus verses that give faith alone a condition for salvation. One could restrict them as being directed either to the apostles alone or also to the tribulation saints who faced or will face special conditions unparalleled by any other groups. If one does not feel convinced by the contexts that these verses are being directed to specialized groups, then the verses are still capable of interpretations that are

---

tural teaching into consideration. The rest of the Bible teaches that believers can fail to admit to others that they have faith. Peter is the outstanding example (John 18:25), and John 12:42 also states there were Pharisees who believed but would not confess the Lord publicly because they feared Jewish authorities. Apparently, a believer can fail to confess Christ on occasions but still have an overall life described as a "confessor." He might admit to faith in safe situations with a pastor, other believers or trusted family and friends. No doubt there are timid believers in Moslem countries in our time who would not dare make a public confession.

On the other hand, Judas' example and Matt. 7:21-23 show that an unbeliever might occasionally confess faith, but his overall description in life would be that of denial. So long as the confession made in Matthew 10 and Luke 12 is understood as being made to other people (not to the Father), it will be necessary to understand the Lord's words as general and loose descriptions qualified by other Scriptures. Most believers usually admit the Savior. Most unbelievers usually deny Him. Keep in mind that the primary intent of Matthew 10 and Luke 12 concerns how believers should handle opposition. Soteriology is not the Lord's primary subject. Thus, He could be describing only the typical behavior of most believers (and unbelievers) without listing every detailed exception. He holds believers to the typical behavior of confessing Him even in times of persecution.

compatible with faith alone. Maybe the subject is the gain or loss of rewards and not salvation (Rewards View). Maybe Christ meant a believer would confess Him to at least some degree while those who consistently deny are unbelievers (Either Extreme View). Another idea would be Christ taught that those who confess Him to the Father in this life before men would avoid denial to the Father in eternity before angels ("Here" vs. "Hereafter" View). Another suggestion would be that the Lord gives usual descriptions of how the saved act instead of conditions to be saved (General Description View). The resulting lessons for the original listeners from at least three of the options end up the same. The disciples had already confessed Jesus to God and would confess Him to others. He wanted them to be true to that confession in time of trouble.

It is not necessary to argue which of the above views is correct. The main point is that they are alternatives to thinking public confession is a condition for salvation in addition to faith.

I. Ask Jesus into Your Heart to Be Saved

This phrase is often used to express a condition for salvation when dealing with children. It can be understood as an equivalent for receiving Jesus as Savior by faith. Therefore, many children have had the gospel communicated by this phrase and have genuinely trusted in Christ.

However, the line "ask Jesus into your heart" is also capable of great misunderstanding. It is even possible for a person to "ask Jesus into your heart" and be completely ignorant of the Savior's death and resurrection or of the idea of trust. Furthermore, Christ's entrance into the heart is a result of salvation rather than a condition for it. The Bible **never** uses such terminology in evangelism, and it should be avoided.

The Greek word for heart is *kardia* from which *cardiac* is derived. It is used between 157-160 times depending upon which manuscripts are counted. The student may consult a concordance to satisfy his own mind that "asking Jesus into ones heart" is **never made a condition for salvation** in the Bible. To state the truth a different way, one could assert people are constantly being saved **without** asking Jesus into their hearts. It simply is not a condition for salvation. The Scriptures do say that one believes with his heart (Luke 24:25; Acts 15:9; Rom.10:9-10), but neither the Gospel of John, nor the evangelistic sermons in Acts, nor in the great theological treatise in Romans, nor anywhere in the New Testament is "asking Jesus into ones heart" made a condition for salvation. **One must not confuse a result of salvation with a requirement for salvation.**

It is possible that asking Jesus into ones heart is viewed as a condition for salvation because of a superficial interpretation of Rev. 3:20.

> "Behold, I stand at the door and knock; if anyone hears My voice and opens the door, I will come in to him, and will dine with him, and he with Me" [Rev. 3:20].

Notice that the word *heart* is not even used in Rev. 3:20. The interpreter also needs to realize that there is a space between the words "in" and "to." This verse is saying the Lord will come **in with** a person not **inside** or **into** a person. The Greek phrase in Rev. 3:20 (*eiserkomai*) is used eight other times in the New Testament, and it never means "inside of" (Mark 7:25; 15:43; Luke 1:28; Acts 10:3; 11:3; 16:40; 17:2; 28:8). In Mark 15:43 Joseph of Arimathea "went in [unto] Pilate and asked for the body of Jesus." He did not go inside of Pilate! He went "in with" or "in unto" Pilate. Likewise, Rev. 3:20 is teaching that Jesus is willing to come unto or "in with" a person to have fellowship with him. Christ's work of indwelling a person's heart is not in view in Rev. 3:20. No verse conditions salvation upon asking Jesus into one's heart.

J. Confess Sins to Obtain Salvation

The confession of sin is a very important Christian doctrine. However, it needs to be viewed in its proper place. Teachings about confession of sin are primarily directed to believers. In His role as Judge, God has already forgiven the believer of all sins (Col. 2:13). In His role as Father, God still can become angry and forgiveness will need to be obtained by the believer through confession (i.e., acknowledgment of sin). Thus, believers are urged to confess their sins to obtain forgiveness from the Father (cf. 1 John 1:9; 1 Cor. 11:31; Matt. 6:12). In its proper place the doctrine of confessing sins is most true and most vital.

However, the Scriptures do not give the confession of sins as a condition for salvation. True, a person who comes in faith to Christ is implicitly admitting his own sinfulness in a general sense, but this is different from a requirement of listing, naming, and confessing specific offences in order to obtain salvation. The latter activity could actually be viewed as a work of penance with salvation being earned by the meritorious act of confessing sins. Consider the fact that a person could list and confess many, many sins without even a basic knowledge of the cross or faith in the person of Jesus Christ. Were not the monasteries of the Middle Ages full of poor wretches who confessed sin after sin but never trusted in Christ to forgive them? Also, consider the truth that nowhere is confession of specific sins made a requirement for salvation. Just as one could confess many sins without trusting in Christ, so also one can trust in Christ without confessing any sin specifically. It is sufficient that a person acknowledge **sinfulness** in a general sense and wants to have deliverance by trusting in Christ. Confession of specific sin is a proper means for a believer to obtain forgiveness from God in His role as Father. However, the means for a sinner to obtain forgiveness from God in His role as Judge is **faith alone**.

A few people use 1 John 1:9 to argue that specific confession of sin is a condition for a lost person to be saved. However, the context and phraseology show that the verse is directed to believers. In 1 John 2:1, John shows he is writing to "little children," i.e., believers. He writes to those for whom Jesus Christ is an Advocate or Comforter. In 1 John 2:2, John distinguished between his readers and the world. It is easy to establish that 1 John 1:9 is directed to believers rather than to unbelievers. The confession of specific sins is not a Biblical condition for salvation. God in His role as Judge forgives sin on the basis of faith in Christ. If a person has genuinely placed his faith in Christ, he has already acknowledged his sin to a degree that is sufficient for salvation.

K. Forgive Others in Order to be Saved

A large church listed "freely forgive as Christ has forgiven you" as a condition for salvation in one of its advertisements for a "revival meeting." The ad specifically said this is one of God's "terms" for salvation. There is no question that the Bible encourages forgiveness, but there are great problems with saying the Bible teaches forgiveness of others as a condition for salvation. First, in the truest sense it is impossible for one who does not know Christ to forgive as Christ does. One must first be saved and experience God's forgiveness in order to truly forgive others. Requiring forgiveness of all others before salvation occurs places an insurmountable barrier upon a person who may want to be forgiven by God but cannot bring himself to forgive those who have victimized him. In fact, even God does not forgive all sins committed against Him! Christians should forgive easily, but if the offense is too great, even a Christian is not required to forgive in the sense of dropping accountability. (See Matt. 18:15-17.) If Christians and even God Himself do not always forgive, it is absurd to make complete forgiveness of others a condition for the lost to meet in order to obtain salvation. Second, requiring forgiveness conditions salvation upon something a person does as opposed to an acceptance of what Christ has done. It adds work to a pure faith that accepts God's pure grace. Third, even if a hypothetical forgiveness of all

others could take place, the person would still be lost in sins. If a natural man could completely forgive others, he still would be unsaved until he learns about and trusts in Christ and His work on the cross. Finally, there is no Scripture whatsoever to support the idea that God demands a person forgive everyone of all things before he can be saved.

Matt. 6:14-15 could be misinterpreted to teach "forgiving others" as a condition for salvation. However, Christ is addressing those who are already saved (v. 9, "...Our Father who art in heaven..."). He is teaching that those believers who hold unforgiving grudges against others will not obtain forgiveness from God in His role as Father. God has already forgiven believers in His role as Judge by virtue of faith in Christ. Yet, if a believer absolutely refuses to forgive another who requests it, that believer will in turn remain unforgiven in the sense that he is not in fellowship with God. Fellowship with God the Father is conditioned upon forgiving those who sincerely request it. However, salvation is conditioned upon faith alone.

L. Deny Self and Forsake All to be Saved

There are several passages where Christ commands complete dedication to Himself. No one will argue the point that Christ requires a complete allegiance and denial of self. However, it is debatable that He requires complete denial of self in order to obtain salvation. There is a distinction between what God requires after salvation and what He requires for salvation.

Before texts that call for self-denial are examined, it will be conceded that they could be interpreted to require utmost sacrifice, self-denial, and obedience to earn salvation. However, they also can be interpreted to harmonize with the clearly Biblical position that salvation is by grace through faith. There is nothing unusual about a teaching that can be taken in more than one sense in isolation from the rest of Scripture. However, logic and the authority of Scripture demand that any interpretation that eliminates contradictions be preferred. Christ told the rich young ruler to give all that he possessed to the poor and to follow (Matt. 19:21-22). Isolated from other Scriptures, this text is capable of teaching that salvation is earned by sacrificial giving. However, it could also be understood that salvation would come by following Christ. Because the man's wealth prevented him from following Christ, it was in his individual case essential that he relinquish that wealth in order to become a believer. Thus, his salvation was to be by faith alone rather than by charitable deeds, but Christ wanted him to remove the barrier that money caused so that he could became a believer. The text itself is capable of both interpretations. However, the correct one is the latter because it harmonizes with the rest of Scripture.

1. Luke 9:23-26

(See also Matt. 16:24-28 and Mark 8:34-38).

> And He was saying to them all, "If anyone wishes to come after Me, let him deny himself, and take up his cross daily, and follow Me. For whoever wishes to save his life shall lose it, but whoever loses his life for My sake, he is the one who will save it. For what is a man profited if he gains the whole world, and loses or forfeits himself? For whoever is ashamed of Me and My words, of him will the Son of Man be ashamed when He comes in His glory, and the glory of the Father and of the holy angels."

To whom does Jesus address these words? Are those listening believers, unbelievers, or a mixture? The context in Luke 9:18 speaks of the disciples (see also Matt. 16:24), but verse 23 uses the word *all*. Mark 8:34 says, "and He summoned the multitude with His disciples." The disciples (apostles) are believers, but many in the crowd are unbelievers. It would not be unusual, then or now, to deliver a sermon to a mixed audience. While Jesus is getting believers ready for persecution, many

unsaved listened to the conversation. The best way to explain this passage is to study what the Lord's teaching in Luke 9:23-26 meant for unbelievers and then to consider what He intended for believers. First, let's be clear on what this passage does **not** teach.

a. Misunderstandings

Luke 9:23 cannot mean salvation comes through self-denial, constant sacrifice, and intense effort. The pursuit of salvation would be a daily process. Either one is never sure when one has done enough to deserve salvation, or one must keep striving to retain salvation. Every day would be a new test.

If we were to follow a similar approach to vv. 24-25, then salvation would come through martyrdom, but then few would be saved. The resulting theology would be like false religions, which promise heaven to fanatics who die for their cause. One could also take vv. 24-25 to refer to the loss of control (authority) over one's own life. While this interpretation has some merit, it would be a serious misunderstanding to then infer salvation would be earned by works. Such conclusions would contradict the more than 150 verses that teach salvation through faith alone.

b. Meaning for Unbelievers: "Believe whatever the cost."

In Luke 9:23 the Lord calls listeners to follow Him without limits. However, many in the crowd had not even begun the process of following. For them the most pressing application would be to take the first step. They had to begin following the Lord with the first step: salvation by faith.

To unbelievers, Luke 9:23 primarily means that if social conditions are such that a person must suffer and take risks in order to become a believer, then he must still believe. Salvation cannot be earned by self-denial, enduring persecution, or accepting risks. However, if placing faith in Christ involves danger, being ridiculed, or leads to pain, then that price must be paid in order to become a believer. Faith alone saves. God the Judge will not accept the excuse; "I could not trust Jesus because doing so would have meant rejection, persecution, or possible martyrdom."

Luke 9:24a warns that those intimidated by fear to the degree that they refuse to believe in Jesus might save their physical lives but would lose eternal life. The seemingly safe decision to reject Jesus preserves this life at the peril of eternal death.

Not only can potential hardship, ridicule, or death threats block faith, but also the world might reward those who turn away from following Christ in initial saving faith (v. 25). When a person yields to pressures not to accept Jesus in faith, he will often find acceptance by the unsaved world system. He may even be blessed and exalted by the world, gaining not only the safe preservation of life but "the good life" as the world defines it.

Jesus warns unbelievers in the multitude not to choose the superficial benefits of rejecting Him to gain the world's acceptance. They might gain socially; however, they will lose genuine life. They forfeit self both eternally and in terms of wasting this life's potential. They can either choose to put their lives in constant ("daily") and mortal jeopardy by faith in Christ, or they can place their souls in eternal jeopardy by safely, comfortably, and perhaps profitably rejecting Him as Savior.

The type of shame in view in verse 26 is a shame that causes one to turn away in unbelief from the Lord. If one is so ashamed of Christ that he rejects Him as Savior, then Christ will reject him in the end. If shame leads a person to unbelief now, the Lord will be too embarrassed and ashamed of that person to have an eternal relationship. To unbelievers, Jesus' words in Luke 9:23 mean they must overcome any fears or allurements from the world and trust Him. Though the call in verse 23 is to follow completely, they must begin to follow by believing in the Lord Jesus. Safety and even gain are a poor trade for eternal death.

The Lord's words warn unbelievers to begin following Jesus whatever it costs. However, His teachings also have meaning for the disciples (apostles) who are already saved. What was the Lord teaching them? How shall we apply the Lord's ideas to believers today?

c. Meaning for Believers: "Don't act like them now", and "The world can persecute but cannot take your eternal life".

Jesus had told the disciples in Luke 9:22 that rejection and suffering was on its way. Though they had already ignored the risks, and had accepted the dangers and threats associated with becoming believers, they still faced pressures not unlike those faced with the risks of initial faith in Christ. Yes, they had chosen the first step. In faith they had begun the process of following, but the choice to follow Christ to a further degree in the face of trouble would have to be made repeatedly through life. Constant danger and hardship was ahead. Risks did not end with faith. The choice to ignore the threats and the temptations to gain by not following would have to be made perpetually. Just as the world pressures the unsaved not to take the first step (faith) in following Jesus, the world threatens conflict and uses enticements to hinder believers from unlimited following. The disciples had not been pushed away from starting to follow Jesus, but would they be stopped from a complete following of Jesus in the critical and high-pressure days to come?

Except for a brief phrase (primarily about martyrdom at the close of Luke 9:24), vv. 24-26 **probably refer to unbelievers.**[59] Still,

---

[59] If one wishes to take Luke 9:23ff. as addressed to **believers only**, then *shame* in v. 26 could refer to loss of rewards. Losing life in v. 24a would then be martyrdom or simply yielding to Christ's authority in life by renouncing ones own control of life. The *saving* of life in vv. 24b would likely include *saving* this life from wasting its potential for God. However, references to *all* (Luke 9:23) and the *multitude* (Mark 8:34) coupled with warnings about the loss of a soul (Matt. 16:26; Mark 8:36) seem to

these truths about unbelievers **apply to the disciples.** Believers can learn from those who choose safety and comfort over faith in Christ. Such are extremely negative examples of how not to think. What does their choice of safety and gain over following Christ in even the first step of faith teach believers who should follow completely?

In v. 24 the Lord uses a *reductio ad absurdum* (reduction to the absurd) method to show the disciples they should not allow the world's opposition to limit how much they would follow Christ. Taken to its extreme, those who wish to save their lives will not even trust Christ. They avoid ridicule. They avoid Christ's cross for salvation and any personal cross of suffering. They also lose eternal life. They gain from the world, but they forfeit themselves eternally. The disciples had not agreed with such logic, or they would not have taken the first step in following, i.e., faith in Christ. They had begun rejecting fearful thinking when they believed. Should they return to a cowardly, worldly, and selfish mind-set now and choose to limit how far they would follow? They had taken risks to begin following Christ; should they now lose courage? The unsaved lose ultimate values by such reasoning. Though the disciples already possess eternal life, nothing good would come from thinking and acting like unbelievers. They had taken risks to start following. They should now choose to follow completely.

The first part of Luke 9:24 describes unbelievers who choose preservation of this life over faith in Christ. The last part of Luke 9:24 describes the disciples. They had already ignored any risk of death for becoming believers. If that decision to start following the Lord in faith (and future decisions/actions consistently arising from continuing to follow) should eventually cost their lives for Christ's sake,

favor that the Lord spoke to a **mixed audience with different applications intended for the saved and the unsaved.**

they would still have eternal life. Eternal life is not earned on the merit of suffering martyrdom. Eternal life came and was guaranteed in the past when the disciples risked in order to believe, but the Lord's present reminder sustains them in ongoing dangers arising from the original choice to trust in Him. Should any part of following Christ (whether the first step in faith or sustained following in obedience) cost physical life, then the believer still has encouragement from his assurance of eternal life.[60] From an eternal view the world can inflict no harm. The Lord's meaning for the disciples is that **no persecution can kill eternal life.**

Jesus reassures His disciples they had made the right choice by refusing to play it safe. Just as they had risked life in order to take the initial step of faith, they should continue to follow now whatever the danger or cost. Whatever drawbacks may come from following Christ (beginning to follow or continuing to follow) are worth the price. Those who have disregarded any possible hardship to start following Jesus should not act like cowardly unbelievers by limiting how far they will follow after salvation. No good comes from an unbeliever's decision to choose safety, comfort, and profit over trusting in the Lord Jesus. No good can arise from believers choosing these same things over following in continued dedication. Following "daily" also saves from losing this life in the sense of wasting it, saving from forfeiting the full potential of this life [vv. 24-25 interpreted not only as restricted to survival versus martyrdom, but also as a con-

---

[60] Efforts to continue following after taking the initial step of faith can be seen as ultimately rooted in the original choice to trust Christ. If there had been no faith, there would not be any danger from persecution caused by on going obedient behaviors. Continuing to follow consistently arises from beginning the process in faith. In this extended sense, the disciple risked death for his fundamental decision to trust Christ in the past (though it would be acts of subsequent obedience in keeping with that original faith which actually would trigger even greater danger).

trast between the stubborn believer who retains ("saves") seeming control over his life and thereby wastes it versus a dedicated believer who gives ("loses") his life's work to Christ and thereby preserves his earthly life by giving it genuine value]. By implication, Luke 9:26 means the Master will be righteously proud (opposite of ashamed) of committed disciples who follow without limits. Luke 9:27 and the following account of the transfiguration remind us that, to the degree we follow now, we will share in the Lord's glory in eternity.

Luke 9:23-26 and parallels can definitely be interpreted compatibly with salvation by faith alone. For unbelievers, it simply means to accept whatever price must be paid in order to initiate following by trusting in Christ. For believers, the passage means to continue to follow regardless of the pressures or temptations to stop along the way. Jesus calls believers to follow even further by pointing to the tragic example of those who favor total safety in this life by refusing to trust in the Savior. Their disastrous example shows believers not to adopt the same cowardly behavior when it comes to following completely. Christians must be careful how they use ideas like self-denial, forsaking, and suffering in evangelistic settings. They have validity only to communicate that **risks might need to be taken in order to trust Christ.** There are no grounds for allowing others to think they can earn salvation by suffering for Jesus.

2. Luke 14:26, 27, 33

(See also Matt. 10:37-39.)

> "If anyone comes to Me, and does not hate his own father and mother and wife and children and brothers and sisters, yes, and even his own life, he cannot be My disciple. Whoever does not carry his own cross and come after Me cannot be My disciple....So therefore, no one of you can be My disciple who does not give up all his own possessions."

In general the word *disciple* means "a learner and/or follower." The term *disciple* seems to have an elastic definition with various shades of meaning. John 6:66 records that some of Christ's disciples permanently abandoned Him. Apparently, one could be a short-term disciple (learner) without being a believer. However, when the disciples are contrasted with the multitudes who listened to Jesus, these must be believers as in the passages covered in the previous section. (See Mark 8:34; Luke 9:18, 20.) In John 8:31, Christ seems to distinguish between *disciples* and *true disciples*. Those who believe are called to deeper discipleship. The gospels include **curious disciples** (only learners), **convinced disciples** (believers), and **committed disciples** (dedicated believers). Which type of disciples does Jesus have in mind in Luke 14:26ff.? The words in Matt. 10:37-39 are given to believers (i.e., the apostles named in Matt. 10:1-2). Luke 14:25 is addressed to the multitudes. Whether the interpreter takes Luke 14 as a call to become a convinced disciple (believer) or a committed disciple (dedicated believer), the words cannot be used to add any condition for salvation beyond faith. We must determine how these teachings could apply to unbelievers and believers (at different stages of spiritual life and development) in ways compatible with salvation by faith.

a. Misunderstandings

Luke 14:26ff. could be misused to teach that salvation comes by commitment and sacrifice. If the Lord is giving a condition for salvation, then salvation seems to be earned only by the most rigorous of works. One must suffer and obey to obtain salvation (v. 27). One must relinquish control of all material possessions (v. 33). However, what becomes of grace and of 150 plus texts that condition salvation upon faith?

b. Meaning for Unbelievers

If Luke 14:26ff. is applied to the unsaved, it is still possible to reconcile the text with the *faith alone* position. If societal conditions are such that in order to become a believer one must alienate family, endure rejection and ridicule, face pain or death threats (i.e., carry the cross) or lose property, one must still choose to place faith in Christ. **If believing brings great hardship, one must still believe**, for salvation comes through faith. Any one among the multitude who had not yet believed had to become a convinced disciple (believer) whatever the cost or risk. Beyond this beginning of life in Christ, the Lord also wants even deeper discipleship. There is a difference between what God requires for salvation (faith) and what God fully requires to those who have begun to follow. Unbelievers in the crowd needed to concentrate first on overcoming fears in becoming formal disciples by accepting Jesus as the Messiah.[61] For them this aspect to discipleship was most important, but there were additional applications in the Lord's message. For those who had already believed, other truths in Jesus' message about discipleship were more pertinent.

c. Meaning for Believers

It is possible that the sermon on discipleship in Luke 14 was directed to a mixed crowd. Unbelievers in the audience would need to begin their convinced discipleship through faith. The initial entrance was the most important response Jesus wanted from them. The apostles were already convinced disciples. For them (and all others who have received salvation), the Lord's words on discipleship hit them at the full commitment level. The Lord calls them to maintain and increase the level of allegiance they had shown by accepting Him in the first place. Christ requires those already saved to give Him primary allegiance over any other human relationship (v. 26). He asks believers to accept suffering for His sake and wants total obedience (v. 27). He requires that all possessions be placed at His disposal (v. 33). The Lord's call for discipleship applies to the apostles (and other believers) at their more advanced level of spiritual life. For unbelievers, response had to begin with taking risks from a dangerous world in order to believe.

One could prefer to limit the interpretation of Luke 14:26-33 in ways that restrict the Lord's comments to **only the unsaved (trust Me whatever the cost)** or **only the saved (give Me total and primary allegiance)**. One cannot, however, use Luke 14:26-33 in ways that suggest salvation comes through personal sacrifice, suffering, or obedience.

M. Lordship Salvation

Saving faith involves acceptance of the fact that Jesus Christ is the Lord (Rom. 10:9; Acts 16:31). Christ must be viewed as God's Son, the Master. This is part of identifying the Biblical Christ. There is also commitment of the soul to Christ for eternal safekeeping. Implied within the act of trusting in Christ for salvation is some desire for deliverance from sin, at the very least a deliverance from sin's penalty. Given that the Old Testament contrasts faith with rebellion, it is unlikely that saving faith can co-exist with an attitude of total rebellion. One who believes Christ is God must also know that he ought to obey Him.

If "Lordship Salvation" involves just these facts, then it could be considered true. However, it is one thing to acknowledge that Christ is the Master and that one ought to obey Him; but it is a vastly different matter to actively obey Him or even promise to obey Him. All Christians would say they should totally obey Christ. None totally obey Christ. Likewise, it is one thing to commit the soul's eternal des-

---

[61] The author has used the awkward phrase *formal disciple* because the crowds are already disciples in the sense of casual learners (as in John 6:66). However, most had not made any decision to follow Christ. In another sense these are not really disciples at all. In Luke 14 the Lord calls for discipleship. For unbelievers, the deepest application of the message would not be germane until they made the initial decision to accept Jesus as Savior. At their level Christ primarily wants them to trust Him. The apostles had already decided to believe in Him. At their level of spiritual development, Christ's message to them is to continue in fully committed discipleship.

tiny to Christ but another to yield every area of life to Him. A sinner could even want to obey Christ but not believe he will be able to do so. It must also be remembered that one who can trust in Christ has already desired deliverance from sin to a degree that is sufficient to obtain salvation.

No one will disagree that a complete obedience to Christ is a logical and consistent corollary to saving faith. If one commits his soul's eternal destiny to Christ, he should commit everything to Him. If one acknowledges that Christ is God and should be obeyed, the next step should be obedience. However, it is a dangerous mistake to make such a complete obedience or a promise to complete obedience a condition to obtain salvation as those who espouse Lordship Salvation often do.

The line, "If Christ is not Lord of all, He is not Lord at all," sounds pious and righteous, but it must be rejected as serious error. First, the New Testament is full of commands to **saved** people urging them to a complete yielding to Christ (e.g., Rom. 6:12-13; 12:1-2; Phil. 3:12-15; James 3:2; 4:8, etc.). Every command implies one could be a believer but not be fully yielded to God. Therefore, it is clear that one can be saved without a complete obedience to Christ (though it is not consistent). Secondly, one must insist upon the distinction between what God requires and what He requires for salvation. There are 150 plus verses conditioning salvation upon faith alone. This means that one who trusts in Christ has already acknowledged His Lordship to a sufficient degree and has obeyed to a sufficient degree to obtain salvation. True, God does require a complete submission to the Lordship of Christ, but faith alone is the requirement for salvation. A third problem with Lordship Salvation is that it is a subtle form of works. Yes, saving faith does involve the attitude that Christ is the Master. Thus, the sinner knows He ought to obey Him. Nevertheless, these aspects of saving faith are simply a realization of the identity of the true Jesus Christ. If one views salvation as contingent upon total obedience to Christ's Lordship

or a vow to yield totally to His Lordship, then salvation is based upon human efforts (great human efforts). If one views salvation as based on a less than total yielding to Christ's Lordship, then what is the problem with the view that faith in Christ involves all the yielding to His Lordship that is necessary to provide salvation? The call to yield to the Lordship of Christ is legitimate **if it is not made a condition for salvation**. When complete "Lordship" is tied to salvation, the result is works, i.e., false doctrine. Finally, Lordship Salvation is ultimately an impossible condition for an unsaved person to fulfill. There is a parallel with the zealous Judaizers who insisted that salvation came from law keeping. Law keeping would be an impossible condition for salvation (Gal. 2:14-16). So is Lordship salvation. To ask for the forsaking of sin (or the promise to forsake sin) and total submission to Christ's authority (or the vow to submit to Christ's authority) before salvation is to ask the impossible of a sinner. The unsaved person can not break the dominion of sin (John 8:34), and saving faith has no confidence in self to assert that it will vow to overcome sin and obey Christ throughout life. Saving faith entails a realization that Jesus Christ is and ought to be Master. Yet, saving faith is also an attitude of utter helplessness relative to overcoming sin. God requires faith in Christ to be delivered from sin, but not faith in self's ability to make a grandiose promise to forsake and totally yield. Saving faith is not trust in self's power to boast of promises to forsake sin and/or totally obey Christ. It is only after salvation that the power comes to make such a commitment. It is only after salvation that one can have any success in the area of forsaking sin and making Jesus Lord.

The drug addict in a rescue mission may have enough faith to trust in Christ. He believes Jesus Christ is the Lord and desires deliverance from sin. However, when a Christian tells him he must forsake his habit and yield totally in obedience to Christ's Lordship, he is asking the impossible of the poor wretch. The addict knows fully that he cannot forsake his sin, or even honestly promise to forsake it. He may even wish he could make Jesus Lord, but the fact is he cannot, and he knows it. That is why he needs a Savior! Ignorant Christians may tell the man he must forsake sin, promise to quit sinning, make Jesus Lord. Yet, God wants the opposite. He wants the man to feel utterly helpless and hopeless. God wants complete despair of hypocritical and/or boastful promises to change. He wants those trapped in sin to realize that such vows cannot be made in good conscience. God wants the addict and all other sinners to feel that sin is so powerful that only the Lord Jesus Christ could deliver from sin's power, as well as, from its penalty. God does not require vows of reformation of life for salvation. The opposite attitude of being hopelessly trapped in sin is more compatible with a faith that recognizes utter dependence on the Lord Jesus Christ for all hope of deliverance (first from sin's penalty, then its power). Satan might want Christian do-gooders to garble the gospel with additional conditions for salvation. He might want misguided evangelists to require faith in self to make boastful empty vows of reformation. **All God requires is that the sinner wants deliverance from sin to the degree of believing in the Lord Jesus Christ and His cross.**

N. Prayer and Saving Faith

Prayer is definitely a God-approved means of expressing faith. In Rom. 10:8 Paul gives his example of how he does evangelism. The phrase, "The word of faith, which we are preaching," could be paraphrased as "The words we use in evangelism to bring about faith." In the following context it is clear that Paul encouraged people to "call upon the name of the Lord" (vv. 12-13) confessing **to God** that Jesus Christ is Lord (v. 9). Probably the best method of evangelism involves instruction that one should pray to express faith in Christ.

However, it is the **faith** expressed by a prayer that saves, not merely prayer. It is not that one can glibly repeat a few lines of some magical prayer to obtain salvation. Apart from the faith expressed by prayer, there is no salvation.

A more fundamental question is "Must there be a prayer in order for there to be salvation?" The key texts that give *faith alone* as the condition for salvation contain virtually no references to prayer. The command is to "believe in Christ" rather than to believe and pray.

Furthermore, a Bible student would be hard pressed to find a point in time when Biblical characters such as Peter, James, and John prayed to obtain salvation. While prayer is the best means to express faith, the condition that brings salvation is **faith** whether a prayer expresses it or not. If a trust in Christ is present, salvation is granted. A prayer expressing this faith is beneficial because it provides assurance to the person that the matter of salvation is settled. However, God knows faith exists in the heart even if it is not directly verbalized by a prayer.

There needs to be balance in the area of prayer and salvation. It is wise to encourage people to pray in order to express faith. However, the fact that a person cannot remember a time of a specific prayer need not be grounds for concluding he or she is unsaved. Many people trust in Christ Jesus for salvation but do not know an exact date or remember a dramatic experience at the beginning of their faith. While it is nice to be able to recall a time when faith began, the matter of overwhelming importance is the presence of faith and not the time it began. If a person can honestly and sincerely maintain he has faith in Christ and His work on the cross, he has salvation. Faith may arise slowly, as it seems to have done with Peter, or faith may arise dramatically as it did with Paul. Salvation is conditioned upon faith. The time of faith's origin and the way it is expressed is secondary to the presence of faith.

O. Conclusion

All these complex studies end in a simple conclusion with a simple gospel: salvation is conditioned upon *faith alone*. "Nothing in my hand I bring, simply to Thy cross I cling." Salvation is not offering to God a full hand of a perfect life. Salvation is an empty hand receiving all grace and mercy from the merits of the Savior and His perfect work on the cross.

The type of faith being commanded by the Bible is trust, dependence, and reliance upon Jesus Christ and His work on the cross. Some might ridicule this doctrine as "easy-believism." The Bible calls it *grace*!

Chapter 9
SOTERIOLOGY
The Doctrine of Salvation

Part III:
The Results of Salvation

OUTLINE

I. Eternal Life
II. Regeneration - New Birth
III. Sonship/Adoption as Sons
IV. Justification
  A. The Definition of Justification: To Make or Declare Righteous?
    1. Justification in Secular Greek
    2. Justification in the Old Testament
    3. Justification in the New Testament
    4. Noting Usage of Greek Words Relating to Justification
  B. Time of Justification: Past or Future?
    1. The Time of Salvation as Background to the Time of Justification
    2. Verbal Uses of *To Justify* in the Past Tense
      a. 1 Cor. 6:11
      b. Titus 3:7
      c. Rom. 5:1, 9
      d. Rom. 6:7
      e. Rom. 8:30
    3. Verbal Uses of *To Justify* in the Present Tense
      a. Acts 13:39
      b. Rom. 3:28
      c. Rom. 3:24
      d. Others
    4. Verses Which Speak of Justification as a Potentiality
      a. Gal. 2:16-17
      b. Gal. 3:8-9
      c. Gal. 3:24-26
    5. Abraham's Example
    6. Noun Forms of *Justification* that Present an Accomplished Fact
      a. Justification

      (1) Rom. 3:22
      (2) Rom. 4:5
      (3) Rom. 5:17
      (4) Rom. 9:30
      (5) Rom. 10:4, 6a, 10a
      (6) 1 Cor. 1:30
      b. Greek Form for a "Just" Person
      (1) The Old Testament Background (Hab. 2:4)
      (2) Paul's Quote of Hab. 2:4
        (a) Rom. 1:16-17
        (b) Gal. 3:11
    7. Conclusion on the Time of Justification
  C. The Basis of Justification: Faith
    1. Texts which Base Justification upon Faith in Christ
      a. Verbal Forms of *to Justify*
      b. The Noun *Justification*
      c. The Noun Form *Just*
    2. Texts that Teach Justification is Freely Given by Grace
    3. Texts that Teach Justification is Not by Works
  D. The Source of the Believer's Righteousness
    1. Old Testament Background for God's Righteousness Being Credited to God's People
    2. The New Testament Teaching about God's Righteousness being Credited to God's People
  E. Conclusions on Justification
V. Good Works
  A. Genuine Salvation Results in Good Works
  B. Genuine Salvation is not Consistent with the Habitual Practice of Sin
  C. Consistency with Doctrines of Eternal Security and Non-eradication of Sin
  D. Practical Considerations
    1. Caution about a Categorical Denial of Salvation Based on Sinfulness

Alone
2. Tentative Doubts
3. Self-examination
4. A Dangerous Reaction to Sinful Professors of Salvation
VI. Sanctification
  A. Sanctification in the Old Testament
  B. Sanctification in the New Testament
    1. Statistics
    2. Usage that Stresses a Position of Being Set Apart
    3. Usages that Stress Moral Separation From Sin
    4. The Past Tense Aspect of Sanctification
    5. The Present Tense Aspect of Sanctification
    6. The Future Tense Aspect of Sanctification
    7. The Sanctifier
    8. The Means of Sanctification
VII. Eternal Security
  A. Evidence for Eternal Security
    1. Viewing the Subject From a Negative Perspective
      a. If a Christian Can Lose His Salvation, Then Christ Must Lose His Righteousness
      b. If a Christian Can Lose His Salvation, Then God is Not All Powerful and the Bible is Wrong on Predestination
      c. If a Christian Loses His Salvation by Misdeeds or Lack Of Works, then Salvation Would be Based on Works
      d. If a Christian Loses His Salvation and Goes to Hell Because of Sin, Then Christ's Atonement Must Not Have Perfectly Dealt With All Sins
      e. If a Christian Can Lose Salvation, Then God the Son Can Fail as an Intercessor or Advocate
      f. If a Christian Loses Salvation, Then the Holy Spirit Fails in His Sealing Ministry
      g. If a Christian Can Lose His Salvation, It Makes the Promises of the Bible Untrue
      h. If a Christian Can Lose His Salvation, Then God has Failed in His Intention to Keep Us
      i. If a Christian Can Lose Salvation, the Bible is Confusing for it Does Not Specify any Causes which Remove Salvation
    2. Viewing the Subject from a Positive Standpoint, Eternal Security is True for the Following Reasons:
      a. Christ's Righteousness Saves; One Cannot Lose Salvation
      b. Election and Predestination Prove Eternal Security
      c. Salvation Not Given or Maintained by Works
      d. Christ's Atonement Perfect and Complete
      e. Christ as Advocate Guarantees Security
      f. Holy Spirit's Seal Cannot be Broken
      g. Many Promises Guarantee Security
      h. God Keeps us by His Power
      i. No Scriptural Grounds for Losing Salvation
  B. Problem Passages Explained
    1. Psa. 51:11
    2. Ezek. 33:12-20
    3. Matt. 24:13
      a. Physical Salvation (Rescue) from the Tribulation
      b. Spiritual Salvation
        (1) Saving Faith
        (2) Tribulational Conditions
    4. Matt. 25:30
    5. John 15:1-8
      a. Judas as the Cut Branch
      b. Warning of Chastisement, Loss of Rewards View
    6. Rom. 11:11-32
      a. The Jew-Gentile Issue
      b. The Original Olive Tree

c. Gentile Relationship to the Olive Tree
d. Conclusion
7. 1 Cor. 6:9-10
8. 1 Cor. 9:24-27
9. 1 Cor. 11:28-32
10. 1 Cor. 15:1-2
11. Gal. 5:1-4
   a. Law Versus Grace
   b. No Benefit in This Life
   c. Severed From Christ
   d. Conclusion on Gal. 5:1-4
12. 2 Tim. 2:12b
13. Warning Passages from Hebrews
   a. The Original Readers of Hebrews
   b. First Passage – Heb 2:1-4
     (1) As Addressed to the Unsaved Among Hebrews
     (2) As Addressed to Believers
     (3) Conclusion
   c. Second Warning Passage – Heb. Chapters 3-4
     (1) As Addressed to Unsaved Among Hebrews
     (2) As Addressed to Believers
     (3) Conclusion
   d. Third Warning Passage – Heb. 6:1-12
     (1) As Addressed to Unbelievers
     (2) As Addressed to Believers
     (3) Conclusion
   e. Fourth Warning Passage – Heb. 10:26-31
     (1) As Addressed to Unbelievers
     (2) As Addressed to Believers
       (a) An Exposition of Hebrews 10:26-31
       (b) An Exposition of Hebrews 10:32-39
     (3) Conclusion
   f. Fifth Warning Passage – Heb. 12:25-29
     (1) As Addressed to Unbelievers
     (2) As Addressed to Believers

     (3) Conclusion
   g. Conclusion to the Warning Passages in Hebrews
14. James 2:18-26
15. James 5:19-20
16. 2 Pet. 1:10-11
17. 2 Pet. 2:20-22
18. 1 John 5:16
19. The Book of Life – Rev. 3:1-6
C. Conclusions on Eternal Security
VIII. Conclusions on Soteriology

Part 3

Results of Salvation

I. Eternal Life

Many familiar Biblical texts promise eternal or everlasting life to one who believes in Christ (John 3:15-16; 4:14; 5:24; 6:40, 47; 10:28; Rom. 6:23; 1 John 5:13).

> "Truly, truly, I say to you, he who hears My word, and believes Him who sent Me, has **eternal life**, and does not come into judgment, but has passed out of death into life" [John 5:24].

> "[A]nd I give **eternal life** to them, and they shall never perish; and no one shall snatch them out of My hand" [John 10:28].

> For the wages of sin is death, but the free gift of God is **eternal life** in Christ Jesus our Lord [Rom. 6:23].

> These things I have written to you who believe in the name of the Son of God, in order that you may know that you have **eternal life** [1 John 5:13].

The words giving the duration of life for those saved are also used of the duration of God's life in verses such as Rom. 16:26; 1 Tim.1:17 and Rev. 4:10. Thus, they refer to a life that never ends. Synonyms such as *never die* (John

11:25-26) and *immortality* (1 Cor. 15:51ff.; 2 Tim. 1:10) confirm this.

Eternal life does refer to length of life, but it is also a quality or kind of life. Christ defines eternal life as knowing God (John 17:3). The life given to a believer is in reality a sharing in Christ's own life. Christ's life is given to a believer. Christ's life never ends. Thus, the believer's life is eternal in duration. Verses which state that the essence of eternal life is a sharing in Christ's life include these:

> "After a little while the world will behold Me no more; but you will behold Me; **because I live, you shall live** also. In that day you shall know that I am in My Father, and **you in Me, and I in you**" [John 14:19–20].

> Therefore we have been buried with Him through baptism into death, in order that **as Christ was raised** from the dead through the glory of the Father, **so we too might walk in newness of life** [Rom. 6:4].

> "I have been crucified with Christ; and it is no longer I who live, but **Christ lives in me;** and the life which I now live in the flesh I live by faith in the Son of God, who loved me, and delivered himself up for me" [Gal. 2:20].

> [T]o whom God willed to make known what is the riches of the glory of this mystery among the Gentiles, which is **Christ in you**, the hope of glory [Col. 1:27].

> And when you were dead in your transgressions and the uncircumcision of your flesh, **He made you alive together with Him,** having forgiven us all our transgressions [Col. 2:13].

> If then you have been **raised up with Christ**, keep seeking the things above, where Christ is, seated at the right hand of God [Col. 3:1].

II. Regeneration – New Birth

Eternal life is initiated by the Holy Spirit (John 3:5ff.; Titus 3:5) using the Word of God. He convicts and enlightens through His own Word (James 1:18; 1 Pet. 1:23) so that faith can be expressed and the new life of Christ imparted. The beginning of sharing in Christ is called regeneration (Titus 3:5) or the new birth (John 3:5ff; 1 Pet. 1:3, 23; 1 John 5:1). Since regeneration is traditionally classified as a work of the Holy Spirit, it will be treated fully in Chapter 10.

III. Sonship/Adoption as Sons

Those who trust in Jesus Christ as Savior are granted eternal life and become part of God's family. Jesus said in Matt. 12:50 (also Mark 3:35 and Luke 8:21) that anyone who does God's will is a part of His family. It is even Scriptural to call Christ a brother (Rom. 8:29; Heb. 2:11-12).

The New Testament authors are in agreement that believers become a part of God's family, and they also differentiate between the sense in which Jesus Christ is the Son of God and the sense in which believers are sons of God. It is interesting that imagery and phraseology vary from author to author but the doctrinal result is the same. The Apostle John writes under the imagery of believers being born into God's family as children. (See *new birth*: in John 1:13; 3:3-8; 1 John 2:29; 3:9; 4:7; 5:1, 4, 18; and *children*: in John 1:12; 11:52; 1 John 3:1, 2, 10; 5:2.) John's way of placing a difference between believers as children of God and Christ as the Son of God is to reserve the Greek word for son (*huios*) for Christ and to stress that He is the "only begotten," i.e., unique Son (John 1:14, 18; 3:16, 18; 1 John 4:9).[62] Believers are born into God's family as children, but Christ is a unique **Son**.

Paul teaches the same truths, but his method is different than John's. Although Paul uses the word *children* (*tekna*) of believers as John does, unlike John, Paul calls believers "sons of

---

[62] The only exception seems to be Rev. 21:7 where *son* refers to believers.

God" *(huios)* (Rom. 8:14, 19; 2 Cor. 6:18; Gal. 3:26; 4:5-7). Paul does not emphasize the picture of a new birth or Christ being an only begotten Son.[63] His way of making a distinction between Christ's sonship and a believer's sonship is to liken a believer's sonship to adoption—a word John never uses. (For adoption at salvation, see Rom. 8:15; Gal. 4:5; and Eph. 1:5.)

These differences are a matter of preferred expression. John teaches that believers are a part of God's family but not in the same sense as Jesus Christ is God's Son. John speaks of a new birth as God's children but calls Christ an only begotten Son with a different sonship than believers. Paul also teaches that believers are a part of God's family but not in the same sense that Jesus Christ is God's Son. Paul speaks of adoption into God's family whereas Christ's sonship is not an adoption. He is God's Son in the fullest sense of the term.

IV. Justification

There are four important issues in developing a Biblical doctrine of justification. First, which is the proper definition of the term *to justify* (*dikaioo* in Greek)? Does it refer to a **process** of becoming more and more righteous? Or does it refer to a **declaration** of a person to be righteous (i.e., a legal declaration that the person is not guilty and has been acquitted)?

A second main factor is the time of justification. Is a person justified over a period of time, as he becomes more and more righteous? Or does justification take place at the moment of placing ones faith in Christ? The first view would mean that justification might not be secured until the final judgment. The second would maintain that justification has already occurred for a person who has faith.

The third issue that needs attention is the basis of justification. What must a human do to be justified? Finally, we must consider the source

of justification, Christ's righteousness.

The definition and timing of justification was a major battleground during the Reformation. The Roman Catholic position that confronted the Reformers contended that justification is a process whereby a person with faith in God could, by the grace conferred through sacraments, undergo a process of becoming more and more righteous in his conduct. The end of this process would be a justification that was viewed to take place eventually at the final judgment. Justification was understood as a goal for which man must strive. It was felt to be a process and a future potentiality.

In opposing the Roman Catholic position, the Reformers insisted that justification is a legal term. It does not mean "to become righteous," rather it means "to declare righteous." They also insisted that justification was not a process but an act and that a person was justified when he placed faith in Christ.

A. The Definition of Justification: To Make or To Declare Righteous?

There is overwhelming evidence that *to justify* (*dikaioo*) is a legal term meaning "to declare righteous, to acquit, to vindicate."

1. Justification in Secular Greek

Moulton and Milligan give these examples from ancient writings: "He **considered it just** that we should repay the capital sum and recover the mortgage" (A.D. 55-65). "The sum was **declared just** by the contract."[64] These two examples show that the Greek term *dikaioo* was a legal term meaning "to declare or consider just."

2. Justification in the Old Testament

The ancient Greek translations of the Old Testament show that ancient Hebrews regarded

---

[63] Paul comes close to the idea of being born again in 1 Cor. 4:15 and then uses the term regeneration in Titus 3:5.

[64] James Hope Houlton and George Milligan, *The Vocabulary of the Greek Testament* (1930: Hodder and Stoughton Limited, 1972) 162. Translations from the Greek are those of this author.

justification as a legal term. Justification is the opposite of condemnation. The Septuagint uses some form of *dikaioo* for these verses:

> "Keep far from a false charge, and do not kill the innocent or the righteous, for I will not **acquit** the guilty" [Ex. 23:7].

> "If there is a dispute between men and they go to court, and the judges decide their case, and they **justify** the righteous and **condemn** the wicked..." [Deut. 25:1].

> [T]hen hear Thou in heaven and act and judge Thy servants, **condemning** the wicked by bringing his way on his own head and **justifying** the righteous by giving him according to his righteousness [1 Kings 8:32].

> He who **justifies** the wicked, and he who **condemns** the righteous, both of them alike are an abomination to the LORD [Prov. 17:15].

> Who **justify** the wicked for a bribe, and take away the rights of the ones who are in the right! [Isa. 5:23].

Justification in the Old Testament is a forensic term. It is used in judicial contexts. It is the opposite of condemnation. English synonyms would be "to declare innocent," "to declare not guilty," "to acquit," "to vindicate." It is perhaps significant that in Dan. 8:14 the causative stem of *zedek*, which means, "to make righteous" is **not** translated by *dikaioo* in the Septuagint. Apparently, justification was not a suitable term for the idea of making righteous. On the contrary, justification means to "declare righteousness."

Not only is justification used in human law courts in the Old Testament, but also it is used of being declared righteous, vindicated before God's tribunal. Old Testament authors made preparation for complete New Testament revelation on the subject of justification. They taught that God will bestow His own right-eousness upon His people or that God will provide righteousness to His people. The Old Testament authors also taught that people will be justified. This means that justification will be based upon a bestowal of God's own right-eousness or in a more general sense a right-eousness that God Himself provides.

> "In the LORD all the offspring of Israel will be justified, and will glory" [Isa. 45:25].

> "I bring near **My righteousness**...And I will grant salvation in Zion, and My glory for Israel" [Isa. 46:13].

> ...My Servant, will justify the many, as **He** will bear their iniquities [Isa. 53:11].

> "...their **righteousness is from Me**," saith the Lord [Isa. 54:17 (KJV)].

> I will rejoice greatly in the LORD, my soul will exult in my God; For He has clothed me with garments of salvation, He has **wrapped me with a robe of righteousness**... [Isa. 61:10]. (See also Jer. 23:6.)

Many times in Isaiah, God's righteousness is said to be coming to bring salvation. The Old Testament is not as clear as the New Testament concerning the doctrine of justification. However, salvation is linked to **God's** coming **righteousness** and a justification was promised to the Old Testament saints. The suffering servant would bring about justification for many, and justification is based in God's own righteousness (Isa. 45:24) or, at least, a right-eousness He Himself provided for His people (Isa. 61:10). All of these truths prepared God's people for a deeper New Testament revelation on the doctrine of justification.

To this point the evidence shows that *justification (dikaioo)* was a legal term meaning "**to declare righteous**" both in secular Greek and in Hebrew thinking. Justification is the **opposite of condemnation**. The Old Testament also contains the idea of God providing righteousness for humans so that they could be justified. Any deviation from such a definition and the concept of God providing righteousness to a sinner would demand the strongest of evidence from the New Testament.

3. Justification in the New Testament

The New Testament usage of *dikaioo* (to justify) confirms the conclusions that have been given thus far. When *justification* is used of God, it is clear that the word means "to declare righteous" not "to make righteous." It is utterly impossible for God to be made more righteous! Thus, the word must mean to **declare** God righteous. Here are examples of God being justified:

> And all the people that heard him, and the publicans, **justified God,** being baptized with the baptism of John [Luke 7:29 (KJV)].

> May it never be! Rather, let **God** be found true, though every man be found a liar, as it is written, "**That thou mightest be justified** in Thy words..." [Rom. 3:4].

> And without controversy great is the mystery of godliness: **God** was manifest in the flesh, **justified in the Spirit**, seen of angels, preached unto the Gentiles, believed on in the world, received up into glory [1 Tim. 3:16 (KJV)].

The New Testament also has examples where justification is contrasted with condemnation. The opposite of condemnation is vindication, acquittal, and declaration of righteousness. In Matt. 12:37 Jesus says, "For by your words you shall be **justified,** and by your words you shall be **condemned**." The contrast of justification with condemnation in a context that speaks of the Day of Judgment testifies to the fact that *dikaioo* is a legal term and means to declare righteous. Paul also contrasts justification with condemnation.

> ...for on the one hand the judgment arose from one transgression resulting in **condemnation**, but on the other hand the free gift arose from many transgressions resulting in **justification** [Rom. 5:16].

> So then as through one transgression there resulted **condemnation** to all men, even so through one act of righteousness there resulted **justification** of life to all men [Rom. 5:18].

> Who will **bring a charge** against God's elect? God is the one who **justifies**; who is the one who **condemns?** [Rom. 8:33-34a].

> For if the ministry of **condemnation** has glory, much more does the ministry of righteousness [justification] abound in glory [2 Cor. 3:9].

The New Testament clearly uses justification as a legal term. This is apparent in Rom. 8:33-34 where Paul writes of **bringing charges** against God's elect. Rom. 2:13-16 speaks of a justification and of the Day of Judgment in close association. Justification has a legal and judicial nuance. It is a word suitable for a courtroom. Rom. 3:19-20 teaches that the Law proves the entire world is guilty before God. Into this legal setting, Paul proceeds to teach about justification. The reference to propitiation in Rom. 3:25 also forces attention upon the wrath of God as judge. There are also legal overtones in Galatians 3 where Paul alternately teaches about justification and a curse due to the Law. Finally, 2 Cor. 5:21 teaches that Christ became sin for us "that we might be made the righteousness (*justification* in Greek) of God in Him." *Righteousness* (justification) in 2 Cor. 5:21 must have a forensic sense because that is the only sense possible in which Christ became sin for us. He certainly did not sin in His actual conduct. Paul is referring to sin that was credited to Christ's account so that he legally took our sins. Likewise, justification must refer to a crediting of Christ's righteousness to believers so that we legally claim His righteous standing before God the Judge. *Justification* is a court-

173

room term. It speaks of being declared right-eous against the demands of a law. It need not actually refer to our doing of righteousness any more than Christ actually sinned.

Luke 10:29 provides a final proof that *to justify* means to declare righteous rather than to make righteous. This is the incident where the scribe asked Jesus about the greatest commandment. Jesus said the first is to love God and the second is to love one's neighbor. The text says, "But he desiring to justify himself said to Jesus, 'And who is my neighbor?' " This man did not act from the motive of wanting to become more and more righteous. He already thought he was plenty righteous. The meaning of *justify* is that the man wanted to vindicate himself. He wanted to declare his own righteousness to Jesus. His goal was to claim innocence of failing to love his neighbors because he did not know their identity. Obviously, *justification* in Luke 10:29 means to declare righteous rather than to become more and more righteous. Other verses where *to justify* equals *to vindicate* include Matt. 11:19; Luke 7:35, and 16:15.

4. Noting Usage of Greek Words Relating to Justification

By noting the usage of the Greek words relating to justification, we can have confidence that the Reformers were correct in their idea of justification. Justification is not a process by which one becomes more and more righteous. It is a judicial term meaning to declare right-eous, to acquit, to vindicate. This is proven by its usage in many judicial contexts, by its contrast with condemnation, and by its use in reference to God Himself (who cannot become more righteous but can be vindicated in His actions). To justify is to declare righteous and to acquit before God's justice. It is a declaration at a point in time; it is **not** a long arduous process. The next question of significance is the time of this declaration. Is justification past? Is it something that must await a final judgment in the future?

B. The Time of Justification: Past or Future?

Does God's acquittal before His justice come in this life, or is it granted at a future judgment when only those who have been persistent are declared righteous? Is justification an accomplished fact for a believer, or is it only a future goal and hope?

1. The Time of Salvation as a Background to the Time of Justification

It will be helpful in determining the time of justification to examine the time of salvation. Several key verses place salvation from sin's penalty in the past for a person with faith. A case could be made that these verses are among the most important in the Bible.

> "Truly, truly, I say to you, he who hears My word, and believes Him who sent Me, has eternal life, and does not come into judgment, but **has passed** [perfect tense, meaning an accomplished reality with continuing results] out of death into life" [John 5:24].

This statement asserts that the one who believes already possesses eternal life. His passage from death into life is a **past** event with results that continue in his present life.

> For by grace you **have been saved** through faith...not as a result of works, that no one should boast [Eph. 2:8-9].

Eph. 2:8 employs a periphrastic construction with a present tense verb and a perfect participle. The resulting teaching is that a person with faith has already been saved and is in an ongoing and abiding state of salvation. It is not surprising that Eph. 2:8-9 is a most cherished verse among Christians.

> He **saved** us, not on the basis of deeds which we have done in righteousness, but according to His mercy...[Titus 3:5].

Titus 3:5 discusses salvation as a past event using an aorist indicative. For a believer, salvation is an accomplished fact, not a future hope. 1 John 5:4 could also be included. It teaches that faith is the victory that "**has over-**

come" the world.

Even the verses that use the present tense of eternal life and of salvation still attest to salvation being an accomplished event for a believer (e.g., John 3:16,18, 36; 5:24 "has eternal life"; 6:40, 47, etc).

This is true because if a person is in the present time a possessor of eternal life, then it must be the case that he has already been saved at some prior point in time. It is also correct logic to assume that if a person has eternal life at the present time, he cannot lose it. If one could lose eternal life, then by definition, he never did possess a life that was truly everlasting. Therefore, for Christ to teach that a believer in Him already has eternal life means that salvation is an accomplished (past) event for a believer. This is why 1 John 5:12-13 assures us that believers can know they have eternal life.

These truths about the time of salvation are germane to the subject of the time of justification. It is inconceivable that one could already have salvation and eternal life without already having justification. It is inconceivable that one could already have a salvation based on faith without also having a justification based in faith. Therefore, as one approaches the texts, which concern the time of justification, there should be an expectation for finding in them the idea that justification is an accomplished fact for a Christian. (This does not rule out a future reaffirmation of a past declaration of righteousness on the Day of Judgment, e.g., Matt. 12:36-37).

2. Verbal Uses of *To Justify* in the Past Tense

The verbal forms of *to justify* (*dikaioo*) which are in the past tense confirm strongly that justification has already occurred for the believer. It is not the end culmination of a long process.

a. 1 Cor. 6:11

    And such were some of you; but you were washed, but you were sanctified, but you **were justified** in the name of

the Lord Jesus Christ, and in the Spirit of our God [1 Cor. 6:11].

Paul taught the Corinthians, a most unspiritual group, that they had already been justified. This declaration of righteousness did not await a future evaluation at the end of a life. The Corinthians already had been declared righteous.

Some might try to blunt the teaching of this verse by claiming that justification refers to being made more righteous rather than to being declared righteous. However, such a definition for the verb *to justify* is not clearly established by the New Testament. The New Testament usage of *to justify* leads to the conclusion that it means "to declare righteous" rather than "to become righteous." The two contexts which might allow the definition "to became righteous" (Rom. 6:7 and Rev. 22:11) can be just as easily interpreted to mean "to be acquitted" or "declared righteous." Furthermore, in the 1 Cor. 6:11 context a meaning of "to become more righteous" would be redundant because of the words *wash* and *sanctify*. There is no basis for altering Paul's definition of *to justify*.

b. Titus 3:7 (NIV)

    [S]o that, **having been justified** by his grace, we might become heirs having the hope of eternal life [Titus 3:7 (NIV)].

In Greek the time of a participle is contingent upon the time of a leading verb in a sentence. Since the Bible teaches that believers are already heirs in anticipation of everlasting life (Rom. 8:16-17; Gal. 4:7; etc.), Titus 3:7 asserts that we have already been justified (aorist passive participle used with an aorist subjunctive passive verb). Believers became heirs in the past and justification took place prior to this (at least in its logical order).

c. Rom. 5:1, 9

    Therefore **having been justified** by faith, we have peace with God through our Lord Jesus Christ....Much more then, **having now been justified** by His blood, we shall be saved from the wrath of God through Him [Rom. 5:1, 9].

Both Rom. 5:1 and 9 use aorist participles. These denote a time prior to the time of the leading verb. The manuscripts differ as to whether the main verb in Rom. 5:1 is indicative (we have peace) or subjunctive (let us have peace), but either way the tense is present. The Romans either had or should have peace with God in the present and justification had already preceded the present. The Romans had already been justified by faith. The declaration of righteousness had already occurred and did not await a future judgment in the after life. This conclusion is reinforced by the word *now* in v. 9. Also, the *therefore* of verse one points back to Romans 4, which teaches that a believer already has justification.

d. Rom. 6:7 (NIV)

> [B]ecause anyone who has died has been freed [lit., has been justified] from sin [Rom. 6:7].

In its context Rom. 6:7 is dealing with the resources that a believer has for overcoming sin. Rom. 6:7 literally says, "For he who dies has been justified from the sin." There is no reason for seeing a new definition for justification in this context. Paul's point is that those who have died with Christ have been declared righteous, acquitted, released from the charges of sin. In the context his reason for saying this is that such a release from the charges of sin also implies a release from sin's power. The courtroom imagery is still appropriate. Because the believer has been legally cleared of the charges of sin, sin has no obligation or inevitable hold on his life. The declaration of acquittal (i.e., justification) has led to a freedom from sin's obligation upon a believer (either its penalty or power). Because of the context, translators usually render "has been justified" as "has been freed." This is fine. The believer's justification was an acquittal or re-

lease from sin's charges that resulted in sin not having any more hold or obligation upon the person. While Rom. 6:7 in context is emphasizing the particular blessing of justification's release from sin's penalty and power, one must still realize that the original word means "has been **justified**." Furthermore, the tense teaches that **justification has already taken place** with continuing results. Justification is not a declaration that awaits the end of life. It has already occurred for every believer.

e. Rom. 8:30

> [A]nd whom He predestined, these He also called; and whom He called, these He also **justified**; and whom He **justified**, these He also glorified [Rom. 8:30].

Viewed strictly from God's own eternal and timeless perspective, the past tense of *to justify* in Rom. 8:30 would teach little about the time of justification in a man's life. From God's timeless perspective justification took place before the world was created, and Rom. 8:30 is giving a logical order rather than a chronological order.

However, it is likely that Rom. 8:30 also is intended to say something about the timing of predestination, calling, justification, and glorification. Certainly, it gives the order of these actions as they were worked out in human time (i.e., predestination in eternity past, next the call, then justification, and finally glorification). Also, the application of these truths in the following verses (i.e., Rom. 8:31-39) seems to indicate that justification had already taken place for the Romans. Verse 34 teaches that Christ is presently at the right hand of God interceding for us. This present ministry of Christ protected the Romans from all charges of sin (v. 33) and all condemnation (v. 34). Justification is the opposite of being charged with sin and of being legally condemned before God. Since Christ's present ministry was keeping the believers in Rome from being charged with sin and condemned before God as judge, it is an inescapable conclusion that Paul was teaching that the Romans had already been justified. Therefore, it is preferable to give the past tense of *to justify* its full force in Rom. 8:30: **believers have already been justified**.

3. Verbal Uses of *To Justify* in the Present Tense

There is a method to the order of the material presented in this study. A study of justification must first carefully define the term *justification*. For generations some confused the Bible's teachings about justification because they had the wrong definition. For them, verses which use *justify* in the present tense, would be especially troublesome.

If justification is viewed as a process of becoming more and more righteous, then a present tense usage seems to teach works. Rom. 3:28 which states, "A man is justified by faith" is taken to mean "a man who has faith is involved in a process of being gradually justified by becoming more and more righteous." Thus, a pre-Reformation Catholic could read a statement about a present justification by faith and miss the whole point. Blinded by a false definition, such words were taken to reinforce a long process of works in order to obtain God's future declaration of an actual righteousness worked out in living instead of an imputation of Christ's righteousness. When Luther and others discovered the truth that *to justify* is a judicial term meaning **to declare righteous** (instead of to make more and more righteous), the dark ages were over. Justification is not a process of becoming more righteous.[65] It is a judicial act wherein God declares one to be legally righteous before Himself as judge. This correct definition revolutionizes the impact of the present tense in the statement, "a man is justified by faith."

The present tense usually signifies an action that is taking place in the present tense and an action that is durative or linear (i.e., **ongoing**

and lasting) in nature. The precise definition of *to justify (diakaioo)* is "to declare righteous"; the definition is not "to make righteous." The present tense cannot possibly signify a process of becoming justified. A declaration is by definition an act rather than a process. A person is either declared righteous in Christ, or he is not declared righteous in Christ. To be in some alleged "process" towards justification is to be unjustified. The statement in Rom. 3:28 that "a man is justified by faith" means a man is **declared righteous** when there is faith. If one denies that a declaration of righteousness occurs at the moment of faith, then he is saying it is possible to have faith but to remain unjustified. Yet, this is a flat contradiction to what the sentence is teaching when the correct definition of justification is maintained.

When the present tense of *to justify* is used in the statement "a man is justified by faith," the meaning can be no other than **a man with faith is in the present declared righteous**. The only proper deduction is that the initial declaration of righteousness must have been simultaneous with an initial faith. When faith became a present reality so did the initial declaration of righteousness. If one desires to push the ongoing aspect to the present tense, then the emphasis is also upon the fact that God continues in the present time to attest to this declaration of righteousness. God initially justifies when faith exists, and He continues to attest to this justification in the present.

There is no basis for the Roman Catholic view of justification being a future goal at the end of a long process that culminates in the judgment day. The past tense usages of *to justify* reveal justification as an accomplished reality. The present tense usage of *to justify* results in the same teaching that justification has already been accomplished (or at least they do so as long as the correct definition of *to justify* is used). Since a declaration of righteousness must be present when faith is present, it is true that justification is a past reality when viewed from the perspective of looking back upon an

---

[65] Such a concept clearly violates the truth that salvation does not come through good works.

initial conversion. Justification first occurred when faith occurred. Thus, it may be considered past. Furthermore, **God in the present still declares the justification of a believer.**

The present tense in the line "a man is justified by faith" does not mean a man is gradually becoming more and more righteous by faith. On the contrary, it is teaching that justification was first present when faith was present. Thus, looking back, a believer views justification as an accomplished fact. The statement also teaches that for believers this declaration of righteousness is **still in force** at any subsequent time up to and including **the present.**[66]

a. Acts 13:39 (NIV)

> Through him everyone who believes is justified from everything from which you could not be justified by the Law of Moses [Acts 13:39 NIV].

When an accurate definition of justification is understood, Acts 13:39 is teaching that one who believes presently possesses a declaration of righteousness before God's justice.

b. Rom. 3:28

> For we maintain that a man is justified by faith apart from works of the Law [Rom. 3:28].[67]

Again this verb would be confusing if *justification* is defined as "becoming or making righteous." Once it is understood that *to justify* is a judicial term meaning to declare righteous, then the verse can be interpreted correctly. Paul is teaching that one who has faith is a present possessor of

God's verdict of acquittal. The one who has faith possesses vindication, i.e., a declaration of righteousness, before God's justice. Obviously this justification first occurred when faith occurred. Thus, justification can be viewed as an accomplished fact. It is also a present reality because God's declaration of righteousness is still presently in force for a believer.

c. Rom. 3:24

> [B]eing justified as a gift by His grace through the redemption which is in Christ Jesus [Rom. 3:24].

The phrase *being justified* in Rom. 3:24 does not speak of a gradual process of justification for an individual. It is best to view the verb corporately as Rom. 3:23 views humanity as one group, "...all have sinned." Any progression in the term *being justified* refers to the process of the elect as a whole gradually obtaining individual justification as each is justified by personal faith.[68] When the human race is viewed as a group, it is true that the outworking of justification for the elect through history is a gradual process. Yet, there is no basis for thinking that justification is gradual for an individual. On the individual level, justification has already occurred in the past and is a present possession for one with faith. The words *gift* and *grace* in this verse also forbid the notion that justification of an individual is based upon a long process of effort.

d. Others

Present tense participles occur in Rom. 3:26; 4:5 and 8:33. All are in reference to God. They mean the "one who justifies" or can be translated as "the justifier."

> ...the justifier of the one who has faith in Jesus [Rom. 3:26].

> But to the one who does not work, but

---

[66] Those who have initial saving faith are kept in the faith in the present. (See 1 Pet. 1:4-5 and 1 John 2:19.) Thus, **believers are still being declared righteous in Christ.**

[67] The Greek form of the word *justify* is a present infinitive. However, it is what is called an infinitive of direct discourse. As such, the present tense infinitive reflects a present tense verb. Thus, translators (KJV, NASV, NIV) translate the infinitive as if it were a present tense verb.

[68] Another option would be to take the present tense as a constant present declaration of righteousness of the individual believer as explained in the preceding section.

believes in Him who justifies the ungodly, his faith is reckoned as righteousness [Rom 4:5].

...God is the one who justifies [Rom. 8:33].

These verses certainly give no encouragement to the idea that justification is a future event based upon the results of a process. God is presently involved in the act of justification. He presently declares as just the person who has faith in Christ. By deduction this also means the verdict of righteousness first occurred at the initial presence of faith and is still in force. Rom. 3:26 could be paraphrased "God is He who declares just the one who has faith in Jesus."

4. Verses Which Speak of Justification as a Potentiality

Sometimes Paul uses a verb form that neither speaks of justification in the past nor in the present tense, but rather speaks of justification as a potential blessing **if** one will meet God's condition. In these verses the verbal tense alone is insufficient to prove justification is a completed act. However, the overall statement does lead to the conclusion that those who have met God's condition, i.e., faith, already have obtained justification.

a. Gal. 2:16-17

[N]evertheless knowing that a man is not justified by the works of the Law but through faith in Christ Jesus, even we have believed in Christ Jesus, that **we may be justified by faith** in Christ, and not by the works of the Law; since by the works of the Law shall no flesh be justified. But if, while seeking to be justified in Christ, we ourselves have also been found sinners, is Christ then a minister of sin?...[Gal. 2:16-17].

Verse 16 teaches that Paul **believed** in order to be justified. Technically, such a verbal tense does not state the time justification occurs. However, in Gal. 2:17 Paul reacts with horror

that one who believed in Christ could still be declared a guilty sinner in a judicial sense before the throne of God's justice. This would imply not only that Christ is a failure but a false prophet. Obviously, Paul is teaching that those with faith are no longer viewed as condemned sinners. The conclusion that Paul regarded justification as an accomplished reality for those who have believed is inescapable.

b. Gal. 3:8-9

And the Scripture, foreseeing that **God would justify** the Gentiles by faith, preached the gospel beforehand to Abraham, saying, "All the nations shall be blessed in you." So then those who are of faith are blessed with Abraham, the believer [Gal. 3:8,9].

The tense of *justify* in v. 8 does not alone give the time of justification. It speaks of justification in potential terms. However, verse 9 teaches that those with faith already share in Abraham's blessings. In the context, the most pronounced blessing is justification. Believers already have justification.

c. Gal. 3:24-26

Therefore the Law has become our tutor to lead us to Christ, that **we may be justified by faith**. But now that faith has come, we are no longer under a tutor. For you are all sons of God through faith in Christ Jesus [Gal. 3:24-26].

The clause, "That we might be justified by faith," does not give the exact time of justification. Yet, following statements indicate that the goal of the Law's instruction (i.e., justification in Christ) has already been obtained for those with faith. The Law can be abrogated because justification by faith is a present reality rather than merely a future goal at the end of a long process.

5. Abraham's Example

Paul's outstanding example of justification is the patriarch Abraham. Abraham certainly did not await the end of his life or a future judgment for justification to occur. Abraham possessed justification when he had faith. Thus, justification was for Abraham, our example, a past decree and a present reality. (Rom. 4:3, 9, 11; Gal. 3:6, 9)

> For what does the Scripture say? "And Abraham believed God, and it was reckoned to him as righteousness" [justification] [Rom. 4:3].

> Even so Abraham believed God, and it was reckoned to him as righteousness [justification] [Gal. 3:6].

6. Noun Forms of Justification that Present an Accomplished Fact

a. Justification

Usually, Greek is more specific than English. However, this is not so with the word *righteousness (dikaiosunee)*. When the reader sees the word *righteousness*, it may refer to an actual righteousness or a declared righteousness, i.e., justification. The word form is identical. Only the context gives a clue to the intended meaning. The reader must be sensitive to whether the context deals with the doctrine of salvation or the doctrine of Christian living. If the topic is salvation, the righteousness probably means declared or imputed righteousness, i.e., justification. If the context is Christian living, then the intended meaning is probably an actual righteousness. One good way to derive the author's intention is to substitute the word *justification* for *righteousness* and see if it fits the context. There are many usages of the word *righteousness* that mean "declared righteousness." These texts also establish the fact that God's declaration of righteousness has already occurred for those with faith.

(1) Rom. 3:22

> ...even the righteousness [justification] of God through faith in Jesus Christ for all those who believe; for there is no distinction [Rom. 3:22].

This statement is teaching that "declared righteousness" comes through faith and belongs to **all** who believe. The immediate context deals with a judicial situation in which the entire world is guilty before God as judge (vv. 19-20). In the extended argument of the book, it is clear that justification is the opposite of condemnation (Rom. 5:16, 18, etc). Thus, the word *righteousness* means *justification*, and it is offered to **all** that believe.

(2) Rom. 4:5

> But to the one who does not work, but believes in Him who justifies the ungodly, his faith is reckoned as righteousness [justification] [Rom. 4:5].

Negatively, Rom. 4:5 teaches that justification is not based upon works. Positively, it is based upon faith. The tense of the verb *is reckoned* establishes that when faith is present so is a declared righteousness. This is perhaps the best section in which to discuss the term *imputation*. The translation of the King James Version in Rom. 4:5 is fine. It reads "is counted." The word basically means "to take into account" mentally. We would say, "to consider, to reckon, to count." A closely related word refers to "putting to one's account" in a financial sense. The best New Testament illustration is Philemon 18. (See also Rom. 5:13.)

> But if he has wronged you in any way, or owes you anything, **charge that to my account** [Philem. 18].

It is very likely Paul has this specific meaning in mind in Rom. 4:5 and similar statements. God credits a declared righteousness to the account of one who believes. Theologians call the transferal of Christ's righteousness to a believer's account "imputation."

(3) Rom. 5:17

> For if by the transgression of the one, death reigned through the one, much more those who receive the abundance of grace and of the gift of righteousness [justification] will reign in life through the One, Jesus Christ [Rom. 5:17].

Romans 5:17 does not give the time of justification, but it states clearly that it is a gift.

(4) Rom. 9:30

What shall we say then? That Gentiles, who did not pursue righteousness [justification], attained righteousness [justification], even the righteousness [justification] which is by faith [Rom. 9:30].

In the context Paul is speaking of the salvation of the Gentiles (Rom. 9:24) and Jews (Rom. 10:1, 12). Righteousness in Rom. 9:30 should be taken to refer to declared righteousness or justification. Those who had faith, even among the Gentiles, had already obtained justification. Justification is something that can be obtained in this life and is not just a future goal or hope.

(5) Rom.10:4, 6a, 10a

For Christ is the end of the law for righteousness [justification] to everyone who believes....But the righteousness [justification] based upon faith speaks thus....for with the heart man believes, resulting in righteousness [justification]...[Rom. 10:4, 6a, 10a].

It would be difficult to miss that the topic of Romans 10 is salvation rather than holy living (Rom. 10:1, 9, 12-13, etc.). Therefore, Paul intends righteousness to be understood as declared or imputed righteousness, i.e., justification. Verse four teaches that justification is a very present reality. It is granted on the basis of faith. Furthermore, it is granted to **everyone** who believes. Also, verse 10 is very clear that justification is something that a believer already possesses rather than something for which he strives to obtain.

(6) 1 Cor. 1:30

But by His doing you are in Christ Jesus, who became to us wisdom from God, and righteousness [justification], and sanctification, and redemption [1 Cor. 1:30].

Righteousness in 1 Cor. 1:30 is best understood as justification, i.e., imputed righteousness. This prevents redundancy with the term sanctification. The verb is in the past tense signifying that justification is already accomplished for a believer.

b. Greek Form for a *Just* Person

The Greek term for a *just* or *righteous* person *(dikaios)* is also capable of meaning one who is "righteous in action" or one who has been "declared righteous." Most of the time it refers to righteous behaviors as in the statement, "Joseph, her husband, was a just man, and not willing to make her a public example" (Matt. 1:19). However, the New Testament quotes Hab. 2:4 three times, and, in these references, *just* refers to "one declared righteous" (Rom. 1:17; Gal. 3:11; Heb. 10:38).

(1) The Old Testament Background (Hab. 2:4)

The prophet Habakkuk was concerned over the Babylonian invasion. He challenged God as to the propriety of allowing Babylon to conquer Israel. Part of God's answer to this challenge is contained in Hab. 2:4: "But the righteous man will live by his faith (or faithfulness)." This statement is capable of two meanings. It could mean the one declared just by faith will continue to have eternal life even in time of trouble. This statement would provide some comfort to the believers in Judah who were going to experience tough times. The line could also mean "a righteous man will survive (live physically through the invasion) due to his faithfulness."[69] Perhaps God

---

[69] Heb. 10:38 takes Hab. 2:4 to mean that a justified person should live a life of faithfulness. The Old Testament saints listed in Hebrews 11 illustrate this interpretation of Hab. 2:4. Paul, in Rom. 1:16-17 and Gal. 3:11, takes Habakkuk's words to refer to justification by faith. It must be that both ideas are compatible with God's intent for the original Old Testament statement. The fact that Heb.10:38 takes Hab. 2:4 to refer to lifelong faithfulness helps explain why this writer felt it necessary to include

intended both ideas for the people of Habak-kuk's time.

(2) Paul's Quote of Hab. 2:4

Although Hab. 2:4 may have also given hope by promising physical life for the faithful and just, Paul definitely either interpreted or applied the passage also to teach that the justified one shall live spiritually because of faith. The phrase alone is capable of either meaning, but it is located in New Testament contexts that definitely refer to spiritual life and definitely refer to declared righteousness instead of actual righteousness.

(a) Rom. 1:16-17

> For I am not ashamed of the gospel, for it is the power of God for salvation to everyone who believes, to the Jew first and also to the Greek. For in it the righteousness [justification] of God is revealed from faith to faith; as it is written, "But the righteous man [the just] shall live by faith" [Rom. 1:16, 17].

Paul's specific meaning of the statement, "the just shall live by faith" is made clear by the argument in the rest of the book. While the words "the righteous man shall live by faithfulness" could be misconstrued to teach works, the rest of the book would never allow such an interpretation. Rom. 1:16-17 is giving one of the theses of Romans. From the rest of the book one knows that Paul in Rom. 1:17a means, "The justified one shall have eternal life because of his faith."

We should consider that the quote of Hab. 2:4 is really just a secondary support to the main statement in Rom. 1:16-17a. The main statement is that "the righteousness [justification] of God is revealed...to [those with] faith." Clearly, the subject is salvation (v. 16). The phrase "righteousness of (or from) God" refers to a justification that He gives based on His

own (Christ's) righteousness (cf. Rom. 3:21-22; 10:4), and one of the key topics in the book is a declared righteousness. Therefore, the first part of verse 17 is dealing with the topic of justification, and so must the quote, "The just shall live by faith." As with all other avenues of evidence, Paul, in Rom. 1:17, is conceiving of justification as a present blessing for a believer rather than something that he hopes to obtain in the future. One satisfactory way to take the phrase "from faith to faith" is to view the ongoing faith to be constant individual conversions throughout human history. The next verse (Rom. 1:18) refers to God's wrath being revealed throughout time against sin. Therefore, Rom. 1:17 could be paraphrased this way: "For by it (the gospel) the declared righteousness of God is revealed through the ages from the faith of one to the faith of the next" (i.e., on and on in progression).

(b) Gal. 3:11

> Now that no one is justified by the Law before God is evident; for, "The righteous man [the just] shall live by faith" [Gal. 3:11].

Rom. 1:17 gives the first statement of a thesis, and so the student must read further to be certain how Paul takes the phrase, "The just shall live by faith." However, Gal. 3:11 lies in the middle of a book and in the middle of an argument. Paul clearly refers to a declared righteousness in Gal. 3:6, (Abraham's imputed righteousness), and he clearly is in a context focusing upon judicial matters (the Law's curse, Gal. 3:10).

Therefore, the "just shall live by faith" must mean that one declared just by faith will continue to have spiritual (eternal) life. Paul either believed this was the consoling hope that bolstered the Hebrews in Habakkuk's day, or at the very least he was led by the Holy Spirit to apply the phrase in this manner.

7. Conclusion on the Time of Justification

The notion that justification is a process that

---

material showing how Paul understood this key Old Testament passage.

occurs over a lifetime is nonsense. Regardless of the angle from which the topic of justification is approached (the past tense of salvation, verbal tenses past and present, verses in which justification is given as a potential, Abraham's example, or uses of the noun), the **Bible teaches justification as an accomplished and settled matter for those with faith**. (See also verses which teach a lack of condemnation: John 5:24; Rom. 8:1, 33-34)

C. The Basis of Justification: Faith

In order to discuss the definition and time of justification, it has been necessary to overlap with the point that the basis of justification is faith. It was deemed best to first define justification before concentrating fully upon its basis. Now attention will be concentrated upon verses that teach justification is based upon faith in Christ. The evidence for justification by faith is so overwhelming that it is difficult to understand how anyone could deny that salvation is by faith alone. There **is no such thing as an unjustified or unsaved believer!** Here are some representative verses with a more complete list of references:

1. Texts Which Base Justification Upon Faith in Christ

a. Verbal forms of *to justify*: Acts 13:39; Rom. 3:26, 28, 30; 4:5; 5:1, 9; Gal. 2:16-17; 3:8; and 3:24

b. The noun *justification*: (i.e., a declared righteousness): Rom. 1:17; 3:22; 4:3, 5, 9, 11, 13, 22-24; 9:30; 10:4, 6, 10; Gal. 3:6; and Heb. 11:7

c. The noun form *just*: Rom. 1:17; Gal. 3:11; and Heb. 10:38

> For we maintain that a man is justified by **faith** apart from works of the Law [Rom. 3:28].

> But to the one who does not work, but **believes** in Him who justifies the ungodly, his **faith** is reckoned as righteousness [Rom. 4:5].

> Therefore, having been justified **by faith,** we have peace with God through our Lord Jesus Christ....Much more then, having now been justified by His blood, we shall be saved from the wrath of God through Him [Rom. 5:1, 9].

> And the Scripture, foreseeing that God would justify the Gentiles by faith, preached the gospel beforehand to Abraham, saying, "All the nations shall be blessed in you." So then **those who are of faith are blessed** with Abraham, the believer [Gal. 3:8-9].

> ...even the righteousness [justification] of God through **faith** in Jesus Christ for **all those who believe**; for there is no distinction [Rom. 3:22]

> For Christ is the end of the law for righteousness [justification] to everyone who **believes** [Rom. 10:4].

> [F]or with the heart man **believes**, resulting in righteousness [justification]...[Rom.10:10a].

2. Texts Which Teach Justification is Freely Given by Grace

> ...being justified as a **gift** by His **grace** through the redemption which is in Christ Jesus [Rom. 3:24].

> For if by the transgression of the one, death reigned through the one, much more those who receive the abundance of **grace** and of the **gift** of righteousness [justification] will reign in life through the One, Jesus Christ [Rom. 5:17].

> [S]o that, having been justified by his **grace**, we might become heirs having the hope of eternal life [Titus 3:7 (NIV)].

3. Texts Which Teach Justification Is Not by Works

a. Verbal forms of *justify*: Acts 13:39; Rom. 3:20; 4:2; Gal. 2:16; 3:11

b. Noun forms of *justification*, i.e., declared righteous: Rom. 4:5; 9:31; Gal. 2:21; 3:21

> Through him everyone who believes is justified from everything **you could not be justified from by the Law** of Moses [Acts 13:39a (NIV)].

> [B]ecause **by the works of the Law no flesh will be justified in His sight**; for through the Law comes the knowledge of sin [Rom. 3:20].

> But **to the one who does not work,** but believes in Him who justifies the ungodly, his faith is reckoned as righteousness [Rom. 4:5].

> Now that **no one is justified by the Law** before God is evident; for, "The righteous man shall live by faith" [Gal. 3:11].

D. The Source of the Believer's Righteousness

When God declares one just on the basis of faith, He is not declaring a lie. He is not declaring righteous that which is unrighteous. It is undeniably true that all humans are unrighteous in their actual deeds. However, the New Testament teaches that Christ's righteousness is credited to the account of a believer. Thus, God looks at Christ's righteousness, not the believer's. On the basis of Christ's righteousness, which is given to a believer, God can truthfully declare that a believer is legally righteous. It is Christ's righteousness that saves, not our own. Since He can never lose this righteousness, a believer can never lose salvation. The believer's legal standing before God is based upon Christ's eternal and unblemished righteousness. This definition of justification must include that the declaration is based upon Christ's righteousness legally credited to a believer, **not self's** righteousness (which is still unrighteousness even at its best, Isa. 64:6).

1. The Old Testament Background for God's Righteousness Being Credited to God's People.

The Old Testament, particularly in the Major Prophets, gives a background to the idea that God would provide His own righteousness to His people and then declare for them a righteous standing before His law. Some verses relate salvation to God's righteousness in a general way (Isa. 45:17; 46:13; 51:5; and 59:16-17). Others teach that God would provide a righteousness for man that he might be considered just (Isa. 53:11; 54:17(KJV); 61:10). Some even teach that God would give His own righteousness to man (Isa. 45:25; Jer. 23:6; 33:16).

2. The New Testament Teaching About God's Righteousness Being Credited to God's People

The phrase *the righteousness of God* refers both to a righteousness that belongs to God and a righteousness that comes from God to men. In the argument of the book of Romans, the phrase *the righteousness of God* can mean God's righteousness that is imputed to believers (Rom. 1:17; 3:21-22; 10:3-4). To be even more specific, Christ's righteousness is credited to a believer's ledger relative to his legal standing with God. (See also our standing **in Him** in Rom. 5:10; Eph. 1:7; 3:12; Col. 2:10).

> For if by the transgression of the one, death reigned through the one, much more those who receive the abundance of grace and of the gift of righteousness will reign in life **through the One**, Jesus Christ. So then as through one transgression there resulted condemnation to all men, even so **through one act of righteousness** there resulted justification of life to all men. For as through the one man's disobedience the many were made sinners, even so **through the obedience of the One** the many will be made righteous [Rom. 5:17-19].

> But by His doing you are in **Christ Jesus,** who became to us wisdom from

God, and righteousness [justification] and sanctification, and redemption [1 Cor. 1:30].

He made Him who knew no sin to be sin on our behalf, that we might become **the righteousness of God in Him** [2 Cor. 5:21].

E. Conclusion on Justification

The above study has considered and classified **all** New Testament references to justification. The term clearly refers to a declaration of righteousness by God as Judge, not a process of becoming more and more righteous. All with faith in Christ have already been justified in the past with assurance that they remain justified in the present. God may reaffirm the believer's justification at the future judgment day. A possible reference is Matt. 12:37, but the context indicates those being addressed will all be condemned because of rejecting Christ. However, any future declaration of justification only repeats and confirms a settled matter. Justification has already taken place for believers. Confidence of one's justification by faith is not an unsettled matter awaiting a future outcome. Justification by faith is a past result of salvation and also a present possession of all believers.

V. Good Works

A. Genuine Salvation Results in Good Works

The New Testament authors are consistent on the point that genuine saving faith results in good works. It is not that faith plus works equals salvation but, rather, that faith equals salvation plus good works. A quote commonly attributed to John Calvin says this: "Faith alone saves, but the type of faith that saves is not alone." Good works are not required before salvation, but they do generally describe one who has been saved.

For by grace you have been saved through faith; and that not of yourselves, it is the gift of God; not as a result of works, that no one should boast.

For we are His workmanship, created in Christ Jesus **for good works**, which God prepared beforehand, that we should walk in them [Eph. 2:8-10].

But someone may well say, "You have faith, and I have works; show me your faith [intellectual faith] without the works, and I will show you my faith [trust] by my works"....For just as the body without the spirit is dead, so also faith without works is dead [James 2:18, 26].

B. Genuine Salvation Is Not Consistent with the **Habitual Practice** of Sin

Or do you not know that the unrighteous shall not inherit the kingdom of God? Do not be deceived; neither fornicators, nor idolaters, nor adulterers, nor effeminate, nor homosexuals, nor thieves, nor the covetous, nor drunkards, nor revilers, nor swindlers, shall inherit the kingdom of God [1 Cor. 6:9-10].

Some may interpret "inherit the kingdom" here as a reference to full rewards. However, the same phrase refers to glorification in 1 Cor. 15:50.

Now the deeds of the flesh are evident, which are: immorality, impurity, sensuality, idolatry, sorcery, enmities, strife, jealousy, outbursts of anger, disputes, dissentions, factions, envying, drunkenness, carousing, and things like these, of which I forewarn you just as I have forewarned you that those who **practice** such things shall not inherit the kingdom of God [Gal. 5:19-21].

For this you know with certainty, that no immoral or impure person or covetous man, who is an idolater, has an inheritance in the kingdom of Christ and God [Eph. 5:5].

Little children, let no one deceive you; the one who practices righteousness is righteous, just as He is righteous; the one who **practices** sin is of the devil....No one who is born of God **practices** sin, because His seed abides in him; and he cannot sin, because he is born of God [1 John 3:7, 8a, 9].

C. Consistency with the Doctrines of Eternal Security and Non-eradication of Sin

The truths that a believer is eternally secure and is still capable of sinning require that the verses in the preceding section are referring to the habitual practice of sin rather than an occasional sin. Paul is not saying in Gal. 5:19-21 that one act of immorality, strife, jealousy, anger, envy, or drunkenness causes a loss of salvation or indicates that a person has never been saved. He is referring to the habitual practice of sin. Modern language might refer to this as a "lifestyle." Those with a lifestyle of wickedness without remorse give indication that they have never been saved. The habitual practice and ongoing nature of sin is also expressed by the word *practice* in Gal. 5:21 and the durative nature of the present tense in 1 John 3. While it is possible for a Christian to commit acts of sin, those who **practice** sin give evidence that they never had a saving faith.

D. Practical Considerations

God obviously intended for the truth that salvation results in good works to have practical applications. However because the eternal destiny of a soul is at stake, there must be great care to make valid applications.

1. Caution About a Categorical Denial of Salvation Based on Sinfulness Alone

Salvation results in good works. How much? When? Genuine salvation does not coexist with habitual sin. What is habitual sin? Once a month? Once a day? Ultimately, we are ignorant on what constitutes the habitual practice of sin. If a person lives for the Lord Jesus Christ for five years and then strays for the next three, is he a practicing sinner? The New Testament definitely teaches that Christians

can be sinners (Rom. 6:12; Gal. 5:17ff.). Although God has given us the overall truths, we must confess ignorance of the specifics. If a person understands the death, burial, and resurrection of Christ; acknowledges Jesus is the Christ, the Son of God; and professes to have sincerely trusted in Him for salvation from sin, it is not possible to categorically and dogmatically deny he is saved based upon a lack of good works. A third party simply does not know exactly what constitutes "habitual sin" in the life of another. Denying all possibility of salvation on the basis of a deficient life alone must be avoided. 2 Tim. 2:19 teaches that, ultimately, "the Lord knows those who are His."

2. Tentative Doubts

What should one's attitude be toward those who profess Christ but do not live as a Christian ought? While we may not have the authority to assert, "You are definitely not saved regardless of your profession," it is certainly proper to have doubts, to express doubts, and to act upon them. There are liars who profess salvation because of social pressures to do so. There are liars who profess faith in order to infiltrate Christ's people. There are also many people who honestly think they are saved but have merely intellectual and/or emotional faith. There is a difference between a dogmatic denial that another is saved and a tentative doubt about their salvation. There is a difference between saying, "I know you aren't saved regardless of what you profess," and saying, "I'm not sure you are saved because of your life." It may not be proper to assert with full confidence another is lost based upon ones evaluation of his life, but it is proper to have doubts and to encourage one who professes faith but lives in sin to examine his life as to whether he really understands salvation. Furthermore, while church leaders should be cautious about telling professing Christians they are not saved, they must also exclude from involvement in positions of authority any in the church whose salvation is in question because of sin.

3. Self-examination

God did not teach that salvation results in good works so that professing Christians could be the final judges of each other's salvation. The primary reason for the Bible stating that a practicing sinner is not saved is that it forces the individual to a self-examination of his own life. Those who are heavily involved in sin should react to the fact that the saved are not practicing sinners with a thorough self-examination as to whether they fully understand the gospel and are sincerely trusting Christ. Others should not so much judge those in sin as being definitely unsaved, but rather their main concern should be to encourage them to a self-examination as Paul did in 2 Cor. 13:5.

> Test yourselves to see if you are in the faith; examine yourselves!...[2 Cor. 13:5].

4. A Dangerous Reaction to Sinful Professors of Christian Faith

It is quite proper to have doubts about the salvation of those engaged in ongoing sin. The correct reaction is to encourage them to self-examination and to a consideration of the gospel. One very dangerous reaction to sinful professing Christians is to change the gospel making it more difficult by demanding a holy life before salvation can be obtained. It is indeed frustrating to observe professing Christians in lives of sin. Yet, there is absolutely no justification for adding works to the gospel in an effort to instill a better morality in others. Salvation by faith alone will result in good works to an unspecified degree and in an unspecified time. We do not need to help God out by altering the gospel of grace in an effort to produce good works in our timing and to our level of satisfaction. The solution to professing Christians who sin is a re-examination of the **same** gospel, not the proclamation of a different one (Gal. 1:6-7).

VI. Sanctification

The original words for *sanctification* are also related to the words for *holy, holiness,* and *saint.*

A. Sanctification in the Old Testament

The Old Testament word forms relating to holiness and sanctification occur over 830 times in the Old Testament (350 in the Pentateuch).[70] The origin is uncertain. Some trace it back to "cut, divide, separate." This may or may not be accurate. However, contexts and usage do illustrate that the basic meaning of *holiness* or *sanctification* is "to set apart to God's service." The Hebrew word *kah-dohsh* is the opposite of *profane* or *common* in 1 Sam. 21:5; Ezek. 22:26; 42:20; 44:23. The best English word to describe *kah-dohsh* in these contexts would be *sacred* as opposed to "secular" or "common." Stress is on the position and relationship, not so much ethical qualities. Stress on the position of being "sacred" or "separated unto God's use" as opposed to moral qualities also appears in the many times inanimate, non-moral objects are said to be "holy." Examples of "holy" objects in the Old Testament include: Israel's camp, heaven, Zion, the burning bush and the ground where Moses stood, Jerusalem, the tabernacle, the temple, the flesh of a sacrifice, vessels, oil, incense, bread, candlesticks, the Sabbath, a "holy" assembly, the year of Jubilee, cloth and garments, "consecration and holiness" for battle. From these examples it seems that the primary meaning of holiness is "to be set apart for God's service." Moral/ethical considerations need not be involved but can be. Context alone must determine whether stress regarding the word *holiness* includes a separation from impurity or whether the stress is simply on a positional separation unto God. Of course, whenever God is said to be holy, there is a stress on separation from sin (Lev. 19:2; 20:7, 8, 26; 21:6, 8, 15, 23; Isa. 6:3-8; Hab. 1:12-13).

B. Sanctification in the New Testament

---

[70] A.S. Wood, "Holiness" in The Zondervan Pictorial Encyclopedia of the Bible (Grand Rapids: Zondervan Publishing House, 1976) 3:174.

1. Statistics

The Greek verb *to sanctify*, *hagaizo*, occurs approximately 29 times in the New Testament. The noun *hagios* meaning "holy" or "saint" occurs approximately 236 times: 94 times of the Holy Spirit, 61 times of believers. The form for "sanctification" occurs 10 times.

2. Usage that Stresses a Position of Being Set Apart

Sometimes members of the *hagiazo* family stress the position of being separated, dedicated, consecrated to God, i.e., separated unto His use, and do not necessarily imply a high degree of moral excellence. As with the Old Testament, this is especially evident in references that concern inanimate objects (the temple - Matt. 23:17, 19; food -1 Tim. 4:5; vessels - 2 Tim 2:21; the holy city - Matt. 4:5, 27:53, Rev. 11:2; 21:2, 10; 22:19; the holy place - Matt. 24:15, Acts 6:13, 21:28, etc.; ground - Acts 7:33, 2 Pet. 1:18). Such objects are not holy in a moral/ethical sense. Their "holiness" consists of being set apart for God's service. Also, sometimes people are said to be holy or sanctified. Yet, it is evident they are not highly spiritual (e.g., the Corinthians - 1 Cor. 1:1-2; 6:11; unsaved people married to Christians are sanctified - 1 Cor. 7:14; children of mixed marriages - 1 Cor. 7:14; all male children - Luke 2:23). Another way to prove that sometimes sanctification stressed primarily position and not "moral holiness" is to` focus on the times when the verb "to sanctify" is used of God Himself. God cannot become more and more holy in moral sense. He cannot possibly undergo any improvement ethically for He is already perfect. Therefore, the verses that speak of Christ being sanctified are not thinking in terms of progress in moral holiness. They cannot refer to the Son becoming less and less evil. They mean Christ is either more exalted positionally or more separated positionally unto a given work for God, (John 10:36; 17:19).[71] All of these considerations show that often the stress in sanctification lies in position instead of in morality. Something can be holy in the sense of separated unto God. It can be holy in the sense of sacred (belonging to God) without much stress on its moral or ethical separation from sin.

3. Usages that Stress Moral Separation from Sin

The above section suggests that in some contexts *sanctification* stresses a position of being separated into God's service rather than implying ethical righteousness. This is not the same as denying that, in other contexts, *sanctification* is closely connected with moral/ethical separation from sin. *To sanctify* means "to set apart." Context will usually indicate whether the setting apart stresses positional holiness or ethical holiness. That the concept of sanctification can and often does contain a prominent idea of separation from sin is most evident from the following verses: Rom. 6:19, 22 where sanctification is the opposite of impurity and lawlessness; 1 Thess. 4:3, 7 where sanctification equals abstaining from immorality and is related to purity and honor; Mark 6:20, Acts 3:14 where holy parallels just or righteous; 1 Pet. 1:14-16 where holiness is the opposite of lust and ignorant living; and Eph. 1:4, 5:27 where holiness is connected with blamelessness. Sanctification may be simply stressing a positional setting apart unto God's service, or it can also refer to practical separation from sin. Probably, both concepts are involved to some degree every time the word is used, but the emphasis does change from one idea to the other depending upon the context. Keeping in mind the various shades of emphasis regarding *sanctification*, one is prepared to understand that there are three tenses of sanctification for a believer.

---

[71] Matt. 6:9; Luke 11:2 and 1 Pet. 3:15 do not refer to God becoming even more pure. He is already infinitely removed from sin. Rather, these are references to God being separated from us in the sense of greater exaltation.

4. The Past Tense Aspect of Sanctification

All believers have already been sanctified. Every believer has been set apart positionally unto God's service. Verses which teach a past tense sanctification include Acts 20:32; 26:18; Rom. 15:16 as well as those given below:

> [T]o the church of God which is at Corinth, to those who **have been sanctified** in Christ Jesus, saints by calling, with all who in every place call upon the name of our Lord Jesus Christ, their Lord and ours [1 Cor. 1:2].

> But by His doing you are in Christ Jesus, who became to us wisdom from God, and righteousness and **sanctification**, and redemption [1 Cor. 1:30].

> And such were some of you; but you were washed, **but you were sanctified**, but you were justified in the name of the Lord Jesus Christ, and in the Spirit of our God [1 Cor. 6:11].

> By this will we **have been sanctified** through the offering of the body of Jesus Christ once for all [Heb. 10:10].

In addition to usage of *sanctify* and *sanctification*, **all believers** are said to be **holy** and are **saints**. This is true of their position, regardless of any low level of practical holiness, e.g., in the Corinthian church. (See Rom. 1:7; 1 Cor. 1:2; 2 Cor. 1:1; Eph. 1:1; Phil. 1:1; Col.1:12-13; 2 Tim. 1:9; Heb. 3:1; 1 Pet. 2:5, 9.)

> [G]iving thanks to the Father, who has qualified us to share in the inheritance of the **saints** in light. For He delivered us from the domain of darkness, and transferred us to the kingdom of His beloved Son [Col. 1:12-13].

> [Y]ou also, as living stones, are being built up as a spiritual house for a **holy** priesthood, to offer up spiritual sacrifices acceptable to God through Jesus Christ....But you are a chosen race, a royal priesthood, a **holy** nation, a peo-

ple for God's own possession, that you may proclaim the excellencies of Him who has called you out of darkness into His marvelous light [1 Pet. 2:5, 9].

Not all believers possess a high degree of purity as is fitting for saints (Eph. 5:3), yet all have been sanctified. This past tense of sanctification must stress the position of being set apart unto God's use. The element of some separation from sin is no doubt included within past tense usages of the believer's sanctification. Every believer has been separated from sin's penalty and every genuine believer has experienced some practical separation from sin. However, the emphasis in the past tense of sanctification must remain in positional separation unto God's service. All believers have been sanctified positionally, regardless of ethical practice. This occurred at the time of salvation and may be viewed as one of the results of salvation.

5. The Present Tense Aspect of Sanctification

Just as there is a present tense aspect of salvation, there is also a present tense aspect of sanctification. Believers were sanctified in the past (position). Yet, believers are also being progressively sanctified in the present (practice). Christians are supposed to undergo ethical/moral improvement and experience greater separation from sin with a deeper dedication to God's service. This progression in growth is taught by many phrases in the New Testament: putting on the new man - Colossians 3 and Ephesians 4; the fruit of the Spirit - Galatians 5; growing in grace and knowledge - 2 Peter 3; pressing on in the race of life - Philippians 3; becoming more and more like the image of Christ - 2 Corinthians 3; and mind transformation - Romans 12. The present tense aspect to sanctification emphasizes both the separation from sin and separation unto God's service.[72] Each Christian

---

[72] See also Eph. 4:12 and 5:3 when the saints are to become even more sanctified. 1 Thess. 3:13 and 5:23 refer to a sanctification process that culmi-

chooses to cooperate or hinder the present sanctification process.

"**Sanctify** them in the truth; Thy word is truth" [John 17:17].

I am speaking in human terms because of the weakness of your flesh. For just as you presented your members as slaves to impurity and to lawlessness, resulting in further lawlessness, so now present your members as slaves to righteousness, resulting in **sanctification** [Rom. 6:19].

Therefore, having these promises, beloved, let us **cleanse** ourselves from all defilement of flesh and spirit, **perfecting holiness** in the fear of God [2 Cor. 7:1].

[T]hat He might **sanctify** her, having **cleansed** her by the **washing** of water with the word, that He might present to Himself the church in all her glory, having no spot or wrinkle or any such thing; but that she should be holy and blameless [Eph. 5:26-27].[73]

For this is the will of God, your **sanctification**; that is, that you abstain from sexual immorality....For God has not called us for the purpose of impurity, but in sanctification [1 Thess. 4:3, 7].

Therefore, if a man **cleanses** himself from these things, he will be a vessel for honor, **sanctified**, useful to the Master, prepared for every good work [2 Tim. 2:21].

Pursue peace with all men, and the **sanctification**...[Heb. 12:14].

As obedient children, do not be conformed to the former lusts which were yours in your ignorance, but like the Holy One who called you, **be holy** yourselves also in all your behavior; because it is written, "You shall be holy, for I am holy" [1 Pet. 1:14-16].

6. The Future Tense Aspect of Sanctification

There is a future tense aspect to sanctification. In the future, believers will be totally separated from sin and totally dedicated to God's service. This future and ultimate "setting apart" from sin unto God will occur when we see Him and are like Him in sinlessness, 1 John 3:2.

[S]o that He may establish your hearts unblamable in **holiness** before our God and Father at the coming of our Lord Jesus with all His saints [1 Thess. 3:13].

Now may the God of peace Himself **sanctify you entirely**, and may your spirit and soul and body be preserved complete without blame at the coming of our Lord Jesus Christ [1 Thess. 5:23].

7. The Sanctifier

Sometimes the Bible presents the Father as the one who sanctifies: John 17:17; 1 Thess. 5:23; and Jude 24-25. The Son sanctifies in other texts: 1 Cor. 1:2; Eph. 5:26-27; and Heb. 2:11. The Holy Spirit sanctifies according to Rom. 15:16; 2 Thess. 2:13; and 1 Pet. 1:2. (The latter 2 texts are dealing with a "setting apart" by the Holy Spirit so that blindness to the gospel may be dispelled.)

8. The Means of Sanctification

Great care should be taken to avoid leaving Biblical doctrine vague and abstract. With the term *sanctification* there must be an explanation as to how the believer becomes sanctified. The past tense setting apart from the world unto God can occur because of the blood, the offering of Jesus Christ (Heb. 9:13-14; 10:10, 14). Those who trust in Christ have been sanctified **by His body** and **by His blood**. The

---

nates in a future and full sanctification. Yet, this process is in progress in the present time.
[73] Eph. 5:26-27 could also refer to positional sanctification. Perhaps it includes all phases of sanctification.

means of the present aspect to sanctification is the **Word of God**. This is very clear both in John 17:17 and Acts 20:32.

"Sanctify them in the truth; Thy **word** is truth"[John 17:17].

"And now I commend you to God and to the **word** of His grace, which is able to build you up and to give you the inheritance among all those who are sanctified" [Acts 20:32].

It is obvious from Gal. 5:1ff. that the **Holy Spirit** produces holiness in the believer's life. However, there are not two ways of sanctification: one by the Holy Spirit and another by the written word. The Sword of the Spirit is the Word of God (Eph. 6:17). Therefore, the Holy Spirit uses His own Word to produce sanctification in the life of the believer who not only hears the Word but does it (James 1:22). The Holy Spirit's work must not be divorced from the written Word of God. The means of present tense sanctification is the written Word of God.

VII. Eternal Security

Because many major soteriological doctrines confirm the eternal security of a believer's salvation, it is logical to cover eternal security after studying more basic doctrines. When one understands doctrines such as predestination and justification by faith, then eternal security follows. It is helpful to organize evidences for eternal security by a method that focuses on the inconsistency of denying it. Here are nine statements that point out the inconsistencies in denying eternal security.

A. Evidences for Eternal Security

1. Viewing the Subject from a Negative Perspective.

a. **If a Christian can lose his salvation, then Christ must lose His righteousness.**

Justification by faith, when correctly understood, supports the eternal security of the believer. When Christ died, our sins were imputed (credited) to His account. When a person trusts in Christ, Christ's righteousness is "imputed" (credited) to the believer's account. God views a believer's position as "in Christ" and covered with **Christ's righteousness**. On this basis, the believer is declared legally just. **It is Christ's righteousness** (not human righteousness and merit) **that is the basis of a believer's acceptance and standing with God.** Self-righteousness did not save in the first place, and it is not a basis upon which salvation is continued. Christ's righteousness brings salvation. So the real issue in a believer's security is not the endurance of human righteousness but the **eternal nature** of Christ's **righteousness**.

A believer cannot lose his righteousness or righteous legal standing before God unless Christ loses His righteousness, and that cannot and will not occur. His righteousness is eternal. Our own human self righteousness is as filthy rags at best and plays no part whatsoever in the gift of salvation (Isa. 64:6). Christ's righteousness, and Christ's righteousness alone, justifies the person who believes (Rom. 4:5). Relative to justification, God never considered our own righteousness or lack of it, rather He looked to Christ's holy perfect righteousness that has been imputed to (credited to) a believer. (See Rom. 5:17-19; 1 Cor. 1:30; 2 Cor. 5:21, and also Eph. 1:6-7; and Col. 2:10.) Maintaining that a believer can lose salvation and become unjustified is the same as believing that Christ can lose His righteousness because it is His righteousness that must be lost in order for one to become "unjustified." A believer cannot lose His justification until Christ loses His righteousness. Even the proposal of the concept is absurd. Christ's death provides salvation, but His life also plays a significant role in the salvation plan. Rom. 5:10 teaches that just as Christ's death saves the believer, so does His life. If trusting in Christ reconciles us to God at a time when we were enemies, how much more secure is the believer's position now that he has been credited with the righteousness of

Christ's holy, perfect, sinless life. Paul confidently asserts, "We shall be saved by **His life**." The merits of Christ's holy, perfect, sinless, righteous life belong to those with faith. His righteous life will never lose righteousness. Thus, Paul can assert that the future outcome for believers is, "We shall be saved," and believers need not worry about the future of their salvation. It is certainly secure.

> For if while we were enemies, we were reconciled to God through the death of His Son, much more, having been reconciled, we shall be saved by **His life** [Rom. 5:10].

> He made Him who knew no sin to be sin on our behalf, that we might become the righteousness of God **in Him** [2 Cor. 5:21].

b. **If a Christian can lose his salvation, then God is not all-powerful, and the Bible is wrong on predestination.**

Regardless of whether one views election as conditional (based on God's foreknowledge of those who have a potential to believe) or unconditional, all must agree that **God's program of predestination extends** far beyond the time of conversion **to future glory in eternity.**

> For whom He foreknew, He also **predestined to become conformed to the image of His Son,** that He might be the first-born among many brethren; and whom He predestined, these He also called; and whom He called, these He also justified; and whom He justified, these He also **glorified** [Rom. 8:29-30].

Everyone who has been justified (i.e., all believers) is so certain of glorification that glory can be spoken of in the **past tense.** The believer (justified one) is predestined to glory by God's decree. The goal of predestination is a conforming to the image of God's Son. This occurs at the rapture. All those predestined (i.e., all believers) **must** obtain that point,

"When He appears, **we shall be like Him**..." (1 John 3:2). In addition, the phrase "predestined us to adoption as sons" in Eph. 1:5 supports a predestination to a future glory.

> He **predestined us to adoption as sons** through Jesus Christ to Himself, according to the kind intention of His will [Eph. 1:5].

The "us" of Eph. 1:5 refers to those "in Him" or "in Christ" as the context of Ephesians proves. Verse 13 establishes that Paul's remarks concern all believers. **Believers,** then, are **predestined to adoption,** or placement as sons. What is Paul's full definition of adoption or "son-placing"? Rom. 8:23 gives the answer:

> And not only this, but also we ourselves having the first fruits of the Spirit, even we ourselves groan within ourselves waiting eagerly for our adoption as sons, the redemption of our body [Rom. 8:23].

Rom. 8:23 teaches that one aspect of this **"son-placing" is the total redemption of the body from the affects and presence of sin.**[74] There is a future aspect of the adoption of sons where the children of God will become mature sons like Christ Jesus and will obtain their inheritance. The ideas of obtaining an inheritance and being redeemed from the curse of sin are all in the context of Romans 8. This

---

[74] "Son-placing" is a literal (admittedly awkward) translation of the Greek word but does have the advantage of showing that the word goes far beyond the initial entrance into the family unlike the English term "adoption". Paul's full definition includes a time of mature sonship when **one already in the family becomes a full son** in the sense of outgrowing status as a minor child and gaining full rights as an adult son. The author knows of no ancient ceremonies of placement as adult sons, but the concept is similar to a bar mitzvah when one already a son becomes acknowledged as a mature son. Believers are predestined not just to entrance into God's family but to become sinless and perfect (mature sons) like the Lord Jesus Christ.

future adoption of Rom. 8:23 equals being mature sons conformed to the image of His Son in Rom. 8:29. Therefore, Romans 8 teaches that **believers are predestined** to a **full adoption as sons** when they will obtain an inheritance, **become like Jesus Christ**, and be redeemed physically from the affects of sin. Being predestined to adoption as sons means believers are predestined to be like the Lord Jesus Christ in glory and sinless perfection. There could not be a stronger evidence of eternal security.

In the context of Ephesians 1, a future aspect to "adoption of sons" must also be intended. Just as in Romans 8, Ephesians 1 deals with inheritance (vv. 11 and 14) and seems to refer to the redemption of the believer's body (v. 14). Ephesians 1 clearly has a future orientation, and there is no reason for missing a parallel with Romans 8. The author is the same and in both places the subject is "adoption as sons" and predestination. **Take careful note that in both Romans 8 and Ephesians 1 a believer is predestined to obtain a full mature sonship.**

Those who deny the eternal security of the believer must disagree that a believer is predestined to glory. They must deny that believers are predestined to obtain a full "adoption as sons." Since God has made the decree that those justified are as good as glorified and has decreed those "in Christ" will obtain adoption as sons (i.e., inheritance, redemption of the body, full sonship after the image of Christ), those who deny security unknowingly deny that God can or will abide by His own promises. If a believer does not obtain glory or full "sonship," then either God contradicted Himself, or He is not able to keep His self-imposed obligation. Either God was mistaken in these teachings about predestination to glory, or He does not have the power or ability to guarantee a full adoption as sons. If a Christian can lose salvation, then God is not all-powerful and the Bible is in error on the topic of predestination.

c. **If a Christian loses his salvation by mis-** **deeds or a lack of works, then salvation would be based upon works**.

Few truths are clearer than the idea that salvation is not granted on the basis of works. The denial that salvation is secure ultimately leads back to a works-salvation. Many who espouse the "insecurity" of the believer claim this is an untrue distortion and misrepresentation of their viewpoint. They would deny salvation by works. They would insist that salvation is initially granted as a free gift through faith, but that subsequent to salvation a person must maintain a certain level of righteousness to maintain salvation. However, this is still a works system.

If God bestows initial salvation without effort but then requires us to perform in order to maintain salvation, then salvation is not a gift at all but is something we must work to have. There is not much difference between such a system and a car dealer who gives a car without cost but expects the recipient to work faithfully or make payments in order to maintain possession of that car. Such a relationship is not that of a free gift; it is a **contract of works**. If a Christian must work at righteousness to maintain possession of salvation, then the possession of salvation ultimately rests on works even if one claims it is initially given freely. **Salvation is a gift**. It is freely given by grace through faith in the Lord Jesus Christ. Works play no role in either obtaining or maintaining the possession of salvation.

> But to the one who does not work, but believes in Him who justifies the ungodly, his faith is reckoned as righteousness [Rom. 4:5].

> For by grace you have been saved through faith; and that not of yourselves, it is the gift of God; not as a result of works, that no one should boast [Eph. 2:8-9].

> He saved us, not on the basis of deeds which we have done in righteousness, but according to His mercy; by the

washing of regeneration and renewing by the Holy Spirit [Titus 3:5].

d. If a Christian loses his salvation and goes to hell because of sin, then Christ's atonement must not have perfectly dealt with all sins.

Again many who deny eternal security would be unaware that their position implies some defect in the cross. However, if a soul can lose his salvation due to sin and spend eternity in hell, then it must also be the case that there are some sins for which the price was not paid. There would be sin for which the ex-child of God would be suffering in hell. If a Christian can lose salvation and suffer punishment because of sins, then somehow Christ's work on the cross must not have completely solved the sin problem as it pertains to those "life-losing" sins. He must have died for some of that believer's sins but not for all of them. There must be some sins that a believer might potentially commit for which he could be liable and be required to suffer.

The idea that the cross did not completely solve the sin problem and that potentially a believer himself might have to pay for some sins is an insult to Christ's work on the cross. It means that there are some potential sins for which redemption has not been paid, but the Scripture speaks of redemption for the believer as involving a complete release from the slave market of sin that has already occurred. (See Gal. 3:13 - past tense; Titus 2:14 - redeemed from all wickedness; Heb. 9:12 - eternal redemption; Eph. 1:7 - redemption already a possession; 1 Pet. 1:18, 19 - redemption past tense.) The possibility of sins existing for which a Christian must spend eternity under God's wrath means that the cross did not fully propitiate God's wrath over sin, but the Scriptures teach otherwise. (See Rom. 3:25; 1 John 2:1-2, 4:10.) Either there has been redemption or there has not been redemption. Either there has been a propitiation of God's wrath or there has not been a propitiation of God's wrath. Either Christ's death finished the sin problem,

or it did not (John 19:30). Either Christ's sacrifice was complete and final or it was partial and tentative. Either it was completely sufficient or it was only partially sufficient. (See Heb. 9:12, 26, 28a; 10:10, 12, 14.) The view that Christ's atonement completely dealt with the sin problem of the human race entails a belief that there are no more sins for which a believer might have to suffer. The view that there are potential sins for which a believer might be liable to punishment entails the idea that the cross's remedy for sin was partial, not total.

> [W]ho gave Himself for us, that He might redeem us from **every** lawless deed and purify for Himself a people for His own possession, zealous for good deeds [Titus 2:14].

> And when you were dead in your transgressions and the uncircumcision of your flesh, He made you alive together with Him, having forgiven us **all** our transgressions [Col. 2:13].

e. If a Christian can lose salvation, then God the Son can fail as an intercessor or advocate.

In John 17:11 Christ prays, "Holy Father, keep them in Thy Name..." In the context, Christ is referring to a keeping, guarding, preserving from perdition (see v. 12), and He is including within the scope of His prayer not just the apostles but all believers (see v. 20). Therefore, Christ has prayed that believers in Him be preserved from destruction. If a believer can ultimately perish, then Christ in John 17 made a request that was out of God's will and Christ failed as an intercessor. He made a petition to God the Father and was turned away.

The Lord Jesus Christ still intercedes on behalf of believers (Rom 8:34; Heb. 7:24-25). He apparently is still asking for a safeguarding of believers. Heb. 7:25 teaches that a Savior who always lives is able to intercede at all times. This constant intercession results in an eternal salvation. God the Father honors

Christ's never-ending petition on behalf of believers. John 11:42 teaches that the Father always hears the Son. Christ's life which never ends results in an intercession which never ends which in turn results in a salvation that never ends. Can we imagine Christ interceding for 2,000 years with a request that is periodically denied because it is not in God will? Of course not. It is within God's will that believers be kept, and He always honors the Son's request to do so.

> [B]ut He, on the other hand, because He abides forever, holds His priesthood permanently. Hence, also, He is able to **save forever** those who draw near to God through Him, since He always lives to make intercession for them [Heb. 7:24-25].

Christ's work as our Intercessor is related to His work as our Advocate. Satan is the accuser of the brethren (Rev. 12:10), but at each accusation of sin Christ our Lord is our defense attorney contending on our behalf (1 John 2:1). His defense does not fail.

f. **If a Christian loses salvation, then the Holy Spirit fails in His sealing ministry.**

> ...who also **sealed** us and gave us the Spirit in our hearts as a **pledge** [2 Cor. 1:22].

> In Him, you also, after listening to the message of truth, the gospel of your salvation—having also believed, you were **sealed** in Him with the Holy Spirit of promise, who is given as a **pledge** of our inheritance, with a view to the redemption of God's own possession, to the praise of His glory [Eph. 1:13-14].

> And do not grieve the Holy Spirit of God, by whom you were **sealed for the day of redemption** [Eph. 4:30].

Several times Paul teaches that the Holy Spirit **seals** a believer (2 Cor. 1:22; Eph. 1:13-14; 4:30). In ancient times a seal with its im-

pressed mark signified ownership and authority. The king's seal on a document meant authority. A seal on an object, such as an oil jar or wine flask, signified ownership. There is also the idea of approval or endorsement (John 3:33). Even today one can hear of a "seal of approval." Finally, sealing spoke of protection. The Lord's tomb was sealed to be protected (Matt. 27:66). A document would be sealed to be protected. The breaking of a seal might subject a document such as a will or title deed to alteration. Therefore, only a person with authority could break a legal seal (Rev. 5:9).

The sealing of the Spirit refers to God's ownership, approval, and protection of a believer. Are there limits to this protection? Eph. 4:30 teaches that believers are **sealed for the day of redemption**, i.e., until the redemption of our bodies when we obtain glory and full inheritance. The Holy Spirit throughout this earthly life seals believers. The duration of the Spirit's protection or time-span of His ownership extends all the way to glorification. If a Christian can lose salvation, then the seal of the Holy Spirit could be broken off long before the day of redemption. If a Christian can lose salvation, then Eph. 4:30 would be an error.

Both 2 Cor. 1:22 and Eph. 1:13-14 mention the Holy Spirit as a pledge in the same sentence that refers to His sealing work. (See also 2 Cor. 5:5.) The Holy Spirit is said to be the earnest, or pledge, of our full inheritance. The King James word *earnest* is somewhat archaic. The phrase "down payment" communicates better. The underlying Greek word means "engagement ring" in modern Greek. The Holy Spirit is like a down payment or engagement ring. He is the pledge, promise or guarantee of greater blessings to come. Another term that expresses the same truth is *first-fruits* (Rom. 8:23). The Holy Spirit is the guarantee and beginning of greater blessing in the future. His role of sealing until the day of redemption means that the Holy Spirit is a secure and certain pledge that future blessing will be obtained. Yet, if a Christian loses salvation, then the Holy Spirit was not the first-fruits of a future blessing, and He was not the down-payment or pledge of a greater inheritance. If the Holy Spirit does indeed seal for the day of redemption and if He is the pledge of a greater inheritance, then eternal security follows.

g. If a Christian can lose his salvation, it makes the promises of the Bible untrue.

The Bible teaches that a believer will not suffer condemnation and is not subject to God's eternal wrath. Yet, if a Christian loses salvation, then he is subject to condemnation and God's eternal wrath.

> "Truly, truly, I say to you, he who hears My word, and believes Him who sent Me, has eternal life, and does not come into judgment, but has passed out of death into life" [John 5:24].

> There is therefore now no condemnation for those who are in Christ Jesus [Rom. 8:1].

> Much more then, having now been justified by His blood, we shall be saved from the wrath of God through Him. [Rom 5:9].

> For God has not destined us for wrath, but for obtaining salvation through our Lord Jesus Christ [1 Thess. 5:9].

If a believer's ultimate salvation is a variable, then John 5:24 ought to read, "He who hears My word and believes Him who sent Me might have eternal life and probably will not come into condemnation but likely has passed out of death into life." Rom. 8:1 ought to say, "There will probably not be condemnation to those who are in Christ."

Heb. 13:5 says, "I will never leave you nor forsake you." If a believer could lose salvation, then Christ would leave him. Heb. 13:5 promises that He will never leave. (The Greek phrase has five negatives.)

John 6:37 says "...the one who comes to Me I will certainly not cast out" (double negative in the Greek for emphasis). Those who teach that a believer can lose salvation should consider what is really being promised here. Indeed, the phrase *has eternal life* is common (e.g., John 6:47). If a person has a life that can end, that life, by definition, was never eternal in the first place. Christ teaches that the one who believes already possesses eternal life. By definition this means his life will not end.

Rom. 8:38-39 says that nothing can separate the believer from the love of Christ. If a Christian can lose salvation, then **something** must cause separation. Likewise, in John 10:28 Christ promises, "They shall never perish" (double negative again). If a believer loses salvation and perishes, then this promise is also wrong. A believer who loses salvation would never have possessed eternal life. He would come into judgment and be subject to God's eternal wrath. God would forsake the ex-child of God, the ex-child would be cast out, be separated from God's love, and would perish. The Bible will not allow these possibilities.

h. If a Christian can lose salvation, then God has failed in His intention to keep us.

> ...to obtain an inheritance which is imperishable and undefiled and will not fade away, **reserved** in heaven for you, who are **protected** by the power of God through faith for a salvation ready to be revealed in the last time [1 Pet. 1:4-5].

> Now to Him who is able to **keep** you from stumbling, and to make you stand in the presence of His glory blameless with great joy [Jude v. 24].

If a Christian can lose salvation, then heaven is not reserved, nor are all believers protected, by God's power. If a Christian can lose salvation, then God does not keep him from stumbling or bring him into glory. Yet, these two passages present a sovereign God whose intention is to protect and preserve believers in the faith and from falling.

i. If a Christian can lose salvation, the Bible is confusing for it does not specify any causes which remove salvation.

There is no teaching in the Bible that lists the kind of sin that removes salvation or that tells what degree of sin exposes one to a risk of loss of salvation. Unless eternal security is true, it would be inconceivable that God would delete all instruction about forfeiture of salvation. He would want His people to be warned of specific perils. Yet, there are no warnings. Instead 1 Cor. 3:15 indicates that all believers, even those who are lacking in good works will be saved at the Judgment Seat of Christ:

> If any man's work is burned up, he shall suffer loss, but he himself shall be saved...[1 Cor. 3:15].

2. Viewing the Subject from a Positive Standpoint, Eternal Security is True

To this point we have viewed the subject of eternal security negatively, looking at the absurdities and inconsistencies that would be true if salvation could be lost. Perhaps it is best to review the same truths phrased from a positive standpoint. In this context, then, eternal security is true for the following nine reasons:

a. Christ's righteousness (not our own righteousness) saves; one cannot lose salvation.

Justification by faith means that Christ's righteousness saves a believer. Since He will never lose His righteousness, a believer can never lose his justification.

b. Election and predestination prove eternal security.

The Bible's teaching on election and predestination prove eternal security. Those whom God has justified are as good as already glorified.

c. Salvation is not given or maintained by works.

Salvation is not initially given because of good works, nor do good works maintain it.

d. Christ's atonement is perfect and complete.

Christ's atonement is perfect and complete. He has paid for all sin. There is no sin that remains for which a believer could ever suffer.

e. Christ as advocate guarantees security.

Christ's ministries as intercessor and advocate guarantee security.

f. The Holy Spirit's seal cannot be broken.

The Holy Spirit has sealed believers until the day of redemption. This seal cannot be broken. He is also our pledge and guarantee of a future inheritance.

g. Many promises guarantee security.

There are many promises that guarantee eternal life without condemnation. Eternal life by the definition of "eternal" cannot end.

h. God is able to keep us from falling.

God says He is able to keep us from falling and that we are kept by His power.

i. There are no Scriptural grounds for losing salvation.

The Bible never gives any grounds for losing salvation. Even believers with unproductive lives and few good works still obtain salvation at the Judgment Seat of Christ.

B. Problem Passages Explained

In theological circles, those who deny eternal security are called Arminians after the Dutch theologian Jacob (James) Arminius (1560-1609). Most groups coming from the Wesleyan tradition such as Methodists are Arminian in that they disagree with eternal security. This issue is not among the fundamentals of the faith, but the security of the believer is among the most important doctrines that divide believers. Thinking Arminians use Bible texts to prove a Christian can lose salvation. However, each of these texts can also be interpreted in ways that are completely compatible with the doctrine of eternal security.

1. Psa. 51:11

(See also Judg. 16:20 and 1 Sam. 16:14.)

> Do not cast me away from thy presence, and do not take thy Holy Spirit from me [Psa. 51:11].

David seems worried that the Holy Spirit would leave him. Under the Law system the Holy Spirit did not indwell every believer (John 7:39) nor had God promised the Holy Spirit would indwell forever (e.g., John 14:16-17). Unlike the Spirit's ministry since Pentecost (Acts 2), the Holy Spirit might depart from a believer under the Law of Moses. This would result in ineffective living and ministry but not a loss of salvation. Another interpretation would take "spirit" as a reference to David's own spirit. He would be saying, "Please do not take the spirit of holiness away from my life". In other words, do not let me loose strong conviction over sin or the desire for holiness in my life. Don't give up on me. Keep convicting me and making me want holiness. Chapter Ten, "Pneumatology", includes detailed studies on the changes in the Holy Spirit's ministry since Pentecost (in Acts 2).[75]

2. Ezek. 33:12-20 (See also Ezek. 3:20; 18:20.)

> "And you, son of man, say to your fellow citizens, 'The righteousness of a righteous man will not deliver him in the day of his transgression, and as for the wickedness of the wicked, he will

not stumble because of it in the day when he turns from his wickedness; whereas a righteous man will not be able to live by his righteousness on the day when he commits sin.' When I say to the righteous he will surely live, and he so trusts in his righteousness that he commits iniquity, none of his righteous deeds will be remembered; but in that same iniquity of his which he has committed he will die" [Ezek. 33:12-13].

Ezekiel's warnings about death from sin involve physical death (either capital punishment as in 18:20, or death in war with Israel's enemies). Ezekiel 33 concerns a predicted attack with a "sword upon the land" (v. 2). God promised deliverance for those living in righteousness at the time of destruction. He warns of death for those living in wickedness. The question of eternal salvation is not the issue here. Death refers to physical death because of sin. Several other references that can be misunderstood may also concern physical life or death.

3. Matt. 24:13

(See also Matt. 10:22; Mark 13:13; Luke 21:19.)

> "But the one who endures to the end, he shall be saved" [Matt. 24:13].

> "By your endurance you will gain your lives" [Luke 21:19].

Salvation in these verses could be physical deliverance or spiritual deliverance. With either interpretation the key to understanding is putting the statement in its **tribulational setting**. The Lord refers to the period of suffering just before the Second Coming. Matt. 24:21 says, "...for then there will be a **great tribulation**, such as has not occurred since the beginning of the world until now, nor ever shall." This absolutely unique period will be a time of great persecution of believers with much loss of physical life. Also, everyone will be forced to demonstrate allegiance to the evil end-time

---

[75] An alternative view would hold that the Holy Spirit did indwell all Old Testament believers. He would also come upon leaders for special empowerment. One could conclude that David fears a loss of this special anointing of the Holy Spirit for leaders.

dictator by accepting a bodily mark. Refusal of the mark is a certain indication of faith in Christ and will result in unavoidable suffering (Rev. 13:16-18). Thus, it can be said that those who endure persecution from the Antichrist gain spiritual salvation. This salvation does not come on the basis of the good work of endurance. Rather the decision to trust in Christ, even though it results in persecution, brings salvation. Endurance of persecution in the Tribulation will not earn or retain salvation, but it does demonstrate it. To believe will mean to endure suffering. To endure will mean to believe. All others will submit to worshiping a false Christ. It is difficult to know whether the Lord intends physical salvation or spiritual salvation.

a. Physical Salvation (Rescue) from the Tribulation

The Lord's words might be taken as encouragement that the tribulation period has limited duration. It will not last indefinitely. Those who are able to endure persecution will find a rescue (physical salvation) by the Lord's return to the earth at the end of the period.[76] These may be words of hope and encouragement to tribulational saints. There will be an end to the ordeal. The Lord will return in power to destroy their tormentors and to rescue (save) believers from further suffering.

b. Spiritual Salvation

The NASB translation of Luke 21:19 seems to favor physical deliverance. In the Luke context v. 19 could even be a promise that those apostles still living in A.D. 70 would survive the destruction of Jerusalem even though some believers would die (v. 16). However, the Greek phraseology in Luke seems harder to limit to physical rescue (salvation) at the end of the tribulation period than is the parallel in Matt. 24:13.

"By your endurance you will gain your **souls**" [Luke 21:19 (literal translation)].

In Luke 21:16 the Lord says, "...they will put some of you to death." Then in v. 18 He says, "Yet, not a hair on your head will perish." This sounds as if Christ intends to contrast physical death with spiritual salvation. "They may kill you, but they cannot really harm you spiritually." Assuming Luke 21:19 refers to a spiritual salvation, it still could not possibly be referring to a loss of salvation. If it does, it would also be teaching good works earn salvation. Clearly, there has to be a better way to understand these two passages. As a background, we must first consider the nature of saving faith and the conditions in the tribulation period.

(1) Saving Faith

Genuine believers are kept in faith. Believers believe. A more complete discussion of this conclusion will occur under a following problem passage (1 Cor. 15:1-2; Col. 1:21-23). Jesus says in John 10:5 that his sheep "do not know the voice of strangers." A Christian might deny faith to others in situations of embarrassment or danger as did Peter. However, Peter never denied Christ to God the Father or denied Christ in his own heart. Genuine believers do not deny Christ is the Son of God or that He died for our sins and rose again. In the conditions of the Tribulation, this means that genuine believers will not worship the Antichrist or accept his mark.

(2) Tribulational Conditions

When the Tribulation begins everyone on earth will be unsaved.[77] After the Antichrist assumes dictatorial powers over the world, he will force all people to choose between worshiping himself or worshiping the true Christ (Matt. 24:15; 2 Thess. 2:4; Rev. 13:15-18). Also, God will indirectly participate in the process. Those who will not receive the truth

---

[76] The *end* in this view refers to the end of the tribulation period. In the next view *end* refers to the end of life.

[77] This, of course, assumes the pretribulational Rapture. See Chapter 12, Eschatology.

of Christ will be blinded so as to believe the Antichrist's lies (2 Thess. 2:11-12). Pressures, both Satanic and divine, will force all people to choose. During the Tribulation, some who began the period as unsaved will turn to faith in Christ (the saints mentioned in Daniel and Revelation, e.g., Rev. 7:9, 14). Virtually no other time in world history will faith be required to be demonstrated in such a permanent and irrevocable way. The decision to accept the beast's mark is a final unchangeable rejection of Christ. All unbelievers will eventually give in to the Antichrist's power and worship him, sealing their choice with a bodily mark. By contrast, only believers and all believers will refuse. A true believer will not be able to reject Christ in such a permanent and final sense. Instead, believers will demonstrate faith by rejecting the mark and incurring the hatred of the Antichrist. **Of the tribulation period it will be true to say that those who are still enduring the beast's persecution at the end are the genuinely saved ones.** They do not earn or keep salvation by perseverance. They reveal or display their faith. Saving faith leads to refusal to worship the beast and accept his permanent mark of allegiance. The individuals who refuse to worship the beast through to the end of the Tribulation are the identical individuals who gain salvation by trusting Christ instead. Because of the choice to trust Christ and thereby reject Antichrist, they have inevitable suffering, but they also have gained salvation. Those who choose faith in Christ will endure suffering and likely death, but will also gain their souls by their choice. Those who choose to worship the beast and accept his mark do not lose salvation; they demonstrate they **never had salvation**. We could paraphrase Jesus' words this way: "those who persevere to the end against the Antichrist are the saved ones." The truth can also be stated, "He that is saved will endure". This gives the same truth but with different emphasis. It would emphasize that every true believer will reject worshiping the Antichrist and suffer for that choice. Instead Jesus wanted to stress the positive. These will gain salvation by their choice

to accept Christ (not Antichrist) even though it will entail persecution and often death.

4. Matt. 25:30

(See also Matt. 8:11-12.)

> "And cast out the worthless slave into the outer darkness; in that place there shall be weeping and gnashing of teeth" [Matt. 25:30].

Here we have a case of a servant ending up in outer darkness. Is this a warning of a Christian losing salvation? The church does not begin until Acts 2. Though many of the Lord's teachings look forward to the church dispensation, many other statements are directed at Israel. In a sense all Jews were servants of God, but not all Jews were saved. Many had no faith. Thus, a Jewish servant of God could end up in punishment. However, this would not be an example of a believer in Christ losing salvation. The context of Matt. 8:12 proves the Lord has unbelieving Israel in mind.

5. John 15:1-8

> "I am the true vine, and My Father is the vinedresser. Every branch in Me that does not bear fruit, He takes away; and every branch that bears fruit, He prunes it, that it may bear more fruit. You are already clean because of the word which I have spoken to you. Abide in Me, and I in you. As the branch cannot bear fruit of itself, unless it abides in the vine, so neither can you, unless you abide in Me. I am the vine, you are the branches; he who abides in Me, and I in him, he bears much fruit; for apart from Me you can do nothing. If anyone does not abide in Me, he is thrown away as a branch, and dries up; and they gather them, and cast them into the fire, and they are burned. If you abide in Me, and My words abide in you, ask whatever you wish, and it shall be done for you. By this is My Father glorified, that you bear much

200

fruit, and so prove to be My disciples" [John 15:1-8].

The cut and discarded branch of John 15 has been taken to be a believer who loses salvation. However, there are other views, which handle the passage in ways that preserve eternal security. It could be an explanation of the departure of Judas from the apostolic company, or it could be a warning about the believer's chastisement in this life.

a. Judas as the Cut Branch

Perhaps John 15 is closely directed to the original listeners. The broken and discarded branch explains Judas' departure earlier that same evening (see John 13:26-30). The call to abide directs the other apostles to remain in the faith and to keep true to Christ during the coming arrest, trial, and death. While lessons can be drawn for all times, many contextual clues show the Lord's teaching is mainly addressed to those from the upper room who had just left the room and were moving towards the garden (cf. John 14:31 with 18:1). Meanwhile, Judas was betraying Jesus and would soon die. Consider the many hints that the Lord is speaking primarily of the apostles:

> "...He (the Holy Spirit) will teach you all things and bring to your remembrance all that I said to you" [John 14:26].

> "...you will bear witness also because you have been with me from the beginning" [John 15:27].

> "They will make you outcasts from the synagogue..." [John 16:2].

> "...And these things I did not say to you at the beginning because I was with you" [John 16:4b].

> "I have many more things to say to you, but you cannot bear them now" [John 16:12].

> "I do not ask in behalf of these alone, but for those also who believe in Me

through their word" [John 17:20].

The Upper Room Discourse seems directed primarily at the disciples. No Christian today was with the Lord "from the beginning" (John 15:27 or 16:4). Even John 17:20, which mentions those in following generations who would believe in Christ because of the apostolic message, reinforces the idea that the Lord's teachings are directed mainly at the apostles. If we view John 15 as primarily directed at the apostles, then the Lord is explaining Judas' departure and commanding the remaining apostles to keep the faith in the dark days immediately ahead.

John 15:2 speaks of a fruitless branch that is taken away.[78] Though it is visibly connected to the vine (as outwardly Judas had been connected to Christ by association), there is no interchange of life from within. Life does not flow from the vine to this dead branch. Therefore, God takes it away (removes it). Though outwardly tied to Christ, Judas had never absorbed life from Christ. He is not an example of a believer who loses salvation. He is an example of one who is outwardly associated with Christianity but had no inward life. Verse two tells the disciples that the fruitless and dead Judas had just been removed from all association with Christ. He would also soon be taken away in death.

The remaining disciples are like the branch that produces some fruit. In addition to mere outward association, they have an inner connection (union) with the Lord Jesus. Life flows from Him to them. They can expect pruning (hardships and chastisement) which will produce more fruit.

---

[78] The phrase *in Me* seems to refer to outward association. There were two kinds of branches in Christ. First, dead branches who had no inner connection and no life. Second, branches with fruit who possessed a living connection on the inside. Only those in the second category could keep the command to abide. Dead branches have visible connection to Christianity but no life. They cannot abide in a relationship they do not possess.

In John 15:4 Jesus commands the remaining apostles to "abide in Me." The command to "abide" includes an appeal to a deeper relationship of keeping all the Lord's commandments. It is a command to absorb more intimate life from the vine. This is the definition of abide in 1 John 3:24. The command to abide includes more than the topic of salvation and encompasses obedience. (See John 15:5, 10.) However, the command to abide does not include less than the topic of salvation either.[79] Abide means remain. While Jesus is telling His apostles to keep His commandments, He is also calling them to remain in the faith during the difficult times just ahead.

Why would one who accepts eternal security think Jesus would need to tell the apostles to remain in faith? One of God's methods for keeping believers in the faith (1 Pet. 1:4-5) is by Scriptural commands to remain in the faith. In a hypothetical sense, one might lose faith and salvation with it were it not for God's work of preserving a believer in the faith. If it were not for Jesus' gracious warning and commands in John 15, perhaps the apostles would have abandoned their faith during this critical period. However, the Lord intended to keep them secure by not letting this happen. The very command for the disciples to remain

(abide) in the faith exhibits God's means of keeping these men in the faith during the dark night and fateful crucifixion day soon to come. Is this not what the Lord means in John 16:1? By application to modern times, we see that Scriptural commands to keep faith are not incompatible with the doctrine of eternal security. Commands to remain in faith in Christ are one means God uses to keep believers secure. When the Lord commanded the apostles to abide, He included both the ideas of remaining in the faith and keeping His commandments.

This command is not really directed to Judas or people like him. Like a dead branch associated by connection to a vine, Judas had been outwardly connected to Jesus without any inner life. Judas will not abide because Judas cannot abide. One cannot keep what one does not have in the first place. Judas could not abide in Christ because He could not remain in a faith that had never begun. He could neither preserve a living union with Christ nor enter a more intimate union by keeping all Christ's commandments. Judas is the dead branch thrown into the fire.

He may illustrate a type of person today who is outwardly tied to Christ by association, such as church membership, but still lacks faith. Without faith there is no spiritual union. Such a person cannot abide because he cannot continue (abide) in a relationship he has not yet begun. He certainly cannot deepen that relationship by keeping the Lord's commandments unless he trusts in Christ. He will eventually, like Judas, be severed from all tenuous links that only appear to be tied to Christ and be thrown into flames.

By interpreting John 15 closely in its original setting, we have found the text need not involve a genuine Christian who loses salvation. Judas is the dead branch. He did not lose salvation. He **never had** salvation. He did not abide and then lose salvation. He could not abide because he could not remain (much less deepen) in a relationship he never possessed. Judas is a warning for all those outwardly as-

---

[79] In 1 John 4:15, "Abide in Him" seems to be the equivalent of being saved, perhaps also 1 John 2:6 (where "abide" equals "in Him" in v.5). In 1 John 3:24 *to abide* means to keep the Lord's commandments. Both ideas may be included in John 15. Jesus is not telling unbelievers to enter salvation (though the text could be applied this way in modern sermons). He is commanding the saved apostles to remain in the relationship they already possess, i.e., keep the faith they have, and also to obey His commandments. It is not the case that Judas stopped abiding. Only the living branches could abide. They would abide by staying in faith and by obedience. There are two types of branches "in Me" (i.e., associated with Christ outwardly). Those connected visibly but lacking fruit are dead. Those connected visibly bearing some fruit are alive. Only the living branches have a union in which they could remain and grow deeper.

sociating with the things of Christ but without real union by faith.

Many who accept eternal security will not accept the above interpretation of John 15. They would prefer that fire not be a reference to eternal punishment. Neither would they understand the command to abide to include an appeal to remain in the faith. For them, fire speaks of loss of rewards and temporal chastisement of the believer. The call to abide is a call to deeper and full obedience that has nothing to do with remaining in the faith. While the author prefers the "Judas View," this second view is worthy of respect.

b. Warning of Chastisement, Loss of Rewards View

Perhaps John 15 is not referring to a "Judas-type" who has associations with Christianity, but no faith. If Christ's words exclusively concern believers, then He is warning believers to abide in a life of obedience and full allegiance. Those who refuse may endure chastisement, even unto physical death, and loss of rewards.

John 15:2 speaks of those "in Me" who bear no fruit and those who bear some fruit.[80] Christians who are void of productivity may be taken away from this world in physical death (cf. 1 Cor. 11:30). Christians who yield some productivity for Christ can expect hardship (pruning) to increase productivity.

The call to abide in v. 4 is a command to keep Christ's commandments.

> "And the one who keeps His commandments abides in Him..." [1 John 3:24].

(See also 1 John 2:28.)

Those who refuse to keep His commandments are like the branch of v. 6. Burning could be an agricultural metaphor. Farmers burn a field to purify it from weeds and increase productivity.[81] Those who will not abide will face God's purifying chastisement. This is not the loss of salvation; rather, these troubles are designed to improve the believer. Also, there could be a reference here to loss of rewards.

1 Cor. 3:15 says that at the judgment seat a believer might find some of his life's work burned up. He himself is still saved but loses rewards. This second possible interpretation of the nature of burning in John 15:6 avoids any contradiction with texts that teach eternal security. It also has the advantage of being simple and includes John's definition of abiding as obedience in 1 John 3:24.[82] The author believes the previous view pays closer attention to the original setting and has a better explanation of the branch in the fire metaphor. Regardless of the interpretation one prefers, it ought to be evident that John 15:1-8 need not contradict eternal security.

6. Rom. 11:11-32

> You will say then, "Branches were broken off so that I might be grafted in." Quite right, they were broken off for their unbelief, but you stand by your faith. Do not be conceited, but

---

[80] Unlike the "Judas View," the chastisement view would interpret both types of branches in v. 2 as saved. Both would have inner spiritual union. There would be saved branches "in Me" with no fruit and other saved branches that produce fruit. However, just as with the "Judas View," the phrase "*in Me*" in v. 2 would not be identical with abiding. It would still be the case that those "in Me" might not be abiding, i.e., keeping the commandments.

[81] The author believes that the burning in Heb. 6:8 does speak of the burning of a believer in chastisement. However, notice that in Hebrews 6 the illustration is of a field. Fire burns off weeds and impurities from a field and improves a field's productivity without destroying it. However, John 15 uses a branch as an illustration. Fire would totally destroy a branch. The "Judas View" has an advantage in taking the warning to be that of hell. Also, if fire equals chastisement in John 15:6 what does the pruning of v. 2 mean? Would it not be better to see chastisement as included in pruning (v. 2) with fire (v. 6) as a reference to an even more severe danger?

[82] By contrast, 1 John 2:5-6 and 4:15 seem to take *abide* as reference to being saved.

fear; for if God did not spare the natural branches, neither will He spare you. Behold then the kindness and severity of God; to those who fell, severity, but to you, God's kindness, if you continue in His kindness; otherwise you also will be cut off. And they also, if they do not continue in their unbelief, will be grafted in; for God is able to graft them in again [Rom. 11:19-23].

a. The Jew-Gentile issue

Paul's question in Rom. 11:1 concerns whether God has rejected Israel. No, He has not rejected Israel because there is a believing remnant. However, because of Jewish unbelief (v. 20) God has suspended His work for Israel as a special people above all others. Now God includes gentiles in His place of blessing. Israel as a nation was cut off from God's place of blessing, but this does not allow gentile arrogance toward Israel. Paul explains that jealousy over gentile blessing may lead some Jews to faith in Christ (vv. 11, 14). In the future millennial Kingdom God will return Israel to a special position (vv. 25-27). In the meantime, gentiles must not feel God's attention upon them comes from superiority over Jews. In explaining the relationship between Jew and gentile, Paul uses the illustration of an olive tree.

b. The Original Olive Tree

The olive tree in Romans 11 is not the church. In a general sense it is the place of God's favor, the place of spiritual opportunity and blessings. More specifically, the olive tree is the place of blessings through Abraham. Since the root is holy (Abraham and the Patriarchs), so are the branches (following generations of Jews, especially those with faith). Gentiles owe all their spiritual benefits to Israel.

Note carefully that the original olive tree (Old Testament Judaism) held branches consisting of **saved and unsaved** Jews. Some of the Jewish branches were believers, but some had no faith (v. 20). Therefore, this tree is **not** the tree

of salvation, but rather a tree that pictures a broad range of spiritual opportunities and blessings. Blessings stemming from Abraham include eternal salvation (only for those with faith). However, blessings from Abraham upon Jews include other areas such as abundant knowledge about God through the Scriptures and prophetic leaders; practical wisdom in terms of family, business, and governmental relationships; and the blessings of ready access to God and living in a nation with many believers. Even the unsaved Israelites enjoyed many advantages.

However, because of unbelief God broke off all unbelieving Jews from the place of special blessing. God abrogated the Law of Moses including Judaism. Removing these unbelieving Jews from a place of God's special attention did not involve a loss of salvation because those without faith never had salvation. The primary definition of "breaking off" a branch is not loss of salvation but rather hardening (see vv. 7-25). The hardening of unbelieving Israel constitutes a breaking off from the place of special blessings for Israel.

c. The Gentile Relationship to the Olive Tree

God removed unbelieving Israel as an object of special opportunity and privilege. God then extended opportunities and special blessings to all nations (gentiles). Just as the original tree had both saved and unsaved Jews, the merger of gentiles to the place of blessing involves saved and unsaved gentiles. In Romans 11, Paul addresses his readers as gentiles (v. 13). The pronoun *you* in his argument addresses the Romans as gentiles. The pronoun *they* refers to Jews. Just as with Judaism, even unsaved gentiles can benefit from Christianity through common blessings. Unsaved gentiles still can have access to truth through the Scriptures and through churches. Cultures which and individuals who adhere to Biblical ethics benefit in terms of the family, business, government, and criminal/judicial affairs. However, permanent blessings from God come only to those with faith. Verse 20 teaches that "you (gentiles) stand only by faith." The gentiles that do have permanent standing within the tree of God's blessing possess their position by faith. No gentile must ever think that God's interest in gentiles has to do with an inherent superiority over Jews. One can see the danger of Romans looking down upon Jews. However, all gentiles have a debt to Israel for truth in Jewish Scriptures, Jewish prophets and a Jewish Messiah (v. 18).

The gentiles who do stand in a permanent place of blessing do so only by faith (v. 20). However, unbelieving gentile Christians can no more be saved than unbelieving Jews. There may be many temporary blessings from Christian influence, and exposure to Christian truth, but gentiles who lack faith will be cut off from eternal blessings. The warning in vv. 20-22 does not involve a loss of salvation. Unbelieving gentiles, who share many blessings by God's work among the gentiles, face a danger of removal from all blessing in this life and eternity. Cutting off would not refer to a loss of salvation. Unbelievers are not saved in the first place. The cutting off refers to a hardening of unbelieving gentiles just as it refers to a hardening of unbelieving Jews (vv. 7 and 25). Continuance of God's kindness comes only by faith (cf. Rom. 2:4 where God's kindness leads to repentance). An unbeliever can experience God's temporary common grace, but only believers have continuance in eternal grace. The danger of being removed from God's blessing comes from unbelief, (v. 20). Being cut off from the place of blessing means removal from temporary blessing such as Christian instruction and blindness to the truth. This is not a loss of salvation but does concern salvation. Unbelieving gentiles who are hardened, i.e., blind to truth, can never believe and, therefore, have no hope of salvation.

d. Conclusion

Rom. 11:11-32 should not be used as an objection to eternal security. Branches cut off the olive tree are unbelievers being removed from exposure to God's blessing and being hard-ened in their unbelief. Common grace extends to all gentiles. However, only those with faith continue in God's grace for eternity (v. 20). Permanent blessings come by faith, not by any superiority of gentiles over Jews.

7. 1 Cor. 6:9-10 (Gal. 5:19-21, See also Eph. 5:5)

These texts have already been studied under Section V of this chapter, "Genuine Salvation Results in Good Works." Paul's words mean that an ongoing **"practice"** of sin without conviction or repentance gives indication a person has never been saved. Christians are indeed capable of isolated involvement in any sin. However, habitual sin is inconsistent with salvation. We do not know God's definition of the practice of sin. Therefore, these warnings end up primarily being a personal warning to people in long-term sins. These people should examine themselves to consider whether they really believe in Christ (2 Cor. 13:5). Relative to evaluating others, a categorical denial of another's salvation should not be made based on their behavior alone if they profess faith. However, a working assumption can be made that a person in lasting sin might not be a genuine believer. In such cases a Christian worker should repeat the gospel of grace. The issue in the above texts is not loss of salvation. It concerns practical evidence that a person has never possessed salvation.

8. 1 Cor. 9:24-27

Do you not know that those who run in a race all run, but only one receives the prize? Run in such a way that you may win. And everyone who competes in the games exercises self-control in all things. They then do it to receive a perishable wreath, but we an imperishable. Therefore I run in such a way, as not without aim; I box in such a way, as not beating the air; but I buffet my body and make it my slave, lest possibly, after I have preached to others, I myself should be disqualified [1 Cor. 9:24-27].

Paul's subject here cannot be salvation. Salvation does not come through human work. The athletic imagery involves rewards for the believer at the Judgment Seat of Christ. Mention of disqualification in v. 27 is not the loss of salvation. Paul is concerned about being disqualified from ministry due to sin. He works hard so as to not be disqualified from gaining a full reward. (Possible references to loss of rewards: Col. 2:18; 2 John 8; Rev. 3:11.)

9. 1 Cor. 11:28-32

> But let a man examine himself, and so let him eat of the bread and drink of the cup. For he who eats and drinks, eats and drinks judgment to himself, if he does not judge the body rightly....But when we are judged, we are disciplined by the Lord in order that we may not be condemned along with the world [1 Cor: 11:28, 29, 32].

There need be no confusion over this communion text. Perhaps the King James translation of "damnation" in v. 29 is the source of the problem. However, the warning to Corinthian believers is of a judgment that is clearly distinguished from the condemnation which the world receives. The danger is not eternal condemnation but rather of temporal chastisement, such as weakness, sickness, or physical death (v. 30).

10. 1 Cor. 15:1-2; Col. 1:21-23 [83]

> ...by which also you are saved, if you hold fast the word which I preached to you, unless you believed in vain [1 Cor. 15:2].

> [I]f indeed you continue in the faith firmly established and steadfast, and not moved away from the hope of the gospel that you have heard, which was proclaimed in all creation under heaven, and of which I, Paul, was made a minister [Col. 1:23].

Biblical calls to continue in the faith are quite consistent with the security of believers. God uses such Scriptural commands to keep believers in the faith and thereby keep them in salvation.

Those with genuine faith might have doubts, or disobey, or even occasionally verbally deny Christianity to others, but genuine believers do not sincerely repudiate the deity, resurrection, or blood of Christ within their own hearts or to God the Father. Jesus says in John 10:4b-5, "...the sheep follow him because they know his voice. And a stranger they simply will not follow, but will flee from him, because they do not know the voice of strangers." 1 John 2:19 teaches that those who renounce Christ and His cross never were saved in the first place: "They went out from us, but they were not really of us, for if they had been of us, they would have remained with us, but they went out in order that it might be shown that they all are not of us." Genuine believers always believe. Though salvation is a past tense matter (e.g., Eph. 2:8, 9; and Titus 3:5, both past tense in the Greek), faith in the Bible is often in the present tense (e.g., John 3:16 "...that whoever believes in Him should not perish..."). Genuine believers always believe because God keeps them in the faith.

> Now to Him who is able to **keep** you from stumbling, and to make you stand in the presence of His glory blameless

---

[83] It is difficult to know whether to include Luke 9:62 in this classification. Jesus is probably saying that the disciple who "looks back" is especially unworthy of God's grace and blessings, but He is not saying he has no salvation. Such a person is unfit for ministry. However, if the topic is salvation not Christian living, then Luke 9:62 teaches one who repudiates Christ never had saving faith as in the line of reasoning given above (1 Cor. 15:1-2 and Col. 1:21-23). A person who visibly follows Jesus and/or even participates in Christian work but falls back to a former repudiation of the cross possesses at best intellectual faith or emotional faith but never trusted Jesus. (See Chapter 9, Part 2:

"Salvation Applied" section II.B.2, p. 133, for explanation of intellectual or emotional faith.)

with great joy…[Jude 24].

[T]o obtain an inheritance which is imperishable and undefiled and will not fade away, reserved in heaven for you, who are **protected** by the power of God through faith for a salvation ready to be revealed in the last time [1 Pet. 1:4-5].[84]

Warnings in the Bible to "keep the faith" are not inconsistent with thinking true believers in fact will keep the faith. One of the ways God keeps believers in the faith is through Biblical commands and warnings. For those with genuine faith, the commands to continue help ensure continuance. Also, such commands warn unbelievers within the visible church. There is a need for ministers to follow Paul's example of warning "to continue." "Test yourselves to see if you are in the faith" (2 Cor. 13:5). Some who think they have saving faith really have only intellectual or emotional faith. (See Chapter 9, Part 2: "Salvation Applied," section II.B., p.133) Paul's warnings in 1 Cor. 15:1-2 and Col. 1:21-23 are concerns that some in New Testament churches lacked trust in Christ. Any definition of faith other than trust constitutes a vain faith that will not last.

---

[84] Peter does not explain whether faith in 1 Pet. 1:5 refers to a past faith, i.e., initial saving faith or an ongoing faith in the present. Those who adhere to eternal security usually see the faith in v. 5 as a past initial act of faith. Initial faith in Christ brings God's protection and causes a reservation in heaven. On the other hand, Arminians naturally see faith in v. 5 as ongoing faith. So long as a person has ongoing faith, he has God's protection of salvation as reservation in heaven. In all fairness, salvation in 1 Pet. 1:5 refers to a future salvation from sin's presence, not a past salvation from sin's penalty. Therefore, faith in v. 5 need not refer to a past act of initial faith in Christ but rather ongoing faith in the Christian life. One who comes to 1 Pet. 1:4-5 already believing in eternal security can agree with Arminians that faith refers to ongoing faith. However, there is no doubt that a believer will continue to believe. **1 Pet. 1:4-5 probably means God's power protects believers by keeping them in faith.**

Thus, Paul's warnings do not concern believers who might lose salvation, but those whose concept of faith does not involve trust (dependence, reliance) in Christ, God the Son, who died and rose again. These would not lose salvation. Instead, they do not have salvation because they lack the kind of faith that saves.

11. Gal. 5:1-4

It was for freedom that Christ set us free; therefore keep standing firm and do not be subject again to a yoke of slavery. Behold I, Paul, say to you that if you receive circumcision, Christ will be of no benefit to you…You have been severed from Christ, you who are seeking to be justified by law; you have fallen from grace [Gal. 5:1,2,4].

a. Law Versus Grace

The debate in the book of Galatians concerns the choice between Law and Grace. Are people saved by Law-keeping (either the Law of Moses or other systems of laws) or are they saved by grace? Paul in Galatians argues for the doctrine of grace instead of Law (e.g., Gal. 2:16; 3:11; etc.). Pages of verses can be quoted that salvation does not come through good works. (See Chapter 9, Part 2: "Salvation Applied," section II.F., p. 142 "Believe and Work to Earn Salvation.") It is inexcusable to add works to faith as a requirement for salvation. However, some Christians from New Testament days to the present have been confused. Many try to merge faith and works. **Faith alone saves.** Works add nothing. When a person trusts in good works or religious rituals, he is definitely unsaved; but how shall we evaluate the spiritual status of one who mixes faith and works, grace and Law? Heresy is confusing. It is wrong to trust in both Christ and Law-keeping for salvation, but many adopt such false thinking.

Likely, millions are really trusting in their own goodness or in their religion without any real faith in Christ and the cross. These are unsaved despite their associations with Christian organizations and rituals.

Nevertheless, Acts 15:5 refers to the "Pharisees who had **believed**" insisting that circumcision and Law-keeping were also essential for salvation. Therefore, it seems possible for genuine Christians to become confused over the conditions for salvation. Even believers can be led astray by false teaching. Paul's writings in the book of Galatians show his concern that saved people can **fall away from the true doctrine of grace**. Those who insist upon Law-keeping for salvation might be saved, or they might be unsaved ("false brethren," Gal. 2:4). Perhaps only God knows whether those with such false ideas have faith in Christ (2 Tim. 2:19). God can tell when one is really trusting his own goodness or trusting a church to save. God can also determine whether some have weak faith in the cross even when they also needlessly do more to "guarantee" salvation because they lack assurance. They are saved but add works to faith as a means of being extra certain to obtain salvation. They keep the Law as an extra measure of precaution. No doubt some with such weak faith will actually be surprised to find they had salvation through grace alone and endured much needless anxiety in this life. While Galatians has a strong message for unbelievers who base salvation on their own goodness, the original recipients were already saved. In Galatians 5 Paul urges them to continue their lives in freedom from the Law. He wants them to continue in grace theology and in a Christian way of life based upon grace theology not to fall away from grace doctrines and a grace-oriented Christian life.

b. No Benefit in This Life (Gal. 5:2)

What happens to believers who trust in the Lord Jesus but then add the idea they must also keep the Law (the Law of Moses or other forms of laws) to either earn or keep salvation?

Paul should not be understood as warning the Galatians they would lose salvation. Yet, by adopting a mixture of Law and grace they would **lose all the benefits of Christ as it pertains to this life**. Believers who abandon the doctrine of grace do not lose eternal life, but they do lose truths that are absolutely necessary to living the Christian life. **Works theology inevitably leads to lack of assurance**. Fear, not gratitude, becomes the motivation for work. As opposed to enjoyment of God's unconditional love and grace, a believer who thinks salvation is in doubt without additional works cannot have the benefits of true Christianity. Christ does not operate through a system of Law. Therefore, in a sense, it is not even possible to live the true Christian life by mixing Law and grace. Believers who try to add Law to grace are not really living a Christian life as taught in the New Testament. When Paul says in Gal. 5:2 that those who mix Law and grace lose the benefit of Christ, he does not mean they lose eternal life. He does mean they lose all benefits of the Christian life in this world. Gal. 5:4 gives the strongest type of warning to believers (the Galatians were believers – Gal. 5:1) who are in danger of falling away from the doctrine of grace.

c. Severed from Christ (Gal. 5:4)

The phrase "fallen from grace" in Gal. 5:4 does not refer to a loss of salvation. Those who place themselves back under a yoke of the Law **fall away from the doctrine of grace** and from the outlook and relationship to Christ based on a system of grace. Being "severed from Christ" means that those who **fall from grace theology and from the Christian life arising from it are cut off from fellowship with Christ**. To abandon the real way of Christian living for an unscriptural way that God will not use means being **severed from opportunities for Christian growth and service**. A person can still be saved though he attempts to add works to grace. However, he cannot really experience Christian living. Also, those with such false doctrines are **totally unqualified to minister to others**. It is the theological equivalent to "malpractice": they harm others spiritually by their error. In addition to being **severed from fellowship** and genuine ministry, they are **severed from Christian growth and activity**. Christ and the Spirit of Christ operate by grace, not by Law. Those who add works to faith cut themselves off from the only way Christ wants to lead them.

d. Conclusion on Gal. 5:1-4

The warnings of Gal. 5:1-4 can be interpreted as consistent with eternal security. Paul does not threaten a loss of eternal life. However, his words are as harsh as possible without implying an eternity in hell. Believers who get mixed-up ideas that salvation requires Law-keeping lose all the benefits of Christ relative to living real Christianity (v. 2). To fall away from the doctrine of grace and the way of Christian living arising from it is to be cut off from fellowship with Christ (v. 4). Since the truths about God's grace are essential to Biblical Christian living, believers who disagree are cut off in terms of potential for growth and ministry (v. 4). Believers who misunderstand grace do not lose salvation, but they do lose the foundation for Christian living. The extreme consequences explain Paul's deep concern for the Galatians.

12. 2 Tim. 2:12b

...if we deny Him, He will also deny us...[2 Tim. 2:12b].

In the context, Paul has told Timothy to "be strong" (v. 1) and to "suffer hardship" (v. 3). Then he gives examples of disciplined lives, a soldier (v. 4), an athlete (v. 5), and a farmer (v. 6).

The statement in 2 Tim. 2:12b is part of an early Christian hymn. While the specific interpretation in each phrase can be difficult, the overall hymn teaches the merits of dedication and discipline.

If "we" is restricted to saved people, then the phrase can mean those who are ashamed to admit they are believers (see 2 Tim. 1:8) will be denied the full rewards God wanted to give them. This would not

be a loss of salvation but a loss of crowns, higher positions in the Kingdom, or a deeper glory in the resurrection body (see 1 Cor. 3:15; Col. 2:18; 1 John 2:28; 2 John 8; Rev. 3:11 for verses that might speak of a believer losing rewards at the Judgment Seat of Christ). Actually, the very next statement is perhaps an assertion that a believer's salvation is secure even if he or she is denied rewards. **"If we are faithless, He remains faithful..."(2 Tim. 2:13a).**

If the "we" in 2 Tim. 2:12b is not restricted to believers and involves people in general, another interpretation results. Those who deny Christ as Savior in this life, i.e., they will not believe on Him, will be denied by the Lord in the future judgment (see Matt. 7:22-23). Then the next verse (v.13) would mean those who are faithless (unbelievers) will face eternal judgment. God will be faithful to His own justice and His warnings of destruction.

The first view fits a context that calls for believers to endure hardship. We will be denied rewards if we disobey. However, the second view also fits the subject in vv. 9-10 (enduring hardship so that the elect obtain salvation and eternal glory). Perhaps 2 Tim. 2:11-12a refers to the saved that obtain life and also rewards. 2 Tim. 2:12b-13 would then refer to those who deny Christ as Savior and are faithless (unbelievers). These will forfeit eternal glory and be denied salvation. By either way of understanding this phrase, it is compatible with the doctrine that a believer does not lose salvation.

13. Warning Passages from Hebrews

The author of Hebrews gives five warning passages in his book: 2:1-4; 3:6-4:11 (especially 3:6, 12, 14, 4:11); 6:4-8; 10:26-31; 12:25-29. Those who deny eternal security point to Heb. 6:4-6 or 10:26-31 as strong evidences for their position. However, all these texts can be better understood in ways compatible with eternal security. Before explaining them, it will be necessary to give an opinion about the original recipients of the book of Hebrews. Were the readers a mixture of saved and unsaved Jews? If so, the warning passages can be read as warnings to the unsaved about placing faith in Christ before being condemned to the fires of hell. If the original readers are strictly believers, then the warnings urge them to avoid the fires of chastisement.[85] Instead of neglecting eternity, believers must work toward obtaining a full reward and share in Christ's coming Kingdom. The exact interpretation of the warning passages depends upon whether one views the recipients as unsaved (evangelistic warnings) or saved (warnings about being unfaithful). However, both options can lead to interpretations consistent with eternal security. After dealing with the identity of the original readers, there will be a study on each warning passage.

a. The Original Readers of Hebrews

The recipients of Hebrews are obviously Jewish. They have affiliated with Christian circles but are being urged to return to Judaism.[86] The author warns against this choice. Obviously, a local church can have members who are unsaved. Could these warnings be directed at unbelievers in Hebrew churches? They would then be evangelistic warnings urging faith in Christ. The other option is that the warnings are directed at genuine believers. They urge believers not to forsake the visible church and return to associations with the synagogue. By an evil choice, they would endure the fires of God's chastisement (hardship in this life but not hell) and loss of full rewards in heaven. Which view is best?

The choice is admittedly difficult. Nevertheless, the author prefers to take the warning texts in Hebrews as directed to believers. The definition of *salvation* in Hebrews gives a slight favor to the idea that these warnings are directed at those already saved. What does the author of Hebrews mean by *salvation*? In the Bible there is a past tense salvation. A believer has already been saved (past tense) from the penalty of sin. If Hebrews intends this definition of salvation, then the warning texts are evangelistic. Nevertheless, the Bible also refers to a future aspect to salvation even for those already saved from sin's penalty. In the future believers will be saved from sin's presence (Rom. 13:11). Christ's future deliverance (salvation) includes all the blessings from His Second Coming (binding the devil, a resurrection body for the church saints, rewards, and positions of authority in the Kingdom).[87] Although all believers will be in heaven, there will be various levels of rewards (crowns), various positions of authority in sharing Christ's rule (Luke 19:17, 19), and even different levels of glory among resurrection bodies (1 Cor. 15:41-42). While no Christian loses admission to heaven, there will be degrees of sharing in the Kingdom. If we take *salvation* in Hebrews to refer to a future deliverance at Christ's coming, then the warning passages apply to believers. They would be warnings about neglecting to live for eternity. Faithlessness will result in a diminished share in the blessings of the future salvation.

Hebrews definitely gives a future outlook; (1) "heir of all things" Heb. 1:2, (2) "He **again** brings the firstborn into the world" Heb. 1:6 i.e., the Second Coming, (3) "the world to come" Heb. 2:5, (4) "bringing many sons to glory" Heb. 2:10, (5) "heavenly calling" Heb. 3:1, (6) "the age to come" Heb. 6:5, (7) "the day drawing near" Heb. 10:25. Even more important, several usages of the term *salvation* show that the author defines it as a future de-

---

[85] Fire would be an agricultural metaphor speaking of purging a field from impurity or a fire that burns away worthless work as a believer forfeits rewards, 1 Cor. 3:15.

[86] We need not concern ourselves here whether the readers are being pulled back to mainstream Judaism or a Jewish splinter sect.

[87] All these topics are covered in Chapter 12, "Eschatology."

liverance from sin's presence and curse (and not just salvation in the past from sin's penalty).

Are they not all ministering spirits, sent out to render service for the sake of those who **will inherit salvation?** [Heb. 1:14].

[S]o Christ also, having been offered once to bear the sins of many, shall appear **a second time for salvation** without reference to sin, to those who eagerly await Him [Heb. 9:28].

The position that takes the warnings in Hebrews as evangelistic warnings to unbelievers about salvation from sin's penalty is a valid position. It preserves the doctrine of eternal security. However, Hebrews probably gives warnings to Christians about missing the full blessings of future salvation. Believers must not live only for this life, neglecting the Lord's return. If so, they could very well miss out on some aspects to future deliverance (salvation). Believers have already been saved from sin's penalty, but can still miss their full potential for rewards and blessings in the future salvation Christ will bring. An illustration about an earthly inheritance should help clarify Hebrews' perspective about our heavenly inheritance. Suppose a man has the potential to obtain a staggering inheritance. The degree to which he could share in the future is beyond understanding. He stands to inherit a blessing greater than anyone in world history. However, suppose through neglect of his benefactor he receives only a small fraction of what he could have inherited. He still obtained a huge benefit. From one point of view he did not miss out on the inheritance. Nevertheless, from another perspective the loss of the potential full inheritance could be viewed as missing out on his inheritance. By neglect he lost out on what he could have possessed.

The Lord will return to bring a complete salvation to this world. There will be salvation from sin's presence (and the curse). All believers have already been eternally saved from

sin's penalty. Yet, there will be various degrees of sharing in the future salvation. No believer will miss out totally. Still, through unfaithfulness and neglect of living with Christ's future rescue in view, many believers will miss the full inheritance that they could otherwise have obtained. All will share in the future deliverance the Lord brings at His Second Coming, but many will miss the full blessing of this salvation. This will be such a huge loss of what they could have possessed, it can be conceived as a loss of the deepest share in salvation. It is not that a believer can go to hell or miss out on entrance into heaven, but a believer can miss out on the full blessings of Christ's future deliverance (rewards, position in the Kingdom, degrees of glory in the resurrection body, etc.). Hebrews probably warns believers against neglecting to live now in ways that obtain a deeper reward in the salvation that is coming. Hebrews probably warns about the fire of chastisement during this life and the loss of rewards.

Now we shall address each warning passage. The first view will give an interpretation based on the assumption the warning is evangelistic (directed at unbelievers). The second view will give an interpretation that results from the assumption that the warning is for believers. Regardless of the exact view adopted, **the main truth must not be lost: there are ways of understanding Hebrews that are consistent with eternal security.**

b. The First Warning Passage: Heb. 2:1-4

[H]ow shall we escape if we neglect so great a salvation? After it was at the first spoken through the Lord, it was confirmed to us by those who heard [Heb. 2:3].

(1) As Addressed to the Unsaved Among the Hebrews

Those who believe the original readers included some unsaved will view this warning as evangelistic. Pay attention to the gospel (Heb. 2:1a). Do not drift through life neglecting the invitation to faith in Christ (Heb. 2:1b). Those who disobeyed the law suffered punishment (Heb. 2:2). Those who neglect salvation (from sin's penalty) offered through faith in Christ will not escape eternal punishment (Heb. 2: 3).

(2) As Addressed to Believers

Those who think Hebrews speaks only to believers will see this as a warning to live for eternity. Salvation refers to a future rescue through the Lord's Second Coming. There will be a future deliverance from this evil world system and from all aspects of the curse (such as sickness and physical death). This future salvation also includes rewards and positions of authority in the millennial Kingdom and eternity. Christians must pay close attention to what the Lord taught about His future deliverance (i.e., Heb. 2:1a - a future salvation). If we want to share a deeper degree of rewards, blessings, and authority in these future aspects of salvation, we cannot just drift through life now (Heb. 2:1b). Some believers are lazy and apathetic about their level of reward and authority in the future Kingdom. They are careless concerning what they have learned about the future rescue (salvation) from the presence of sin and from this world system. Believers who live only for this present time neglecting Christ's teaching about His future salvation will receive chastisement now and loss of rewards later (v. 2 – "just recompense"). Those who pay attention to what Christ taught about the future will not just drift through this life. They will not neglect the future salvation that is coming with degrees of sharing in rewards, positions in the Kingdom, and the glory of the resurrection body. They will live now so as to obtain the fullest possible share when Christ comes to save us out of and from this sinful and transitory world.[88] They will take action in this world that will be of benefit in "the world

to come" (v. 5).

Viewing salvation from a future angle probably seems unusual to Christians who read the Bible today. Our thinking emphasizes salvation from sin's penalty. However, the warning in Heb. 2:1-4 is sandwiched between two references to future salvation. Hebrews 1:14 clearly uses salvation to encompass all future blessings. Also, Heb. 2:5 is tied to the arguments of 2:1-4. Heb. 2:5 tells of the "world to come." While living in this world, believers must pay attention to how they can obtain a larger reward and a deeper share in the rule, power, and glory of the world to come.

(3) Conclusion

The first warning passage is not teaching that believers can lose salvation from sin's penalty by drifting away or neglect. We have given two alternative interpretations. The above section reveals the author's preference for one view over another. However, both interpretations supply the need for an understanding of Heb. 2:1-4 that is compatible with eternal security.

c. The Second Warning Passage: Hebrews Chapters 3-4

> [B]ut Christ was faithful as a Son over His house whose house we are, if we hold fast our confidence and the boast of our hope firm until the end [Heb. 3:6].

> Take care brethren, lest there should be in any one of you an evil, unbelieving heart, in falling away from the living God [Heb. 3:12].

> For we have become partakers of Christ, if we hold fast the beginning of our assurance firm until the end [Heb 3:14].

> Let us therefore be diligent to enter that rest, lest anyone fall through following the same example of disobedience [Heb. 4:11].

---

[88] The Lord will save believers **out of** this world at the Rapture. This is also a salvation from the suffering, persecution, and temptation **from** the world (i.e., caused by living in a world dominated by Satan and a world system opposed to Christ).

(1) As Addressed to the Unsaved Among the Hebrews

One earlier conclusion from this study was that genuine saving faith keeps faith. God keeps a believer believing. A person who trusts Christ as Savior will not renounce the deity, blood, or resurrection of Christ. (See VII.B.10., p.206 of this section, which deals with 1 Cor. 15:1-2). The type of faith that saves (trust) leads to an ongoing faith. Other types of faith such as intellectual faith in certain facts about God (James 2:19) or emotional faith that Jesus can save from temporal difficulties (without an interest in salvation from sin [e.g., Luke 8:13] do not save, see Part 2, II.B.2., p. 133 of this chapter). The warnings in Hebrews 3-4 may be addressed to unbelievers who have associated with Jewish churches. These do not possess the type of faith that saves and one that lasts (holds fast) By this understanding *house* in Heb. 3:6 refers to being part of God's family, and *partaker* in Heb. 3:14 refers to saving union with Christ. Heb. 3:6 is a warning to examine whether some among the readers might not have saving faith (the kind that continues to believe). Heb. 3:12 warns against being an unbeliever who falls away from God. They would fall away by rejecting God's appeals to trust Jesus. The Hebrew readers are being invited to leave the church and return to the synagogue. Again, in Heb. 3:14, the author may be urging the readers to make sure they have personal faith in Christ. (**Personal** in the sense of **trust** rather than just intellectual faith in facts about Jesus or emotional faith that He can help with temporal problems). The type of faith that saves keeps believing. Other definitions of faith do not involve saving faith. The author is not worried that a believer has lost salvation. He is worried that some readers, though joined to a church, might not have ever trusted in Christ. Heb. 4:11 becomes another evangelistic appeal to enter salvation by resting through faith in Christ and resting from works as a way of earning salvation (4:10).

(2) As Addressed to Believers

The warnings in Hebrews 3-4 can also be understood as warnings to believers to remain active in worship/service, to keep working in an active partnership with Christ, and to enter a full inheritance (reward). Remember the Hebrews are struggling with the temptation to forsake the visible church and return to association with Judaism. The "houses" in Hebrews 3 do not seem to refer to the family of God. Moses' house in Heb. 3:5 refers to the worship/service system in the tabernacle. Only priests could serve in the "house of God" as limited to the priestly functions within the holy place and holy of holies. In the Old Testament one could still be saved without active participation in God's house (the place and system of priests). Christ's house in v. 6 probably also refers to active participation in priestly worship. Unlike the Law where only a minority could be priests, all believers under the New Testament (covenant) have standing as priests with God; but some withdraw from involvement in the activity of worship and service. Christians can never drop out of the family of God, but they can refuse to participate in God's system of worship and service. They can remove themselves from God's house by refusing to assemble with other believer-priests as they worship. The familiar call to assemble in Heb. 10:25 is preceded by a statement in Heb. 10:21 that Christ is the great priest over the house of God. Thus, the command not to forsake church equals a warning to remain in God's house. Heb. 3:6 is probably a warning for Jewish believers to not drop out of God's house (which is not a church building but is, rather, the assembly of believer-priests as they worship) and return to the synagogue.[89] A person can be saved and be

---

[89] Moses' house in Heb. 3:5 refers to the tabernacle (the house of God) with its holy place and also refers to the function of the Old Testament priesthood that offered worship and service in that place. The definition of *house* in Heb. 3:6 includes both the **place** of worship and also the **participants** (priests in their roles of worship and service). By Christ's "house" the author of Hebrews means the

a part of God's family but depart from involvement with the church, the house of worship. Heb. 3:6 encourages remaining active in "Christ's house."

Assuming the author addresses the saved, Heb. 3:12 would be referring to the ongoing faith of Christian living. A saved person has believed in the cross but must also constantly believe the commands and teaching of the Bible. It would exhibit a great lack of faith for a Jewish Christian to forsake the church out of social pressures and return to associations with Judaism. Leaving the church might not cause a loss of salvation but it does break fellowship with God and can be called "falling away from the living God" (v. 12).

Heb. 3:14 can be taken as a warning totally restricted to believers. Perhaps understanding *partakers* as a saving union with Christ misses the intent of the warning. Luke 5:7 uses the same Greek word of business partners in a joint fishing business. The definition of "partners" or "co-laborers" also fits the usage in Heb. 1:9 ("companions," NASB) and 3:1 ("partners in the heavenly calling or heavenly work"). The stress need not be on spiritual union but upon active participation as co-laborers with Christ in the work of ministry. Just as the concept of the "house" in Heb. 3:6 warns of dropping out of activity in God's system of worship, so Heb. 3:14 warns against failing to be a working partner with Christ in service. Believers who are active partners with Christ's work in this world will share in a more full partnership in His power and glory later. We must both remain in Christ's house of worship (the church) and remain active partners with Him to realize full potential for inheritance.

If addressed to believers, Heb. 4:11 is a command to diligently strive for the fullest possible inheritance. The concept of rest may not seem to have anything to do with inheritance until we realize the context and the Jewish way of thinking. For them *rest* is closely linked with inheritance. After God **rested** from His creative work, He could **enjoy the inheritance** He had made for Himself. Those in the Exodus generation were called to conquer the Promised Land. Then they could enter the **rest** and **enjoy the inheritance**. Notice the connection between rest and inheritance in Deut. 3:18-20 and 12:9-11.

> [F]or you have not as yet come to the **resting** place and the **inheritance** which the LORD your God is giving you. When you cross the Jordan and live in the land which the LORD your God is giving you to **inherit,** and He gives you **rest** from all your enemies around you so that you live in security... [Deut. 12:9-10].

The author of Hebrews teaches that not even Joshua led God's people to full rest and inheritance in the land (Heb. 4:8). The greatest rest and inheritance still lies in the future. Believers have not yet entered rest from labor. Now is the time to work. Rest and inheritance are coming.

Someday we will cease earth's labors (at death or the Rapture). However, the present is not a time of rest but rather of labor, even warfare as implied by the Old Testament parallels of fighting to obtain full inheritance in the Promised Land. Heb. 4:11 is certainly not an appeal to earn salvation from hell by diligent work. The command in Heb. 4:11 tells believers to be diligent to enter the inheritance God wants to give them. The author's definition of *inheritance* is not just minimal deliverance from eternal punishment but the full possession of rewards and blessings that God wants bestowed. When the term inheritance is strictly defined as "a **full** possession or inheritance," it is possible to miss out on the inheritance and obtain only a rescue from damnation. This is a

---

heavenly tabernacle and its holy place (the presence of God on His throne) with a New Testament **priesthood** of worship and service to God. A believer always has the position as a priest but can drop away from the functions of service and worship.

huge blessing but not the full inheritance that can be possessed by diligence. All believers will enter eternal rest in the common meaning of that phrase, rest from earthly troubles. Yet, some will inherit more rewards and blessings than others. All believers will be citizens and residents of God's Kingdom, but many will miss the (complete) inheritance God wanted to give them. Just as many in the Exodus generations were saved but did not obtain their inheritance in the Promised Land, so believers can be saved from hell but miss the full inheritance God wants to give. Just as believers in Joshua's generation were saved from hell but did not obtain the full inheritance God wanted to give, there is a danger of a believer today going to heaven but missing the full inheritance God wanted to give. If *inheritance* is viewed as the potential for the greatest possible blessing, it is possible for a believer to miss out on the promised rest by a lack of diligence. Heb. 4:11 warns to obey and work now to enter full inheritance and rest in the future.

All the warnings in Hebrews 3-4 can be taken as warnings to believers without implying a loss of salvation from eternal punishment: (1) "Remain in God's house" (Heb. 3:6) i.e., remain in the church assembly as a system of priestly worship and service; (2) "Do not fall away from fellowship with the living God by returning to ties with Judaism" (Heb. 3:12). (3) "Keep your partnership in working for Christ" Heb. 3:14; (4) "Do not rest yet. Be diligent and obedient so you do not miss out on any part of the rest (the complete inheritance) God wants to give you" (Heb. 4:11). Believing Hebrews would not lose salvation by dropping out of the church. However, they could withdraw from God's house (system of worship, v. 6). They could fall away from fellowship with God (v. 12). They could cease to be active partners in Christ's work (v. 14). Like the Hebrews of Old Testament days (many of whom were also saved), they could fail to enter the inheritance (rest) God wanted to give them (4:11). They would have salvation from hell, but God wanted to give more.

If they forsake the church and return outwardly to Judaism, they will miss the rest (inheritance) God wants them to have (but not miss heaven itself).

(3) Conclusion

The second warning passage may urge unbelievers affiliated with the church to come to faith in Christ. It may urge believers to remain diligent and involved to obtain the complete inheritance God wants for them. It does not contradict the basic doctrines of Scripture that teach the eternal security of the believer.

d. The Third Warning Passage: Heb. 6:1-12

> For in the case of those who have once been enlightened and have tasted of the heavenly gift and have been made partakers of the Holy Spirit, and have tasted the good word of God and the powers of the age to come, and then have fallen away, it is impossible to renew them again to repentance, since they again crucify to themselves the Son of God, and put Him to open shame. For ground that drinks the rain which often falls upon it and brings forth vegetation useful to those for whose sake it is also tilled, receives a blessing from God; but if it yields thorns and thistles, it is worthless and close to being cursed, and it ends up being burned [Heb. 6:4-8].

If a person comes to this text already thinking that believers can forfeit salvation, he will interpret these verses as confirmation. However, assuming that is the correct view, then Heb. 6:6 would be teaching **once lost always lost**. It says that for those who fall away "it is impossible to renew them again to repentance." The true interpretation of Hebrews 6:1-12 lies in another direction. Again, the precise outcome depends on whether one thinks the author directs his warning to unsaved people associated with the visible church or strictly to believers. If the words are to unbelievers, this is a warning to place faith in Christ. They must press on to maturity, i.e., out of Judaism to full Christianity (Heb. 6:1). The curse and burning of v. 8 would be a reference to hell. On the other hand, this warning could be aimed at believers. Then the burning of v. 8 would be a metaphor for burning a field to remove impurities (weeds) and produce fertility. Notice the actual figure employed is of a field. Burning would refer to God's chastisement of a believer in this life and perhaps the loss of rewards at the Judgment Seat (1 Cor. 3:15). While the precise interpretation varies depending on the conclusion about the recipients, **in neither case does Hebrews 6 need to be understood as dealing with Christians who lose salvation.** Now we will look at the passage in detail.

(1) As Addressed to Unbelievers

Suppose the author directs his warnings to unbelievers who assemble within the Hebrew churches. Leaving elementary teaching and pressing on to maturity would be a call to permanently leave all forms of Judaism and enter by faith into God's more advanced system, Christianity. It might not be possible for this to happen. The impossible renewal of Heb. 6:6 may mean that some of the Hebrews have rejected Christ to the point of no return, or maybe this means nothing further the author can say or do will produce saving repentance. However, God can change hearts (v. 3). The strongest evidence for thinking unsaved people are in view comes from the phrase in v. 6, "crucify to themselves the Son of God," and v. 9, "things that accompany salvation." If a person actually believes Jesus was a false messiah who deserved to die, he is indeed unsaved. Also, by saying he expected better things of the readers, "things that accompany salvation," maybe the author implies his previous words describe the unsaved. Maybe the picture in vv. 4-6 refers to persons who have been exposed to Christian people and truths but have not placed faith in Christ. In current language, we would call them "seekers." They are considering faith in Christ. They have moved away from Judaism but not yet to Christian

faith. They have some truths about the Lord Jesus (enlightenment, v. 4). They have had some experience of what salvation means because they have associated with the saved (tasting or sampling the heavenly gift of salvation, v. 4). They have had some participation with the Holy Spirit's convicting ministry (partakers, v. 4). They have sampled (tasted) the blessings of the Scripture and had seen miracles (v. 5). However, there was pressure upon those Jewish people to fall away from the church and thereby reject any further influence to the possibility of faith in Christ. If they return to the conclusion that Jesus was a false christ who deserved death (crucify to themselves the Son of God, v. 6), they might experience blindness and reprobation. At the very least nothing the author could do would ever change their minds (i.e., renew repentance, v. 6). God alone could change this serious falling away (v. 3), and, unless reversed, the end would be burning (v. 8). Heb. 6:1-8 can be interpreted as a warning for unbelievers (seekers) to come to faith in Christ and to not return to Judaism. The result squares with eternal security. Another option would be the idea that the warning is for believers with the fire of v. 8 being severe chastisement for falling away from the church.

(2) As Addressed to Believers

The descriptions "again crucify to themselves the Son of God" (v. 6) and "things that accompany salvation" (v. 9) need not rule out the view that Hebrews 6 is addressed to those already saved. Suppose the description of "crucify Christ" does not speak of a deliberately expressed theological position. Instead, it might be an inadvertent, unconscious, and unintended description of one who falls away (*forsake* – Heb. 10:25) from the church and returns to associations with Judaism. The description, "crucify Christ," might not give a true heart-felt theological conviction but rather a sociological behavior. Anyone who falls away from a Christian assembly to listen to false teachers from a Judaistic cult sides with Christ's killers by actions and associations without realizing it. A genuine Christian who falls away from the church can side with Christ's enemies by association. The author would not be classifying the readers as unsaved. He would be using "guilt by association" tactic. In theological beliefs they had not agreed with the crucifixion, but, by affiliation with Christ's enemies, their actions are inconsistent with their beliefs. Christians must not return to the religious circles that killed Christ. If they drop out of the church and return to involvement in Judaism, they would be assisting the very group whose leaders wanted Jesus killed as a false messiah. Most likely the Hebrew readers never realized the true picture of what it would mean to fall away from Christian circles and a return to their old friends in Judaism. Perhaps they thought it would be a simple innocent change. The author wants them to see that, even without intent and without realization, those who forsake the church for a return to Judaism would be siding (in association but not belief) with those who killed Jesus as a false messiah. Dropping fellowship with the church might be a more serious matter and might make God angrier than the Hebrew believers ever realized. If the phrase (crucifying the Son of God) is interpreted as sociological behavior and not theological belief, it can still refer to genuine Christians.

Likewise, the phrase "things that accompany salvation" (Heb. 6:9) need not imply the readers are unbelievers. Salvation in the book of Hebrews has a future tense emphasis. Christ will return to save believers both out of and from this world and from the curse of sin. This deliverance involves degrees of rewards, co-ruling with Christ in various ranks of authority, and levels of glory in the resurrection body. All believers will have a share in this future type of salvation. Some will have a greater and more glorious degree of sharing than others. Jewish believers who fall away from the church for a return to Judaism could still be saved from sin's penalty in eternal hell. However, they would miss out on the deepest

blessing of future salvation upon the Lord's return. "Things that accompany salvation" in v. 9 equals "pressing on to maturity" in vv. 1-3. It also equals the description in vv. 11-12. In Heb. 6:11-12, the author calls for diligence and avoidance of sluggishness. The outcome will be the realization of the full hope for believers. With faith and endurance in this life, believers can have the full inheritance and full realization of all promises about the future deliverance (salvation) at the Lord's return. The issue is not whether believers are saved from hell and go to heaven. The issue is whether the saved readers will fall away from the church and miss out on the full rewards of the future aspects of salvation.

The phrases that seem to prove Hebrews 6 concerns unbelievers can also fit believers. A saved Jew could not crucify Christ in the sense of theological beliefs, but he could assist Christ's enemies by falling away from the church and returning to affiliation with Judaism. "Things which accompany salvation" probably refers to a believer pressing on to maturity as he shares the fullest blessings of Christ's **future salvation** brought at His return. Once those key phrases can be explained to refer to believers, other clues can be discovered in Heb. 6:4-6 which indicate the author writes to believers. The readers have been "once enlightened." In Heb. 10:32 the author uses "enlightenment" of saving faith. The word *once* speaks not of the Holy Spirit repeatedly convicting a lost person but of a once-for-all penetration of blindness that leads to saving faith in Christ. The word *taste* in Heb. 2:9 does not mean "sample"; it means a full experience. Christ tasted death for every man. We must interpret words by an author's own definition. Therefore, tasting the heavenly gift in Heb. 6:4 refers to a full experience of salvation (the gift); it does not refer to an unbeliever indirectly sampling salvation by attending church. It is preferable to see the warning in Heb. 6:4-6 as a warning to saved Jews not to fall away from the church by returning to social/religious ties with Judaism. If they do so, it will be impossible for Christian leaders to say or do anything to convince them to repent of their departure (v. 4).[90] Only God could change their minds (v. 3). Such a departure, causing shame to Christ (v. 6) by ties with those who hate Christ, would not leave a believer's relationship with God unaffected. Instead of maturity, they could expect severe chastisement. The picture in vv. 7-8 is not that of eternal hell. It is the picture of a field. The field yields an abundant crop and blessing from God one season (v. 7), but the next harvest season the same field is worthless relative to fruit (v. 8). It is close to being cursed (but not fully cursed). The farmer burns the weeds and impurities from the field so it can return to a productive season. One can burn thorns and thistles (as in John 15:6), but one cannot really destroy a field by burning. Such purging actually improves the field. Jewish Christians who fall away from the church towards Judaism reject the process of maturity. They should not think God would be unconcerned. Instead He will burn them in the sense of trial and chastisement in this life (but not hell) in order to improve them. The warning does not concern a loss of salvation but of God's anger over believers who ignore maturity and spend their lives in association and friendship with those who hate Christ.

(3) Conclusion

Regardless of the above options as to the exact meaning of Heb. 6:1-12, there is no need to view the statement as a warning that believers can lose salvation from eternal punishment. We have demonstrated valid alternatives to thinking Hebrews 6 contradicts eternal security. Given that the basic doctrines of Scripture support eternal security, **any** view is superior to thinking Hebrews 6 supports Arminianism.

e. The Fourth Warning Passage: Heb. 10:26-

---

[90] A good sermon title for Heb. 6:6 would be "What More Can I Say?" The author of Hebrews means he can say and do nothing more to change the minds of his readers if they reject the warnings he gives them in the epistle.

31

> For if we go on sinning willfully after receiving the knowledge of the truth, there no longer remains a sacrifice for sins, but a certain terrifying expectation of judgment, and the fury of a fire which will consume the adversaries. Anyone who has set aside the Law of Moses dies without mercy on the testimony of two or three witnesses. How much severer punishment do you think he will deserve who has trampled under foot the Son of God, and has regarded as unclean the blood of the covenant by which he was sanctified, and has insulted the Spirit of grace? For we know Him who said, "Vengeance is mine, I will repay." And again, "The Lord will judge his people." It is a terrifying thing to fall into the hands of the living God [Heb. 10:26-31].

Heb. 10:26-31 seems to teach that a Christian can lose salvation. The difficulty can be solved easier than many think. It is important to **interpret first** and **only then apply** a Biblical text. In the rush to make relevant sermons, a minister can bypass careful interpretation. Hebrews is written to readers who are being tempted to return to Judaism (or a splinter Judaistic cult). Heb. 10:26-31 must be interpreted against a background of the transition from Judaism to Christianity.

Those who assert that Heb. 10:26-31, the fourth warning passage, concerns a loss of salvation will also have to struggle with the phrase "no more sacrifice for our sins." If Heb. 10:23-31 supports Arminianism, then it also teaches "once lost always lost." Something is wrong with such an interpretation.

(1) As Addressed to Unbelievers

One view takes the warning as directed to unbelievers mixed within the Hebrew church. These "seekers" may have been on the verge of faith in Christ, but relatives and friends are also encouraging a return to Judaism. The decision to withdraw from consideration of faith in Christ would lead to a "terrifying expectation of judgment" (Heb. 10:27).

Heb. 10:29 seems to refer to unbelievers. If a person believes the Son of God should be trampled, if he thinks Christ's blood is unclean, if he completely insults the convicting work of the Spirit, he is indeed unsaved. Assuming the warning is directed to Jewish unbelievers within the church (Jewish seekers), then the warning of judgment would be warning about hell.

This warning would not involve a believer who loses salvation but a Jewish unbeliever who toys with faith in Christ and even assembles with the church. The deliberate sin of Heb. 10:26 has been defined in v. 25 (forsaking a church for a return to Judaism). "After receiving knowledge of the truth" (the gospel), some decide to keep rejecting the Messiah (i.e., go on willfully sinning), and return to Judaism. The author of Hebrews will not let these think such rejection of Christ and forsaking the influence of the Hebrew church towards faith in the Jewish Savior is only a minor decision. They must not think both views about Jesus are acceptable to God. The willful sin of rejecting Jesus and dropping away from a seeker standing in the church will lead to judgment. If a person knows the truth and willfully sins by rejecting Christ, "there remains no longer a sacrifice for sins" (v. 26). In general this statement warns that the cross is the only answer for sins. The specific meaning, however, lies in v. 18, "there is no longer any offering for sin." The early part of Hebrews 10 assumes that Old Testament animal sacrifices were only a temporary fix to man's sin. (See Heb. 10:4.) Christ's one time death is God's complete solution to sin (Heb. 10:10, 12, 14). Now that God offers forgiveness in Christ, He no longer respects animal sacrifice for sin. The precise meaning of the phrase "there is no longer any sacrifice for sin", (v. 26) is that God has set aside animal sacrifice. Jewish people who sin by rejecting the Messiah must not think the animal sacrifices in the temple

would be an alternative way of being right with God.

By paying close attention to the argument of the book, we can avoid the mistake of thinking Hebrews 10 teaches a loss of salvation. One alternative is that the author warns Jewish unbelievers who have attended the church assembly and have heard the truth about Christ. If they willfully sin by rejecting Him (v. 26) and by forsaking the truth offered by the church and return to Judaism (v. 25), they must not think God still covers sin through animal sacrifices (v. 26). The choice to refuse faith in Christ and return to Judaism would lead to God's fury, judgment, and vengeance (vv. 29-31).

(2) As Addressed to Believers

(a) An Exposition of Heb. 10:26-31

Previous material on the warning passages has given evidence that they are directed to believers. Heb. 10:26-31 can be interpreted as a warning to Jewish Christians to not drop away from the church by returning to involvement with Judaism. Heb. 10:29 supplies the strongest support for thinking of the recipients as unbelievers. By definition, a believer in Christ could not agree with the theological positions expressed in v. 29. Yet, in sociological involvement, a believer who helped and encouraged first century Judaism would be in effect supporting the persecution of the Savior and the cross. Without even realizing the full implications, the readers were being influenced to return to and support a movement that did "trample under foot the Son of God, regard Christ's blood as unclean, and insult the Holy Spirit's offer of grace" through faith. While a Christian cannot believe such things, believers are quite capable of defection from the true church and giving finances and friendship to groups that despise the Lord Jesus. Those that do so participate in actions and associations contrary to their beliefs. Often they do so inadvertently without thinking. To use the Lord's phrase "they know not what they do." Once we see that Heb. 10:29 could refer to believers, then it is easier to spot additional support from Chapter 10 for thinking that Heb. 10:26-31 warns genuine Christians as follows:

The readers are sanctified (Heb. 10:10).

The readers are perfected in their standing before God (Heb. 10:14).

The readers are brethren (Heb. 10:19).

The readers should hold fast a confession of hope (i.e., remain with the church, v. 25) to give a witness or confession of Christ to their unbelieving Jewish friends (Heb. 10:23).

The author applies the danger to himself by using the pronoun "we." The author of Hebrews is certainly a believer (Heb. 10:26).

The fire need not refer to hell (Heb. 10:27). The original quote in Isa. 26:11 can speak of physical death. Also, "the fury of a fire" is a figure for a "blaze of intense anger." Zeph. 1:18 tells of the "fire of His jealousy."

The penalty in mind here is physical death rather than eternal death (Heb. 10:28).

Even the verse which offers the best support for taking the warning as directed at unbelievers says that those addressed have been "sanctified" (Heb. 10:29).

"The Lord will judge **His people**" (Heb. 10:30).

By being sensitive to the arguments in Hebrews, one can take the warnings in Chapter 10 as addressed to Christians without implying a loss of salvation. Perhaps because Hebrews 10 gives such stern warnings, many who adhere to the doctrine of eternal security think the warning is for unbelievers. It might be better to think that God is furious at believers who forsake the Bible-believing church and associate with groups that insult the cross.

Assuming this warning pertains to saved people, an exposition results that still agrees with eternal security. The recipients have received the knowledge of the truth and are saved (v. 26). Should they now willfully sin by defect-

ing from the church (vv. 25-26) and returning to associations with Judaism, they must not think animal sacrifices will continue to cover their sins and give fellowship with God (v. 26, see v. 18, which defines the cessation of sacrifice.) Believer's sins are already forgiven before God in His capacity as Judge (justification by faith). However, believers also need daily forgiveness from God in His role as Father. The Christian readers of Hebrews must not think they can drop out of the assembly and return to involvement with Judaism without guilt. Jewish Christians who will not assemble with believers, but, instead, return to affiliation with Judaism will incite a blaze of fury from God (v. 27). Those who set aside the Old Covenant deserved to die. Believers who set aside the practice of the New Covenant are more worthy of an even more horrible or painful death (or lingering death) than stoning. Though a genuine believer could not believe the theology expressed in v. 29, a believer who drops out of the church could promote these views by involvement with a false group (such as Judaism). If these Jewish believers withdraw from the church and return to Judaism, they face God's wrath.[91] It will be "a certain terrifying expectation of judgment" (v. 27). God will exhibit fiery fury (v. 27).[92] Such defection and cooperation with a system opposed to Christ deserves a horrible physical death through God's chastisement, called vengeance in v. 30 (vv. 28-31).[93] The warning passage itself can be understood as directed to believers without concerning a loss of salva-

---

[91] Please do not take this exposition of Hebrews 10 as bearing any Anti-Semitic feeling. As with the Apostle Paul, it is possible to love Israel but disagree with its rejection of the Messiah (Rom. 9:1-5, 10:1).

[92] The "fury of fire" in v. 27 could just be a description of "fiery wrath." Chastisement is like fire. The loss of rewards at the Judgment Seat is also like the burning away of worthless works (1 Cor. 3:15).

[93] Other cases of God's chastisement leading to physical death include Acts 5:1-11; 1 Cor. 11:30; and 1 John 5:16.

tion. The following section has been included to show how this interpretation is consistent with, and even supported by, the rest of Hebrews 10.

b. An Exposition of Heb. 10:32-39

The close of Hebrews 10 also fits the above view that the warning concerns believers who face God's severe chastisement. Instead of forsaking the Christian assembly, Jewish believers must follow the teachings in the rest of Hebrews 10. In v. 35 they should not throw aside their boldness (confidence) in the things of Christ. Continuance in commitment to Christ by remaining in the assembly would lead to "great reward" in eternity (v. 35). Endurance brings the rewards that have been promised (v. 36). From an eternal view persecution would only last "a very little while" before Christ's return (v. 37). In the meantime saved people should live their entire lives by faith (v. 38a).[94] (Hebrews 11 builds on this argument by giving numerous illustrations of justified people living out their lives by faith. They did not allow persecution or peer-pressure to cause them to withdraw from a life of faith.) God will be disgusted with the one who shrinks from (forsakes) the assembly (v. 25) and returns to participation in the synagogue (v. 38b). The author speaks for himself in v. 39, but he also assumes other Jewish believers will remain faithful after they understand the full implication and dangers of for-saking the church. We must not shrink from the New Covenant and the church. That would lead to the ruin (destruction) of this life either through wasting this life by being out of God's will or through a chastisement unto death.[95] Instead, those who live their lives by faith will preserve their soul. This could simply mean they face no danger of premature death.[96] However, it may be better to include the non-material aspects to man in the author's definition of *soul* in v. 39. Those who lead lives of faith, including not forsaking assembly with the saints, do preserve their psyche (Greek for soul) from much danger and pain.[97] The purposes for which a person's soul has been brought into this world can only be preserved by a life of faith. By lifelong faith, a believer can preserve his soul (existence) from being a waste during its time on earth. (1 Tim. 4:16 has a similar thought.) The opposite would not be an eternal loss of the soul, but a ruin of God's plan for a soul being in this world. A life of faith gives the soul meaning as illustrated by the lives of faith in Chapter 11. All the heroes of faith preserved the purpose and the meaning for which God created their souls and placed them in this world. The Hebrew believers are expected to follow their example and not throw away the opportunities that God has for them in this life. The Book of Hebrews should not be used to deny eternal security. A modern application for preaching is that God is furious over believers forsaking Bible-believing churches in order to associate with groups that insult the Savior and the cross.

---

[94] The familiar quote in Heb. 10:38 is capable of more than one interpretation in its original context in Habakkuk 2. "The just shall live by faith" does mean justification is by faith as Paul teaches (Rom. 1:17; Gal. 3:11). Yet, in Habakkuk 2 these words also mean God expects those who are saved to face the coming Babylonian invasion by having faith that God would keep His promises. The author of Hebrews understands the phrase, "The just shall live by faith," to mean, "saved people must live out their entire lives in ongoing faith." All of Chapter 11 illustrates what the author means. Jewish believers must not allow persecution or pressures to hinder a life of faith as shown by the great Old Testament saints in Hebrews 11.

[95] The word translated "destruction" in Heb. 10:39 is the same word translated "waste" in Mark 14:4.

[96] The Greek word *psyche* means "soul" but often refers to physical life in the New Testament, e.g., in Matt. 2:3-20 where Herod sought the Christ child's life (soul).

[97] The author's doctoral dissertation surveys evangelical relatives of those with schizophrenia. One main factor which correlates with low scores or emotional adjustment is **withdrawing from church**. See Steven Waterhouse, *Families of the Mentally Ill*, diss., Dallas Theological Seminary 1995.

(3) Conclusion

Whether the author intends to warn unbelievers or believers, Heb. 10:26-31 must be interpreted in its original setting. The "willful sin" of v. 26 is "forsaking our own assembling" in v. 25. The phrase "there no longer remains a sacrifice for sins" (v. 26) means that the animal sacrifices of Judaism no longer cover sins after Christ's final and perfect sacrifice (v. 18). One view is that the author warns unbelievers (seekers who assemble with the church) not to reject Christ and return to Judaism. Those who commit this sin must not think the sacrifices of the temple will save them. Another more probable view is that the author warns believers about dropping out of the church and returning to involvement with the synagogue. These Hebrew Christians may not realize that such a move would give assistance in promoting views they do not accept. Also, God would respond to their disloyalty with fiery anger and chastisement even unto death.

If one still thinks Heb. 10:26-31 disproves eternal security, he must be prepared to deal with the phrase "there remains no more sacrifice for sins" after "willful sin." If this warning concerns loss of salvation, it is teaching salvation cannot be regained. The author has personally counseled believers who were thinking of suicide because of such unfortunate and needless interpretations.

f.　The Fifth Warning Passage: Heb. 12:25-29

> See to it that you do not refuse Him who is speaking. For if those did not escape when they refused him who warned them on earth, much less shall we escape who turn away from Him who warns from heaven [Heb. 12:25].

The final warning passage of Hebrews does not contain language as controversial as previous warnings. Whether one thinks the warning applies to believers or unbelievers, it is easy to see the words do not contradict eternal security.

(1) As Addressed to Unbelievers

If the author has unsaved readers in mind, he is warning them not to refuse the invitation to trust in Christ.

(2) As Addressed to Believers

If the author addresses believers, he is telling Christians not to refuse obedience to God. Instead of pulling away from the church (Heb. 10:25) and returning to involvement with Judaism, believers must "show gratitude" and "offer to God an acceptable service with reverence and awe" (v. 28). Those who do not heed the warning will find that God can severely chastise them. The reference to "fire" is that of the chastisement of the believer. (See Heb. 12:5-13.)

g.　Conclusion to the Warnings in Hebrews

Any student of the book of Hebrews struggles over the identity of the original readers. Are they unbelievers mixed within the Hebrew churches? Are they strictly Jewish Christians? Ones precise understanding of the warning passages will be influenced by his conclusion as to the spiritual status of the readers. However, **both options can yield interpretations that do not involve warnings about a loss of salvation**. The author might be giving evangelistic warnings to unbelieving Hebrews. Maybe these Hebrews are seeking the truth and have assembled with the church to consider the claims of Christ. Of course, Jewish friends are urging them to return to the synagogue. If the recipients are unsaved, the author would be warning them to trust Christ to escape the fires of hell.

More likely the warnings of Hebrews are directed to believers. These Christians are being urged to drop out of the church and return to social ties with the synagogue. While they would still believe in Jesus, they face the danger of associating with those who oppose Christ. The author warns that a Hebrew believer who abandons the church will face God's fiery anger in chastisement during this life and loss of rewards at the Judgment Seat of Christ. With either interpretation, one can consistently maintain eternal security.

14. James 2:18-26

> But someone may well say, "You have faith, and I have works; show me your faith without the works, and I will show you my faith by my works. You believe that God is one. You do well; the demons also believe, and shudder....For just as the body without the spirit is dead, so also faith without works is dead" [James 2:18, 19, 26].

(Additional study on James 2 is found in Chapter 9, Part 2: "Salvation Applied," section II. F., p. 142, "Believe and Work to Earn Salvation.") The key to understanding James 2 is that James defines faith as **only intellectual faith** in orthodox doctrine (e.g., v. 19).[98] That type of faith does not save. Genuine faith results in some level of good works at some time. If a person never has good works, it reveals he has never placed trust in Christ rather than that he has lost salvation.

It is virtually impossible to know how God would define a complete absence of good works; but James' warning urges an examination as to whether one has actually trusted Christ or just has intellectual faith in certain true theological facts. If a Christian worker notices a pattern of unrepentant sin in another's life, it may be proper to give him the gospel, assuming as a working hypothesis that

---

[98] Also, James seems to have a definition of *justification* that differs from Paul's. *Justification* means "to declare righteous." Paul writes of justification by God. Before God as Judge a person is justified by faith alone. However, James seems to refer to a declaration of righteousness by other people. How do others know whether a man or woman is saved? Other people declare a person righteous based on both faith and observable good works. Because of both faith and good works other people could declare that Abraham was righteous both in the sense of justified before God (saved) and righteous in living. Based on both faith and good works other people could call Abraham "the friend of God" (v. 23).

such a person has not really trusted Christ. However, it would not be true to think the person has lost salvation. The situation in James would be that of one who has never been saved because his type of faith is only intellectual and not a personal trust in Christ as Savior.

15. James 5:19-20

> My brethren, if any among you strays from the truth, and one turns him back, let him know that he who turns a sinner from the error of his way will save his soul from death, and will cover a multitude of sins [James 5:19, 20].

The Greek word for soul (*psyche*) can refer to physical existence in this life. While most Bible students would take a phrase about a soul dying to mean spiritual death, the Bible often compares physical death to the loss of a soul. Sample references include the original language in Matt. 2:20; Acts 15:26 and 27:22. James 5:20 encourages turning back Christians from errors in doctrine and morals. Those who rescue straying believers can preserve a life from **physical death**. God's chastisement can lead to removal from this world (1 Cor. 11:30; 1 John 5:16). In addition, various sins naturally lead to physical death even without God directly causing death (immorality, suicide, alcoholism, crimes, etc). Proverbs constantly warns about the relationship between sin and physical death. (See Prov. 2:18; 5:5; 14:12; 21:16.)

The context in James 5 includes the possibility that some sickness comes because of sin. Thus, confession of faults may be a factor in God restoring health (5:15b-16). James closes his book with an extension of these ideas. One who leads a believer to repentance may very well be prolonging his physical life. The issue in James 5 is a possible loss of physical life but not a loss of eternal life.

16. 2 Pet. 1:10-11

> Therefore, brethren, be all the more diligent to make certain about His call-

ing and choosing you; for as long as you practice these things, you will never stumble; for in this way the entrance into the eternal kingdom of our Lord and Savior Jesus Christ will be abundantly supplied to you [2 Pet. 1:10, 11].

Peter's words are definitely addressed to Christians (v. 3). However, some Christians forget all the blessings that God has given. 2 Pet. 1:9 is a picture of senility. In comparison to old age, one who has been saved for many years can grow near-sighted to Christian blessings and responsibilities and can forget the blessings of his initial conversion to Christ.

In vv. 10-11, Peter warns against spiritual senility. Verse 10 uses a verb in the middle voice. It can be translated "make for yourselves your calling and election sure." As an objective fact, a believer's election is already certain. God will bring the believer to heaven. However, some Christians do not have the feeling of assurance over the security they possess. Diligence in the Christian life does not make a believer secure, but it can deepen inward assurance. One way to overcome nagging and needless doubts over salvation is to grow in the faith unto being like the Lord Jesus Christ in character. A life close to the Holy Spirit increases assurance of salvation (Rom. 8:16; 1 John 5:7, 10-11). 2 Pet. 1:10 urges believers to deepen their subjective assurance of salvation by diligence. By this a believer will not stumble into doubts or the practical dominion of sin. A believer will not stumble away from a life of fellowship with Christ.

2 Pet. 1:11 gives the blessing of such diligence. Peter is not offering an entrance into heaven by good works, but rather he tells of an **abundant** entrance. Some believers will be saved but have little reward (they minimally enter God's Kingdom but will not enjoy an abundant entrance, 1 Cor. 3:15). Others who follow Peter's command will have an abundant entrance into God's Kingdom. The alternatives in 2 Peter 1 are not salvation or the

loss of salvation. The alternatives are assurance of salvation or doubts. They are mere arrival in heaven versus an abundant entrance.

17. 2 Pet. 2:20-22

For if after they have escaped the defilements of the world by the knowledge of the Lord and Savior Jesus Christ, they are again entangled in them and are overcome, the last state has become worse for them than the first. For it would be better for them not to have known the way of righteousness, than having known it, to turn away from the holy commandment delivered to them. It has happened to them according to the true proverb, "A dog returns to its own vomit," and, "A sow, after washing, returns to wallowing in the mire" [2 Pet. 2:20-22].

Peter is definitely writing about unsaved people. The chapter begins with a reference to "false prophets" who "deny the Master" (v. 1). Other clues that these are unsaved occur throughout the entire argument. In v. 9 these are kept "for the Day of Judgment." Verse 12 mentions "destruction" and v. 14 says those under consideration are "accursed children." The description of being "without water" (v. 17) reminds us of lacking the water of life (John 4:14). The same verse says those under consideration have a reservation for black darkness (v. 17). Jude gives a parallel to Second Peter. In Jude 19 the false teachers are "devoid of the Spirit." Obviously, Peter's comment concerns unsaved people. He should be interpreted as discussing those who have never trusted in Christ (not believers who have lost salvation). These unsaved false prophets did experience a temporary escape from deep moral defilement through knowledge of the Lord Jesus. Knowledge here does not mean knowing Christ as Savior in the sense of trusting Him. They had factual knowledge about Christ and His teaching that led to moral improvement but not true regeneration through faith in Christ. Many unsaved people experience moral improvement by contact with Christian teaching. They know the Ten Commandments, the Golden Rule, the parable of the Good Samaritan, etc. Such knowledge alone is not saving faith but can improve morality.

However, Peter observed that those who experience ethical improvement without saving faith end in a worse situation should they return to their old sinful habits.[99] One who repudiates knowledge of God's holy commandments without ever trusting in Christ is worse off in at least three respects. First, he will probably be harder to reach with the gospel in subsequent encounters. A rejection of the gospel often causes hardening to future invitations to trust in Jesus. Second, those who repudiate the ethical standards of Christianity often swing their moral pendulum to even worse defilement than before contact with Christian standards. A rejection of the gospel along with a rejection of commandments for holiness can lead to deeper rebellion and wickedness. Finally, those who reject Christ against great knowledge of the truth will receive greater eternal punishment. The Lord seems to teach this in Matt. 10:15; 11:20-24; Luke 10:12, 14; and Luke 12:47-48. Those who turn away in unbelief and sin despite much exposure to God's truth will experience worse eternal punishment than those lacking such opportunities.

18. 1 John 5:16

> If anyone sees his brother committing a sin not leading to death, he shall ask and God will for him give life to those who commit sin not leading to death. There is a sin leading to death; I do not say that he should make request for this [1 John 5:16].

The subject in 1 John 5:16 is prayer for a brother in serious sin.

Only God knows the nature or degree of sin

that might lead to a Christian's removal from this life, but God will sometimes take sinful Christians home. John's words might be better understood without the article *a*: "There is sin (i.e., unspecified sin) leading to death."

Sometimes God chastens a believer with swift physical death (as in Acts 5:1-11). The phrase "I do not say that he should make request for this" (i.e., this situation, swift death) is not a prohibition against prayer. Rather it is a special exemption from the command to pray for sinning brethren. One could paraphrase, "I do not mean you are responsible and accountable to pray for brethren who sin in secret and then die suddenly, but you are accountable to pray for (living) brethren in known and serious sin."

The death of a friend can bring irrational feelings of false guilt. John does not want anyone to suffer false guilt when a believer dies suddenly, apparently through God's chastisement because hidden sins are revealed after the brother's death. Sensitive souls might think a friend's death has something to do with their failure to pray even if they had no knowledge of involvement in serious sin. In situations of the unexpected death of a believer in secret sin, John wants his readers to know God would never hold them responsible to pray for a brother when they did not even know about his sins. They should consider themselves exempt from the command in 1 John 5:16, to pray for brethren in sin.

In most cases a believer in serious sin does not die suddenly. Other Christians have time to show concern and to pray for their brother's repentance. Though the believer still lives, he literally risks his life by continuance in sin. (1 Cor. 11:30; James 5:19-20). Perhaps God's patience will end. Other times sin leads to a premature death through a slow wasteful process (Prov. 10:27, 11:19, 13:14, 19:16, 21:16). In situations where an erring brother does not experience sudden death, other Christians aware of the evil are under John's command to pray. Obviously, in these cases it is not too

---

[99] The same truth can be drawn by application from the Lord's teaching in Matt. 12:43-45.

late for repentance though stubborn sin does endanger life. Since John's subject is the risk of losing physical life, 1 John 5:16 cannot be used as a warning over the loss of spiritual salvation.

19. Rev. 3:1-6 – The Book of Life

In Rev. 3:1-6, the Lord Jesus addresses the church at Sardis. Many in this church are dead (v. 2, unsaved). Other aspects to church life are about to die (e.g., remnants of true doctrine and ethics). A few are saved, clothed in Christ's righteousness (v. 4). In Rev. 3:5 the Lord Jesus promises that overcomers will not be erased from the book of life. The same author, the Apostle John in 1 John 5:4 defines overcoming as possessing faith in Christ (note the past tense). Therefore, Rev. 3:5 is promising those who have faith will **not** be blotted from the book of life.

> "He who overcomes shall thus be clothed in white garments; and I will not erase his name from the book of life, and I will confess his name before My Father, and before His angels" [Rev. 3:5].

A verse which promises that believers will **not** be blotted out of the book of life does not make a good proof text that believers can lose eternal life.

The Old Testament contains additional references to a name being blotted out of the book of life. Moses asks that his name be blotted from the book of life in Ex. 32:32. The Psalmist prays that his persecutors be blotted out of the book of life in Psa. 69:28. One interpretation is that the Old Testament may be referring to a book of physical life. The Bible speaks of God's books in the plural (Dan. 7:10; Rev. 20:12). The Lamb's book of life is definitely a book of eternal life. However, it is possible that the book of life in the Old Testament is a book of physical life. If so, Moses is asking to die. The Psalmist is asking for death for those who persecute the Messiah. (Psalm 69 is definitely Messianic).

A second approach maintains that the book of life in the Old Testament is a book of eternal life not physical life. However, Moses' request in Exodus 32 is viewed as an impossible demand. God obviously declined Moses' rash and impossible request. Moses' words would be similar to Paul's thoughts in Rom. 9:1-3. If it were possible, Paul would trade his own salvation for Israel's salvation. Psa. 69:28 can also be viewed as concerning a book of eternal life. Suppose every soul is originally recorded in the book of life as having a potential for salvation. However, at death God blots out the names of unbelievers but keeps His promise not to blot out the names of those with faith. If the book of life begins with everyone's name included, then Psa. 69:28 could be a request that those who directly killed the Messiah be eternally condemned. (See Psa. 69:21.) These may have been hardened so that they had no further hope of ever believing. Thus, when they died without Christ, their names would be blotted from the book of life.

There are many references in the Bible to God's books (Ex. 32:32-33; Psa. 56:8; 69:28; Dan. 7:10; 12:1; Mal. 3:16; Luke 10:20; Phil. 4:3; Heb. 12:23; Rev. 3:5; 13:8; 20:12-15). The author believes it is best to conceive of many kinds of records and to take each passage in its own context without trying to see them as referring to a single book. It ought to be apparent that references about names being blotted from God's books need pose no problem for eternal security. They either refer to loss of physical life or to an unbeliever at death being erased from all potential for eternal life. Regardless, believers are **not** blotted out of the Lamb's Book of eternal life.

C. Conclusion on Eternal Security

This study has been an honest effort to address common objections to the doctrine of eternal security of the believer. Support for eternal security rests on the most basic and clear teachings of the Bible (justification by faith, predestination, sealing of the Spirit, etc.) Objections to the believer's security are based upon verses that can readily be interpreted in ways compatible with the security of believers. The doctrine of eternal security enables a servant of God to teach and counsel others with truth and without fear. Assurance of salvation is foundational to an accurate view of God and self. Only from the basis of the believer's security can we experience God's full blessing in the Christian life.

VIII.   Conclusions on Soteriology

The Holy Trinity has provided and applied "so great salvation" (Heb. 2:3). As the angels study the church, they learn about the depths of God's wisdom and praise Him for it (Eph. 3:10). On the cross the Lord Jesus Christ paid the redemption price for sin, propitiated God's wrath, and made a means of full reconciliation of man to God. This salvation is applied to individuals by grace through faith alone in Christ alone. Believers are blessed beyond imagination with realities such as being clothed in Christ's righteousness (justification by faith) and eternal security. After salvation there are opportunities of Christian life and service many of which come from the Holy Spirit.

CHAPTER 10
PNEUMATOLOGY
Doctrine of the Holy Spirit

PART 1:
THE DOCTRINE OF THE HOLY SPIRIT

OUTLINE

(ii). Filled With
Spirit
(iii). Filled In Spirit
(4). Conclusion, Obtaining
More of Holy Spirit

THE DOCTRINE OF THE
HOLY SPIRIT

I. Introduction

The Scriptures contain much teaching relative to the Third Person of the Trinity, the Holy Spirit. Because some texts are capable of referring either to the human spirit (lower case *s*) or to the Holy Spirit (capital *S*), it is not possible to be totally dogmatic on the exact number of uses. There are approximately 75 references to the Holy Spirit in the Old Testament and approximately 220-230 references to Him in the New Testament (92-94 times the New Testament uses the word *holy* with Spirit depending upon which Greek manuscripts are counted). The concept of a Spirit gives trouble to those who deny the reality of the invisible. Therefore, some who do not regard the Bible with high esteem teach that the Holy Spirit is not a person but an impersonal force or influence. They would view the Holy Spirit in a similar vein to the "fighting spirit" of an athletic team or to the "Christmas spirit." Studies on Pneumatology, therefore, often begin with a treatment of the Holy Spirit's personhood.

II. The Personhood of the Holy Spirit

A. Grammar and the Personhood of the Spirit

Sometimes a little knowledge is dangerous. A relevant case is the contention by some that the Holy Spirit cannot be a person because the Greek word (*pneuma*) is neuter.

Those who study the Greek language discover that there are three main declensions (endings) to its nouns. Because many clearly feminine objects tend to have the same ending, all the words with that pattern are called feminine. Because many clearly masculine objects seem to have the same ending, all the words with that pattern are called masculine. However, these are general designations and do not at all imply that every item in the one group is a man or that every item in the other group is a woman. The Greek words *road* and *epistle* are feminine. They are not ladies! The Greek words *fruit* and *world* are masculine. They are not men! The word *spirit* is indeed neuter. It is simply the Greek word for *wind* (we derive pneumonia from it). Authors commonly used this neuter word for *wind* to refer to invisible (as wind is invisible) elements or beings. Humans are spirits. Angels are spirits. Demons are unclean or evil spirits. Likewise, God is Spirit (John 4:24). When the Biblical authors chose to make the word *spirit* into a proper name, the *Holy Spirit*, they were not trying to deny personhood any more than when a human is called a spirit. Likely, the term is intended to express His invisible nature and His power (as the wind).

The student of the Holy Spirit should also realize that there are plenty of references to Him that are not neuter but rather masculine. The word *Comforter* (*helper* in the NASB) or *Advocate* is masculine. Christ said the Holy Spirit would be "another comforter" (John 14:16, 26; 15:26; 16:7) i.e., another of the same kind as the Lord Himself. Just as the Lord Jesus Christ is a person, so must the Holy Spirit be a person. Furthermore, masculine personal pronouns are used of the Holy Spirit in many places (John 15:26– *ekeinos*, 16:7–*auton*, 16:8–*ekeinos*, 16:13– *ekeinos*, 16:14–*ekeinos;* Eph 1:14–*ekeinos*).

B. Elements of Personhood

Theologians usually define a person as a being with intellect, emotion, and will. The Holy Spirit is portrayed in the Scripture as possessing all of these elements of personhood.

1. Intellect

The Holy Spirit searches the deep truths of

God (1 Cor. 2:10-11). According to Rom. 8:27, He has a mind.

> For to us God revealed them through the Spirit, for the **Spirit searches all things**, even the **depths of God**. For who among men knows the thoughts of a man except the spirit of the man, which is in him? Even so the thoughts of God no one **knows** except the Spirit of **God** [1 Cor. 2:10-11].

> [A]nd He who searches the hearts knows what the **mind of the Spirit** is, because He intercedes for the saints according to the will of God [Rom. 8:27].

2. Emotions

Since the Holy Spirit may be grieved, He must possess emotions.

> And do not **grieve** the Holy Spirit of God, by whom you were sealed for the day of redemption [Eph. 4:30].

3. Will

The Holy Spirit decides what gift or gifts to bestow upon each believer. He definitely has a will.

> But one and the same Spirit works all these things, distributing to each one individually just **as He wills** [1 Cor. 12:11].

C. Holy Spirit Performs Personal Actions

1. He teaches (John 14:26)

2. He speaks (Acts 13:2; 21:11; Gal. 4:6; 1 Tim. 4:1; Rev. 2:7, 11, 17, 29)

3. He reproves (Gen. 6:3; John 16: 8ff.)

4. He prays or intercedes (Rom. 8:26)

5. He leads (Acts 16:6; Rom. 8:14; Gal. 5:18)

6. He testifies (John 15:26; Rom. 8:16)

7. He gives life (John 3:6; Titus 3:5)

8. He commands and appoints (Acts 13:1-4; 20:28)

9. He fellowships (2 Cor. 13:14)

D. Holy Spirit Treated as a Person

1. He may be grieved and resisted (Gen. 6:3; Isa. 63:10; Eph. 4:30)

2. He may be lied to (Acts 5:3)

3. He may be tested (Acts 5:9)

4. He may be insulted (Heb. 10:29)

5. He may be blasphemed (Matt. 12:31)

E. The Trinity and Personhood of the Holy Spirit

All the evidence for the deity of the Holy Spirit and the doctrine of the Trinity also establishes the personhood of the Holy Spirit. (See below and Chapter 2, "Theology Proper: The Doctrine of God.")

III. The Deity of the Holy Spirit

A. Statements of Deity

> But Peter said, "Ananias, why has Satan filled your heart to **lie to the Holy Spirit**, and to keep back some of the price of the land? While it remained unsold, did it not remain your own? And after it was sold, was it not under your control? Why is it that you have conceived this deed in your heart? You have not lied to men, but to God"[Acts 5:3-4].

> Now the **Lord is the Spirit**; and where the Spirit of the Lord is, there is liberty [2 Cor. 3:17].

> And the angel answered and said to her, "The **Holy Spirit** will come upon you, and the power of the **Most High** will overshadow you; and for that reason the holy offspring shall be called the Son of God" (Deity of the Holy Spirit implied) [Luke 1:35].

> Do you not know that you are a temple of God, and that the Spirit of God

dwells in you? (Deity of the Holy Spirit implied) [1 Cor. 3:16].

B. Proofs for the Trinity

Every evidence for the Trinity is also a proof for the deity of the Holy Spirit. Theology proper is the best sub-section in which to completely discuss the Trinity. (See Chapter 2, "Theology Proper: The Doctrine of God" for greater details.) The following are some common New Testament Trinitarian formulas: Matt. 3:16-17; 28:19; John 14:16-17; 15:26; 16:7-15; Rom. 8:14-17; 15:30; Gal. 4:4-6; Eph. 1:3-14; 4:4-6; 1 Cor. 12:4-6; 2 Cor. 1:21-22; 13:14; Heb. 9:14; 1 Pet. 1:2. Note that the Holy Spirit is listed first in Eph. 4:4-6 and second in Rom. 15:30.

C. The God of the Old Testament as the Holy Spirit of the New Testament

Several times a reference in the Old Testament to God is said to be speaking of the Holy Spirit by a New Testament author. Compare Isa. 6:8-10 with Acts 28:25-27; Psa. 95:7-11 with Heb. 3:7-11; and Jer. 31:31-34 with Heb. 10:15-17.

D. The Holy Spirit and Attributes/Works of Deity

1. Omnipresence (Psa. 139:7-10)

2. Eternality (Heb. 9:14)

3. Omniscience (1 Cor. 2:10-11)

4. Creator (Gen. 1:2; Job 33:4; possibly Job 26:13 and Psa. 104:30)

5. Life giver (John 3:6; Titus 3:5; resurrection in Rom. 8:11)

6. Author of Scriptures (2 Sam. 23:1-2; 2 Pet. 1:21)

7. Blasphemy against the Spirit is more serious than blasphemy against God the Son (Matt. 12:31-32)

IV. Symbols of the Holy Spirit

A. Dove (Matt. 3:16; Mark 1:10; Luke 3:22)

As a dove, the Holy Spirit should be associated with love, peace, and gentleness.

B. Water (Ezek. 36:25, 27; Isa. 44:3; John 7:37-39; Titus 3:5)

As water, the Holy Spirit brings life, fullness, refreshment, and purity. Scripture sometimes speaks of the Spirit being "poured out."

C. Fire (Matt. 3:11; Luke 3:16; Acts 2:3)

Fire in the Bible can portray the presence of God (Ex. 3:1ff.), the power of God (1 Kings 18:38-39), the protection of God (Ex.13:21), and the purging judgment of God (Heb. 12:29).

D. Wind (John 3:3-8; Acts 2:2ff.; 2 Peter 1:21; the word *moved* is used of wind in a boat's sails in Acts 27:15, 17)

In the Hebrew (*ruach*) and the Greek (*pneuma*), the term for *Spirit* is the same as the term for *wind*. As wind, the Spirit is invisible and powerful. Also, God's breath is linked with creation—the creation of man (Gen. 2:7), the re-creation of the nation Israel (Ezek. 37), the regeneration or new birth (John 3:3-8), and the creation or "breathing out" of the Scriptures (2 Tim. 3:16 and 2 Pet. 1:21).

E. Oil

The Bible associates oil with the Holy Spirit and uses the word *anoint* in connection with the Spirit (see 1 Sam. 10:1, 6; 16:13; Isa. 61:1; Luke 4:18; Acts 10:38; 2 Cor. 1:21, 22; 1 John 2:20, 27). Oil is related to healing (Luke 10:34; James 5:14), the blessings of God such as joy and comfort (Psa. 23:5; 45:7; 104:15; Joel 1:10; 2:24), inauguration unto a new task (Ex. 29:7; 1 Sam. 10:1, 16:13, etc.) and light (Psa. 119:105, i.e., oil lamp). The Holy Spirit heals us spiritually by bringing life. He provides joy and gladness. He gives truth, and He is the source of power for our service for God.

F. Wine (Luke 1:15; Acts 2:13; Eph. 5:18)

The Holy Spirit is contrasted with wine. He

provided a different (beneficial) kind of control and true joy.

G. Seal

The Holy Spirit is likened unto a seal. This is covered elsewhere (see pp. 195-96, 248).

H. Down Payment or Pledge

This subject has been covered in the section on eternal security (see pp. 195-96).

V. The Procession of the Spirit

The Holy Spirit has been sent into the world by both the Father and Son. This is the clear teaching of John 15:26 and 16:7. The doctrine of the Spirit's procession is hardly notable except for its impact upon church history. The Roman Catholic and Greek Orthodox churches split in the year 1054 over the Holy Spirit. The Roman Catholic position is that the Spirit comes from both Father and Son, while the Orthodox position is that the Spirit comes from only the Son.

VI. The Work of the Spirit under the Law Administration

A. The Importance of Distinguishing the Spirit under Law from the Spirit under Grace.

The greatest mistake in studies of the Holy Spirit is an ignorance and/or neglect of the differences between the Holy Spirit's work under the Law and His work under grace. The student who ignores the great change at Pentecost (Acts 2) from Judaism to the Church (from Law to grace) will likely never understand the works of the Holy Spirit. **The pattern for the Holy Spirit's work under the church system is not found in the Old Testament or gospels**. There is little excuse for missing the announcements in the Gospels that a great change in the Holy Spirit's work was impending. John the Baptist constantly referred to Spirit baptism as something future (Matt. 3:11; Mark 1:8; Luke 3:16). Even at the ascension, Christ told His followers that the Spirit baptism was future and would occur shortly (Acts 1:5). By the time of Acts 11:15-16, this Spirit baptism had already occurred. Thus, at Pentecost the predicted change occurred. **The Holy Spirit's work after Pentecost is not the same as before.** Therefore, one cannot look to the Old Testament or Gospels as giving the Spirit's pattern or work for today.

There are other indications in the Gospels that a major change in the Holy Spirit's work was coming. John 7:37-39 teaches that all believers would be indwelt by the Holy Spirit, but it just as clearly teaches that this work of the Holy Spirit would commence **after** Christ's glorification. Likewise, the Upper Room Discourse on the night before the Lord's death (John 14:16) is replete with anticipation that the Holy Spirit would begin brand new ministries after Christ's departure.

Those who look to the Old Testament and/or Gospels as giving the normative operation for the Holy Spirit in this age have only themselves to blame for their confusion. There are plenty of indications that the Spirit's work would radically change after the Lord's resurrection and ascension. While it is correct that Old Testament saints (the disciples included) obtained the Holy Spirit subsequent to the time of salvation, this is not the way the Holy Spirit works under the church system. The differences between the Spirit's work under Judaism and the Spirit's work under the church must be understood in order to have a Biblical view of the Holy Spirit. The differences will now be listed, and the Holy Spirit's work under the Old Testament explained.

B. The Old Testament Recipients of the Holy Spirit

Under the Law system the Holy Spirit usually "comes upon" or "fills" a person long after salvation, and He works in the lives of **only a few outstanding individuals rather**

Pneumatology: Part 1: The Doctrine of the Holy Spirit

than in all believers.[1] Under grace the Holy Spirit works in the life of **every believer** and begins to work at the time of salvation (John 7:37-39; Rom. 8:9; 1 Cor. 12:13; Gal. 3:2; 1 John 4:13).

Those who properly note this change in the Spirit's work at Pentecost object to the idea of a "Second Blessing" where the Holy Spirit supposedly enters into a believer's life at a crisis or maturation point after salvation. They also correctly object to a theology that makes some believers have the Holy Spirit and some to be without Him. The doctrine that some believers have had a "Second Blessing" and, therefore, have the Holy Spirit while others do not is based upon a Law pattern. This is not the way the Holy Spirit works in the church. Old Testament examples where the Holy Spirit came upon only a few outstanding leaders (not all believers as during the church age) at a time **subsequent to salvation** (not at the time of salvation as during the church age) include the following:

- Bezalel – the tabernacle craftsman (filled with Spirit, Ex. 31:3; 35:31)

- Moses and the 70 Elders of Israel, whom the Holy Spirit rested upon, (Numbers 11:17-29)

- Joshua – whom the Spirit indwelt (Num. 27:18)

- Othniel – the Spirit came upon (Judges 3:10)

- Gideon – the Spirit came upon (Judges 6:34)

- Jephthah – the Spirit came upon (Judges 11:29)

- Samson – the Spirit came upon and stirred (Judges 13:25; 14:6, 19; 15:14)

- Saul – the Spirit came upon (1 Sam. 10:6, 10; 11:6)

- David – the Spirit came upon (1 Sam. 16:13; see also 2 Sam. 23:2)

- Amasai, one of David's officers – the Spirit came upon (1 Chron. 12:18)

- Azariah the prophet – the Spirit came upon (2 Chron. 15:1)

- Jahaziel the prophet – the Spirit came upon (2 Chron. 20:14)

- Zechariah the son of Jehoiada the prophet – the Spirit came on (2 Chron. 24:20)

- Ezekiel – the Spirit fell on (Ezek. 11:5)

- Micah - filled with the Spirit (Micah 3:8)

C. The Old Testament Duration of the Holy Spirit's Ministry in a Person

The first difference between the work of the Spirit under Law and His work under Grace lies in the persons with whom He works. Under the Law the Spirit came upon only a few select individuals (not all) and at a time after salvation. The second major distinction between His work in the Old Testament versus His work in the New Testament concerns the duration of His work in a life. Under the church system the Holy Spirit abides **forever** in a believer's life (see John 14:16-17 and Eph. 4:30). However, under the Law system He would come and go. It is a serious mistake to confuse the two distinct systems and think that the Holy Spirit might depart a believer today or that His continued presence is contingent upon a believer's holiness. Such grave misunderstandings result in unbiblical notions of pleading for the Spirit to reenter a life or not to depart. The total removal of the Holy Spirit's pres-

---

[1] One view is that the following Old Testament references to the Holy Spirit's work only involved His blessing for leadership abilities upon a few. They involved anointing for service, not indwelling. By this view, these Old Testament passages would become even less a pattern for how the Holy Spirit works in the life of every believer since Pentecost. By either interpretation of Old Testament information, a study of the Holy Spirit must stress texts concerning His works after Pentecost.

ence from a believer's life pertains strictly to the Law administration. The Holy Spirit did leave Samson and Saul; and David was concerned about the possibility of the Spirit's removal.[2]

> And she (Delilah) said, "The Philistines are upon you, Samson!" And he awoke from his sleep and said, "I will go out as at other times and shake myself free." But he did not know that **the LORD had departed from** him [Judges 16:20].

> **Now the Spirit of the LORD departed** from Saul...[1 Sam. 16:14a].

> Do not cast me away from Thy presence, and do not take Thy Holy Spirit from me [Psa. 51:11].

VII. The Work of the Spirit under the Church Administration

A. The Holy Spirit's Work Relative to Unbelievers

1. Conviction

It is common in Christian circles to use the word *conviction* in reference to the Holy Spirit pricking the conscience of a believer concerning personal sins. This is legitimate, as the Word of God gives "reproof, for correction" (2 Tim. 3:16). No doubt the Holy Spirit does use the Word to convict believers of faults. Nevertheless, explicit Scriptural teachings about the Holy Spirit and the work of His conviction are directed to the lost rather than to believers. John 16:7-11 is the key text.

> "But I tell you the truth, it is to your advantage that I go away; for if I do not go away, the Helper shall not come to you; but if I go, I will send Him to you. And He, when He comes, will convict the world con-

cerning sin, and righteousness, and judgment; concerning sin, because they do not believe in Me; and concerning righteousness, because I go to the Father, and you no longer behold Me; and concerning judgment, because the ruler of this world has been judged" [John 16:7-11].

a. The Need for the Holy Spirit's Convicting Ministry

Previous materials in this study have explained that Satan blinds the unsaved mind. No unbeliever can understand the gospel without enlightenment caused by the Holy Spirit (see John 6:44; Acts 16:14; 26:18; 1 Cor. 1:18; 2:14; 2 Cor. 4:3-4 and Chapter 4, pp. 46-47; Chapter 6, p. 63; and especially election, Chapter 9, pp. 126-30). God knows that without the Holy Spirit's efforts to penetrate Satanic blindness no one could ever comprehend the significance and value of the gospel. The catastrophic result would be that no one would ever believe. Therefore, God has a program of election. All those foreknown to have a potential for faith are chosen to be recipients of the Holy Spirit's work to dispel darkness so that their faith can be expressed. This "setting apart" unto conviction/enlightenment by the Holy Spirit is taught by the word *sanctification* in 2 Thess. 2:13 and 1 Pet. 1:2.

b. The Holy Spirit's Tools for Convicting the World

There can be no doubt that the Word of God is a primary tool used by the Holy Spirit to bring about conviction (see James 1:18; 1 Pet. 1:23; Rom. 10:14-17). Since human agents spread the Word of God, it is also correct to think in terms of believers as a source for bringing conviction to the world. Believers convict the world by a verbal message (Acts 5:32; 1 Cor. 14:24; Eph. 5:11) and by righteous living (Matt. 5:16; Phil. 2:15-16; 1 Pet. 2:12, 15).

c. Primary Areas of the Spirit's Convicting Work

---

[2] Sometimes the Holy Spirit would work in the lives of sinful people. There may even be cases of the Holy Spirit's temporary influence upon unbelievers (Num. 24:2; 1 Sam. 19:20-24).

Although the Holy Spirit through the Word and through believers does undoubtedly convict the world of specific personal sins (John 3:20), personal sins are **not the primary focus** of the Holy Spirit's convicting ministry. The narrow restriction of the Holy Spirit's convicting work to a work on the conscience about drunkenness, or pornography, or bad temper, is an error that hinders appreciation of the Spirit's true goal in conviction. We must notice that the word **sin** in John 16:8-9 is **singular** and that it is defined as **a failure to believe** in John 16:9[3] The Holy Spirit mainly strives to convict the world of the one and major sin of unbelief. All other aspects of His conviction are quite secondary to this overriding concern. The sin of unbelief is the only sin that is unforgivable and sends a person to eternal doom. The goal of the Holy Spirit's convicting ministry is not moral reformation of some wicked habit. He desires to enlighten the unsaved mind as to the value of the gospel by dispelling Satanic blindness, and He desires to convict the unregenerate conscience of the terrible sinfulness in rejecting Jesus Christ and thereby persuade the person that he should believe. The Holy Spirit's main work toward the lost is soteriological rather than ethical. Any conviction of personal sins is a "secondary contribution" to a conviction about the wickedness of unbelief.

Furthermore, the Holy Spirit's conviction about righteousness is also for purposes of salvation. The inability of the world to see Christ in person makes the Holy Spirit's work of convicting the world of righteousness necessary (according to John 16:10). Therefore, the type of righteousness of which the Holy Spirit convicts the world is **Christ's own righteousness**. The Holy Spirit is less interested in promoting righteousness in the sense of morality at a pre-salvation stage than in convicting the unbeliever of Christ's righteousness. The Holy Spirit seeks to impress upon the unsaved conscience the attractiveness of Christ's righteousness and the need to be justified by faith in Him, (thus obtaining a claim to His righteousness) and the wickedness of treating Christ as an unrighteous deceiver.

The last element of the Holy Spirit's convicting ministry in John 16:7-11 is judgment. The cross rendered Satan's doom quite certain. By the cross God can justly save men from Satan's domain because the Lord Jesus took the judgment for our sin, enabling a just release from Satan. Believers are justly freed from Satan and from sin's penalty. When the last elect one is saved, God will dispense with the devil. The Holy Spirit convicts (persuades) the world of the judgment that will await those guilty of the sin of unbelief in Christ ignoring the truth of and attraction in His righteousness.

d. Questions Concerning What Should be Included as "Conviction"

It does seem from the use of the word *world* in John 16:8 and from experience that the Holy Spirit convicts many people who ultimately reject the truth. He enlightens them by penetrating Satanic blindness. They understand the significance of the gospel, the wickedness of unbelief, the fact of Christ's righteousness, and the danger of judgment for rejecting Him. Yet, they still refuse to believe. This leads to a couple of questions relative to the extent of the Holy Spirit's convicting work. Does the Holy Spirit convict every person ever born into the world, or does John 16:8 mean that the Holy Spirit is at work in the "world system" (*cosmos*) without necessarily teaching that He will convict each individual in this system? Linked to this question is the issue of whether the Holy Spirit convicts in the absence of written revelation, for many people live without a formal proclamation of the Bible.

The answers to such questions really do not affect our knowledge of what the Holy Spirit is actually doing among the unsaved world.

---

[3] The Greek word, *hoti*, in John 16:9, can be translated "that". The main sin is **"that they believe not on Me"**.

The scope and extent of His work is the same regardless of whether we choose to group all of it under the category of "conviction."

It is undeniably true that people who reject truths from creation (Job 12:7-9; Psa. 19:1-3; Rom. 1:19-20), from a moral conscience (Rom. 2:14-15), and from an inborn belief (2 Pet. 3:5 KJV) in God are guilty enough to be doomed without any explicit gospel presentation from the Bible. God the Holy Spirit does prompt the hearts of the lost through natural revelation (Rom. 10:18). The only real issue in the extent of "conviction" is whether one thinks that enlightenment by means of natural revelation (as opposed to written) should be classified as "conviction" or should be named a separate work of the Holy Spirit.

If one chooses to view Christ's promise of the Holy Spirit's convicting work in John 16 as a brand new ministry, then there would be a tendency to place enlightenment by natural revelation in a different category than specific conviction about the person of Christ. Conviction then would be seen as totally limited to this age and as something that requires an explicit gospel presentation. It would be something the Holy Spirit does in the "world" but not necessarily to each individual.

However, one could also choose to view the work discussed in John 16 as an extension of the Holy Spirit's prior work that would just be made much more specific after the ascension. Thus, *conviction* would be seen as including both enlightenment by natural revelation (which occurred before the ascension) and since the ascension a more specific enlightenment about the person of Christ. If enlightenment by natural revelation is included under the classification of convicting, then literally every mature person in the world is convicted by the Holy Spirit.

Again, the scope of the Holy Spirit's work is the same either way. The only problem is whether to label enlightenment by natural revelation as conviction by the Holy Spirit or whether to make it a separate work. The Holy Spirit can definitely work in the hearts of the lost without written words. He did so in the days of Noah (Gen. 6:3). There are probably many workings of the Holy Spirit upon the hearts of the lost that are not known by us (John 3:8).

2. Restraining

The world seems dreadfully wicked. Yet, given the potential depths of baseness in the human heart, it is actually surprising that world conditions are not far worse. The measure of civilization that exists in the world is totally due to God's grace.

The Scriptures teach that a period of tribulation is coming in which unimaginable horrors will plague the earth. Although some of the suffering will be caused by God's wrath, much of it man will bring upon himself. The world has yet to see the full misery that man can bring upon himself due to uncontrolled and unrestrained sin. 2 Thess. 2:6-7 teaches that someone is restraining lawlessness in the world at the present time. The Restrainer prevents the rise of the "man of sin" (the Antichrist) who would otherwise control the world before God's time for him to rise.

> And you know what restrains him now, so that in his time he may be revealed. For the mystery of lawlessness is already at work; only **he** who now restrains will do so until **he** is taken out of the way [2 Thess. 2: 6-7].

The Restrainer mentioned in 2 Thess. 2:6-7 must have supernatural power as only such force could oppose Satan's goal of world domination through the man of sin. Verse 7 uses a masculine form ("He who now restrains"). Thus, the Restrainer is a person. The best interpretation that can be given to this text is that the Holy Spirit presently restrains lawlessness in the world system. If he did not, there would be a tremendous increase of man's inhumanity to man, and the Antichrist would rise to power shortly. The view that the Holy Spirit is the Restrainer also helps explain why a neuter is used in v. 6. Since the word *Spirit* is neuter, Paul used a neuter in v. 6. However, wishing to stress His personhood he used a masculine in v. 7.

The restraining work of the Holy Spirit provides a secondary support for the pretribulational Rapture. Likely, the Holy Spirit uses the universal church to curtail wickedness in the world. Bible-believing Christians have influenced the world toward less wickedness than would exist in the absence of the church. The Antichrist cannot appear until the Holy Spirit's work through the church ceases, and the church's work on earth ceases only at the Rapture.

B. The Holy Spirit's Work Relative to Believers

1. Regeneration

Regeneration is the supernatural, instantaneous, and direct act of God whereby He imparts eternal life to all that trust in Christ. Most of the time, verses pertaining to the topic of regeneration or the new birth do not include a reference to the Holy Spirit. However, two key passages make it clear that the Holy Spirit is involved in giving new life to one who believes.

> Jesus answered and said to him, "Truly, truly, I say to you, unless one is born again, he cannot see the kingdom of God"....Jesus answered, "Truly, truly, I say to you unless one is born of water and the **Spirit**, he cannot enter into the Kingdom of God. That which is born of the flesh is flesh, and that which is **born of the Spirit** is spirit. Do not marvel that I said to you, 'You must be born again.' The wind blows where it wishes and you hear the sound of it, but do not know where it comes from and where it is going; so is everyone who is **born of the Spirit**" [John 3:3, 5-8].

He saved us, not on the basis of deeds which we have done in righteousness, but according to His mercy, by the washing of **regeneration and renewing by the Holy Spirit** [Titus 3:5].

Most of the following verses do not mention the Holy Spirit directly. However, because they do pertain to regeneration, they are teaching about a work that the Holy Spirit performs in regeneration. The Holy Spirit causes a "new birth" for one who believes (John 1:12-13; John 3:3-8; 1 Cor. 4:15; 1 Pet. 1:3, 23; 1 John 5:1). Physical birth brings a child into a family. The new birth also brings a person into a family, God's family (see Chapter 9, pp. 170-71, and also John 1:12-13; Rom. 8:14-19; Gal. 3:26; 4:4-7; 1 John 3:1-2). New birth, of course, also means new life. More specifically, the Holy Spirit provides a believer with eternal life (see Chapter 9, pp. 169-70, also John 3:16; 4:14; 5:24; 6:40, 47; 10:28; Rom. 6:23; 1 John 5:13). The Bible uses other terms to convey the same truth as regeneration, new birth, and eternal life. Sometimes it refers to regeneration by the terminology of a new resurrection life (see John 5:21, 25; 14:19-20; Rom. 6:4, 11, 13; Gal. 2:20; Eph. 2:5; Col. 1:27; 2:12-13; 3:1-2). The regeneration that the Holy Spirit causes brings a sharing in Christ's resurrection life. It is easy to see that such life must be eternal in duration because Christ's life obviously never ends.

Another way the Bible expresses regeneration is to call it a new creation resulting in a new nature (a possible interpretation of 2 Cor. 5:17; also Gal. 6:15; Eph. 2:10; 4:24; 2 Pet. 1:4).[4] Thus, the doctrine of regeneration

---

[4] 2 Cor. 5:16 states that a believer looks at people differently after salvation. An unbeliever who knew Christ personally obviously viewed the Lord much differently after salvation. Therefore, 2 Cor. 5:17 may be primarily referring to a person's new outlook and assessment of others after salvation. Also, a recent convert has a new relationship to those who had preceded him in faith.

ought to be linked in thought to the idea of the new birth, sonship, new and eternal life, resurrection life that shares Christ's life, and with a new nature (i.e., behavioral mechanism).

The Scriptures sometimes speak of the Holy Spirit causing the new birth, but other times speak of the Word of God causing new birth. These two aspects to regeneration should be united. The Holy Spirit is the ultimate author of Scripture (2 Sam. 23:1-2; 1 Tim. 4:1; 2 Pet. 1:20-21). He brings about new life by using His own Word (James 1:18; 1 Pet. 1:23). He convicts and dispels Satanic darkness by the Word so that a person can understand and believe the gospel.

Because both Spirit baptism and regeneration concern a union with Christ, it is likely that these two topics should also be viewed as closely linked. Baptism in the Spirit means that Christ places a believer in the Spirit of Christ, and thus in union with Himself. The union with Christ's life is a new life, i.e., regeneration. The terms *regeneration* and *baptism in the Spirit* sound very different, but in reality both concern union with Christ and sharing His life. Baptism in the Spirit creates the union with Christ's life that may be called regeneration. Conviction makes faith possible so that baptism in the Spirit occurs. Thus, the Holy Spirit's works of conviction, baptism, and regeneration are interrelated.

2. Indwelling

Indwelling is the ministry of the Holy Spirit during the church administration whereby at the moment of salvation He takes up permanent residence in the believer. All the various aspects to this definition will be established in the following treatment.[5]

Christians view a new brother or sister differently than if the person were still lost. Conversion causes them to see the person as a new person, a "new creature."

[5] The work of anointing is not given a separate category because it seems to be tied to the in-

dwelling of the Spirit (during the grace dispensation). In the Old Testament, "anointing" is associated with the call or installment in an office or work. Priests were anointed with oil (Ex. 29:7; Num. 3:3) as were political rulers (1 Sam. 9:16; 16:12; 2 Sam. 12:7; 1 Kings 1:34).

Sometimes the word *anoint* was used in connection to the Holy Spirit initially indwelling a person, usually a leader, to empower him for a task (1 Sam. 10:1, 6, 10; 16:13). Thus, anointing and the initial coming of the Holy Spirit are associated. Yet, the only Person under the Law for whom the Scriptures directly indicate "Spirit anointing" is the Anointed One, the Messiah (see Isa. 61:1; Luke 4:18; Acts 10:38). It is probably safe to infer that others, such as David, were also anointed with the Holy Spirit (although Scripture does not directly teach this). Such Spirit anointing seems to be a reference to the initial indwelling of the Holy Spirit setting apart a leader and empowering him for a task. In Old Testament times, the Holy Spirit indwelt and, therefore, anointed only a few people and these subsequent to salvation. Thus, His anointing work under the Law would **not** be a precise pattern for today under grace.

Under the church system the Holy Spirit indwells all at the time of salvation. Therefore, we would expect any New Testament teaching about Spirit-anointing to include all believers and to begin at the time of salvation. This seems to be the case.

2 Cor. 1:21, which could be apostolic but probably includes all believers, and 1 John 2:20, 27 are the only New Testament texts mentioning anointing by the Holy Spirit. They make such anointing to be the possession of every believer (as every believer has been indwelt). There is no Biblical basis for pleading, praying, or striving for some Spirit-anointing at salvation. Now all believers have already been set apart (sanctified) for the Lord's work and, thus, all believers have been anointed by the Spirit with power to carry out their responsibilities.

It may be possible to use the word "anoint" to refer to a believer today being led by God into a certain work and being blessed with a special ability to do that work (e.g., one might refer to ordination as an anointing). While there is nothing wrong with such language, and it does parallel the Old Testament example of anointing bringing power for a special task, it seems that New Testament Spirit-anointing is even more

a.   Whom Does the Holy Spirit Indwell?

Those who fail to see a distinction between Law and Grace, between Judaism and the Church, will fail to understand the doctrine of the Holy Spirit's indwelling for the present time. Christ, in John 7:37-39 and John 14:16-17, taught that there would be a great change in the operation of the Holy Spirit after His glorification and departure. If one looks to the Old Testament or even the gospels as giving the normative work of the Holy Spirit for the church administration, the end result will be confusion. From the time of Christ's glorification (including His ascension), **all that believe are indwelt by the Holy Spirit.** The Holy Spirit indwells all that belong to Christ.

"He who believes in Me, as the Scripture said, 'From his innermost being shall flow rivers of living water.' " But this He spoke of the Spirit, whom **those who believed** in Him were to receive; for the **Spirit was not yet given, because Jesus was not yet glorified** [John 7:38-39].

...But if anyone does not have the Spirit of Christ, he does not belong to Him. (Likewise, anyone who **does belong** to Christ **has been indwelt** by the Holy Spirit [Rom. 8:9b].

1 Cor. 12:13b says, "we were **all** made to drink of one Spirit." In its context, the reference is to all that have union with Christ, and this in turn is a reference to all that be-

lieve.[6] The word *drink* causes one to think of an internal work. Thus, Paul is teaching that all believers have been indwelt by the Holy Spirit.

The same conclusion follows from the truth that all who obtain the resurrection are indwelt by the Holy Spirit (Rom. 8:11)[7] and all who are sons of God have been indwelt by the Holy Spirit (Gal. 4:6; Rom. 8:14 correctly understood).[8]

> ...He who raised Christ Jesus from the dead will also **give life** to your mortal bodies **through His Spirit** who indwells you [Rom. 8:11b].

> And **because you are sons**, God has **sent forth the Spirit** of His Son into our hearts, crying, "Abba! Father!" [Gal. 4:6].

When Paul writes to the carnal-like Corinthians, he makes no distinction between some whom the Holy Spirit indwells and others whom He does not. He makes a blanket statement to all that the Holy Spirit resides within them.

> Or do you not know that **your body is a temple of the Holy Spirit** who is in you, whom you have from God, and that you are not your own?

---

closely tied to the initial empowerment of the Holy Spirit in an individual's life. Under the Law this initial reception might come after salvation (as with David). Yet, **every believer under the grace dispensation has already been anointed by the Spirit for special ministry.** All have been set apart (sanctified) for Christian service. All have resources from the Holy Spirit to minister (1 Cor. 12:7; Eph. 4:12). Therefore, it is needless for Christians to plead for an anointing that has already been bestowed by virtue of the indwelling presence of the Spirit in every believer's life.

[6] All believers have union with Christ (Eph. 2:4-9; Gal. 3:26-28). Therefore, it must be that all believers have been indwelt by the Spirit because the Spirit's indwelling work (and baptizing work) is a cause of union with Christ (1 Cor. 12:13). There is no room for the idea of a Christian who does not possess the Holy Spirit.

[7] All believers have eternal life (John 5:24; 11:25). Since the Holy Spirit is the one who gives life (Rom. 8:11), it must be that the Holy Spirit has indwelt all. There is no room for the idea of a Christian who does not possess the Holy Spirit.

[8] All believers are sons of God (John 1:12-13; Gal. 3:26). Since the Holy Spirit creates this sonship (Gal. 4:6; Rom. 8:14), it is absurd to think of a believer who does not have the Holy Spirit. There is no room for the idea of a Christian who does not possess the Holy Spirit.

[1 Cor. 6:19].

Several times the New Testament presents the indwelling of the Holy Spirit as an accomplished reality for a believer (see Rom. 5:5; 2 Cor. 5:5; 1 John 3:24; 4:13). There is never any command in this dispensation for a believer to seek or strive to obtain the indwelling of the Holy Spirit.

b. How and When Does One Obtain the Holy Spirit's Indwelling?

Since the Holy Spirit indwells all believers, it is obvious that **one obtains the Holy Spirit by believing and that He indwells at the time of faith.** John 7:38-39 and Gal. 3:2 are especially clear that the Holy Spirit is given on the basis of faith in Christ. There can be no such thing as one who has faith but does not have the Spirit. Thus, the Holy Spirit indwells on the basis of faith in Christ and at the time such faith begins.

> "He who believes in Me, as the Scripture said, 'From his innermost being shall flow rivers of living water.' " But this He spoke of the Spirit, whom **those who believed in Him were** to receive; for the Spirit was not yet given, because Jesus was not yet glorified [John 7:38-39].

> This is the only thing I want to find out from you: did you receive the Spirit by the works of the Law, or by hearing with **faith**? [Gal. 3:2].[9]

Again, all those who are the Sons of God are indwelt by the Spirit (Gal. 4:6; Rom. 8:14). Since a person becomes a child of God by faith and at the time of faith, the Holy Spirit's indwelling must also come at the

time of faith. Likewise, those who have union with Christ are indwelt by the Holy Spirit (Rom. 8:9b; 1 Cor. 12:13b). Since a person obtains this union with Christ by faith, the Holy Spirit's indwelling must come about by faith. Faith in Christ brings eventual resurrection (John 6:40, 47) and the Holy Spirit who will "give life to your mortal bodies" (Rom. 8:11). **All lines of evidence indicate that the Holy Spirit indwells on the basis of faith and that this indwelling begins at the time faith is placed in Christ.** Acts 10:44 gives an example of this. While Peter preaches the gospel, some believed. Even before the sermon is finished, and long before they are water-baptized, they obtain the Holy Spirit.

c. How Long Does the Holy Spirit Indwell?

Unlike conditions under the Law when the Holy Spirit would indwell and then might leave, Christ told his disciples that, under the new ministry of the Holy Spirit, He would remain forever. On the same occasion, He also made it clear that His words were intended for all of His people rather than just the Apostles.

> "And I will ask the Father, and He will give you another Helper, that He may be with you **forever**; that is the Spirit of truth whom the world cannot receive, because it does not behold Him or know‑Him, but you know Him because He abides with you, and will **be in you**...."Jesus answered and said to him, "If **anyone** loves Me, he will keep My word; and My Father will love him, and We will come to him, and make Our abode with him" [John 14:16-17, 23].

Although Eph. 4:30 technically refers to sealing and not indwelling, it establishes the point that the Holy Spirit's work in a believer's life is permanent. He indwells believers and will continue to work in them throughout their lifetimes.

---

[9] See also Eph. 1:13. If the participle in this verse is taken as causative, it reads, "Because of having believed, you were sealed in Him with the Holy Spirit..." While Eph. 1:13 might also be able to be compatible with the idea that the Holy Spirit comes after the time of salvation, other clearer texts that base reception of the Holy Spirit by faith establish that the translation in this footnote be preferred.

And do not grieve the Holy Spirit of God, by whom you were sealed for the day of redemption [Eph. 4:30].

Actually, the duration of the Holy Spirit's indwelling is intertwined with the doctrine of eternal security. Since the Holy Spirit indwells those who are the sons of God (Gal. 4:6), and those in union with Christ (1 Cor. 12:13b), and those who will be raised (Rom. 8:11); and since believers will never cease to be children of God, or lose union to Christ, or fail to be resurrected; the Spirit's indwelling must also be permanent.

Those who view the Holy Spirit as coming and going, those who teach that one must strive, plead, beg, or seek the Holy Spirit's residence do so in ignorance of what Scripture teaches about the Holy Spirit's work under the church dispensation.[10]

---

[10] Luke 11:13 is often used as a proof-text for the idea of pleading for the Holy Spirit. However, it was given under the Law dispensation when very few believers possessed the Holy Spirit. Christ invited His disciples to ask for the Holy Spirit. Even though the Holy Spirit's indwelling work in all believers would not commence until after Christ's glorification (John 7:38-39), God would have granted the Holy Spirit to some who followed Christ in His early ministry. Yet, there is no record that any of them ever asked for the Holy Spirit. Different conditions prevail during the Church dispensation than were operative when Luke 11:13 was given. At present everyone who believes already has the Holy Spirit without asking. While Luke 11:13 may have contemporary applications, the Holy Spirit now works differently than in the time of the gospels before the church began.

John 20:22 is another text that some claim gives precedent for people obtaining the Holy Spirit long after salvation. However, once again the change from Law to Grace, from Judaism to the Church, is a factor. It should be quite clear that this transition had not yet occurred since at His ascension Christ still was teaching that Spirit baptism was future (Acts 1:5). John 20:22 occurred before the church administration had begun, and thus it says nothing about the way the Holy Spirit operates now.

Furthermore, John 20:22 is an obscure text. One view is that Christ is merely giving His pre-authorization and a blessing for the Spirit baptism that would shortly occur. Another idea is that He is offering the apostles a measure of temporary blessings from the Holy Spirit to support them in the difficult and fearful days just after the crucifixion. Still another view is that the Lord is pre-authorizing His apostles to obtain divine revelation and inspiration from the Holy Spirit. Finally, even if one takes John 20:22 to be granting an indwelling to the apostles; it still would not provide a pattern for how God would work with all believers under grace. In sum, John 20:22 is just not a text that can be used to overthrow the conclusion that all believers in the Church dispensation are indwelt by the Holy Spirit.

Acts 19:2 is sometimes used to show that the Holy Spirit comes into a life after salvation. However, the problem is simply one of translation. The King James Version reads, "Have you received the Holy Spirit **since** you believed?" This translation gives the impression that believers normally receive the Holy Spirit subsequent to salvation. It is true that the Holy Spirit comes after faith in Christ. However, He comes **immediately** after faith. The grammar of Acts 19:2 allows a translation which does not imply any measurable length of time between belief and reception of the Holy Spirit. They happen virtually at the same time.

Dana and Mantey say, "...the aorist [participle] frequently expresses **contemporaneous**... action [H.E. Dana and Julius R. Mantey, *A Manual Grammar of the Greek New Testament* (Toronto: Collier-Macmillan, Ltd., 1955, 230)]. Moulton writes, "...there are numerous examples of the aorist participle denoting **coincident** action" [(James Hope Moulton and Nigel Turner, *A Grammar of New Testament Greek*, 3 vols. (Edinburgh: T. and T. Clark, 1963, 3:79)]. The newer translations, therefore, are superior. They translate Acts 19:2 to read that belief and reception of the Holy Spirit are virtually simultaneous. The New American Standard Bible reads, "Did you receive the Holy Spirit **when** you believed...". The New International Version translation is identical. These superior translations eliminate any implication that the Holy Spirit comes subsequent to salvation.

Acts 8:14-17 is probably the most difficult passage in Pneumatology. It concerns the evangelization by Philip of the Samaritan people. De-

3. Baptism in the Holy Spirit

a. Introduction and Definition

spite all the evidence above that all believers have been indwelt by the Holy Spirit (John 7:38-39; Rom. 8:9; 1 Cor.12:3b, etc.), the Samaritans did not immediately possess the Holy Spirit at the time they believed. Rather, it took official recognition by the Apostles Peter and John before the Samaritans obtained the Holy Spirit.

A theology student has two choices with this example of the Holy Spirit coming upon believers after salvation: either it is a contradiction or a special exception to the way the Holy Spirit normally works. One critical of the Bible could charge it with a contradiction. John 7:38-39; Rom. 8:9; 1 Cor. 12:13b, etc. teach that all who believe are indwelt by the Spirit of God, but Acts 8:14-17 provides an example of some who believed but did not immediately have the Spirit. (Note: Acts 9:17 concerns filling, not indwelling, and Acts 10:44 provides the normal example of reception of the Holy Spirit at the time of faith).

The contradictory view should be quite unacceptable to those who respect the Scripture's integrity. Obviously, the situation in Acts 8:14-17 is abnormal. In this situation involving Samaritans, it is easy to infer a logical reason that they should be an exception to the way the Holy Spirit normally works. First, this is the first time in the church's short history that the gospel was preached to non-Jews. Secondly, the Jews and Samaritans hated each other (see John 4:9). Temporarily withholding the Holy Spirit from the Samaritans eliminated the danger of a break between Jewish Christians and Samaritans who still distrusted and hated each other. The Jewish apostles were forced to recognize publicly the legitimacy of the Samaritan's conversion. They could attest to the Holy Spirit's coming. Likewise, the Samaritans by obtaining the Holy Spirit through the apostles were forced to recognize the authority of the Jewish apostles. Given the cultural and sociological conditions that existed between Jews and Samaritans, it is best to view Acts 8:14-17 as a planned exception to the general way the Holy Spirit works rather than thinking the Bible gives two contradictory methods of His operation. The Holy Spirit indwells every believer at the moment of salvation. However, in the first conversions of Samaritans, He delayed His indwelling long enough so that the two inimical groups could recognize their mutual salvation in Christ.

Although the Spirit's baptism is not the most difficult of topics concerning the Holy Spirit, it is among the most widely misunderstood. One can search the New Testament exhaustively and never find any command to strive for the baptism of the Holy Spirit. One can search the Old Testament exhaustively and never even find references to Spirit baptism.

Spirit baptism is not a feeling or an initiation into a plateau of Christian experience where the pressures and temptations of life cease. Rather than a feeling or experience, Spirit baptism is fundamentally a **position**. Both of the following definitions are accurate:

"The act of the Holy Spirit, whereby, during this age, He places a believer 'in Christ' at the moment of salvation."[11]

Spirit baptism occurs as Christ submerges, envelops, places a believer into the Spirit in order to produce a union with the Spirit of Christ, which is ultimately a union with Himself and all other believers.[12]

These definitions express the same conclusion with different phraseology. The first views Christ more in the role of "sending" the Spirit. The second as "using" the Spirit. However, both yield the conclusion that baptism in the Spirit refers to being placed into a position of "union in Christ." The basis for this definition will be established in coming sections.

b. Spirit Baptism and the Church System

The gospels present the work of Spirit baptism as something that had not yet occurred. John the Baptist constantly referred to Spirit baptism as a **strictly future** work of the Messiah, "and He Himself **will** baptize you in the Holy Spirit" (Luke 3:16; see also Matt. 3:11; Mark 1:8). Furthermore, Christ placed the work of Spirit baptism beyond the time of His ascension in Acts 1:5, "and

---

[11] Don Phillips, Class Lecture Notes, Grand Rapids School of the Bible and Music, fall 1975.

[12] This is the author's own definition.

you **shall** be baptized with the Holy Spirit not many days from now." Thus, we should not look to Old Testament or gospel texts concerning the Holy Spirit's work as providing truths on the doctrine of Spirit baptism. Prior to Christ's ascension, there had never been any such thing as a "baptism in the Spirit." The first baptism in the Spirit occurred "not many days" after the ascension. Peter shows that by the time of Acts 11:15-16 the work of the Spirit baptism had already been operative. We are forced to conclude that the first work of Spirit baptism in the world occurred on Pentecost in Acts 2. This should not be too surprising. If the above definition of Spirit baptism is correct, then Spirit baptism creates the union of believers in Christ, which is the church. Thus, the work of Spirit baptism began at the same time the church began at Pentecost, Acts 2.

c.   Spirit Baptism and Union in Christ

In John 14:20, Christ predicted a coming relationship of "**you in me** and I in you." The "you in me" aspect comes through believers being placed (baptized) into the Spirit of Christ. ("I in you" refers to indwelling.)

A basic starting point for understanding the precise meaning of Spirit baptism lies in a parallel that is repeated **six times in the New Testament. John the Baptist baptized "in, with, or by water." Christ will baptize in, with or by the Holy Spirit** (see Matt. 3:11; Mark 1:8; Luke 3:16; John 1:33; Acts 1:5, 11:16).[13] John is the actor. Baptize

---

[13] The Greek word is often *en* or a dative case when used with *water* followed by *en* in parallels concerning the Holy Spirit. This chart gives the original:

Verse	Water	Spirit
Matt. 3:11	en	en
Mark. 1:8	dative	en
Luke 3:16	dative	en
John 1:33	en	en
Acts 1:5	dative	en
Acts 11:16	dative	en
1 Cor. 12:13	----	en

is the action. Water is the *agent* or *element* that John uses to baptize. Likewise, in Spirit baptism, Christ is the Actor; baptize is the action. The Holy Spirit is the *agent* or *element* that Christ uses to baptize. Technically, therefore, Spirit baptism is a work of Christ. The Spirit is the element "in which," "by which," or "with which" Christ baptizes. However, because Christ uses the Holy Spirit to baptize, Spirit baptism is commonly classified under the works of the Spirit as in this study.

Although the Greek preposition *en,* which is used in all six of the above passages, may be translated "in," "by" or "with," a good case can be made for preferring the translation, "**Baptism *in* the Spirit.**" A figurative meaning should be interpreted to be based upon a literal. Since the literal meaning of baptism means, "to place into something," this definition should be transferred to the doctrine of Spirit baptism. Baptism *"in"* the Spirit best parallels the idea of John's baptism in water. Secondly, the topic of Spirit baptism made Paul think of water as is shown by his use of the word *drink* in 1 Cor. 12:13. This also shows that baptism **in** the Spirit is similar to the relationship of baptism **in** water. The strongest argument for translating the phrase "baptism **in** the Spirit" is that Spirit baptism creates a oneness, a union "in Christ." It creates the oneness between the believer and Christ and between a believer and all other believers in the body of Christ, the church. The argument of 1 Cor. 12:12-13 is clear that Spirit baptism creates oneness in Christ: "...all the members of the body, though they are many, are one body. For [because] [in, by, or with] one Spirit we were all baptized **into** one body...." Gal. 3:27 also teaches that Spirit baptism produces union in Christ: "For all of you who were baptized **into** Christ..."[14] The doctrine

---

[14] The idea of baptism "in" also best fits the texts in which it is difficult to tell whether the author intends Spirit baptism or water baptism (Rom. 6:3; Eph. 4:5; Col. 2:12; 1 Pet. 3:21.

that Spirit baptism creates oneness and union is a primary truth. However, as a secondary point the translation *in* seems to better
communicate the formation of a union than
does *with* and much better than *by*. This
would also parallel the common phrase "in
Christ" where the **same** preposition is employed and the phrase "you in me" in John
14:20 which also uses the **same** proposition.

Regardless of the preferred translation of the
phrase, the definition of Spirit baptism ought
to be clear from 1 Cor. 12:12-13. Spirit baptism ought to be viewed primarily as a position. Christ "inundates, submerges, envelops, surrounds, places a believer in (with or
by) the Spirit." Since He is the "Spirit of
Christ," this is the equivalent of uniting a
believer with or in Christ (you in me, John
14:20). Furthermore, since all believers are
placed into the Spirit of Christ, all are united
in the same position. There is a oneness in
Christ. It might be pictured like this:

(1). Baptism in the Spirit Makes Union in
Christ ("You in me," John 14:20)

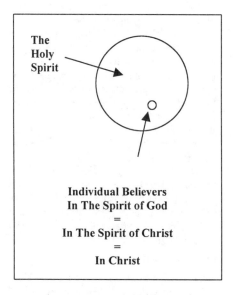

Individual Believers
In The Spirit of God
=
In The Spirit of Christ
=
In Christ

(2). This union in Christ also joins a believer
to all other believers.

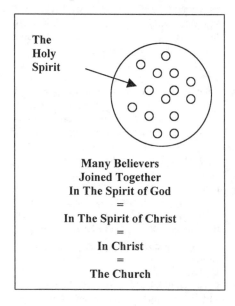

Many Believers
Joined Together
In The Spirit of God
=
In The Spirit of Christ
=
In Christ
=
The Church

d. The Recipients of Spirit Baptism (Who,
When, and How?)

(1). Those Who Receive Baptism in the
Spirit

There are not two classes of believers in
respect to Spirit baptism. It is not true that
some believers have been baptized in the
Spirit and others have yet to obtain baptism
in the Spirit. 1 Cor. 12:13a leaves no doubt
as to a universal baptism in the Holy Spirit
for **all** believers: "For by [or in] one spirit
we were **all** baptized into one body."

It is Biblically unthinkable that there could
be such a condition as a believer who has
not yet been baptized in the Spirit. Since
Spirit baptism produces union in Christ and
creates oneness in the Church, a "spiritually
unbaptized" believer would be the same
thing as a believer who is not in Christ and
who is not a part of His body, the Church.

By reasoning in the other direction, it ought to be plain to see that all those who are in Christ and part of the church (i.e., **all believers**) must have been baptized in the Spirit (for Spirit baptism creates the position of being in Christ and oneness in the Church!).[15] There can be no such thing as a believer who is not in Christ, a believer who is not in the Church. Therefore, there can be no such thing as a believer who is not baptized in the Holy Spirit.

(2). The Time of Spirit Baptism

Several lines of thought point to the inevitable conclusion that every believer is baptized in the Spirit at the time of salvation.

First, the fact that **all** believers have undergone Spirit baptism (1 Cor. 12:13) means that Spirit baptism must be traced back to a common experience, faith in Jesus Christ. Since all believers have been baptized in the Spirit, this means that, whether one has been saved five minutes or has been saved only five seconds, he has already been "Spirit baptized." The universal nature of Spirit baptism leaves only one option: Spirit baptism occurs at the moment of salvation.

Secondly, Spirit baptism must occur at the time a Christian is united to Christ and made one in the body of Christ, the Church. The question, "When does Spirit baptism occur?" is the same question as "When is a believer united to Christ?" Spirit baptism occurs at the time of union with Christ, which is the time of faith. Salvation from its beginning involves a position of being in Christ (2 Cor. 5:21; Eph. 2:4ff; Gal 3:26-28, etc.). God views a believer as being in Christ

and declares a believer to be justified by virtue of sharing in Christ's righteousness. Since a believer shares in the merits of Christ's death and resurrection at the very moment of salvation, it must be true that Spirit baptism, which creates a sharing in Christ's life, must exist at the very moment of salvation.

(3). The Means of Obtaining Spirit Baptism

An exhaustive study of all references to the Holy Spirit in the entire New Testament will reveal that **there is no command whatsoever associated with Spirit baptism**. We are never told to pray for or seek Spirit baptism. We are never commanded to strive for it or to try to obtain a certain level at which the "baptism" happens.

Spirit baptism is presented as a sovereign work of God, which He does automatically. 1 Cor. 12:13 views Spirit baptism as a work in the past tense that has already occurred in the life of **all** believers. Spirit baptism concerns what Christ does in order to make a union in Him. It does not concern anything we do.

(4). The Duration of Spirit Baptism

John 14:16-17 teaches that indwelling is forever. Eph. 4:30 teaches that sealing is permanent. Thus, the Holy Spirit's work in a believer does not cease. We can, therefore, safely infer baptism in the Spirit is permanent.

The doctrine of Eternal Security relates to the permanence of Spirit baptism. If Spirit baptism ceases, then so does a believer's union in Christ and his inclusion in the church. On the other hand, if a believer is eternally secure in his position in Christ, then baptism in the Spirit that forms this union must also be permanent.

(5). Conclusion

When the Scriptures wish to stress the **Holy Spirit's presence in believers**, they use the idea of **indwelling**. When the Scriptures wish to stress the **presence of a believer or**

---

[15] All believers are "in Christ" (2 Cor. 5:21; Eph. 1:6-7, 2-4ff.; Col 1:10). Thus **all** must have undergone the spiritual operation that creates this union, Spirit baptism. All believers are part of the universal church, Christ's body (Rom. 12:5; 1 Cor. 12:13). Thus, all must have undergone the spiritual operation that creates the body of Christ, Spirit baptism.

of all believers in the Holy Spirit, then they use the idea of **baptizing**.

The doctrine of baptism in the Spirit can be summed up in three words, "Union in Christ." At salvation a believer is placed into the Spirit of Christ. This makes him or her one with Christ and all other believers. If Spirit baptism were understood as a position, much confusion could be avoided.

4. Sealing

The Holy Spirit is the guarantee or pledge of greater blessings to come (2 Cor. 1:22; 5:5; Eph. 1:13-14). His work "seals" a believer until the day of redemption. In ancient times a seal conveyed thoughts of ownership, approval, and protection. The sealing of the Spirit (2 Cor. 1:22; Eph. 1:13-14; 4:30) guarantees the eternal security of the believer and has been more thoroughly treated under that subject in Chapter 9, pp.195-96.

> [W]ho also **sealed** us and gave us the Spirit in our hearts as a pledge [2 Cor. 1:22].

> In Him, you also, after listening to the message of truth, the gospel of your salvation—**having also believed, you were sealed** in Him with the Holy Spirit of promise, who is given as a pledge of our inheritance, with a view to the redemption of God's own possession, to the praise of His glory [Eph. 1:13-14].

> And do not grieve the Holy Spirit of God, by whom you were **sealed** for the day of redemption [Eph. 4:30].

5. Filling

Filling is the only major work of the Holy Spirit concerning believers that involves a repeated process. His other works typically involve a one-time event that is not repeated. Also, it is the only major work that involves a command for human cooperation. The command in Eph. 5:18 to "be filled with or by the Spirit" is passive. The Holy Spirit does the work, but a Christian must cooper-

ate in the process.

Because some issues involving the Spirit's filling are simple and clear and others are complex and difficult, this study will be divided between truths that are certain and speculations that are unclear.

a. Firm Conclusions

(1). Filling Equals Control and Influence

We can feel safe in concluding that the main idea behind filling in, with, or by the Spirit is a control or influence by the Holy Spirit. To be controlled by the Spirit equals being filled by the Spirit. Such control may be initiated by a crisis experience but filling is not so much a crisis experience as a constant process whereby the believer is controlled by the Holy Spirit.

The Scriptures often contrast filling by the Spirit with a filling by wine (Luke 1:15; Acts 2:4, 15; Eph. 5:18). Wine controls and influences those filled by it. Instead of being under the influence of wine, Christians should allow the Holy Spirit to influence and control (Eph. 5:18).

The Scriptures use the word "filling" in connection with many different attitudes and behaviors (filled with **rage**, Luke 4:28; filled with **fear**, Luke 5:26; filled with **rage** or **folly**, Luke 6:11; filled with **wonder** and **amazement**, Acts 3:10; filled with **jealousy**, Acts 5:17, 13:45; filled with **confusion**, Acts 19:29; filled with **joy** and **peace**, Rom. 15:13; filled with **knowledge**, Rom. 15:14; filled with **comfort**, 2 Cor. 7:4; filled with **fruits of righteousness**, Phil. 1:11). Most of these phrases convey the idea of control or influence. To be filled with anger or jealousy means anger or jealousy permeates and influences behavior. A city filled with confusion is a city whose behavior is controlled by confusion.

To be filled with or by the Spirit must involve a control by the Spirit. The next section discusses the way the Holy Spirit controls believers.

(2). The Holy Spirit Controls by His Own Word

Letters written at the same time usually have similarities. This is certainly true with Ephesians and Colossians. Both books were written while Paul was in a Roman prison. There are many parallels.

Eph. 5:18ff. commands the Ephesians to be filled by the Spirit with the results of "speaking to one another in psalms and hymns and spiritual songs, singing and making melody with your heart to the Lord always giving thanks." Then Paul discusses the subjects of authority and submission. In Col. 3:16ff. Paul commands: "let the Word of Christ richly dwell within you." The results are "teaching and admonishing one another with psalms and hymns and spiritual songs, singing with thankfulness." Then Paul discusses the subject of authority and submission. **By comparing Eph. 5:18 with Col. 3:16, it is evident that being filled with the Spirit equals letting the Word of Christ dwell in us**. The Holy Spirit influences and controls believers by the Word of God. This should not be too surprising since "the sword (tool) of the Spirit is the Word of God" (Eph. 6:17). The Holy Spirit is the author of Scripture. He moved the prophets along in the writing process, 2 Pet. 1:21. Thus, when the Word speaks, the Holy Spirit speaks. Filling by the Spirit sounds esoteric and mysterious. In reality the Christian whose life is controlled by the Word of God is a Christian who is filled (controlled) by the Spirit. It is that simple.

There is great danger in divorcing the Holy Spirit from the Scriptures. There are not many ways of Christian growth as though some Christians mature by following "the Word," while others mature by following "the Spirit." **Let all beware of closing the mind to the Word and equating this with following the Spirit.** This is nothing other than following fleshly impulses and subjectively rationalizing that our actions must be acceptable because we call impulse "Spirit."

There is a sound Biblical basis for forging an inseparable union between the Holy Spirit and the Word of God. Christ is inseparably linked with the Word of God (John 1:1; and Rev. 19:13). There ought not to be any trouble in viewing the Holy Spirit as linked with the written Word. Again, Eph. 6:17 teaches that the Holy Spirit uses the Word, and 2 Pet. 1:21 teaches that the words of the Scriptures are the words of the Holy Spirit. Filling with the Spirit is the equivalent of letting the Word of Christ control one's life (Eph. 5:18; cf. Col. 3:16). Furthermore, consider the pattern in regeneration. The Holy Spirit brings about new birth (John 3), but He uses the Word of God to do it (Rom. 10:17; James 1:18; 1 Pet. 1:23). In other words, the Holy Spirit uses His own Word to do His work. There is every reason that this pattern for bringing about salvation is also true for the Holy Spirit's work in the area of sanctification. He uses His Word to do His work.

Consider the absurd situation that results from separating the filling by the Spirit from control by the written Word. In reality this amounts to thinking that growth can occur without the Word of God. Those who think they can become mature Christians without submission to and practice of the Word of God need to consider the Bible's own admonition (see also, Josh. 1:8; Psa. 1:2,3; 1 Tim. 4:13-15; 2 Tim. 2:15; 4:2).

> But He answered and said, "It is written, 'Man shall not live on bread alone, but on every word that proceeds out of the mouth of GOD' " [Matt. 4:4].

> All Scripture is inspired by God and profitable for teaching, for reproof, for correction, for training in righteousness [2 Tim. 3:16].

> [L]ike newborn babes, long for the pure milk of the word, that by it you may grow in respect to salvation [1 Pet. 2:2].

Christian growth simply **cannot** occur without the written Word, and this must mean that the Holy Spirit invariably uses the written Word to fill us. There will be no progress without the Spirit (Zech. 4:6), but it is equally true there will be no progress without the written Word. One of the Spirit's major works is illumination. There is much discussion of Christian growth as mind renewal. Both of these concepts suggest that the Holy Spirit works through the mind. This in turn supports the idea of uniting the filling work of the Spirit to the written Word.

(3). Definition of Filling:

The continuous ministry of the Holy Spirit in this present age whereby He controls the believer who is yielded to Him.[16]

(4). A Description of the Filling Process

Unless there are strong indications to the contrary, one would assume that the Bible presents only one maturation process for the believer.[17] Though the New Testament uses different phrases or pictures for the process of Christian growth, these really describe the same process. Whether the way of growth is called transformation (as in Romans 12) or filling/walking by the Spirit (as in Eph. 5:18 and Gal. 5:16-18), the same process is under consideration. **The Holy Spirit uses the Bible to cause believers to become more like the Lord Jesus.**

This conclusion is confirmed by a comparison of Biblical teaching about the sanctification process. Whether a Biblical author speaks of "renewal" or "filling" or some other term, the mechanism for Christian growth seems to be the same. The following sections will examine the Bible's teachings

about renewal (transformation) and about Spirit filling. It should be observed that both involve an **active-dependent mechanism** whereby the believer actively strives to obey but at the same time depends upon the indwelling Spirit's power to obey (compare Gal. 5:22-23 with 1 Tim. 6:11. In 1 Timothy, believers are told to work at the same characteristics which are said to be **produced** by the Holy Spirit in Gal. 5:22-23).

Furthermore, regardless of terms used to describe the path to growth, **all** involve both the Holy Spirit and the Word of God. Finally, the results are the same: mind renewal (transformation) results in the fruit of the Spirit, which is Christ-likeness.

It will be obvious that there is only one underlying process to Christian maturity. Therefore, even if some verses on sanctification do not specifically use the word "filling," they still give insight into how the Holy Spirit controls and changes a life.

(a). The Holy Spirit's Control Described as Mind Renewal (or Transformation)

Several key passages concerning Christian growth compare it to mind renewal or transformation.

> I urge you therefore, brethren, by the mercies of God, to present your bodies a living and holy sacrifice, acceptable to God, which is your spiritual service of worship. And do not be conformed to this world, but **be transformed** by the renewing of your mind, that you may prove what the will of God is, that which is good and acceptable and **perfect** [Rom. 12:1-2].

> But we all, with unveiled face beholding as in a mirror the glory of the Lord, are **being transformed** into the same image from **glory** to glory, just as from the Lord, the **Spirit** [2 Cor. 3:18].

> [A]nd that you **be renewed** in the

---

[16] Don Phillips, Class Lecture Notes, Grand Rapids School of the Bible and Music, 1975.

[17] The most recent believer can be controlled by the Holy Spirit through the Bible and thereby be spiritual. Maturity, however, takes time and never ends (1 Thess. 4:9-10 "to excel still more...", Phil. 1:9; 3:13-16).

spirit of your mind [Eph. 4:23].

In all three texts, transformation is passive, not active. In other words, the believer does not so much make the transformation as allow it to be made. Some outside agency does the primary work. The 2 Cor. 3:18 passage clearly identifies this agent as the Holy Spirit. It also teaches that the Spirit uses truths that come as through a mirror to transform us. James 1:23-24 identifies the Word of God as a mirror. Also, the context of 2 Corinthians 3 is a contrast between the Old Covenant (Testament) and the superior New Covenant (Testament), which allows a greater revelation of God's glory. The emphasis upon a transformation of the mind also causes one to think of the Bible's affect upon the mind. These indications, coupled with the Holy Spirit's typical use of Scripture in His saving ministry, leave one confident that **mind transformation** comes about through the **Holy Spirit using Scripture**.

The goal to which this transformation tends is said to be the image of Christ (2 Cor. 3:18), the image of God (Eph. 4:24, cf. Col. 3:10). In other words, the Holy Spirit uses truths from the Word to produce Christlikeness in believers. Rom. 12:1-2 stresses the same result viewed from the opposite direction of the process. Those transformed into Christ-likeness become very much unlike the world.

A step-by-step format to the transformation process is something like this:

i. A believer confesses sin and is dedicated to being a living sacrifice as stipulated in Rom. 12:1. Without this initial condition all growth stops.

ii. The believer sees the glory of God in Christ as he studies the mirror of the Word with a view to **practicing** it. The believer actively studies but also depends upon the Holy Spirit to illuminate his mind as to the personal significance and relevance of the Word.

iii. The Holy Spirit uses His own Word, the Scripture, to show the glory of Christ's character and thus the flaws, deficiencies, errors, and sins in a believer's life.

iv. At this point the believer can choose to be a "hearer only" or acknowledge faults and sins. Ideally, he will confess shortcomings and strive to model Christ's character as revealed in the Word. At the same time as the person tries to improve, there must also be a dependence upon the power from the indwelling Spirit for strength to accomplish the change and dependence upon the Spirit to resist temptation towards un-Christ-like behavior.

v. Over the course of time, the Holy Spirit seeks to use the Word to reveal Christ's character point by point and a believer's defects point by point. If a believer responds to this ministry, he or she will become little-by-little, point-by-point, area-by-area, more like the Lord Jesus Christ and less like the world.

This process of mind renewal or transformation is not mysterious, or vague, or spooky. Now we shall discover that it is the same as Spirit-filling.

(b). The Holy Spirit's Control Described as Filling

There are only five commands in all of the Scriptures addressed to the Church that pertain to the Holy Spirit. Four of them involve individual responsibility for Christian growth and are usually grouped together under the "Filling of the Spirit."[18] At the very least, all must concede these commands are all related to the role of the Holy Spirit in the maturation process. Furthermore, they end up describing the same process as passages that speak in terms of transformation.

i. Be Filled by the Spirit (Eph. 5:18)

---

[18] The fifth command is addressed corporately to the church to guard the treasure of truth that has been entrusted to us (2 Tim. 1:14). There are no commands to seek indwelling or baptizing by the Spirit.

And do not get drunk with wine, for that is dissipation, but be filled with the Spirit [Eph. 5:18]. [19]

This verse speaks of a control of the believer by the Holy Spirit. The parallel passage in Col. 3:16 shows that the Spirit uses His own Word to bring about this control. There is no reason to think filling (control, influence) by the Spirit is any different than the Spirit using the mirror of the Word to influence (transform) a believer.

ii. Walk by the Spirit (Gal. 5:16,25) [20]

But I say, walk by the Spirit, and you will not carry out the desire of the flesh....If we live by the Spirit, let us also walk by the Spirit [Gal. 5:16, 25].

When we walk by means of our legs, we depend upon them for strength and power. Also, in the motion of walking there is a forward momentum that would cause us to fall if a leg were not out in front of the body. We unconsciously trust first one leg and then the other to support our bodies when we walk. Both of these ideas parallel the principles of a spiritual walk by the Spirit. To walk by the Spirit means to live in dependence upon Him for the strength and power to keep moving forward. Also, the Christian who walks by the Spirit is continually in the process of trusting the Spirit. He will trust the Holy Spirit not only for strength but also for guidance. While there is some room for believing in a subjective guidance from the Holy Spirit where He guides individuals in matters not contained in the Scriptures, the primary means of the Holy Spirit's guidance is through His own written Word. He shows believers God's will in the Word of God. Those who walk by

the Spirit trust in these instructions to keep them from "falling" spiritually. They also depend upon the power of the indwelling Spirit for strength to obey instruction from the Holy Spirit that comes in the Bible.

Another angle of understanding comes by the phrase "walk after the Spirit" (Rom. 8:4, KJV). While "walking by the Spirit" and "walking after the Spirit" are obviously related, they seem to have different emphases. The preposition "after" is a key. In Rom. 8:4 it means "after the standard of" or "according to." Christ said in John 8:15 (KJV), "You judge after the flesh." This means the Pharisees judged according to the standards of the flesh. When Paul says in 1 Cor. 1:26 (KJV) that not many "wise **after** the flesh" were Christians, he does not mean most Christian are fools in an objective sense. The phrase means that those who judge by the standards of the flesh do not consider many Christians to be wise. To walk after the Spirit means to live under the standards of the Holy Spirit. What are the standards of the Holy Spirit? This ought not to be made overly complicated. The Scriptures give to us the standards by which God wants believers to live. Technically, all **believers walk after or according to the Spirit at all times** in the sense that the Word of God is always our standard for conduct (even at times when we are not in compliance with our standard, i.e., not walking by the Spirit). [21]

---

[19] This verse could be translated "be filled in, by or with the Spirit." (See the forthcoming section, "the meaning of Eph. 5:18, pp. 266-67".)
[20] The Greek words for "walk" are not the same in these two verses though this may just be a different writing style.

[21] Galatians 5:18 teaches that **all believers are led by the Spirit** in the sense that no believer is under the Law as a standard for living ("But if you are led by the Spirit [and you are], you are not under the Law" [and indeed you are not]). When taken in context, Rom. 8:14 also teaches that **all believers are led by the Spirit of God.** It is saying all who are sons are led by the Spirit. Then the next few verses teach all believers are sons. The Spirit is at all times positionally our leader (primarily by His written Word) even if we do not always practice following (walking by) Him. Romans 8 seems to contrast the position of a believer who is "in the Spirit" and has ability to do righteousness with unbelievers who are "in the

The command to walk by the Spirit simply means to practice our position of being subjugated to the Word of God as a standard for living. The believer who depends upon and complies with the Holy Spirit's writings for a standard is walking by the Spirit. Once again the way to Christian maturity is the same whether it be spoken of in terms of Spirit filling, or in terms of mind transformation. The Holy Spirit uses the Word to guide and to change believers toward increasing Christ-likeness.

iii. Quench Not the Spirit (1 Thess. 5:19)

> Do not quench the Spirit; do not despise prophetic utterances [1Thess. 5:19-20].

The command not to quench the Holy Spirit must be studied in conjunction with the following verse that forbids a disregard of prophecy. The subject of promptings and impressions made by the Holy Spirit upon a

---

flesh" and have no ability to do righteousness. Despite the common view that Romans 8 contrasts a struggle within each believer (a struggle taught in Galatians 5), Paul's own definition of his terms in Rom. 8:9a shows that he intends the phrase "in the flesh" to describe one devoid of the Holy Spirit. i.e., an unbeliever. Likewise, in the context of Romans 8 all believers are "in the Spirit." "...you are **not in the flesh** but in the Spirit, **if** indeed **the Spirit of God dwells in you**..."(Rom. 8:9a). Given Paul's own definitions for "in the flesh" and "in the Spirit" in Rom. 8:9, it is best to understand Rom. 8:4 as describing a believer's position. **All** believers walk "after" or "according to the Spirit" at all times in the same sense that the Holy Spirit leads all believers at all times. He, not the Law, is our standard for conduct. Therefore, all believers walk "after" or "according to" the Spirit in a positional sense at all times. The Holy Spirit is constantly our leader as He commands and guides through the Scriptures. He gave the commands for the Church (not the Mosiac system). Though all believers constantly walk "after" or "according to" the Spirit, each must still obey the command to "walk by the Spirit" in terms of constant trust and actual obedience to the standard by which the Spirit always leads us (Gal. 5:25).

believer's heart is found on pp. 261-62. No doubt such promptings should be included within the scope of this command. When a spiritual believer is prompted by the Holy Spirit to do something, he should obey.

However, we should not major on minors. A carnal-like believer can confuse and rationalize so that he interprets fleshly desire as direction by the Spirit. The Spirit's primary means of instruction is in the Bible. Only those who are practiced in following the Holy Spirit's written Word will ever learn to discern and distinguish His subjective promptings from a fleshly impulse. The primary way the Holy Spirit leads is by the Word of God. Even though there are no prophets today, a believer despises prophecy whenever he defies the Word of God. The main way a modern believer can quench the Spirit is to ignore commands and responsibilities that are given by the Holy Spirit in divine revelation. The Holy Spirit uses His Word to guide and to transform believers. Those who despise this written "prophecy" are quenching the Spirit.

iv. Grieve Not the Spirit (Eph. 4:30)

> And **do not grieve the Holy Spirit** of God, by whom you were sealed for the day of redemption [Eph. 4:30].

Paul assumes his readers will know behaviors that cause grief to the Holy Spirit. It should not be too difficult to conclude that a primary way of bringing sorrow to the Holy Spirit is to defy the Scriptures He has given. Christians who obey the written Word of God will please God the Spirit.

v. Results of the Spirit-Controlled Life: The Fruit of the Spirit

> But the fruit of the Spirit is love, joy, peace, patience, kindness, goodness, faithfulness, gentleness, self-control; against such things there is no law [Gal. 5:22-23].

A believer who follows the Holy Spirit's

guidance (i.e., the Word written by the Holy Spirit) will exhibit the characteristics listed in Gal. 5:22-23. Anyone who is concerned about the "feeling" of the Holy Spirit's filling should take note that the Holy Spirit produces "love, joy, peace, patience, kindness, goodness, faithfulness, gentleness and self-control." These personality traits exemplify Christ-likeness and are the "experience" that the Holy Spirit wants to produce in a believer's life. Those who would belittle the privilege of experiencing Christ-likeness and demand other experiences from the Spirit are making a poor choice. Those who are discontent and dissatisfied with Christ-likeness (the fruit of the Spirit) are inevitably going to be discontent with any other "spiritual experience." The Holy Spirit wants to produce Christ-likeness in a believer. This is true spirituality, and there is no spirituality without Christ-likeness regardless of claims to mysterious or exciting experiences. The primary "feeling of the filling" is the fruit of the Spirit. We could also add that Spirit-filling gives the feeling of the presence of the Holy Spirit as an indwelling reservoir of power to obey the Word. Power to obey (not power to perform amazing tricks) coupled with the fruit of the Spirit is the experience of a Spirit-filled believer. There is nothing wrong or inferior with the real blessings that the Holy Spirit wants to bestow. What can be inferior about Christ-likeness?

(c). Summary and Conclusions About a Description of Spirit-filling

Although the terminology varies, the ideas presented show that there is only one sanctification process in the Bible. Whether it is taught by the wording of "renewal" or Spirit-filling" the process is identical. From the Holy Spirit's side, growth is brought about by using the Spirit's sword, the Word of God. A believer must live in active dependence upon the Spirit's Word to be a trustworthy guide. He or she actively strives to obey it, but at the same time depends upon the Holy Spirit's power for sufficient strength to obey. The results of this process may be called transformation or the fruit of the Spirit. By either terminology its goal is Christ-likeness.

Filling of the Spirit (control by the Spirit) is better viewed as an ongoing process of considerable duration, not a crisis experience. A believer in compliance with the Word of God (authored by the Spirit) is being controlled (filled) by the Spirit. A believer who is in violation to any known Biblical principle is not being controlled (filled) by the Spirit. Confession of sin is the avenue to reassertion of the Spirit's control over a life (see 1 John 1:9).[22] The process of control constitutes Spirit-filling and not necessarily crisis experiences or euphoric emotional states. If a car is out of gear, it needs to be put into gear in order to move again. There need not be anything dramatic about it.

In saying this, it is acknowledged that a crisis may bring about the desire for a believer initially to resubmit to the Holy Spirit's Word.[23] Also, if there is a deep and prolonged period of rebellion, it may take a dramatic experience to bring confession and restoration. However, if it took a crisis to bring about every confession, then life would be a constant crisis, for confession of sin should be a daily occurrence. The more normal experience is that the Holy Spirit's control is restored by a simple and routine act of confession. Once submission to the Word of God is restored, then so is Spirit-filling (control). A believer should not expect a crisis/dramatic experience or a "sign" to prove that the Spirit has again filled. After

---

[22] The Spirit's filling is predicated upon confession of known sin and a humble dependence upon the Bible as the source of truth for living. Spirit-filling (control) is incompatible with quenching or grieving the Spirit by violating His Word and refusing to confess it as sin.

[23] The idea of a major turning point in life that leads to submission and dedication to God is Scriptural (Rom. 6:11ff., Rom. 12:1-2). This point may or may not be brought about by a crisis.

sin is confessed and a believer is again in submission to the Holy Spirit's guidance by the Word, he or she is by definition "filled" whatever the accompanying emotions or experiences. It is likely an insult to God for an ignorant believer to continue pleading for the Spirit's filling after confession has taken place. This is similar to the annoying experience a parent might have when a child keeps whining for a dessert that has already been set before him. If there has been confession and a restoration to yieldedness to the Spirit's control through the Bible, then Spirit-control or Spirit-filling has already taken place. It will continue as long as there is an active dependence upon the Spirit's tool, the Word of God. At that point, one who continues to beg for a refilling of the Spirit is asking for something God has already given.[24] It is similar to a believer repeatedly asking for salvation when he has already obtained it by faith alone. Both types of prayers must annoy God, for they indicate a failure to believe God's Word at face value. Those who are under the Spirit's control through the Word are Spirit-filled. The demanding of constant spectacular signs of the Spirit's filling reveals that the person does not really believe God's Word is a sufficient guide. The Bible defines Spirit-filling as being richly indwelt by the Word of Christ. However, those who seek additional phenomena to evidence Spirit-filling act as though they do not believe this. Also, they are concentrating their energies on obtaining something they already possess and thus are sidetracked from what God really wants to do in their lives. The filling of the Spirit is viewed as a repeated process in Eph. 5:18. When conceived as the control of the Spirit through His Sword (the Word of God), it is

easy to see why Spirit-filling is a repeated occurrence. The believer must be repeatedly brought to control by the Scriptures through confession.

If a believer does not knowingly quench or grieve the Spirit (by disobeying His Word), if a believer walks by the Spirit (i.e., is guided by the Spirit's Word), then he is undergoing a gradual process of transformation. This transforming process is Spirit-filling. It is not granted on the basis of pleading but yielding. It is occurring in the life of one in submission to the Spirit's Sword, the Word of God, and it occurs even in the absence of strange and inexplicable experiences. The study and practice of the Word of God is the essence of God's method for Spirit-filling. This process may be less spectacular and dramatic and may be slower than impatient people desire, but it is God's way for growth. The results far surpass those of any other unbiblical method for Christian maturity, for the fruit of the Spirit, Christ-likeness, is more precious than any alleged "powers" or "experiences" that supposedly come by unbiblical avenues promising "spirituality."

(5). Optimal Results for the Spirit-filled Life

A Biblical study on the optimal results for the Spirit-filled life will help separate reality from fiction (possible from impossible) in the area of Christian living. The Scriptures are the source for what is and what is not obtainable by the believer in this life. By studying the Scriptural results for a Spirit-filled life one can determine what benefits can legitimately occur from being under the Holy Spirit's control. Just as important, it also exposes exaggerations and phony claims of those who are ignorant or who seek attention by pretending to obtain levels of "Spiritual" experiences that are clearly not obtainable in this life.

(a). Artificial and Contrived "Results" to Spirit Filling

The Bible does not give any comfort to

---

[24] Filling (or control) by the Spirit obviously relates to other New Testament phrases involving commands about the Holy Spirit. One who is filled (controlled) by the Spirit is not grieving or quenching the Spirit through disobedience to the Word. He or she walks by the Spirit in the sense of trust and obedience to the Words of the Spirit, the Scriptures.

those who view optimal Christian living in the Spirit-filled life as an initiation into an unreal world without troubles. Those who claim to seek an unscriptural "spirit-filling" after their own desires in which a plateau without suffering or struggles is achieved are headed for a great disappointment when they wake up to Scriptural and experiential reality. The Bible simply does not promote utopian bliss in this life. Spirit-filled living, even at its optimal level, does not involve invincibility relative to sin or invincibility relative to suffering. There will be a continual struggle with sin and temptation (Gal. 5:17; Heb. 2:18; 4:15; 1 John 1:8-9). Spirit filling may give power to break the inevitable dominion of the sin nature, but it does not eradicate sin or the need to struggle with it. Christian living, even at its optimal level, still includes pain and sickness (Rom. 8:18, 22-23; 2 Cor. 5:2-4; 12:7-9). Those who claim that "Spirit-filling" initiates them into a level of spirituality where life is easy and problem-free are either deceived or self-deceived. The Bible is more realistic than this! "For we know that the whole creation groans and suffers the pain of childbirth together until now... we [believers] ourselves... groan..." (Rom. 8:22-23).

Selfish people demand instant gratification in everything, but there is no such thing as instant Christian maturity. Christian growth is a daily process that involves duration in dedication (Phil. 3:13-16). Those who claim that a special filling work of the Spirit has transformed them instantaneously into spiritual giants are either insecure, attention-seekers, or wish to claim spiritual authority over others without being qualified to do so. Those who claim Spirit-filling leads to apostolic powers and a life in which miracles are constant and normal are also claiming levels that the Bible does not allow in optimal Christian living.

The New Testament gives examples of godly people being poor (Matt. 8:20; Luke 16:20; 2 Cor. 8:1-5,9), and wicked people having wealth (Luke 12:16ff.; 16:19ff.;

Matt. 19:21ff.). Spirit-filled living might tend to material blessing, but it does not guarantee it. It is even true that optimal Christian living does not guarantee big ministries with large followings, as is evidenced from the life of Noah, Elijah, Isaiah, Jeremiah, and others to whom few listened.

Believers should have sober and, more importantly, **Scriptural** expectations of what optimal Christian living does and does not bring. The Spirit-filled life is a blessed life but not necessarily an easy one and certainly not a problem free one. In fact, maturity will not come without some God-controlled measure of suffering (James 1:2-3; 1 Pet. 4:12-13; 5:10).

(b). Actual Results to Spirit-Filled Living

Optimal Christian living produces many wonderful benefits. A believer who is content with these legitimate results from Spirit-filling will be most blessed.

The main product of the Spirit is Christ-likeness. The "fruit of the Spirit" (see Gal. 5:22-23, Phil. 1:11) brings no small stability and contentment to life. Spirit filling brings the power of the Spirit (Acts 1:8; Rom. 15:13; Col. 1:11; 1 Thess 1:5). Such power is legitimately viewed not as a power to perform the spectacular, but a power to obey. The Spirit-filled believer can draw upon the Holy Spirit as a constant and sufficient source for the power to obey the Word of God.[25]

Optimal Christian living may not guarantee that one will be instrumental in "harvesting souls." However, it is legitimate to make the winning of souls a general tendency that usually arises from spirituality (e.g., John 15:5), and increased witnessing **does** arise from spirituality (Acts 1:8).

Likewise, prayer in the Spirit (one praying in the context of a life that is properly re-

---

[25] God the Holy Spirit is our strength (see Old Testament verses on God being the believer's strength, Ex. 15:2; Psa. 46:1; 118:14; Neh. 8:10).

lated to the Holy Spirit, Eph. 6:18, Jude 20) will increase effectiveness in prayer. Spirituality does not guarantee affirmative answers to every prayer. However, those who obey His commands do obtain greater results in prayer (1 John 3:22; James 5:16b). Spiritual people tend to eliminate prayers that are selfish or known to be outside God's will (James 4:3; 1 John 5:14-15). Furthermore, a life that is not controlled by the Spirit leads to ineffective prayer (Psa. 66:18; 1 Pet. 3:12). Thus, Spirit-filling, while it may not guarantee an affirmative answer to every prayer, does in a general sense greatly increase effectiveness in prayer.

Assurance of salvation is another area of blessing that arises from optimal Christian living. While a study of apologetics produces objective data to support Christianity, there must also be a subjective assurance that comes from the Holy Spirit in order to arrive at absolute certainty. The Holy Spirit produces assurance of salvation in the hearts of those under His control (see Rom. 8:16; Gal. 4:6; 1 John 5:7,10).

A complete discussion of God's specialized will cannot be included here. However, one of the results of walking by the Spirit is a greater ability to discover God's will. Phil. 2:13 teaches "for it is God who is at work in you both to will and to do of His good pleasure." God does direct our paths (Prov. 3:5-6; 16:9; Psa. 37:5-6). The transformation process which the Holy Spirit wants to work in a believer's life leads to "proving what is that good, and acceptable, and perfect will of God" (see Rom. 12:1-3, cf. 2 Cor. 3:18 for the Spirit's role in the process). There is ¬lso a measure of confidence ("faith", Rom. 12:3) as to one's spiritual gifts and even personalized convictions about issues of Christian liberty (Rom. 14:23). Spirit-filled believers are not going to be ignorant of either God's general or specific will (see Eph. 5:17 just before the command to be filled by the Spirit). Those believers who are not controlled by the Spirit have not met the conditions to know God's will.

Illumination is part of the process by which the Holy Spirit fills (controls) a believer. The Holy Spirit illuminates not so much the factual content (which can be learned by study 2 Tim. 2:15 etc.) but the spiritual significance and relevance of Scripture. He seeks to teach believers the personal importance of the Scriptures. This is a part of His transformation of our minds into the image of Christ.

However, increasing illumination of the Scripture can also be classified as a result of Spirit-filling. The Spirit controls (fills) by the written Word, but also in the process He continually teaches the one who is controlled even more about the Word. Thus, Spirit-filled living results in a greater appreciation and practical understanding of God's Word (1 Cor. 2:15; 1 John 2:20, 27). Illumination is an important ministry by the Holy Spirit and receives separate treatment in the next section.

The Spirit-filled life results in great blessedness. There are those who do not appreciate true spiritual values and are, therefore, discontent with what optimal Christian living can realistically offer. They seek more. They would desire Spirit-filling that produces results that they subjectively consider desirable.

Nevertheless, believers who have a correct sense of spiritual priorities will recognize the invaluable treasures of those blessings that God wants to offer. They will be content with the Biblically legitimate results of optimal Christian living because they understand their infinitely superior value to the baubles offered by proponents of a warped and fleshly Pneumatology. The blessings that God wants to give are far more precious than those that unspiritual Christians (not to mention just plain charlatans) want to receive. The fruit of the Spirit, the presence of the Holy Spirit as a source of power to obey, soul winning, increased effectiveness in prayer, assurance of salvation, guidance in God's will for a life, illumination of the

Scriptures, and more are the Biblical results of Spirit filled-living. It is hard to understand why some are discontent and seek additional "manifestations" of the Spirit that are in reality not more spiritually valuable but less, and in reality not more miraculous but less, and are actually excluded from the scope of what the Bible teaches can happen in Christian living even at its optimum.

(6). Topics Related to the Spirit's Filling (Control)

(a). Illumination

The Holy Spirit is a teacher and illuminator of the truth. Illumination from the Holy Spirit may be viewed as either one of the main steps in the process of the Spirit's control (filling) or also as a continued result of the Spirit's filling. The Holy Spirit illuminates the understanding of believers as to the Word of God in order to control (fill) by the Word of God. Yet, where a life is so controlled there is still additional illumination of truth.

Filling involves more than understanding. There must also be a response (i.e., submission) to that Word in order to be filled (controlled). Thus, filling and illumination are not synonyms. There is more involved in filling than just illumination. Yet, illumination must occur as a necessary step to the filling (control) process. The Spirit illuminates in order to fill (control).

Although the author believes such passages as John 14:26; 15:26-27; 16:12-14 and 1 Cor. 2:6-13 concern the Holy Spirit's ministry of giving divine **revelation** to the **apostles** and **not** the topic of **illuminating ordinary believers**, there is still ample evidence to show the Holy Spirit teaches all believers.

> But a natural man does not accept the things of the Spirit of God; for they are foolishness to him, and he cannot understand them, because they are spiritually appraised. But he who is spiritual appraises all things yet he himself is appraised by no man [1

Cor. 2:14-15].

> But you have an anointing from the Holy One, and you all know....And as for you, the anointing which you received from Him abides in you, and you have no need for anyone to teach you; but as His anointing teaches you about all things, and is true and is not a lie, and just as it has taught you, you abide in Him [1 John 2:20, 27].

There is a danger of giving a mistaken emphasis to the illuminating ministry of the Holy Spirit. A Mormon once told the author that Mormonism had to be the truth because the "Holy Spirit gave such a good feeling about it!"

We need to realize that illumination is not revelation, it is not inspiration, and it does not primarily concern the intellectual aspects of Bible study. Revelation is God's imparting of truths that man would otherwise never know. God revealed truths to the apostles and prophets. Inspiration is God's supervision of the process of recording His revelation so that it was recorded without error and passed on to all of God's people. Illumination is God's work of enabling His people to understand inspired revelation. Illumination does not concern the bestowal of new revelation or the inspiration that records such new revelation. It concerns the understanding of what has already been revealed and recorded without error (inspiration), namely the Bible. Even the concept of "understanding" should be qualified.

The ministry of the Holy Spirit does relate to an intellectual comprehension of the Scriptures. He gives the self-control (discipline) that is needed to understand the Holy Bible (Gal. 5:22-23). The Holy Spirit generates the hunger and thirst for the truth that leads a believer in the diligence that is needed for factual understanding of the Bible. Yet, it is also true that the emphasis in illumination lies in another direction, not so much toward the intellect but the emotions and will.

The Scriptural doctrine of illumination does not cancel out the equally Scriptural command to study in order to understand the facts of Scripture. (Ezra 7:10; Psa. 1:2-3; Matt. 4:4; 1 Tim. 4:13 and 15; 5:17; 2 Tim. 2:15; 1 Pet. 2:2). The Holy Spirit will not teach the factual content of the Bible to those believers too apathetic to study the precious Word. Also, it is true that one can understand the facts of the Bible without any illumination. This occurs whenever an unsaved historian correctly reports the facts of Christianity or a liberal scholar correctly understands Luther's teachings on justification by faith. Intellectual understanding without illumination also occurs when a seminary student studies the Bible with a bad attitude and still gets an "A", or a minister makes a doctrinally precise sermon just to obtain a paycheck. The Scriptures which concern the topic of illumination define a failure to understand not so much as failure of the intellect as a failure of the emotions to see the beauty and value of Scripture and a failure of the will to obey.

> For the word of the cross is to those who are perishing **foolishness**, but to us who are being saved it is the power of God [1 Cor. 1:18].

> But a natural man does not accept the things of the Spirit of God; for they are **foolishness** to him, and he cannot understand them, because they are spiritually **appraised**. But he who is spiritual appraises all things, yet he himself is appraised by no man [1 Cor. 2:14-15].

1 Cor. 1:18 does not deny that an unbeliever can understand the facts of the gospel. He might intellectually understand that Christ claimed to be the Son of God. He knows what the words "death, burial, and resurrection" mean. The problem is not with understanding the facts. It lies in the area of appreciating and evaluating these facts. To the unbeliever the gospel is not incomprehensible. It is rather "foolishness" (Greek word

related to "moron"). It is irrelevant, absurd, and ridiculous.

1 Cor. 2:14 teaches that unbelievers do not accept and cannot correctly appraise Scriptural truths. The word "accept" means "to welcome" (see Matt. 10:14,40; 18:5). The problem is not one of an inability to understand the facts but one of an inability to evaluate them properly. Simple Christian truths may be mentally understood by an unbeliever. Yet, he does not accept or welcome them because he is totally unable to assess these truths. The intellect may understand but the emotions do not desire and the will does not appreciate. While the unsaved may mentally understand, his emotions and will evaluate Scriptural truths as being absurd, ridiculous, distasteful, and complete irrelevant nonsense.

The word "appraise" or "discern" in 1 Cor. 2:14 also shows that illumination does not so much concern the intellect as the emotions and will. It is a judicial term meaning to judge (Acts 4:9; 12:19; 17:11; 24:8). A man without illumination might be able to understand the gospel or Christian doctrine and ethics, but he lacks the ability to judge, evaluate, appraise, and assess these truths with any objectivity and sense. He might intellectually comprehend the Bible, but he does not welcome or appreciate it. He does not choose with his will to follow it.

Believers should view the Holy Spirit's work of illumination as going far beyond a mental understanding of Bible facts. The Holy Spirit desires to illuminate in the sense of showing a believer the significance, the beauty, the glory, the personal relevance, the preciousness, the vital nature and importance to the Scripture. A carnal-like Christian can intellectually understand Bible facts. A Christian being taught by the Spirit also understands the personal impact of these facts, the changes that should be made in life and the personal benefit in compliance. A carnal-like believer can intellectually understand the meaning of a sentence for theology. A spiritual believer appreciates the same Scriptural line both for its impact upon doctrine and also upon life and God's work in the present and real world.

Although the Holy Spirit does play a role in the academic understanding of the Bible, His teaching work extends far beyond that point. Illumination occurs when the Holy Spirit teaches the spiritual man to understand the spiritual significance, spiritual glory, and spiritual wisdom of the Bible.

(b). Individual Guidance by the Holy Spirit

All believers are led by the Spirit in the sense that He seeks to control us by the standards of His Word (Rom. 8:14; Gal. 5:18). Primarily, the Holy Spirit teaches, guides, and controls through the Scriptures. Does His ministry include any guidance beyond the direct teaching of Scripture? Does He ever specifically guide an individual?

Some maintain there is no such thing as an individualized guidance by the Holy Spirit for each person. They would limit the Spirit's guidance only to that which is directly taught by the Scripture. While recognizing the dangers of ignorant or deliberate abuse of the concept of being prompted by the Spirit, the author feels that a total elimination of the idea of individualized guidance is an extreme reaction. It would be better to try to curtail abuse by careful instruction on the subject.

i. Guidance by Audible Voices

Can God the Holy Spirit ever guide by audible voices or visions during the church age? One must be careful about putting God in a box and insisting He cannot act in a certain way. While God might and possibly does communicate verbally, there are some Scriptural truths that must control our understanding of such communication happening.

First, there are no apostles and prophets today. Apostles had to have seen the resurrected Lord (see Acts 1:21-22; 1 Cor. 9:1).

Paul was absolutely the last man to qualify (1 Cor. 15:8). Apostles and prophets were part of the founding period of the church (Eph. 2:20). They were the instruments by which revelation was given to the church (see John 14-16; Eph. 3:5). In order to be included in the New Testament canon a book had to have been written by an apostle or under the authority of an apostle. Because there are no apostles or prophets, there can be no such thing as modern revelation that is binding upon the whole church. While a **strictly personal** revelation in an audible sense might be possible, there can be no such thing as an authoritative revelation from the Holy Spirit that is binding in authority upon others. Thus, anyone claiming to have obtained new revelation and new authority as a leader who can give divine revelation for others should be quickly dismissed. If audible divine revelation is still possible, it would have to be a strictly personal communication. Authority for the church comes from the apostolic and prophetic New Testament. Christian people should not blindly submit to another who claims to have new revelation about God's will for them. It is a deception.

Another consideration is that while the Holy Spirit might give a direct (but highly personal) revelation, this would not be expected as a normal, common way for Him to work. **His primary way of leading is by the Scripture.** Secondarily, He also gives **inaudible promptings and impressions** (see next section, ii). While audible personal revelations might occur, they are not the Holy Spirit's normal way of working, and they should be expected to be a very rare phenomenon as we are no longer in the apostolic age. The author feels obligated to dismiss most claims to God directly speaking as confusion, attention-seeking devices, or rationalizations for dubious behavior (e.g., evangelists claiming God "told" them to raise "dollars").

After the qualifications that any audible revelation must be a strictly personal mes-

260

sage and that such revelation must be extremely rare, there still is some room for the possibility that the Holy Spirit could speak audibly today. The author does not feel obligated to deny all such claims. If a person claims a message binding on others, he is a fraud. If he claims God talks with him frequently, he is also not to be trusted. Yet, there may be credibility for an isolated and strictly personal communication. Paul's example as one who obtained such personal revelations is that he did not boast about the experience. In fact he did not talk about it for 14 years and even then would not go into details (2 Corinthians 12). The claim to have an audible revelation by the Holy Spirit is belied by an eagerness to brag about it quickly and extensively. Such revelation must be contained to personal messages that are so intensely personal that the one so favored is reluctant to draw attention to himself or to the experience. Not all claims to a verbal message by the Holy Spirit must necessarily be treated as phony. Yet, those which are used to claim authority over others are as illegitimate as are those that obviously contradict God's Word. Also, claims which are made frequently and which seem to involve a desire to draw attention to self are dubious at best. Another factor in credibility is the reliability of a person's judgment of Biblical truth. If he has a faulty judgment relative to Bible interpretations, it is unlikely that his judgment can be trusted in the area of experiences.

ii. Inaudible Promptings and Impressions by the Holy Spirit

There is a greater Scriptural basis for believing that the Holy Spirit gives inaudible promptings and impressions in order to guide a believer than for belief in the possibility of audible voices. However, this area is just as capable of abuse and misunderstandings as the topic of audible revelations or visions.

Warnings against a rationalizion that confuses fleshly impulses with "Spirit-leading" cannot be given in too strict terms. Internal promptings, impressions, burdens, convictions, are only reliable in a context of a life that consistently follows clear teaching by the Holy Spirit from the Bible. If a person ignores clear guidance from the Holy Spirit by the Word, he dare not presume to be able to discern the Spirit's individual guidance in any specific matter. Internal feelings are only reliable if they arise from a heart that is submitted to God in every area that is already revealed in the Scriptures. Otherwise, there is much room for rationalization and manipulation. Promptings and impressions, unrestrained by submission to Scripture, are a very poor basis for decision-making or behavior. Remember, the filling of the Spirit is the same as being filled with the Word of Christ (cf. Eph. 5:18, Col. 3:16).

Having given this warning it still is true that the Bible encourages the idea that the Holy Spirit can and does guide **spiritual** people by promptings and impressions. Such inaudible guidance never contradicts the written Word (Isa. 8:20). It never leads to any secret of Christian living that is not already contained in the Bible or gives a person some resource for living not available to other believers. The Scriptures alone contain all essential promises for godly living (2 Pet. 1:3) and all equipment for Christian service (2 Tim. 3:16-17).

However, Christianity has some very personal and individual aspects. It is almost necessary to include some ministry of individual guidance by the Holy Spirit into knowledge of God's specific and personal will in these areas. Not all believers have the same convictions about behaviors not covered in the Bible. Thus, apparently there must be some individualized guidance from God in developing personal standards in areas of Christian liberty. Rom. 14:22-23 indicates that individual believers will have a differing confidence (faith) as to the propriety or impropriety of actions in the area of Christian liberty. It is logical to assume the Holy Spirit wants to develop such convictions by promptings, impressions, burdens as to individual convictions about various issues of Christian liberty in the life of spiritual believers. Likewise, every believer has a spiritual gift, but not all have the same gift. Thus, there apparently must be some guidance by which an individual can discern the identity of his gift(s). It is very likely that the Holy Spirit gives a measure of confidence (i.e., faith, Rom. 12:3) to the **spiritual** person as to what he or she should be doing in God's work. The Holy Spirit prompts (only spiritual people) in the areas of personal convictions and identity of spiritual gifts. Furthermore, there is evidence that the Holy Spirit gives promptings and impressions to **spiritual people** as a way of guiding them into making decisions according to His specific will (Phil. 2:13).[26] The Bible does not seem to restrict God's guidance to a generalized leading for all Christians at all times directly given in the Scriptures (Prov. 3:5-6; Psa. 32:8; 37:4-5; 73:23-24). Apparently God also gives individualized guidance.

Some might criticize these ideas about the Holy Spirit's promptings and impressions as being too subjective. True, there can be abuse by the unspiritual. However, ultimately the inclusion of promptings as a ministry of the Holy Spirit's guidance rests in a trust in the objective Scriptures. The Bible teaches that God the Holy Spirit resides within. It teaches that He works in the mental faculties of spiritual people (Phil. 2:13) giving burdens, convictions, and guidance about matters of His individual will (such as in areas of Christian liberty, Rom. 14:22-23, or spiritual gifts, Rom. 12:3). If an unspiritual person trusts his promptings and impressions, he ends up in sin by confusing selfish impulses for the "Spirit's leading." This can even be done by deliberate distor-

tion and manipulation of an otherwise legitimate doctrine. Yet, the spiritual person who trusts promptings and impressions is in reality expressing faith in the teaching of Scripture that God does operate in a certain way in a godly heart. For the spiritual person to trust an impression is not an involvement in self-deluded subjectivity. It is a trust in those Scriptures that teach God lives within and that He guides individually into a knowledge of differing convictions, burdens, gifts, and decisions. While possible abuse exists in the area of promptings by the Holy Spirit, this does not mean the whole idea of such guidance should be rejected. When promptings and impressions arise from a life of spirituality, they should be viewed as a legitimate means by which the Holy Spirit gives individual guidance.

(c). Prayer in the Spirit

> With all prayer and petition pray at all times **in the Spirit**... [Eph. 6:18].

> But you, beloved, building yourselves up on your most holy faith; **praying in the Holy Spirit** [Jude 20].

Prayer in or by the Holy Spirit is an area that could be classified as a part of the Spirit's controlling (filling) process, but it also could be viewed as an ongoing result of the Spirit's control over ones life.[27] Prayer "in or by the Spirit" is mentioned in Eph. 6:18 and Jude 20. Eph. 2:18 also teaches that the Holy Spirit is a channel through which prayers are directed to the Father (see the Holy Spirit's title, "Spirit of Supplication" in Zech. 12:10).

At the very least the phrase "prayer in the Spirit" means that believers must be rightly related to the Holy Spirit in order to have effective prayer. Grieving or quenching the Spirit is not consistent with a healthy basis

---

[26] The Bible gives many reasons that God might allow sickness or suffering in a believer's life. Is it not reasonable to think the Holy Spirit could give conviction as to the purpose behind a specific hardship a believer has endured?

[27] In other words, one is not filled by the Spirit unless the Spirit controls the area of prayer. Yet, the Spirit's control will result in increased ability to pray by the Spirit.

for prayer because sin renders prayer non-effective (Psa. 66:18; 1 Pet. 3:7,12; James 4:3), while obedience to God's commandments increases effectiveness in prayer (1 John 3:22; James 5:16). Furthermore, it is likely that the Holy Spirit gives burdens, promptings, and impressions in the area of subjects for prayer. Part of the filling process is a correct relationship to the Spirit that fosters prayer. Yet, this filling also results in an increased sensitivity to the Spirit's prompting to additional prayers.

Due warning must be given against taking the concept of prayer in or by the Spirit to unscriptural excesses. The phrase does not refer to prayer seizures or trances. 1 Cor. 14:15 and Matt. 6:7 teach that prayer should be offered in understandable languages. 1 Cor. 14:32 gives a general principle that when God works in His people they still retain control of their mental faculties.

> "And when you are praying do not use meaningless repetition, as the Gentiles do, for they suppose that they will be heard for their many words" [Matt. 6:7].

> What is the outcome then? I shall pray with the spirit and **I shall pray with the mind also**....and the spirits of prophets are subject to prophets; for God is not a God of confusion but of peace, as in all the churches of the saints [1 Cor. 14:15a; 32-33].

Rom. 8:26-27 does not so much concern believer's prayers by the Holy Spirit as it does prayers that the Holy Spirit Himself makes for believers. This is another ministry of the Holy Spirit as it relates to prayer. Yet, it is not the same as "praying in the Spirit" which concerns conscious thoughts (often audible words) that the believers pray. The Holy Spirit prays in a mysterious and **inaudible** way interceding to God the Father on behalf of believers. We are not aware or conscious of when or how He intercedes.

(d). Assurance

Assurance of salvation is brought about by the Holy Spirit in the hearts of believers who are submissive to His filling (control). This is a result of salvation and has already been covered (see Rom. 8:16; Gal. 4:6; 1 John 5:7,10).

(e). Fruit of the Holy Spirit

Likewise, the fruit of the Spirit is a result of the filling (control) of the Spirit. The topic of the Spirit's fruit is worthy of extended treatment, but this would extend beyond the scope of this more limited study. The fruit of the Spirit is listed in Gal. 5:22-23.

> But the fruit of the Spirit is love, joy, peace, patience, kindness, goodness, faithfulness, gentleness, self-control; against such things there is no law [Gal. 5:22-23].

It would be good to note here that these characteristics are supposed to deepen and grow in a Christian's life. The most recent convert may be spiritual (i.e., controlled by the Spirit) and exhibit the fruit to some degree immediately. However, maturity takes time, as over the course of a lifetime a person becomes more and more like Christ in character. The New Testament clearly teaches that love, for example, is supposed to deepen in time. Phil. 1:9-11 refers to a deepening of love, knowledge, discernment, and righteousness. Eph. 3:16ff. includes mention of the Holy Spirit and "fullness." It teaches that believers grow deeper in the love of Christ and in knowledge. 1 Thess 4:8-10 shows that while the Spirit produces love in all, there is a need "to excel still more" in love.

> [T]hat He would grant you, according to the riches of His glory, to be strengthened with power **through His Spirit** in the inner man; so that Christ may dwell in your hearts through faith; and that you, being rooted and grounded in love, may be able to comprehend with all the saints what is the breadth and length

and height and depth, and to **know the love of Christ which surpasses knowledge**, that you may be filled up **to all the fullness of God** [Eph. 3:16-19].

And this I pray, that **your love may abound still more and more** in real knowledge and all discernment, so that you may approve the things that are excellent, in order to be sincere and blameless until the day of Christ; having been filled with the fruit of righteousness which comes through Jesus Christ, to the glory and praise of God [Phil. 1:9-11].

Consequently, he who rejects this is not rejecting man but the God who gives His **Holy Spirit** to you. Now as to the love of the brethren, you have no need for anyone to write you, for you yourselves are taught by God to love one another; for indeed you do practice it toward all the brethren who are in all Macedonia. But we urge you, brethren **to excel still more** [1 Thess. 4:8-10].

While spirituality with its fruit of the Spirit is accessible to all believers, maturity takes time. All believers can be spiritual. Yet, viewed strictly from the immediate present, not all can be mature. The maturation process takes time, and there are no short cuts in producing depth. There is danger in rejecting God's more strenuous and lengthy program of growth for easy, quick and thoroughly unscriptural notions that maturity can be achieved instantaneously by some crisis initiation into the realms of spiritual giants. All may have the fruit of the Spirit. All may be spiritual. However, a deepening of this fruit takes time and effort (active-dependence). There is no other way.

b. Mysteries concerning Spirit-filling

In John 3:8 the Lord taught that the work of the Spirit is as mysterious as the wind. Therefore, it should not be very surprising if some aspects to His work are not well understood. This section on Spirit-filling covers an area where there possibly is no final answer. Sometimes it is helpful to know that the Bible is unclear on an issue. This acknowledgement of ignorance can help us in distinguishing between important doctrine and Bible trivia, between pursuits that should be at the core of our efforts and no. speculation. If a truth is not clearly taught by Scripture, then Christians have no business to "major on minors" by focusing their spiritual energies in a direction which does not have firm Biblical support.

Several questions naturally arise from the phrase "Spirit-filling." Can a believer obtain more of the Spirit at one time in His life than at another? Can one believer obtain more of the Holy Spirit than another? This study is going to conclude that we do not know with certainty the answers to these questions. The conclusion of ignorance can be very important for it makes this particular aspect of "Spirit-filling" as irrelevant as the medieval argument of how many angels can occupy the area of a pinhead.

We do know what we must do in order to be Spirit-filled and we do know the optimal results of Spirit-filled living. Thus, both the Christian's responsibility and expectations have been revealed. Actually, it makes little practical difference what the Spirit is invisibly doing in secret. Such activity is unperceived by us anyway. There are no commands in the Bible to seek or plead for more of the Spirit. Our task is to mind our own business by not quenching or grieving the Spirit and by walking by the Spirit. Energies spent in trying to obtain more of the Spirit are wasted. We know our tasks. What the Spirit does is His business, and ultimately it is not our concern. We do not know whether we can obtain more of Him or not. From the Christian perspective it makes absolutely no practical difference either in efforts or outcome. Regardless of whether "filling" includes more of the Spirit, our work is the same and the optimal results are the same.

Those who are not content with what God has revealed about the Holy Spirit and our responsibilities to Him are likely to become sidetracked by speculation and pursuits to obtain more of the Spirit. Such pursuits are not even mentioned (to say nothing of the absence of commands) in the Word of God. Such efforts are really a digression from Biblically revealed efforts toward maturity, or at the least a circular movement.

The way of maturity involves rejoicing and contentment in what is known and concentrating on what we know God wants us to do (not rejection of clear teachings for speculation on mysteries that we do not either control or even perceive).

(1). Reasons for Ambiguity About Obtaining More of the Spirit

Verses that refer to "full", "fullness", or "filled by the Spirit", are virtually all contained in the writings of Paul and Luke. However, there are differences between the two authors. First, the Greek verb "fill" is **not** the same word in Luke and Acts as it is in Eph. 5:18. Secondly, Luke and Paul use different prepositions. Luke writes of being "filled **of** the Spirit" (usually genitive case without actual preposition) while Paul writes of being filled "**in, with,** or **by** the Spirit.**" The argument as to whether the differences are just stylistic or reflect an actual change in subject is endless. Various options will now be listed. **Remember the point of this material is to show we likely do not know the answer**. Ignorance will be easy to establish.

(2). Filled of the Spirit in Luke and Acts

Luke uses some form of being filled of the Spirit in many places (John the Baptist, Luke 1:15; Elizabeth, Luke 1:41; Zacharias, Luke 1:67; Pentecost, Acts 2:4; Peter, Acts 4:8; early Christians, Acts 4:31; Saul, Acts 9:17; 13:9).[28] This phrase is capable of sev-

eral meanings. Also, its relationship to Paul's command to be "filled by the Spirit" in Eph. 5:18 can be understood in different ways. Here are some various options. It is hard to prove which view is correct.

(a). Luke intended the phrase "filled of the Spirit" to refer to a filling that the Spirit accomplishes, not to refer to obtaining more of Him (similar to a subjective genitive). The Spirit fills, but He fills with the Word. A good understanding would be "filled by the Spirit" (but with the written Word).

Furthermore, this can be understood as the same thing as commanded in Eph. 5:18. There Paul commands believers to be "filled by the Spirit." The Spirit fills but not with Himself. He fills with the Word of God (see Col. 3:16). Believers **never** obtain **more** of the Spirit.

View one is a popular approach in non-charismatic church circles. It is defensible but not absolutely certain.

(b). A second approach to Luke's phrase "filled of the Spirit" sees the filling in Luke's writings to be different than the filling in Paul's writings and something limited to apostolic times. Perhaps Luke is referring to obtaining more of the Spirit. The phrase "filled of the Spirit" might refer to a filling whose content is the Spirit Himself (a filling that consists of the Spirit, similar to genitive of content).[29]

However, one could argue that John the Baptist's family and the early church are special cases. They did obtain more of the Spirit, but their experience is recorded only as historical events (not models whom we are commanded to follow). It does not directly concern life today and could not happen beyond apostolic times. The historical books of Luke and Acts merely record some people who obtained a special measure of

---

[28] Uses of the noun "fill" by Luke include: Luke 4:1 (Christ), Acts 6:3,5; 7:55 (Stephen) and 11:24 (Barnabas).

[29] The genitive could also be a genitive of description, i.e., a spiritual filling, or we could take the Greek case to denote source, means, or reference.

the Spirit. [30]There is no command for us to try to obtain a similar experience.

The only command concerning Spirit-filling is Eph. 5:18. There Paul uses a different verb and a different preposition. He is not referring to obtaining more of the Spirit, but rather a filling by the Spirit with the Word. Thus, Luke writes of historical examples, but he gives no commands for living today. Today no one can obtain more of the Spirit. Eph. 5:18 refers to a different experience.

(c). Like the second view, a third understanding distinguishes between Luke's phrase "filled of the Spirit" and Paul's phrase "filled (different word) in, by or with the Spirit." However, unlike view number two it is possible to maintain that the bestowal of an extra measure of the Spirit need not be limited to apostolic times.

Eph. 5:18 is commanding believers to "be filled by the Spirit," but refers to the Spirit's filling us with the written Word. This is the only command relative to Spirit-filling. However, God might sovereignly bestow an extra portion **of the Spirit** (Luke's phrase) to one today as it pleases Him. This would not be something we should seek or request, but it is something God might do. The only difference between views two and three is that the latter's proponents feel that an extra measure of the Spirit is not something limited to the early church.

(d). A final view of Luke's phrase "filled of the Spirit" treats it the same as Paul's phrase "filled by the Spirit." However, unlike view one, it maintains that both phrases do involve obtaining more of the Spirit. Eph. 5:18 commands us to "be filled by the Spirit." This means not only that He does the filling but also He is the content of the filling. We can obtain more of the Spirit. A greater level of the Spirit is not just restricted to apostolic times, nor is it just something that God might sovereignly bestow upon a few today.

He desires this more complete bestowal of the Spirit for all.

This final view is the most radical departure from typical non-charismatic theology. However, there still need be no difference whatsoever in the practice of Christian living from the views given above. If Eph. 5:18 does speak of gaining more of the Spirit, then the way to go about it is still the same as described previously. A believer's responsibility is still to be controlled by the Spirit through the Word. There is no difference in responsibilities or outcome. The only difference would be in speculation as to the Spirit's unseen work and whether a believer can obtain more of the Spirit.

(3). The Meaning of Ephesians 5:18

Eph. 5:18 has as many interpretive options as does Luke's phrase "filled of the Spirit." It is extremely difficult to know whether one can obtain more of the Spirit or not. Yet, this makes little difference for Christian living.

(a). Some interpreters do not think that Eph. 5:18 even refers to filling by the Holy Spirit. They would take "Spirit" to refer to the human spirit and would translate the preposition as "in" as follows: "And do not get drunk with wine, for that is dissipation, but be filled in spirit, speaking to one another in psalms, hymns, and spiritual songs, singing, and making melody with your heart to the Lord."

The word "spirit" can refer to the Holy Spirit or the human spirit. A reference to the human spirit fits the following context nicely. Paul would be speaking of a human spirit with a joyous disposition. Furthermore, there would be a nice parallel with Col. 3:16, which refers to "letting the Word of Christ dwell in you," i.e., in the human spirit. The preposition can be translated "in" (the author argues for "in" being the best translation of the same preposition in the phrase "baptism in the Spirit", see pages 245-46).

Proponents of this view would argue for a

---

[30] Compare John 3:34.

big difference between Paul in Ephesians 5 and Luke's use of the phrase "filled of the Spirit." Luke, they would say, does speak of a Holy Spirit-filling. Paul, in Eph. 5:18, does not. [31]

This uncommon interpretation of Eph. 5:18 would not cancel out the need to be controlled by the Spirit. Christian living would remain about the same. There would still be commands to "walk by the Spirit," "grieve not," "quench not." However, one might be hesitant to call it the doctrine of "Spirit-filling."

This first view of Eph. 5:18 is a minority view, but it cannot be dismissed as erroneous. It actually deserves more credence than has been traditionally given it.

(b). Filled In, By, or With the Spirit

The preposition employed in Eph. 5:18 is capable of being translated "in," "by," or "with." Each translation has its affects upon the issue of whether a believer could ever obtain more of the Spirit. However, grammar and context do not favor one over the other. The only recourse is to translate in accordance with a preconceived theology and be charitable to others who differ.

(i). Be Filled **By** the Spirit

This translation will be favored by those who think it is impossible that a believer could ever obtain more of the Spirit. It would be maintained that believers are to be "filled by the Holy Spirit" but with the Word of God (Col. 3:16). The Spirit is viewed as the agent but not the content of filling.

However, even the translation "by" need not rule out a greater portion of the Spirit. Perhaps believers are "filled by the Spirit" both in the sense that He is the One who does the filling, and He is the content with which we are filled.

(ii). Be Filled **With** the Spirit [32]

Those who believe one can obtain more of the Spirit will likely prefer to translate the command "Be filled **with** the Spirit". The Spirit is the agent who does the filling, but He may also be the content of filling.

(iii). Be Filled **In** the Spirit

Those who take *spirit* to refer to human spirit will most likely prefer the translation "*in*." However, one can take the reference to the Holy Spirit and still prefer "*in*." The meaning is "Be filled *in* the sphere of the Holy Spirit," "Be filled *in* the realm of the Holy Spirit." After all, the same preposition can be translated "*in*" in reference to "a baptism in the Spirit".

(4). Conclusion on Obtaining More of the Spirit

The author is neutral on the point as to whether believers can obtain more of the Holy Spirit. Along with this openness, however, there is an attitude that the matter is quite trivial. The matter concerns the Holy Spirit's business, not ours. Either way, there is no difference in the human experience. Believers are told what they should do relative to the Holy Spirit. The Bible reveals optimal results for Spirit-filled living. If, in the process, we obtain more of the Spirit, we are unaware of it. [33] If, in the process, we do not obtain more of the Spirit, we are likewise unaware of it. Our responsibilities are the same either way, and they do not include any sidetrack of seeking or pleading for more of the Spirit. Such would be detrimental to the known path to maturity. Our re-

---

[31] Other verses with the idea of filling the human soul or spirit could be Eph. 3:19; Phil.1:11; Col.1:9-10.

[32] See C.F.D. Moule, *An Idiom Book of New Testament Greek*, 2nd Ed., (Cambridge University Press, 1959), p.79. Here Moule teaches the preposition *en* can be a description meaning "consisting of".

[33] Perhaps God wanted to eliminate all the smugness and pride that could come by comparing levels of possession of the Holy Spirit. It is best for us not to know some things.

sources for Spirit-filled living are the same regardless of whether in a mysterious way we at times have more of the Spirit than at other times. No believer has more resources than any other believer does, although some use them better. Finally, the results of Spirit-filling are going to be the same whether we obtain more of Him or not. The issue of whether believers can obtain more of the Spirit is a moot point relative to Christian living. This is exactly the point of this whole final section. Since there is no absolute evidence either in favor of or against the concept, it should be given a low priority in a believer's thinking. It really does not matter to either our responsibility or to the outcome of Spirit-filled living. There are certainly no commands to seek or plead for more of the Spirit. If He does come in a greater fullness, our lives are the same as if He does not. Therefore, it is a great mistake to focus attention and energies upon pursuing more of the Spirit when the basis for doing so is so Scripturally weak. The Bible teaches what we need to do to be rightly related to the Spirit. This ought to be our concern. The mysteries of the Spirit should be left to the Spirit (Deut. 29:29).

PNEUMATOLOGY:

The Doctrine of the Holy Spirit

PART II

THE GIFTS OF THE HOLY SPIRIT

OUTLINE

F. Miscellaneous Teachings About
    Gifts
    1. Gifts should be Developed
    2. Gifts can Be Neglected
    3. Gifts can Be Abused
    4. Gifts are Irrevocable
G. Definitions for the Gifts
    1. Romans 12:6-8
        a. Prophecy
        b. Service
        c. Teaching
        d. Exhortation
        e. Giving
        f. Leading
        g. Mercy
    2. Ephesians 4:11-12
        a. Apostleship
        b. Prophet
        c. Evangelist
        d. Pastor/teacher
    3. 1 Peter 4:10-11
    4. 1 Corinthians 12:8-10
        a. Word of Wisdom
        b. Word of Knowledge
        c. Faith
        d. Healings, Miracles
        e. Discerning of Spirits
        f. Interpretation of Languages
        g. Helps
        h. Administration
VIII.   Conclusion to Pneumatology

THE GIFTS
OF THE HOLY SPIRIT

I. Introduction

The Holy Spirit's ministry as the gift-giver
deserves its own comprehensive study as
there is a deep rift among conservative
Christians as to His present work. The origin
and growth of the charismatic movement
necessitates a detailed study on the issue of
the cessation of sign gifts before there can be
a study about gifts in general.

While many charismatics are indeed believers in the Person of Christ and His work on
the cross, this does not diminish great differences between the typical charismatic and
typical non-charismatic schools of thought.
The two camps are usually civil and sensible
enough to acknowledge brotherhood where a
genuine faith in Christ exists. However, deep
differences in theology and ecclesiastical
philosophy usually require some limitations
in intimate and continuous joint ministries,
especially teaching and counseling. Few
issues in Pneumatology could be considered
fundamentals of the faith where the matter is
one of deep apostasy that necessarily separates Christians from infidels. Yet, beliefs
that divide typical charismatics from
non-charismatics can be among the most
important of the "secondary" doctrines. Actually, the cessation of sign gifts is a minor
difference compared to the more important
doctrines, such as whether the Holy Spirit's
indwelling is for all believers or some,
whether Spirit baptism is a position or crisis
experience, whether one should strive or
plead for more of the Spirit, whether there
are prophets and apostles who obtain revelation for the church, whether new Scriptures
could be written. These more major topics
have already been treated in this study. Charismatics are typically confused on them,
and this raises some question as to whether
their judgment can be trusted in their exegesis of more specialized topics (not to mention their interpretation of experiences). At
the very least, charismatic theology ought
not to be considered immune from scrutiny
from the Bible. If it has made errors in major
areas of Pneumatology, one cannot just accept every pronouncement charismatics
make without Scriptural validation. Christians have every right to question experiences, for experiences may be of human
origin or even Satanic origin. Indeed, Christians have a responsibility to test and evaluate every claim to truth by the standard for
truth, the Scriptures.

To the law and to the testimony! If they do not speak according to this word, it is because they have no dawn [Isa. 8:20].

Now these were more noble-minded than those in Thessalonica, for they received the word with great eagerness, examining the Scriptures daily, to see whether these things were so [Acts 17:11].

But examine everything carefully; hold fast to that which is good [1 Thess. 5:21].

Beloved, do not believe every spirit, but test the spirits to see whether they are from God; because many false prophets have gone out into the world [1 John 4:1].

Since many areas of conflict between charismatics and non-charismatics have already been studied, concentration will only be focused on the area of gifts.

II. Cessation of Sign Gifts:

A. Cessation of Sign Gifts as Scripturally Probable

It would be unfair to assert that the argument for the cessation of sign gifts is as ironclad as that for Biblical inspiration or the deity of Christ. However, it is fair to conclude that Biblical evidence would lead one to anticipate a cessation of sign gifts at the close of the apostolic age. If sign gifts did not cease with the apostles, then the Bible's portrayal of this age would be confusing and misleading. While the Bible does not explicitly teach "sign gifts will cease with the apostles," the idea of cessation of sign gifts is a logical deduction that can reasonably be made from what the Bible does teach. Biblical evidence suggests that the sign gifts would probably cease with the end of the apostolic age. Non-charismatics should not be faulted for probing this inference. The historical fact that certain gifts did cease supports that it is a correct line of reasoning.

1. Precedent for Cessation of a Gift

It is difficult to challenge the point that the gift of apostleship has ceased. One of the qualifications for apostleship was that one had to be an eyewitness of the resurrected Lord. Acts 1:21-22 is giving qualifications for one to become an apostle and a replacement for Judas Iscariot.

"It is therefore necessary that of the men who have accompanied us all the time that the Lord Jesus went in and out among us - beginning with the baptism of John, until the day that He was taken up from us - one of these should become a **witness with us of His resurrection.**" And they put forward two men, Joseph called Barsabbas (who was also called Justus), and Matthias. And they prayed, and said, "Thou, Lord, who knowest the hearts of all men, show which one of these two Thou hast chosen to occupy this ministry and **apostleship** from which Judas turned aside to go to his own place" [Acts 1:21-25].

...Am I not an **apostle**? Have I not **seen Jesus** our Lord?... [1 Cor. 9:1].

Paul in 1 Cor. 15:1-10 is listing the resurrection appearances of Christ. In v. 8 he says that he was the **last of all** to have a resurrection appearance and that the timing of his seeing the resurrected Christ was unusual, unusually late. Paul saw the Lord last of all at an unusually late time. In v. 9 he immediately ties this witnessing of the resurrected Lord into the subject of apostleship.

[A]nd **last of all**, as it were to one untimely born, [unusually late] He appeared to me also. For I am the least **of the apostles,** who am not fit to be called an **apostle,** because I persecuted the church of God [1 Cor. 15:8-9].

Since no one in the present time lived during the post-resurrection period and no one has witnessed the resurrected Lord, there can be no such thing as an apostle today. This is a very important point as it eliminates the possibility of anyone having the authority to compose additional Scripture. To be a part of the New Testament, a writing had to be apostolic (either written by an apostle or under the supervision of an apostle). The absence of apostles necessitates the close of the canon of Scripture.

Eph. 2:20 should end all debate as to whether the gift of apostleship has ceased. It clearly places apostles within the founding period of the church.

> [H]aving been built upon the foundation of the apostles and prophets, Christ Jesus Himself being the corner stone...[Eph. 2:20].

The idea of a gift ceasing is not unscriptural. Apostleship ceased. Interpreters should not lightly dismiss the idea that other gifts (especially those associated with the apostles) have also ceased.

2. Sign Gifts as Associated with the Apostles

Scripture associates sign gifts (such as tongues, healings, miracles, etc.) with the apostles. The fact that non-apostles such as Stephen (Acts 6:8), or Philip (Acts 8:6), or even the Corinthian believers performed signs does little to break the strong association that the Bible makes between sign gifts and apostles. The exercise of powers by non-apostles could still be a factor in the confirmation of God's approval of the apostles. If, for example, those led to the Lord by Peter and/or those who ministered under Peter's supervision had wonderful gifts, this reflected back upon Peter as a sign that God had indeed made Peter an apostle (one sent by God with a special commission). Furthermore, it is even possible to assume that the ability for non-apostles to perform sign gifts had to be bestowed by an apostle (Rom.

1:11; 1 Tim. 4:14; 2 Tim. 1:6). If this was so, then performance of sign gifts by non-apostles was still the same as a confirmation of an apostle.

Regardless of the details, it is possible to maintain both truths. Non-apostles did perform sign gifts. Yet, it is still true that the Scriptures link sign gifts to the apostles. Paul refers to the signs of an apostle in 2 Cor. 12:12.

> The **signs** of a true **apostle** were performed among you with all perseverance, by signs and wonders and miracles [2 Cor. 12:12].

If sign gifts are the sign of an apostle, then one would not expect them to endure past the apostolic times. Otherwise, they would be serving to confirm people who were not apostles and who had no personal relationship with the apostles (either possessing gifts bestowed by an apostle, or having been converted through an apostle, or ministering under the personal authority of an apostle). Though this is an inference, it is valid logic. The Bible leads one to expect that the sign gifts would cease when the apostleship ceased because the purpose of such gifts was to confirm apostles (either directly or indirectly).

Paul is not the only New Testament author to associate sign gifts with apostleship. Sign gifts and the apostles are tied together throughout the book of Acts.

> And everyone kept feeling a sense of awe; and many wonders and **signs** were taking place through the **apostles** [Acts 2:43].

> And at the hands of the **apostles** many **signs** and wonders were taking place among the people... [Acts 5:12].

> Therefore they spent a long time there speaking boldly with reliance upon the Lord, who was bearing wit-

ness to the word of His grace, grant-ing that **signs** and wonders be done by their hands. But the multitude of the city was divided; and some sided with the Jews, and some with the **apostles** [Acts 14:3-4].

Paul, stressing his apostleship, used his abili-ties in the area of sign gifts to bolster his authority over the Roman church (see con-text Rom. 15:15-16 and also Rom. 1:1-5, 11:13).

For I will not presume to speak of anything except what Christ has ac-complished through me, resulting in the obedience of the Gentiles by word and deed, in the power of signs and wonders, in the power of the Spirit; so that from Jerusalem and round about as far as Illyricum I have fully preached the gospel of Christ [Rom. 15:18-19].

Finally, the author of Hebrews places God's confirmation by sign gifts in the past.

[H]ow shall we escape if we neglect so great a salvation? After it was at the first spoken through the Lord, it was confirmed to us by **those who heard**, God also bearing witness **with them**, both **by signs** and won-ders and by various miracles and by gifts of the Holy Spirit according to His own will [Heb. 2:3-4].

In Greek the time of a participle is contin-gent upon the time of the sentence's leading verb. In this Hebrews 2 passage, this means that "God...bearing witness" took place at the same time as the action "was confirmed." Thus, both God's work of confirmation and bearing witness are **past**. He in the past, the author of Hebrews says, confirmed those who were eyewitnesses of Christ's earthly teaching ministry. God, in the past, con-firmed and bore witness to them by signs.

Note also that the purpose for these signs was to confirm those who knew the Lord

personally. While the context alone would not limit this group to only the apostles, surely the author of Hebrews knew his read-ers would think of the apostles as the pri-mary men who learned under the Lord's personal teaching and the primary group to whom the Holy Spirit gave confirmation by signs. At the very least the apostles ought to be given the prominence in this past confir-mation ministry. All of the above verses that associate signs with apostles might even cause the interpreter to think Hebrews is also referring exclusively to the apostles as the ones who heard the Lord.

Either way the confirmation by signs is **past**, and no one today fits in the category of ei-ther apostle or eyewitness of the Lord's teaching work. Thus, one would not expect sign gifts to continue as God's normal way of working during the present time.

There is little excuse for failing to associate the sign gifts with the apostles. Furthermore, since the purpose of sign gifts, including tongues, (cf. 1 Cor. 14:22 where tongues are called a sign) was to confirm apostles, it is reasonable to conclude that the sign gifts would cease when the gift of apostleship ceased.

3. The Sign of Languages and Israel

In 1 Cor. 14:21-22 Paul teaches that the sign gift of tongues (foreign languages) ought to have a special interest for Jewish people.

In the law it is written, "**By men of strange tongues** and by the lips of strangers **I will speak to this people**, and even so they will not listen to Me," says the Lord. So then tongues are for a sign, not to those who be-lieve, but to unbelievers; but proph-ecy is for a sign, not to unbelievers, but to those who believe [1 Cor. 14:21-22].

Verse 21 is a quote from Isa. 28:11. Isaiah's point is that because Israel would not listen to God in her own language (tongue) that

God would get the nation's attention by forcing them to hear the voice of a foreign language, the Assyrians, who would conquer the ten northern tribes of Israel. In Isaiah's day foreign languages were a sign of judgment for Israel.

Paul quotes Isaiah not so much as a prophecy that found fulfillment but as an illustration. Just as foreign languages had been a sign of God's disappointment with Israel in the past, so too this pattern was repeating itself in the early church. The ability to speak foreign languages that one had not learned was one sign gift that confirmed the apostles. [34] Yet, in the very process of confirming the apostles, God was showing His displeasure with and judgment upon Israel. The two purposes for sign gifts are complementary. By beginning to work through the apostles and the church, God was removing His work through the priesthood and Judaism. The signs of confirmation of the apostles as the foundation of the church were also signs of judgment upon the temple/priesthood and Levitical system that would now be removed as the means by which God works in the world.

1 Cor. 14:21-22 teaches that tongues (languages) are a sign for unbelievers. This should not be limited to Jews exclusively. Christ taught that there would be no special signs for Israel (see Matt. 16:4; Mark 8:12, etc.) and clearly the sign gifts confirmed the apostles in areas far from Israel (Rom. 15:19-20). However, Jewish people are a primary subset in the category "unbelievers." Paul taught that tongues were a sign for unbelievers, and one major application is that it was a sign for those Jews who refused to believe (not a sign for Jews by way of exclusion but by way of emphasis). Sign gifts and languages in particular should have caused unbelieving Jews to think in terms of judgment just as did foreign languages in Isaiah's

day. These signs to confirm the apostles were at the same time signs of rejection and judgment for unbelieving Judaism. God approved the apostles' work in founding the church. God was also angry with Israel.

The reader may be wondering how this fits under the category of the cessation of sign gifts. Given that one of the purposes for the sign gift of languages was to show God's rejection of Judaism, there is no longer any purpose for such a sign. In A.D. 70, the Romans under General Titus totally destroyed the temple. Since then, there has been no priesthood as the genealogy rolls were destroyed. There has been no altar and no animal sacrifices. Judaism after the pattern of the Old Testament and Judaism as it was known during the period of the gospels and early church is defunct and has been since A.D. 70. There is no longer any need for a sign that had as one of its purposes the lesson that God was no longer working through the temple, priesthood, altar, and sacrifices. There simply is no need for a sign with such a purpose when the temple, priesthood, and sacrifices do not exist. God was obviously done with that system when the system went out of existence. Since a partial purpose for tongues (languages) was to show that God was displeased with Israel and would no longer work through the temple system, one would anticipate that tongues would no longer be operative when the temple system was no longer operative. To state the point negatively, one would expect tongues to cease when the temple did. This is a reasonable inference from what the Bible teaches. It may only be a secondary point in the overall discussion about sign gift cessation, but still its validity is strengthened by the historical facts supporting the gradual cessation of sign gifts in the time after the destruction of the Levitical system.

4. Biblical Patterns in the Frequency of Miracles

---

[34] The definition of "tongue" as "language" will be established in pp. 276-78.

The Bible presents a pattern of time periods during which the miraculous is common-place alternated by time periods in which the miraculous is more rare. There were increased miracles during the times of Moses, Elijah and Elisha, and Christ and the apostles.

At such times many miracles occurred. Yet, in between these times, the miraculous was possible but infrequent. In the majority of Biblical time periods miracles have been infrequent. Even during the most intense period of miracles, miracles were not performed in a wide geographical area and did not occur for everybody. Millions of sick people suffered during Christ's earthly ministry in places such as China, India, Arabia, etc. Christ Himself did not wish to heal all people in all places at all times while He was on earth.

> "But I say to you in truth, there were many widows in Israel in the days of Elijah, when the sky was shut up for three years and six months, when a great famine came over all the land; and yet Elijah was sent to none of them, but only to Zarephath, in the land of Sidon, to a woman who was a widow. And there were many lepers in Israel in the time of Elisha the prophet; and none of them was cleansed, but only Naaman the Syrian" [Luke 4:25-27].

Many who claim the ability to perform signs and wonders today actually claim to surpass Christ in terms of frequency and extent of miracles. The pattern of Biblical miracles does not suggest that God wants to do miracles for all times in all places. In fact, we would expect that the present is just as the majority of Biblical history, a time when miracles may be possible but are infrequent.

B. Cessation of Sign Gifts as Historically Certain

The Bible gives an impression that sign gifts would cease with the close of the apostolic age. The historical fact that they did cease proves that the deduction of cessation at the close of the apostolic age is a valid one. The Bible indicates sign gifts would cease with the apostles. Because they did in fact cease, we can have confidence that we have interpreted the Scripture correctly on this issue. For too long the burden of proof has been placed upon non-charismatics to prove that the sign gifts have ceased. The historical fact is that they did cease. Therefore, the burden of proof should be upon charismatics to prove that the sign gifts would begin again in the 20th Century.[35] What Bible texts teach that there will be a second Pentecost during the church dispensation?

It is undeniable that sign gifts as the common normative way God works have ceased for the bulk of church history. If that had not been the case, there would be no debate today. Although the cessation of sign gifts is only a logical inference from the Scriptures and not a direct teaching, the fact that they did cease shows that the inference is based upon sound reasoning. The Bible seems to teach the sign gifts will cease with the apostles. Because the cessation did in fact happen, non-charismatics are not misreading the Bible.

---

[35] Historians often trace the claim of a revival of sign gifts to Topeka, Kansas in 1901 and the Azusa Street revival in California in 1906 (see Grant Wacker, "The Pentecostal Movement" in *Eerdmans Handbook of Christianity in America*, edited by Mark P. Noll, Nathan O. Hatch, George M. Marsden, David F. Wells, John D. Woodbridge (Grand Rapids: Eerdmans Publishing Co., 1983), p. 336-339. Bible texts that refer to great outpouring of the Holy Spirit have contextual references to end time events (e.g., Ezekiel 36-39 and Joel 2-3). For discussion about these verses pertaining to future spiritual blessings see Chapter 12, Section XIII, F5e, "Great Outpouring of the Spirit", pp. 523-24.

It is easy to show from church history that sign gifts did cease.[36] It is impossible to show from the Bible that they would start again until the Second Coming and millennial Kingdom. Chrysostom, Patriarch of Constantinople (345-407), considered sign gifts a thing of the past. In writing on 1 Corinthians 12, he remarks that the people of his day no longer understood the passage well because of the cessation of sign gifts.

"This whole place is very obscure; but the obscurity is produced by our ignorance of the facts referred to and by their cessation, being such as then used to occur but now no longer take place. And why do they not happen now? Why look now, the cause too of the obscurity hath produced us again another question: namely, why did they then happen, and now do so no more?" [37]

Augustine lived from A.D. 354-430 and was the Bishop of Hippo in North Africa. Apparently, the sign gifts had ceased not only in Constantinople but also in Africa.

"In the earliest times the Holy Ghost fell upon them that believed: and they spoke with tongues, which they had not learned, as the Spirit gave them utterance. These were signs adapted to the time. For there behooved to be that betokening of the Holy Spirit in all tongues, to show that the gospel of God was to run through all tongues over the whole earth. That thing was done for a betokening and it passed away... If then the witness of the presence of the Holy Ghost be not now given through these miracles, by what is it given, by what does one get to know that he has received the Holy Ghost?" [38]

Scripture seems to portray the sign gifts as associated with the apostles. One would expect, therefore, sign gifts to pass away when they were no longer needed to confirm the apostles. The fact that the sign gifts did pass away shows the soundness of such reasoning. Biblical inference coupled with historical fact leads to a negative evaluation of charismatic claims that miraculous gifts are a normal means for God's work today.

A second major area in evaluation of charismatic claims lies in the nature of the sign gifts. Not only must we study the evidence for thinking sign gifts have ceased, we must also determine whether the phenomena claimed by charismatics do or do not match the genuine gifts as defined by Scripture. Here the study must divide between tongues and healings. What was the nature of the Biblical gift of tongues? Do modern "tongues" equal Biblical tongues?

III. The Nature of Tongues

The Biblical gift of tongues was the miraculous ability to speak a foreign language that one had never learned. The Biblical gift of interpreting tongues was the ability to translate a language that one had never learned.

A. Tongues as Languages

1. Secular Greek

A detailed study of non-Christian Greek literature is beyond the scope of this study. However, it is important to give the conclusion of such research. The Greek word for

---

[36] By cessation of a gift the author does not rule out occasional examples of the miraculous. To say the sign gifts have ceased means God does not give a person the ability to perform signs as a continuous and normal part of life. It is one thing, for example, to believe He has granted people to be faith healers by giving them a gift. It is another to believe God can heal directly in response to prayer. After the apostolic age there may indeed have been occurrences of the miraculous, but these definitely did not occur with routine frequency as in the life of Jesus and the apostles.

[37] Chrysostom, *Homilies in First Corinthians*, Homily XXIX, in *The Nicene and Post-Nicene Fathers*, reprinted ed. (Grand Rapids: Wm. B. Eerdmans Publishing Co., 1979) Vol. 12, p. 168.

[38] Augustine, *The Epistle of St. John*, VI, 10, in *The Nicene and Post-Nicene Fathers*, reprint ed., (Grand Rapids: Wm. B. Eerdmans Publishing Co., 1979) Vol. 7, pp. 497-498.

tongue is *glossa* (from which we derive glossary). It means either the physical organ or language. There is no basis for concluding that the Greek word "tongues" ever meant ecstatic speech, gibberish, or babbling.

"It is apparent, as far as the evidence we have, that the ancient Greeks did not use glossa to mean unintelligible, ecstatic speech. This is not due to a lack of references to such utterance, since there are numerous references in Greek literature".[39]

Because secular Greek did not use "tongue" to refer to gibberish, there should be a prejudice against adopting such a definition when the word is used in the Bible. Unless there is strong evidence to the contrary, the New Testament word "tongue" should be understood as "language". Actually, this does not present any problem whatsoever. The New Testament itself clearly proves that "tongue" means "language."

2. Tongues in New Testament Greek

a. Tongues in the Book of Acts

Luke could hardly have made the point that tongues are languages any clearer. He uses the Greek word *dialectos* twice (from which we derive dialect). Also, he lists 16 ethnic groups who had traveled to Jerusalem for the Pentecost holiday. All of them understood the gospel in their own language!

Now there were Jews living in Jerusalem, devout men, from every nation under heaven. And when this sound occurred, the multitude came together, and were bewildered, because they were each one hearing them speak in his own **language**. And they were amazed and marveled, saying, "Why, are not all these who are speaking Galileans? And how is it that we each hear them in our own **language** to which we were born?

Parthians and Medes and Elamites, and Libyan residents of Mesopotamia, Judea and Cappadocia, Pontus and Asia, Phrygia and Pamphylia, Egypt and the districts of Libya around Cyrene, and visitors from Rome, both Jews and proselytes, Cretans and Arabs - we hear them in our **own tongues** speaking of the mighty deeds of God" [Acts 2:5-11].

Visitors from around the world understood God's message in their own languages by these "tongues" on Pentecost. They were amazed that Galileans had the miraculous ability to speak in their **languages**.

b. Tongues in the Book of Revelation

The word "tongue" can hardly mean anything other than languages in Revelation. It is often grouped in lists that classify people.

And they sang a new song, saying, "Worthy art Thou to take the book, and to break its seals; for Thou wast slain, and didst purchase for God with Thy blood men from every tribe and tongue [language] and people and nation" [Rev. 5:9].

After these things I looked, and behold, a great multitude, which no one could count, from every nation and all tribes and peoples and tongues, [languages] standing before the throne and before the Lamb, clothed in white robes, and palm branches were in their hands [Rev. 7:9].

And they said to me, "You must prophesy again concerning many peoples and nations and tongues [languages] and kings" [Rev. 10:11].

And those from the peoples and tribes and tongues [languages] and nations will look at their dead bodies for three and a half days, and will not permit their dead bodies to be laid in a tomb [Rev. 11:9].

---

[39] Thomas R. Edgar, *Miraculous Gifts*, (Neptune, New Jersey, Loizeaux Brothers, 1983), p. 114.

And it was given to him to make war with the saints and to overcome them; and authority over every tribe and people and tongue [language] and nation was given to him [Rev. 13:7].

And I saw another angel flying in midheaven, having an eternal gospel to preach to those who live on the earth, and to every nation and tribe and tongue [language] and people [Rev. 14:6].

And he said to me, "The waters which you saw where the harlot sits, are peoples and multitudes and nations and tongues [languages]" [Rev. 17:15].

Tongue means language in Acts. Tongue means language in Revelation. Furthermore, there are indications that tongue means language in 1 Corinthians.

c. Tongues in 1 Corinthians

1 Cor. 14:21 is a quote from Isa. 28:11. Paul teaches that the tongues of Isaiah's day illustrate a truth about the gift of tongues in New Testament times. The tongues to which Isaiah refers are the foreign languages of those who conquered Israel. Thus, if tongues means languages in 1 Cor. 14:21, why should it be given a different meaning in 1 Cor. 14:22? Furthermore, if tongues means languages in 1 Cor. 14:22, it should be understood as languages throughout the entire context.

Another point that shows that the tongues in 1 Corinthians are languages concerns use of the Greek word *idiotes* in 1 Cor. 14:16 and 23. English derives the word "idiot" from the original. A good translation is "unlearned" (see KJV). The only reason one might not be able to understand tongues was that he or she was "unlearned" in the study of that tongue. This supports the concept that the gift of tongues was the miraculous ability

to speak a foreign language that one had not learned. [40]

When the King James Bible was translated in the 1600's the word "tongue" meant language. This is clear from the way it translated Rev. 9:11, "And they had a king over them, who is the angel of the bottomless pit, whose name in the Hebrew tongue is Abaddon, but in the Greek tongue hath his name 'Apollyon' ". "Hebrew tongue" and "Greek tongue" equal "Hebrew language" and "Greek language." Clarity would be served if modern translators would actually use the word "language" and drop the archaic use of "tongue" (meaning language).

It is ironic that liberals were the first to interpret tongues as gibberish. Denying the supernatural, they could not accept the view that the gift of tongues involved real languages. Charismatics, most of whom are conservative in their attitude toward Scripture, usually adopt this unbiblical definition for tongue as opposed to viewing the gift as languages. The Biblical gift of tongues was ability in languages. The claims of charismatics do not match the gift of tongues as Biblically defined.

B. Modern Claims to Tongues

The ability to speak gibberish in a state of frenzy ought not to be regarded as the genuine miraculous gift of tongues. The experience which charismatics wish to have accepted as a gift from the Holy Spirit parallels more closely false religions than genuine Biblical tongues (languages).

1. Studies on Modern "Tongues"

When the charismatic movement was making great gains in the mid-twentieth century, several studies were done by linguists to determine the nature of modern tongues-speaking. The conclusions were that modern

[40] A missionary such as Paul would be greatly blessed by the ability to work in foreign languages without years of study (1 Cor. 14:18).

tongues speakers do not speak in languages (see also Christianity Today, Sept. 13 and Nov. 8, 1963).

"A scientific study of *glossolalia* concludes that utterances of people tested did not have the characteristics regarded as essential to human language, and in a tape experiment, tongues speakers were found to disagree on the meaning of what the others said... The study showed that the tendency of tongues speakers is 'to be more submissive, suggestible, and dependent in the presence of authority figures. It is generally not the speaking in tongues that brings the great feelings, of euphoria (buoyancy) that these people experience; rather, it is the submission to the authority of the leader.' The research project was initiated at the Lutheran Medical Center in Brooklyn, New York. The findings were based largely upon tests and interviews conducted with twenty-six people who spoke in tongues and thirteen who did not. Linguist William Samarin stated that where certain prominent tongues-speakers had visited, whole groups of glossolalists would speak in his style of speech... The report listed features that linguistic experts say characterize human language and argued that recordings of people speaking in tongues did not display enough of these features to warrant the conclusion that the utterances were any kind of human language, known or unknown, living or dead." Christianity Today, June 4, 1971

"Although some of the theologians of the Pentecostal groups have recognized that the Biblical gift of tongues is the miraculous ability to speak in foreign languages, none have validated such experiences, and the overwhelming majority do not even claim to speak human languages." [41]

2. Parallels with Heathenism

Babbling in an ecstatic state would have served little to confirm the apostles. The ancient world was full of religious groups who gibbered in trance-like states. In fact, it still is! It is amazing that Christians would claim a phenomenon is from the Holy Spirit when unbelievers can do the same thing. Did the ancient pagan Greeks or more modern Mormons obtain their abilities to gibber by the power of the Holy Spirit? Here are some quotes concerning ecstatic speech among non-Christians:

"She attained her ecstatic state and speech in a haunted cave where drafts and winds made weird sounds and music. When she became united in spirit with the god Apollo, she began to speak in tongues, sometimes understood, sometimes incoherent." (Virgil, 1st century B.C. commenting of the priestess on the Isle of Delos). [42]

"In a trance, perhaps induced by narcotic herbs, she sat on a tripod and raved. Priests enriched themselves by translating her incoherent cries into rhymed prophecies." (National Geographic on the priestess at Delphi). [43]

Speaking of this same priestess at Delphi, Chrysostom, a 4th Century Christian, wrote: "... This same Pythoness then is said to be female, to sit at times upon the tripod of Apollos astride, and thus the evil spirit ascending from beneath and entering the lower part of her body, fills the woman with madness, and she with disheveled hair begins to play the bacchanal and to foam at the mouth,

---

[41] Edgar, *Miraculous Gifts* p. 283. Again, even if one could document occasions of supernatural ability to work in an unknown language, it ought to be clear this ability is not being bestowed as a gift (i.e., a normal pattern of a gifted person's

life). If such ability is given as a gift, then charismatic speakers should never need translators when ministering to those of a different language.
[42] Cited by John Miles, *The Subject of Tongues, an Introduction to Christian Doctrine: An Outline Course*, (Grand Rapids; Grand Rapids School of the Bible and Music, 1974), p. 2.
[43] *Greece and Rome: Builders of Our World*, National Geographic Society, 1968), p. 171.

and thus being in frenzy to utter the words of her madness." [44]

Incoherent speech is not limited to ancient religions. The early Mormons spoke in tongues. Joseph Smith commanded: "Arise upon your feet, speak or make some sound, continue to make sounds of some kind, and the Lord will make a language or tongue of it." [45]

Brigham Young also spoke in "tongues" (if by tongues we mean non-languages): "Shouting, jerks, and dancing were common in their services, and Brigham Young not only spoke in unknown tongues but interpreted his messages to his hearers." [46]

Many books document the presence of "tongues" (i.e. trance-like babbling) among non-Christians. Included are examples of pagan priests, shamans, and medicine men. Ecstatic babbling takes place in a broad range of false religions. There are documented reports of occurrences among ancient Phoenicians, Greeks, Moslems, Mormons, American Indian cults, Eskimo religions, Tibetan and Chinese religions, North Borneo cults, etc. [47] America produces examples of people who speak in "tongues" (i.e. gibberish) before they are believers in Christ.

"Now before you sit down and write me a letter telling me how real your experience with tongues is, let me tell you about mine. I've spoken in tongues on several occasions. I've walked down aisles, I've prayed through at the altar, I've followed the instructions of the spiritual leaders who were telling me how to speak in tongues, and I

spoke in tongues. It was very real. It happened. There was nothing unreal about it. But it was not of the Holy Spirit! How do I know? I wasn't even saved at the time. That's how I know. I became convinced by the preaching I heard that I must speak in tongues to be right with God. I was determined to do it, and I did it." [48]

The author's wife knows personal friends who spoke in "tongues" at charismatic services before they trusted in Christ. All of these examples show that speaking in gibberish need not be a sign of gifts from the Holy Spirit. Whereas the Biblical gift of tongues was the ability to speak a language that had never been learned, modern practices of charismatics are more akin to false religions than Biblical Christianity relative to the nature of tongues. This statement does not mean charismatic Christians are unsaved. Assuming faith in Christ, they are very definitely brethren. However, non-charismatics should not be faulted for being unimpressed and unconvinced by charismatic gibberish. Such is not the Biblical gift of tongues as correctly defined. If gibberish is a gift of the Holy Spirit, then must we also assume that many heathen have the Holy Spirit also?

3. The Bible on Heathen Gibberish

There seems to be at least at least one reference to heathen gibberish in the Bible. It is not viewed favorably. As we shall see, Paul would not even permit the use of untranslated **languages** in the church and probably not even in prayer. Certainly, he would not have allowed gibberish.

> "And when you pray, **do not keep on babbling** like pagans, for they think they will be heard because of their many words..." [Matt. 6:7 (NIV)].

What is the outcome then? I shall pray with the spirit and I shall pray **with the mind** also; I shall sing with

---

[44] Miles, *Introduction to Christian Doctrine*, p. 2.
[45] Joseph Dillow, *Speaking in Tongues* (Grand Rapids: Zondervan Publishing House, 1975), p. 173.
[46] Edgar, *Miraculous Gifts*, p. 255.
[47] See Dillow, *Speaking in Tongues*, p. 171ff.; Edgar, *Miraculous Gifts*, p. 252ff.; and Donald W. Burdick, *Tongues: To Speak or Not to Speak*, (Chicago: Moody Press, 1969), p. 65ff.

[48] Miles, *Introduction to Christian Doctrine*, p. 3.

the spirit and I shall sing **with the mind** also [1 Cor. 14:15].

4. Conclusion

There are Biblical grounds for thinking that sign-gifts have ceased. Yet, beyond this conclusion there must also be an evaluation as to whether the experiences of modern charismatics represent *bona fide* New Testament gifts. Relative to tongues they do not. The Biblical gift of tongues was an ability to speak a foreign language that had not been studied. Modern charismatics do not have the genuine gift of tongues. This fact is made obvious by their need to preach through interpreters when conducting services in foreign lands.

IV. Biblical Regulations Concerning the Practice of Tongues

There is a Biblical foundation for believing that the sign gifts, including tongues, have ceased. Furthermore, incoherent speech is not the genuine New Testament gift of tongues. Even if we assume that the sign gifts are for today and that modern charismatics possess the genuine gift of tongues, we still would have to evaluate whether their practice conforms to Biblical regulations for such gifts. In all fairness it should be realized that some more biblically-oriented charismatics do try to follow these standards. However, many do not; and none adhere consistently to all of them.

A. Tongues Should Have a Low Priority in the Assembly

In the listings of gifts in 1 Cor. 12:28 and 30, tongues, or the interpretation of tongues, is placed last. Such an order is more than mere literary style. Paul, especially in 1 Cor. 12:28, is listing gifts in order of their importance. Therefore, even if tongues were being given as gifts today; they should not be given greatest prominence in the assembly. Often charismatic zeal causes such a focus on experiences that the more weighty matters of the faith must be relegated to a lesser and unscriptural priority.

And God has appointed in the church, first apostles, second prophets, third teachers, then miracles, then gifts of healings, helps, administrations, various kinds of tongues. All are not apostles, are they? All are not prophets, are they? All are not teachers, are they? All are not workers of miracles, are they? All do not have the gifts of healings, do they? All do not speak with tongues, do they? All do not interpret, do they? [1 Cor. 12:28-30].

B. Edification by Teaching Should Have Highest Priority in the Assembly

One cannot read 1 Corinthians Chapters 12-14 without being impressed by the priority of teaching in the assembly. This should not be too surprising, as the need for instruction is taught elsewhere (Eph. 4:11ff.; 1 Tim. 4:13; 2 Tim. 2:2; 3:16-17; 4:2). Although there are no prophets today, the church may still stress prophecy by teaching the prophetic writings of Scripture. Untranslated languages were not allowed in the early church (and surely not gibberish) because its stress was on edification. Many charismatic churches are negligent in the area of Bible teaching. They exalt experiences and diminish the value of serious Bible study.

Even if their "gift of tongues" were valid, this would not be an excuse to develop a church philosophy that stresses sign gifts and minimizes Bible study and exposition.

But one who prophesies speaks to men for edification and consolation. One who speaks in a tongue edifies himself; but one who prophesies edifies the church....So also you, since you are zealous of spiritual gifts, seek to abound for the edification of the church....however, in the church **I desire to speak five words with my** mind, that I may instruct others also, rather than ten thousand words in a tongue [1 Cor. 14:3-4, 12,19].

C. Not All Will Have the Gift of Tongues

Many charismatics claim that tongues-speaking is the necessary or inevitable sign that a person has been baptized or indwelt by the Holy Spirit. Also, many charismatics encourage others to seek the gift of tongues and view those without such experiences as second-class Christians. However, the Bible is clear on the point that all believers have been baptized and indwelt by the Holy Spirit (see pp. 241-48). It is also clear on the point that God never intended all Christians to have the gift of tongues. Paul's rhetorical questions demand a negative answer.

All do not have gifts of healings, do they? All do not speak with tongues, do they? All do not interpret, do they [1 Cor. 12:30].

D. The Idea That Christians Should Seek Other Gifts, Including the Gift of Tongues, is Weak.

One of the main points of 1 Corinthians 12 is that God bestows gifts sovereignly as He deems best (1 Cor. 12:7,11,18,24,28). This means it is not His will for all to have the same gift, including tongues. Another main point is that believers should be content with the gift they have. There should be no self-pity about the absence of a gift nor jealousy toward others who have a different gift (1 Cor. 12:15ff.). It is difficult to reconcile the idea of "coveting" another gift with these two emphases. God distributes gifts as it pleases Him. We are to be content with what He does.

Verses that seem to suggest the propriety of seeking other gifts can be interpreted differently. 1 Cor. 12:31 says, "But earnestly desire the greater gifts." The Greek word for "earnestly desire" is *zeelao,* and it could be better translated "zeal." "Be zealous for the

greater gifts." Also, the verb form is plural. Thus, Paul is telling the church **as a whole** to be zealous of greater gifts. The church should be emphasizing the greater gifts, such as prophecy and teaching, in its corporate ministry and worship. 1 Cor. 12:31 need not be understood as giving warrant for individuals to be discontent with the gift that God has bestowed and seek or covet another. Given the context, which stresses God's sovereign bestowal of gifts and our responsibility to be content with our position in the body of Christ, it is far better to take the command of 1 Cor. 12:31 as a corporate command for the whole church, not just for the individual. Thus, the case for one to seek another gift is weak. [49]

If one should persist in the notion of seeking individual gifts, let him take note that such an interpretation of 1 Cor. 12:31 would still not be an endorsement to seek inferior gifts like tongues. The best modern application that could be made from taking 1 Cor. 12:31 as an individual command would be to seek the gift of teaching.

E. The Case For a Devotional Use of Tongues is Weak

Many charismatics advocate "tongues" as a prayer language or feel their "gift" is for private use. Yet, it would be hard to establish such claims as valid from the Bible. It has already been pointed out that Matt. 6:7 forbids gibberish in prayer. Also, 1 Cor. 14:15 discourages the practice of praying in

---

[49] Some take 1 Cor. 12:31 as a statement, not a command. This is possible grammatically and also eliminates the idea of individuals seeking gifts. However, the Corinthians were in fact **not** seeking the greater gifts such as prophecy and teaching. Also, the parallel phrase in 1 Cor. 14:1 almost has to be taken as a command. Since 1 Corinthians 13 is parenthetical, this means 1 Cor. 12:31 and 14:1 are parallel texts. Therefore, since 14:1 is a command, 12:31 should also be understood as a command (imperative, not indicative). The key is seeing Paul's command as addressed to the whole church (plural), not to individuals.

words that are not understood by the mind. Since this holds true for legitimate foreign languages that are not understood, can there be any doubt that Paul would have forbidden incoherent speech in prayer?

Although personal benefit may be one of the results of a gift, the purpose for all gifts is to benefit others (1 Cor. 12:7). It is unlikely that any gift was ever given to be used for private benefit. Also, the gifts are to be exercised in love (1 Corinthians 13). This also indicates that gifts are for the benefit of others, not private use. In 1 Cor. 14:22 tongues are specifically said to be for unbelievers. It would be hard for this gift to benefit unbelievers if it were given for private/devotional use. All of these factors militate against the idea of God giving anyone tongues for private use.

Finally, verses which charismatics use to support private "prayer languages" are better interpreted in another way. 1 Cor. 14:1 teaches that tongues are inferior to prophecy. Verse 2 begins with "for", meaning "because". Thus, v. 2 is not endorsing the private use of tongues. It is making a negative statement in support of the thesis in verse 1 that tongues are inferior. We might summarize the teachings of 1 Cor. 14:1-2 this way: "Tongues are inferior to prophecy because only God can understand the one who speaks in an untranslated language." 1 Cor. 14:2 does not support the private use of tongues. It is giving a criticism of the use of untranslated tongues. Only God knows what such languages mean!

Likewise, Paul's statement in 1 Cor. 14:4 is not an endorsement of the private use of tongues. It is a criticism of using untranslated languages. The first part of the verse says, "The one who speaks in a tongue edifies himself." Self-edification or self-enhancement in this context is not commendable. It is worthy of criticism. The next line teaches that prophecy is superior because it edifies the whole church. (See Greek

in 1 Cor. 8:10 for a negative aspect to the word "edify."). There is in reality no endorsement for devotional tongues in 1 Cor. 14:4.

1 Cor. 14:28 can also be made compatible with the view that tongues were never given for personal use. It commands a tongues speaker to be silent in the church if there is no interpreter. The last part of the verse says, "and let him speak to himself and to God." Perhaps this simply means that the tongues-speaker should not speak in tongues publicly without an interpreter but should spend the service time in quiet meditation and prayer in his own native language. The verse need not be taken as any endorsement for the use of tongues in prayer.

In summary, the Bible does not clearly endorse the devotional use of tongues. All believers are priests and have equal access to God without any need for special prayer gifts (Eph. 2:18; 1 Pet. 2:9; Rev. 1:6; 5:10). If a language was not understood, it was not recommended for prayer (1 Cor. 14:15). Incoherent speech that was not at all part of a genuine language (i.e., not genuine tongues) is not permitted in prayer (Matt. 6:7).

F. Tongues are Supposed to Be a Sign for Unbelievers

1 Cor. 14:22 teaches that tongues are a sign for unbelievers. In the modern charismatic movement tongues are used almost exclusively in the church and are used very little in outreach to the lost.

G. Tongues Speakers Should Be in Full Control of Their Facilities

1 Cor. 14:32 teaches, "and the spirits of the prophets are subject to the prophets." This means that the exercise of the New Testament gift of prophecy did not involve any trance-like ecstatic state where the person was out of control. By application one would assume that the same conditions held true while the gift of tongues was being exer-

cised. Yet, many charismatics endorse the idea of a trance-like hypnotic state as being spiritual.

H. Only Intelligible Speech May Be Allowed in the Church

This standard is violated by many charismatic groups. Untranslated languages were simply not allowed in the early church (1 Cor. 14:7-12,28). It was reasonable for outsiders to consider the use of untranslated foreign languages to be deranged (1 Cor. 14:23). Emphasis upon use of languages not understood displays an immature childish understanding (1 Cor. 14:20).

Even during the period when the legitimate gift of tongues was being given, languages that were not understood were excluded from the church. It ought not be difficult to reason that babbling, which does not belong to any real language group, would likewise be barred from church.

I. There Could Be no More Than Two or Three Tongues Speakers in a Service, and They Could Only Speak One at a Time (1 Cor. 14:27).

These guidelines ought to be easy enough to follow. However, some charismatic services fail to do so.

J. Services Must Be Orderly and Without Confusion (1 Cor. 14:33, 40).

Some charismatic groups do not follow this basic principle for the operation of a church.

K. Summary of Biblical Regulations of Tongues

The charismatic movement spans a wide diversity of people from those with radical practices to those who are very mild in charismatic practices. However, even when we assume sign gifts have not ceased and we assume charismatics have genuine gifts, many are still deficient in compliance with Biblical standards concerning the regulation of tongues.

All types fail to follow the principle that languages that are not understood may not be used in church (1 Cor. 14:28). If this were true for legitimate foreign languages, it would certainly have been true for ecstatic gibberish. Incoherent speech, babbling, or gibberish would not have been allowed in the early church.

The charismatic movement in its violation of some or many of the regulations for tongues is indicative of an overall attitude that diminishes the Bible's authority and exalts experience and flashy leaders in its place. If one cannot trust charismatic judgment on basic teachings such as baptism in the Spirit, indwelling by the Spirit, or regulation of tongues speaking, why should there be any confidence that they understand the Bible on detailed doctrines such as the cessation of sign gifts? If the written Word is so little understood or regarded, how can there be any credibility in charismatic interpretations of experiences?

There are Biblical reasons for believing that the sign gift of tongues ceased with the apostles. Furthermore, the gibberish of contemporary charismatics is not the same as the legitimate gift of tongues. Finally, even if it were the *bona-fide* gift of tongues, charismatics often do not obey Biblical regulations of the gift. The charismatic movement should be evaluated negatively from all three of these angles. It also fails in the area of its beliefs and practices on healing.

V. The Bible on Miraculous Healing

> Is anyone among you sick? Let him call for the elders of the church, and let them pray over him, anointing him with oil in the name of the Lord; and the prayer offered in faith will restore the one who is sick, and the Lord will raise him up, and if he has committed sins, they will be forgiven him [James 5:14-15].

A. Healings vs. Healers

James 5:14-15 teaches that prayer is a means of bringing health to the sick. Given the Biblical examples of godly people who were sick, it is best to understand James to be giving a general principle and not an inevitable promise. In other words, prayer often, customarily, and usually, is an asset in regaining health. It is not unusual for God to grant requests about health, but He is not obligated to cause complete health for all believers at all times. Furthermore, the passage does not specify whether the healing will be instantaneous or gradual. How and when healing occurs is up to God. Virtually all Bible-believing churches believe that prayer is a factor in healing. There is, however, a difference between believing that prayer can heal and believing that there is such a thing as faith healers.

It is interesting that James does not tell believers in the early church to seek out a faith healer when they are ill. They are told rather to call for the elders of the church to pray. This fact in itself is an indication of the rarity of those with gifts of healing. Also, it probably shows that the sign gifts were more for use with those outside the church. The typical response of every believer to sickness was to ask others to pray. Non-charismatic churches adhere to this practice. While they do believe God can and does heal, they do not agree with the theology that God still has faith healers in the world today.

B. Sign Gifts and Healings

The whole argument for believing that sign gifts ceased with the end of the apostles need not be repeated here (See pp. 271-76). All that need be done is to show that healing is a sign gift. This is not difficult to establish. Many texts in Acts that refer to signs have miracles of healing in the context.

> [W]hile Thou dost extend Thy hand to **heal**, and **signs** and wonders take place through the name of Thy holy servant Jesus [Acts 4:30].

> And at the hands of the apostles many **signs** and wonders were taking place among the people; and they were all with one accord in Solomon's portico....to such an extent that they even carried the **sick** out into the streets, and laid them on cots and pallets, so that when Peter came by, at least his shadow might fall on any one of them. And also the people from the cities in the vicinity of Jerusalem were coming together, bringing people who were sick or afflicted with unclean spirits; and they were all being **healed** [Acts 5:12, 15-16].

Healing is certainly a "sign" gift. Since signs were to confirm the apostles, one would expect that the gift of healing would cease with the apostles. This need not exclude God from healing by prayer, and it need not exclude the occurrence of miracles. However, it does mean that there are no faith healers or miracle workers. We should make a distinction between healings and healers, between miracles and miracle workers. One is possible. The other is not.

C. Charismatic Claims vs. Healing and Biblical Teachings on Health

1. Frequency of miracles

It should be noted that it is common for charismatics to claim a greater frequency of miracles than even occurred in Biblical history including the earthly ministry of Christ and the apostles.[50] There have been three periods of intensive miracle workings on earth: the times of Moses and Joshua, the times of Elijah and Elisha, and the times of Christ and the apostles. At other times, even within Bible days, miracles were very rare.

---

[50] John 14:12 may not mean the apostles would do greater miracles than Jesus in terms of physical healings. It may mean they would experience greater results in terms of conversions than did the Lord Jesus in His earthly ministry.

The Lord did not heal everyone, and His ministry was not wide in geographical extent. In the New Testament times there still were very many sick people around the world who were never miraculously healed. Miracles have always been limited in time periods and geographical extent.

> "But I say to you in truth, there were many widows in Israel in the days of Elijah, when the sky was shut up for three years and six months, when a great famine came over all the land; and yet Elijah was sent to none of them, but only to Zarephath, in the land of Sidon, to a woman who was a widow. And there were many lepers in Israel in the time of Elisha the prophet and none of them was cleansed, but only Naaman the Syrian". And all in the synagogue were filled with rage as they heard these things [Luke 4:25-28].

> These twelve Jesus sent out after instructing them, saying, "Do not go in the way of the Gentiles, and do not enter any city of the Samaritans; but rather go to the lost sheep of the house of Israel" [Matt. 10:5, 6].

Modern faith healers make claims that extend even beyond Biblical examples of miracles in terms of frequency of miracles, duration of miracles, and location of miracles. The normal pattern during the years of Bible history was that miracles were infrequent and occasional. They have never been common, long lasting in duration, or wide in locality.

2. Biblical Patterns of Sickness

Often faith healers claim that it is God's will for every believer to be well all of the time. For them physical infirmity is an indication of spiritual problems as well. This idea cannot be supported from Biblical examples. The Apostle Paul was sick even though he was very dedicated to God's will in his life.

And because of the surpassing greatness of the revelations, for this reason, to keep me from exalting myself, there was given to me **a thorn in the flesh**, a messenger of Satan to buffet me – to keep me from exalting myself! Concerning this I entreated the Lord three times that it might depart from me. And He has said to me, "My grace is sufficient for you, for power is perfected in weakness" [2 Cor. 12:7-9a].

Other devout Christians in the early church faced physical ailments. It simply is not true that faithful Christians are always healthy.

> No longer drink water exclusively, but use a little wine for the sake of your stomach and your **frequent ailments** [1 Tim. 5:23].

> But I thought it necessary to send to you Epaphroditus, my brother and fellow worker and fellow soldier, who is also your messenger and minister to my need; because he was longing for you all and was distressed because you had heard that he was **sick**. For indeed he was **sick to the point of death**… [Phil. 2:25-27].

> Erastus remained at Corinth, but Trophimus I left **sick** at Miletus [2 Tim. 4:20].

It ought to be evident that many spiritual believers have become sick and have died. Both Luther and Calvin, especially Calvin, were sickly. It is both theological and experiential nonsense to assert that God's will always involves health. Such false teaching ends up damaging Christianity's reputation. Those who become infirm but believe that God always desires perfect health can react in several negative ways. They might view themselves with self-hatred and self-recrimination despite the fact that the illness may not be a judgment from God for spiritual failure. This leads to feelings of false guilt, pressure, and worthlessness. There also might be doubts of God's love.

Sickness for one who believes in "health theology" might affect views of self. However, it might also warp one's view of God. God might appear to be cruel and morally vindictive for causing affliction when there has been no special wrongdoing in a person's life. On the other hand, God might appear to be weak if He is supposed to guarantee health but cannot seem to do so. Even worse would be the response that there is no God at all.

The false theology that God wants all believers healthy all of the time is appealing to many, but it is neither Biblical nor beneficial in the advancement of the faith. God can use sickness, and He does not eliminate it entirely from a believer's experience. The Bible gives many good reasons that God might allow suffering even in the life of a spiritual believer.

3. God's Plan for Permitting Suffering

The idea that God wants believers to be immune from suffering, including sickness, is false. Although personal sin can be a cause for sickness (see John 5:14; 1 Cor. 11:30), God permits suffering for a variety of reasons. In fact, Scripture teaches that Christians are predestined to undergo sufferings (Phil. 1:29; 1 Thess. 3:3; 2 Tim. 2:12; 3:12; 1 Pet. 4:12-13). Trials, whether from sickness or from other types of problems, are part of God's program for Christian growth. Those who tend to view all suffering as due to the devil or due to personal sin have an unbiblical theology of suffering. God does allow righteous people to suffer (Psa. 34:19).

Trials may make one more sympathetic to others and better able to minister to others with a similar problem (2 Cor. 1:3-4). Suffering helps build strength and endurance for the future rigors of life (James 1: 2-3). It also can produce examples of faithfulness for

other Christians (Job's example, see Job 13:15) or a witness for unbelievers (see John 11:4; 12:10-11). Hardships force us to become or remain dependent upon God whereas ease might cause us to forget God (2 Cor. 12:6-9; Deut. 6:10-12; 8:3). They also teach us to pray. There are many Biblical examples in which pressures created intense prayer (1 Sam. 23:1ff.; Isa. 37:1; Matt. 26:36-45; Acts 4:29; 12:5). The Scripture commonly refers to Christ's experience as one of suffering followed by glory (Luke 24:26; Phil. 2:8-10; 1 Pet. 1:11).

Here is an intended pattern in the Christian's life. God wants believers to endure some suffering so that they can become more like Christ. Eventually, He will bring believers into glory (1 Pet. 2:21; 4:13; 5:1,10). God's plan for believers involves suffering that He deems beneficial. A theological system that teaches it is never within God's will to permit suffering or that all suffering is a direct attack from the devil or that suffering indicates spiritual failure conflicts with Scriptural teachings on the purpose of trials.

4. Biblical Patterns for Healings

The practices and teachings of modern faith healers need to be compared with Biblical incidents of healings. This exercise shows that modern faith healers do not come close to having the genuine gift of healing as practiced by Bible characters.

a. Healing Those Without Faith

Biblical healings did not ultimately depend upon the faith of the sick person. It is very true that the Lord and the apostles often responded to the presence of faith or declined to heal those lacking faith. Yet, they, as genuine healers, possessed the ability to bless even in the absence of faith. Certainly, the demon-possessed did not have faith before their healing (Matt. 8:28-29; Mark 1:23-26). In several incidents Jesus healed people who did not even know Him. The paralyzed man at the pool of Bethesda did not know who had caused him to walk (John 5:13). The man born blind did not believe in Christ until after his sight was restored (John 9:25,35-36). Neither of these men had any faith before they were healed. Nine of ten lepers never returned to offer thanks to Christ for His blessing (Luke 17:11-19). Surely, their faith was either weak or non-existent. The lame man at the temple gate neither asked for healing nor expected healing. He asked for money, and Peter gave him health (Acts 3:2-8).

Those with the genuine gift of healing **ought to be able to heal those without any faith.** This contrasts with modern faith healers who assert any failures in healing are due to a lack of faith on the part of the infirm. The inability to heal regardless of the sick person's faith shows that such do not really possess the genuine gift of healing.

b. Success Rate of Biblical Healings

It is true that sometimes Christ and the apostles declined to heal certain parties. However, whenever they decide to heal they were always successful. [51] Deut. 18:21-22 instructed Israel to evaluate a prophet as a fraud if he failed in just one prediction. It is reasonable to make a similar standard for those who claim to have the genuine gift of healing. There should never be a case where they attempt to heal but fail, including the healing of those without faith.

---

[51] This statement holds true for the Lord Jesus at all times and for the apostles after the Holy Spirit had come upon them to give them the gift of healing. Prior to Pentecost, before the apostles enjoyed either the indwelling of the Spirit or His bestowal of gifts, the apostles did fail to heal on one occasion (Matt. 17:16; Mark 9:17; Luke 9:40). However, this is not an example of one gifted with healing experiencing a failure to heal. It is rather an example of ineffective prayer on the part of those who still lacked the gift of healing. Later after Pentecost the apostles would be gifted to heal.

c. Distance as no Hindrance to Healing On Several Occasions

On several occasions Christ healed people who were not physically present (Matt. 8:5-13; John 4:49-53). Those with the genuine ability to heal should be able to stand in their church buildings and heal the sick in a distant hospital. There should not be any need to have special meetings at which the sick are brought to the healer. He should be able to just speak a healing word with resulting health coming upon even those not actually present. It ought to be apparent that modern claims to having the gift of healing cannot be fairly placed in the same category as genuine Biblical healing.

d. Spontaneous, Unexpected, and Public Healings

Healings in the New Testament were not restricted to private and specially called meetings. There were no "healing services" to which only the believers and expectant were invited. Biblical healings occurred at unexpected times and were spontaneous and public. Christ raised the dead both from a funeral procession (Luke 7:11ff., see also Matt. 9:23-25) and from a cemetery (John 11:43-44). Paul raised Eutychus after a totally unexpected accident (Acts 20:7ff.). Furthermore, Biblical healings were so impressive that even the enemies of Christ could not deny their validity (John 11:47-48; Acts 2:22; 4:16; 5:13). When have modern faith healers emptied emergency rooms by unexpectedly healing all patients? Have they ever gone to a funeral or a cemetery to "heal" one who is acknowledged as dead by unbelievers? Are their healings so unexpected as to be convincing even to Christ's enemies? Modern healers pale in comparison to genuine Biblical examples of the gift of healing. In fact, they are exposed as lacking the genuine gift.

5. Complete Health as a Future Promise

The main purpose of the cross was to bring about spiritual healing. Peter quotes Isaiah 53 to show this (1 Pet. 2:24-25). Yet, there should be no problem in seeing that physical healing was also one aspect of the atonement. Penalties for sin involve both spiritual and physical suffering. It is only reasonable that Christ paid for sin in such a way as to release humanity from all of its curses, including sickness. The Hebrew words in Isa. 53:4 can include the idea of Christ dying for our sicknesses. The verse could be translated, "Surely, He has borne our sicknesses and carried our pains."

Charismatics and non-charismatics can agree that Christ's death on the cross has important implications for physical health. However, the issue is one of time. The cross is the solution to sickness, but when will complete healing occur?

There were partial foretastes of the health that will exist in the Millennium given during Christ's earthly ministry (Matt. 8:17, perhaps also Heb. 6:5). The King was present on earth, and there were samples of healing that He could bring during the Kingdom. However, the King was rejected, and His Kingdom postponed. Thus, these foreshadowings of healing do not teach anything about health conditions once the Kingdom has been postponed.

Although Christ's death has indeed laid the foundation for the eventual elimination of sickness, many Scriptures teach that the present time will not be one of universal health. Rom. 8:22-23 and 2 Cor. 5:2ff. have already been quoted to establish that at the present .1e people of God can expect a certain amount of bodily "groaning." Healing is in the atonement, but its full application awaits the future. The fact that the Bible promises a future wiping of tears and a future eradication of sickness and death in Rev. 21:4 is confirmation that sickness and death will not be eliminated until then. Just as the doom of Satan was guaranteed by the cross but has

not been executed, so too the basis for destroying sickness has been accomplished by the cross but has not yet been put into affect. The issue is not whether the cross has provided victory over sickness but when such victory happens. The promise for the complete removal of sin is future. Although spiritual healing occurs for those who trust in Christ, it ought to be apparent that many of the physical curses of sin are still in force (see Gen. 3:14ff.). Snakes still crawl. Thorns still grow. Man still must work to survive. Childbirth is still painful. People still die. The curse will be reduced (Isa. 11:6-9; 65:25) but not fully eliminated during the Millennium (Isa. 65:20). Even death will still occur. The complete cessation of all sickness awaits the Eternal State, i.e., heaven, (Rev. 21:4). Until then, sickness is going to be a common human problem despite the claims of faith healers.

6. Summary on Healing

Virtually all Bible teachers maintain that God heals in response to prayers, but healing by God and healing by faith healers are two different matters. Healing was a primary sign gift. Sign gifts to confirm the apostles would likely cease with the apostles. It is an historical fact that they did.

Charismatic theology fails to synthesize all of the Bible's teachings about sickness and suffering. Godly people do become sick, and God has good reasons for allowing hardships in the lives of His children. Furthermore, the claims and experiences of modern faith healers simply do not parallel the genuine New Testament gift of healing. While God may chose to heal in response to prayer, He is not raising up healers in our time. The complete removal of sickness will not transpire until the Eternal State, heaven.

VI. Conclusions on the Charismatic Movement

Christianity by definition believes in the supernatural. God still can and does perform miracles. However, this is not the same as maintaining that God's work normally involves miracles. While there are isolated and rare occurrences of genuine miracles, they are not God's usual means of operation. This study leads to the conclusion that while periodic miracles may still occur, God no longer gives miraculous gifts (occurrences of miracles, yes; gifts of miracles, no).

Such a negative evaluation of the charismatic movement raises a number of questions. If the movement is not from the Holy Spirit, what it its origin? Why is charismatic Christianity so popular? How should non-charismatic Christians relate to their charismatic brethren?

The charismatic movement is large and an attraction to many, but size and popularity does not establish truth. The Bible alone determines truth. Much of the appeal in charismatic theology is emotion. It "feels" good to many. They just simply enjoy the "excitement." Others are attracted by the promise of instant spiritual or material success. They are not content with the more gradual sanctification process that the Bible teaches. In addition, the claim to instant spiritual maturity and to spiritual power feels good to those who want authority over others or who want excuses to defy legitimate authority. The charismatic system also attracts the insecure and those who have difficulty coping with the pressures of life. Rather than trusting in God for grace to endure hardships, they create a god after their own liking who is obligated to perform miracles to make life easier. A system that promises miraculous relief from trials is appealing.

Another factor that explains involvement of individuals in the charismatic movement is shallowness of faith or what might also be called misdirection of faith. One's faith or satisfaction in God should not need to be bolstered by continuous experiences or miraculous signs that "prove" the supernatural

to the skeptical. Christian faith should be directed to the Person of Christ and the Bible (John 4:48; Luke 16:31; Rom. 10:17; 2 Cor. 5:7). Faith should not depend upon signs and wonders to remain strong. Many charismatics seem to have a wrong object of faith. They believe because of their experiences, not because of the credibility of the Scriptures and of Christ.

Satan is probably another factor that explains the popularity of some types of charismatic groups. A close relationship exists between radical charismatics and some occult practices. The practice of diminishing Biblical authority and focusing attention upon listening to the "spirit" is similar enough that it ought to be frightening to believers.

There is a broad spectrum of beliefs and practices under the charismatic "umbrella." It would not be consistent with Christian charity and brotherhood to insist that all types of fellowship with all types of charismatics would be improper. Differences between charismatics and non-charismatics are great enough that permanent association in joint ministries would be difficult (for example, adding charismatic missionaries to a non-charismatic church's mission program or trying to mix both systems on a church staff). However, this does not mean charismatic believers need be completely shunned or treated as unbelievers. Personal friendship and mutual recognition of the brotherhood in Christ should be extended to all who genuinely believe.

VII. Legitimate Spiritual Gifts

After a critique of charismatic excesses, it is important to study the topic of spiritual gifts from a more positive angle. How does the Holy Spirit function today relative to spiritual gifts?

A. Recipients of Spiritual Gifts

The Bible is very clear that every believer has a spiritual gift(s).

But to **each one** is given the manifestation of the Spirit for the common good [1 Cor. 12:7].

But to **each one** of us grace was given according to the measure of Christ's gift [Eph. 4:7].

As **each one** has received a special gift, employ it in serving one another, as good stewards of the manifold grace of God [1 Pet. 4:10].

B. The Time of Obtaining a Spiritual Gift

If every believer has a spiritual gift, it stands to reason that all believers must obtain some sort of gift at the time of salvation. If all believers have gifts, then one who has been saved only a few seconds has already been given a gift. This does not rule out the idea that a gift may be originally bestowed in a germ form with a need to be gradually developed to its potential. Also, even though some form of gift must be granted at the time of salvation, it is probably true that additional gifts may be given at a later time. Paul seems to have bestowed gifts upon Timothy (see Rom. 1:11; 1 Tim. 4:14; 2 Tim. 1:6)

C. Relationship Between Spiritual Gifts and Natural Ability

It is clear that unbelievers do not have either the Holy Spirit or gifts from the Holy Spirit. Since unbelievers do have natural abilities in teaching, or administration, or music, a distinction must be made between strictly natural abilities and spiritual gifts. The natural abilities of the unsaved are not spiritual gifts. This much is certain. However, it is likely that sometimes the Holy Spirit transforms a purely natural ability by channeling it into God's work after conversion to Christ. In other cases, the Holy Spirit probably bestows brand new aptitudes, interests, and abilities.

D. The Purpose for Spiritual Gifts

God does not give spiritual gifts to believers for personal enjoyment, or competition, or spectacular display. They are not for rivalry or self-elevation. God, the Holy Spirit, gives gifts so that they may be used to bless and edify other believers.

Let no one seek his own good, but that of his neighbor [1 Cor. 10:24].

But to each one is given the manifestation of the Spirit **for the common good** [1 Cor. 12:7].

Gifts are supposed to be used in love (1 Cor. 13) with a view to edification (1 Cor. 14:4; 12,17; 1 Pet. 4:10). The goal in using a gift should be the glory of God and the benefit of other believers. The distinction between purpose and result needs to be remembered. Self-enrichment is not the purpose for spiritual gifts, but it can be a result. One of the mysteries of the Christian life is that those who lose self benefit self. If one uses a spiritual gift with the goal of self-enrichment, he will harm himself. If one uses that same gift with the goal of glorifying God and benefiting others, self will benefit as a result.

E. Identification of One's Gift

Romans 12 seems to be the only place in Scripture that gives directions relative to finding ones spiritual gift.

I urge you therefore, brethren, by the mercies of God, to present your bodies a living and holy sacrifice, acceptable to God, which is your spiritual service of worship. And do not be conformed to this world, but be transformed by the renewing of your mind, that you may prove what the will of God is, that which is good and acceptable and perfect. For through the grace given to me I say to every man among you not to think more highly of himself than he ought to think; but to think so as to have sound judgment, as God has allotted to each a measure of faith. For just as we have many members in one body and all the members do not have the same function, so we, who are many, are one body in Christ, and individually members one of another. And since we have gifts that differ according to the grace given to us, let each exercise them accordingly: if prophecy, according to the proportion of his faith; if service, in his serving; or he who teaches, in his teaching; or he who exhorts, in his exhortation; he who gives, with liberality; he who leads, with diligence; he who shows mercy, with cheerfulness [Rom. 12:1-8].

In this passage Paul first discusses Christian living in general (vv. 1-2a). Then he refers to knowing God's will. Finally, in vv. 3-8 he covers spiritual gifts. A step by step process of identifying one's gift(s) might be as follows:

1. Become Dedicated and Undergo Mind Renewal (Rom. 12:1-2a)

With contemporary emphasis upon spiritual gifts it is easy to confuse priorities and approach spiritual gifts with a cart-before-the-horse attitude. It is not true that the Christian who is unsure of his or her spiritual gift(s) should remain inactive in the Lord's work. It is not the case that until a believer can pinpoint his spiritual gifts he should not serve. While the doctrine of spiritual gifts is important, the doctrine of servanthood is even more basic. One who does not know his or her spiritual gift should still present himself as a "living sacrifice" and allow himself to be transformed by the Holy Spirit's teaching in the Word of God (see previous section on mind renewal, p. 250). He should obey the commands, given to all believers generally, and should submit to the transforming Word of God. The true order is not first find a gift and then serve, but rather first serve in order to know God's "good and acceptable and perfect will" (v. 2b), including the specific knowledge of spiritual gifts (v. 3ff.). Knowledge of specific interests

arises out of a living context of servanthood. Specific direction in the Lord's work arises from general involvement in that work. First things should be placed first in Christian living. The best advice that could be given to those who are uncertain as to their gift(s) is to get busy serving and growing in the areas that are known to be God's will for all Christians in general, i.e., obey Rom. 12:1-2a first. Knowledge of God's will concerning spiritual gifts will follow.

2. Think Soberly and Objectively With a View to Determining the Measure of Faith (confidence) Concerning Various Gifts

The first step in determining one's gift is to become dedicated as a living sacrifice and to become committed to undergo mind renewal by the Holy Spirit through the Scriptures. Next Paul tells us to think soberly about self, i.e., assess self objectively. The type of self-appraisal being commanded in Rom. 12:3 is one in which there is humility without any self-delusion whatsoever. The last part of Rom. 12:3 links the act of objective self-assessment with a view to determining the measure of faith (confidence) that God has given. Verses 4-8 directly connect to v. 3 as a subordinate section and show that the "measure of confidence" in v. 3 concerns spiritual gifts. Each believer who meets the condition of being dedicated and undergoing transformation should make an objective self-assessment with a view to determining his measure of confidence about various spiritual gifts. As a practical suggestion, one should begin this assessment by considering the spiritual gifts listed in the Scriptures (making certain, of course, that these gifts are properly defined and with the sign gifts omitted from consideration). The fact that every Biblical listing of spiritual gifts is different adds weight to the argument that the Bible does not intend to give an exhaustive list of all the spiritual gifts that the Holy Spirit might bestow. Therefore, an assessment of one's confidence for involvement in spiritual gifts should begin with the Biblical lists for gifts but should also expand to all the various aspects of Christian service. If a person follows the counsel of Rom. 12:1ff., he will eventually know God's perfect will, including the possession of a measure of confidence relative to spiritual gifts. When a person tries to follow Paul's advice in Romans 12, but still is unable to identify his/her gift(s), then the best course is to remain patient and faithful to the concepts of being a living sacrifice and undergoing mind renewal. First, serve in the areas that are known to be God's will for all believers. Then knowledge of His specific will concerning gifts will come at some future self-assessment in God's good timing. [52]

F. Miscellaneous Teachings About Gifts

1. Gifts Should Be Developed

Since all saved people have spiritual gifts, then a six-year-old Christian has a spiritual gift. Yet, it is obvious that a child's gift needs to be nurtured and developed. This truth does not just rest on observation of people but has Scriptural support in 2 Tim. 1:6.

> And for this reason I remind you to kindle afresh the gift of God which is in you through the laying on of my hands [2 Tim. 1:6].

---

[52] Sometimes one might have a large measure of confidence (faith) that God wants him or her to exercise a certain gift. With other gifts there might be great confidence that one should **not** participate in certain aspects of ministry (some should not sing or teach). There may be many areas of ministry in which there is no measure of confidence either way. While there is no special burden for involvement, there seems to be no prohibition either. These areas may not be a person's primary area of ministry in life, but being adaptable and humble as a good servant one should consider temporary involvement in them as the church needs help. Then when another with the gift arises, one should be willing to step aside.

Apparently, "giftedness" does not cancel out the need for hard work and discipline in developing and applying ministry skills.

2. Gifts Can Be Neglected

1 Tim. 4:14 implies that a spiritual gift can be neglected.

> Do not neglect the spiritual gift within you, which was bestowed upon you through prophetic utterance with the laying on of hands by the presbytery [1 Tim. 4:14].

A gift can be neglected by deliberate failure to obey God's commands to serve Him. It might be possible to inadvertently neglect a gift by failing to have vision in considering the full options for Christian ministry. Christians should avoid the mistake of thinking that Christian service occurs only within the walls of a church building and only on Sunday. We should not neglect gifts for service by confining service for the Lord only to a special place at special times. 1 Cor. 12:4-6 teaches that the Holy Spirit gives a variety of gifts. The same gift can be used in a variety of ministries. Teaching, for example, can be used in ministries to children, teens, elderly people, seminary, missionary work, and so forth. The same type of ministry has different effects, e.g., one church might be traditional and especially appeal to professional people, but another might be more contemporary and appeal to a different group. The same gift can be used in many various ways. Christians should be cautious about neglecting gifts due to a nearsighted view of what constitutes Christian service, as well as, through sin and laziness.

3. A Gift Can Be Abused

1 Cor. 1:7 shows that the most unspiritual person can have great gifts (i.e., the carnal Corinthians). Christians abuse their gifts when they use them for selfish and sinful pursuits and not for God's glory or the edification of others in the body of Christ.

4. Gifts are Irrevocable

Rom. 11:29 says, "The gifts and calling of God are irrevocable." In its context this line specifically teaches that God's promises to Israel will not be withdrawn. Yet, as a general principle it lends some support to the idea that God intends for a spiritual gift to be given and used for a lifetime. This does not exclude the truth that a man may disqualify himself from church leadership by failing to meet the standards of 1 Timothy 3 and Titus 1. There is a difference between God arbitrarily withdrawing a gift and a person disqualifying himself by sin.

G. Definitions for the Gifts

An effort to find precise definitions of spiritual gifts is not just academic trivia. If Christians are to identify their own spiritual gifts, they must have accurate definitions for the gifts listed in Scripture. Furthermore, the gifts must be defined so that those that are sign gifts can be eliminated from consideration as options for gifts today. It is sad that the current emphasis upon gifts has not been accompanied by a carefulness to correctly define them.

There are four lists of spiritual gifts given in the New Testament: Rom. 12:6-8; Eph. 4:11; 1 Pet. 4:10-11; 1 Cor. 12:8-10, 28-30.

1. Romans 12:6-8

"And since we have gifts that differ according to the grace given to us, let each exercise them accordingly: if prophecy, according to the proportion of his faith; if service, in his serving; or he who teaches, in his teaching; or he who exhorts, in exhortation; he who gives, with liberality; he who leads, with diligence; he who shows mercy, with cheerfulness."

a. Prophecy

Many teach that the gift of prophecy refers to the "forthtelling" of God's message. This makes prophecy similar to any preaching or teaching. While prophets did speak God's message, this contemporary definition makes an error by failing to include all that was involved in prophecy.

A prophet in the Old Testament obtained a message by divine revelation and could predict the future. This is evident from many Old Testament passages, especially the book of Deuteronomy. In Deut. 18:18 a prophet is defined as one in whom God placed "My words." Deut. 18:22 shows that there was a predictive element to prophecy.

> "I will raise up a prophet from among their countrymen like you, and I will put **My words in his mouth**, and he shall speak to them all that I commanded him" [Deut. 18:18].

> "When a prophet speaks in the name of the LORD, **if the thing does not come about or come true**, that is the thing which the LORD has not spoken. The prophet has spoken it presumptuously; you shall not be afraid of him" [Deut. 18:22].

All of the authors of the New Testament except Luke were Jews whose thinking would naturally be heavily influenced by the Old Testament. We, therefore, must insist upon very strong evidence before modifying the Old Testament concept of a prophet. In fact, there is no evidence at all for thinking the New Testament authors had a different definition of prophecy than did the Old Testament writers. In Mark 14:65 members of the Sanhedrin slapped Christ and challenged Him to prophesy the identity of those who struck Him while He was blindfolded. Clearly, they are asking Christ to convey supernatural revelation as to the identity of the culprit. Zacharias gives a prophecy in Luke 1:67 about his son, John the Baptist. From the context it is obvious he gave a divinely revealed prediction about the future. The Book of Acts also shows how the early church viewed prophecy. David was deemed a prophet because he foretold of Messiah's resurrection (Acts 2:30-31). Agabus, a New

Testament prophet, foretold a famine (Acts 11:27-28) and that Paul would suffer in Jerusalem (Acts 21:10-11).

It ought to be plain from Old Testament references to prophecy that it involved more than giving a message as when a minister delivers a sermon. Prophets obtained direct divine revelation from God and often predicted the future. Eph. 3:5 shows that prophets obtained revelation. 1 Cor. 14:29-30 gives instructions for using the gift of prophecy in the early church. It says that when the next **prophet** received a **revelation**, it was time for the previous speaker, to sit down and remain quiet.

> And let two or three **prophets** speak, and let the others pass judgment. But if a **revelation** is made to another who is seated, let the first keep silent [1 Cor. 14:29-30]

> [W]hich in other generations was not made known to the sons of men, as it has now been **revealed** to His holy apostles and **prophets** in the Spirit [Eph. 3:5]

It is true enough that a prophet was a spokesman for God, but there is distinction between a prophet and a minister in the pulpit. A prophet obtained his message by direct divine revelation, not from the Scriptures. In fact, prophets wrote the Scriptures! When the written revelation was complete, there was no longer any need for the gift of prophecy. We study prophecy whenever we read the Bible; and thus, it is still possible to be zealous for prophecy as 1 Corinthians 14 commands. However, Eph. 2:20 links the gift of prophecy with the apostles and the founding period of the church. God does not bestow the gift of prophecy today.

> So then you are no longer strangers and aliens, but you are fellow citizens with the saints, and are of God's household, having been built upon the **foundation of the apostles and**

prophets, Christ Jesus Himself being the corner stone [Eph. 2:19-20].

b. Service (KJV, ministry)

The original word here is one from which "deacon" is derived. This is a broad term and refers to many aspects of service. A medical missionary, a church treasurer, a nursery worker, might all be considered to have gifts of service. All Christians should serve. God intends for some to specialize and emphasize works that can be classified as general services.

c. Teaching

Teaching is different from prophesying. Teachers do not obtain direct divine revelation. They instead explain truths that have already been placed into the Scriptures. There are many phases of God's work where the gift of teaching may be applied (children, women, youth, pulpit ministry, etc.) The gift of teaching should probably not be limited to just pastors. Although a pastor/elder has more responsibilities than teaching alone, he must be able to teach (1 Tim. 3:2; Titus 1:9). All elders must be able to teach, but some specialize in it (1 Tim. 5:17). Since the gifts of apostle and prophet are no longer being given today, the gift of teaching remains the most important of gifts (1 Cor. 12:28).

d. Exhortation (NIV, encouraging)

All believers should be an encouragement to each other and should bolster each other in life's pressures (Heb. 10:25). Some are especially gifted to sustain and to support others. They enjoy and are adept at giving motivation and inspiration to other believers. Exhortation might take place in a formal speech but exhortation can take place just as easily in informal conversations. It is logical to view musicians as having the ability to exhort by their music ministry.

e. Giving (NIV, contributing)

All Christians should give. The gift of giving means that some will be especially sacrificial and will be devoted to meeting the needs of other Christians. One need not be rich in money to display a sacrifice of love and concern. Above all else a giver is unselfish in his thought of and interest for other Christians. In the following context (Rom. 12:13) Paul mentions hospitality. Those with the gift of giving do not just throw money around. They use their resources to show hospitality and love to other believers.

f. Leading (KJV, ruling)

The gift of leading will be studied in conjunction with the gift of administration (1 Cor. 12:28, see pp. 298-99).

g. Mercy

All believers should display mercy. Again some will have special interests for involvement with the poor, the infirm, the weak, etc. They will want to devote major energies to helping those in pitiable conditions.

2. Eph. 4:11-12

"And He gave some as apostles, and some as prophets, and some as evangelists, and some as pastors and teachers, for the equipping of the saints for the work of service, to the building up of the body of Christ"

a. Apostleship

The gift of apostleship has already been covered in the material on the cessation of sign gifts (pp. 271-72). Apostles were witnesses to the post resurrection ministry of Christ (Acts 1:21-22; 1 Cor. 9:1). The word "apostle" means that these have been sent by Christ with a special commission. Paul was the last one to become an apostle (1 Cor. 15:8-9). Apostleship was for the founding period of the church (Eph. 2:20). If someone believes that he is an apostle, he has not assessed himself with sufficient humility as Rom. 12:3 commands.

b. Prophet

The gift of prophecy was studied above (pp. 294-95) under the Romans 12 list of spiritual gifts.

c. Evangelist

The Greek word *euangel is* composed of *eu* meaning good (as in euthanasia, "good" death) and the word from which "angel" is derived meaning "message". The evangelist gives "the good message" of the gospel. All Christians should be involved in evangelism, even those whose main gift lies in another area (2 Tim. 4:5). However, some will be especially interested in majoring in the work of proclaiming the gospel An evangelist need not be one who constantly travels to conduct "revivals." Missionaries are evangelists. Furthermore, one who does personal work without any public speaking can still be an evangelist.

d. Pastor/teacher

It is difficult to tell from the original language whether Paul intends two gifts, pastors and teachers, or just one gift, pastor/teacher. Many conclude that the Granville Sharp rule of Greek grammar mandates that there be one gift. Yet, this rule of Greek grammar does not apply to plurals. [53] Therefore, it is difficult to know whether Paul intends one gift or two.

Regardless of what this particular verse intends, the overall teaching of Scripture suggest that one can be a teacher without being a pastor. Nevertheless, to be a pastor one must be able to teach (1 Tim. 3:2, Titus 1:9). There seems to be two kinds of pastor/elders, those who rule and have some ability to teach and those who rule and specialize in teaching (see p. 295 and 1 Tim. 5:17). Often these are classified as "ruling elders" and "teaching elders." [54]

---

[53] Granville Sharp, *Remarks On the Uses of the Definitive Article in the Greek Text of the New Testament*, 3rd ed. (Philadelphia: B. B. Hopkins and Co., 1807), pp. 3-7.

[54] For a deeper study on elders see Chapter 11.

3. 1 Pet. 4:10-11

"As each one has received a special gift, employ it in serving one another, as good stewards of the manifold grace of God. Whoever speaks let him speak, as it were, the utterances of God; whoever serves, let him do so as by the strength which God supplies; so that in all things God may be glorified through Jesus Christ, to whom belongs the glory and dominion forever and ever. Amen."

This passage from 1 Peter 4 does little in the way of listing specific gifts. However, it does give two general categories of gifts. There are **speaking** gifts, and there are **serving** gifts. If the gifts were to be classified topically, the outline "sign gifts, speaking gifts, service gifts" would be a good way to group them.

4. 1 Cor. 12:8-10,28-30

"For to one is given the word of wisdom through the Spirit, and to another the word of knowledge according to the same Spirit; to another faith by the same Spirit, and to another gifts of healing by the one Spirit, and to another the effecting of miracles, and to another prophecy, and to another the distinguishing of spirits, to another various kinds of tongues, and to another the interpretation of tongues....And God has appointed in the church, first apostles, second prophets, third teachers, then miracles, then gifts of healings, helps, administrations, various kinds of tongues. All are not apostles, are they? All are not prophets, are they? All are not workers of miracles, are they? All do not have gifts of healings, do they? All do not speak with tongues, do they? All do not interpret, do they?"

a. Word of Wisdom

Any time a concept is used sparsely it becomes more difficult to define. The gift of wisdom as a spiritual gift is mentioned just once. In this case the definition that is selected affects whether wisdom should be

considered a gift for today or belongs to those sign gifts that have ceased.

Many charismatics define the word of wisdom as a special, direct, and immediate revelation from God. They might claim a revelation that detects one in the audience has a certain sickness as being a "word of wisdom." If this is the definition of word of wisdom, then it should be viewed as a sub-category of direct divine revelation and be viewed as something germane to the days of the apostles and prophets.

A better case can be made that the gift of wisdom simply involves the ability to find wisdom from the Scripture and to convey good counsel to others. In 1 Cor. 2:6-7 and in other places in 1 Corinthians, Paul uses "wisdom" as a reference to the possession of prudent and sound judgment. There is no reason to change his definition for wisdom when it appears in a list of gifts in 1 Corinthians 12. Also, the ability to obtain revelation is contained within the gift of prophecy. Word of wisdom would seem to be something else. Likely, a good Christian counselor possesses the gift of wisdom as may many older saints in any church. If this second definition for wisdom were adopted, then there would be no reason to think the gift of wisdom has ceased.

b. Word of Knowledge

Many of the above statements about the gift of wisdom also apply to the gift of knowledge. If one thinks it refers to some aspect of divine revelation, e.g., the direct voice of God, then the gift should be limited to the days of the apostles and prophets. However, knowledge in 1 Cor. 8:1ff. seems to refer to just brute intellect, and the gift of prophecy already includes the ability to obtain revelation. Perhaps "word of knowledge" refers to a special ability to understand complex Biblical truths and to help others do the same. If Bible scholars or theologians be viewed as having the gift of knowledge in a less mystical sense, then there would be no reason to limit the gift of knowledge to the days of direct divine revelation to the apostles and prophets.

c. Faith

All Christians by definition possess faith. Those with the gift of faith possess a deep trust in God in the midst of difficult surroundings. Missionaries in dangerous areas must have a special gift of faith to impel them to leave material comforts and face hardship for Christ's sake.

d. Healings/miracles

The gift of miracles is more extensive than the gift of healings, but both can be studied together. Earlier sections of this study gave support for believing that sign gifts ceased with the apostles. There is no difficulty in proving that gifts of healing and miracles must be classified as sign gifts (see Acts 5:12-15) Thus, there are no gifts of healing and miracles today. There may be periodic occurrences of healings and miracles that God performs independently of any humans with such gifts. There may be occurrences of healings and miracles, but there are no healers and miracle workers. These gifts are signs. Sign gifts ceased with the close of apostolic times (see Sections II-V, above, especially pp. 271-76 and 285-89).

e. Distinguishing of Spirits (KJV, discerning)

Here is another gift that presents difficulty as to its precise definition. If it were understood as the ability to detect the invisible presence of demons, then there would be some question to whether it is a sign gift or a service gift.

The distinguishing of spirits may just refer to a special ability of detecting moral or doctrinal error. 1 John 4:1 encourages all Christians to discern the spirits, but in the context this refers to the false teaching of the false prophets who are in reality the agents of the "spirits." Perhaps the gift of "discerning

spirits" simply means the ability to recognize falsehood (See also, Acts 17:11; 1 Thess. 5:21).

Heb. 5:14 teaches that those Christians who are skilled in the "Word of righteousness" (Heb. 5:13) develop abilities to discern good from evil. The church needs those who can ferret out error and evil. Perhaps those who are especially sensitive and quick to detect doctrinal/moral error have the gift of discerning spirits.

f. Languages/Interpretations of Languages

In apostolic times God gave the ability to speak foreign languages that one had never learned. He also gave the ability to interpret languages that one had never learned. The genuine gift of tongues involved real languages, not incoherent gibberish (see Acts 2:6,8 and Section III of this Chapter, pp. 276-78). Tongues are among the sign gifts according to 1 Cor. 14:22. Signs were to confirm the apostles (2 Cor. 12:12). The apostles have ceased and so have tongues. There is no longer any gift of languages or gift of interpretation of languages (pp. 271-76).

g. Helps (1 Cor. 12:28)

The Greek for "helps" is different from the Greek words for "service" in the Romans 12 list. A distinction is probably intended. Maybe those who "serve" do so to minister to others. "Helps" may be more specific. Those who "help" free others to exercise their gifts more effectively. A church secretary does not so much do service to meet the needs of church leaders as she does help them to perform their gifts more effectively. Every wife should help her husband's ministry for Christ.

h. Administration (KJV, government)

The Greek word for administration in 1 Cor. 12:28 is different from the Greek word for leading (ruling) in Rom. 12:8. Again this may indicate a distinction. One might be able to be an administrator without ruling. There is a difference between helping with organization and being one who has authority in decision-making. Those with the gift of ruling have final authority for church policy and programs, but they may delegate implementation of the actual work to one gifted with administration. The elders may lead, but, for example, they will want to find someone with the gift of administration to direct a given project.

VIII. Conclusion to Pneumatology:

It is unfortunate that there is so much confusion relative to the Holy Spirit. There is irony that so many self-centered and fleshly pursuits are attributed to the Holy Spirit. Nevertheless, the Holy Spirit is a precious companion and wants to effect growth for and bestow blessings upon believers. This can occur if there is a hunger for and submission to what the Holy Spirit teaches in His own Word, the Bible.

Chapter 11
ECCLESIOLOGY
Doctrine of the Church

a. Different Perspectives on Baptism
   (1) The Sacramental View
   (2) Baptismal Regeneration
   (3) The Reformed View
   (4) No Baptism
   (5) The Baptist View of Baptism
b. The Meaning of Water Baptism
   (1) Shows Believer Wishes Obedience to Christ's Command
   (2) Symbolizes Sharing In Christ's Death, Burial, Resurrection
   (3) Symbolizes Spirit Baptism
   (4) Public Identification with the Church
   (5) Summary
c. The Mode of Baptism
   (1) Ancient Secular Greek and the Words *Bapto/Baptizo*
   (2) The Septuagint and *Bapto/Baptizo*
   (3) *Bapto/Baptizo* in the New Testament
   (4) Symbolism as an Argument for Immersion
   (5) Prepositions As Evidence for Immersion
   (6) Church History and Baptism by Immersion
d. Conclusions of Water Baptism
E. Purity of the Church
   1. Ecclesiastical Separation
      a. Commands to Separate
         (1) Separation from False Doctrine
         (2) Separation from Divisive Persons
         (3) Separation from Immorality
         (4) General Disobedience to the Scripture
      b. Contemporary Theological Schools of Thought
         (1) Liberalism
         (2) Fundamentalism
         (3) Neo-evangelicalism
      c. The Specifics of Separation
         (1) Submissive vs. Believing Attitude toward the Bible
         (2) Circles of Fellowship
   2. Church Discipline
      a. Biblical Commands for Exercise of Discipline
      b. Biblical Reasons for Exercise of Discipline
      c. Offenses that Merit Discipline
      d. Administration of Church Discipline
         (1) The Persons in Authority
         (2) Points of Procedure
      e. Conclusions on Church Discipline
F. Church History - Denominations
G. Conclusions on the Study of the Church

ECCLESIOLOGY: THE DOCTRINE OF THE CHURCH

I. Introduction and Definition

The Greek word for church is *ekklesia* from which we derive *ecclesiastical*. It is a compound formed from the preposition *ek* meaning "out of" and *kaleo*, meaning "to call." The church is a group of people called out from the world unto God. It is an assembly of "called out" ones. James, in Acts 15:14, refers to God's work for this age as being that of "taking from among the gentiles a people for His name." God is calling out a people, the gentiles, for Himself. They are united with Jews to form a new group, the *church,* or church of God. (See Eph. 3:6, 10 and 1 Cor. 10:32 which give three categories of people, Jew, gentile, and church of God, and 1 Pet. 2:9 which refers to "a people for God's own possession.")

Bible students discover that the Bible uses the word *church* in two different senses. *Church* might refer to the universal church or a local church. The universal church is the entire group of believers in the Lord Jesus (between Pentecost and the Rapture to be precise). The universal church includes people who have died and are in heaven, as well as, believers who remain on earth. The Bible likens it not to an organization but to an organism, "Christ's body." Several passages refer to this universal church. (See 1 Cor. 12:28; 15:9; Eph. 5:23, 24, 32.)

> "And I also say to you that you are Peter, and upon this rock I will build My **church**; and the gates of Hades shall not overpower it" [Matt. 16:18].

Christ speaks here of a massive body of people of which a local church is only a small section. This large group is the church.

> Give no offense either to Jews or to Greeks or to the **church of God** [1 Cor. 10:32].

Church in the above verse refers to a **whole class** of people.

> [F]ar above all rule and authority and power and dominion, and every name that is named, not only in this age, but also in the one to come. And He put all things in subjection under His feet, and gave Him as head over all things to the **church**, which is **His body**, the fullness of Him who fills all in all [Eph. 1:21-23].

Note that *church* is identified with the body of Christ.

> [T]o be specific, that the Gentiles are fellow heirs and fellow members of the body, and fellow partakers of the promise in Christ Jesus through the gospel....in order that the manifold wisdom of God might now be made known through the **church** to the rulers and the authorities in the heavenly places [Eph. 3:6, 10].

Verse six refers to a group formed by the believing Jews and Gentiles. Verse 10 identifies this **massive group as the church**.

> Husbands, love your wives, just as Christ also loved the church and gave Himself up for her; that He might sanctify her, having cleansed her by the washing of water with the word, that He might present to Himself the church in all her glory, having no spot or wrinkle or any such thing; but that she should be holy and blameless [Eph. 5:25-27].

Here *church* refers to the whole group of believers rather than just a local organization.

> He is also head of **the body**, the **church**; and He is the beginning, the firstborn from the dead; so that He Himself might come to have first place in everything....Now I rejoice in my sufferings for your sake, and in my flesh I do my share on behalf of **His body** (which is the **church**) in filling up that which is lacking in Christ's afflictions [Col. 1:18, 24].

In both above verses, *church* is equated with Christ's *body*.

> [T]o the general assembly and church of the first-born who are enrolled in heaven, and to God, the Judge of all, and to the spirits of righteous men made perfect [Heb. 12:23].

All these "**enrolled in heaven**," i.e., all those saved, **are members of the church**.

Ultimately, the church in its entirety is invisible. It includes both the living and the dead. It can never be brought to assembly at one place or at the same time before the Rapture. By contrast, the local church is the visible manifestation of the universal church. Obviously, the local church excludes that portion of the universal church that has died and gone to be with the Lord. Unlike the universal church, the local church can have unbelievers associated with it. A majority of the approximately one hundred fifteen uses of the word *ekklesia* in the New Testament refer to a local church or local churches (e.g., the church in Jerusalem, Acts 8:1; 11:22; the churches of Galatia, 1 Cor. 16:1; the church of Macedonia, 2 Cor. 8:1; the churches of the Thessalonians, 1 Thess 1:1, etc.).

Our study considers the universal church first, then the local church.

II. Word Pictures of the Universal Church

The New Testament gives many figures that teach of the relationship between Christ and the church or describe the nature of the church.

A. The Shepherd and the Sheep

The Old Testament pictures the people of God as sheep, with the LORD being their shepherd (Psa. 23:1; 74:1; 78:52; 79:13; 80:1; 95:7; 100:3; Isa. 40:11; Jer. 23:1; Ezek. 34; Zech. 13:7). In the lesson of the good shepherd Christ teaches that He was bringing His sheep out of the fold (Judaism) and that He had other sheep of a different fold (gentiles). These would be united to form a new flock (see John 10:16). Christ is the head of this new flock, called the *church* (see Acts 20:28). Jesus is the Chief Shepherd (1 Pet. 5:4; see also 1 Pet. 2:25), and the Great Shepherd (Heb. 13:20). Pastors (shepherds) are His representatives (Acts 20:28; Eph. 4:11; 1 Pet. 5:2-3).

The picture of a shepherd and sheep teaches that Christ is the authority over the church. He offers protection, guidance, and nurture to believers. Believers, as sheep, tend to wander and need our Shepherd's wisdom and strength.

"And I have other **sheep**, which are not of this fold; I must bring them also, and they shall hear My voice; and they shall become one flock with one **shepherd**" [John 10:16].

Be on guard for yourselves and for all **the flock**, among which the Holy Spirit has made you overseers, to shepherd the **church of God** which He pur-

chased with His own blood [Acts 20:28].

Now the God of peace, who brought up from the dead **the great Shepherd of the sheep** through the blood of the eternal covenant, even Jesus our Lord [Heb. 13:20].

[S]hepherd **the flock of God** among you, exercising oversight not under compulsion, but voluntarily, according to the will of God; and not for sordid gain, but with eagerness; nor yet as lording it over those allotted to your charge, but proving to be examples to **the flock**. And when the **Chief Shepherd** appears, you will receive the unfading crown of glory [1 Pet. 5:2-4].

B. The Head and Body

A second common Biblical figure for the church is that of a body with Christ as the Head. (See 1 Cor. 10:17; Eph. 2:16; 3:6; 4:4, 12, 16; 5:23, 30; 6:15-16; Col. 2:19; 3:15.)

[S]o we, who are many, are **one body in Christ**, and individually members one of another [Rom. 12:5].

For even as the body is one and yet has many members, and all the members of the body, though they are many, are **one body**, so also is Christ. For by one Spirit we were all baptized into **one body**, whether Jews or Greeks, whether slaves or free, and we were all made to drink of one Spirit....Now you are **Christ's body**, and individually members of it. [1 Cor. 12:12-13, 27].

And He put all things in subjection under His feet, and gave Him as head over all things to **the church, which is His body**, the fullness of Him who fills all in all [Eph. 1:22-23].

He is also **head of the body, the church**....Now I rejoice in my sufferings for your sake, and in my flesh I do my share on behalf of **His body** (which is **the church**) in filling up that which is lacking in Christ's afflictions [Col. 1:18a, 24].

As a body the church is both diverse and united. Every part affects the whole. There should be no feelings of jealousy towards others or inferiority towards others or vanity towards others, just as each part of a body is necessary but at the same time dependent upon all other parts. The imagery of the body teaches that we should allow other believers to be different and yet feel a sense of solidarity with them. Believers should rejoice when other believers are blessed and sorrow with other believers in their grief.

As the Head of this body, Christ supplies direction and wisdom. He is the authority that directs all the work of the body.

C. The Bride and Groom

The Old Testament likens the relationship between God and Israel as one of husband and wife. Usually, there is a mention of Israel being an unfaithful wife with the promise that she will eventually be restored (see Isa. 50:1; Jer. 2:2; 31:32; Ezek. 16:32; Hosea 2:2ff.; Isa. 54:5-8; 62:4-5).

> "For **your husband** is your Maker, whose name is the LORD of hosts; and your Redeemer is the Holy One of Israel, who is called the God of all the earth. For the LORD has called you, **like a wife** forsaken and grieved in spirit, even **like a wife of one's youth** when she is rejected," says your God. "For a brief moment I forsook you, but with great compassion I will gather you. In an outburst of anger I hid My face from you for a moment; but with everlasting lovingkindness I will have compassion on you," says the LORD your Redeemer [Isa. 54:5-8].

> It will no longer be said to you, "Forsaken," nor to your land will it any longer be said, "Desolate," but you will be called, "My delight is in her," and

your land, "**Married**"; for the LORD delights in you, and to Him your land will be married. For as a young man marries a virgin, so your sons will marry you; and **as the bridegroom rejoices over the bride**, so **your God** will rejoice over you [Isa. 62:4-5].

The imagery of the bridegroom occurs repeatedly in the Gospels. Christ assumes the figure of the groom while His followers, particularly John the Baptist, have the role of friends of the groom. (See Matt. 9:15; 25:1-13; Mark 2:19-20; Luke 5:34-35; John 3:29.)

> And Jesus said to them, "The attendants of the **bridegroom** cannot mourn as long as the **bridegroom** is with them, can they? But the days will come when the bridegroom is taken away from them, and then they will fast" [Matt. 9:15].

> John answered and said, "A man can receive nothing, unless it has been given him from heaven. You yourselves bear me witness, that I said, 'I am not the Christ,' but, 'I have been sent before Him.' He who has the bride is the **bridegroom**; but the **friend of the bridegroom**, who stands and hears him, rejoices greatly because of the bridegroom's voice. And so this joy of mine has been made full" [John 3:27-29].

Through the Scriptures addressed to the church, it becomes clear that Christ is as a groom who is engaged to His bride, the church. In Jewish culture, a betrothal was much more binding than is a modern engagement. Nothing can ever break the covenant between Christ and His church. The church is now betrothed to Christ, and this is a relationship that cannot be broken. It culminates in the marriage of the Lamb in the heavenly city.

> So then if, while her husband is living, she is joined to another man, she shall be called an adulteress; but if her husband dies, she is free from the law, so

that she is not an adulteress, though she is joined to another man. Therefore, my brethren, you also were made to die to the Law through the body of Christ, that you might be **joined to another**, to Him who was raised from the dead, that we might bear fruit for God [Rom. 7:3-4].

For I am jealous for you with a godly jealousy; for I **betrothed** you to **one husband**, that **to Christ** I might present you as a pure virgin [2 Cor. 11:2].

Wives, be subject to your own husbands, as to the Lord. For the husband is the head of the wife, as Christ also is the head of the church, He Himself being the Savior of the body. But as the church is subject to Christ, so also the wives ought to be to their husbands in everything. **Husbands, love your wives, just as Christ also loved the church** and gave Himself up for her; that He might sanctify her, having cleansed her by the washing of water with the word, that He might present to Himself the church in all her glory, having no spot or wrinkle or any such thing; but that she should be holy and blameless. So husbands ought also to love their own wives as their own bodies. He who loves his own wife loves himself; for no one ever hated his own flesh, but nourishes and cherishes it, just as Christ also does the church, because we are members of His body. For this cause a man shall leave his father and mother, and shall cleave to his wife; and the two shall become one flesh [Eph. 5:22-31].

"Let us rejoice and be glad and give the glory to Him, for **the marriage of the Lamb** has come and His **bride** has made herself ready." And it was given to her to clothe herself in fine linen, bright and clean; for the fine linen is the righteous acts of the saints. And he said to me, "Write, 'Blessed are those who are invited to the marriage supper of the Lamb.' " And he said to me, "These are true words of God" [Rev. 19:7-9].

And I saw the holy city, new Jerusalem, coming down out of heaven from God, made ready **as a bride** adorned for her husband....And one of the seven angels who had the seven bowls full of the seven last plagues, came and spoke with me, saying, "Come here, I shall show you the **bride**, the **wife of the Lamb**" [Rev. 21:2, 9].

And the Spirit and the **bride** say, "Come..." [Rev. 22:17].

The relationship between Christ and the church is supposed to parallel that of a Christian husband and wife. Christ loves the church with an unselfish and sacrificial love. The church is to be in submission to Him as a wife to her husband. It is interesting that the Hebrew has a word that means both master and husband. References to the holy city as a bride probably include the truth that this city is the eternal home of Christ's bride, the church.

D. The Temple, Household, or Building with Christ as the Cornerstone

There are probably different shades of truth intended by these overlapping figures. The comparison of a church to a temple conveys the truth that God Himself through the Holy Spirit indwells the church just as God took up residence in the Old Testament tabernacle. 1 Cor. 3:16-17 gives a strong warning that God promises to destroy those who destroy the church (or local churches).

Do you not know that you are a **temple of God**, and that the Spirit of God dwells in you? If any man destroys the **temple of God**, God will destroy him, for the **temple of God** is holy, and that is **what you are** [1 Cor. 3:16, 17].

(See also 2 Cor. 6:16 and Eph 2:19-22 for references to God indwelling the church as a temple.)

Other texts liken the church to a building with Jesus Christ being the cornerstone. Psalm 118:22ff. refers to a "stone which the builders rejected (that) has become the chief corner stone." Christ claimed that Psalm 118 teaches about Himself (Matt. 21:42ff.; Mark 12:10ff.; and Luke 20:17). Peter also found the fulfillment of Psalm 118 in the Lord Jesus Christ (Acts 4:11). Christ is the cornerstone. The apostles and prophets are the foundation. The church, i.e., believers, is the building.

> For we are God's fellow workers; **you are** God's field, **God's building.** According to the grace of God which was given to me, as a wise master builder I laid a foundation, and another is building upon it. But let each man be **careful how he builds** upon it. For no man can lay a foundation other than the one which is laid, which is Jesus Christ [1 Cor. 3:9-11].

> So then you are no longer strangers and aliens, but you are fellow citizens with the saints, and are of **God's household,** having been built upon the **foundation of the apostles and prophets, Christ Jesus** Himself being the **corner stone,** in whom **the whole building,** being fitted together is growing into a **holy temple** in the Lord; in whom **you also are being built** together into a dwelling of God in the Spirit [Eph. 2:19-22].

> And coming to Him as to a **living stone,** rejected by men, but choice and precious in the sight of God, **you** also, as **living stones, are being built up as a spiritual house** for a holy priesthood, to offer up spiritual sacrifices acceptable to God through Jesus Christ [1 Pet. 2:4-5].

The imagery of a building teaches us that the church is comprised of interdependent individuals just as a building is made of many individual stones. Also, the church is constantly progressing in its construction process. It is a building that is being built as new people trust in Christ and as believers "edify" one another. Another basic lesson from the picture of a building is that Christ is the only legitimate and lasting foundation for the church or a church (cf. the story of the wise man building on a rock, Matt. 7:24 ff.).

The comparison of the church to a "household of faith" is closely related to the figure of a temple or building. Sometimes all the terms are included in the same passage (e.g., Eph. 2:19-22: household, v. 19; building, v. 21; temple, v. 21). The concept of a household speaks of unity and a family relationship.

> So then, while we have opportunity, let us do good to all men, and especially to those who are of the **household of faith** [Gal. 6:10].

> [B]ut in case I am delayed, I write so that you may know how one ought to conduct himself in the **household of God,** which is **the church** of the living God...[1 Tim. 3:15a].

> For it is time for judgment to begin with the **household of God**...[1 Pet. 4:17].

E. A Priesthood with Christ as the Great High Priest

The doctrine of the priesthood of believers was one of the three major tenets of the reformation, along with justification by faith alone and the doctrine that Scripture alone and not church tradition is the final authority. Protestants objected to the Roman Catholic practice of giving confession to a human priest or praying to some dead saint as intermediary between God and a believer. Also, they objected to the philosophy that Scripture should only be studied in ancient languages by a class of priests. They believed that God wanted common people to study the Bible in their own language. (This did not, however, mean the

Reformers believed scholarship was unnecessary or that every man should have equal authority in governing the church or teaching it doctrine). All believers are priests.

The book of Hebrews stresses that Jesus Christ is a Great High Priest for believers. He is the perfect and final mediator between God and man (see 1 Tim. 2:5). He offered the perfect sacrifice to end all sacrifices and bring about a lasting relationship between God and man without any further need for continual animal sacrifices or a special priesthood. (See also Heb. 2:17; 5:5-6, 10; 7:17, 26; 9:11; 10:11-12, 21.)

> Therefore, holy brethren, partakers of a heavenly calling, consider **Jesus**, the Apostle and **High Priest** of our confession [Heb. 3:1].

> Since then we have a **great high priest** who has passed through the heavens, **Jesus the Son of God**, let us hold fast our confession. For we do not have a **high priest** who cannot sympathize with our weaknesses, but One who has been tempted in all things as we are, yet without sin [Heb. 4:14-15].

> [W]here **Jesus** has entered as a forerunner for us, having become a **high priest** forever according to the order of Melchizedek [Heb. 6:20].

> Now the main point in what has been said is this: we have such a **high priest**, who has taken His seat at the right hand of the throne of the Majesty in the heavens [Heb. 8:1].

At the time of the Law's introduction, God promised to make Israel a Kingdom of Priests "if you will indeed obey my voice..." (Ex. 19:5-6). However, Israel broke the Old Covenant (The Law of Moses) and, therefore, lost the privilege of becoming a kingdom of priests. Later she rejected her Messiah. Based upon the blood of Christ, God offers a new covenant that is now in force with the church (and will be eventually ratified with the nation of Israel). All in the church, i.e., all believers, have been made a kingdom of priests with Christ as the High Priest.

> [Y]ou also, as living stones, are being built up as a spiritual house for a **holy priesthood**, to offer up spiritual sacrifices acceptable to God through Jesus Christ....But you are a chosen race, a royal **priesthood**, a holy nation, a people for God's own possession, that you may proclaim the excellencies of Him who has called you out of darkness into His marvelous light [1 Pet. 2:5, 9].

> [A]nd He has made us to be a kingdom, **priests** to His God and Father; to Him be the glory and the dominion forever and ever. Amen. [Rev 1:6].

> And they sang a new song, saying, "Worthy art Thou to take the book, and to break its seals; for Thou wast slain, and didst purchase for God with Thy blood men from every tribe and tongue and people and nation. And Thou has made them to be a kingdom and **priests to our God**; and they will reign upon the earth" [Rev. 5:9-10].

> Blessed and holy is the one who has a part in the first resurrection; over these the second death has no power, but they will be **priests of God** and of Christ and will reign with Him for a thousand years [Rev. 20:6].

Because all believers are priests, they all have the privilege of direct access to God without any need to pray through a human mediator (Eph. 2:18). Furthermore, it is God's will that all believers have access to His Word in their own respective languages in order to develop personal convictions and validate doctrines from teachers in the church (e.g., Acts 17:11; 1 John 4:1).

Priests have the obligation to offer sacrifices. The New Testament mentions at least three sacrifices that believer-priests should offer. First, we should offer ourselves as a living sacrifice (Rom. 12:1). Next God wants us to offer up our wealth to advance His work (Phil. 4:18). Finally, believer-priests are to render a sacrifice of praise and worship (Heb. 13:15-16).

> I urge you therefore, brethren, by the mercies of God, to present **your bodies** a living and holy **sacrifice**, acceptable to God, which is your spiritual service of worship [Rom. 12:1].

> But I have received everything in full, and have an abundance; I am amply supplied, having received from Epaphroditus **what you have sent**, a fragrant aroma, an **acceptable sacrifice**, well pleasing to God [Phil. 4:18].

> Through Him then, let us continually offer up a **sacrifice of praise** to God, that is, the fruit of lips that give thanks to His name. And do not neglect **doing good and sharing**; for with **such sacrifices** God is pleased [Heb. 13:15-16].

F. The Pillar of Truth

> [B]ut in case I am delayed, I write so that you may know how one ought to conduct himself in the household of God, which is the **church** of the living God, **the pillar and support of the truth** [1 Tim. 3:15].

The imagery of the church as a pillar of truth ought to be very dear to those in Bible teaching churches. A local church has a responsibility to preserve the truth in the midst of a dark world (see Phil. 2:15). One of the foremost responsibilities of the church is that of teaching the Scriptures.

III. The Origin of the Universal Church

In Matt. 16:18, the Lord considered the church to be a future institution: "I will build My church." In John 17:11 and 21, Christ prayed that all believers would become one. According to 1 Cor. 12:12-13, the oneness in the body of Christ, the church, comes about by Spirit baptism. Therefore, the origin of the

church must be traced back to the beginning of the Holy Spirit's baptizing ministry.

Throughout the gospels Spirit baptism is presented as a future work (see Pneumatology, p. 234). At the ascension, the Lord said that Spirit baptism would occur "not many days from now" (Acts 1:5). Peter in Acts 11:15-16 teaches that Spirit baptism had already occurred and did so "at the beginning." Therefore, the church was formed not long after the events in Acts 1:5 but long before the times of Acts 11:15-16. Also, the foundation of the church involved Peter and the other apostles. All lines of evidence point to Pentecost in Acts 2 as being the time of the first Spirit baptism and hence the time of the church's origin.

IV. The Church as a Unique Work of God:

A. The Importance of "Dispensationalism"

Dispensationalism is a school of thought that maintains that God's work in the world has been operated by different systems or administrations. This study will work towards a more refined definition later. The immediate goal is simply to argue that God's program has been or will be implemented by at least three main administrations (dispensations): Law or Judaism, Grace or Church, and Kingdom or Millennium.

While it is true that a person can be orthodox in the essentials of the faith without adopting the dispensational view, it is also true that a thorough and consistent understanding of the Bible must be based upon dispensationalism. Those who confuse God's various administrations will make serious mistakes in secondary areas of doctrine. Those who do not realize that the Holy Spirit works differently in the church administration may, for example, believe that Luke 11:13 teaches we must plead with God in order to obtain the Holy Spirit. This verse, however, pertains to the disciples who were living under the Law dispensation when not all believers were indwelt by the Holy Spirit. Denominations that call clergy "priests" confuse the difference between Judaism and the church. There was a priesthood under the Law of Moses, but all believers are priests under the Grace system. Under the Law, believers **had** a priesthood. Under the church, believers **are** a priesthood. Furthermore, it is important to realize that the "servants" in the gospels who are cast into outer darkness (e.g., Matt. 8:12; 25:30; Luke 12:46, etc.), refer to unbelieving Israelites under the Law of Moses, not to believing servants in the church. Thus, the doctrine of eternal security need not be compromised. Example after example could be given to show errors that will result from a failure to distinguish between the dispensations (administrations), especially between the dispensations of Law, Church, and Kingdom.

B. Evidence for Dispensationalism

Anyone who does not bring a sacrifice to church or celebrate the feast of tabernacles by living in huts made of palm branches is, in practice, a dispensationalist, although in theory he might deny it. The evidence that God has worked by various administrations or systems of management is conclusive.

1. Law vs. Grace, or Judaism vs. the Church

Scriptures clearly speak of the abrogation of the Law of Moses. It has been rescinded and is no longer binding upon believers unless a given point is repeated in Scripture pertaining to the church. That is why we no longer have a temple, a priesthood, sacrifices or other rituals of Judaism.

To say that the Law of Moses has been set aside is not the same as affirming its destruction (Psa. 119:89; Matt. 5:17). While the Church is not under the Law, this does not mean the Law has been destroyed or that Christians disparage the Old Testament. Because God does not change in His attributes, everything that the Old Testament taught about God's nature is still valid (Mal. 3:6; James 1:17). Old Testament verses and Old Testament stories may be used to either prove or apply truths that were carried over into (i.e.,

repeated in) the Scriptures for the church (Rom. 15:4; 1 Cor. 10:6, 11; 2 Tim. 3:16). The Law of Moses still proves man's guilt (Rom. 3:20; 1 Tim. 1:8 ff.). The Law also contains many unfulfilled prophecies and teaches about God's dealings with gentile nations. Furthermore, the Old Testament is rife with ideas that may not be strictly binding upon the whole church but might serve as a source for developing personal convictions in areas of Christian liberty (e.g., not lending at interest to a poor believer). Dispensationalists do not disregard the Old Testament. They just use it properly. See 1 Tim. 1:8: "...the Law is good, if one uses it **lawfully**."

There is little excuse for failure to grasp the change from Law to grace. It is one of the fundamental teachings of the New Testament.

For the **Law** was given **through Moses; grace** and truth were realized through **Jesus Christ** [John 1:17].

For sin shall not be master over you, for you are **not under law**, but under **grace** [Rom. 6:14].

Therefore, my brethren, you also were made **to die to the Law** through the body of Christ, that you might be joined to another, to Him who was raised from the dead, that we might bear fruit for God [Rom. 7:4].

For Christ is **the end of the law** for righteousness to everyone who believes [Rom. 10:4].

But if the ministry of death, in **letters engraved on stones**, came with glory, so that the sons of Israel could not look intently at the face of Moses because of the glory of his face, fading as it was, how shall the ministry of the Spirit fail to be even more with glory?....For if that which **fades away** was with glory, much more that which remains is in glory [2 Cor. 3:7, 8, 11].

Therefore **the Law** has become **our tutor** to lead us to Christ, that we may be justified by faith. But now that faith has come, **we are no longer under a tutor** [Gal. 3:24-25].

[B]y **abolishing** in His flesh the enmity, which is **the Law** of commandments contained in ordinances, that in Himself He might make the two into one new man, thus establishing peace [Eph. 2:15].

[H]aving **canceled** out the certificate of debt consisting of **decrees** against us and which was hostile to us; and He has taken it out of the way, having nailed it to the cross [Col. 2:14].

Now if perfection was through the Levitical priesthood (for on the basis of it the people received the Law), what further need was there for another priest to arise according to the order of Melchizedek, and not be designated according to the order of Aaron? For when the priesthood is changed, of necessity there takes place a **change of law** also. For the one concerning whom these things are spoken belongs to another tribe, from which no one has officiated at the altar. For it is evident that our Lord was descended from Judah, a tribe with reference to which Moses spoke nothing concerning priests. And this is clearer still, if another priest arises according to the likeness of Melchizedek, who has become such not on the basis of a law of physical requirement, but according to the power of an indestructible life. For it is witnessed of Him, "Thou art a priest forever according to the order of Melchizedek." For, on the one hand, there is a **setting aside of a former commandment** because of its weakness and uselessness (for **the Law** made nothing perfect), and on the other hand there is a bringing in of a better

hope, through which we draw near to God....so much the more also **Jesus** has become the guarantee of a **better covenant** [Heb. 7:11-19, 22].

For if that **first covenant** had been faultless, there would have been no occasion sought for a **second**....When He said, "A **new covenant**," He has made the **first obsolete**. But whatever is becoming obsolete and growing old is ready to disappear [Heb. 8:7, 13].

2. The Coming Kingdom

It is amazing that anyone could read the Bible and not believe that it promises a future earthly Kingdom centered in the nation of Israel. Scriptural evidence is more than conclusive. God has changed administrations from Law to the Church, and He will one day change from a church administration to that of a political kingdom with Christ sitting on the Davidic throne in Jerusalem.

God promised that the land of Palestine would belong to Abraham's seed eternally. The word eternal occurs both in the original promise and in reaffirmations of it in coming centuries. **This promise of a land to Abraham's seed must be kept.** Israel **will** have a Kingdom.

> [F]or all **the land** which you see, I will **give it to you** and to your descendants **forever** [Gen. 13:15].

> "And I will establish My covenant between Me and you and your descendants after you throughout their generations for an **everlasting covenant**, to be God to you and to your descendants after you."....But God said, "No, but Sarah your wife shall bear you a son, and you shall call his name **Isaac**; and I will establish My covenant with him for an **everlasting covenant for his descendants** after him" [Gen. 17:7, 19].

> [T]he covenant which He made with **Abraham**, and His oath to Isaac. He

also confirmed it to Jacob for a statute, to Israel as an **everlasting** covenant [1 Chron. 16:16-17].

He has remembered His **covenant forever**, the word which He commanded to a thousand generations, **the covenant** which He made **with Abraham**, and His oath to Isaac. Then He confirmed it to Jacob for a statute, to Israel as an **everlasting covenant** [Psa. 105:8-10].

"Nevertheless, I will remember **My covenant with you in the days of your youth** [either with Abraham or Moses] and I will establish an **everlasting covenant** with you. Then you will remember your ways and be ashamed when you receive your sisters, both your older and your younger; and I will give them to you as daughters, but not because of your covenant. Thus, I will establish My covenant with you, and you shall know that I am the LORD" [Ezek. 16:60-62].

"And **they shall live on the land** that I gave to **Jacob** My servant, in which **your fathers** lived; and they will live on it, they, and their sons, and their sons' sons, **forever**; and David My servant shall be their prince forever. And I will make a covenant of peace with them; it will be an **everlasting covenant** with them. And I will place them and multiply them, and will set **My sanctuary in their midst forever**" [Ezek. 37:25-26].

What I am saying is this; the Law, which came four hundred and thirty years later, **does not invalidate a covenant** previously ratified by God, **so as to nullify the promise** [Gal. 3:17].

For when God made the **promise to Abraham**, since He could swear by no one greater, He swore by Himself....In

the same way, God, desiring even more to show to the heirs of the promise the **unchangeableness of His purpose**, interposed with an oath, in order that by two **unchangeable** things, in which it is impossible for God to lie, we may have strong encouragement, we who have fled for refuge in laying hold of the hope set before us [Heb. 6:13,17-18].

God promised David that his seed would have a right to rule and would eventually rule over Israel **forever**. Yet, David's children have not ruled over Israel since the exile. (King Herod was neither of David's line nor even truly Jewish.) The promise of an eternal throne for David's son must be fulfilled in the ultimate Son of David, Jesus Christ. **He must someday come to enjoy a literal rule over the Davidic Kingdom,** a rule that will be both 1,000 years according to Rev. 20:4-6 (hence called the Millennium) but also eternal in the sense that the Millennium will merge with the Eternal State. The original promise to David was stated to be eternally binding. Just as with the Abrahamic Covenant, the Davidic Covenant is reaffirmed throughout Scripture as being irrevocable and eternal in nature. In the future, the church dispensation will end and the Kingdom will begin.

"When your days are complete and you lie down with your fathers, I will raise up your descendant after you, who will come forth from you, and I will establish his kingdom. He shall build a house for My name, and I will establish **the throne of his kingdom forever**. I will be a father to him and he will be a son to Me; when he commits iniquity, I will correct him with the rod of men and the strokes of the sons of men, but My lovingkindness shall not depart from him, as I took it away from Saul, whom I removed from before you. **And your house and your kingdom shall endure before Me forever, your** throne shall be established forever" [2 Sam. 7:12-16].

"I have made a **covenant with My chosen**; I have sworn to **David** My servant, I will establish **your seed forever**, and build up **your throne to all generations**" [Psa. 89:3-4].

"My lovingkindness I will keep for him **forever**, and My covenant shall be confirmed to him. So I will establish **his descendants forever**, and his **throne as the days of heaven**" [Psa. 89:28-29].

"But I will **not break off** My lovingkindness from him, nor deal falsely in My faithfulness. My covenant I will not violate, nor will I alter the utterance of My lips. Once I have sworn by My holiness; I will not lie to **David**. His **descendants** shall **endure forever**, and his **throne as the sun** before Me. It shall be **established forever** like the moon, and the witness in the sky is faithful" [Psa. 89:33-37].

"Incline your ear and come to Me. Listen, that you may live; and I will make an **everlasting covenant** with you, according to the faithful **mercies shown to David**" [Isa. 55:3].

"And it shall come about on that day," declares the LORD of hosts, "that I will break his yoke from off their neck, and will tear off their bonds; and strangers shall no longer make them their slaves. But they shall serve the LORD their God, and **David their king**, whom I will **raise up** for them" [Jer. 30:8, 9].

For the sons of Israel will remain for many days without king or prince, without sacrifice or sacred pillar, and without ephod or household idols. Afterward the sons of Israel will return and seek the LORD their God and **David their king**; and they will come

trembling to the LORD and to His goodness **in the last days** [Hos. 3:4-5].

"In that day I will **raise up** the fallen booth of **David,** and wall up its breaches; I will also raise up its ruins, and rebuild it as in the days of old" [Amos 9:11].

The Old Testament prophets also spoke of a New Covenant that would be made with Israel. The New Covenant is based upon Christ's blood (Matt. 26:28). It is in force with the church but will eventually also be ratified with the nation of Israel (see also Heb. 8:7-13). This New Covenant is unconditional. It cannot be broken, and thus, guarantees a future for Israel. This means a Kingdom dispensation will follow a church dispensation.

"Behold, days are coming," declares the LORD, "when I will make a **new covenant with the house of Israel and with the house of Judah,** not like the covenant which I made with their fathers in the day I took them by the hand to bring them out of the land of Egypt, My covenant which they broke, although I was a husband to them," declares the LORD. "But this is the covenant which I will make with the house of Israel after those days," declares the LORD, "I will put My law within them, and on their heart I will write it; and I will be their God, and they shall be My people. And they shall not teach again, each man his neighbor and each man his brother, saying 'Know the LORD,' for they shall all know Me, from the least of them to the greatest of them," declares the LORD, "for I will forgive their iniquity and their sin I will remember no more." Thus says the LORD, who gives the **sun** for light by day, and fixed order of the **moon** and the stars for light by night, who stirs up the sea so that its waves roar; The LORD of hosts is His name: "**If this fixed order departs from before**

Me," declares the LORD, "Then the offspring of Israel also shall cease from being a nation before Me forever." Thus says the LORD, "If the heavens above can be measured, and the foundations of the earth searched out below, then I will also cast off all the offspring of Israel for all that they have done," declares the LORD [Jer. 31:31-37].

"And I will make an **everlasting covenant** with them that I will not turn away from them, to do them good; and I will put the fear of Me in their hearts so that they will not turn away from Me" [Jer. 32:40].

"For I will take you from the nations, **gather you from all the lands,** and **bring you into your own land.** Then I will sprinkle clean water on you, and you will be clean; I will cleanse you from all your filthiness and from all your idols. Moreover, I will give you a new heart and put a new spirit within you; and I will remove the heart of stone from your flesh and give you a heart of flesh" [Ezek. 36:24-26].

"Therefore prophesy, and say to them, 'Thus says the Lord God, "Behold, I will **open your graves** and cause you to come up out of your graves, My people; and I will **bring you into the land of Israel.** Then you will know that I am the LORD, when I have opened your graves and **caused you to come up out of your graves,** My people. And I will put My Spirit within you, and you will come to life, and I will place you on your own land. Then you will know that I, the LORD, have spoken and done it," declares the LORD' "[Ezek. 37:12-14].

"And I will make a **covenant of peace** with them; it will be an **everlasting** covenant with them....and will set **My sanctuary in their midst forever**"

[Ezek. 37:26] (This reference in Ezekiel 37 helps prove those in Ezekiel 36 also refer to the New Covenant ratified with Israel).

The Old Testament promises that Israel will be the center of a worldwide and enduring Kingdom. Unless we are to believe that either God is a liar or is too weak to keep His promises, **we must maintain that there is coming a future Kingdom for Israel.** (See also Jer. 31:3.)

Now it will come about that in the **last days,** the mountain of the **house of the LORD will be established** as the chief of the mountains, and will be raised above the hills; and **all the nations will stream to it.** And many peoples will come and say, "Come let us go up to the mountain of the LORD, to the house of the God of Jacob; that He **may teach** us concerning His ways, and that we may walk in His paths." For **the law will go forth from Zion,** and the word of the Lord from Jerusalem. And He will **judge between the nations,** and will render decisions for many peoples; and they will hammer their swords into plowshares, and their spears into pruning hooks. Nation will not lift up sword against nation, and **never again** will they learn war [Isa. 2:2-4].

"And nations will come to your light, and kings to the brightness of your rising....Then you will see and be radiant, and your heart will thrill and rejoice; because the abundance of the sea will be turned to you, the **wealth of the nations will come to you**" [Isa. 60:3, 5].

"And foreigners will build up your walls, and their kings will minister to you; for in My wrath I struck you, and in My favor I have had compassion on you. And **your gates will be open continually;** they will not be closed day or night, so that **men may bring to you** the wealth of the nations, with their kings in procession" [Isa. 60:10-11].

"You will also suck the milk of nations, and will suck the breast of kings; then you will know that I, the LORD, am your Savior, and your Redeemer, the Mighty One of Jacob. Instead of bronze I will bring gold, and instead of iron I will bring silver, and instead of wood, bronze, and instead of stones, iron. And I will make peace your administrators, and righteousness your overseers. Violence will not be heard again in your land, nor devastation or destruction within your borders; but you will call your walls salvation, and your gates praise. No longer will you have the sun for light by day, nor for brightness will the moon give you light; but you will have the LORD for an everlasting light, and your God for your glory. Your sun will set no more, neither will your moon wane; For you will have the LORD for an everlasting light, and the days of your mourning will be finished. Then all your people will be righteous; they will possess the land forever, The branch of My planting, the work of My hands, that I may be glorified [Isa. 60:16-21].

But you will be called the priests of the LORD; you will be spoken of as ministers of our God. You will eat the wealth of nations, and in their riches you will boast [Isa. 61:6].

On your walls, O Jerusalem, I have appointed watchmen; all day and all night they will never keep silent. You who remind the LORD, take no rest for yourselves; and give Him no rest until He establishes and makes Jerusalem a praise in the earth [Isa. 62:6-7].

"At that time they shall call Jerusalem 'The Throne of the LORD,' and all the nations will be gathered to it, to Jerusalem, for the name of the LORD;

nor shall they walk anymore after the stubbornness of their evil heart" [Jer. 3:17].

And it will come about in the last days that the mountain of the house of the LORD will be established as the chief of the mountains. It will be raised above the hills, and the peoples will stream to it. And many nations will come and say, "Come and let us go up to the mountain of the LORD and to the house of the God of Jacob, that He may teach us about His ways and that we may walk in His paths." For from Zion will go forth the law, even the word of the LORD from Jerusalem. And He will judge between many peoples and render decisions for mighty, distant nations. Then they will hammer their swords into plowshares and their spears into pruning hooks; nation will not lift up sword against nation, and never again will they train for war [Micah 4:1-3].

"Thus says the LORD of hosts, 'It will yet be that peoples will come, even the inhabitants of many cities. And the inhabitants of one will go to another saying, "Let us go at once to entreat the favor of the LORD, and to seek the LORD of hosts; I will also go." So many peoples and mighty nations will come to seek the LORD of hosts in Jerusalem and to entreat the favor of the LORD.' Thus says the LORD of hosts, 'In those days ten men from all the nations will grasp the garment of a Jew saying, "Let us go with you, for we have heard that God is with you" ' " [Zech. 8:20-23].

And the LORD will be king over all the earth; in that day the LORD will be the only one, and His name the only one [Zech. 14:9].

And people will live in it, and there will be no more curse, for **Jerusalem will dwell in security** [Zech. 14:11].

And Judah also will fight at **Jerusalem**; and the **wealth of all** the surrounding **nations will be gathered**, gold and silver and garments in great abundance [Zech. 14:14].

Then it will come about that any who are left of **all the nations** that went against Jerusalem will **go up from year to year to worship the King, the LORD of hosts**, and to celebrate the Feast of Booths. And it will be that whichever of the families of the earth does not go up **to Jerusalem** to worship the King, the LORD of hosts, there will be no rain on them [Zech. 14:16-17].

All these promises (covenants) find their ultimate fulfillment in the Lord Jesus Christ who will return to give Israel her eternal right to the land and her eternal Davidic throne. Many verses focus upon Messiah's role in a coming Kingdom.

"But as for Me, I have installed **My King upon Zion**, My holy mountain" [Psa. 2:6].

For **a child will be born to us**, a son will be given to us; and the government will rest on His shoulders; and His name will be called Wonderful Counselor, Mighty God, Eternal Father, Prince of Peace. There will be **no end to the increase of His government** or of peace, **on the throne of David and over his kingdom,** to establish it and to uphold it with justice and righteousness from then on and **forevermore**. The zeal of the LORD of hosts will accomplish this [Isa. 9:6-7].

"Behold, the days are coming," declares the LORD, "when I shall raise up for David a **righteous Branch**; and **He will reign as king** and act wisely and do justice and righteousness in the land. In His days Judah will be saved, and Israel will dwell securely; and this is His name by which He will be called, 'The LORD our righteousness' " [Jer. 23:5-6].

"I kept looking in the night visions, and behold, with the clouds of heaven one like a **Son of Man** was coming, and He came up to the Ancient of Days and was presented before Him. And **to Him was given dominion**, glory and a **kingdom**, that **all the peoples, nations**, and men of every language might **serve Him**. His dominion is an **everlasting dominion** which will not pass way; and His kingdom is one which will not be destroyed" [Dan. 7:13-14].

And the **LORD will be king** over all the earth; in that day the LORD will be the only one, and His name the only one [Zech. 14:9].

These conclusions about a future for Israel should in no way be construed to mean that believers, who are a part of the church, will have no role in the Kingdom. Believers are the "Sons of Abraham" and can be called the "true circumcision." (See Rom. 4:13-16; Gal. 3:7, 9, 14; Phil. 3:3, 9, and pp. 498-501) Yet, the fact that the church will share in millennial blessing does not cancel out the equally Biblical truth that Israel has a future and that Christ's rule over David's throne must culminate in a political and earthly rule (as opposed to merely a spiritual rule through the church as under present conditions). Promises for an earthly Kingdom centered in Israel with Christ as King are not restricted to only Old Testament literature. The New Testament teaches the same. **Just as the Law Dispensation ended, so the Church Dispensation will give way to the millennial Kingdom.**

And Jesus said to them. "Truly I say to you, that **you who have followed Me,** in the regeneration when the Son of Man will sit on His glorious throne, you also **shall sit upon twelve thrones**, judging the twelve tribes of Israel" [Matt. 19:28].

"He will be great, and will be called the Son of the Most High; and the Lord God will give Him the **throne of His father David**; and He will reign over the house of Jacob forever; and **His kingdom will have no end**" [Luke 1:32-33].

For I do not want you, brethren, to be uninformed of this mystery, lest you be wise in your own estimation, that **a partial hardening has happened to Israel until the fullness of the Gentiles** has come in; and thus **all Israel** will be **saved**; just as it written, "The **Deliverer will come** from Zion, He will **remove ungodliness from Jacob**. And this is My covenant with them, when I take away their sins" [Rom. 11:25-27] .

And I saw thrones, and they sat upon them, and judgment was given to them. And I saw the souls of those who had been beheaded because of the testimony of Jesus and because of the word of God, and those who had not worshipped the beast or his image, and had not received the mark upon their forehead and upon their hand; and they came to life and **reigned with Christ for a thousand years**. The rest of the dead did not come to life until the thousand years were completed. This is the first resurrection. Blessed and holy is the one who had a part in the first resurrection; over these the second death has no power, but they will be priests of God and of Christ and will **reign with Him for a thousand years** [Rev. 20:4-6].

3. Logic and Additional Dispensations

The Scripture itself insists there has been a change in administration from **Law to Grace**, from **Judaism to the church**. Just as **clearly** it predicts **there will be a change** from **church to** a literal political **Kingdom** at Christ's return to earth. Therefore, there are at least three dispensations (administrations or management systems) clearly taught by the Bible: **Law, Church, Kingdom**.

It is not fair to assert there is as clear Scriptural evidence for additional dispensations, but logic suggests that we should add several dispensations in God's program with man during the earliest of times. It is reasonable to think that God's plan for mankind was different after the Fall than it was before; that it was different after the flood as opposed to before the flood; and that it was different again after the beginning of the nation of Israel, through Abraham, than before the existence of Israel.

Although it is perhaps not fair to insist that another believe in the typical dispensational view with its seven dispensations, such a view does have merit. Usually, dispensationalists list God's various administrations as follows:

Innocence - before the Fall (Gen. 1:28-3:6)

Conscience - after the Fall but before the Flood (Gen. 3:7-8:14)

Human Civil Government - after the Flood but before the promise to make a great nation from Abraham (Gen. 8:14-11:32)

Promise - after Abraham's call and the beginning of Israel but before the giving of the Law of Moses at Mt. Sinai (Gen. 11:32 - Exodus 18)

Law - The Law was in force from its revelation at Mt. Sinai until the Holy Spirit formed the church at Pentecost (Exodus 19 - Acts 2; some Scriptures in the gospels, however, give teachings about the then future church).

Grace or Church - God has been working His program on earth through the church since the time of Pentecost and will continue to do so until the church's removal at the Rapture (Acts 2 to Rapture).

Kingdom - Christ will rule on earth for 1,000 years. The millennial Kingdom will commence with His Second Coming.

4. The Church as a Mystery

a. Tracing Mysteries Revealed by New Testament Truths

The dispensational view can be proven by following the Bible's own transition from Law to the church and by noting its unconditional promise of a coming Kingdom. However, this is not the only line of reasoning that proves the validity of dispensational thinking.

In the New Testament, the word *mystery* does not refer to a truth that is so difficult that it is virtually impossible to understand. A *mystery* is a truth that had been secret or hidden. As one traces the uses of the word *mystery* through the New Testament, it becomes clear that the church was a brand new aspect to God's work in the world. Truths about the church were completely unknown to the Old Testament saints who lived under the Law of Moses. This establishes that a great distinction exists between Israel and the church. When God inaugurated the church, He was initiating a completely new administration in His divine government.

Many texts speak of the new truths being given to the apostles as being a mystery in general terms. They, in a general sense, were unknown under the Law (Rom. 16:25-26; 1 Cor. 2:7; 4:1; Eph. 1:9; 6:19; Col. 2:2; 4:3; 1 Tim. 3:9).

> Now to Him who is able to establish you according to my gospel and the preaching of Jesus Christ, according to the **revelation of the mystery** which has been kept **secret for long ages past**, but **now is manifested**, and by the Scriptures of the prophets, according to the commandment of the eternal God, has been **made known** to all the nations, leading to obedience of faith [Rom. 16:25-26].

More pertinent to the topic of dispensationalism are the verses that give the specific truths that were hidden mysteries to the Old Testament saints but were revealed in apostolic times. When the cumulative points from these verses are considered together, it creates the same view of God's program as espoused by "Dispensationalism." We study these in their logical, but not necessarily Scriptural, order.

The Jews expected a Messiah Who would curse their enemies and usher in a worldwide dominion of perfect righteousness, peace, and prosperity. When they rejected their King, He lectured to them on the "mysteries of the Kingdom of heaven" (Matt. 13:11ff.; Mark 4:11; Luke 8:10). **One of the mysteries** that was totally hidden to the Old Testament saints under the Law was that **there would be two comings of the Messiah with a period intervening in which good and evil would be mixed,** as in the parable of the wheat and tares and of the dragnet. Instead of bringing in an immediate earthly and political kingdom with perfect justice, the Messiah was going to allow a period in which a spiritual, but nonpolitical, aspect of the Kingdom on earth prevailed. Good and evil would be mixed until the end of the age when the Son of Man would return to sort out the bad from the good and begin His Kingdom in a more political manner (e.g., Matt. 13:39-43, 47-50). The doctrine of two advents with a time of good mixed with evil between was a brand new teaching that had been a mystery to the Old Testament saints. It is also expressed in 1 Tim. 3:16. The Messiah came, but He also ascended to await the establishment of a literal Kingdom on earth at another time.

> And by common confession great is the **mystery** of godliness: He who was **revealed in the flesh**, was vindicated in the Spirit, beheld by angels, proclaimed among the nations, believed on in the world, **taken up in glory** [1 Tim. 3:16].

Another mystery that had been unknown to the Old Testament saints is the truth that **Israel would be temporarily set aside and then restored at a later time** in God's program.

> For I do not want you, brethren, to be uninformed of this **mystery**, lest you be wise in your own estimation, that a **partial hardening has happened to Israel until the fullness of the Gentiles has come in**; and thus all Israel will be saved; just as it is written, "**The Deliverer will come** from Zion, **He will remove ungodliness from Jacob**. And this is My covenant with them, when I take away their sins." From the standpoint of the gospel they are enemies for your sake, but from the standpoint of God's choice they are beloved for the sake of the fathers; for the gifts and the calling of God are irrevocable [Rom. 11:25-29].

The Old Testament saints never dreamed there would be two Messianic advents with a time period in between them. They did not know God would cease working through Israel for a time. Additional references to the mystery show the **mystery that the church was a brand new revelation and that the church did not exist under the Law** (this is the essence of dispensationalism).

> [I]f indeed you have heard of the **stewardship of God's grace** which was given to me for you; that by **revelation** there was **made known** to me the **mystery**, as I wrote before in brief. And by referring to this, when you read you can understand my insight into the **mystery of Christ,** which in **other generations was not made known** to the sons of men, as it **has now been revealed** to His holy apostles and prophets in the Spirit; to be specific, **that the Gentiles are fellow heirs** and fellow members of the body, and fel-

low partakers of the promise in Christ Jesus through the gospel [Eph. 3:2-6].

God began a **brand new work** when He **instituted a body composed of both Jews and gentiles**. No longer did He work through Judaism, but all believers became one in Christ. Take note that the context calls this new union of believers "the *church*" (Eph. 3:10) and that Paul said this new revelation (*mystery*) brought to light a new administration that had been secret. The words for *stewardship* in Eph. 3:2 and *administration* in Eph. 3:9 mean *dispensation*. They are the same Greek word. (See chart, page 322.)

Another mystery that was unknown under the Law was that **God Himself would indwell** this group of believers comprised of both Jews and gentiles. Under the Law only a few believers were indwelt by the Holy Spirit (see "Pneumatology", pp. 234-35). Most Old Testament saints did not experience an actual union with God. Once again the church is shown to be a new work of God in great distinction from Israel under the Law. Note the word *stewardship* in Col. 1:25 means "dispensation."

> Of this church I was made a minister according to the **stewardship** (*dispensation*) from God bestowed on me for your benefit, that I might fully carry out the preaching of the Word of God, that is, **the mystery which has been hidden from the past ages** and generations; but has now been manifested to His saints, to whom God willed to make known what is the riches of the glory of **this mystery** among the Gentiles, which is **Christ in you,** the hope of glory [Col. 1:25-27].

> [B]ecause **we are members of his body.** For this cause a man shall leave his father and mother, and shall cleave to his wife; and the two shall become one flesh. This **mystery** is great; but I am speaking with reference to **Christ and the church** [Eph. 5:30-32].

Most people would interpret the mystery in 1 Cor. 15:51-52 to be the resurrection of the body.

> Behold, I tell you a **mystery; we shall not all sleep,** but **we shall all be changed,** in a moment, in the twinkling of an eye, at the last trumpet; for the trumpet will sound, and the dead will be raised imperishable, and we shall be changed [1 Cor. 15:51-52].

The problem with equating the resurrection with Paul's *mystery* is that the doctrine of bodily resurrection was not a secret under the Law (Job 19:25-27; Isa. 26:19; Ezek. 37:12; Dan.12:2). Thus, it is difficult to conclude that Paul would be calling the resurrection a mystery. A more careful reading of what is actually being said leads to the conclusion that the **new revelations** in this verse are that **not all believers would experience death** and that all, whether dead or alive, would experience an **instant transformation** at the trump of God. Students of the New Testament will immediately equate these ideas with 1 Thess. 4:13-18 and the doctrine of the Rapture. The **mystery**, unknown under the Law, was **that Christ would return to the clouds** (not yet all the way to the earth) **and would immediately transform all who have believed in Him**. Those who had died would be resurrected and glorified, but some would never die, and these would be instantly glorified without even experiencing death.

The **last "mystery"** that was revealed in apostolic times is the **mystery of lawlessness** in 2 Thess 2:7. It will help to give some of the context.

> Let no one in any way deceive you, for it will not come unless the apostasy comes first, and the man of lawlessness is revealed, the son of destruction, who opposes and exalts himself above every so called god or object of worship, so that he takes his seat in the temple of God, displaying himself as being God. Do you not remember that while I was

still with you, I was telling you these things? And you know what restrains him now, so that in his time he may be revealed. For the **mystery of lawlessness** is already at work; only he who now restrains will do so until he is taken out of the way. And then that lawless one will be revealed whom the Lord will slay with the breath of His mouth and bring to an end by the appearance of His coming; that is, the one whose coming is in accord with the activity of Satan, with all power and signs and false wonders, and with all the deception of wickedness for those who perish, because they did not receive the love of the truth so as to be saved [2 Thess. 2:3-10].

The "Man of Sin" in 2 Thessalonians 2 sits in the temple claiming to be God (v. 4). He ought to be equated with Christ's warning of the "abomination that makes desolate" (Matt. 24:15 etc.). The "Mystery of lawlessness" refers to Satan's program whereby he would like to control the world by the "Antichrist." However, there is at present (during the church administration) a restrainer who prevents the lawless one from coming to power until the time of God's plan for world history.

Some commentaries view government as being the restraint that hinders lawlessness. However, the personal pronoun "He" is used in v. 7. Furthermore, governments are not powerful enough to control Satan, nor do they always restrain lawlessness; at times they cause it. Others think that the church restrains lawlessness. This is a better guess. Yet, the church is also unable to oppose Satan, and it is also an unlikely candidate to qualify as an "He."

The best solution to the identity of the restrainer is that it is the Holy Spirit. God alone is powerful enough to restrain Satan's most ardent ambitions. Also, the Holy Spirit is a person and would qualify as "He" in v. 7; but the Greek word for "Spirit' is neuter, and this would explain the neuter reference to "what restrains" in v. 6.

Reasoning that the Holy Spirit is present in a special way in the church (by indwelling every believer and baptizing them into one body), it is difficult to think of the Holy Spirit's special presence being withdrawn while the church remains. 2 Thess. 2:6ff. yields the idea that the Holy Spirit will restrain the rise of the Antichrist until the church is removed (and with the church goes the witness and special presence of the Holy Spirit in the world). The church's removal at the Rapture will make possible the rise of the "Man of Sin," the Antichrist.

b. Conclusions about Mysteries Revealed in the New Testament

Anyone at all familiar with the dispensational school of thought will realize that **the "mysteries" of the New Testament give the dispensational system**. There will be a time period in between the first and second comings during which good and evil exist side by side (Matt. 13:11ff.; Mark 4:11; Luke 8:10; 1 Tim. 3:16). Israel will be set aside during this time, and God will work through a new administration called the church, which is composed of both Jews and gentiles united in Christ (Rom. 11:25-29; Eph. 3:2-6, 5:30-32; Col. 1:25-27). Eventually, this church will be raptured and all, both dead and living, will obtain a glorified body (1 Cor. 15:51-52). With the church's removal the Antichrist can arise (2 Thess. 2:3-10). Yet, this man of sin will ultimately be slain at the Lord's coming, when He will separate the good from the evil at the time of beginning a Kingdom on earth when God will again choose to work through Israel. It is impossible to deny that the "mysteries" of the New Testament prove that there are at least three administrations or dispensations: Law, Church, and Kingdom.

5. Evidence for a Change of Administrations

The gospels give plenty of indications that there would be a dramatic change in the way

God worked after Christ's departure from earth. The greatest changes occurred in the ministry of the Holy Spirit. (This is covered in Chapter 10, "Pneumatology, pp. 234ff.")

Christ promised the disciples that the Holy Spirit would come in a unique way after His ascension (John 16:7-13 etc.). Unlike the Law system, the **Holy Spirit** would **indwell all** believers and indwell them **permanently** beginning at the time of salvation (John 7:37-39; 14:16-17; Rom. 8:9; 1 Cor. 12:13, etc.). Also, the baptism of the Spirit which John the Baptist predicted (Matt. 3:11; Mark 1:8; Luke 3:16; John 1:33) occurred after the Lord's departure (Acts 1:5) to form the body of Christ (1 Cor. 12:13).

These changes in the ministry of the Holy Spirit prove that there was a great change between Law and the church and support the idea of dispensationalism. It should also be stressed that the **church was future** to Matt. 16:18 when Christ said; "I **will** build my church." Much of Christ's teaching was **preparatory for the change from Judaism to the church**.

Finally, the change in a day of worship from the Sabbath (Saturday) to Sunday also establishes that there has been a fundamental change in administrations from Law to church. (See section on local church, pp. 328-29.)

6. Is *Dispensation* a Biblical Term?

Dispensation is more of a Scriptural term than is *Trinity* or *rapture*. *Dispensation* is an old English word that the King James translators used to translate the Greek term *oikonomia* from which we derive our word *economy*. This is a compound term formed from *oikos* meaning "house" and *nomos* meaning "law" (as in Deuteronomy, "second law"). Thus, it refers to the law of the household or the system of rules by which a household is governed. We should think of a large rural estate with many sons, daughters, servants, and temporary hired help. There might also be accountants and merchants who buy for the household's needs and sell the estate's products. The system by which this large household's business operation was managed, or administered, was called an "economy." Modern translators have dropped the archaic term *dispensation* and used other translations as the following chart reveals:

REFERENCE	NASB	NIV
Luke 16:2	Management	Management
Luke 16:3	Management	My Job (as manager)
Luke 16:4	Management	My Job (as manager)
1 Cor. 9:17	Stewardship	The trust
Eph. 1:10	Administration	(Not translated)
Eph. 3:2	Stewardship	Administration
Eph. 3:9	Administration	Administration
Col. 1:25	Stewardship	Commission
1 Tim. 1:4	Administration	God's Work

The KJV used *dispensation* to translate "economy" four times. *Dispensationalism* takes its name from this older word. However, several contemporary synonyms include the same concept.

"Economy" is a system of trade. The United States is a capitalistic dispensation; the Soviet Union was a communist dispensation. An "administration" is a system of management that gives direction to a government. Washington, Jefferson, Lincoln, Roosevelt, et al, have served in various political dispensations or administrations of the government. A stewardship is a trust or commission to manage property or assets. Joseph had a dispensation to manage Potiphar's household. At its basic form a dispensation involves a system of management, rules for a system's organization. Thus, a "dispensation" is a system of management, an administration, a stewardship, trust, or commission whereby God gives man certain tasks to fulfill. Dispensationalism simply means God has imposed different systems as to how He wants His household of faith to live and work. These various administrations do not involve differing ways of salvation, for salvation has always been by faith alone (Gen.

15:6; Hab. 2:4). The dispensations vary responsibilities and tasks that God wants His people to do in order to fulfill His will and His plan for working in the world.

Of the nine occurrences of *dispensation* in the Bible, Ephesians 3 and Colossians 1 are the strongest relative to supporting that the church is a new administration in great contrast to the old administration of Law. Because the King James Version uses the word *dispensation*, it will be quoted in support of the theological system bearing its name.

> For this cause I Paul, the prisoner of Jesus Christ for you Gentiles, if ye have heard of the **dispensation of the grace of God** which is given me to you-ward: how that by **revelation he made known** unto me the **mystery**; (as I wrote afore in few words, Whereby, when ye read, ye may understand my knowledge in the **mystery of Christ) which in other ages was not made known** unto the sons of men, as it is now revealed unto His holy apostles and prophets by the Spirit; that the **Gentiles** should be fellowheirs, and of **the same body**, and partakers of his

promise in Christ by the gospel: whereof I was made a minister, according to the gift of the grace of God given unto me by the effectual working of his power. Unto me, who am less than the least of all saints, is this grace given, that I should preach among the Gentiles the unsearchable riches of Christ; and to **make all men see** what is the fellowship (**dispensation**) of the mystery, which **from the beginning of the world hath been hid in God**, who created all things by Jesus Christ: to the intent **that now** unto the principalities and powers in heavenly places **might be known by the church** the manifold wisdom of God, according to the eternal purpose which he purposed in Christ Jesus our Lord: In whom we have boldness and access with confidence by the faith of him [Eph. 3:1-12 KJV].

Who now rejoice in my sufferings for you, and fill up that which is behind of the afflictions of Christ in my flesh for his body's sake, which is **the church**: Whereof I am made a minister, **according to the dispensation of God** which is given to me for you, to fulfill the word of God; even the **mystery which hath been hid from ages** and from generations, but now is made manifest to his saints: to whom God would make known what is the riches of the glory of this **mystery among the Gentiles**; which is **Christ in you**, the hope of glory [Col. 1:24-27 KJV].

In both passages Paul says that he was given the revelation of a new administration or dispensation, the church. This new dispensation was "hidden" and "unknown" to the Old Testament saints, but had been recently revealed to the apostles and the New Testament prophets. Unlike the prevailing condition under the Law administration, the church is composed of Jew and gentile united into one body, the church. Another difference between these dis-

pensations, or administrations, was the union of all believers with the indwelling Christ. Note carefully that Eph. 3:9 teaches that God gave Paul the task of helping all men to understand this new dispensation. It is amazing that some segments of the professing church are so ignorant of the Scriptures as to classify dispensationalism as a strange cult!

7. Various Dispensational Details

One of the major misunderstandings about dispensationalism is that some think it teaches different ways of salvation. This is simply not true. Old Testament saints were saved by faith (Gen. 15:6; Hab. 2:4; Rom. 4:6). Old Testament saints were well aware of the fact that sacrifices alone could not save. It was the faith expressed by the offering of a sacrifice that saved. (See 1 Sam. 15:22; Psa. 40:6; 51:16; Prov. 15:8; 21:27; Isa. 1:11ff.; Hosea 6:3-6; Micah 6:6ff.; Heb. 9:12; 10:3.)

Dispensations may represent different systems for doing God's work, different modes of operation for fulfilling His will, different responsibilities and requirements for managing God's household of faith as it labors in the world, but **dispensationalism does not teach different ways of salvation.**

Just as the United States has had only one government under the Constitution but has been managed by more than forty administrations, so too God has only one divine government; but He has structured various administrations by which to manage it. God's attributes do not change. The way of salvation does not change. Yet, God can and has varied His governing relationship with His people by altering His works through them. Although dispensations involve time, time is only a secondary matter. A dispensation is a distinct system by which God ordains that His household of faith operates. Just as it is better to refer to a communist system or capitalistic system as opposed to communistic or capitalistic times, so it is more precise to refer to the Law system or church system and not the Law age or the church age.

Just as regulations from previous presidential administrations are still in force unless they have been specifically rescinded, so too, regulations from previous administrations should be considered binding under the church dispensation unless they have been rescinded.

Thus, we are no longer obligated to offer blood sacrifices. However, the dispensation of human government has never been rescinded by later Scriptures. Thus, such truths as capital punishment (Gen. 9:6) are still very much in force. Again time is only a secondary factor in dispensations. Systems of management or administrations are the main idea. It is better to think of the regulations from the previous dispensations as cumulative (unless rescinded) as shown by **Charts A** and **B**, below.

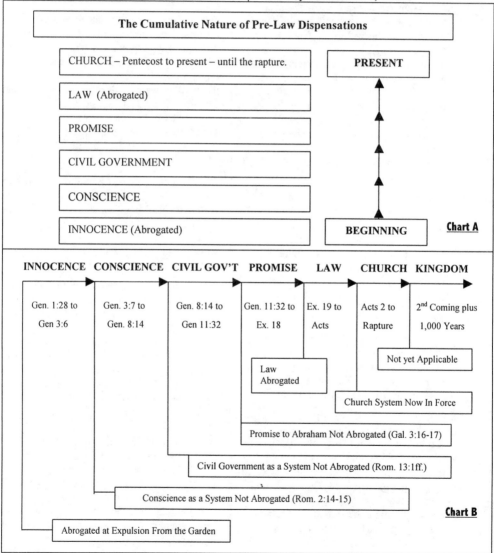

The Cumulative Nature of Pre-Law Dispensations

CHURCH – Pentecost to present – until the rapture.

LAW (Abrogated)

PROMISE

CIVIL GOVERNMENT

CONSCIENCE

INNOCENCE (Abrogated)

PRESENT

BEGINNING

Chart A

INNOCENCE	CONSCIENCE	CIVIL GOV'T	PROMISE	LAW	CHURCH	KINGDOM
Gen. 1:28 to Gen 3:6	Gen. 3:7 to Gen. 8:14	Gen. 8:14 to Gen 11:32	Gen. 11:32 to Ex. 18	Ex. 19 to Acts	Acts 2 to Rapture	2nd Coming plus 1,000 Years

Not yet Applicable

Law Abrogated

Church System Now In Force

Promise to Abraham Not Abrogated (Gal. 3:16-17)

Civil Government as a System Not Abrogated (Rom. 13:1ff.)

Conscience as a System Not Abrogated (Rom. 2:14-15)

Abrogated at Expulsion From the Garden

Chart B

8. Conclusion

The church is a unique system of administration in God's government. Bible students who fail to understand the great difference between Law and Grace and the future millennial Kingdom will never understand the details of the Bible. Without dispensationalism, large segments of Scripture will at best remain hidden or obscured. At worst they will be used to develop false ideas.

V. The Local Church

A local church is a gathering of people who are professed believers in Jesus Christ. Like the universal church, it is a "called out group." Yet, unlike the universal church, a local church may contain people who have not actually trusted in Christ. Thus, one can be a member of a local church but not the universal church. Also, the universal church involves believers who have died and are with Christ. Thus, all the local churches combined do not contain all the members of the true church, many of whom are in heaven. One can be a member of the universal church but not a participant in any local church.

A. The Purpose for the Local Church

The overall purpose for the local church is the same as the universal church. The church exists to glorify (i.e., honor, praise, worship, reverence, give homage to) God.

> "Teacher, which is the great commandment in the Law?" And He said to him: "You shall **love the Lord your God** with all your heart, and with all your soul, and with all your mind. This is the **great and foremost commandment**" [Matt. 22:36-38].

> Now may the God who gives perseverance and encouragement grant you to be of the same mind with one another according to Christ Jesus; that with one accord you may with one voice **glorify the God** and Father of our Lord Jesus Christ [Rom. 15:5-6].

> For I say that Christ has become a servant to the circumcision (Israel) on behalf of the truth of God to confirm the promises given to the fathers, and for the Gentiles **to glorify God** for His mercy; as it is written, "Therefore I will give praise to Thee among the Gentiles, and I will sing to Thy name" [Rom. 15:8-9].

> He predestined us to adoption as sons through Jesus Christ to Himself, according to the kind intention of His will, **to the praise of the glory of His grace**, which He freely bestowed on us in the Beloved [Eph. 1:5-6].

> [T]o the end that we [Jews] who were the first to hope in Christ should be to the **praise of His glory**. In Him, you [Gentiles] also, after listening to the message of truth, the gospel of your salvation— having also believed, you were sealed in Him with the Holy Spirit of promise, who is given as a pledge of our inheritance, with a view to the redemption of God's own possession, to the **praise of His glory** [Eph. 1:12-14].

> [A]nd to bring to light what is the administration of the mystery which for ages has been hidden in God, who created all things; in order that the **manifold wisdom of God** might now be **made known through the church** to the rulers and the authorities in the heavenly places....to **Him be the glory in the church** and in Christ Jesus to all generations forever and ever. Amen [Eph. 3:9-10, 21].

> He is also **head of** the body, **the church**; and He is the beginning, the firstborn from the dead; so that **He Himself** might come to have **first place** in everything [Col. 1:18].

[I]n order that the name of our **Lord Jesus may be glorified** in you, and you in Him, according to the grace of our God and the Lord Jesus Christ [2 Thess. 1:12].

But you are a chosen race, a royal priesthood, a holy nation, a people for God's own possession, that you may **proclaim the excellencies of Him** who has called you out of darkness into His marvelous light [1 Pet. 2:9].

Whoever speaks, let him speak as it were, the utterances of God; whoever serves, let him do so as by the strength which God supplies; **so that in all things God may be glorified** through Jesus Christ, to whom belongs the glory and dominion forever and ever. Amen [1 Pet. 4:11].

"Worthy art Thou, our Lord and our God, **to receive glory and honor and power**; for Thou didst create all things, and because of Thy will they existed, and were created [Rev. 4:11].

This general purpose of honoring God occurs through several important church functions. While the format may change from culture to culture and generation to generation, fundamental doctrine and these essential church functions may not change. They are not listed in any order of importance. All are important, and they need to be implemented with **balance** to fulfill God's intention for a local church.

1. Teaching/Doctrine

Sometimes Christians forget that teaching is a major component of the great commission. "**Teaching** them to observe all that I commanded you" (Matt. 28:20). Many texts support the statement that a non-teaching church is not in compliance with the Bible. Teaching should be construed to involve not just theology but also ethics and Christian ser-

vice. The church as a pillar of truth (1 Tim. 3:15) must teach the Word of God. (See also Eph. 4:11-12.)

And they were **continually devoting themselves to the apostles' teaching** and to fellowship, to the breaking of bread and to prayer [Acts 2:42].

So also you, since you are zealous of spiritual gifts, seek to abound for the **edification of the church** [1 Cor. 14:12].

...Let all things be done for **edification** [1 Cor. 14:26].

[H]aving been firmly rooted and now being built up in Him and established in your faith, just as you were **instructed**, and overflowing with gratitude [Col. 2:7].

Until I come, **give attention** to the **public reading** of Scripture, to exhortation and **teaching** [1 Tim. 4:13].

And the things you have heard from me in the presence of many witnesses, these entrust to faithful men, who will be able to **teach** others also [2 Tim. 2:2].

All Scripture is inspired by God, and profitable for **teaching,** for reproof, for correction, for training in righteousness; **that the man of God may be adequate, equipped for every good work** [2 Tim. 3:16-17].

[P]**reach the word;** be ready in season and out of season; reprove, rebuke, exhort, with great patience and **instruction** [2 Tim. 4:2].

2. Observance of the Ordinances

A local church is supposed to carry out the great commission by baptizing new believers and is supposed to create a reminder of Christ's sacrificial love by observing the Lord's Supper. Both baptism and communion are addressed in detail at a later point (see pp. 340-352).

"Go therefore and make disciples of all the nations, **baptizing** them in the name of the Father and the Son and the Holy Spirit" [Matt. 28:19].

And they were continually **devoting themselves** to the apostles' teaching and to fellowship, to the **breaking of bread** and to prayer [Acts 2:42].

For I received from the Lord that which I also delivered to you, that the Lord Jesus in the night in which He was betrayed took bread; and when He had given thanks, He broke it, and said, "This is my body, which is for you; do this in remembrance of Me." In the same way He took the cup also, after supper, saying, "This cup is the new covenant in My blood; do this, as often as you drink it, in remembrance of Me." For as often as you eat this bread and drink the cup, you proclaim the Lord's death until He comes [1 Cor. 11:23-26].

3. Prayer

Prayer is one of the primary functions of a local church. It may not be relegated beneath teaching, evangelism, worship or any other facet of church life. Although the doctrine of prayer is relevant to individuals, it is also a practice that ought to be observed corporately. Prayer helps forge unity among believers. It is foundational for evangelism. Most important is the truth that prayer pleases God and tends to bring about His favor and blessings. No church dare minimize the role of prayer as a necessary ingredient to a healthy church. Notice that the apostles viewed prayer and the ministry of the Word as priorities (Acts 6:4).

Now He was telling them a parable to show that **at all times they ought to pray** and not to lose heart [Luke 18:1].

And they were continually **devoting themselves** to the apostles' teaching and to fellowship, to the breaking of bread and to **prayer** [Acts 2:42].

So Peter was kept in the prison, but **prayer** for him was being made **fervently by the church** to God [Acts 12:5].

With all prayer and petition **pray at all times** in the Spirit, and with this in view, be on the alert with all perseverance and petition for all the saints [Eph. 6:18].

[P]ray without ceasing [1 Thess. 5:17].

First of all, then, I urge that **entreaties and prayers, petitions and thanksgivings**, be made on behalf of all men, for kings and all who are in authority, in order that we many lead a tranquil and quiet life in all godliness and dignity [1 Tim. 2:1-2].

Is anyone among you sick? Let him call for the elders of **the church**, and **let them pray** over him, anointing him with oil in the name of the Lord; and the prayer offered in faith will restore the one who is sick, and the Lord will raise him up, and if he has committed sins, they will be forgiven him [James 5:14-15].

4. Evangelism (Includes Missionary Outreach)

While it is true that the Great Commission was addressed to the apostles, the Lord clearly envisioned that it would be a work carried on through those who believed the apostolic message "even unto the end of the age." Thus, it is still God's will for the church to be involved in proclaiming the gospel of salvation by faith in Christ. Individuals witness, but, in another sense, the whole church can be a witness to God's saving grace. In addition to proclaiming God's glory in its own locality, a church should be separating and sending missionaries to other regions.

"Go therefore and **make disciples of all the nations**, baptizing them in the name of the Father and the Son and the Holy Spirit, teaching them to observe all that I commanded you; and lo, I am with you always, even to the end of the age" [Matt. 28:19-20].

[A]nd He said to them, "Thus it is written, that the Christ should suffer and rise again from the dead the third day; and that repentance for forgiveness of sins should be proclaimed in His name to **all the nations**, beginning from Jerusalem" [Luke 24:46-47].

So **the church** throughout all Judea and Galilee and Samaria enjoyed peace, **being built up**; and going on in the fear of the Lord and in the comfort of the Holy Spirit, it **continued to increase** [Acts 9:31].

And while they were ministering to the Lord and fasting, the Holy Spirit said, "**Set apart for Me** Barnabas and Saul for the work to which I have called them." Then, when they had fasted and prayed and laid their hands on them, **they sent them away** [Acts 13:2-3].

So the **churches** were being strengthened in the faith: and were **increasing in number** daily [Acts 16:5].

How then shall they call upon Him in whom they have not believed? And **how shall they believe in Him whom they have not heard**? And how shall they hear without a preacher? And how shall they preach unless they are sent? Just as it is written, "How beautiful are the feet of those who bring glad tidings of good things!" [Rom. 10:14-15].

(See also John 4:35ff.; Matt. 9:37-38).

For the word of the Lord has sounded forth from you not only in Macedonia and Achaia, but also **in every place your faith toward God has gone forth** [1 Thess. 1:8].

But you are a chosen race, a royal priesthood, a holy nation, a people for God's own possession, that you may **proclaim** the excellencies of Him who has called you out of darkness into His marvelous light [1 Pet. 2:9].

5. Worship

The commandment to "remember the Sabbath" (Ex. 20:8) is the only one of the ten commandants not repeated for the church. There is a command to assemble (e.g., Heb. 10:25), but there is no prescribed day of worship for the church (Rom. 14:5-6; Col. 2:16). However, by tradition the early churches assembled on the first day of the week, Sunday, in order to commemorate the Lord's resurrection on the first day of the week (John 20:1). His two appearances to the disciples in the upper room on the first day of the week (John 20:19, 26), and Pentecost, the birthday of the church, also occurred on a Sunday. By tradition the church has assembled to worship on Sunday from the New Testament times (see Acts 20:7; 1 Cor. 16:2) until the present time.

And on the **first day of the week**, when we were gathered together to break bread, Paul began talking to them, intending to depart the next day, and he prolonged his message until midnight [Acts 20:7].

On the **first day of every week** let each one of you put aside and save, as he may prosper, that no collections be made when I come [1 Cor. 16:2].

Modern believers from Bible-teaching churches would have felt comfortable in early church gatherings. There was Bible teaching (Acts 2:42; 1 Cor. 14:19, 26; 1 Tim. 4:13; 2 Tim. 4:2), singing (1 Cor. 14:26; Eph. 5:19; Col. 3:16), collections (Rom. 15:26; 1 Cor. 16:2; 2 Corinthians 8 and 9), prayer (Acts 2:42), fellowship including love-feasts (Heb. 10:24-25; Jude 12) and communion (Acts 20:7). Services were conducted in homes (1 Cor. 16:19; Col. 4:15, etc.) and were conducted in orderliness without confusion (1 Cor. 14:32, 40). 1 Cor. 14:26 comes the closest to giving an order of service.

> What is the outcome then brethren? When you assemble, each one has a psalm, has a teaching, has a revelation, has a tongue (languages), has an interpretation. Let all things be done for edification [1 Cor. 14:26].

Justin Martyr lived A.D. 100-167, in Israel. His account of the early worship services shows how little things have changed:

"And on the day called Sunday, all who live in cities or in the country, gather together to one place, and the memoirs of the apostles or the writings of the prophets are read, as long as time permits; then, when the reader has ceased, the president verbally instructs, and exhorts to the imitation of these good things. Then we all rise together and pray, and, as we before said, when our prayer is ended, bread and wine and water are brought, and the president in like manner offers prayers according to his ability, and the people assent saying Amen....And they who are well to do, and willing, give what each thinks fit; and what is collected is deposited with the president, who succours the orphans and widows, and those who, through sickness or any other cause, are in want, and those who are in bonds and the strangers sojourning, among us, and in a word takes care of all who are in need." [1]

6. Benevolence

A church has an obligation to provide for those honestly poor. Assistance is not exclusively for believers but is especially for them:

> ...while we have opportunity, let us do good to all men, and especially to those who are of the household of the faith [Gal. 6:10].

The New Testament presents many examples of Christians helping the brethren. It also gives commands for Christians to help other Christians in need (Acts 2:44-45; 4:32-38; 11:28-30; Gal. 2:10; 1 John 3:17-18; James 1:27; 2:15-16). The early church was particularly involved in a formal ministry to widows (Acts 6:1-6; 1 Tim. 5:3-16). This seems to have been a system of permanent support as opposed to temporary assistance that could be given to anyone. There were strict guidelines that had to be met in order to qualify for any support, especially for widows who wanted help of an ongoing nature (2 Thess. 3:10; 1 Tim. 5:4, 9-11).

B. Government for the Local Church

There are three common structures for church government: episcopal, presbyterian, and congregational.

1. Episcopal

The episcopal form of government is followed by the Roman Catholic, Anglican, Episcopalian, and Methodist churches. It is one in which there is a hierarchy of authority with power at the top. The Roman Catholic system begins with the pope, then there are cardinals, archbishops, bishops, priests, deacons, and lay people.

One could read the Bible forever without finding the precise church government that is employed by those groups with the episcopal

---

[1] Justin Martyr, *The First Apology of Justin*, in *The Anti-Nicene Fathers*, ed. Alexander Roberts and James Donaldson, reprinted., 10 vols. (Grand Rapids: Wm. B. Eerdman Publishing Co., 1969, 1:186. *(First Apology of Justin 67)*.

method. Yet, episcopal government does pattern the Biblical example of power from the top down. There can be no question that the apostles had complete authority over the early church.

> "And I also say to you that you are **Peter, and upon this rock I will build My church**; and the gates of Hades shall not overpower it" [Matt. 16:18].

> If anyone thinks he is a prophet or spiritual, let him recognize that **the things which I write to you are the Lord's commandment** [1 Cor. 14:37].

> [H]aving been built upon the **foundation of the apostles** and prophets, Christ Jesus Himself being the corner stone [Eph. 2:20].

> [T]hat you should remember the words spoken beforehand by the holy prophets and the **commandment of the Lord and Savior spoken by your apostles** [2 Pet. 3:2].

> But you, beloved, ought to remember the words that were spoken beforehand by the **apostles** of our Lord Jesus Christ [Jude 17].

In Acts 15 the church wrestles over the issue of gentile circumcision. At this conference, authority rested with the apostles and elders (see Acts 15:2, 6), not so much the whole congregation. Also, in Titus 1 and 1 Timothy 3 the Apostle Paul is the one who grants authority to select elders for every church. Thus, the early church did have an authority structure that was hierarchical and in which power came from the top down: apostles, elders, deacons, congregation.

It is impossible to return completely to the early church's system of government. Since no one alive has seen the risen Lord, there are no apostles (Acts 1:21-22; 1 Cor. 9:1). In the absence of apostolic authority, it would seem that the next closest system to the New

Testament pattern would be elder rule with each church possessing autonomy.

2. Presbyterian

Presbyterian church government can be found in churches of the Presbyterian and Reformed tradition, as well as, in some Bible churches.

The highest authority in the early church was apostolic. However, elders were grouped along with apostles (see Acts 15:2, 6). Many verses teach obedience to church leaders. This fits well with the conclusion that *presbyterian* (from the Greek word for "elder," *presbuteros*) government is the closest to the Scriptural example after the passing of the apostles.

Another support for the concept of elder rule is that of "implied powers." An assigned task implies the power to do that task. It is most reasonable to assume that if God gives a responsibility, He also gives the authority to fulfill that responsibility. The Bible gives elders the responsibility to lead and protect the church. We may safely assume He also gives them the authority that they need to carry out their tasks.

> "Be on guard for yourselves and for all the flock, among which the Holy Spirit has made you **overseers,** to shepherd the church of God which He purchased with His own blood" [Acts 20:28].

> But we request of you, brethren, that you appreciate those who diligently labor among you, and **have charge over you** in the Lord and give you instruction [1 Thess. 5:12].

> [B]ut if a man does not know how to **manage** his own household, how will he **take care of the church of God?** [1 Tim. 3:5].

> Let the **elders who rule** well be considered worthy of double honor, es-

pecially those who work hard at preaching and teaching [1 Tim. 5:17].

Obey your leaders, and **submit** to them; for they keep watch over your souls, as those who will give an account. Let them do this with joy and not with grief, for this would be unprofitable for you [Heb. 13:17].

Therefore, I exhort the elders among you, as your fellow elder and witness of the sufferings of Christ, and a partaker also of the glory that is to be revealed, **shepherd the flock** of God among you, **exercising oversight** not under compulsion, but voluntarily, according to the will of God, and not for sordid gain, but with eagerness [1 Pet. 5:1-2].

It is best to view the leadership style in the early church (minus the apostles as a factor) similar to a board that might administer a modern seminary or mission. Existing elders chose new leaders as a self-perpetuating body.

Do not neglect the spiritual gift within you, which was bestowed upon you through prophetic utterance with the laying on of hands by the **presbytery** [1 Tim. 4:14].

Elders also rebuked and/or removed colleagues who disqualified themselves from church leadership.

Do not receive an accusation against an elder except on the basis of **two or three witnesses. Those who continue in sin, rebuke** in the presence of all, so that the rest also may be fearful of sinning [1 Tim. 5:19-20].

There is room for congregational participation in the selection of leaders and major decisions of the church, as elders are commanded not to "lord it over" the church (1 Peter 5:3). Still, authority in the New Testa-

ment church was from the top down. The result of the cessation of apostolic authority would probably be elder rule.

3. Congregational

Congregational government could be expected to be popular in a democracy. Early American churches in New England were congregational, and this has been carried on to this day in many groups, particularly Baptists and many Bible churches.

No one wishes to classify full congregational government as doctrinal heresy, but, of the three forms of church government, it is the least like the New Testament church. Can we seriously assert, for example, that the Corinthian congregation could take a vote and overrule Paul's authority? Furthermore, congregational rule is very impractical. Even if all church members were highly spiritual (which is seldom the case), it is difficult for a large group to be well enough informed to make intelligent decisions. This is especially the case when a matter is sensitive and would be better handled as privately as possible. Church discipline by a congregational vote is almost inevitably a disaster.

Biblical examples that are used to support congregational rule do not, in reality, give examples of complete congregational power. Some argue that Acts 6:1-6 gives precedent for congregational control. The apostles made this offer to the church in Jerusalem; "...select from among you, brethren, seven men of good reputation, full of the Spirit and of wisdom, whom we may put in charge of this task." A close examination of this incident shows that the apostles retained ultimate power. First, they gave their permission to the church to make selections, but they would have done nothing wrong in making the selections without congregational help. Also, the apostles were ultimately the authority that installed these men into office. They could have vetoed the congregational selections. Thus, while the apostles did permit congregational involvement, (a wise precedent), they still retained ultimate authority. Even though the Acts 6:1-6 passage contains congregational involvement, it is actually another example of the apostles having ultimate authority in the early church.

Other examples of supposed congregational government are also unconvincing. The apostles had ultimate power in the early church and, after them, the elders. The presbyterian system would be the closest to the Biblical pattern once the apostles were removed.

4. Conclusions on Church Government

Any form of church government is going to be a complete fiasco if power resides with unspiritual people. Certainly, congregational rule by spiritual people is superior to presbyterian rule by wicked elders. Yet, power in the New Testament church was from the top down, not from the people to the leaders. As long as elders meet the qualifications in 1 Timothy 3 and Titus 1, their authority comes from God, and not from the people. This pattern is the Biblical example in both Old and New Testaments.

C. Officers for the Church

The Scripture definitely mentions two church officers, elders and deacons, with a third, deaconess, that is less certain.

1. Equivalence of Elder, Pastor, Bishop

The Greek text yields three words for the spiritual leader of a local church: *episkopos,* from which we derive *episcopal,* means "overseer"; *epi* means "upon", as in *epidermis* (outer skin); and *skopos* refers to seeing (e.g., microscope, telescope, etc.). The King James Version translates *episkopos* "bishop." The spiritual leaders of a church are also called *poimeen,* which means "shepherd" and would be translated into English as *pastor.* A third word is *presbuteros,* from which we derive the word *presbyterian.* This means elder. It is easy to show that the New

Testament uses the terms *bishop, pastor,* and *elder* quite interchangeably. It does not view these three as different offices or ranks of authority.

> ...and appoint **elders** [the singular is *presbuteros*] in every city as I directed you, namely, if any man be above reproach, the husband of one wife, having children who believe, not accused of dissipation or rebellion. For the **overseer** [*episkopos*] must be above reproach as God's steward...[Titus 1:5-7, cf. 1 Tim. 3:1ff.].

> And from Miletus he sent to Ephesus and called to him the **elders** [*presbuteros*] of the church...."Be on guard for yourselves and for all the flock, among which the Holy Spirit has made you **overseers**, [*episkopoi*] to **shepherd** [pastor] the church of God which He purchased with His own blood" [Acts 20:17 and 28].

> To the **elders** [*presbuteros*] among you, I appeal as a fellow elder, a witness of Christ's sufferings and one who also will share in the glory to be revealed: Be **shepherds** [pastors] of God's flock that is under your care, serving as **overseers**...[*episkopos*] [1 Pet. 5:1-2 NIV)].

Scripturally, there is no difference between the terms *pastor, elder, overseer* and *bishop.* It is important to add that contemporary church governments often give the responsibilities of an elder to men without calling them elders. Likewise, churches may call a position "elder" when it bears little resemblance to the New Testament function of an elder. It would be best to call a position "elder" when the qualifications and responsibilities model those of 1 Timothy 3 and Titus 1.

2. Qualifications for Elders

The New Testament gives qualifications for elders. There is more involved than being a male member of the church over the age of 18.

> It is a trustworthy statement: if any man aspires to the office of overseer, it is a fine work he desires to do. An overseer, then, must be above reproach, the husband of one wife, temperate, prudent, respectable, hospitable, able to teach, not addicted to wine or pugnacious, but gentle, uncontentious, free from the love of money. He must be one who manages his own household well, keeping his children under control with all dignity (but if a man does not know how to manage his own household, how will he take care of the church of God?); and not a new convert, lest he become conceited and fall into the condemnation incurred by the devil. And he must have a good reputation with those outside the church so that he may not fall into reproach and the snare of the devil [1 Tim. 3:1-7].

> For this reason I left you in Crete, that you might set in order what remains, and appoint elders in every city as I directed you, namely, if any man be above reproach, the husband of one wife, having children who believe, not accused of dissipation or rebellion. For the overseer must be above reproach as God's steward, not self-willed, not quick-tempered, not addicted to wine, not pugnacious, not fond of sordid gain, but hospitable, loving what is good, sensible, just, devout, self-controlled, holding fast the faithful word which is in accordance with the teaching, that he may be able both to exhort in sound doctrine and to refute those who contradict [Titus 1:5-9].

a. General Qualifications

"Above reproach" - An elder should be without serious moral blemishes that would impair the reputation of the church. This does not mean a man must be perfect or sinless, but no one should be able to come forward with a serious accusation that can be proven true to the damage of the church.

b. Moral Qualifications

"The husband of one wife" - It is best if Christians allow tolerance for diversity of views but in general conclude that there must be high moral values at the time a man is a candidate for elder. The literal phrase in the Greek is "one woman man." Some would stress quantity and argue that an elder must not have been divorced and/or remarried. Others stress quality. This means an elder must have a "one woman philosophy" and behavior. By this view a man would be disqualified if he does not love his wife even if he has never been divorced. Also, one divorced in the past may subsequently become a "one-woman man". The author considers the phrase, "one-woman-man", qualitative.

c. Mental Qualifications

"Temperate, prudent, respectable, able to teach"

"Temperate" - An elder must have clear, objective, vigilant, conservative judgment when it comes to decision making or determining the truth. He will not allow his judgment to be clouded by emotionalism, his personal interest, popularity, or worldly views and fads. We might say an elder must be "level headed" and vigilant for the truth of the Word (cautious, conservative, incapable of being influenced by winds of doctrine or fads).

"Prudent" (NIV *self-controlled*, KJV *sober minded*) - This word has a range of meanings. The basic word means "sound mind." This leads to a translation like "prudent." However, one becomes wise and prudent through discipline and "self control." We might say a pastor/elder must be serious and disciplined about his life and work. He is a serious thinker about Christ's work; his goal is not just to have a "good time." He is not a "clown" as he approaches church work, but rather he has a serious, sensible, rational mindset that pursues wisdom.

"Respectable" - The original word is related to our word for "cosmetic." This does relate to a "respectable" demeanor. However, the word also gives the idea of order, as the "cosmos" is an organized system. An elder should have an organized, methodical approach to ministry. He is not only "respectable" in appearance, but he can organize time and can administer the ministry. He meets deadlines, keeps appointments, and prefers order to chaos.

"Able to teach" - This qualification does not demand that every elder's main function be public speaking. According to 1 Tim. 5:17, there are both teaching elders and administrative elders. Yet, even administrative elders must be able to teach at least to a degree of competence that enables them to defend and explain the church's doctrine. Also, every elder must be skillful in handling the Word of God in both informal settings and conversations even if he is not a polished speaker. In short, men who do not thoroughly know the Scriptures should not be elders.

d. Personality Qualifications

"Hospitable, not addicted to wine, not pugnacious, gentle, uncontentious, free from the love of money"

"Hospitable" - The Greek word means "love of strangers." Those in the early church had occasion to shelter Christian refugees from persecution. They did special good to Christians but also displayed kindness to unbelievers (Gal. 6:10). We may apply this to our times by saying elders should be quick to extend hospitality to traveling Christian workers or to the deserving poor, and they should be interested in welcoming newcomers and visitors to church.

"Not given to wine" - This qualification may not demand abstinence, but it does demand strict sobriety. An elder should understand Christian liberty and be willing to restrict his liberties when it will help immature believers (see Rom. 14:21).

"Not pugnacious" - A loose paraphrase might be "not a bully." The word denotes a quick-tempered individual who strikes with his fists when annoyed.

"Gentle" - Although an elder must not be one who compromises essential doctrine or ethics, he should have a tendency to yield rather than to cause divisions over minor issues. Relative to annoyances, criticism, and insults, an elder should be patient and forbearing. He tries to avoid unnecessary contention.

"Uncontentious" - This means a "noncombatant." Such a person will not insist on having his own way or being overly aggressive in promoting personal ideas and goals. An elder should not be "pig-headed."

"Free from the love of money" - If a man gives evidence of dishonesty, he ought not to be tempted by handling church funds. Also, teaching elders must not be mercenary, those who serve only for money without real love for either Christ or His people.

e. Domestic Qualifications

"Manages household well, children in subjection" - An acceptable level of behavior for children is a subjective matter. However, Titus 1:6 makes it clear that an elder must have Christian children. Also, those children at home must not be the kind who flaunt rebellion against their parents or against God.

f. Christian Experience Qualification

"Not a new convert" - New believers may not qualify for the office of elder. Maturity

334

takes time. Also, a man's commitment must be tested with time. A premature elevation to authority can lead to vanity.

g. Reputation Qualification

"A good report with those outside" - If a particular man's past reputation would subject the church to mockery or slander, someone else should be selected.

3. Number of Elders

The Bible gives a uniform precedent for a plurality of elders. This does not mean quality must be sacrificed for quantity. Under some Baptist systems, the pastor is regarded as the only elder. For churches where only one man qualifies (1 Timothy 3; Titus 1), only one man should be considered an elder. However, the Biblical example of a plurality of elders is an ideal and should be followed when a church does possess a sufficient number of men who meet the qualifications (see Acts 14:23; 15:2, 6, 22; 20:17, 28; Phil. 1:1; 1 Thess. 5:12; 1 Tim. 5:17; Titus 1:5; James 5:14).

> And when they had appointed **elders** for them in every church...[Acts 14:23].

> Paul and Timothy, bond-servants of Christ Jesus, to all the saints in Christ Jesus who are in Philippi, including the **overseers** and deacons [Phil. 1:1].

> Is anyone among you sick? Let him call for the **elders** of the church...[James 5:14].

4. Distinctions Among Elders

1 Tim. 5:17 distinguishes between ruling elders and teaching elders. Ruling elders must be "apt to teach." Teaching elders must still participate in shepherding and oversight. Elders have the same authority but differ in gifts, as do all Christians. Although each elder should have equal authority, it is only natural that an elder will tend to have more

influence in areas of his giftedness and expertise. This means teaching elders will have special influence in doctrinal matters, as teaching is the most important gift bestowed today (see 1 Cor. 12:28).

> Let the **elders who rule** well be considered worthy of double honor, especially **those who work hard at preaching and teaching** [1 Tim. 5:17].

5. Responsibilities of Elders

The responsibilities of elders parallel those of a shepherd. The elders are "to feed," "to oversee," and "to protect" the flock. Feeding involves teaching and "pastoral care." Overseeing involves church administration. Protection of the church might concern church discipline to expel those who would destroy the church and also involves refuting those who are enemies of Christian truth.

6. Duration of Elder's Office

The practice of two or three year terms for elders does not have Biblical precedent. Since "elder" and "pastor" are the same, they are best given the same duration in office, i.e., indefinite. The presbytery should be considered a lifelong office unless a man disqualifies himself by heresy, unethical conduct or negligence (see Rom. 11:29).

7. Selection of Elders

a. Source

Although Scripture does not prohibit calling an elder/pastor from outside the group, this was not the New Testament pattern. New Testament churches found their additional elders from among their own body. One could argue that this example was necessary for that early time but is not a command for today. Probably, this is true. Still it is best to select new elders from the group itself. It insures that the one selected has a proven record of faithfulness and meets the qualifications of 1 Timothy 3 and Titus 1.

And when **they had appointed** elders for them in every church, having prayed with fasting, they commended them to the Lord in whom they had believed [Acts 14:23].

For this reason I left you in Crete, **that you might set in order** what remains, and appoint elders in every city **as I directed you** [Titus 1:5].

b. Method

As one would not expect sheep to choose their shepherd, so in the selection of elders in the New Testament the authority resides at the top. First, the apostles had ultimate authority to ordain elders (Acts 14:23; 1 Tim. 3:1; Titus 1:5ff.). Next, a verse concerning Timothy indicates that existing elders had a major voice in the selection of new elders.

Do not neglect the spiritual gift within you, which was bestowed upon you through prophetic utterance with the **laying on of hands by the presbytery** [those already elders] [1 Tim. 4:14].

Elders are given the responsibility to be overseers and to protect the flock from wolves (Acts 20:28ff.; 1 Pet. 5:1ff.). It would be virtually impossible for elders to protect a group from infiltration if they do not also have authority over leadership in a church. If God told elders to protect from "wolves," then we may safely assume elders must have been given the authority to keep wolves from becoming elders! The early presbytery (elder board) recognized new elders like Timothy and could exclude those it regarded as unqualified. The closest modern structure would be a self-perpetuating board just as most Christian colleges or missions have. Existing board members decide on any new members.

This does not rule out congregational participation, although it perhaps is best not viewed as an absolute right. Elders are warned against "lording it over the flock" (1 Pet. 5:3). Wisdom dictates that they must consider views from the entire church in the matter of choosing new elders. At the Jerusalem Council in Acts 15, the apostles and elders held ultimate authority (see Acts 15:2, 6). Nevertheless, it was desirous to have "the whole church" agree in such an important matter (Acts 15:22). After all, it is a Biblical principle to obtain a multitude of counselors (Prov. 15:22), and there is precedent for authority figures delegating some power in the matter of choosing officers (Acts 6:1-6 certainly, and possibly 2 Cor. 8:19).

Several procedures could be devised that combine the principle of existing elders recognizing new elders with the principle of sensitivity to all people and congregational unity. Existing elders could have power of nomination with the congregation being asked to give or withhold consent; or the elders could have veto power to confirm or deny a group's choice for elders. The latter would probably result in greater problems. Whatever the procedure, existing elders must have a primary voice in determining the qualifications of any potential new elder. If either the congregation or the existing elders do not think a man is qualified, that should end consideration.

Then it seemed good to the apostles and the elders, **with the whole church**, to choose men from among them...[Acts 15:22].

8. Removal of Elders

Christian leaders have great responsibility and great accountability. They should be judged by a higher standard than other believers (Luke 12:48; James 3:1).

Acts 20:28 gives existing elders "police" powers in a church to keep outsiders or even one of their own number from destroying the whole church. Because leaders are a special target for lies and slander, charges against them must not be entertained without a sufficient basis (2 or 3 witnesses, see 1 Tim. 5:19). However, those who are guilty must be rebuked and/or removed. Elders are expected by the Lord to have a prior allegiance to Him so that if necessary they can and will discipline a friend. Those who do not meet the qualifications of 1 Timothy 3 and Titus 1 may not serve as elders unless and until their lives are put back in order.

> "...And from everyone who has been given much **shall much be required**; and to whom they entrusted much, of him they will ask all the more" [Luke 12:48].

> Let not many of you become teachers, my brethren, knowing that as such we shall incur a **stricter judgment** [James 3:1].

> "Be on guard for yourselves and for all the flock, among which the Holy Spirit has made you overseers, to shepherd the church of God which He purchased with His own blood. I know that after my departure savage **wolves** will come in among you, not sparing the flock; and **from among your own selves men will arise**, speaking perverse things, to draw away the disciples after them [Acts 20:28-30].

> **Do not receive an accusation against an elder except on the basis of two or three witnesses**. **Those who continue in sin**, rebuke in the presence of all, so that the rest also may be fearful of sinning. I solemnly charge you in the presence of God and of Christ Jesus and of His chosen angels, to maintain these principles without bias, doing nothing in a spirit of partiality [1 Tim. 5:19-21].

9. Deacons

A second church office taught in the New Testament is that of deacon. This term is related to the Greek term for "service."

Thus, deacons work in service related capacities but do not make overall policy for a church. Although the execution of details may be delegated to deacons (and here wisdom is a requirement, see Acts 6:3), they do not have control of church government as do "ruling elders" (see 1 Tim. 5:17).

The New Testament does not explain details about the position of deacons. Apparently, a deacon could administer a given ministry alone, or there might be a group acting as a board or committee. Actually, only two passages clearly mention "deacon" as an official position, Phil. 1:1 and 1 Tim. 3:8ff., with a third, Acts 6:1-6, that probably refers to deacons.

Because of scant information it is best not to become overly rigid or dogmatic about the topic of deacons. It perhaps refers to any man who works in a permanent position of service in a local church as directed by that church's elders.

Acts 6:1-6 does not use the word *deacon*, but it does use the verb *"diakoneo"* twice and the word service or ministry (*diakonia*) once. The apostles allowed the church to participate in the selection of the deacons in Acts 6. However, the apostles retained the right of final screening and appointment. The deacons of Acts 6 were involved in administering the "money" tables of the church, i.e., they directed the benevolence ministry to widows. These men did not need to be teachers, but they did need to be honest, Spirit-filled, and wise. They did not initiate policy but were trusted with much responsibility as to the execution of ministries.

It would be a mistake to take Acts 6 as teaching that the ministries of deacons are limited to benevolence or that control of church finances should belong to a board of deacons. If elders are to have "oversight," they must also have some control of finances. Whatever a deacon does with funds ought to be at the direction of superiors. Also, 1 Tim. 3:8ff. does not limit deacons to the sole function of handling money. Again, **it is possible to view all men in permanent positions of service as deacons.**

1 Tim. 3:8-10, 12-13 give qualifications for deacons. Here is the list with brief definitions.

> **Deacons** likewise must be men of dignity, not double-tongued, or addicted to much wine or fond of sordid gain, but holding to the mystery of the faith with a clear conscience. And let these also first be tested; then let them serve as deacons if they are beyond reproach [1 Tim. 3:8-10].

> Let **deacons** be husbands of only one wife, and good managers of their children and their own households. For those who have served well as deacons obtain for themselves a high standing and great confidence in the faith that is in Christ Jesus [1 Tim. 3:12-13].

"Men of dignity" - Deacons ought to be serious about fulfilling tasks. They should have earned respect for following through on assigned tasks.

"Not double-tongued" - A "double-tongued" person says one thing and does another or says one thing to one person but the opposite to the next. A deacon's words must be consistent, and he must not betray confidences or incite disrespect for other leaders.

"Not addicted to much wine" - A deacon may not need be an abstainer, but he must always be sober. This phrase suggests that wine is not a priority with him. Although he may feel liberty to indulge, alcohol is not one his great interests.

"Not fond of sordid gain" - Deacons should have good business ethics and have complete honesty in handling money, either personal money or church money. They should never be involved in pursuing dishonest gain.

"Holding the mystery of the faith with a clear conscience" - A deacon need not be a teacher, but he does need to know what he believes. Deacons should be doctrinally sound and uphold their church's doctrine with a clear conscience.

"First tested" - Christ taught that those who are faithful in lesser matters can be entrusted with greater responsibilities (Luke 16:10). Following this principle Paul commands that deacons should be first tested before placed in permanent service. A practical means of testing is to place a man in temporary and/or substitute position. Just as an elder should not be a new convert, so too a period of time after conversion gives time for a deacon to be tested.

"Beyond reproach" - Just as elders should have a reputation that will not bring ridicule upon the church, so too deacons must have a reputation for integrity.

"Husband of only one wife" - The Greek phrase is "one woman man." Here again there is a difference of opinion as to whether this means quality or quantity. If it is quantity, then divorced men should not be made deacons. If it is quality, then Paul is teaching a man must be of a one-woman character to qualify as a deacon. If he is married, he must be devoted to his wife.

"Good managers of children and house" - Deacons should have stable families without rebellion among their children.

10. Deaconess

A case can be made for thinking the New Testament refers to a position of deaconess. However, the facts are not conclusive. Rom. 16:1 calls Phoebe a "deaconess." It is impossible to know whether this is an official position or whether Paul simply intends the meaning of "female servant."

Some interpret the reference to "women" in 1 Tim. 3:11 as meaning "deaconess" because it occurs in a context teaching about deacons. This is possible. Yet, the women of 1 Tim. 3:11 might also be deacon's wives or women who assisted the deacons. It is best to be charitable to believers who have diverse attitudes about the office of deaconess. A greater issue is whether a woman can be a pastor/elder or teacher in the church.

11. The Role of Women in the Church

Bible believers are not so concerned with the popularity of an idea as they are with its conformity to the Word of God. Although the Bible views the sexes as equal in person and worth (Gal. 3:28), women are subordinate to men in their position and work relative to church leadership. The issue is not so much "why" has God structured the church this way, but rather "will His people submit" to His stipulations.

1 Tim. 2:11-12 prohibits women from teaching men. There can be no alternative interpretation that remains faithful to the Scripture.

> Let a woman quietly receive instruction with entire submissiveness. But **I do not allow a woman to teach or exercise authority over a man**, but to remain quiet [1 Tim. 2:11-12].

The New American Standard Bible has correctly rendered this passage with indefinite articles. It does not say: "I will not allow **the** woman to teach or have authority, over **the** man." This would be a Greek way of asserting wives may not teach their own husbands. Yet, the limitation goes beyond a wife having authority over her own husband. Paul did not allow **any** woman to have authority over **any** man. There may be some flexibility as to what constitutes a position of authority, e.g., a woman being the choir director. Likewise, there must be some interpretation as to when boys are "men" (e.g., having a woman teach in a youth group). In addition, the Bible does not seem to exclude women from "teaching" men in an informal conversation (such as Priscilla instructing Apollos

in private, see Acts 18:26). However, there ought not be any gray area relative to a woman being a pastor/elder or teacher of adult men. The Bible simply does not permit it, and God does not explain His reasoning for the prohibition. We can presume it has nothing to do with lack of intelligence. It may involve either internal church stability or the ability for effective witness to men in the world.

It is clear from the qualifications for pastor/elder in 1 Tim. 3: 1 ff. and Titus 1:5ff. that women were not considered for the pastor/elder/overseer position.

> Let **the women keep silent in the churches**; for they are not permitted to speak, but let them subject themselves, just as the Law also says. And if they desire to learn anything, let them ask their own husbands at home; for it is **improper for a woman to speak in church** [1 Cor. 14:34-35].

1 Cor. 14:34 commands women to "keep silent in the churches." This does not seem to refer to total silence, as only three chapters earlier Paul wrote of women praying or prophesying in the church if there was a head covering (see 1 Cor. 11:2-16). Although the context has reference to tongues speaking or prophesying, 1 Cor. 14:34 does not seem to be prohibiting women in the early church from these because the Bible mentions several prophetesses (Miriam - Ex. 15:20, Num. 12:1-2, and Micah 6:4; Deborah - Judges 4:4; Huldah - 2 Kings 22:14-15, and 2 Chron. 34:22-23; Anna - Luke 2:36; Philip's daughters - Acts 21:9; and 1 Cor. 11:2-16).

It is best to interpret 1 Cor. 14:34 by 1 Tim. 2:11-12. When Paul says: "Let the women keep silent," he is not forbidding all speech but only when speaking in the role of pastor/elder or teacher. Women must not speak in a way that gives them authority over men in a local church. The main point of 1 Cor.

14:35 seems to be that women should not question, especially in the sense of "challenging" a male teacher in the formal setting of a church assembly.

Although the Bible limits the role of women relative to leadership over men in a local church, it also gives examples of women contributing to a local church's ministry. The passage in Titus 2:3-5 gives women the task of ministry to other women, and there are certainly examples of women teaching children (2 Tim. 1:5; 3:15).

> Likewise, teach the older women to be reverent in the way they live, not to be slanderers or addicted to much wine, but to teach what is good. Then they can train the younger women to love their husbands and children, to be self-controlled and pure, to be busy at home, to be kind, and to be subject to their husbands, so that no one will malign the word of God [Titus 2:3-5 NIV].

Other examples of women being involved in ministries include music (Ezra 2:65 and Neh. 7:67), hostesses for the tabernacle (Ex. 38:8), charity and benevolence (Luke 8:3 and Acts 9:36ff.), and general service (Rom. 16:1 and 1 Tim. 3:11).

D. Church Ordinances

1. Communion

Many Christians are aware that the great continental denominations to arise from the Reformation are the Reformed church (Presbyterian) and the Lutheran church. An initial attempt was made to merge the two groups in a common defense against Roman Catholicism. Zwingli and Luther met each other. Together with other eminent theologians they sat down at Marburg to hammer out a common doctrinal statement. They agreed on fourteen of fifteen doctrinal points but could not agree on the nature of communion.

Luther took chalk and wrote on the table, "This is my body." Zwingli believed that the communion elements were memorials. Thus, the colloquy ended without agreement or common defense against Catholicism. Two years later Zwingli and many Swiss Reformed believers were killed at the battle of Kappel.[2]

This anecdote shows that the very ordinance that is supposed to establish oneness among believers has been the source of tragic discord. However, with a Biblical understanding of the essentials and with tolerance for diverse secondary practices, the Lord's supper can be a practice that draws believers closer to Christ and closer to each other by a recognition of our oneness in Christ pictured by the bread and by the cup.

a. Early Optional Practices

There are several practices associated with communion that are **Biblical examples** but not necessarily **Biblical commands**. They are recorded as practices which New Testament Christians did (or may have done) but are not phrased as commands which believers of all times must follow.

(1). Love Feasts

At least three New Testament verses indicate that the early church had an entire meal, the love feast, before it practiced communion. These love feasts also have ample attestation in early church history.

> Therefore when you meet together, it is not to eat the Lord's Supper, for in your eating each one takes his own supper first; and one is hungry and another is drunk. What! Do you not have houses in which to eat and drink? Or do you despise the church of God, and shame those who have

---

[2]   Roland H., Bainton, *Here I stand: A Life of Martin Luther*, reprinted. (Nashville: Abingdon, 1978), pp. 249-251.

nothing? What shall I say to you? Shall I praise you? In this I will not praise you [1 Cor. 11:20-22].

The above passage refers to the perversion of the meal before communion. It is obvious that the Corinthians held a substantial meal in conjunction with the communion ordinance.

> They will be paid back harm for the harm they have done. Their idea of pleasure is to carouse in broad daylight. They are blots and blemishes, reveling in their pleasures while they **feast** with you [2 Pet. 2:13 NIV].

> These men are blemishes at your **love feasts**, eating with you without the slightest qualm—shepherds who feed only themselves. They are clouds without rain, blown along by the wind; autumn trees, without fruit and uprooted— twice dead [Jude 12 NIV].

While a love feast before communion might not be a requirement, it seems to have been the example of the early church. It can be a good means of bringing the entire church together.

(2). Communion Wine

Although grape juice qualifies as "the fruit of the vine" (see Matt. 26:29; Mark 14:25; Luke 22:18), there can be little doubt that the New Testament church used real wine for communion. The Lord made wine (John 2:1ff.) and consumed wine (Luke 7:33-39). The practice of that time was to mix two, three or four parts water with wine. The Corinthian church must have used real and undiluted wine because they became drunk (1 Cor. 11:21).

If the example of the early church was to use wine in communion, does this mean the modern church is required to do the same? It does not seem so. Beyond the offense to the parents of small children who would be in-

troduced to alcohol at church, the use of real wine could be a stumbling block to those with a background of alcohol problems. Rom. 14:21 can be used for a justification for substituting juice as an alternative "fruit of the vine" which can also symbolize blood. 1 Cor. 10:31-32 is also pertinent and comes in a context that has dealt with communion.

> It is good not to eat meat or to drink wine, or to do anything by which your brother stumbles [Rom. 14:21].

> Whether, then, you eat or drink or whatever you do, do all to the glory of God. Give no offense either to Jews or to Greeks or to the church of God [1 Cor. 10:31-32].

Churches which use real wine in communion would be following more closely the example in the early church. However, churches that use juice as a "fruit of the vine" consider the early church's practice more an example than a command. A case can be made that they follow the spirit of the New Testament where great care is taken to avoid creating needless offense or temptation. They view the matter as one of Christian liberty (of example rather than command) and judge that it is more important to avoid giving offense or temptation than to follow the early church's pattern, especially while the substitute also qualifies as "fruit of the vine" and nicely symbolizes blood.

(3). Frequency of Communion

The New Testament church practiced communion at least weekly and maybe even daily. Again, this is an example of how communion was celebrated but not necessarily a command that it must be conducted this way today.

> And they were **continually devoting themselves** to the apostles' teaching and to fellowship, to the **breaking of bread** and to prayer [Acts 2:42].

And on the **first day of the week**, when we were gathered together to **break bread**, Paul began talking to them, intending to depart the next day, and he prolonged his message until midnight [Acts 20:7].

(4). Last Supper Practices

In Matt. 26:30, Christ closed the Last Supper with a hymn. This may not have been intended to be an essential part of communion but rather something the Lord preferred to do on that particular occasion as it fits the Jewish custom of closing the Passover meal (i.e., singing of the second half of the Hallel, Psalms 115-118). Although singing is not mentioned as mandatory in 1 Corinthians 11, it is a nice optional feature that can be used to close communion.

Foot washing is a far more controversial practice. There is no debate that the Lord washed the disciples' feet at the Last Supper. But there is great argument as to whether He intended this for only the apostles (or for only that one occasion), or whether He desired foot washing to be an integral part of communion for all believers at all times.

> Then He poured water into the basin, and began to wash the disciples' feet, and to wipe them with the towel with which He was girded. And so He came to Simon Peter. He said to Him, "Lord, do You wash my feet?" Jesus answered and said to him, "What I do you do not realize now, but you shall understand hereafter"....And so when He had washed their feet, and taken His garments, and reclined at the table again, He said to them, "Do you know what I have done to you? You call Me Teacher and Lord; and you are right, for so I am. If I then, the Lord and the Teacher, washed your feet, you also ought to wash one another's feet. For I gave you an example that you also should do as I did to you" [John 13:5-7, 12-15].

Some of the most Biblically oriented small denominations practice foot washing along with the communion service, e.g., Grace Brethren. At the very least it is fair to say that if one wants to be safe about compliance, then it is wise to include foot washing along with communion (especially v. 14). Still, a case can be made that the Lord did not intend for this practice to be universal in extent or continuing in time. Perhaps He intended this lesson only for the apostles, the actual participants in the Last Supper. They were supposed to wash each other's feet. If the practice was supposed to be universal, it is odd that foot washing is not mentioned in the other three gospel accounts of the Last Supper nor as a church ordinance in the epistles, especially in primary sections about communion in 1 Corinthians 10 and 11.

Furthermore, there is some question as to what precisely Christ means when He commands in John 13:15, "do as I did to you." Does this refer to foot washing or to the significant lessons on humility and forgiveness that He portrayed by His example? It would be possible to wash another's feet but still not have humility or display love toward him or her. Certainly, the "deeds" of real importance being taught by the Lord in John 13 extend beyond a ritual of foot washing. The disciples could see that the Lord was washing their feet, but in John 13:6-7, Christ insists that what He was really "doing" was something else, something with a deeper meaning that would take some time to grasp. Thus, the command to "do as I did" may not even refer to foot washing, but to what Christ really did, i.e., model humility and forgiveness. It is possible to view John 13:14 as a command to wash each other in the sense of "forgive each other and serve each other."

Hopefully, believers can be charitable with each other in their disagreement over foot washing. Some feel uncomfortable in not following the example of the Last Supper more strictly. Others, noting that foot washing as an ordinance is not taught elsewhere, feel just as uncomfortable in making a practice binding when it is based on a single passage capable of alternate interpretations.

b. Mandatory Communion Practices

1 Cor. 11:23-32 gives essential practices that are binding upon the church relative to communion practices. (See also Matt. 26:26-29; Mark 14:22-25; Luke 22:17-20).

> For I received from the Lord that which I also delivered to you, that the Lord Jesus in the night in which He was betrayed took bread; and when He had given thanks, He broke it, and said, "This is My body, which is broken for you; do this in remembrance of Me." In the same way He took the cup also, after supper, saying, "This cup is the new covenant in My blood; do this, as often as you drink it, in remembrance of Me." For as often as you eat this bread and drink this cup, you proclaim the Lord's death until He comes. Therefore whoever eats the bread or drinks the cup of the Lord in an unworthy manner shall be guilty of the body and the blood of the Lord. But let a man examine himself, and so let him eat of the bread and drink of the cup. For he who eats and drinks, eats and drinks judgment to himself, if he does not judge the body rightly. For this reason many among you are weak and sick, and a number sleep. But if we judged ourselves rightly, we should not be judged. But when we are judged, we are disciplined by the Lord in order that we may not be condemned along with the world. [1 Cor. 11:23-32].

The pattern of communion laid down in 1 Cor. 11:23, mandates that thanks be given first, before the bread and then before the cup. It is best to follow this pattern of prayer before partaking and the order of the bread first and then the cup.

The passage allows freedom in the frequency of observance ("...as often as..." in 1 Cor. 11:25). The early church held communion weekly (Acts 20:7) and probably even daily (Acts 2:42 and 46). This is understandable given the situation of persecution. Frequent communion would be a means of bolstering the early church faced with harsh threats and onslaughts of her enemies. For the most part the modern church does not suffer similar pressures. Communion should be observed frequently enough to prevent forgetfulness of the Lord's sacrifice and to provide regular occasions for a reminder to confess our sins. Yet, communion should not be so frequent as to become a trite, meaningless ritual. Since the Bible allows flexibility as to the frequency of communion, the elders of a church should decide what frequency best serves these goals.

Beyond the order of the ritual, 1 Cor. 11:28 (also v. 31) requires self-examination before participating in the Lord's Supper. Verse 27 refers to drinking in an "**unworthy manner.**" This is an adverb stressing unworthy manner of observance, not so much unworthiness of a person. In the ultimate sense no one is worthy to take communion. Christ's sacrifice on our behalf was pure grace. Paul, in this context, is mainly concerned that participants in communion "discern or judge the body" correctly, i.e., that they observe with the respect and honor due to the seriousness of the ordinance. The Corinthians were observing in a disrespectful manner to the point of gorging themselves at the "love feast" and even getting drunk. The point in the context is not that one who observed communion with unconfessed sin will drop over dead. The warning of judgment is specifically directed to those who made a mockery of the Lord's Supper. These are the objects of the warnings about God's judgment. Still, it is wise that a general examination of all aspects of Christian living take place along with the specific examination of one's attitude toward the Lord's Supper during its actual observance. Most would draw the conclusion that if God becomes angry over unholy attitudes toward communion, He would also be displeased for one to share in communion while other categories of sins remain unconfessed. We know from other Scriptures that God might chastise believers for other sins as well.

c. The Meaning of Communion

(1). Transubstantiation

In 1215 at the Lateran Council, the Roman Catholic Church adopted transubstantiation as its official view of communion. Transubstantiation means that as a priest consecrates the elements they became the actual body and blood of Christ.

Reasoning that the body and blood of Christ are necessary to salvation, the Catholic Church could terrorize medieval nations by withholding mass from their populations. This practice of "interdiction" often brought fearful and ignorant people to revolt against kings who displeased a pope. The transubstantiation view was also the basis for denying the cup to the laity. They might profane the service by spilling some of the "blood of Christ."

With complete unity, Protestants rejected the transubstantiation view of communion as heresy. The biggest objection is that transubstantiation views Christ as being sacrificed again and again contrary to the New Testament which teaches His was a complete sacrifice that never needs repetition. (See Chapter 9, Part 1, pp. 123-24)

> By this will we have been sanctified through the offering of the body of Jesus Christ **once** for all....For by **one** offering He has perfected for all time those who are sanctified [Heb. 10:10, 14].

Another heresy fostered by the transubstantiation view is that of works-salvation. Contrary to the Bible, transubstantiation makes our religious deeds and rituals the basis of salvation (Rom. 4:5; Eph. 2:8-9; Titus 3:5).

Those who espouse transubstantiation utterly fail to do justice to the phrase "this is My body." Clearly, the Lord was speaking metaphysically because He was sitting right there in flesh and blood while He spoke these words! Literal interpretation means that words should be taken in the most normal, customary, usual meaning given the laws of language, the customs of the times, and the context. With Christ present in the body, the phrase, "this is my body" should be interpreted the same way as "I am the door," or "I am the vine," or "I am the light." This is "My body" means this "represents My body."

True participation in Christ's broken flesh and shed blood is defined in John 6. The Lord in vv. 35 and 48 claims to be "the bread of life." In John 6:55 He teaches that His flesh is food and His blood is drink. **It is helpful to remember that the ordinance of the Lord's Supper had not yet been given at the time of John 6.** Thus, in the context, eating Christ's flesh and drinking His blood has nothing to do with communion. Rather it refers to a personal appropriation of the benefits of Christ's broken body and shed blood as **the Lord Himself explains in the context.**

> "...I am the bread of life; he who **comes to me** shall not hunger and he who **believes in Me** shall never thirst" [John 6:35].

> "Truly, truly, I say to you, he who **believes** has eternal life. I am the bread of life" [John 6:47-48].

It must be noted that the last parts of John 6:40 and John 6:54 are clearly parallel and that "**believes in Him**" is the **equivalent of** "**eats My flesh**" and "**drinks My blood.**" Communion is not the subject of John 6. Christ is teaching personal appropriation by faith in His broken body and shed blood.

(2). Consubstantiation

The Lutheran view rejects the notion that the elements become the actual body and blood of Christ. It maintains that the body and blood of Christ are present in a mystical sense along with the literal bread and cup.

Providing one believes in the finished work of Christ and justification by faith alone (as most conservative Lutherans do), consubstantiation is much less objectionable than transubstantiation. Since Christ is spiritually present inside each believer (Rom. 8:9) and present when two or three gather together in His Name (Matt. 18:20), it is possible to think **the Lord may be spiritually present in the communion elements**. One can heartily agree with the Lutheran view that the gospel is proclaimed in every communion service. Although the elements themselves do not save, the realities of the broken body and shed blood do save; and even the elements symbolically teach the means of salvation to all who understand the observance (see 1 Cor. 11:26, "proclaim the Lord's death").

(3). The Memorial View

Churches in the Reformed, Presbyterian, and Baptist traditions generally adhere to the memorial view of communion. This means that the elements are not the actual or mystical body and blood of the Lord, but rather they are symbols to assist in remembrance. Several phrases reveal that this is one intent of the communion service: "do this **in remembrance of Me**" [Luke 22:19], "do this **in remembrance of Me**" [1 Cor. 11:24], "For as often as you eat this bread and drink this cup, you proclaim the Lord's death until He comes" [1 Cor. 11:26].

Having established that the Lord's Supper should be considered a memorial, it is logical to study the specifics of the memorial. What does God want His people to remember? This can be nicely classified by the three terms used for this ordinance: Eucharist, Communion, and the Lord's Supper.

(a). Eucharist

The term *Eucharist* is not just an ecclesiastical term that is the property of specific denominations. It is a form of the Greek word for **"thanksgiving."** The observance of the Eucharist should cause us to remember with deep gratitude the sacrifice of Christ's broken body and shed blood. Christ gave His life voluntarily out of sacrificial love (John 10:18; Matt. 26:53; Heb. 12:3), and He deserves eternal thanks. The Eucharist assists us so that we never forget to be mindful of His death and the benefits of His broken body and shed blood.

(b). Communion

Communion has a Latin derivation and refers to having something in common. The Greek word translated as *communion* in the English New Testament means "fellowship."

The communion service should remind believers of their fellowship, union, oneness, with Christ and with all other believers. By partaking of "one bread" and sharing of "one cup" in communion, we remember our sharing with and union in Christ's life and of the union of all believers in the church.

1 Cor. 10:16-17 associates communion with both a union with Christ's life (specifically the benefits of His shed blood) and union with all other believers in the body of Christ.

> Is not the cup of blessing which we bless a sharing in the blood of Christ? Is not the bread which we break a **sharing in the body of Christ**? Since there is one bread, **we who are many are one body**; for we all **partake of the one bread** [1 Cor. 10:16-17].

(c). Lord's Supper

The *Lord's Supper* reminds us that He is the unseen host of the observance. Also, more

345

than the other terms, it points back to the origin of the ordinance at the time of the Last Supper before the cross. It is the Lord's Supper because He is the one who originated it. In observing the Lord's Supper we should remember that Last Supper, and especially Christ's promise to come again and partake with us in His Kingdom. Although the ritual forces attention to the past death on the cross and to the present union with Christ and all other believers, it should also cause us to remember the promise that Christ shall return.

> "But I say to you, I will not drink of this fruit of the vine from now on **until that day** when I drink it new with you **in My Father's kingdom**" [Matt. 26:29].

> ...you proclaim the Lord's death **until He comes** [1 Cor. 11:26b].

(4). Summary

The Lord may, indeed, be spiritually present in communion. At the very least, it is certain that communion is a memorial service. It is intended as a reminder of Christ's past sacrifice, of the present union with Him and all other believers, and of the promise to return in the future to share a feast with His own in the Kingdom. All of these blessed thoughts should come to mind when the Lord's Supper is observed.

2. Baptism

It ought to become apparent that the Baptist view of baptism is Scriptural both as to meaning and mode. However, other views will be listed so as to cover the topic more completely.

a. Different Perspectives on Baptism

(1). The Sacramental View

The word *sacrament* comes from a Latin Word that means: "token, pledge, or down payment." Some view the baptism of an infant as a sacrament that regenerates a baby,

making the child a living member of the body of Christ. The infant is safe from eternal perdition should it die. It is further assumed that salvation is a process. Thus, the infant has been initiated into the covenant path of growing in grace with the view of hoping eventually to retain and/or earn eternal life.

(2). Baptismal Regeneration

Baptismal regeneration as used in this section may be distinguished from the sacramental view if we restrict the former to those who believe in "adult baptism." The Church of Christ and other similar groups do not practice infant baptism, but they do believe that baptism is a necessary means of salvation. Faith alone is not enough. The believer must also submit to baptism to be saved. (This is covered extensively in part 2, pp. 144-151, Chapter 9, "Soteriology.")

(3). The Reformed View

Those with the Reformed/Presbyterian view believe that baptism has replaced circumcision as a sign that one is a part of the covenant community. Just as those who were a part of Abraham's seed were required to undergo circumcision in infancy, so too those who are baptized as infants show that they are a part of the church's covenant community. Infant baptism also creates a covenant between the parents and God that they will rear the child in the Christian faith. While infant baptism allows advantages in belonging to the covenant of faith (a Christian home), biblically-informed adherents within these groups would insist that salvation rests on faith alone. They would maintain that the infant must profess faith in Christ as he grows into an adult. Otherwise, there is no salvation.

(4). No Baptism

Some Protestants do not practice baptism at all. The Salvation Army, for example, views baptism as unimportant since it is not a matter of salvation. Also, there are some Bible churches in the "Grace Gospel Fellowship" that do not practice baptism because they are "hyper-dispensational." They do not feel the church started in Acts 2. Some say Acts 9, or 13, or even 28. Those on the extreme fringes follow only the prison epistles of Paul, and therefore, do not believe baptism is for the church.

(5). The Baptist View of Baptism

Baptists, unlike Catholics, Lutherans, Presbyterians, Methodists, Reformed, etc., do not practice infant baptism. Unlike the Church of Christ, they do not believe baptism is essential to salvation. Yet, Baptists do stress baptism as a necessary observance to obey the commands of Christ.

The Baptist understanding is that only those who already believe may be candidates for baptism. This excludes infants who are unable to believe. It also views baptism as occurring after salvation.

It ought to be obvious to any unbiased Bible student that the Bible never commands nor gives examples of infant baptism. The Scriptures uniformly give salvation by faith as the condition in order to be baptized. Without faith a person is unsaved regardless of whether he has been baptized. If faith is present, he is saved even if he has not submitted to baptism. The following texts prove that baptism is only for believers, and thus, it is for those already saved and those old enough to exercise faith in Christ.

> "Go therefore and make disciples of all the nations, **baptizing** them [**the disciples**] in the name of the Father and the Son and the Holy Spirit" [Matt. 28:19].

> And Peter said to them, "**Repent, and** let each of you **be baptized** in the name of Jesus Christ for the forgiveness of your sins, and you shall receive the gift of the Holy Spirit...." So then, **those who had received his word** were **baptized**; and there were

added that day about three thousand souls [Acts 2:38 and 41].

> But **when they believed** Philip preaching the good news about the kingdom of God and the name of Jesus Christ, **they were being baptized**, men and women alike [Acts 8:12].

> "Of Him all the prophets bear witness that through His name **everyone who believes** in Him receives forgiveness of sins." While Peter was still speaking these words, the **Holy Spirit fell upon all** those who were **listening to the message**.... "Surely **no one can refuse the water for these to be baptized** who have received the Holy Spirit just as we did, can he?" And he ordered them to be baptized in the name of Jesus Christ...[Acts 10:43-44; 47-48].

The Bible teaches that only believers obtain the baptism of the Holy Spirit (John 7:37-39; Rom. 8:9). These, in Acts 10, believed in the gospel message that Peter was preaching, and, therefore, obtained the Holy Spirit. Notice that **after they believed** they were qualified candidates for water baptism.

> And a certain woman named Lydia, from the city of Thyatira, a seller of purple fabrics, a worshiper of God, was listening; and the Lord **opened her heart to respond** to the things spoken by Paul. And when **she and her household had been baptized**... [Acts 16:14-15].

> [A]nd after he brought them out, he said, "Sirs, what must I do to be saved?" And they said, "**Believe in the Lord Jesus**, and you shall be saved, you and your household." And they spoke the word of the Lord to him together with all who were in his house. And he took them that very hour of the night and washed their

wounds, and **immediately he was baptized**, he and all his household [Acts 16: 30-34].

And Crispus, the leader of the synagogue, **believed in the Lord** with all his household, and many of the Corinthians when they heard were **believing and being baptized** [Acts 18:8].

The Bible teaches believer's baptism with baptism occurring after salvation, not as a contribution toward salvation. Only those old enough to believe may be baptized. It is ironic that the following quotes occur in a section designed to prove infant baptism. Here is Louis Berkhof, a former president and professor of theology at Calvin Seminary and champion of conservative Reformed theology:

"It may be said at the outset that there is no explicit command in the Bible to baptize children and that there is not a single instance in which we are plainly told that children were baptized. But this does not necessarily make infant baptism un-Biblical."[3]

"There is no explicit command that children must be baptized. This is perfectly true, but it does not disprove the validity of infant baptism."[4]

"...there is no example of infant baptism in the New Testament. It is perfectly true that the Bible does not explicitly state that children were baptized..."[5]

b. The Meaning of Water Baptism

(1). Baptism shows that the new believer wishes to be **obedient** to Christ's command.

___

[3] Louis Berkhof, *Systematic Theology* (Grand Rapids: Wm. B. Eerdmans Publishing Co., 1939) p. 632.

[4] Ibid., 636.

[5] Ibid., 637.

It also shows the obedience of the church to carry out an ordinance that Christ expected to be valid "until the end of the age" (Matt. 28:20).

"Go, therefore, and make disciples of all the nations, **baptizing them** in the name of the Father and the Son and the Holy Spirit, teaching them to observe all that I commanded you; and lo, I am with you always, even **to the end of the age**" [Matt. 28:19-20].

(2). Water baptism symbolizes a **sharing in Christ's death, burial, and resurrection**. A case can be made that Rom. 6:3-4 is referring to Spirit baptism, the more important baptism that water baptism symbolizes. Regardless of whether baptism in Rom. 6:3-4 is taken as Spirit baptism which comes by faith or a water baptism based in a genuine faith, the passage shows that baptism pictures a sharing in Christ's death, burial, and resurrection. This point will surface again under the point that immersion is the proper mode for baptism.

(3). **Water baptism symbolizes** the more important **Spirit baptism**. Although John's baptism is different from Christian baptism (see Acts 19:3-5), John the Baptist's statements can be used to show that Spirit baptism is far more important than the ritual of water baptism (Matt. 3:11; Mark 1:8; Luke 3:16; John 1:33; Acts 1:5; 11:16).

There must be some connection between the more important Spirit baptism and the lesser water baptism, for Eph. 4:5 speaks of "one baptism," and Acts 10:47 gives Spirit baptism as a qualification for water baptism. Indeed, there are passages where good Bible scholars disagree as to whether the author means Spirit baptism or water baptism, e.g., Rom. 6:3-4; Gal. 3:27; Col. 2:12. Water baptism must symbolize the more important Spirit baptism.

Actually, this point overlaps with the previous one but extends beyond it. According to

1 Cor. 12:13, believers have been baptized (submerged, enveloped, inundated) in the Spirit of Christ. The position of being in the Spirit of Christ unites a believer to Christ, especially in the area of sharing in the benefits of His death, burial and resurrection. Thus, to say water baptism symbolizes Spirit baptism includes the previous point that it symbolizes a sharing in Christ's death, burial, and resurrection. Yet, the symbolism as it portrays Spirit baptism goes further. Baptism in the Spirit unites a believer to the Holy Spirit as well as to Christ. It also unites a believer to all other believers in the body of Christ. Thus, water baptism symbolizes identification with Christ's death, burial, and resurrection; and it also shows that the person has been placed in the Spirit united with the church.

(4). Water baptism is a **public identification with the church**. Just as water baptism symbolizes a baptism in the Spirit that unites a believer with the universal church, it also publicly identifies a believer with the visible church. In many cultures where non-Christian religions dominate, baptism marks the final break with a false religion and proves affiliation with the church. In Acts 2:41; the idea of addition speaks of addition to the church.

> So then, those who had received his word were baptized; and there were added that day about three thousand souls [Acts 2:41].

(5). Summary

Baptism speaks of a sharing in Christ's death, burial, and resurrection. Sharing in Christ's life comes about through Spirit baptism into the Spirit of Christ. Thus, baptism in water also pictures baptism in the Spirit and union with the universal church. The one who undergoes baptism displays obedience to Christ's command and identifies with the visible church. It also seems reasonable to think that baptism symbolizes the cleansing (forgiveness) which comes through faith in

Christ. (See Acts 2:38 where *for* means *because of*, and also Acts 22:16).

c. The Mode of Baptism

Various denominations baptize by different modes: pouring, sprinkling, or immersing. Although some conservatives baptize by sprinkling or pouring because of their denominational heritage, it appears that the New Testament mode for baptism was immersion.

(1). Ancient Secular Greek and the Words *Bapto/Baptizo*

Standard references for Greek words give the definition of *bapto/baptizo* as used in secular Greek[6] as "to dip, to dye, to sink, to drown, to suffer shipwreck, to be overwhelmed." Plutarch used the word *baptizo* when he described the soldiers of Alexander on a riotous march, as by the roadside dipping (lit., baptizing) with cups from huge wine jars and mixing bowls, and drinking to one another.[7] Josephus writes of wicked King Herod baptizing Aristobulus, the high priest. He drowned him![8]

Herodotus uses *baptizo* saying that if an Egyptian "touches a swine in passing with his clothes, he goes to the river and dips himself in it."[9] Ancient secular literature

---

[6] Albrecht Oepke, "Bapto" in *Theological Dictionary of the New Testament*, edited by Gerhard Kittel, translated by Geoffrey Bromiley (Grand Rapids: Wm. B. Eerdmans Publishing., 1964), 1:529-30.

[7] Augustus H. Strong, *Systematic Theology* (Old Tappan, NJ: Fleming H. Revell Co., 1907), p. 934.

[8] Josephus, *Josephus Complete Works*, translated by William Whiston, reprint ed. (Grand Rapids, Kregal Publications, 1960), p. 317. (Antiquities 15:3:3).

[9] Herodotus, *The Histories*, translated by Aubrey De Selicourt, revised ed. (Middlesex, England: Penguin Books, 1982), p. 148. (Histories 2:47).

indicates that baptism is immersion. Evidence from the Septuagint is even more impressive.

(2). The Septuagint and *Bapto/ Baptizo*

The Septuagint uses the word *baptizo* a total of sixteen times. Following are important references:

Ex. 12:22 - The hyssop was to be dipped in blood and applied to the doorposts of the Hebrews.

Lev. 4:6, 17; 9:9; 14:16 - These references in Leviticus refer to a priest dipping his finger in either blood or oil.

Num. 19:18 - Often there is a distinction made between "dipping" into the blood and then "sprinkling" or "pouring" it on the altar or on a cleansed person.

Joshua 3:15 - The priests carrying the ark dipped their feet into the Jordan and it parted.

Ruth 2:14 - Boaz invited Ruth to dip her bread into some vinegar.

1 Sam. 14:27 - Jonathan dipped the end of his staff into some honey.

2 Kings 8:15 - In this verse, a servant assassinates a sick king by smothering him with blankets that had been immersed in water.

Pedo-baptists, (those who baptize infants either by pouring or sprinkling) point to Dan. 4:33 (LXX 30) and Dan. 5:21 as evidence that *bapto* can mean sprinkling. These verses say that Nebuchadnezzar was "drenched" with the dew of heaven during the time of his madness. It may be proper to think of him as being sprinkled by dew. However, the idea of being drenched, virtually immersed, fits the context just as well.

Baptizo occurs two times in the Septuagint. Isa. 21:4 is a figurative usage: "Horror overwhelms me." 2 Kings 5:14 is very perti-

nent to the definition of *baptizo*. Elisha told Naaman to dip (*baptizo*) in the Jordan River seven times.

So he went down and **dipped** himself seven times in the Jordan... [2 Kings 5:14].

(3). *Bapto/Baptizo* in the New Testament

Bapto occurs four times in the New Testament. In all passages the meaning of "to dip or to dye" fits nicely.

"And he cried out and said, 'Father Abraham, have mercy on me, and send Lazarus, that he may **dip** (*bapto*) the tip of his finger in water and cool off my tongue; for I am in agony in this flame' " [Luke 16:24].

Jesus therefore answered, "That is the one for whom I shall **dip** (*bapto*) the morsel and give it to him." So when He had **dipped** the morsel... [John 13:26].

And He is clothed with a robe **dipped** (*bapto*) in blood...[Rev. 19:13].

Pedo-baptists might assert that Rev. 19:13 refers to Christ's robe "sprinkled" with blood. Nevertheless, there is no absolute reason to change from the established meanings of "to dip or to dye."

References where some feel the meaning of the "*bapto*" word-family is "to pour" or "to sprinkle" should be mentioned. Mark 7:4, Luke 11:38, Heb. 6:2 and 9:10 use various words related to baptism in reference to ceremonial washings. Some claim that in these texts words related to baptism are used to mean sprinkling or pouring. This is possible, but the meaning of immersion is equally valid. Mark 7:4 and Luke 11:38 speak of Pharisaical traditions of washing before a meal. This might refer to pouring water over ones hands, but it might also refer to immersing hands in water or even taking an entire bath. The same point is valid for Mark

7:4 where it also refers to cleaning cups, pitchers, and pots. Utensils may be cleaned by immersion. Thus, these verses present a weak support upon which to argue that baptism means something other than immersion.

A word study of *bapto/baptizo* shows that immersion is either a required meaning or a possible meaning in virtually every context. While pouring or sprinkling might fit some contexts, dipping or dyeing is an equally suitable meaning. There should be little doubt that the Bible means immersion by the word baptism.

(4). Symbolism as an Argument for Immersion

Rom. 6:3-4 teaches that baptism is supposed to portray identification with the death, burial, and resurrection of Christ. It would seem that immersion fits this symbolism whereas sprinkling or pouring does not.

Objectors might say that the ancient Jews did not bury under ground but rather "sideways" into caves. That is true. Nevertheless, going down in the water still better symbolizes the posture of death and coming up out of the water still better symbolizes being raised up in new life.

(5). Prepositions as Evidence for Immersion

Sometimes Greek prepositions have a wide range of meanings. They often have a common meaning in most contexts with secondary (more remote) meanings that are intended when a specific context or doctrinal truth demands it. The normal meanings for prepositions employed in baptismal narratives show that baptism was by immersion. If strong evidence existed that baptism was by sprinkling or pouring, then some of the prepositions could be given secondary meanings. However, no strong evidence for sprinkling or pouring exists. Therefore, we need not and should not take baptismal narratives as referring to anything but immersion.

Many texts speak of baptism in water or in the Jordan (Matt. 3:6ff.; Mark 1:5, 9; John 1:26, 31, 33). Baptism in a river favors immersion! In fact, John the Baptist preferred to work in an area with much water (see John 3:23).

The following texts strongly support immersion being the New Testament mode of baptism.

> And after being baptized, Jesus went immediately up **from the water**... [Matt. 3:16].

> And immediately coming **up out of the water**... [Mark 1:10].

> And he ordered the chariot to stop; and they both went **down into the water**, Philip as well as the eunuch; and he baptized him. And when they came **up out of the water**, the Spirit of the Lord snatched Philip away...[Acts 8:38-39].

The normal way to interpret all of these baptismal narratives is to understand that baptism was by immersion. Word studies on *bapto* and *baptizo*, the symbolism of death and resurrection, and the prepositions in baptismal narratives, all establish that immersion is the Biblical mode for baptism. Church history is secondary to the Bible, but it can be helpful.

(6). Church History and Baptism by Immersion

While the early church allowed baptism by other means in special cases, there can be little debate that immersion was the primary and preferred way to baptize. The Didache (c. A.D. 120) gives permission for pouring but makes immersion obligatory whenever the means for it are available:

"And concerning baptism, thus baptize ye, having first said all these things baptize into the name of the Father, and of the Son, and of the Holy Spirit in living [running] water. But if thou have not living [running] water,

351

baptize into other water and if thou canst not in cold, in warm. But if thou have not either, pour out water thrice upon the head into the name of the Father and Son and Holy Spirit."[10]

Grace Brethren immerse but do so face forward and three times. The following quote shows that thrice immersion has a very old heritage. It just as clearly shows in somewhat amusing fashion that thrice immersion goes beyond the Lord's requirement to be immersed only once. Tertullian, who lived between A.D. 145-220, said:

"When we are going to enter the water, but a little before, in the presence of the congregation and under the hand of the presidents [the elders], we solemnly profess that we disown the devil, and his pomp, and his angels. Hereupon we are thrice immersed, making a somewhat more ample pledge than the Lord has appointed in the Gospel."[11]

d. Conclusions on Water Baptism

Baptism is for believers only. Thus, only those old enough to profess faith are suitable candidates for baptism. The ritual contributes nothing to salvation. It shows identification with Christ's death, burial, and resurrection; pictures baptism in the Spirit including the union in Christ with the universal church; identifies one publicly with the visible church; displays obedience to Christ's commands; and pictures cleansing. Immersion is the Biblical mode for baptism. The government of each church must decide whether it

will recognize a past baptism by another mode as valid. It should, however, insist that one was a believer at the time of baptism.

E. Purity of the Church

The Bible develops two closely related doctrines that concern the purity of the church. Ecclesiastical separation helps prevent falsehood and evil from entering the church.

Where falsehood or evil does gain a foothold in the church, the Bible teaches a doctrine of church discipline to purge it. Naturally, some texts concern both separation and discipline.

1. Ecclesiastical Separation

Separation has been likened to walking a tightrope. One wants to hold the unity of the faith with genuine believers (Eph. 4:3). Yet, obedience to God, preservation of the truth, and a pure church demand separation from error. The most difficult issue involves identification of doctrinal and ethical points that are serious enough to warrant a withdrawal of fellowship. When is a doctrine a basic and non-negotiable truth? When is an idea a secondary and non-essential point so that fellowship may continue in a spirit of toleration for flaws in other believer's thinking?

a. Commands to Separate

Those who have allegiance to the Bible will submit to its commands relative to non-cooperation with groups that are anti-Christian in thinking and behavior. Ecclesiastical separation does not mean hatred towards unbelievers or that Christians may not have unsaved friends. It does mean that believers may not join in "religious" endeavors with those who are working in opposition to Biblical Christianity.

The imagery of being "yoked together" shows that the emphasis in separation is upon joint efforts with those who actually pull against Christ. A church, for example, might befriend Jews, or Muslims, or Hindus, but it must not form a religious alliance with

---

[10] "The Teaching of the Twelve Apostles", in *The Ante-Nicene Fathers,* ed. by Alexander Roberts and James Donaldson, reprint ed., 10 vols. (Grand Rapids: Wm. B. Eerdmans Publishing Co., 1979), 7:379. (Didache 7:1-3).

[11] Tertullian, "The Chaplet on De Corona" in *The Ante-Nicene Fathers*, edited by Alexander Roberts and James Donaldson, reprint ed., 10 vols. (Grand Rapids: Wm. B. Eerdmans Publishing Co., 1973), 3:94.

them or tolerate the promotion of a false religion's errors within the church. The Bible forbids joint "worship," "ministries," or "mergers" with groups in error. There is a difference between ministry to and cooperation with unbelievers. Not only would a religious alliance with the lost corrupt the church, it gives the world a false sense of security that false religions are acceptable.

The church or denomination that ignores the Scriptural command to remain separate will sooner or later (usually sooner) be so corrupted as to lose distinctiveness as a Christian body. The proof of this statement lies in the histories of most American Protestant denominations in the 20th Century. When separation was ignored, corruption so spoiled the church as to be heartbreaking to those within it who adhered to Biblical authority.

The Bible gives several areas in which the principle of separation should be applied.

(1). Separation from False Doctrines

> **Do not be bound together with unbelievers**; for what partnership have righteousness and lawlessness, or what fellowship has light with darkness? Or what harmony has Christ with Belial, or what has a believer in common with an unbeliever? Or what agreement has the temple of God with idols? For we are the temple of the living God; just as God said, "I will dwell in them and walk among them; and I will be their God, and they shall be My people. Therefore, come out from their midst and be separate," says the Lord. "And do not touch what is unclean; and I will welcome you. And I will be a father to you and you shall be sons and daughters to Me," says the Lord Almighty [2 Cor. 6:14-18].

Both the context and the use of Old Testament quotes show that one of the most famil-

iar passages on separation involves a separation from false religious doctrines and practices. 1 Cor. 5:9ff. allows friendship and ministries to unbelievers; but the 2 Corinthians 6 passage forbids joining the temple of God (the church) with idols (the major false religions of the day). Paul does not forbid love towards the heathen, but he does forbid "yoking together," that is cooperative work as if the church and the pagan temple are on the same side and working for the same cause. Paul argues with three rhetorical questions that ultimately state that it is not even possible for a faithful church to have "partnership" (v. 14), "harmony" (v. 15), or "agreement" (v. 16) with unbelievers. The two parties in this unequal yoke pull in different directions. Any such superficial union will destroy the distinctiveness of the church so that it will not be a partnership but a takeover!

Consider also that 2 Corinthians repeatedly mentions false teachers who were damaging the Corinthian church (3:1-2; 11:13ff.; 12:19ff.; and 13:1-5). This separation commanded in Chapter six no doubt includes separation from false teachers.

> Anyone who goes too far and **does not abide in the teaching of Christ**, does not have God; the one who abides in the teaching, he has both the Father and the Son. If anyone comes to you and does not bring this teaching, **do not receive him** into your house, and **do not give him a greeting**; for the one who gives him a greeting participates in his evil deeds [2 John 9-11].

2 John 9-11 commands separation from religious workers who do "not abide in the teachings of Christ." The phrase "teachings of Christ" might refer to "teachings about Christ," i.e., the main doctrines of His virgin birth, deity, atonement, resurrection, Second Coming; or it may refer to teachings that Christ gave. By either interpretation the pas-

sage commands a lack of cooperation and withdrawal of fellowship from those who promote doctrinal error.

For those who might think that the doctrine of separation is unloving, John insists that love involves keeping "His commandments" and love is the opposite of the works of deceivers (antichrists in philosophy).

> And **this is love,** that we **walk according to His commandments. This is the commandment,** just as you have heard from the beginning, that you should walk in it. For **many deceivers have gone out into the world,** those who do not acknowledge Jesus Christ as coming in the flesh. This is the deceiver and the antichrist [2 John 6-7].

It is certainly legitimate to apply Rom. 12:2 to the practice of separation from doctrinal error. Paul commands believers to separate from conformity to the world, especially in the area of the mind.

> And do not be conformed to this world, but be transformed by the renewing of your **mind,** that you may prove what the will of God is, that which is good and acceptable and perfect [Rom. 12:2].

(2). Separation from Divisive Persons

The church is to separate from persons and/or groups that cause needless division. Doctrinal or ethical deviations are major causes of division, but they are by no means the only causes. Often churches experience trouble from doctrinally orthodox persons who are proud, bitter, jealous, slanderous, etc.

> But shun foolish controversies and genealogies and strife and disputes about the Law; for they are unprofitable and worthless. **Reject a factious** [Greek, *heretic*] man **after a first and second warning,** knowing that

such a man is perverted and is sinning, being self-condemned [Titus 3:9-11].

> Now I urge you, brethren, keep your eye on **those who cause dissensions** and hindrances contrary to the teaching which you learned, and **turn away from them** [Rom. 16:17].

(3). Separation from Immorality

Every verse that teaches church discipline for immorality also teaches separation from it. Obviously, if immorality within the church must be removed, then it is correct to forbid its entrance in the first place. (See also Psalm 1; Prov. 1:10ff.; 13:20; 1 Cor. 15:33.)

> I wrote you in my letter not to associate with immoral people; I did not at all mean with the immoral people of this world, or with the covetous and swindlers, or with idolaters; for then you would have to go out of the world. But actually, I wrote to you **not to associate with any so-called brother if he should be an immoral person,** or covetous, or an idolater, or a reviler, or a drunkard, or a swindler— not even to eat with such a one [1 Cor. 5:9-11].

> And **do not participate** in the unfruitful deeds of darkness, but instead even expose them [Eph. 5:11].

(4). General Disobedience to the Scripture

While there can be toleration for differences and weakness in others (Phil. 3:15), flagrant violation of any major Biblical doctrine, ethical standard or attitude can be grounds for separation.

> Now we command you, brethren, in the name of our Lord Jesus Christ, that you keep **aloof from every brother who leads an unruly life and not according to the tradition which you received from us....And**

if anyone does not obey our instruction in this letter, take special note of that man and **do not associate with him,** so that he may be put to shame. And yet do not regard him as an enemy, but admonish him as a brother [2 Thess. 3:6, 14-15].

b. Contemporary Theological Schools of Thought

The above verses establish the principle of separation. A study of various theological trends will help in the practice of separation.

(1). Liberalism

Liberalism can be a vague term. The quotes below by J. I. Packer list the tenets of religious liberalism.[12]

"God's character is one of pure benevolence."

Liberals believe that all people are the children of God. He is a God of pure love who would never submit any human to eternal punishment.

"There is a divine spark in every man."

Humans do not so much need salvation as they need the right environment and right encouragement to cause their natural goodness to be expressed.

"Jesus Christ is man's Savior only in the sense that He is man's perfect Teacher and Example."

He was not God nor born of a virgin, but He did express great moral principles. The crucifixion was an unfortunate twist of history that cut short the career of a wise teacher. Christ did not rise from the dead.

"Just as Christ differs from other men only comparatively, not absolutely, so Christianity differs from other religions not generically, but merely as the best and highest type of religion that has yet appeared."

The goal of foreign missions, therefore, ought not to be to convert those in other religions but to enrich their understanding of Christianity and to provide social/humanitarian help.

"The Bible is not a divine record of revelation, but a human testament of religion."

The Bible does not give us the Word of God. It is a record of the religious insight and experiences of wise men of bygone times.

(2). Fundamentalism

One needs to make a great distinction between the classical theological definition of "fundamentalism" and contemporary use of the term in the media.

The term fundamentalism arose in the early part of the 20th Century. It is now used in a derogatory sense of any religious maniac. However, "fundamentalism," as a term has a definite meaning and a noble heritage.

In 1909 Lyman and Milton Stewart, two oil millionaires from California, sponsored the publication of a series of twelve paper bound books called "The Fundamentals." The authors included James Orr, B.B. Warfield, W.H. Griffith-Thomas, R.A. Torrey, A.T. Pierson, and G. Campbell Morgan. These books were sent free of charge to over three million Christian workers. The goal was to send these studies to every pastor, missionary, theological student, and Sunday school superintendent in the English-speaking world.[13]

---

[12] J. I. Packer, *Fundamentalism and the Word of God,* reprint ed. (Grand Rapids: Wm. B. Eerdmans Publishing Co., 1977), pp. 25-26. The material in quotes comes from Dr. Packer. Additional comments give my own paraphrase following Packer's thoughts closely.

[13] See Torrey, R. A., ed. *The Fundamentals: The Famous Sourcebook of Foundational Biblical Truths,* reprint ed. (Grand Rapids, Kregal Publications, 1990).

From a conference held at Niagra in 1895 and from debates in the General Assembly of the Northern Presbyterian Church in 1910 came a general agreement as to five fundamentals of fundamentalism: the infallibility of the Bible, the deity of Christ, His virgin birth and miracles, Christ's atoning and substitutionary death, and His physical resurrection and personal return. The fundamentalists also believed in salvation by faith, in the existence of heaven for believers and hell for unbelievers, and most rejected evolution.[14] Because the term *fundamentalism* is so misunderstood at the present time, it is well to explain what definition is intended before using it in conversation with others. In its historical definition, *fundamentalist* is basically synonymous with evangelical, conservative, and orthodox.

(3). Neo-evangelicalism

The term New or Neo-evangelical was coined in addresses at Fuller Seminary in 1948.[15] The neo-evangelical position is supposedly a compromise between fundamentalism and liberalism. Early advocates of neo-evangelicalism were personally conservative but believed in accommodation with liberals. Those with such a mentality are also often called "moderates." Neo-evangelicals either deny the inerrancy of Scripture or are willing to cooperate with those who do. The infallibility of the Bible is not considered a doctrine of ultimate importance. Neo-evangelicals or evangelicals or moderates do not take a stand on literal creation or the Genesis Flood. They may or may not be personally committed to some form of theistic evolution, but they will join forces with those who deny a literal interpretation of Genesis. Neo-evangelicals often stress cooperative evangelistic campaigns among groups of all beliefs. Neo-evangelicals have an excessive concern for acceptance by liberal "scholarship." They do not believe in separation. Many neo-evangelicals believe in greater involvement with social and political issues (e.g., the ordination of women).

c. The Specifics of Separation

(1). Submissive Versus Rebellious Attitude Toward the Bible

In the practice of separation, a church (or an individual) should distinguish not only differences in doctrine but also differences in attitude toward the Scripture.

A liberal's attitude is that he may stand in arrogant judgment upon the Bible with the freedom either to choose or reject a Biblical statement. The liberal might think, "The Bible says that there is a place called hell; but I do not believe it."

On the other hand, **conservatives** believe what they do **because they think the Bible teaches it**. Even when they believe a doctrinal error, they do so because they think the Bible teaches their error; and **they want to be in submission to the Scripture**. A conservative might erroneously believe that one can lose salvation or that the gift of healing exists today. However, he believes those things because he can find Bible verses that seem to teach them. **Even if one cannot totally agree with a mistaken interpretation, at least the attitude of submission to Biblical authority** and viewing it as the final source for doctrine can **be heartily commended**.

---

[14] For additional details about church history in the early 20th Century, see Packer, J. I. *Fundamentalism and the Word of God.* (Grand Rapids: Wm. B. Eerdmans Publishing Co., 1977) or Cairns, Earle E. *Christianity Through the Centuries,* Revised ed. (Grand Rapids: Zondervan Publishing Co., 1967), or Marsden, George, *Fundamentalism and American Culture.* (Oxford: Oxford University Press, 1980).

[15] Robert P. Lightner, *Neoevangelicalism Today* (Schaumberg, Il: Regular Baptist Press, 1978), p. 44.

In the difficult area of practicing separation, it seems that a church must take into consideration the huge difference between those who place themselves above the authority of the Bible by denying its clear and repeated teachings, and those who place themselves under what they believe to be the Bible's teaching, even if they do make mistakes concerning secondary doctrines.

Some doctrines are so clearly and repeatedly taught that all those who are yielded to Biblical authority agree on them. These are the fundamentals recognized by Bible believers in all denominations. They include the following cardinal tenets: the creation of man, the Trinity, virgin birth, deity of Christ, physical resurrection, Second Coming, substitutionary atonement, salvation by faith alone without works, the infallibility of the Bible, and the realities of heaven and hell. Regardless of mistakes on other doctrines, those in submission to the Bible will believe these things because these are so clearly and repeatedly taught in Scripture. The only excuse for denying one or more of them is that the person has a liberal attitude toward Scripture by which he gives his own mind the authority to reject what the Word of God clearly teaches.

Adherence to these fundamentals displays an attitude of submission to the Word of God. Despite interpretive errors in other areas, people who adhere to the fundamentals ought to be considered brothers and sisters in Christ. Even when they do believe in other less serious errors, it is because they sincerely think the Bible teaches it. Thus, if the particular error is blameworthy, the underlying allegiance to Christ and treatment of His Word is still worthy of approval. It is best to have a philosophy of separation which is flexible enough for a church to recognize the good points of other theological heritages while at the same time pursuing and promoting its own doctrinal distinctiveness on the issues which divide sincere Bible-believers. It is better to view separation in terms of widening circles (Chart A) than by an area divided by a line (Chart B).

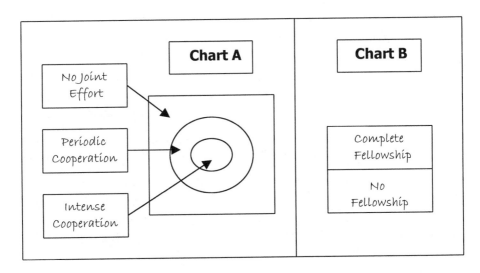

(2). Circles of Fellowship

There should be no ecclesiastical union or joint cooperation with groups who deny any of the fundamentals. In most cases such alliances would be with unbelievers. In all cases those who would deny any of the fundamentals are different in outlook from those who make innocent interpretive mistakes. They are in rebellion against Christ by their attitude of placing their own minds above the authority of the Bible. Uniting with such reveals dishonor toward Christ and disobedience to His Word.

Intense cooperation between conservatives of various theological camps is not practical because of clashes that inevitably would arise in teaching (e.g., eternal security, infant baptism, spiritual gifts). Yet, love, humility, and forbearance demand that a distinction be made between Bible-rejecting liberals and Bible-believing conservatives. We want to love those who are faithful to the fundamentals. (See John 13:35; Eph. 4:3; Col. 3:13-14.)

A church adopting the basic doctrinal view contained in this book should maintain its doctrinal accuracy in all details by reserving church leadership and probably even church membership to those who agree with all its details in doctrine. However, it should also feel free to recognize other conservatives as brethren and cooperate with them as considered wise by those with authority for church government. Intense fellowship (e.g., calling one to serve on the staff or the elder board or to teach Sunday school) should be reserved for complete doctrinal agreement. However, less close and binding fellowship with other conservatives should be considered an option so long as it does not imperil the whole doctrinal position of the church (e.g., cooperation among conservative Bible churches, Baptists, Presbyterians, charismatic groups, etc., in joint ministries such as supporting a Crisis Pregnancy Center, a Bible distribution effort, or a Christian radio outreach).

2. Church Discipline

The topics of separation and church discipline do overlap, but they are also different. Separation is a principle that helps prevent impurity entering the church. Church discipline is a principle that removes impurity from the church after it has infiltrated or arisen from within. Furthermore, the goal of church discipline is more remedial. Discipline occurs with a view that fellowship should be restored. Separation means that no fellowship is possible.

a. Biblical Commands for Church Discipline

Several verses give a clear basis for the discipline of a professing Christian in serious and unrepentant sin. As most of these verses will be given in full in following sections, only key phrases occur here.

...those who **cause dissensions...turn away** from them [Rom. 16:17].

I wrote you in my letter **not to associate** with **immoral people** [1 Cor. 5:9].

But actually, I wrote to you **not to associate** with any **so-called brother** if he should be an immoral person...[1 Cor. 5:11a].

...**Remove the wicked man** from among yourselves [1 Cor. 5:13].

...**keep aloof from** every brother who leads **an unruly life**...[2 Thess. 3:6].

And if anyone does **not obey our instruction** in this letter...**do not associate** with him so that he may be put to shame. And yet do not regard him as an enemy, but **admonish him as a brother** [2 Thess. 3:14-15].

Reject a factious man after a first and second warning, knowing that such a man is perverted and is sinning, being self-condemned [Titus 3:10-11].

358

The Scripture not only gives permission for discipline, it commands it. A typical objection is that discipline is not compatible with love. However, God Himself disciplines those whom He loves (Heb. 12:5ff.). True love speaks the truth (Eph. 4:15), it rejoices in righteousness and truth (1 Cor. 13:6), and it keeps God's commandments (2 John 6). In fact, those who love another will desire correction so that their lives will not be harmed by sin. Just as God's correction shows love and is for our ultimate good (Heb. 12:10-11) and just as parental discipline is ultimately for a child's welfare, so church discipline is for the good of an offender.

b. Biblical Reasons for the Exercise of Discipline

The discipline process and/or the removal of a church member nearly always elicits protest from some in the church. Therefore, it is important to understand the necessity of church discipline. The first reason that discipline must be practiced is that God commands it. That ought to be a sufficient basis for its practice in modern times. However, secondly, Paul gives an ancient equivalent to the "one good apple spoils the whole barrel" maxim to both the Corinthians and the Galatians.

Your boasting is not good. Do you not know that **a little leaven leavens the whole lump of dough**? Clean out the old leaven, that you may be a new lump...[1 Cor. 5:6-7].

A little leaven leavens the whole lump of dough [Gal. 5:9].

Negligence in the area of church discipline can be fatal to a church's holiness. Neither gross sin nor serious doctrinal error may be tolerated in the church because of its corrupting effect. It is true in any time period, ancient and modern, that rebels arise to test the moral backbone of the church. When the church backs down time and again, it not only loses its credibility, it leaves the impression (especially upon the upcoming generation) that any behavior will be tolerated. A church that will not discipline runs the risk of becoming a "moral zoo" where just about anything goes. When the church backs down on point A, someone will assuredly test point B. If no sin is too bad to obtain rebuke and condemnation, then every sin will occur by someone who says he is a "Christian."

A third reason that discipline must occur is that it can be beneficial to the offender. Admittedly, the fact that other churches will often accept a disciplined party with "no questions asked" tends to reduce the hope that discipline will produce a moral change. Still, God rules in the heart, and He uses discipline as a means of bringing about repentance.

Brethren, even if a man is caught in any trespass, you who are spiritual, **restore such a one in a spirit of gentleness**; each one looking to yourself, lest you too be tempted [Gal. 6:1].

All discipline for the moment seems not to be joyful, but sorrowful; yet to those who have been trained by it, **afterwards it yields the peaceful fruit of righteousness** [Heb. 12:11].

Stripes that wound **scour away evil** ...[Prov. 20: 30].

Faithful are the **wounds of a friend**...[Prov. 27:6].

The goal of church discipline is not punishment; it is restoration. When a church refuses to discipline, its failure can only make matters worse. The offender is less likely to repent. Others are more likely to test whether the church will compromise on other sins. Lacking moral fiber, respect for the church is lost. Even unbelievers expect the church to have a strong moral stand. Worse than all of the above is a disobedience toward God that diminishes His favor.

c. Offenses that Merit Discipline

Now I urge you, brethren, keep your eye on **those who cause dissensions** and hindrances contrary to the teaching which you learned, and turn away from them. For such men are slaves, not of our Lord Christ but of their own appetites; and by **their smooth and flattering speech they deceive** the hearts of the unsuspecting [Rom. 16:17-18].

I wrote you in my letter **not to associate with immoral people**; I did not at all mean with the immoral people of this world, or with the covetous and swindlers, or with idolaters; for then you would have to go out of the world. But actually, I wrote to you **not to associate with any so called brother if he should be an immoral person, or covetous, or an idolater, or a reviler, or a drunkard, or a swindler**— not even to eat with such a one....**Remove the wicked man** from among yourselves [1 Cor. 5:9-11, 13].

Now we command you, brethren, in the name of our Lord Jesus Christ, that you **keep aloof** from every brother who leads an **unruly life** and **not according to the tradition** which you received from us....And if anyone **does not obey our instruction in this letter**, take special note of that man and **do not associate** with him, so that he may be put to shame. And yet **do not regard him as an enemy, but admonish him as a brother** [2 Thess. 3:6,14-15].

Reject a **factious man** after a first and second warning, knowing that such a man is perverted and is sinning, being self-condemned [Titus 3:10-11].

Offenses that make one liable to discipline include these: immorality, covetousness, idolatry, reviling (slander), drunkenness, being a swindler, being divisive, living an unruly life, disobedience to apostolic instruction. It must be noted that the Bible does not include murderers, drug dealers, or abortion clinic operators on the list of those to be removed from fellowship. It seems that the Apostle Paul is giving representative cases where discipline should be enforced without trying to make an exhaustive list. There is no complete list of offenses that warrant disciplinary measures by the church. Apparently, the basis for discipline must remain somewhat subjective. In general any serious and unconfessed sin may be grounds for discipline depending on whether, in the judgment of church authority, it constitutes a serious enough sin to withdraw fellowship.

d. Administration of Church Discipline

(1). The Persons in Authority

The actual practice of church discipline is nearly always a nightmare that causes trauma for a church (unless there is immediate repentance). It will be even worse if a church has not agreed upon a basic procedure. This will just tend to increase the usual charges of partiality and the confusion that accompanies discipline. While integrity demands that one operating under a constitution and by-laws follows its procedure (as far as it is compatible with Scripture), there are reasons, both Scriptural and practical, for placing responsibility for church discipline in the hands of qualified elders. The Bible makes elders "overseers" and gives them the responsibility to protect the flock from "wolves" (see Acts 20:28ff.). How can elders protect from wolves if they do not also have the authority to remove wolves! Again the concept of implied powers comes into play. Given that God wants the elders to protect the church from evildoers, it must be that He wants them to have the authority to remove evildoers.

Beyond this Scriptural point, there are practical considerations for elders having the authority to discipline. Church discipline involves the courage to make tough decisions and suffer the consequences for them. Many people in any church lack the emotional detachment to make objective judgments involving friends. Furthermore, there is only the remotest of possibilities that an entire congregation can debate a disciplinary case and retain church unity. While the Bible teaches discipline as a general principle, it obviously does not give guidance in specific cases. Someone must determine whether or not the person was guilty. Someone must determine whether or not the sin is serious enough to deserve discipline. Someone must determine whether or not repentance has occurred. Someone must determine whether or not public confession will be required. Someone must determine the exact nature of discipline. Seldom are these decisions easy even when a small group of godly leaders makes them after a thorough investigation of the facts. It can be next to impossible for hundreds of church members to be well enough informed to make fair judgments and just as unlikely that a whole congregation can administer church discipline without bitterness and/or divisions. When Matt. 18:17 commands to take a grievance to the church, it can mean to take the matter to the authority representing the church (the elders) and need not demand congregational judgment.

(2). Points of Procedure

The Bible commands that discipline must occur without partiality. There must not be extra harshness towards some in a spirit of vindictiveness, nor can there be leniency toward a favorite party who may be able to engage in serious sin without being challenged.

> These also are sayings of the wise. **To show partiality in judgment is not good** [Prov. 24:23].

Those who continue in sin, rebuke in the presence of all, so that the rest also may be fearful of sinning. **I solemnly charge you** in the presence of God and of Christ Jesus and of His chosen angels, **to maintain these principles without bias**, doing **nothing in a spirit of partiality** [1 Tim. 5:20-21].

Matt. 18:15-17 does not technically involve a case of church discipline that is initiated by church authority against a member in deep sin. It concerns a situation of a private grievance of one believer against another that is eventually brought to the church for consideration. Therefore, it may not be mandatory for church discipline to be conducted with the exact procedure in Matthew 18 for all cases. In very serious situations a church may be split in the course of a week, and the leadership needs to have the option to move with speed. Also, the practice of an initial private encounter without witnesses can be a poor device when the offender might possibly lie about the conversation in order to disrupt the church. Nevertheless, the Matt. 18:15-17 passage may be applied to cases of church discipline and should be followed if at all possible.

> "And if your brother sins, go and **reprove him in private**; if he listens to you, you have won your brother. But **if he does not listen** to you, **take one or two with you** so that by the mouth of two or three witnesses every fact may be confirmed. And if he refuses to listen to them, tell it to the church; and if he refuses to listen even to the church, let him be to you as a Gentile and a tax-gatherer" [Matt. 18:15-17].

If there is a serious sin without repentance or even the charge of such sin, it is possible for an elder to act the role of the offended party and try to elicit a confession in private. Hopefully, the private encounter will yield genuine confession of sin and cessation of its practice so that no further procedure is necessary.

If the sin did occur and there is no confession after the first private encounter, then a second effort should be made prior to withdrawal of fellowship. Regardless of whether the procedure of a one-on-one meeting is adopted, there should always be a second warning (see Titus 3:10) even if the second contact occurs relatively soon after the first. Also, the Bible gives a principle of having two or three witnesses before a charge may be deemed credible (see Num. 35:30; Deut. 19:15; 2 Cor. 13:1; 1 Tim. 5:19). It is unclear whether the two or three witnesses in Matt. 18:16 are witnesses to the guilt of the offender or witnesses to the second attempt to secure repentance. Both types of witnesses should be present in a case of church discipline. There must be ample evidence as to guilt so that discipline is not based upon slander. Also, witnesses to the discipline procedure can attest that a loving attempt was made to secure repentance before any removal of fellowship, and they can bear testimony to what was and what was not said at the encounter.

Although the congregation need not be the governing body in church discipline cases, it will need to be notified when discipline has occurred. If elders want to protect sheep from wolves, they must identify them. Without clear warning, unsuspecting believers may be duped by the smooth words of one who is in reality very wicked in nature (see Psa. 28:3, Prov. 26:25).

Not only must a congregation be warned when someone is guilty and unrepentant of a serious sin, it must participate in the discipline by withdrawal of fellowship. Ancient Jewish custom was that one under discipline could only attend the synagogue for purposes of spiritual counsel in private conversation with the rabbis. Other than coming to the synagogue for purposes of restoration, the offender was not welcome in the services and

normal social ties were cut. Members directed him to the spiritual leaders for counsel.

Paul seems to have adopted a similar view to one under discipline. All interactions must be made with civility and gentleness with one who is not an enemy but an erring brother (2 Thess. 3:15). Still, there is an attitude of firm insistence that the wrong must be changed and normal relationships cannot resume until the sin is genuinely confessed.

There should be some flexibility as to whether the offender must be required to make public confession. The primary consideration is that confession must be made to God. If such occurs, then public confession may or may not be considered necessary. A wise general rule is that to the degree a sin is known and to the degree that it does damage, to the same extent it must be confessed. Certainly, one who is genuinely repentant should at least confess to the direct victims of a serious sin. Also, church leaders need to be sensitive to the fact that public confession can be a very good therapy for the offender. Rather than being a humiliating punishment, it can help remove guilt and restore respect in the sight of all church members. It helps remove doubts about the sincerity of the confession.

Something should be said about relatives of those under discipline. The Bible does not seem to address this problem. Yet, since the goal of discipline is not to punish but to correct, it seems that relatives of those disciplined should be allowed and encouraged to meet their family obligations and keep lines of communication open. As an example, this means that the physical brother of one disciplined for drunkenness should still be an exemplary brother. The mother of a son under discipline for immorality should not be required to sever her relationship to him as a mother. Such relationships may be strained and hard to maintain, and perhaps the family relationship will be severed by serious sins. The point here is that a church should encourage a family unit to fulfill responsibilities to a relative under discipline, (unless it would be dangerous, such as cases of child abuse or crimes.) If the family can work out the problem, the church should not view that withdrawal of fellowship from the offender inevitably requires family members to disassociate from their "black sheep" the same way another church member should. Although the sin may be serious enough to destroy family ties, officially the church should view such disruption as an optional family matter, not a matter of church business.

e. Conclusions on Church Discipline

Eccl. 8:11 teaches that discipline must follow soon after an infraction or else it loses any benefit in curtailing additional evils. The Bible requires church discipline for sins that are serious and unconfessed. Discipline should be enacted as speedily as fairness permits.

F. Church History - Denominations

Any detailed study on church history would be inappropriate here. However, it can be helpful to have some basic knowledge of various denominations. This is not only a matter of academic interest but assists a local church in the matter of separation.

It is true that the early church was catholic (meaning *universal*) for the first few centuries. However, it was assuredly not Roman Catholic. There were originally several cities that became centers of Christian authority: Jerusalem, Antioch, Constantinople, Alexandria, and Rome. As the barbarian hordes overran Italy, the church leaders in Rome stepped into the power vacuum with increasing secular authority. Furthermore, Rome's dominance was enhanced by Moslem conquests or threats to other cities where Christian leaders could challenge Rome's power.

Antioch, Alexandria, and Jerusalem came under Moslem domination. Constantinople was weakened but never did totally yield to Rome.

Protestant historians would disagree as to the starting point of the Roman Catholic Church. The church in Rome no doubt began in apostolic times. Some might see this as the beginning of Catholicism. However, it is also clear that Rome gained priority in Christendom only after the Islamic conquest of rival centers of Christianity in the east. Many would not consider the Roman Catholic Church in its present form to have begun until it became the world's most powerful church due to the destruction of the other Christian centers.

The Protestant church arose against a corrupt Roman Catholic system on three basic points: *sola fide* (salvation by faith alone), *sola Scriptua* (the Bible alone) rather than church tradition as final authority, and the priesthood of the believer (meaning that all believers had equal access to God with no need of a human intermediary or confessor).

There were four main branches to the Reformation: Lutheran, Calvinist, Anglican (the Church of England), and Anabaptists (Mennonites and Baptists). The main reason that the United States is home to so many denominations is that it is a melting pot for so many ethnic groups. The Europeans brought their denominations with them, and many are still distinct not only along doctrinal but ethnic lines (e.g., the Dutch Reformed and the Orthodox Presbyterian churches often agree on doctrine but are still separate. One is Dutch. The other is Scots-English).

The following chart shows the historical ties of Protestant churches coming from the Reformation:

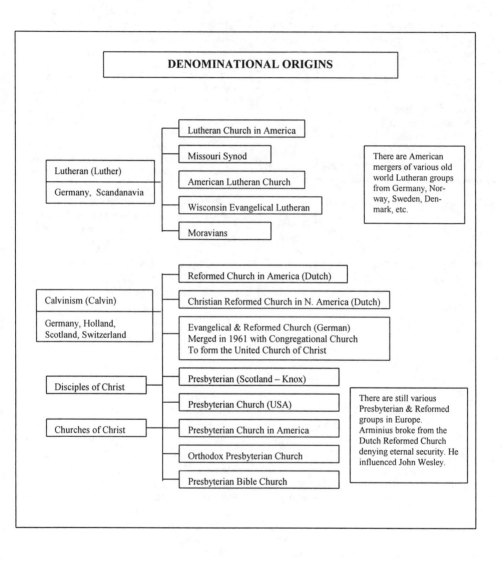

DENOMINATIONAL ORIGINS

Lutheran (Luther)

Germany, Scandanavia

- Lutheran Church in America
- Missouri Synod
- American Lutheran Church
- Wisconsin Evangelical Lutheran
- Moravians

There are American mergers of various old world Lutheran groups from Germany, Norway, Sweden, Denmark, etc.

Calvinism (Calvin)

Germany, Holland, Scotland, Switzerland

- Reformed Church in America (Dutch)
- Christian Reformed Church in N. America (Dutch)
- Evangelical & Reformed Church (German) Merged in 1961 with Congregational Church To form the United Church of Christ

Disciples of Christ

Churches of Christ

- Presbyterian (Scotland – Knox)
- Presbyterian Church (USA)
- Presbyterian Church in America
- Orthodox Presbyterian Church
- Presbyterian Bible Church

There are still various Presbyterian & Reformed groups in Europe. Arminius broke from the Dutch Reformed Church denying eternal security. He influenced John Wesley.

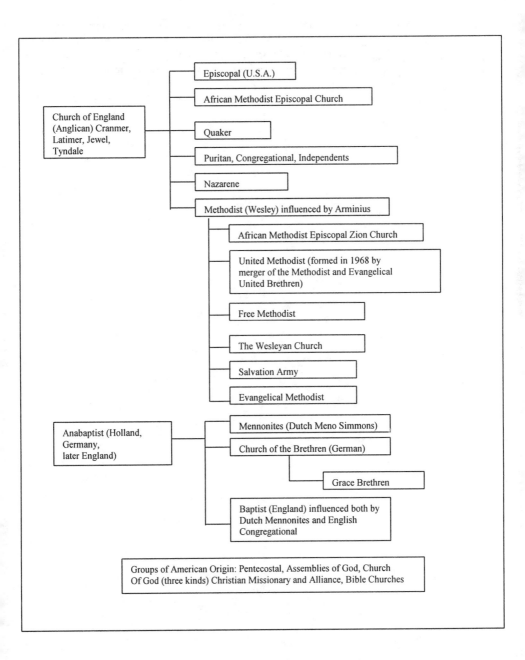

G. Conclusion on the Study of the Church

Believers in Christ, regardless of denomination, are permanent members of the universal church. At the Rapture, God will unite the universal church for a blessed eternity as the bride of Christ. Until then, part of the church resides in heaven, while those who are "alive and remain" must remain faithful to truth and must try to fulfill God's mission for the church. Encouragement and hope come from the Lord's promise: "I will build **My church**; and the gates of Hades will not overpower it" (Matt. 16:18).

Chapter 12
ESCHATOLOGY
The Doctrine of Future Events

(c) Angels
(d) Saved, All Dispensations
(e) Summary

ESCHATOLOGY
The Doctrine of Future Events

I. Introduction:

There can be no doubt that God wants His people to know about future events. One-quarter of Biblical books are prophetic with fully one-fifth of all Biblical material being prophetic in content.

The study of prophecy can be discredited by those who go beyond the Bible's statements about the future. It is clear that some things God has simply not revealed to man (Deut. 29:29; Matt. 24:36; Mark 13:32; Acts 1:7). Nevertheless, the Bible teaches much about the future even if it does not teach all about the future. Whatever it says is certainly a valid area for study and must not be neglected. The early church, for its first three centuries, understood the importance of eschatology. However, detailed Biblical knowledge about future events was lost during the dark ages. The Reformers were too busy at soteriological battlefronts to research eschatology. It is only within the last two centuries that Bible students have renewed concentration upon eschatology.

One story is illustrative of a previous neglect. Dr. Dabney was one of the most respected of American theologians of the 19th century. "Dr. R. L. Dabney, the honored theologian of the South, when asked by a former student whether certain interpretations of prophecy were correct, replied, 'you are probably right. I have never looked into the subject.' " [1]

The excesses of those who go beyond the Bible in prophetic assertions must not force the church to a return to its traditional neglect and/or ignorance of future events. The Lord told us that the Holy Spirit would "show you things to come" (John 16:13), and there is a special blessing for those who read and understand prophecy (Rev. 1:3). Knowledge of eschatology is not only intellectually rewarding but also spiritually enriching. The Bible teaches this repeatedly.

Knowledge of future judgment may bring a person to salvation by faith in Christ. The following passage ties knowledge about the Second Coming and judgment to a person finding **salvation** for his soul.

"For what will a man be profited, if he gains the whole world, and forfeits his soul? Or what will a man give in exchange for his soul? For the Son of Man is going to come in the glory of His Father with His angels; and will then recompense every man according to his deeds" [Matt. 16:26-27].

For those who are already believers, the study of future events should purify their lives. The following verses link the Lord's coming to believers and **holiness** in life.

Let your forbearing spirit be known to all men. The Lord is near [Phil. 4:5].

When Christ, who is our life, is revealed, then you also will be revealed with Him in glory. Therefore consider the members of your earthly body as dead to immorality, impurity, passion, evil desire, and greed, which amounts to idolatry. For it is on account of these things that the wrath of God will come [Col. 3:4-6].

Now may the God of peace Himself sanctify you entirely; and may your spirit and soul and body be preserved complete, without blame at the com-

---

[1] Quoted by Lewis Sperry Chafer, *Systematic Theology* (Dallas Theological Seminary Press, 1948), IV: 256.

ing of our Lord Jesus Christ [1 Thess. 5:23].

For the grace of God has appeared, bringing salvation to all men, instructing us to deny ungodliness and worldly desires and to live sensibly, righteously and godly in the present age, looking for the blessed hope and the appearing of the glory of our great God and Savior, Christ Jesus [Titus 2:11-13].

Since all these things are to be destroyed in this way, what sort of people ought you to be in holy conduct and godliness [2 Pet. 3:11].

Beloved, now we are children of God, and it has not appeared as yet what we shall be. We know that, when He appears, we shall be like Him, because we shall see Him just as He is. And everyone who has this hope fixed on Him purifies himself, just as He is pure [1 John 3:2-3].

Knowledge of the future helps produce what the Bible calls "sobriety of life". Believers who ponder the future know that life has a serious side to it with responsibilities for serious pursuits. Sobriety of perspective overlaps with an awareness of the need for purity, but it also includes an awareness of the need for **service**. Eschatology should make believers sense the **urgency of their work**. (See also in addition to the following printed texts: Matt. 25:14ff.; Luke 12:42ff.; 19:12ff.; 1 Thess. 5:4-9).

"Blessed is that slave whom his master finds so doing when he comes" [Luke 12:43].

"We must work the works of Him who sent Me, as long as it is day; night is coming, when no man can work" [John 9:4].

And this do, knowing the time, that it is already the hour for you to awaken from sleep; for now salvation is nearer to us than when we believed. The night is almost gone, and the day is at hand. Let us therefore lay aside the deeds of darkness and put on the armor of light. Let us behave properly as in the day, not in carousing and drunkenness, not in sexual promiscuity and sensuality, not in strife and jealousy [Rom. 13:11-13].

Therefore also we have as our ambition, whether at home or absent, to be pleasing to Him. For [because] we must all appear before the judgment seat of Christ, that each one may be recompensed for his deeds in the body, according to what he has done, whether good or bad [2 Cor. 5:9-10].

I solemnly charge you in the presence of God and of Christ Jesus, who is to judge the living and the dead, and by His appearing and His kingdom: preach the word; be ready in season and out of season; reprove, rebuke, exhort, with great patience and instruction [2 Tim. 4:1-2].

Therefore, gird your minds for action, keep sober in spirit, fix your hope completely on the grace to be brought to you at the revelation of Jesus Christ [1 Peter 1:13].

The end of all things is at hand; therefore, be of sound judgment and sober spirit for the purpose of prayer [1 Pet. 4:7].

Therefore, I exhort the elders among you, as your fellow elder and witness of the sufferings of Christ, and a partaker also of the glory that is to be revealed, shepherd the flock of God among you, exercising oversight not under compulsion, but voluntarily, according to the will of God; and not for sordid gain, but with eagerness; not yet as lording it over those allotted to your charge, but proving to be examples to the flock. And when the Chief Shepherd appears, you will receive the unfading crown of glory [1 Peter 5:1-4].

In addition to stimulating purity and providing motivation for work, knowledge of future events gives **comfort in suffering** and in times when believers face the ridicule of the world. The informed believer need fear neither his personal future nor premature world destruction.

"Let not your heart be troubled; believe in God, believe also in Me. In My Father's house are many dwelling places; if it were not so, I would have told you; for I go to prepare a place for you. And if I go and prepare a place for you, I will come again, and receive you to Myself; that where I am, there you may be also. And you know the way where I am going." Thomas said to Him, "Lord, we do not know where You are going, how do we know the way?" Jesus said to him, "I am the way, and the truth, and the life; no one comes to the Father, but through Me" [John 14:1-6].

For I consider that the sufferings of this present time are not worthy to be compared with the glory that is to be revealed to us [Rom. 8:18].

Therefore do not go on passing judgment before the time, but wait until the Lord comes who will both bring to light the things hidden in the darkness and disclose the motives of men's hearts; and then each man's praise will come to him from God [1 Cor. 4:5].

For momentary, light affliction is producing for us an eternal weight of glory far beyond all comparison [2 Cor. 4:17].

And let us not lose heart in doing good, for in due time we shall reap if we do not grow weary [Gal. 6:9].

But we do not want you to be uninformed, brethren, about those who are asleep, that you may not grieve, as do the rest who have no hope. For if we believe that Jesus died and rose again, even so God will bring with Him those who have fallen asleep in Jesus. For this we say to you by the word of the Lord, that we who are alive, and remain until the coming of the Lord, shall not precede those who have fallen asleep. For the Lord Himself will descend from heaven with a shout, with the voice of the archangel, and with the trumpet of God; and the dead in Christ shall rise first. Then we who are alive and remain shall be caught up together with them in the clouds to meet the Lord in the air, and thus we shall always be with the Lord. Therefore, comfort one another with these words [1 Thess. 4:13-18].

Therefore, do not throw away your confidence, which has a great reward. For you have need of endurance, so that when you have done the will of God, you may receive what was promised. For yet in a very little while, He who is coming will come, and will not delay [Heb. 10:35-37].

Be patient, therefore, brethren, until the coming of the Lord. Behold, the farmer waits for the precious produce of the soil, being patient about it, until it gets the early and late rains. You too be patient; strengthen your hearts, for the coming of the Lord is at hand [James 5:7-8].

[T]hat the proof of your faith, being more precious than gold which is perishable, even though tested by fire, may be found to result in praise and glory and honor at the revelation of Jesus Christ [1 Peter 1:7].

[B]ut to the degree that you share the sufferings of Christ, keep on rejoicing; so that also at the revelation of His glory, you may rejoice with exultation [1 Peter 4:13].

God intends that the study of eschatology be spiritually stimulating, intellectually satisfying and psychologically stabilizing. In order to build a foundation for the intelligent study of eschatology it is best to define some common terms. Also, one will have to understand the typical pretribulational/premillennial time chart before it can be intelligently defended and discussed. Here are some basic eschatological terms with the prophetic time line that will be taught in the course of this study.

Eschatology - This term is from two Greek words *(eschatos* - last, and *logos* - word). Eschatology means a word or study about last things, meaning the future.

Rapture - This word is the Latin translation of the phrase "caught up" in 1 Thess. 4:17. It refers to Christ coming in the clouds to take all believers with Him.

Tribulation - As a technical term "tribulation" refers to a time of great suffering which Jesus predicted in Matt. 24:21 (see also Jer. 30:7, Dan. 12:1). Dan. 9:27 indicates the period will be 7 years long (a "week" here means a seven-year cycle). The last half of the Tribulation is called the Great Tribulation and is 3 1/2 years long. (See Daniel 7:25; 12:7; Rev. 12:14; "time, times, dividing of time;" Rev. 11:2; 13:5; "forty-two months;" Rev. 11:3; 12:6; "1260 days").

Pretribulational Rapture - The view that believers will not have to go through the Tribulation but will be raptured before it begins. This is the best view.

Partial Rapture - The view that Christ will remove "spiritual" Christians before the Tribulation but allow others to remain to face the Tribulation.

Midtribulation Rapture - The view that believers will be on earth for the first 3 1/2 years of the Tribulation but will be raptured before the Great Tribulation (i.e., the last 3 1/2 years).

Posttribulation - The view that believer's must go through the entire 7 year Tribulation. Then Christ will come again. (With this view there is no difference between Rapture and Revelation or Second Coming. Both would occur at the same time).

Judgment Seat of Christ - This judgment pertains only to Christians. It occurs after the Rapture while there is the Tribulation on the earth. Christians will be judged on the basis of works for rewards. Salvation is not the issue (2 Cor. 5:10; Rom. 14:10; 1 Cor. 3:14-15).

Marriage of the Lamb - The church is the bride of Christ in the sense of being engaged to Him (2 Cor. 11:2). Revelation 19 places the wedding itself in heaven just before the Revelation, or Second Coming.

Revelation or Second Coming - Though the phrase "Second Coming" is used loosely to refer to either Rapture or Revelation, technically the terms "**Second Coming**" and "**Revelation**" refer to Christ's coming **to the earth with His saints at the end of the Tribulation**. (The **Rapture** refers to His coming **in the clouds for His saints before the Tribulation**.). There are 7 years between the Rapture and the Revelation. At the Revelation, Christ is coming to destroy the Antichrist at Armageddon and to set up His Kingdom on earth (Jude 14-15).

Judgment of The Nations - This is the judgment that takes place after the Revelation when the Lord is beginning to set up His rule on earth. The word "nations" comes from the word *ethna* (ethnic) in Matt. 25:32, and it should be understood to mean a judgment of individuals who are of different ethnic groups. Christ will start His Kingdom by removing all non-believers to judgment (v. 46) and permitting those who have been saved in the Tribulation to enter the Kingdom (v.34).

Kingdom or Millennium - After the Revelation of Christ, the Lord will remove all of the unbeleivers and rule on the throne of David in Jerusalem for 1,000 years. The word *mille* is the Latin word for 1,000, and it comes from Rev. 20:1-8.

Premillennialism - The belief that Christ will come before the 1,000 year period and

will be present to rule over the earth from Jerusalem. This is the best view.

Amillennialism - The position that there will be no earthly rule of Christ over the Jews from Jerusalem. One basic view among amillennialists is that the Jews rejected their King and, therefore, are not entitled to have the Old Testament promises fulfilled.

Dominion Theology, Reconstructionism, Neo-postmillennialism - These are all terms for a movement that teaches the church should and eventually will dominate the world. Those in this movement believe in political involvement with the goal and the expectation that the world will become

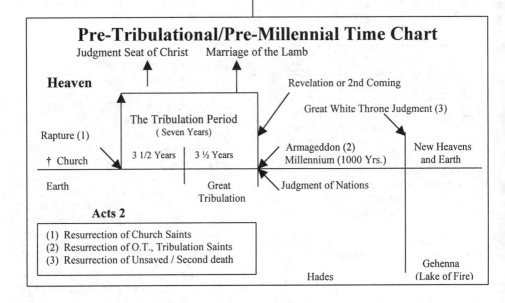

Pre-Tribulational/Pre-Millennial Time Chart

Judgment Seat of Christ   Marriage of the Lamb

Heaven

Revelation or 2nd Coming

Great White Throne Judgment (3)

The Tribulation Period
(Seven Years)

Rapture (1)

Armageddon (2)

New Heavens
and Earth

† Church   3 1/2 Years | 3 ½ Years   Millennium (1000 Yrs.)

Earth   Great
Tribulation   Judgment of Nations

Acts 2

(1) Resurrection of Church Saints
(2) Resurrection of O.T., Tribulation Saints
(3) Resurrection of Unsaved / Second death

Gehenna
(Lake of Fire)

Hades

better and better spiritually. With postmillennialism there will be a 1,000-year Christian kingdom on earth **before** the Second Coming.

Great White Throne Judgment - At the end of the Millennium the unsaved dead will be raised to stand trial and to be formally condemned for not receiving the Lord Jesus Christ as Savior (Rev. 20:11-15).

Eternal State - At the end of the 1,000 years the Kingdom on earth merges with the Kingdom in heaven. The Eternal State is the same as heaven.

There are several good ways to organize a study on eschatology. One could profit from building a prophetic system logically (as opposed to chronologically), reasoning from clear truths to the more complex points. First, it is relatively easy to prove that the Bible promises Israel a Kingdom on earth (see Section XIII "Christ's Kingdom on earth", pp. 471ff.). Next Christ, in the Olivet Discourse, clearly teaches that His coming to the earth will precede this Kingdom and that prior to His arrival there will be a period of tribulation (e.g., Matt. 24:21,29-31). The next step would be to explain that texts which refer to Christ's Second Coming seem to involve two phases of that coming (one in which He comes in the clouds for His saints to receive them to heaven and another in which He comes all the way to the earth with His saints and remains here for a Kingdom). A final step would be to argue that there must be a time span between these two phases and that the first aspect occurs prior to the Tribulation. Advanced students would probably benefit more from this strictly logical approach to building an eschatological system. However, the same approach could be very confusing to beginners. This study will follow the more chronological approach for the sake of those who may not be familiar with Biblical eschatology.

II. Scriptural Expectations for the Course of the Church System

With the evident decline in morals and spirituality, the call for Christian political action is quite valid. All Christians can agree that "righteousness exalts a nation" (Prov. 14:34). Virtue for virtue's sake alone is good, and all Christians should be sensitive to their civic responsibilities.

However, modern Christians view political involvement from widely divergent philosophical grounds. Some believe that the primary mission of the church is to rescue individuals from the world through the gospel. These would make political and social efforts to be at best secondary projects. They maintain that the best a government can do for the Church is to leave it alone (cf. "peace" in 1 Tim. 2:1-2), granting the freedom to fulfill its mission. The government is accountable to God for the promotion of basic natural law (Rom. 2:14-15), but Christians should not desire the imposition of the entire Law of Moses on society, and they certainly do not want a theocratic state with compulsion to worship, believe, or give.

Other Christians approach political/social action with different expectations. They believe that Christians can actually reconstruct society through dominating its social/political institutions. They believe that the end result will be a Christian society (essentially a theocracy ruled by Biblical law including the Law of Moses) which is prepared to receive its King at His Second Coming. This later school of thought goes by various names, "theocratic postmillennialism", "reconstructionism" or "dominion theology." It is growing among charismatics who tend to transfer their belief in individual miracles to hope for a miraculous transformation of the whole society. Also, it is strong in conservative Reformed/Presbyterian circles.

While all conservatives have far more similarities than differences, it is proper to criticize the unrealistic expectations of dominion theology and to point out the dangers of sidetracking the church from its more important goal, evangelization. The bringing in of the Kingdom is not the task of the church. While tolerant relationships between church and state can enhance the furtherance of the gospel, those who think society can be transformed by law and politics will experience disillusionment. The Bible does not picture the church age as one of complete triumph of the gospel, nor does it teach that the spiritual condition of the world must be or will be at a high point for the Second Coming of Christ. [2] It pictures the opposite as will be evident in the course of this study. In addition, while the church is a form of the Kingdom of God, God will work through Israel in the future, not the church in the present, to bring in the period of peace, righteousness, and holiness which the Bible promises.

It is true that the world will not extinguish the church during the present dispensation (Matt. 16:18). It is just as true that the church will not "conquer" the entire world either spiritually or politically. There will be **a mixture of good and evil**. This is the whole point of several of Christ's most notable parables.

> Then He left the multitudes, and went into the house. And His disciples came to Him, saying, "Explain to us the parable of the tares of the field," And He answered and said, "The one who sows the good seed is the Son of Man, and the field is the world, and **as for the good seed, these are the sons of the kingdom; and the tares are the sons of the evil one**; and the enemy who sowed them is the devil, and the harvest is the end of the age; and the reapers are angels. Therefore just as the tares are gathered up and burned with fire, so shall it be at the end of the age. The Son of Man will send forth His angels, and they will gather out of His kingdom all stumbling blocks, and those who commit lawlessness, and will cast them into the furnace of fire; in that place there shall be weeping and gnashing of teeth. Then the righteous will shine forth as the sun in the kingdom of their Father. He who has ears, let him hear" [Matt. 13:36-43].

> "Again, the kingdom of heaven is like a dragnet cast into the sea, and gathering fish of every kind; and when it was filled, they drew it up on the beach; and they sat down, and gathered the good fish into containers, but the bad they threw away. **So it will be at the end of the age; the angels shall come forth, and take out the wicked from among the righteous**, and will cast them into the furnace of fire; there shall be weeping and gnashing of teeth" [Matt. 13:47-50].

In this same sermon the Lord teaches that His Kingdom will indeed make progress during the period between His first and second comings. Consider the parables of the mustard seed and leaven (Matt. 13:31-33). Nevertheless, even at the end of the age the world will be a mixture of good and evil.

The church can be optimistic relative to delivering individuals from the world by the gospel (and every soul is important, see Luke 15:7,10). There should be no fear of the church failing (Matt. 16:18; Acts 1:8). Christians should pray for and work toward

---

[2] Texts that predict that the gospel will permeate the world before Christ returns need not pertain to the church dispensation. While the gospel should go throughout the world during the church dispensation, it is possible that predictions of a worldwide presentation of the gospel will be fulfilled only in the tribulation period, not the church period. Verses like Matt. 24:14 technically involve the tribulation period. The gospel will be presented to the world in the Tribulation by means of two witnesses (Rev. 11:3-12), a flying angel (Rev. 14:6) and probably the 144,000 witnesses who are sealed (i.e., protected from death, Rev. 7:3-8).

regional and temporal revivals, for they are most certainly possible. Nevertheless, despite these hopes for limited success, the Bible simply does not present the church age as one in which the world will be brought into submission to Christ; and it certainly would not encourage Christians to view God's work as involving the imposition of the Law of Moses upon society in order to transform it.

> "Enter by the narrow gate; for the gate is wide, and the way is broad that leads to **destruction**, and **many** are those who enter by it. For the gate is small, and the way is narrow that leads to **life**, and **few** are those who find it [Matt. 7:13-14].

> But realize this, that **in the last days difficult times will come**. For men will be lovers of self, lovers of money, boastful, arrogant, revilers, disobedient to parents, ungrateful, unholy, unloving, irreconcilable, malicious gossips, without self control, brutal, haters of good, treacherous, reckless, conceited, lovers of pleasure rather than lovers of God; holding to a form of godliness, although they have denied its power; and avoid such men as these.... And indeed, all who desire to live godly in Christ Jesus will be persecuted. But **evil men and impostors will proceed from bad to worse**, deceiving and being deceived [2 Tim. 3:1-5, 12-13].

III. The Rapture as a Valid Concept:

Despite the fact that some have ridiculed the concept of a "secret rapture," the Bible does seem to give two phases or elements to Christ's return. The first phase has been customarily called the "Rapture" after the Latin translation in 1 Thess. 4:17 meaning, "to snatch away." The KJV phrase is "caught up." Oddly enough "rapture" and "rape" are related in origin. Both include the notion of snatching away.

After laying some foundational points to enhance understanding of the issue, this section will develop the propositions that there are two phases to Christ's return and that the first of these, called the Rapture, occurs before the Tribulation and is the very next prophetic event. Nothing needs to be fulfilled before the Rapture can occur. We will follow a question-answer format.

A. How do we know that there is a Future "Tribulation Period"?

The Scriptures predict a time of great trouble for the earth. Jer. 30:7 mentions "a time of Jacob's trouble" with deliverance from it. This pertains to a future time because v. 9 teaches God will "raise up" David to be king as a part of the deliverance. Also, Jer. 30:24 says, "In the latter days you will understand this." Daniel 12 also teaches about a time of great trouble for Israel.

> "Now at that time Michael, the great prince who stands guard over the sons of your people, will arise. And there will be a **time of distress** [tribulation] such as has never occurred since there was a nation until that time; and at that time your people, everyone who is found written in the book, will be rescued" [Dan. 12:1].

The New Testament is just as clear as the Old on the point that the earth will experience a time of deep horrors in the end times. Christ's teachings are conclusive proof for the existence of a tribulation period (see Matt. 24:15-30; Mark 13:1-37: Luke 21:1-38). Note that the Lord equates this dreadful time with teachings from the book of Daniel (cf. Matt. 24:15 and Dan. 9:27, 11:36ff.).

> "Therefore when you see the ABOMINATION OF DESOLATION which was spoken of through Daniel the prophet, standing in the holy place (let the reader understand), then let those who are in Judea flee to the

mountains; let him who is on the housetop not go down to get the things out that are in the house; and let him who is in the field not turn back to get his cloak. But woe to those who are with child and to those who nurse babies in those days! But pray that your flight may not be in winter, or on a Sabbath; **for then there will be a great tribulation**, such as has not occurred since the beginnings of the world until now, nor ever shall be. And unless those days had been cut short, no life would have been saved; but for the sake of the elect those days shall be cut short. Then if anyone says to you, 'behold, here is the Christ,' or 'there He is' do not believe him. For false Christs and false prophets will arise and will show great signs and wonders, so as to mislead, if possible, even the elect. Behold, I have told you in advance" [Matt. 24:15-25].

The Apostle Paul refers to a time when sudden destruction will overtake those on earth who think that all is "peace and safety" (1 Thess. 5:1ff.). He also taught that conditions would degenerate to the point of great apostasy and the wicked man of sin demanding worship as God (2 Thess. 2:3-12).

Finally, any literal interpretation of the Book of Revelation leads to the conclusion that the events of Chapters 4 through 19 have not yet occurred and are not in progress. The miseries described in Revelation 4-19 are future and pertain to a time of tribulation.

Specific teachings about the tribulation period must await further sections. The immediate task is merely to establish that a tribulation period is a Biblical concept. Thus, it makes sense to argue over whether the Rapture occurs before or after it.

B. Why do Many Theologians View the Tribulation as a 7-year period?

In Matthew 24:15ff. Jesus identifies the future tribulation period with the period of time spoken of in Daniel 9:27. Daniel refers to a one "week" period, and he also gives significance to the middle of the week as being another sub-division of time. An evil prince who is coming will violate his peace pact with Israel in the middle of the "week." He will cause sacrifices in the temple to cease and desire that he be honored as God (see also Daniel 11:36; 2 Thess. 2:4ff.).

> "Therefore when you see the **ABOMINATION OF DESOLATION** which was spoken of through Daniel the prophet, standing in the holy place (let the reader understand), then let those who are in Judea flee to the mountains" [Matt. 24:15-16].

> "And he will make a firm covenant with the many for **one week**, but in **the middle of the week** he will put a stop to sacrifice and grain offering; and on the wing of **abominations** will come one who makes **desolate**, even until a complete destruction, one that is decreed, is poured out on the one who makes desolate" [Daniel 9:27].

The word translated "week" in Daniel 9 simply means a group or cycle of seven and does not by itself give the unit of time. Jewish people were just as accustomed to seven year cycles as we are to seven day weekly cycles. They were supposed to work their land for six years and then give it rest in the seventh (Lev. 25:3-4). The Hebrews had failed to observe the seventh year of rest for a period of 490 years. Therefore, God imposed a 70-year captivity upon them to recover the neglected sabbatical years (2 Chron. 36:21). The context of Dan. 9:27, specifically v. 2, concerns this 70 year punishment and leads one to believe that the "weeks" in Daniel 9 refer to cycles of seven years, not cycles of seven days. When the "weeks" are interpreted as cycles of seven years, then a very specific and accurate prediction for the time of Messiah's first coming unfolds.[3] This confirms the interpretation of Daniel's weeks as weeks of seven years.

The "one week" period of Daniel 9:27, which Christ associates with the Tribulation in Matt. 24:15, must be a period of seven years, not just seven days.

Other time notations concerning the Tribulation clearly give a period of 3 1/2 years. The phrase "time, times and dividing of time" means "one year plus two years plus 1/2 year" or 3 1/2 years. It occurs in Dan. 7:25, 12:7, and Rev. 12:14. This time corresponds to the second half of the Tribulation. In Revelation the holy city is desecrated for 42 months, and the Beast speaks blasphemy for 42 months (see Rev. 11:2 and 13:5). Forty-two months equals 3 1/2 years and also corresponds to the time from the middle of the week to its end in Daniel 9:27. Thus, the entire "week" must be seven years. The two witnesses in Rev. 11:3 will prophesy for 1,260 days (which equals 3 1/2 years of 42 months of 30 days), and the woman in Rev. 12:6, Israel, will also undergo deep persecution for 1,260 days. The latter period corresponds to the last half of Daniel's week (9:27).[4]

All lines of evidence indicate that the period from the middle of the Tribulation to the end is 3 1/2 years (time, times, and a dividing of time, or 42 months or 1,260 days). The entire period will be approximately seven years in duration.

There will be a tribulation period. It will be seven years long. Furthermore, it will precede the Second Coming and the millennial Kingdom.

C. Why do we place this coming tribulation period prior to Christ's return to the earth to set up His millennial Kingdom?

Both the Gospels and the Revelation present the tribulation period as ending with the King's return to destroy His enemies and set up a Kingdom. Matt. 24:15-25 teaches about the Tribulation, with vv. 29-31 stressing that it will end at the Son of Man's return. On the same occasion Christ taught that He would judge the nations at His return and initiate a Kingdom into which only His own sheep can be admitted (Matt. 25:31ff.).

The Book of Revelation also teaches that the time of tribulation precedes and will be ended by Christ's coming to earth (Rev. 19:11ff.). Following the Lord's return there will be a complete destruction of His adversaries and a reign that is 1,000 years in duration (see Rev. 19:19-20:6. *1,000 years* occurs six times in Rev. 20:2-7).

Although **a more complete defense for the concept of premillennialism is forthcoming**, this material should be enough to prove that the following segment of the prophetic time line is very much Scriptural. *Rapture* is not included in the following chart since evidence for the time of the Rapture is presented later in the text.

---

[3] For an excellent study on Daniel's 70 weeks as it relates to Messianic prophecy, see Harold W. Hoehner, *Chronological Aspects of the Life Of Christ* (Grand Rapids, Zondervan Publishing Co., 1977), pp. 115-39.

[4] Dan. 12:11-12 also mentions 1,290 days and 1,335 days. This could mean the Great Tribulation ends on day 1,260 while it takes 30 more days to judge and cleanse the world and still 45 more days to install the millennial Kingdom.

Prophetic Time Line		
Church	7-Year Tribulation	Second Coming 1,000 Year Kingdom

Now we must study whether the Bible presents two distinct phases to the Lord's return and whether the first of these occurs prior to the Tribulation.

D. Why should a distinction be drawn between the Rapture and the Revelation of Christ? Careful students of the Bible note that the Scriptures indicate there will be two phases or aspects to Christ's Second Coming. Teachings about various details of the Lord's return seem to be in conflict unless some sort of distinction is drawn. When used in a technical sense, "Rapture" refers to one aspect of the Lord's return, and "Revelation" refers to another aspect. The following contradictory propositions ought to show the wisdom of concluding there are two phases to the Lord's return. In each of the five examples, contrast statement "a" with statement "b".

1. Contrast One

a. The Lord will return to take saints unto Himself up to the clouds and/or to heaven. **Saints do not remain on earth** after Christ's return.

> "In My Father's house are many dwelling places; if it were not so, I would have told you; for I go to prepare a place for you. And if I go and prepare a place for you, I will come again, and **receive you to Myself**; that where I am, there you may be also" [John 14:2-3].

> Then we who are alive and remain shall be **caught up together with them in the clouds** to meet the Lord in the air, and thus we shall **always be with the Lord** [1 Thess. 4:17].

b. When the Lord returns, He and His **saints will remain on the earth to enjoy the Kingdom.**

> "But when the Son of Man comes in His glory, and all the angels with Him, then He will sit on His glorious

throne....Then the King will say to those on His right, 'Come, you who are blessed of My Father, **inherit the kingdom** prepared for you from the foundation of the world' " [Matt. 25:31, 34].

It ought to be obvious, especially to premillennialists, that these two future truths concern two different aspects to the Lord's return. In one phase He will come to take believers away with Him. In another phase He will come and remain with believers on earth. Admittedly, we could merge these two details into one occasion if we adopt a "heavenly yo-yo" view where Christians are raptured up to the sky to peep at the heavenly mansions only to return immediately to earth for the Kingdom. However, it is preferable to understand these Scriptures to refer to different events. Both are true. One time Christ will return to take His followers up and **away from the earth.** Another time He will return and **keep His followers on the earth for a Kingdom.** At the Rapture believers leave the earth. At the Revelation believers stay on the earth.

2. Contrast Two

a. **The Lord's return can happen at any time** and is the next event the church should anticipate.

> [S]o that you are not lacking in any gift, awaiting **eagerly** the revelation of our Lord Jesus Christ [1 Cor. 1: 7].

> If anyone does not love the Lord, let him be accursed. Maranatha (Our Lord, come!) [1 Cor. 16:22].

> For our citizenship is in heaven, from which also we **eagerly await** for a Savior, the Lord Jesus Christ...[Phil. 3:20].

> Let your forbearing spirit be known to all men. The Lord is **near** [Phil. 4:5].

[A]nd **to wait for His Son** from heaven, whom He raised from the dead, that is Jesus, who delivers us from the wrath to come [1 Thess. 1:10].

[L]ooking for the blessed hope and the appearing of the glory of our great God and Savior, **Christ Jesus** [Titus 2:13].

You too be patient; strengthen your hearts, for the coming of the Lord is **at hand** [James 5:8].

In the future there is laid up for me the crown of righteousness, which the Lord, the righteous judge, will award to me on that day; and not only to me, but to all who have **loved His appearing** [2 Tim. 4:8].

"And behold, I am coming **quickly.** Blessed is he who heeds the words of the prophecy of this book"....He who testifies to these things says, "Yes, I am coming **quickly.**" Amen. Come, Lord Jesus [Rev. 22:7, 20].

b. **The Lord's return cannot take place until many signs and wonders are fulfilled** including the proclamation of the gospel to the whole world.

And as He was sitting on the Mount of Olives, the disciples came to Him privately, saying, "Tell us, when will these things be, and what will be the sign of Your coming, and of the end of the age?" And Jesus answered and said to them, "See to it that no one misleads you. For many will come in My name, saying 'I am the Christ,' and will mislead many. And you will be hearing of wars and rumors of wars; see that you are not frightened, for those things must take place, but **that is not yet the end**. For nation will rise against nation, and kingdom against kingdom, and in various places there will be famines and

earthquakes. But all these things are merely the beginning of birth pangs. Then they will deliver you to tribulation, and will kill you and you will be hated by all nations on account of My name. And many false prophets will arise, and will mislead many. And because lawlessness is increased, most people's love will grow cold. But the one who endures to the end, he shall be saved. And this gospel of the kingdom shall be preached in the whole world for a witness to all the nations, and then the end shall come....even so you too, **when you see all these things**, recognize that **He is near**, right at the door." [Matt. 24:3-14,33].

"**And there will be signs** in sun and moon and stars, and upon the earth dismay among nations, in perplexity at the roaring of the sea and the waves, men fainting from fear and the expectation of the things which are coming upon the world; for the powers of the heavens will be shaken. And then they will see the Son of man coming in a cloud with power and great glory. But when **these things begin to take place**, straighten up and lift up your heads, because **your redemption is drawing near**" [Luke 21:25-28].

How shall we reconcile these details about the Lord's return? In one sense it must be the very next thing to occur. The church must look for the "Blessed Hope", Christ Himself, to return at any possible moment. It need not wait for any more wars or famines than have already occurred. It need not wait until the gospel goes any further than it has at the present. Yet, in another sense the Lord's return can not take place until the gospel penetrates the world and until many signs come to pass.

Either we leave the Scriptures in confused contradiction, or we conclude there must be two phases to Christ's return. The first aspect of His return is imminent. It can transpire at any moment without need for any sign to be fulfilled. Another aspect of His return can not occur at any moment for many signs must yet come to pass, including worldwide proclamation of the gospel. It is nonsense to try to merge these contradictory points in one event. If Christ cannot return until the gospel goes into the entire world, then it was foolish for the early church to look for His return. It would still be foolish for us to look for the Lord's return for the gospel still must penetrate the whole world. This would be true unless, of course, there are indeed two aspects to that return. The early church anticipated the Rapture. After the Rapture will come to pass the signs and wonders and the world-wide proclamation of the gospel (by the 144,000 in Rev. 7:4ff., by the two witnesses in Rev. 11:3ff., even by an angel flying in heaven in Rev. 14:6ff.). After these signs, the second aspect to the Lord's return, the Revelation, will take place. Tribulational saints are commanded to look for signs of the Lord's return. The church is commanded to look for the Lord Himself. There are two phases or aspects of the Lord's return.

3. Contrast Three.

a. The Lord will return **to the clouds in the air.**

> Then we who are alive and remain shall be caught up together with them in the clouds **to meet the Lord in the air**, and thus we shall always be with the Lord [1 Thess. 4:17].

b. The Lord will return **all the way to the earth**.

> And in that day **His feet will stand on the Mount of Olives**, which is in front of Jerusalem on the east; and the Mount of Olives will be split in its middle from east to west by a very large valley, so that half of the mountain will move toward the north and the other half toward the south [Zech. 14:4].

The first point in this section concerns the location of the saints. Some texts say Christ will return, and saints will leave the earth. Others say He will return, and saints will remain on earth. This third point concerns the location of the Lord. Why does the Bible stress in some places that Christ will return to the earth? To be specific, He must return to the Mt. of Olives near Jerusalem. Yet, in other places Christ comes in the clouds but not all the way to the earth. Some might suggest that He comes and meets believers in the air only to bring them immediately back to earth (the heavenly yo-yo again). The next point will show this can not be true. It is better to view the Lord's return as involving **two distinct aspects.** In one phase He comes in the air to the clouds. In another phase He comes completely to the earth.

4. Contrast Four.

a. At the time of the Lord's return **believers will receive glorified bodies** like the Lord's. For them there will be **no more marriage or children.**

> Beloved, now we are children of God, and it has not appeared as yet what we shall be. We know that, **when He appears, we shall be like Him**, because we shall see Him just as He is [1 John 3:2].

> Behold, I tell you a mystery; we shall not all sleep, but **we shall all be changed**, in a moment, in the twinkling of an eye, at the last trumpet; for the trumpet will sound, and the dead will be raised imperishable, and **we shall be changed** [1 Cor. 15:51-52].

> "[B]ut those who are considered worthy to attain to that age and **the res-**

urrection from the dead, neither marry, nor are given in marriage; for neither can they die anymore, for they are like angels, and are sons of God, being sons of the resurrection" [Luke 20:35-36; also Matt. 22:30; Mark 12:25].

These texts prove that at the Lord's return all believers, dead and living, will obtain glorified bodies. After the return those in the church will no longer marry or produce children.

b. At the Lord's return He will establish a Kingdom, and **saints will repopulate the earth** after the destruction of the tribulation period.

"No longer will there be in it an infant who lives but a few days, or an old man who does not live out his days; for the youth will die at the age of one hundred and the one who does not reach the age of one hundred shall be thought accursed. And they shall build houses and inhabit them; they shall also plant vineyards and eat their fruit. They shall not build, and another inhabit, they shall not plant, and another eat; for as the lifetime of a tree, so shall be the days of My people, and My chosen ones shall wear out the work of their hands. They shall not labor in vain, or **bear children** for calamity; for they are the offspring of those blessed by the LORD, and their **descendants** with them. It will also come to pass that before they call, I will answer; and while they are still speaking, I will hear. The wolf and the lamb shall graze together, and the lion shall eat straw like the ox; and dust shall be the serpent's food. They shall do no evil or harm in all My holy mountain," says the Lord [Isaiah 65:20-25 (see also Deut. 30:9)].

These observations illustrate the difficulty of trying to merge all the details of the Lord's return into one event. Those who maintain that there should be no distinction between the Rapture and the Revelation are going to have trouble explaining how the same people who have been raptured and glorified can immediately return to the earth to repopulate it.

Clearly, it is better to view a distinction between two phases of the Lord's return with a time interval separating them. In the first phase all believers obtain the glorified state. Then before the second phase occurs more people trust in Christ. These are the ones who are still able to produce children after the final aspect of the Lord's return.

5. Contrast Five.

a. The Lord will return **to meet His saints**.

"Let not your heart be troubled; believe in God, believe also in Me. In My Father's house are many dwelling places; if it were not so, I would have told you; for I go to prepare a place for you. And if I go and prepare a place for you, **I will come again, and receive you to Myself**; that where I am, there you may be also. And you know the way where I am going." Thomas said to Him, "Lord, we do not know where You are going, how do we know the way?" Jesus said to him, "I am the way, and the truth, and the life; no one comes to the Father, but through Me" [John 14:1-6].

But we do not want you to be uninformed, brethren, about those who are asleep, that you may not grieve, as do the rest who have no hope. For if we believe that Jesus died and rose again, even so God will bring with Him those who have fallen asleep in Jesus. For this we say to you by the word of the Lord, that we who are alive, and remain until the coming of the Lord, shall not precede those who have fallen asleep. For the Lord Himself will descend from heaven with a shout, with the voice of the archangel, and with the trumpet of God; and the dead in Christ shall rise first. Then we who are alive and remain shall be caught up together with them in the clouds **to meet the Lord in the air**, and thus we shall always be with the Lord. Therefore, comfort one another with these words [1 Thess. 4:13-18].

b. The Lord will return **with His saints**.

[S]o that He may establish your hearts unblamable in holiness before our God and Father at the coming of our Lord Jesus **with all His saints** [1 Thess. 3:13].

Some would interpret "saints" in 1 Thess. 3:13 and Jude v. 14 as angels (holy ones), but Paul uses the term saints of **believers,** not angels (e.g., 1 Cor. 1:2 and many other places). Also, the return with saints may refer to the souls of departed Christians coming with Christ in order to obtain resurrection bodies. Such a returning of saints with Christ is even taught in the 1 Thessalonians 4 passage (v. 14 - "even so will God bring with Him those who have fallen asleep in Jesus"). Yet, the word "all" in 1 Thess. 3:13 does not favor the view that "all His saints" refers only to the souls of departed Christians coming at the Rapture, for they constitute some, but not **all** the saints. It is better to conclude that one aspect of the Lord's return is **for His saints**. Another is "**with** *all* **His saints**."

The contrast between coming for His saints and coming with all His saints can be considered important **if** the distinction between Rapture and Revelation can be proven by other means. Those who are convinced by other Scriptures that there must be two aspects to the Lord's return can justifiably point to the difference between "coming for

His saints" and "coming with His saints" as another support for their view. In the first phase Christ comes for His saints. In the next phase He comes with **all** His (church) saints. Given that the Rapture/Revelation distinction has other stronger evidence, this interpretation just adds more credibility to it.

Bible students cannot be faulted for thinking that the Lord's return involves two different phases, the **Rapture**, as distinct from the **Revelation**. It is virtually impossible to blend all of the specific details about the Lord's return into a single event. It is difficult to see how Christ can return to take saints away from the earth and also remain with the saints on the earth unless there are two phases to His return. It is impossible that the Lord's return can be at any moment without intervening events and yet can not transpire until many signs come to pass (including worldwide proclamation of the gospel) unless there are two aspects to His coming. It is just as impossible to think that Christ will return to give believers glorified bodies, but they at the same time will repopulate the earth after the decimation caused by the Tribulation. There must be a time interval between two distinguishable aspects to His return. Finally, it is best to place a distinction between the Lord coming in the clouds to meet His saints and the Lord coming all the way to the earth with His saints.

The distinction between Rapture and Revelation as two phases to the Lord's return is credible to say the least. Specific teachings about the Lord's return force it upon Bible students.

At this point it is established that there is coming a seven-year tribulation period followed by the Lord's return to the earth to set up His Kingdom. Therefore, there is no debate as to the time for the second phase of the Lord's return, the Revelation. It occurs at the close of the Tribulation. When does the

Rapture occur? A credible case can be made for a pretribulational Rapture.

IV. The Pretribulational Rapture

An argument can be weakened by the multiplication of tenuous supports. There is wisdom in adopting the strategy of emphasizing only the very best arguments, and then letting the position stand or fall on its own merits. Some books will give fifty or more arguments for the pretribulational Rapture. There simply are not fifty **good** supports for pretribulationism. However, there are about six primary points that do add weight to other "secondary" proofs (Such classifications are admittedly subjective).

A. Primary Support for the Pretribulational Rapture

1. The Rapture is Imminent

The Bible presents the Rapture as an impending event that need not wait for any intervening events. Therefore, theologians should not place any intervening events before the Rapture. Since the Rapture could take place at any possible time, it ought to be the first event of a prophetic time chart.

The Bible commands Christians to await the Lord's return with eager anticipation. How can this be a realistic command if the Rapture cannot take place for at least seven more years? Seven years surely blunts anticipation. Furthermore, if the Rapture is posttribulational, then the majority in the church will be slaughtered before the Rapture. This would also tend to reduce eager anticipation for the Lord's return (see point 4). These verses support an imminent Rapture:

> And this do, knowing the time, that **it is already the hour** for you to awaken from sleep; for now salvation is nearer to us than when we believed. The night is almost gone, and **the day is at hand**. Let us therefore lay aside the deeds of darkness and put on the armor of light [Rom. 13:11-12].

> [S]o that you are not lacking in any gift, **awaiting eagerly** the revelation of our Lord Jesus Christ [1 Cor. 1:7].

> If anyone does not love the Lord, let him be accursed. **Maranatha** (Our Lord come!) [1 Cor 16:22].

> For our citizenship is in heaven, from which also we **eagerly await** for a Savior, the Lord Jesus Christ [Phil. 3:20].

> Let your forbearing spirit be known to all men. **The Lord is near** [Phil. 4:5].

> [A]nd **to wait for His Son** from heaven, whom He raised from the dead, that is Jesus, who delivers us from the wrath to come [1 Thess. 1:10].

> [L]ooking for the blessed hope and the appearing of the glory of our great God and Savior, **Christ Jesus** [Titus 2:13].

> You too be patient; strengthen Your hearts, for **the coming of the Lord is at hand** [James 5:8].

> And he said to me, "Do not seal up the words of the prophecy of this book, for **the time is near**"....He who testifies to these things says, "Yes, I am coming **quickly**." Amen. Come, Lord Jesus [Rev. 22:10,20].

Paul himself expected to take part in the Rapture (note the plural "we" in 1 Cor 15:51 and 1 Thess. 4:17). The New Testament church looked to Christ Himself as being the next eschatological event. Placing all of the tribulational events (signs, wonders, judgments, and battles) before the Rapture destroys the doctrine of the Rapture's imminence. Thus, it is best to view the Rapture as the next (and the very first) prophetic event without any intervening events that must occur before the Rapture can take place.

2. Separation of sheep from goats sensible only with pretribulational Rapture.

If the Rapture is posttribulational and occurs along with the Revelation, then there would be no need to separate the "sheep" from the "goats" upon the Lord's return to earth (Matt. 25:31-46). Suppose for the sake of argument that the Rapture in which believers are snatched away to the clouds occurs at the same time as the coming of Christ to the earth at the end of the Tribulation. If all believers on earth had been taken to Christ in the clouds, then believers have already been separated from unbelievers. This would make the separation during the Judgment of the Nations in Matt. 25:31-46 nonsense. (The only other post-tribulational alternative scheme would be to view the Judgment of the Nations as taking place in the clouds at the same time as the Rapture, but this clearly contradicts 1 Thess. 4:14, which limits the rapture to believers. Also, the Judgment of Israel that separates believers from unbelievers definitely takes place on earth not in the clouds, Ezek. 20:35-38. Joel 3:2 and 14 appear to place the Judgment of the Nations in a valley on earth.)

This line of reasoning shows that there must be a time interval between the Rapture and the Revelation and that the Rapture does not take place at the end of the tribulation period in conjunction with Christ's descent to the earth.

The same argument can be made for the judgment that separates believing Israel from unbelieving Israel (Ezek. 20:34-38). A posttribulational Rapture would make such a separation unnecessary and is, therefore, an incorrect view.

3. Only the pretribulational view allows remaining saints who can repopulate the world.

If the Rapture is posttribulational, then there would be no remaining saints in a non-glorified state who could repopulate the earth during the Kingdom. This point has already been covered on pp. 385-86. This truth makes it difficult to place the Rapture at the end of the Tribulation.

4. The Rapture is supposed to be a "Blessed Hope."

> "Let not your heart be troubled; believe in God, believe also in Me. In My Fathers house are many dwelling places; if it were not so, I would have told you; for I go to prepare a place for you. And if I go to prepare a place for you I will come again, and receive you to Myself; that where I am, there you may be also" [John 14:1-3].

> Therefore, comfort one another with these words [1Thess. 4:18].

> [L]ooking for the blessed hope and the appearing of the glory of our great God and Savior, Christ Jesus [Titus 2:13].

How can the Rapture be a time of comfort and a blessed hope if believers face seven years of terror and probably horrible deaths before it can occur? If the Rapture is posttribulational, then the present generation would be better off if the Lord delayed His return until the next generation. A posttribulational Rapture would give believers grounds for hoping that Christ does not return within their lifetimes! It turns the blessed hope in to a dreaded horror and thoughts of comfort into worries about impending catastrophe. The Biblical portrayal of the Rapture as a blessed hope and as a comforting thought definitely favors the pretribulational view.

5. Revelation 3:10 promises that the Church will be kept from the Tribulation.

> "Because you have kept the word of My perseverance, I will **keep you**

from the hour of testing, that hour which is about to come upon the whole world, to test those who dwell upon the earth" [Rev. 3:10].

This promise concerns a period of testing for those "who dwell upon the earth." This phrase also occurs in Rev. 6:10, 13:8 and 17:8 and definitely refers to people in the coming tribulation period.

Although Rev. 3:10 addresses the church at Philadelphia, it should not be construed as a promise restricted to the Philadelphian church. No one would think of restricting Rev. 3:20 to Laodicea. Furthermore, the early chapters of Revelation give constant invitation for all to apply the message to the seven churches (2:7,11,17,29; 3:6,13,22). In fact, what sense would there be in restricting application to only the Philadelphian church when all believers of the 1st Century Philadelphian church died long before the Tribulation?

Thus, Rev. 3:10 promises some sort of immunity for the whole church from the Tribulation. Posttribulationalists maintain that Rev. 3:10 promises that the church will be kept "through" the Tribulation. Noah provides a parallel. He was not taken **out of** the flood but rather kept safe **through** the flood. Nevertheless, Rev. 3:10 does not say kept "**through**" the hour. It says kept "**from**" or "**out of.**" Greek for "through" is *dia* (as in diameter, the measure through a circle). Greek for "out of" is *ek* (as in exit or exodus, a way out). Rev. 3:10 promises the church will be kept "**out of**" the Tribulation. Notice the important point that the verse provides a keeping from the time period, the hour of tribulation. The promise is not so much that the church will be delivered through suffering. It will be **kept from the time period** of such suffering. In fact, in order to be protected from suffering, the church has to be removed. Those who believe after the Rapture will most definitely suffer during the Tribulation. Thus, the analogy with Noah

would not be accurate. Tribulation saints will not be totally protected from the Tribulation. Rev. 3:10 cannot be interpreted as opponents of pretribulationism might wish.

"I kept looking, and that horn was waging war with the saints and overpowering them" [Dan. 7:21].

"And he will speak out against the Most High and wear down the saints of the Highest One…"[Dan. 7:25].

And when He broke the fifth seal, I saw underneath the altar the souls of those who had been slain because of the word of God, and because of the testimony which they had maintained; and they cried out with a loud voice, saying, "How long, O Lord, holy and true, wilt Thou refrain from judging and avenging our blood on those who dwell on the earth?" [Rev. 6:9-10].

"And they overcame him because of the blood of the Lamb, and because of the word of their testimony, and they did not love their life even to death…."And the dragon was enraged with the woman, and went off to make war with the rest of her offspring, who keep the commandments of God and hold to the testimony of Jesus [Rev. 12:11, 17].

And it was given to him to make war with the saints and to overcome them; and authority over every tribe and people and tongue and nation was given to him….If anyone is destined for captivity, to captivity he goes; if anyone kills with the sword, with the sword he must be killed. Here is the perseverance and the faith of the saints….And there was given to him to give breath to the image of the beast, that the image of the beast might even speak and cause as many as do not worship the image of the beast to be killed….and he provides that no one should be able to buy or to sell, except the one who has the mark, either the name of the beast or the number of his name [Rev. 13:7,10,15,17].

The posttribulationalist way of handling Rev. 3:10 makes the Bible contradict itself. It simply is not true that God's people will be delivered safely through the horror of the Tribulation. The only means of immunity from the Tribulation is a removal from it. That is the promise of Rev. 3:10 for the church.

B. Evaluation of Secondary Supports for the Pretribulation Rapture

The following points alone would probably not be convincing for a pretribulational Rapture. However, taken in conjunction with stronger evidence, they do help confirm the pretribulational viewpoint.

1. The Church is Immune to God's Wrath.

Pretribulationalists usually contend that since believers are not subject to God's eternal wrath or to condemnation, they will be removed before the time God pours out His wrath on the earth. Although this argument has weaknesses, it is valid as a secondary point if the pretribulational position can be secured on other more firm grounds. The following verses teach that all believers are immune from God's wrath.

"Truly, truly, I say to you, he who hears My word, and believes Him who sent Me, has eternal life, and does not come into judgment, but has passed out of death into life" [John 5:24].

Much more then, having now been justified by His blood, we shall be saved from the wrath of God, through Him [Rom. 5:9].

There is therefore now no condemnation for those who are in Christ Jesus [Rom. 8:1].

[A]nd to wait for His Son from heaven, whom He raised from the dead, that is Jesus, who delivers us from the wrath to come [1 Thess. 1:10].

For God has not destined us for wrath, but for obtaining salvation through our Lord Jesus Christ [1 Thess. 5:9].

The tribulation period will definitely be a time of God's wrath. In addition to the wrath of the dragon (Rev. 12:12), the Tribulation is a time of the Lamb's wrath (Rev. 6:16). Posttribulationalists counter by saying that the church will indeed be protected from God's wrath but must endure the time of Satan's wrath. The fact that some believers (tribulational saints from the pretribulational viewpoint, church saints from the posttribulational viewpoint) will be on earth during the time of the Tribulation undercuts the philosophical premise that those under Christ's blood could not possibly remain on earth during a time of God's judgment. Thus, the doctrine of immunity from God's wrath cannot by itself establish the pretribulational Rapture. [5] That is the reason for placing it in the category "secondary supports."

Nevertheless, even after a realization of its weakness it remains true that believers' immunity from God's judgment fits nicely with the pretribulational view. Since pretribulationalism is credible on other more solid

---

[5] Some try to pinpoint a time in the Tribulation when the wrath of God begins. Then they claim a pre-wrath Rapture. The author believes the time for the Rapture must be determined on other grounds than the time for God's wrath. Obviously, believers (even if only those called tribulational saints) can reside in the world during a time of God's wrath. Thus, all arguments for the time of the Rapture which are based upon the time for God's wrath are weak. It is better to argue for the timing of the Rapture on stronger grounds then to classify immunity from God's wrath as a secondary point.

grounds, the point that believers are not subject to God's judicial wrath (as opposed to His paternal wrath as a Father) favors the view that the church will not be present in the time of the Lamb's wrath.

The 1 Thessalonians 5 passage deserves special attention. Verse 9, quoted above, says that believers are delivered from the wrath to come. The context refers to the Tribulation. Sudden destruction will come as a "thief in the night" (vv. 3-4). The promise of 1 Thess. 5:4 is most relevant to the time of the Rapture.

> But you, brethren, are not in darkness, that **the day** (likely, the time period) overtake you like a thief [1 Thess. 5:4].

A thief brings unexpected peril and destruction. One might be able to say all this verse promises is that the Tribulation will not be a surprise to the church. Yet, it is also reasonable to think in terms of a promise to Paul's readers of deliverance from the time period of the Tribulation's destruction as a thief (by way of a pretribulational Rapture).

2. The word *church* does not occur in Revelation Chapters 4-18.

The word "church" occurs 19 times in Revelation 1-3. Then it disappears throughout the portion of Revelation that gives details about the tribulation period. Posttribulationists will interpret "saint" as a reference to those in the church, and it occurs many times in materials about the Tribulation (Rev. 11:18, 13:7, 10, 16:6 etc.). However, the concentrated use of the word *church* in Revelation 1-3 followed by its abrupt absence starting in Chapter 4 can be best explained by a pretribulational Rapture. In its early chapters Revelation gives constant appeals for the church to listen. Rev. 13:9 presents a noticeable change. Since the pretribulational view has stronger supports, the absence of the word *church* in Revelation Chapters 4-18

may be legitimately used to strengthen the pretribulational position.

3. The church was not involved in the first 69 weeks of Daniel. It should not be placed in the 70th.

Dan. 9:24-27 contains Daniel's prediction of 70 weeks (i.e., weeks of years). The first 69 weeks occurs before the death of the Messiah. The 70th week is the tribulation period (Matt. 24:15ff.; Daniel 9:27). The church obviously did not play a role in the first 69-week period before the crucifixion. Thus, it is probable the church will not play a role during the 70th week, the tribulation period.

This point does favor a pretribulational Rapture. Still, arguments from silence should remain secondary.

4. If the 24 elders in Rev. 4:4 represent the church, then the church will be in heaven before the Tribulation. [6]

> And around the throne were twenty-four thrones; and upon the thrones I saw twenty-four elders sitting, clothed in white garments, and golden crowns on their heads [Rev. 4:4].

It is likely that the elders of Rev. 4:4 do represent the church in heaven. These elders seem to be human as distinguished from angelic creatures with four faces and six wings. Elder is a term used of church leaders, and many of the descriptions of these 24 elders are appropriate for church saints (enthroned, Rev. 3:21; dressed in white, Rev. 3:5; 19:8; crowns, 2 Tim. 4:8).

---

[6] Rev. 5:9-10 was not used in this study to help identify the elders because it has textual variants. Rev. 5:10 in the New American Standard Bible uses the third person, meaning the elders are speaking about others and do not necessarily include themselves as part of the church. "And Thou has made **them** to be a kingdom of priests to our God, and **they** will reign on the earth."

However, pretribulationalism cannot stand by this verse alone. Would it not be possible for dead and departed church elders to be around God's throne in heaven while living church saints are still on earth? Are there not many church leaders in heaven at this very moment? Those who come to Revelation Chapter 4 already believing in the pretribulation Rapture find that it fits their system well as a confirmation that they are on the right track. It is fair to list the elders in heaven as a secondary but not a primary evidence for pretribulationism.

5. The Restrainer Must Be Removed Before the Tribulation.

It is difficult to conceive of the Holy Spirit's removal without the church's removal.

> Let no one in any way deceive you, for it will not come unless the apostasy comes first, and the man of lawlessness is revealed, the son of destruction, who opposes and exalts himself above every so called god or object of worship, so that he takes his seat in the temple of God, displaying himself as being God....And you know **what** restrains him now, so that in his time he may be revealed. For the mystery of lawlessness is already at work; only **he** who now restrains will do so until **he** is taken out of the way. **And then that lawless one will be revealed** whom the Lord will slay with the breath of His mouth and bring to an end by the appearance of His coming [2 Thess. 2:3-4,6-8].

2 Thessalonians 2 teaches that God restrains the rise of the man of sin, the Antichrist, until the appointed time. Some have interpreted the restraint to be human government. Yet, human government is not powerful enough to withstand Satan's program, nor does it always try to resist the rise of evil. Even more damaging to the view that takes the restrainer as human government is the

masculine form of the participle in v. 7, "**he** who restrains." Government is not a person.

It is best to interpret the restrainer as a person. Only God Himself is powerful enough to withstand Satan's program of world domination. The neuter of v. 6, "what", indicates that Paul has the Person of the Holy Spirit in mind, for although He is a person, the word "spirit" is grammatically neuter. In some sense the Holy Spirit will remove Himself before the Tribulation begins. This does not refer to absolute removal, as the Spirit is omnipresent, but there will be a termination of His special presence relative to the work of restraining evil.

Is it possible to think that the Holy Spirit might remove His influence for restraint while the church remains on the earth? Pretribulationists should concede such a possibility. It is only fair because all must agree that the Holy Spirit will be present and operative in other ministries among tribulational saints (e.g., convicting the lost).

It would be possible for the Holy Spirit to remove His presence relative to restraint but still continue to work in other areas among God's people.

Yet, the church does act as a primary instrument through which God curtails evil. It is as the "salt of the earth" and the "light of the world" (Matt. 5:13ff.; Phil. 2:15-16). It may not be impossible to conceive of the Holy Spirit's removal of restraint without a removal of a primary instrument of restraint, the church; but it is difficult to conceive of such. The cessation of one of the church's primary functions implies a cessation of all the church's work on earth. If one views the pretribulational position as correct before coming to 2 Thessalonians 2, he finds that it fits the proposed scheme of events nicely and enhances his view.

6. The Bible gives examples of God removing believers before inflicting temporal judgments upon the world.

Doctrine should not be built upon types or examples alone. Yet, if a doctrine can be established by other teachings, examples or types may be used as secondary confirmation or illustrations.

The examples of Noah, Lot, and Rahab show that God does not judge believers with unbelievers. This supports a pretribulational position. However, posttribulationalists have a point when they note that God protected these individuals from His own wrath but did not remove them from the world. Maybe God would protect believers from His own wrath in the Tribulation (as distinct from the devil's wrath) but would do so without removing them from the world.

7. The coming of Christ is not as much a purifying hope if it is at least seven years away.

1 John 3:3 says that Christ's return has a purifying effect. Perhaps a seven-year delay would not totally eliminate any purifying effect of the Rapture, but it would reduce it. An imminent Rapture produces a more intense purifying effect.

C. Summary on the Pretribulational Rapture.

Pretribulationists have been guilty of using arguments that are weak and unconvincing to those inclined to belief in a posttribulational Rapture. They do themselves no favor by arguing boldly for weak points. It is best to bring forward the strongest of arguments, and then let the case stand or fall on its own merits. Having pursued this strategy, the author must conclude that the pretribulational case is credible enough that it should be viewed as correct doctrine. Secondary supports that may not prove pretribulationalism alone still have a role in confirming that the pretribulational scheme fits well with known Biblical facts.

V. Posttribulational Arguments Refuted

A good defense is part of a good offense. Therefore, the pretribulational position can be strengthened by meeting challenges posed by posttribulationalists.

A. Posttribulationalists Often Employ an *Ad Hominem* Approach.

They may assert pretribulationalism is based upon a spineless and cowardly attitude, or they use guilt by association tactic where pretribulationalism appears wrong because one with heretical views in other areas might say he is a pretribulationalist. Propaganda is not evidence. The fact that a isolated pretribulationalist holds false views in other areas has nothing to do with the validity of the Biblical case for a pretribulational Rapture. Likewise, the assertion that pretribulational theology rests in cowardice is absurd. Posttribulationalists must deal with the issues and arguments without name-calling or propaganda techniques.

B. Posttribulationalists Charge that Pretribulationalism is Relatively Recent.

Again the age of a position is not the final indication of its truth. Do we want to assert that truths maintained before the Reformation are superior to those taught after the Reformation? Actually, it is only a half-truth to teach that pretribulationalism is relatively recent. Early church writings indicate that the church believed in the imminent return of Christ. It also tended not to have any definite views about the Tribulation. Thus, the church after the apostolic age was **neither pretribulational nor posttribulational** in the modern conception of these two terms. Both are relatively new as developed systems. The real issue is the position of the original New Testament church. It clearly believed that the Rapture was imminent and that the Tribulation was a future time period. Thus, pretribulationalists are compatible with the eschatological views of the early N.T. church. That is what ought to matter.[7]

---

[7] See John Walvoord, *The Rapture Question*, rev. ed. (Grand Rapids: Zondervan Publishing Co., 1979), pp. 150-57.

C. Posttribulationalists Deny the Doctrine of Christ's Imminent Return.

Despite the fact that many Bible verses present the Rapture as the next event on God's timetable, posttribulationalists deny that the New Testament church believed Christ could return at any moment. They raise the following typical objections:

1. The early church could not have believed in an imminent Rapture because Peter had to grow old before the Lord's return (John 21:18-19).

The obvious rebuttal to this objection is that Peter was older by the time the epistles were written with their teachings about Christ's imminent return. Peter was old enough and could have been martyred anytime without the majority of Christians across the world having any news of such an event. Therefore, the prediction that Peter would live to be old is quite compatible with the early Church's belief (based in the epistles) that Christ could return at any moment.

2. The parables speak of a nobleman on a long journey (Luke 19:11-27, see also Matt. 25:14-30).

Therefore, the New Testament church expected Christ to be gone a long time and must not have adhered to an imminent view of the Rapture.

> He said therefore, "A certain nobleman went to a distant country to receive a kingdom for himself, and then return" [Luke 19:12].

Here is another very weak argument. By the time the epistles were written with their teachings about Christ's imminent return, the Lord had been gone nearly 20 years. By any standard a 20-year trip qualifies as a "long journey." Nothing in the parable of the nobleman's long journey would have prevented the early church from believing in an imminent Rapture. The early church expected Him back at any time.

3. The early church could not have believed in an imminent Rapture because Jerusalem had to be destroyed before Christ's return.

> "But when you see Jerusalem surrounded by armies, then recognize that her desolation is at hand" [Luke 21:20].

By hindsight we understand that Luke 21:20 refers to the destruction of Jerusalem by the Romans in A.D. 70. However, for all the early church knew such a destruction would occur after the Lord's imminent Rapture but before His return all the way to earth (i.e., in the tribulation period).

Posttribulationalists use several other points to skirt the idea of Christ's imminent return. The fact remains, however, that the early New Testament church expected Christ to return at any moment without intervening events. This is among the strongest of supports for a pretribulational Rapture.

D. Revelation 3:10 does not promise removal from the tribulation period but rather a protection during it.

The posttribulational view of Rev. 3:10 is covered in pp. 389-391. Its promise is not just to be kept from the suffering of the Tribulation. It is to be kept "from" or "out of the **hour**" of the Tribulation. The only way of preserving a body of saints from suffering during the Tribulation is to remove them out of it. Otherwise, they will suffer (Dan. 7:21, 25; Rev. 6:9-10; 12:11, 17; 13:7,10,15,17).

Rev. 3:10 clearly supports a pretribulational Rapture. Attempts to circumvent it are subjective and unsatisfying.

E. Since a resurrection occurs after the Tribulation (Dan. 12:1-2; Isa. 26:16-19; Rev. 20:4-5) and since the Rapture occurs at a time of resurrection, (1 Thess. 4:13ff.; 1 Cor. 15:51ff.), then the Rapture must occur at the end of the Tribulation.

This is one possible conclusion. However, pretribulationalists also include resurrection as a factor at the close of the Tribulation. They usually place the resurrection of Old Testament saints and martyred tribulational saints at the end of the Tribulation in accordance with Dan. 12:1-2; Isa. 26:16-19; and Rev. 20:4ff.

Pretribulationism is not incompatible with placing some kind of resurrection at the close of the Tribulation. It just maintains that the church is resurrected before the Tribulation while verses speaking of resurrection at the close of the Tribulation refer to either Israel or the martyred tribulational saints. Placing a resurrection of some at the close of the Tribulation has no bearing on whether the church could or could not be resurrected before the Tribulation.

In fact, it is the posttribulational view concerning the time for resurrection that leads to serious problems. If one lumps the resurrection and glorification of all saints, dead and living, at the end of the Tribulation, then no saints remain in an unglorified state to repopulate the world in the Millennium. It is better to place the Church's resurrection and glorification before the Tribulation with a resurrection for Old Testament and martyred tribulational saints after the Tribulation. Those believers who survive the Tribulation continue in the Kingdom in their natural bodies. They are the ones who repopulate the world during the Millennium.

F. The order of events in the Gospels is the Tribulation, Second Coming, and then Kingdom.

Pretribulationalists agree with the order of the gospels, i.e., Tribulation, Second Coming to the earth, then Kingdom, but they maintain a distinction between Rapture and Revelation. The Rapture was a "mystery" (1 Cor. 15:51ff., 1 Thess 4:13ff.) which means it is a truth that had been hidden but was revealed to the church. At the time of the Olivet Discourse, God had not revealed anything about the Rapture. One should not expect teachings about the Rapture to be in-

cluded in the gospels. Christ taught that the Tribulation would end in the Second Coming and the Kingdom. The pretribulational system abides by this teaching just as well as does the posttribulational system. The difference is that pretribulationists are sensitive to more complete revelation on the subject of eschatology, and they try to make all Biblical teachings consistent.

G. The Book of Revelation Portrays Saints as Present on Earth during the Tribulation.

Groups which tend not to distinguish Israel from the church (Old Testament saints from church saints) also have a hard time conceiving of the possibility that the Scriptures refer to more than one kind of "saint." Both theological camps agree that there will be believers on earth during the Tribulation (Daniel 7; Matthew 24 and 25; Revelation 7 and 13). The issue is whether they are church saints or tribulational saints.

Pretribulationists find significance in the observation that Revelation **does not use the word** *church* in conjunction with the "saints" in its teachings about the tribulation period.

H. The Church is Promised Tribulation.

There is a difference between experiencing sorrow or persecution and passing through the tribulation period. The Bible indeed warns Christians of the world's hatred (John 15:18-19; 16:1-2,33; Acts 14:22; Phil. 1:29; 1 Thess. 3:3; 2 Tim. 3:12), but this has no relevance as to whether the church will endure a period of God's wrath upon the world.

I. The Rapture takes place at the last trump (1 Cor. 15:52) and the last trumpet recorded in Scripture occurs at the end of the tribulation period (Matt. 24:31).

If a posttribulational Rapture could be proven on other clearer grounds, this point about the trumpet call could be a confirming factor. However, by itself it is not enough to prove posttribulationalism. When a school-boy talks about the "last bell," he means the last bell in the series for the day, not absolutely the last bell that will ever ring in world history. To a pretribulationalist the "last trump" of 1 Cor. 15:52 has reference to the last trump of the church age, not to the absolutely last trumpet call for all eternity. Actually, it is unreasonable to suppose that there never could be a trumpet sound in heaven for an eternity. Therefore, "last" in "last trump" should be viewed as last for a time period. Pretribulationalists think it is the last trump of the church age. Posttribulationalists think it is the last trump of the Tribulation. By itself the idea of the last trump has no bearing on the time of the Rapture.

J. Summary

Posttribulational objections to pretribulational arguments do not stand up under scrutiny. There are many valid reasons for placing a distinction between the Rapture and Revelation, and there are several strong reasons for believing the Rapture will take place before the Tribulation. While the issue is ultimately a secondary one relative to fellowship between believers, the pretribulational view has superior evidence and does a better job of synthesizing all Biblical facts into a harmonious system. Most who have a definite view of the subject are going to fall into either the pretribulational or posttribulational camp. Only a small number adhere to either a midtribulational or partial Rapture.

VI. The Midtribulational Rapture Theory.

The Bible does indeed note a distinction in time at the mid-point of the Tribulation. Virtually all time notations concerning the tribulation period refer to the last three and one-half years (see pp. 381-82, "Why do many theologians view the Tribulation as a seven-year period?") The only clear exception is Dan. 9:27, and even this verse shows the tribulation period is divided in half.

The midtribulational view contends that Christ will rapture the church after the first three and one-half years of the Tribulation. Next to the pretribulational view a midtribulational position is the second most acceptable position. Indeed, Charles Ryrie has written, "...midtribulationalism is sometimes described as a form of pretribulationalism." [8]

If one places all the distinctive events of the Tribulation in the last half, then it is conceivable the church could endure three and one-half years of terrible conditions before anyone would even realize the Tribulation has begun. World history has been replete with wars, rumors of wars, famines, pestilence, and earthquakes. Thus, from an earthly viewpoint a midtribulational Rapture need not necessarily cancel out the idea of an imminent Rapture. Christians at such times could still expect an imminent Rapture because they would not be certain when the Tribulation began. For all they know the conditions would just be a troublesome time in world history. However, many prophecies concerning the last three and one-half years are so unique and unmistakable that their fulfillment would destroy the concept of imminency (e.g. a world dictator demanding worship in a rebuilt temple, a Russian invasion of Israel with supernatural destruction, the mark of the beast, etc.). Fulfillment of such things would be impossible without identifying the time period as the Tribulation. It would be impossible for the church to go through such things without destroying the imminence of the Rapture. Thus, the church could not pass through the last three and one-half years (so often described as time, times, dividing of time, or 42 months, or 1260 days).

Thus, while a posttribulational Rapture would destroy the doctrine of imminency, a midtribulational Rapture would not necessarily do so. If one places all the unique hor-

---

[8] Charles C. Ryrie, *Basic Theology*, (Wheaton, Il; Victor Books, 1986), p. 497.

rors in the Great Tribulation, (the last three and one-half years), then a midtribulational view is possible. It is interesting that a leading pretribulational scholar, John Walvoord, interprets all the details of Revelation Chapters 6-18 as pertaining to the last three and one-half years. [9] To preserve imminency a midtribulationalist should agree and see all unique predictions about the Tribulation as taking place in the last three and one-half years (Rev. 6:8, 1/4 of world dies; Rev. 8:7, 1/3 of the earth burned). [10] Then from a human perspective imminency is preserved. If one interprets the time in the phrase "kept from the hour" (Rev. 3:10) as the hour of the Great Tribulation, the last three and one-half years, then a midtribulation Rapture is possible. In essence midtribulationalism is an option if it is conceived **as a form of pre-**

---

[9] John F. Walvoord, *The Revelation of Jesus Christ* (Chicago: Moody Press, 1966), p. 123; see also John Walvoord, "Revelation" in *The Bible Knowledge Commentary* (Wheaton, Il: Victor books, 1983), p. 947.

[10] Some midtribulationists place the Rapture in Revelation 11. Thoughts about the Rapture would not occur to most people who read Revelation 11. There are some superficial similarities, but there is no basis for equating the events of Revelation 11 with the Rapture.

1 Cor. 15:52 associates the "last trump" with the Rapture. Pretribulationalists contend this is the last trump of the church age and not the last trump in all of eternity. It is true that Rev. 11:15 gives the last angelic trumpet in the book of Revelation, but if one insists that "last" means "absolute last in time", then the last trumpet of the Bible occurs at the close of the Tribulation (see Matt. 24:31) not the middle of it. Another difference between the doctrine of the Rapture and Revelation 11 concerns the order of resurrection and the sound of the trumpet. In Revelation 11 the dead rise, and later the seventh trumpet sounds. At the Rapture there will be a trumpet sound followed by the resurrection (1 Cor. 15:51ff.;1 Thess. 4:13ff.). Revelation 11 only involves a special raising of two witnesses from the dead (vv. 3,7, and 11). Clearly, the special resurrection of two men cannot be equated with the Rapture of the entire church.

tribulationalism as far as the human perspective is concerned.

VII. The Partial Rapture View

The partial Rapture view divides spiritual Christians from unspiritual Christians. Those who adhere to a partial Rapture maintain that spiritual Christians will be raptured before the Tribulation, but unspiritual Christians must endure the Tribulation. This is sort of an evangelical purgatory.

A. The Partial Rapture and Rev. 3:10

Because you have kept the word of My perseverance, I also will keep you from the hour of testing, that hour which is about to come upon the whole world, to test those who dwell upon the earth [Rev. 3:10].

Rev. 3:10 definitely promises some sort of removal prior to the tribulation period. It is a major argument against a strictly posttribulational Rapture. However, when studied in isolation, Rev. 3:10 could support either a pretribulational Rapture or a partial Rapture. It clearly teaches a Rapture before the Tribulation, but the next issue is whether this Rapture is for all or part of the church. Partial rapturists feel that the phrase "Because you have kept the word of my perseverance" limits the promise of a pretribulational Rapture to only spiritual Christians. This would be a possible interpretation **if Rev. 3:10 were the only verse in the Bible**. However, other Biblical facts show that the pretribulational Rapture will involve the whole church. This makes it preferable to take the phrase "have kept the word of my perseverance" to refer to all who have believed in Christ despite the hostility or persecution that comes from the world toward believers.

Rev. 3:10 teaches a pretribulational Rapture. In isolation it is compatible with either a partial Rapture or the Rapture of all the church. The latter is the correct view as the following section shows.

B. Inclusive Statements about the Rapture

The typical pretribulationalist will not accept a partial Rapture because Scripture presents the Rapture as an all-inclusive event. 1 Cor. 15:51-52 teaches "we shall **all** be changed" at the Rapture. 1 Thess. 4:13ff. includes all church saints in the Rapture. The only condition is "if we believe that Jesus died and rose again" (v. 14). Those in this class can be divided into those sleeping (v. 14) and those who are alive and remain (vv. 15 and 17). However, Paul does not further divide the "alive and remain" category into spiritual and unspiritual. At the Rapture all that are alive and remain go to be with the Lord.

Near the end of the Bible, Christ promises that He will return quickly and then make judgment in order to give rewards to "every" believer (Rev. 22:12).

> "Behold, I am coming quickly, and My reward is with Me, to render to **every** man according to what he has done" [Rev. 22:12].

The Judgment Seat of Christ follows the Rapture, and it involves every believer (see 1 Cor. 3:13; 2 Cor. 5:10). Any partial Rapture theory creates serious problems for doctrines about the Judgment Seat of Christ. If a partial Rapture occurred, then many (most?) church saints would not be present at the Judgment Seat of Christ which follows the Rapture. The serious problems of a partial Rapture view ought to be evident.

C. The Promise of 1 Thess. 5:9-10

If one comes to 1 Thessalonians 5 with a pretribulational theology (and in a sense a partial rapturist does), then 1 Thess. 5:9-10 becomes a promise that directly refutes a partial Rapture.

> For you yourselves know full well that the day of the Lord will come just like a thief in the night. While they are saying, "Peace and safety!" then destruction will come upon them suddenly like birth pangs upon a woman with child; and they shall not escape. But you, brethren, are not in darkness, that the day overtake you like a thief....For God has not destined us for wrath, but for obtaining salvation through our Lord Jesus Christ, who died for us, that whether we are awake or asleep, we may live together with Him [1 Thess. 5:2-4, 9-10].

The key word in the statement of 1 Thess. 5:10 is the word "sleep." If it refers to the "sleep of death," then 1 Thess. 5:10 would be saying all Christians, whether alive or sleeping in death, will live together with Christ at the Rapture. By such an interpretation 1 Thess. 5:10 is parallel to 1 Thess. 4:13-14. All Christians whether awake (living) or asleep (dead) will participate in the Rapture.

However, Greek students know that the Greek word for "sleep" in 1 Thess. 4:13-14 is not the same Greek word for "sleep" as in 1 Thess. 5:10. Furthermore, taking 1 Thess. 5:10 to mean the sleep of death is not the only or the best alternative. The word Paul uses for sleep in 1 Thess. 5:10 seems to mean death 3 times in the New Testament but in approximately 17 cases it means either physical sleep or the drowsiness of one who is lazy or inactive. The same word occurs in Eph. 5:14 where it definitely speaks of spiritual laziness.

> For this reason it says, "Awake sleeper, And arise from the dead, And Christ will shine on you" [Eph. 5:14].

Even more significant is Paul's usage of this same word for *sleep* in the context of 1 Thessalonians 5:6.

> [S]o then let us not sleep as others do, but let us be alert and sober [1 Thess. 5:6].

Sleep in 1 Thess. 5:6 does not refer to death but to spiritual laziness or inactivity. It is contrasted with one who is spiritually active, vigilant, and alert. Unless there are very strong reasons to the contrary, "sleep" and "awake" in 1 Thess. 5:10 should be given the same meaning that they clearly have in 1 Thess. 5:6. *Awake* in v. 6 does not refer to one who is merely living but to one who is spiritually active and vigilant. *Sleep* in v. 5 cannot mean the sleep of death but refers to the stupor of spiritual inactivity and drowsiness. Thus, 1 Thess. 5:10 should be paraphrased "whether we are spiritually active or spiritually lazy, we shall live together with Him." This verse supports eternal security. Yet, given that the previous verse, (v. 9), likely refers to deliverance from the tribulation period of God's wrath, then v. 10 also promises that **all** Christians, spiritually active or spiritually lethargic, will enjoy life together with Christ at the Rapture. If one comes to 1 Thessalonians 4 and 5 with a belief in the pretribulational view, then the best interpretation to 1 Thess. 5:10 is that it promises **rapture for all** the church, not a partial Rapture.

D. The Full Scope of Salvation by Grace, not Works

When most Christians hear the word "salvation" they think exclusively in terms of salvation from sin's penalty. Yet, there is a future tense aspect to salvation. Future deliverance from the very presence of sin is an aspect to salvation. The Bible associates the Lord's return as bringing this fullest sense of salvation to believers.

> And this do, knowing the time, that it is already the hour for you to awaken from sleep; for now salvation is nearer to us than when we believed. The night is almost gone, and the day is at hand…[Rom. 13:11-12].

> [S]o Christ also, having been offered once to bear the sins of many, shall appear a second time for salvation without reference to sin, to those who eagerly await Him [Heb. 9:28].

The Rapture with its associated glorification of believers is actually a part of salvation. At the Rapture believers will obtain their glorified bodies which are not subject to the sin nature. The Rapture is ultimately the "day of redemption" (Eph. 1:14; 4:30; cf. Rom. 8:23).

If the partial Rapture view were true, then those Christians who work hard enough will be rewarded with their full salvation before the Tribulation. Those who do not work hard enough do not obtain the salvation promised by Christ's return but must suffer martyrdom or endure the "Protestant purgatory." The partial Rapture view makes one aspect of salvation dependent upon works, and, therefore, must be rejected as error.

E. Summary.

The arguments for either the post-tribulational or partial Rapture views are weak. It is preferable to accept either pretribulationalism or a form of mid-tribulationalism in which the church is raptured before any of the unique features of the Tribulation period come to pass. This ends up being a form of pretribulationalism as far as the Christians living in that time will be able to tell. Again, the author does not regard any of these views as heretical, for they do not concern a core issue of the faith. The next point concerns a topic upon which evangelicals find greater agreement, the believer's resurrection.

VIII. Believer's Resurrection

Although the resurrection of Old Testament believers and also martyred tribulational saints will occur at the end of the Tribulation, 1 Thess. 4:13ff. and 1 Cor. 15:51ff. teach that the resurrection of church saints (also the glorification of those who have not died) occurs at the Rapture. Thus, a chronological study of eschatology best covers resurrection along with the Rapture.

A. General Promises of Resurrection

Many verses guarantee the bodily resurrection of believers. The majority of promises about resurrection occur in the New Testament. Yet, the Old Testament also contains ample material on the subject of the believer's resurrection.

"Even after my skin is destroyed, Yet **from my flesh I shall see God**" [Job 19:26].

Your dead will live; Their corpses will rise. You who lie in the dust, awake and shout for joy, for your dew is as the dew of the dawn, and the earth will give birth to the departed spirits [Isa. 26:19].

"And many of those who sleep in the dust of the ground will **awake**, these to everlasting life, but the others to disgrace and everlasting contempt" [Dan. 12:2] (see also Heb. 11:19 for an Old Testament saint's understanding of resurrection).

"For **in the resurrection** they neither marry, nor are given in marriage, but are like angels in heaven. But regarding the resurrection of the dead, have you not read that which was spoken to you by God, saying, 'I am the God of Abraham, and the God of Isaac, and the God of Jacob'? **God is not the God of the dead but of the living.**" [Matt. 22:30-32] (see also Mark 12:24-27, Luke 20:35-38).

"Truly, truly, I say to you, an hour is coming and now is, when the dead shall hear the voice of the Son of God; and those who hear shall live. For just as the Father has life in Himself, even so He gave to the Son also to have life in Himself; and He gave Him authority to execute judgment, because He is the Son of Man. Do not marvel at this; for an hour is coming, in which **all who are in the tombs shall hear His voice, and shall come forth**; those who did the good deeds to a resurrection of life, those who committed the evil deeds to a resurrection of judgment" [John 5:25-29].

"For this is the will of My Father, that every one who beholds the Son and believes in Him, may have eternal life; and **I Myself will raise him up on the last day**" [John 6:40].

Jesus said to her, "I am the resurrection and the life; **he who believes in Me shall live even if he dies**, and everyone who lives and believes in Me shall never die. Do you believe this?" [John 11:25-26].

Behold, I tell you a mystery; we shall not all sleep, but we **shall all be changed,** in a moment, in the twinkling of an eye, at the last trumpet. For the trumpet will sound and **the dead will be raised** imperishable, and we shall be changed. For this perishable must put on the imperishable, and this mortal must put on immortality. But when this perishable will have put on the imperishable, and this mortal will have put on the immortality, then will come about the saying that is written, "Death is swallowed up in victory. O death, where is your victory? O death, where is your sting?" The sting of death is sin, and the power of sin is the law; but thanks to God, who gives us the victory through our Lord Jesus Christ. Therefore, my beloved brethren, be steadfast, immovable, always abounding in the work of the Lord, knowing that your toil is not in vain in the Lord [1 Cor. 15:51-58].

[W]ho will **transform the body of our humble state** into conformity with the body of His glory, by the exertion of the power that He has even to subject all things to Himself [Phil. 3:21].

But we do not want you to be uninformed, brethren, about those who are asleep, that you may not grieve, as do the rest who have no hope. For if we believe that Jesus died and rose again, even so God will bring with Him those who have fallen asleep in Jesus. For this we say to you by the word of the Lord, that we who are alive, and remain until the coming of the Lord, shall not precede those who have fallen asleep. For the Lord Himself will descend from heaven with a shout, with the voice of the archangel, and with the trumpet of God; and **the dead in Christ shall rise first**. Then we who are alive and remain shall be caught up together with them in the clouds to meet the Lord in the air, and thus we shall always be with the Lord. Therefore, comfort one another with these words [1 Thess. 4:13-18].

Beloved, now we are children of God, and it has not appeared as yet what we shall be. We know that, **when He appears, we shall be like Him**, because we shall see Him just as He is [1 John 3:2].

Blessed and holy is the one who has a part in the first resurrection; over these the second death has no power, but they will be priests of God and of Christ and will reign with Him for a thousand years [Rev. 20:6].

B. The Nature of the Resurrection Body

There are at least three angles to approach a study about the resurrection body. One can study Christ's resurrection body in order to infer various points about the resurrection body of believers. Of course, several passages teach directly on the nature of the glorified state.

Finally, several truths about our resurrection bodies can be gleaned from materials that describe heaven.

1. The Resurrection Body as Patterned after Christ

The Bible promises that believers are going to obtain a body like Christ's resurrected body. Therefore, it is fair to draw truths about our eventual resurrection from facts about His historical resurrection.

> The first man is from the earth, earthy; the second man is from heaven....And just as we have borne the image of the earthy, we shall also bear **the image of the heavenly** [1 Cor. 15:47,49].

> [W]ho will transform the body of our humble state into **conformity with the body of His glory,** by the exertion of the power that He has even to subject all things to Himself [Phil. 3:21].

> Beloved, now we are children of God, and it has not appeared as yet what we shall be. We know that, when He appears, **we shall be like Him**, because we shall see Him just as He is [1 John 3:2].

a. Ability to Eat

The Lord consumed food on at least two occasions after His resurrection. In the glorified state believers will eat not from necessity due to physical exhaustion (as there will be no weakness, see 1 Cor. 15:43) or hunger pains Rev. 21:4, but for pure enjoyment.

> And while they still could not believe it for joy and were marveling, He said to them, "have you anything here to eat?" And they gave Him a piece of a broiled fish; and He took it and ate it before them [Luke 24:41-43].

> And so when they got out upon the land, they saw a charcoal fire already

laid, and fish placed on it, and bread ....Jesus said to them, "Come and have breakfast." None of the disciples ventured to question Him, "Who are You?" knowing that it was the Lord. Jesus came and took the bread, and gave them, and the fish likewise [John 21:9,12-13].

In addition to Christ's example, many verses confirm the practice of eating will continue in the glorified state (taking of the vine in the Kingdom, Luke 22:16,18; the wedding supper of the Lamb, Rev. 19:9; and the river of the water of life and tree yielding 12 kinds of fruits, Rev. 2:7; 22:2,17). The resurrection body may not need food, but it can and will enjoy it.

b. Tangible with Flesh and Bones

The resurrection body is a spiritual body (1 Cor. 15:44), but this should not conjure up ideas of being a ghost or phantom. It refers to a body that is spiritual in the sense of being suited to a sin-free environment, a body that is suited to dwelling in the presence of a holy God. [11] Christ Himself had a resurrection body composed of flesh and bones. He could show Thomas the marks in His hands and side and had to command eager followers to stop clinging to Him. The glorified state is not going to involve the absence of a body but rather perfection for the body.

> And behold, Jesus met them and greeted them. And they came up and took hold of His **feet** and worshiped Him [Matt. 28:9].

> "See My hands and My feet, that it is I Myself; touch Me and see, for a spirit does not have **flesh and bones** as you see that I have" [Luke 24:39].

---

[11] It is interesting that Jesus describes Himself in Luke 24:39 as having "flesh and bones." 1 Cor. 15:50 says, "flesh and blood cannot inherit the kingdom of God." Will the resurrection be without blood?

Jesus said unto her, "Stop **clinging to Me**, for I have not yet ascended to the Father..."[John 20:17].

> Then He said to Thomas, "Reach here your finger, and see My **hands**; and reach here your hand, and put it into My **side**; and be not unbelieving, but believing" [John 20:27].

c. Rapid Transportation without Barriers

The Lord made a deep impression upon His disciples during His post-resurrection ministry. He walked through walls (John 20:19,26; Luke 24:36). He vanished on the Emmaus Road (Luke 24:31). He defied gravity at His ascension (Acts 1:9).

While these abilities could pertain to His deity and not humanity, many conservative theologians feel that believers in a glorified state will virtually travel at the speed of thought without any subjection to hindrance by physical objects or gravity.

Hebrews 2 implies that believers will someday be superior to angels. With the curse lifted and with Christ Himself as our teacher, it stands to reason that the true mental, as well as, physical capacities of humanity will obtain fruition in heaven. Believers will not become "gods," as some cults teach, but the Bible presents a glorified state that we cannot now begin to imagine.

2. Direct Teachings about the Resurrection

a. Continuity yet Change

In the resurrection our bodies will be different and yet bear similarities to our present bodies. The repeated illustration of resurrection being like a seed implies these points.

> But someone will say, "How are the dead raised? And with what kind of body do they come?" You fool! That which you sow does not come to life unless it dies; and that which you sow, you do not sow the body which is to be, but a bare grain, perhaps of

wheat or of something else. But God gives it a body just as He wished, and to each of the seeds a body of its own [1 Cor. 15:35-38].

And Jesus answered them, saying, "The hour has come for the Son of Man to be glorified. Truly, truly, I say to you, unless a grain of wheat falls into the earth and dies, it remains by itself alone; but if it dies, it bears much fruit" [John 12:23-24].

In 1 Cor. 15:36, Paul expresses very little patience with those who would deny the resurrection of believers. He calls them fools and asks them to consider the nature of seeds. No one fully understands how a seed works, but everyone knows that it does. Even seeds found in Egyptian tombs that appear dead for thousands of years can sprout new life. The fact that we do not understand every detail and can not answer every question about resurrection does not make its eventual occurrence ridiculous. The inability to explain resurrection no more eliminates the fact of resurrection than does the inability to explain seed decay and growth cancel out the obvious fact that it happens. If one plants an apple, it will result in something similar to an apple but also with roots, branches, and leaves. The result of a seed's "death" is both dramatic change and continuity with the past. A kernel planted yields a root, stalk, leaves, husk, and additional kernels of grain. There is both dramatic change and continuity with the past.

Just as in the natural seed process, so believer's resurrection bodies will be similar to our present bodies: similar but not identical! Consider Christ's resurrected body. It was similar to the old but yet different. All who saw Him recognized Him as human. His glorified body had normal human features. He walked, talked, and ate food. However, despite the similarity with the past, He was also very different. While others immedi-

ately recognized Him as human, they did not immediately recognize Him as the same Jesus. [12] This came only with time. There was at the same time a large degree of continuity with the past but also drastic differences.

The nature of seeds and the nature of Christ's glorified body cause us to expect that our future resurrection bodies will have some similarities with our present bodies. Yet, there will also be drastic changes for the better. The transformation to physical perfection will be such a great alteration from our present state that there will be a faint or vague recognition of each other as opposed to an immediate and obvious recognition (Luke 24:16,31; John 20:14-16; 21:4,12).

b. Individuality and Diversity

> But God gives it a body just as He wished, and to **each** of the seeds a **body of its own.** All flesh is not the same flesh, but there is one flesh of men, and another flesh of beasts, and another flesh of birds, and another of fish. There are also heavenly bodies and earthly bodies, but the glory of the heavenly is one, and the glory of the earthly is another. There is one glory of the sun, and another glory of the moon, and another glory of the stars; for star differs from star in glory. **So also is the resurrection** of the dead... [1 Cor. 15:38-42a].

Just as there are many kinds of bodies on earth and varieties of stellar bodies, so there will be diversity and individuality to resurrection bodies in the future. Heaven will not be inhabited by clones. It will not be populated by those who all came off the same assembly line or printout. There will be diversity and also individuality. There is even reason to believe that the human race will retain ethnic diversity in the glorified state

---

[12] In the Lord's case this involved a God-imposed blindness to recognition (Luke 24:16,31,35).

(see following Section 3, a, "Ethnic Diversity", p. 407).

c. Perfection in Duration: an Imperishable Body

...It is sown a perishable body, it is raised an **imperishable** body [1 Cor. 15:42b].

Bible teachers make a valid distinction between restoration and resurrection. Although the terms are loosely interchangeable, it is true that there is a great difference between those whom a prophet, apostle, or Christ raised from the dead and those who are raised in the end time resurrection unto life. The former died again. The latter are immortal. Funerals, cemeteries, bereavement will never again be a part of our human experience.

[B]ut those who are considered worthy to attain to that age and the resurrection from the dead, neither marry, nor are given in marriage; for **neither can they die anymore**, for they are like angels, and are sons of God, being sons of the resurrection [Luke 20:35-36].

For if we have become united with Him in the likeness of His death, certainly we shall be also in the **likeness of His resurrection**....knowing that Christ, having been raised from the dead, is **never to die again**; death no longer is master over Him [Rom. 6:5,9].

The last enemy that will be abolished is death....But when this perishable will have put on the **imperishable**, and this mortal will have put on **immortality** then will come about the saying that is written, "Death is swallowed up in victory. O Death, where is your victory? O Death, where is your sting?" The sting of death is sin, and the power of sin is the law; but thanks be to God, who gives us the victory through our Lord Jesus Christ [1 Cor. 15:26, 54-57].

"[A]nd He shall wipe away every tear from their eyes; and there shall be **no longer be any death**; there shall be no longer be any mourning, or crying, or pain; the first things have passed away" [Rev. 21:4].

d. Perfection in Appearance: a Glorious Body

[It] is sown in dishonor, it is raised in **glory**... [1 Cor. 15:43a].

"And many of those who sleep in the dust of the ground will awake, these to everlasting life, but the others to disgrace and everlasting contempt. And those who have insight will **shine brightly like the brightness of the expanse of heaven**, and those who lead the many to righteousness, **like the stars** forever and ever" [Dan. 12:2-3].

"Then the righteous will **shine forth as the sun** in the kingdom of their Father. He who has ears, let him hear" [Matt. 13:43].

[T]hrough whom also we have obtained our introduction by faith into this grace in which we stand; and we exult in hope of the **glory** of God [Rom. 5:2].

For I consider that the sufferings of this present time are not worthy to be compared with the **glory that is to be revealed to us**....For we know that the whole creation groans and suffers the pains of childbirth together until now. And not only this, but also we ourselves, having the first fruits of the Spirit, even we ourselves groan within ourselves, waiting eagerly for our adoption as sons, **the redemption of our body** [Rom. 8:18, 22-23].

When Christ, who is our life, is revealed, then you also will be **revealed with Him in glory** [Col. 3:4].

All humans have some defect in appearance.
No one looks good in death. Ravaging diseases, old age, accidents, wars, all result in
bodies that die in a dishonorable appearance.
Yet, no believer will remain in a decayed,
mangled, shrunken condition, for the resurrection brings glory, perfection in appearance. Believers will be free from all defect,
flaw, or blemish. (Christ Himself, seems to
be the only exception as He bears evidence
of His sacrificial love in His scars, which are
regarded as marks of love and victory not
flaws.)

It is probable that some believers will have a
greater capacity to reflect God's glory than
others. This point overlaps with that of rewards. In 1 Cor. 15:41 Paul teaches that
"star differs from star in glory", and then
adds, "so also is the resurrection of the
dead" (v. 42). Dan. 12:2-3 also compares the
glory of the resurrection body to stars. All
those who trust in Christ will obtain glorious
resurrection bodies. However, it is best to
include the probability that individual believers will not possess the same amount of
glory, just as stars do not have the same
amount of glory. Believers who obtain
greater reward will probably be given a
greater glory in their resurrection bodies.
Such increased glory will not lead to pride.
Humans were created to bring glory to God
(Rev. 4:11). Increased ability to reflect
Christ's glory will be considered a very
prized reward and a wonderful privilege in
heaven. Unlike the present world's warped
values where almost anything - money, possessions, appearance, popularity, - is deemed
more important than glorifying Christ,
heaven will have true priorities with glorifying Christ at the top of the list. No one will
then care who was rich and popular on earth.
Glorifying Christ will not sound unappealing
or receive a low evaluation in heaven.

All believers will obtain a glorious body. It
will be truly dazzling, full of splendor and
light. We will shine like the sun sharing "His
glory" (Col. 3:4). If we were able to see it
now, we probably could not bear the experience (Rev. 1:17). However, those who live
to glorify Christ on this earth will be privi-
leged to reflect His glory even more by their
glorified bodies in heaven. Such individuals
will be very glad that they lived to glorify
Christ on earth.

e. Perfection in Endurance: a Powerful Body

...it is sown in weakness, it is raised
in **power** [1 Cor. 15:43b].

The Greek word for *weakness* could be
translated infirmity and includes the idea of
sickness (Rom. 8:22; 2 Cor. 5:2). By contrast the resurrection body is totally incapable of sorrow and pain (Rev. 21:4). It will
never be low on energy. It will never be un-
healthy. The handicapped or deformed will
be raised whole. It is probable that infants
will be raised as adults, and the elderly will
be raised in a condition of youthful vigor.
Hospitals, nursing homes, and health-care
professionals will not exist in eternity.

f. Perfection in Spirituality: a Spiritual Body

[I]t is sown a natural body, it is raised
a **spiritual** body... [1 Cor. 15:44].

While 1 Cor. 15:44 teaches that the resurrection body will be a spiritual body, this does
not mean believers will be disembodied spirits as ghosts or phantoms. Christ specifically
denied that this was the nature of His resurrected condition.

And while they were telling these
things, He Himself stood in their
midst. But they were startled and
frightened and thought that they were
seeing a spirit. And He said to them,
"Why are you troubled, and why do
doubts arise in your hearts? See my
hands and My feet, that it is I Myself;
touch Me and see, for a spirit does

not have flesh and bones as you see that I have" [Luke 24:36-39].

By the phrase "spiritual body" Paul means a body that is perfectly adapted to spirituality, i.e., one suitable for living in sinless perfection. The natural body suits this earthly environment where it is surrounded by wickedness and quite capable of yielding to it. After resurrection a believer's body will no longer be permeated with a sinful behavioral mechanism. It will be a spiritual body as opposed to one capable of carnal-like behavior.

g. Marriage and Children

Despite the claims by false religions and cults that heaven will be similar to a harem, the Bible is very clear that marriage is an earthly relationship that is broken by death (e.g., Rom. 7:3; 1 Cor. 7:39). Undoubtedly, our family ties from days on earth will not be forgotten and love for relatives will increase rather than diminish. Yet, believers in heaven will in reality be part of one family. There will be no marriage, no conception, and no childbirth in heaven.

> And Jesus said to them, "The sons of this age marry and are given in marriage, but those who are considered worthy to attain to that age and the resurrection from the dead, **neither marry, nor are given in marriage**" [Luke 20:34-35] (see also Matt. 22:30).

3. Inferences about the Resurrection from Texts on Heaven

Revelation 21 and 22 give the Bible's most extensive teaching on heaven. Some of its details have implications for the nature of the resurrection body of believers.

a. Ethnic Diversity

The Greek word for nations is *ethna* from which we derive the word *ethnic*. It is likely that resurrected humanity will still be divided into various ethnic groups.

> And the **nations** shall walk by its light, and the kings of the earth shall bring their glory into it....and they shall bring the glory and the honor of the **nations** into it....And on either side of the river was the tree of life, bearing twelve kinds of fruit, yielding its fruit every month; and the leaves of the trees were for the healing of the **nations** [Rev. 21:24,26; 22:2].

b. No Need for Rest

The fact that night will not exist in the Eternal State seems to imply that those in glory will not need rest.

> And there shall be **no longer be any night**; and they shall not have need of the light of a lamp nor the light of the sun, because the Lord God shall illumine them; and they shall reign forever and ever [Rev. 22:5].

c. The Lord's Name

Several verses indicate that Christ's name will be written upon glorified believers in some manner.

> "He who overcomes, I will make him a pillar in the temple of My God, and he will not go out from it anymore; and **I will write upon him the name of My God**, and the name of the city of My God, the new Jerusalem, which comes down out of heaven from My God, and My new name" [Rev. 3:12].

> [A]nd they shall see His face, and **His name shall be on their foreheads** [Rev. 22:4].

d. Work

The fact that the heavenly city never closes its gates implies that resurrected believers will be busy coming and going in some unspecified work assignments.

And in the daytime (for there shall be no night there) its gates shall never be closed [Rev. 21:25].

IX. The Judgment Seat of Christ:

Following the Rapture (with its simultaneous resurrection/glorification), the next event for believers will be the Judgment Seat of Christ. This judgment is sometimes called the "Bema Seat" using the Greek word found in Rom. 14:10 and 2 Cor. 5:10. This word occurs in reference to several historical trials and spectacles that are recorded in the New Testament (Christ before Pilate, Matt. 27:19 and John 19:13; Herod's speech from the "rostrum", Acts 12:21; Paul before Gallio, Acts 18:12,16,17, and before Festus, Acts 25:6,10,17). While athletic imagery does play a role in the subject of the judgment of believers (the word for crown in 1 Cor. 9:24ff. is an athlete's wreath worn on the winner's head), one should not restrict the Judgment Seat of Christ to imagery of handing out trophies to celebrating victors. The word *bema* in the New Testament is primarily used of courts of justice involving a critical evaluation.

This is not to say that believers need to fear a loss of salvation at the Judgment Seat, but they should know that the Lord's evaluation might well involve some criticism and some unpleasant aspects. Although God in grace will find something desirable in every believer's life (1 Cor. 4:5), the Judgment Seat of Christ will not be just a victory party and celebration for those believers who have wasted life on earth.

A. The Time for the Judgment Seat of Christ

There is more than ample evidence to make a conclusion as to the time for the Judgment Seat.

"But when you give a reception, invite the poor, the crippled, the lame, the blind, and you will be blessed, since they do not have the means to repay you; for you will be **repaid at the resurrection** of the righteous" [Luke 14:13-14].

Therefore do not go on passing judgment before the time, but wait **until the Lord comes** who will both bring to light the things hidden in the darkness and disclose the motives of men's hearts; and then each man's praise will come to him [1 Cor. 4:5].

[I]n the future there is laid up for me the crown of righteousness, which the Lord, **the righteous Judge, will award to me on that day**; and not only to me, but also to all who have loved **His appearing** [2 Tim. 4:8].

"Behold, I am coming quickly, and **my reward is with Me** to render to every man according to what he has done" [Rev. 22:12].

Luke 14:14 associates resurrection with reward. Therefore, one may conclude that reward follows resurrection. For church saints this means that the Judgment Seat of Christ occurs after the Rapture. 1 Cor. 4:5 and 2 Tim. 4:8 seem to link the Lord's return with judgment and reward. Finally, Rev. 22:12 is probably the clearest verse on the time for reward. Since the Lord's return brings a reward, Bible teachers usually place the Judgment Seat of Christ as the next event after the Rapture (i.e., the next event for the church. There is, of course, a tribulation period on earth). [13]

B. The Place for the Judgment Seat of Christ

The Bible does not specifically indicate the place for the tribunal. Since Christ's return will bring believers to heaven (John 14:1 ff.), many Bible teachers place the judgment in heaven. It is safe to say it will not be on earth.

C. The Judge

[13] Other verses seem to link the Lord's return with an evaluation or reward (1 Cor 1:8; 2 Cor 1:14; 1 Thess. 2:19; 1 John 2:28).

Obviously, the Judge at the Judgment Seat of Christ is Christ.[14]

> For we must all appear before the **judgment seat of Christ**, that each one may be recompensed for his deeds in the body, according to what he has done, whether good or bad [2 Cor. 5:10].

> Whatever you do, do your work heartily, as for the Lord rather than for men; knowing that **from the Lord you will receive the reward** of the inheritance. It is the Lord Christ whom you serve [Col. 3:23-24].

This could be inferred even if it were not specifically taught because God the Father has delegated all judgment to the Son.

> "For not even the Father judges anyone, but He has given **all judgment to the Son**" [John 5:22].

D. Those Judged

The Judgment Seat of Christ is for believers only. It must not be confused with The Great White Throne Judgment which is for unbelievers, i.e., the "dead" (see Revelation 20:11-15).[15] In both the context of Romans 14 and 2 Corinthians 5 the term "we" has reference to believers. Thus, the scope of the Judgment Seat should be restricted to believers in Rom.14:10 and 2 Cor. 5:10.

> But you, why do you judge your **brother**? Or you, again, why do you regard your **brother** with contempt? For **we** shall **all** stand before the judgment seat of God [Rom. 14:10].

> For **we** must **all** appear before the judgment seat of Christ, that each one may be recompensed for his deeds in the body, according to what he has

done, whether good or bad [2 Cor. 5:10].

When God judges believers, it will be at a judgment that is exclusively for believers. All at the Judgment Seat of Christ are saved.

> If any man's work is burned up, he shall suffer loss; but **he himself shall be saved,** yet so as through fire [1 Cor. 3:15]

One should not conceive of the Judgment Seat as a group judgment with a mob of nameless Christians from many nations and centuries being judged in mass. Although "time" in heaven is probably different than time on earth, and it is difficult to conceive of Christ spending the time to judge millions of believers individually, the Bible clearly teaches that the Judgment Seat of Christ is some kind of **individual** judgment.

> But you, why do you judge your brother? Or you, again, why do you regard your brother with contempt? For we shall all stand before the judgment seat of God....So then **each one** of us shall give **account of himself** to God [Rom. 14:10,12].

> Now he who plants and he who waters are one; but **each** will receive his own reward according to **his own** labor [1 Cor. 3:8].

> [E]ach man's work will became evident; for the day will show it, because it is to be revealed with fire; and the fire itself will test the quality of **each** man's work. If any man's work which he has built upon it remains, he shall receive a reward. If any man's work is burned up, he shall suffer loss; but he himself shall be saved, yet so as through fire [1 Cor. 3:13-15].

> Therefore do not go on passing judgment before the time, but wait until the Lord comes who will both bring to light the things hidden in the

---

[14] Heb. 9:27-28 also teaches that Christ will judge at His coming.

[15] Rev. 20:11-15 even uses a different word for the tribunal. There we find *thronos* not *bema*.

darkness and disclose the motives of men's hearts; and then **each** man's praise will come to him from God [1 Cor. 4:5].

For we must all appear before the judgment seat of Christ, that **each** one may be recompensed for his deeds in the body, according to what he has done, whether good or bad [2 Cor. 5:10].

For **each** one shall bear his own load [Gal. 6:5].

E. The Basis for the Judgment

1. Non-Issues at the Judgment Seat

It is very important to understand that salvation or entrance into heaven is not the issue at the Judgment Seat of Christ. All those being judged are believers. Since salvation comes through believing, all those at the Judgment Seat of Christ are saved. In fact, they are probably already in heaven. The Bible teaches that believers cannot face any condemnation for sin and are not subject to God's judicial wrath. Sins are not the issue at the Judgment Seat. 1 Cor. 3:15 specifically teaches that all those at the Judgment Seat of Christ are saved.

"Truly, truly, I say to you, he who hears My word, and believes Him who sent Me, has eternal life, and does **not come into judgment**, but has passed out of death into life" [John 5:24].

Much more then, having now been justified by His blood, we shall be **saved from the wrath of God** through Him [Rom. 5:9].

There is therefore now **no condemnation** for those who are in Christ Jesus....Who will bring a charge against God's elect? God is the one who justifies; who is the one who condemns? Christ Jesus is He who died, yes, rather who was raised, who is at the right hand of God, who also intercedes for us [Rom. 8:1,33-34].

If any man's work is burned up, he shall suffer loss; **but he himself shall be saved**, yet so as through fire [1 Cor. 3:15].

And you were dead in your transgressions and the uncircumcision of your flesh, He made you alive together with Him, **having forgiven us all** our transgressions [Col. 2:13].

"And their **sins** and their lawless deeds **I will remember no more**" [Heb. 10:17].

For God has **not destined us for wrath**, but for obtaining salvation through our Lord Jesus Christ [1 Thess. 5:9].

And we have come to know and have believed the love which God has for us. God is love, and the one who abides in love abides in God, and God abides in him. By this, love is perfected with us, that **we may have confidence in the day of judgment**; because as He is, so also are we in this world. There is no fear in love; **but perfect love casts out fear, because fear involves punishment**, and the one who fears is not perfected in love [1 John 4:16-18].

There is no double jeopardy in God's system of justice. While believers can and do sin against God in His role as Father, and while this may bring temporal chastisement, all sin has been forgiven relative to God in His role as Judge. The issues at the Judgment Seat of Christ are not salvation or entrance into heaven, nor will that judgment be for sins that have already been forgiven. The verdict of "justification by faith" means that no charge will ever by entertained in God's courtroom against any believer.

2. Works Done on Earth

a. Works in General

The issues at the Judgment Seat are not salvation, entrance into heaven, or even sins on earth. The purpose for the Judgment Seat of Christ is to determine reward or loss of reward based upon works done on earth. Paul stresses works as the basis for judgment.

> Now he who plants and he who waters are one; but each will receive his own reward according to his own **labor** [1 Cor. 3:8].

> [E]ach man's **work** will become evident; for the day will show it, because it is to be revealed with fire; and the fire itself will test the quality of each man's **work**. If any man's **work**, which he has built upon it, remains, he shall receive a reward. If any man's **work** is burned up, he shall suffer loss; but he himself shall be saved, yet so as through fire [1 Cor. 3:13-15].

> For we must all appear before the judgment seat of Christ, that each one may be recompensed for his **deeds** in the body, according to what he has done, whether good or bad [2 Cor. 5:10].

b. Specifically Quality not Quantity of Work

The word translated "bad" in 2 Cor. 5:10 is not the normal Greek word for evil. It means "worthless." [16] The Judgment Seat of Christ will evaluate not so much whether ones works have been good versus evil (for condemnation due to sin is not the issue) but whether they have been good in the sense of worthy or bad in the sense of worthless. Notice that the stress in the contrast is not even between works done and works undone. The work has been done. The judgment determines whether it is **worthy** or **worthless**.

Christ will be more interested in the quality of work than the quantity (though it must be said that quality and quantity may be related in some people's lives). The Judgment Seat will evaluate works as to quality, especially whether they were done to glorify Christ or for some other goal such as enhancing self (see 1 Sam. 16:7). God is more interested in the quality of a faithful, obedient and, yes, loving heart than in popular or sensational results. Noah was a preacher of righteousness for 120 years (2 Pet. 2:5, Gen. 6:3), but the quantitative results were meager. Few listened to Isaiah (Isa. 6:9-10) or Jeremiah (Jer. 1:19, 15:15,17; 20:7-10). In fact, the Messiah was despised and rejected of men (Isa. 53:3; John 1:11). While results are desirable and a blessing, God-honoring faithfulness (with or without results) is the main criteria for judgment at the Judgment Seat of Christ.

> According to the grace of God which was given to me, as a wise master builder I laid a foundation, and another is building upon it. But let each man be careful **how** he builds upon it....each man's work will be evident; for the day will show it, because it is to be revealed with fire; and the fire itself will test the **quality** of each man's work [1 Cor. 3:10,13].

> Therefore do not go on passing judgment before the time, but wait until the Lord comes who will both bring to light the things hidden in the darkness and disclose the **motives** of men's hearts; and then each man's praise will come to him from God [1 Cor. 4:5].

> In this case, moreover, it is required of stewards that one be found **trustworthy** [1 Cor. 4:2].

c. Works that Especially Please God When Accompanied by a Loyal Heart

---

[16] See Richard C. Trench, *Synonyms of the New Testament*, reprint ed. (Grand Rapids: Wm. B. Eerdmans Publishing Co., 1976), pp. 317-18.

There are some questions about the various crowns offered as rewards that the Bible does not answer. Perhaps God wants His people to focus attention more on the nature of their responsibilities than the exact nature of potential rewards. Rather than dwelling on the precise nature of what we can obtain, God wants believers to concentrate more on what they should be doing. A following section will address the nature of the rewards offered by the "crowns" of the Bible. Here we look into what must be done in order to obtain these crowns. Remember again that a reward comes not just from doing but from doing that arises from a pure heart, a heart whose goal is to honor, love, and please God Himself.

(1). Imperishable (Incorruptible) Crown

> Do you not know that those who run in a race all run, but only one receives the prize? Run in such a way that you may win. And everyone who competes in the games exercises **self-control** in all things. They then do it to receive a perishable wreath, but we an imperishable. Therefore, I run in such a way, as not without aim; I box in such a way, as not beating the air; but I buffet my body and make it my slave, lest possibly, after I have preached to others, I myself should be disqualified [1 Cor. 9:24-27].

There is a special reward for those who exhibit **discipline, dedication, and self-control** in their Christian experience just as an athlete in training. Christ is central to their lives, and they strive to be and to do as He directs through His Word.

(2). Crown of Exultation (rejoicing)

> For **who is our** hope or joy or **crown** of exultation? Is it not even **you**, in the presence of our Lord Jesus at His coming? For **you** are our glory and joy [1 Thess. 2:19-20].

God is especially interested in rewarding those who work to **lead others to salvation** in Christ. Daniel 12:3 also associates "leading the many to righteousness" with future glory. Paul's Thessalonian converts would be his crown of rejoicing.

(3). Crown of Righteousness

> [I]n the future there is **laid up for me the crown** of righteousness, which the Lord, the righteous Judge, will award to me on that day; and not only to me, but also to all who have **loved His appearing** [2 Tim. 4:8].

It is fair to say that those who love Christ's appearing love the Person of Christ. Furthermore, those who love Christ do not love the world. Rather than conformity with the world they choose conformity to Christ. Thus, **loving Him and His return** goes together with **righteous living** (see 1 John 3:2-3). There is a special reward for believers who work at righteousness while they wait for His return. In fact the phrase "crown of righteousness" can be interpreted as a crown that comes from righteousness.

(4). Crown of Life

> Blessed is a man who **perseveres under trial**; for once he has been approved, he will receive the **crown** of life, which the Lord has promised to those who love Him [James 1:12].

> Do not fear what you are about to **suffer**. Behold, the devil is about to cast some of you into prison, that you may be tested, and you will have tribulation ten days. **Be faithful until death**, and I will give you the **crown** of life [Rev. 2:10].

It is easy to let spirituality slip in times of pressure and crisis. Yet, pressure tests character. God gives a special reward to those who **endure temptations, trials, persecution, or death for His sake**. He especially appreciates those who remain faithful in hardship.

(5). Crown of Glory

> And when the Chief Shepherd appears, you will receive the unfading crown of glory [1 Peter 5:4].

The crown of glory awaits Christian leaders who are faithful as undershepherds. There is a special **reward for Christian leaders** but also a more strict judgment (Luke 12:48; James 3:1; Heb. 13:17)

d. Contributions to the Lives of Other Believers

1 Cor. 3:12-13 says that God will evaluate whether one builds "gold, silver, precious stones" or "wood, hay, straw" upon the "foundation". [17] In the context the church is God's building (v. 9). Therefore, the building materials must be people. One way that God will evaluate a believer is to look at his works relative to **building up or tearing down other believers** within his sphere of influence. This is certainly true of leaders (see Heb. 13:17) although it is ultimately true that every Christian is accountable to God for his own faithfulness or lack thereof (Rom. 14:12; 1 Cor. 4:5; Gal. 6:5). Each Christian is responsible for efforts to influence other Christians for good. He or she must try to bring about enduring permanence, value, and spiritual quality in the lives of other Christians rather than transitory cheapness (i.e., the character of precious stones as opposed to stubble). There is no guilt if others rebel or fail after we have tried to help, but the failure to show any interest in the spiritual welfare of other believers is a serious sin of omission. There is a special reward for Christians who use their lives to edify, enrich, and benefit others.

> Now we who are strong ought to bear the weakness of those without strength and not just please ourselves. Let each of us please his neighbor for his good, to his edification [Rom. 15:1-2].

> Do nothing from selfishness or empty conceit, but with humility of mind let each of you regard one another as more important than himself; do not merely look out for your own personal interests, but also for the interests of others. Have this attitude in yourselves which was also in Christ Jesus [Phil. 2:3-5].

3. Standards for Judging Believer's Works

One of the lessons in the parable of the laborers in the vineyard (Matt. 20:1-16) is that there will be great surprises when God gives rewards. There is no way that we can presently anticipate the level of reward a particular believer will obtain. If we were to guess, we would be wrong. Some who expect to receive a great reward will have a more modest one. Others anticipate little but will obtain much. Will the pastor of a church with 5,000 members or a godly mother with five children receive greater praise at the Judgment Seat of Christ? There is no way to know during the present time. We do know that God has full knowledge of all circumstances and will judge fairly. We also know some of the standards He will employ.

a. God will judge Christian leaders by a stricter judgment.

One of Paul's points in 1 Cor. 9:14-17 is that his great missionary efforts were part of his calling. His labors were only a duty not something of special merit. His attitude was that expressed by the Lord's parable in Luke 17:7-10. Paul felt that given his calling, he would have to work extra hard to do something meritorious. James is clear on the point

---

[17] Perhaps Paul's instructions in 1 Cor. 3:10ff. are aimed primarily at Christian leaders who must be careful how they build the people of the local church. By application, God is concerned that every believer contributes to the spiritual advancement of other believers in his or her life.

that God judges teachers by a higher standard than others.

> "So you too, when you do all the things which are commanded you, say, 'We are unworthy slaves; we have done only that which we ought to have done' " [Luke 17:10].

> For if I preach the gospel, I have nothing to boast of, for I am under compulsion; for woe is me if I do not preach the gospel [1 Cor. 9:16].

> Let not many of you become teachers, my brethren, knowing that as such we shall incur a stricter judgment [James 3:1].

b. God takes advantages and disadvantages into account in His judgment.

Unlike man, God can judge with perfect judgment. He will take into account those with advantages or disadvantages in areas like salvation at an early age, backgrounds in Christian or non-Christian homes, advantages to learn of God in a good church, natural aptitudes, and spiritual gifts. God not only sees the results in a life but also any special struggles or handicaps. At the Judgment Seat some of the first will be last and the last first. God is aware of all factors and will make a completely fair judgment.

> ...And from everyone who has been given much shall much be required and to whom they entrusted much, of him they will ask all the more [Luke 12:48b].

c. God will judge works but with an emphasis upon character. Jonah led a great revival but with a bad attitude. From a human perspective he may seem to deserve a great reward for his ministry, but God's standards for judgment are different from man's standards (1 Sam. 16:7).

Eph. 6:6 and Col. 3:22 mention those who work hard only to please men and contrast those who work "as to the Lord." Both con-texts go on to mention God's evaluation (Eph. 6:8; Col. 3:24). At the Judgment Seat of Christ, God will judge each believer's works to determine reward or loss of reward. However, He will place heavy emphasis upon the motivation for a person's works, whether to please man or to please Christ. The Sermon on the Mount addresses those whose religious deeds arose from a motive to be seen of man as "pious." Twice Christ says of them, "they have their reward in full" (Matt. 6:2,5, see also John 12:43). All their religious deeds were done to gain attention from men. They got the reward they sought but will have none from God. There are likely some Christians today who are faithful only when watched, or others who work hard but do so only to be noticed or praised without any special love for God. The focus of judging a believer's works is upon the inner spirit that led to those works (see 1 Cor. 4:5).

F. The Nature of Future Rewards

One cannot stress enough that the Judgment Seat of Christ concerns rewards or loss of rewards, not salvation or entrance into heaven or even personal sins. God has not told us everything about the nature of the rewards that He will bestow, but we do know some important facts.

1. Degrees of Rewards

God in His grace is going to find something praiseworthy in every believer's life (1 Cor. 4:5). However, one of the Lord's parables indirectly teaches that God rewards His servants in varying degrees (Luke 19:11-19).

2. Glory in the Resurrection Body

Dan. 12:3; Matt. 13:43; Rom. 8:16-17; Phil. 3:21; Col. 3:4 and several verses in 1 Peter (1 Pet. 4:13; 5:1,10) mention the prospect of believers having a glorious resurrection body and sharing in Christ's glory. In a context that concerns the resurrection body, Paul in 1 Cor. 15:41-42, seems to teach that there will be various degrees of glory in the resurrection body of believers: "There is one glory of the sun, and another glory of the moon, and another glory of the stars; for star **differs** from star in glory. **So also is the resurrection** of the dead."

Based upon this text, many Bible teachers believe that God will reward believers with different degrees of glorification. All will obtain a glorified state, but perhaps some will have a greater ability to praise and honor God, and some will have resurrection bodies that are more resplendent and brighter than others. Since God created man to glorify Himself (1 Pet. 2:9; Rev. 4:11), a greater capacity to glorify God either by increased ability to praise or increased service and an greater capacity to reflect Christ's visible glory in ones body would be a truly desirable reward (cf. 2 Cor. 3:18).

3. Positions of Service and Authority

Christ told the apostles, the founders of the church (see Eph. 2:20), that they would sit on thrones, judging the twelve tribes of Israel in the coming Kingdom (Matt. 19:28). The Bible does not restrict participation in ruling over Christ's future Kingdom to only the apostles.

> If we endure, we shall also **reign** with Him… [2 Tim. 2:12a].

> [A]nd He has made us to be a **kingdom**, priests to His God and Father; to Him be the glory and the dominion forever and ever. Amen [Rev. 1:6].

> "And Thou hast made them to be a kingdom and priests to our God; and they will **reign** upon the earth" [Rev. 5:10].

> …and they came to life and **reigned** with Christ for a thousand years….Blessed and holy is the one who has a part in the first resurrection; over these the second death has no power, but they will be priests of God and of Christ and will **reign** with

Him for a thousand years [Rev. 20:4c, 6].

In Luke 19:11ff., the nobleman who returns as a king gives one of his servant's "authority over ten cities" (v. 17) and another servant authority "over five cities" (v. 19). It is safe to conclude that God rewards believers with different positions of authority in the Millennium and probably also in the Eternal State. Increased position and increased service for God will not be deemed a burden but an honor.

4. Crowns

The Bible promises various crowns as rewards for believers. With the exception of the "golden crowns", which the 24 elders in heaven wear on their heads (Revelation 4), it is preferable to interpret these crowns as figurative symbols for unspecified rewards that are valuable and noticeable. The word employed is s*tephanos* (the name Steven), and it does not refer to a gem-filled crown of a monarch but to a laurel made of ivy worn by a victorious athlete. It is a garland as opposed to a diadem. Do we seriously want to conclude that believers will be wearing green laurels for eternity in heaven? It does seem these crowns are better interpreted as figurative. In fact, 1 Cor. 9:25 makes a specific contrast with a literal "wreath" or "crown" and eternal rewards. 1 Thess. 2:19-20 provides even more impressive evidence that the Biblical crowns are figurative. The Thessalonian believers themselves are Paul's crown (see also Phil. 4:1).

> For who is our hope or joy or crown of exultation? Is it not even **you**, in the presence of our Lord Jesus at His coming? For **you** are our glory and joy [1 Thess. 2:19-20].

The "crown" in 1 Thess. 2:19 is obviously figurative. This bolsters the argument that the rest are also intended as figures. They speak of victory, reward, and visible honors that God will give believers at the Judgment

Seat of Christ. It is difficult to be any more precise than this.

God wants believers to focus not so much on the nature of future rewards but on the basis for these rewards (particularly the quality of their hearts). Our main pursuit is to love Christ and work to honor Him. Any rewards obtained are incidental and secondary to a deeper satisfaction in pleasing Him and contributing to His exaltation. Therefore, it is best for us at the present to worry less about the nature of coming rewards and more upon what pleases God and thus the bases for those rewards: the imperishable crown for discipline, dedication, self-control; the crown of rejoicing for evangelism; the crown of (or from) righteousness for loving His appearing and thus loving Him, not the world; the crown of life for enduring trials and temptations; the crown of glory (appositional genitive, meaning glory will be the crown) for being a faithful leader.

5. Loss of Reward/ Shame

God will reward work done from the devoted heart with a higher degree of glory, with increased authority in the Kingdom, and with crowns. There is, however, another possible outcome to the Judgment Seat, shame and loss of reward. All believers will obtain salvation (1 Cor. 3:15). All believers will obtain glorification in some degree (1 Cor. 15:51). God will give some praise to every believer (1 Cor. 4:5). Yet, some will find their works "burned up" by Christ's judgment. The Bible presents the possibility of shame and of loss of reward.

And now, little children, abide in Him, so that when He appears, we may have confidence and not shrink away from Him in **shame** at His coming [1 John 2:28].

Let no one keep **defrauding you of your prize** by delighting in self-abasement and the worship of angels... [Col. 2:18].

Watch yourselves, that you might **not lose** what you have accomplished, but that you may **receive a full reward** [2 John 8].

"I am coming quickly; hold fast what you have in **order that no one take your crown**" [Rev. 3:11].

G. Future Evaluation and Present Competition

A word should be given about the relationship between the future judgment of believers and present competition among believers. God did not teach us about future rewards so that we could entertain rivalry in the present. Real love for Christ involves the attitude that we are delighted when another excels at honoring Him. While self-evaluation is a part of Christian living, a spirit of competition between Christians does not please God even if the work that is generated is in itself legitimate.

So then neither the one who plants nor the one who waters is anything, but God who causes the growth. Now he who plants and he who waters are one...[1 Cor. 3:7-8].

...when they measure themselves by themselves, and compare themselves with themselves, they are without understanding [2 Cor. 10:12b].

But let each one **examine his own work**, and then he will have reason for boasting in regard to himself alone, and not in regard to another [Gal. 6:4].

Competition and comparison leads to pride, envy, possibly laziness, coveting another's abilities, and bitterness (maybe even bitterness against God). A better method for self-evaluation is to judge ones own efforts against ones own potential and also to measure present progress over past performance.

H. Positive and Negative Incentive from the Judgment Seat

The Bible teaches that the coming judgment of believers is both a negative and positive incentive for diligence in the present. Negatively, Christians will want to avoid the possibility of shame. Positively, we will be glad on the judgment day if we serve faithfully now. Just as an examination is terrifying to an unprepared student but brings promotion to a diligent one, so too ones experience at the future Judgment Seat of Christ will depend upon his degree of faithfulness and preparedness now. Paul viewed the coming judgment as giving both negative and positive incentives for service.

> Therefore, also we have as our ambition, whether at home or absent, to be pleasing to Him. For (because) we must all appear before the judgment seat of Christ, that each one may be recompensed for his deeds in the body, according to what he has done, whether good or bad. Therefore knowing the fear of the Lord, we persuade men... [2 Cor. 5: 9-11a].

> I have fought the good fight, I have finished the course, I have kept the faith; in the future there is laid up for me the crown of righteousness, which the Lord, the righteous Judge, will award to me on that day; and not only to me, but also to all who have loved His appearing [2 Tim. 4:7-8].

X. The Marriage Supper of the Lamb

A. Introduction

There were three main aspects to a Jewish wedding. The engagement (betrothal) was considered binding and caused the couple to be viewed as husband and wife. It took a formal divorce to break a betrothal (see Matt. 1:18-19). The church is Christ's bride in this first sense. She is betrothed to Christ, but the actual wedding has not yet taken place (see also John 3:29; Rom. 7:3-4; Eph. 5:22ff.; Rev. 19:7ff.; 21:2,9; New Jerusalem is Christ's bride in the sense that the church dwells there, Rev. 22:17).

> For I am jealous for you with a godly jealousy; for I betrothed you to one husband, that to Christ I might present you as a pure virgin [2 Cor. 11:2].

One may view the Holy Spirit as a token of a promised future relationship. He is like an engagement ring (2 Cor. 1:22; 5:5; Eph. 1:14) (The meaning of the word translated "earnest" or "pledge" in modern Greek is "engagement ring").

In the second phase of a wedding the groom would come to the bride's home to take her in a procession back to his home for an official wedding ceremony. This seems to correspond to the Rapture, in which Christ comes to lead His bride in a procession to His home in heaven for the actual wedding. It is best to place the marriage of the Lamb and the church in heaven at a time after the Judgment Seat of Christ. Rev. 19:8 identifies the bride's white garments as the "righteous acts of the saints" (righteous in Greek is plural). Apparently, the fact that the bride is clothed in white indicates that her righteous deeds have already been evaluated at the Judgment Seat.

The third phase of a wedding was the wedding feast or supper. Some students of prophecy distinguish between the wedding, which occurs in heaven (during the tribulation period on earth), and the wedding feast or supper that occurs back on earth after the Tribulation. Others think that both the wedding and wedding feast occur in heaven before Christ's Second Coming to earth. This disagreement is not a major one in overall theology, but it does affect teachings about the place, time, and nature of the marriage feast. Is it in heaven or earth? Does it occur during the tribulation period or at the beginning of the Kingdom? Is the feast itself a celebration around fellowship with Christ in heaven, or a celebration that the King finally rules on earth?

B. Evidence for Marriage in Heaven with a Marriage Feast on Earth

Although most passages that concern the marriage supper of the Lamb can be explained by either view, it is better to distinguish between the **marriage** of Christ and the church **in heaven** and the marriage **feast** which takes place **on earth** after the Second Coming. Indeed, the marriage feast may in actuality be a celebration throughout the entire 1,000 years.

> And the LORD of hosts will prepare a lavish banquet for all peoples **on this mountain** (i.e., on earth in Israel); a banquet of aged wine, choice pieces with marrow, and refined, aged wine [Isa. 25:6].

> "[F]or I say to you, I will not drink of the fruit of the vine from now on **until the kingdom of God comes**" [Luke 22:18].

Although Christ is the groom and the church is the bride, a wedding feast could be expected to involve guests who are not actual participants. The best interpretation of the parable of the ten virgins is that the girls represent Israel (Matt. 25:1ff.). Indeed, John 3:29 likens John the Baptist, definitely Jewish, to a friend of the groom. If Israel participates in the wedding feast for Christ and the church, it is best to place this feast back on earth because the resurrection of Old Testament saints occurs after the Tribulation (Isa. 26:19; Dan. 12:1-2; Ezek. 37:12-13)

Several parables give even stronger evidences that while the marriage of the Lamb may take place in heaven, the marriage feast seems to have an earthly setting. In Matthew 22 the Lord speaks of a wedding feast that the king gives for his son. The setting is definitely earthly. Some who are invited refuse to come. Although one might argue the parable refers only to Israel's treatment

of Christ at His first coming, there do seem to be eschatological overtones in such phrases as "outer darkness" and "weeping, and gnashing of teeth" (Matt. 22:13).

> "The kingdom of heaven may be compared to a king, who gave a wedding feast for his son. And he sent out his slaves to call those who had been invited to the wedding feast, and they were unwilling to come. Again he sent out other slaves saying, 'Tell those who have been invited, "Behold, I have prepared my dinner; my oxen and my fatted livestock are all butchered and everything is ready; come to the wedding feast."' "But they paid no attention and went their way, one to his own farm, another to his business, and the rest seized his slaves and mistreated them and killed them. But the king was enraged and sent his armies, and destroyed those murderers, and set their city on fire. Then he said to his slaves, 'The wedding is ready, but those who were invited were not worthy. Go therefore to the main highways, and as many as you find there, invite to the wedding feast.' "And those slaves went out into the streets, and gathered together all they found, both evil and good; and the wedding hall was filled with dinner guests. But when the king came in to look over the dinner guests, he saw there a man not dressed in wedding clothes, and he said to him, 'Friend, how did you come in here without wedding clothes?' And he was speechless. "Then the king said to the servants, 'Bind him hand and foot, and cast him into the outer darkness; in that place there shall be weeping and gnashing of teeth' [Matt. 22:2-13].

If the teachings of Matt. 22:1ff. extend beyond the single point of Christ's rejection at His first coming, then it presents a future

418

wedding feast on earth after the Second Coming. The parable fits well with the supposition that invitations to the Kingdom will be presented through the "gospel of the Kingdom" during the Tribulation (Matt. 24:14; Rev. 14:6). All who reject the invitation will be excluded from the joy of the wedding celebration (by the Judgment of Israel and the Judgment of the Nations). If the marriage feast takes place in heaven, who are those who refuse to come and are cast out? While we can envision exclusion from Christ's Kingdom on earth, we should rule out an interpretation in which some unsaved sneak into heaven and must then be tossed out.

Matt. 25:1ff. gives even stronger evidence for the distinction between a marriage in heaven and a marriage feast on earth. It definitely refers to the Kingdom of heaven (v. 1) and is future (all of Matthew 24, Matt. 25:31, etc). References to the Lord's coming involve His revelation at the end of the Tribulation (see Matt. 24:21, 29-31). Matt. 25:10 clearly places the "feast" on earth after the groom's return.

> "And while they were going away to make the purchase, **the bridegroom came**, and those who were ready went in with him **to the wedding feast**; and the door was shut" [Matt. 25:10].

The parable of the ten virgins pictures a wedding feast on earth after the groom's return. Therefore, the doctrinal point involves a marriage feast on earth after Christ's return at the close of the Tribulation. Those in Israel who are prepared are welcome. Those unprepared are excluded. If the marriage feast is in heaven, who are those removed from it? [18]

---

[18] Those who accept eternal security can hardly take the virgins to be Christians who lose their welcome at the wedding feast. Also, the church is the bride. Wedding guests are best viewed as Israelites. Some are saved. Some are unsaved.

The parable of Luke 14:16-24 refers to a man giving banquet invitations to all after those initially invited decline to come. Yet, the word for "wedding feast" does not occur, nor is there any imagery of the king's son being married or a groom returning. It would be hard to prove that Luke 14:16-24 is an exact parallel to Matt. 22:1-13. Yet, there are some indications that Christ also has the future in mind in giving this parable. Luke 14:14 mentions rewards for the resurrection of the righteous, and v. 15 shows that the parable is about the "Kingdom of God." If we view the "parable of the dinner" as teaching about future events, as well as the rejection of Christ by His own generation, then it also presents a feast on earth and gives a secondary support to the idea of the marriage supper occurring on earth.

C. Texts Compatible with the Marriage Supper in Heaven or on Earth

The single factor that creates the most confusion about the marriage supper is that the Greek word (*gamos*) can mean either "wedding" or "wedding feast." Only the context, or additional descriptions, make it clear which is intended.

Luke 12:36ff. could be fairly used to teach that the wedding supper occurs in heaven before Christ's return (v. 40). He comes to earth **from** the wedding feast.

> "And be like men who are waiting for their master when he **returns from the wedding feast**, so that they may immediately open the door to him when he comes and knocks" [Luke 12:36].

Luke 12:36 is capable of two translations. He returns from either the wedding feast (NASB, NIV) or the wedding itself (KJV).

This mixture of the two can only occur in an earthly setting not heaven. Therefore, the wedding may take place in heaven after the Rapture, but it seems best to locate the wedding feast back on earth after the Second Coming.

Yet, it is probably better to translate as the KJV does. The understanding of the KJV translators was that the Master returns **from the wedding** (in heaven) and then has a banquet on earth for His servants (Israel, vv. 36-37).

To translate, "from the wedding feast" (NASB, NIV) means Christ returns to earth after the wedding feast. This is also legitimate translation of the word (if we consult no other passages, wedding feast is perhaps even preferable given that the word is plural). [19] Nevertheless, because Matt. 25:10 clearly teaches that the groom returns to the wedding feast and given that Luke 12:36 is capable of a compatible translation, it is probably better to translate as the KJV does. The understanding given by the King James Version translation would be that the Master returns from the wedding (in heaven) and then has a banquet on earth for His servants (Israel, v. 37).

> "And ye yourselves like men that wait for their lord, when he will return from the wedding [not wedding feast]; that when he cometh and knocketh, they may open unto him immediately. Blessed are those servants, whom the lord when he cometh shall find watching; verily I say unto you, that he shall gird himself, and make them to sit down to eat, and will come forth and serve them....Be ye, therefore, ready also; for the Son of man is coming at an hour you do not expect" [Luke 12:36-37,40] (KJV New Scofield)

The parable of Luke 12:35ff. does not prove that the marriage supper of the Lamb occurs on earth, but it can be legitimately translated to fit that conclusion if one has been swayed in that direction by Matt. 22:1-13, 25:1-13; Luke 14:16-24.

Rev. 19:7-9 is another text that is capable of placing the marriage supper of the Lamb either in heaven before the Second Coming or on earth after the Second Coming.

> "Let us rejoice and be glad and give the glory to Him, for the marriage of the Lamb has come and His bride has made herself ready." And it was given to her to clothe herself in fine linen, bright and clean; for the fine linen is the righteous acts of the saints. And he said to me, "Write, 'Blessed are those who are invited to the marriage supper of the Lamb.' " And he said to me, "These are true words of God" [Rev. 19:7-9].

Verse seven says that the wedding of the Lamb has already taken place (aorist). This statement occurs before the discussion about the Second Coming in v. 11. Nearly all agree that the actual marriage takes place in heaven before Christ's return. Verse 8 indicates that the righteous acts of the church have already been judged and rewarded. Thus, most place the actual marriage of Christ and the church in heaven at some point after the Judgment Seat of Christ but before the Second Coming.

John adds the word "supper" after marriage in v. 9. There is no vagueness as to the event discussed, but his statement lacks references to time. It says those who are invited to the marriage supper are blessed. Does this mean those in heaven who have already participated in the marriage supper are blessed? Or is this a heavenly announcement of blessings upon those who will be soon enjoying a

---

[19] The standard Greek lexicon states the plural of *gamos* is generally used when a "wedding celebration" is in view. However, Matt. 22:8 is singular; but the context clearly involves a feast. Also, the same lexicon says, "sg. an. pl. are oft. used interchangeably w. no difference in mng." See Walter Bauer, *The Greek-English Lexicon of the New Testament and Other Early Christian Literature,* translated by Wm. F. Arndt and F. Wilber Gingrich (Chicago, University of Chicago Press, 1957), p. 150.

sharing in the marriage supper after the Second Coming, which takes place in vv. 11ff.? Those who want to place the marriage supper of the Lamb in heaven will take v. 9 as a statement of blessing already enjoyed in heaven. Those who want to place the marriage supper of the Lamb on earth will take v. 9 as an announcement that will soon take place back on earth after the Second Coming. Rev. 19:7-9 is capable of fitting either view.

D. Conclusions on the Distinction between a Marriage in Heaven and a Marriage Feast on Earth

While the issue is relatively minor, it is best to see a distinction between the marriage of the Lamb as taking place in heaven and the marriage supper as occurring on earth. The marriage between Christ and the church occurs while the Tribulation rages on earth. The marriage feast probably occurs as a part of the transition from the Tribulation to the Kingdom after the Second Coming. The unsaved survivors of the tribulation period who had declined the invitation to the wedding celebration are excluded from the Kingdom by the Judgment of Israel and of the Nations. Perhaps some change their minds and want to enter the celebration when they see others admitted to glory (Matt. 25:34), but the King will exclude them (Matt. 25:41, 22:11-14). The survivors of the Tribulation who believed in "the gospel of the kingdom" (Matt. 24:14) are welcome to the marriage feast which may include a celebration for the entire 1,000 years.

XI. The Tribulation Period

After the Rapture (with its simultaneous resurrection) the church undergoes the Judgment Seat of Christ and the Marriage of the Lamb (again the marriage feast may be after the Second Coming). While the church enjoys its rewards and union with Christ, the Tribulation brings unimaginable horror to the world. Major sections of the Bible discuss this coming tribulation period (e.g., Ezekiel 38-39; Daniel 9-11; Matthew 24-25 and parallels; 1 Thess. 5; 2 Thessalonians 2; Revelation 6-18). It will be impossible to cover every detail in this topical study, but the main truths about the Tribulation may be classified under "Major Gentile World Powers During the Tribulation," "The Antichrist", "Battles in the Tribulation", and "God and the Saints in the Tribulation."

A. Major Gentile World Powers during the Tribulation

The purpose for this section is simply to identify the major players in the world during the Tribulation. Following sections attempt to give a chronology of tribulational battles.

1. Revived Rome (A European confederation of ten kings that soon turns into a dictatorship).

The surge in Arab economic power has caused some interpreters to drop the idea of a revived Roman Empire in favor of taking the Babylon of Revelation 17-18 as literal Babylon and not a revived Rome. This interpretation of Revelation 17-18 has merits, but it need not exclude the concept of a revived Roman Empire. The case for a revived Rome does not depend on Revelation 17-18.

a. The 69th week of Daniel's prophecy (9:24-27) ended with Rome as a world power. Since the intervening church age is not in view, we would anticipate that Rome will also be a major power during the 70th week (which is the Tribulation as identified in Matt. 24:15).

b. Daniel 9:26 predicts that the people of the (evil) prince to come will destroy Jerusalem after the Messiah is "cut off" (i.e., crucified). The Romans destroyed Jerusalem after Christ's death. Therefore, the (evil) prince that shall come is the leader of Rome, and the Antichrist should be leading a revived Roman Empire (see also Luke 21:20ff. where the destruction of Jerusalem in A.D.

70 by Rome also seems blended with similar conditions of the end time.)

"Then after the sixty-two weeks the Messiah will be cut off and have nothing, and the people of the (evil) prince who is to come will destroy the city and the sanctuary. And its end will come with a flood; even to the end there will be war; desolations are determined. And he (the evil prince) will make a firm covenant with the many for one week, but in the middle of the week he will put a stop to sacrifice and grain offering; and on the wing of abominations will come one who makes desolate, even until a complete destruction, one that is decreed, is poured out on the one who makes desolate" [Dan. 9:26-27].

c. Dan. 2:36-45 and 7:2-14 speak of four gentile world powers that arise before Christ sets up His Kingdom. The book identifies the first three as Babylon (Dan. 2:38), Medo-Persia (Dan. 5:28, 8:20, 11:2) and Greece (8:21, 11:2). The fourth empire from Daniel's own time in terms of the chronological sequence of ancient history was Rome. It was theoretically possible for Christ the King to have set up His Kingdom at His first coming. The fourth kingdom that Christ would have had to destroy in the first century was Rome (Dan. 2:44-45, 7:11-14; 8:11, 23-27). It is likely that the power Christ will destroy at His Second Coming will also be Roman.

d. The Nature of Revived Rome

(1). The confederation begins with 10 kings in association. This is the symbolism behind 10 toes (Dan. 2:41), and 10 horns (Dan. 7:7, 20, 24; Rev. 12:3; 13:1 and 17:12). This is the Bible's own explanation.

"...As for the **ten horns**, out of this kingdom **ten kings** will arise" [Dan. 7:24a].

"And the **ten horns** which you saw are **ten kings**..."[Rev. 17:12].

Revived Rome is usually viewed as a Western European confederation because the ancient Roman Empire was centered in Europe. Other nations such as Iran, Turkey, Libya, and Ethiopia, and possibly east Europe seem to be allied with Russia in the Tribulation (see below and Ezek. 38:5-6).

(2). The little horn (the Antichrist) destroys three of the ten kings and assumes dictatorship. It seems that he replaces the three kings and continues to rule over an empire with ten kings as subordinates.

"While I was contemplating the horns, behold, another horn, a little one, came up among them, and **three of the first horns were pulled out by the roots** before it; and behold, this horn possessed eyes like the eyes of a man, and a mouth uttering great boasts....As for the ten horns, out of this kingdom ten kings will arise; and another will arise after them, and he will be different from the previous ones and will **subdue three kings**" [Dan. 7:8,24] (see also 7:20).

"And the ten horns which you saw are **ten kings**, who have not yet received a kingdom, but they receive **authority as kings with the beast** for one hour. These have one purpose and they give their power and authority to the beast" [Rev. 17:12-13].

The time at which the Antichrist gains full control over revived Rome is not certain. However, he dominates the entire earth for the last 3 1/2 years of the Tribulation.

And there was given to him a mouth speaking arrogant words and blasphemies; and authority to act for **forty-two months** was given to him. And he opened his mouth in blasphemies against God, to blaspheme His name and His tabernacle, that is those who dwell in heaven. And it was given to him to make war with the saints and to overcome them; and authority over every tribe and people and tongue and nation was given to him [Rev. 13:5-7].

Daniel 9:27 teaches that this evil ruler will make a peace treaty to protect Israel for the first 3 1/2 years. However, at the middle of the Tribulation he breaks the treaty and begins to persecute both Israel (Dan. 12:1; Rev. 12:1-6, 13-17) and all believers (Dan. 7:21; Rev. 13:7).

It is logical to assume that many of the international "wars and rumors of wars" (Matt. 24:6) in the Tribulation take place during the first half because no one will be able to oppose the Antichrist during the second half (The Great Tribulation, Rev. 13:4). The final half, however, will be worse because of God's judgments upon the world and worse in terms of persecution for Israel and the saints. The Antichrist is studied in greater detail on pp. 429-440.

2. The Kings of the East

Rev. 16:12 mentions "the kings of the east." These are apparently in an alliance with the Antichrist as he controls the whole world at this time (Rev. 13:7-8). The kings of the east come to assist the Antichrist and battle the Lord Jesus Christ at Armageddon. (Despite the titles in many study Bibles, Rev. 9:13ff. seems to describe a demonic horde and not the armies of the east. Unless they are highly figurative, vv. 17 and 19 are not describing a human army, and the first part of Chapter 9 definitely concerns demons from the abyss.)

And the sixth angel poured out his bowl upon the great river, the Euphrates; and its water was dried up, that the way might be prepared for the kings from the east. And I saw coming out of the mouth of the dragon and out of the mouth of the beast and out of the mouth of the false prophet, three unclean spirits like frogs; for they are spirits of demons, performing signs, which go out to the kings of the whole world, to gather them together for the war of the great day of God, the Almighty....And they gathered them together to the place which in Hebrew is called Har-Magedon [Rev. 16:12-14,16].

3. Gog and Magog (Russia and Allies)

Ezekiel 38-39 teaches about the end time invasion of Israel by Gog of the land of Magog. These names also occur in Rev. 20:8. The invasion will be studied separately. The present purpose is to identify "Gog of the land of Magog" (Ezek. 38:2).

And the word of the LORD came to me saying, "Son of man, set your face toward Gog of the land of Magog, the prince of Rosh, Meshech, and Tubal, and prophesy against him, and say, 'Thus says the Lord God, "Behold, I am against you, O Gog, prince of Rosh, Meshech, and Tubal. And I will turn you about and put hooks into your jaws, and I will bring you out, and all your army, horses and horsemen, all of them splendidly attired, a great company with buckler and shield, all of them wielding swords; Persia, Ethiopia, and Put with them, all of them with shield and helmet; Gomer with all its troops; Beth-togarmah from the remote parts of the north with all its troops - many peoples with you" [Ezek. 38:1-6].

a. Several times Ezekiel says that Israel's enemy is from the "remote parts of the North." This phrase alone is enough to suggest that the prophet has in mind the area that we now call "Russia."

"Gomer with all its troops; Beth-togarmah **from the remote parts of the north** with all its troops

423

- many peoples with you" [Ezek. 38:6].

"And you will come from your place out of the remote **parts of the north...**" [Ezek. 38:15].

"[A]nd I shall turn you around, drive you on, take you up from **the remotest parts of the north**, and bring you against the mountains of Israel" [Ezek. 39:2].

b. Magog

Gog is the leader of Magog. It is interesting that Bible teachers identified Magog as Russia long before Russia was a superpower. Lindsey mentions a British bishop who taught that Magog was Russia in 1710. [20]

Ancient sources identify Magog with the "Scythians" who are the peoples north of the Black Sea, i.e., modern Russia (see Col. 3:11). Josephus, the 1st century Jewish historian writes:

"Magog founded those that from him were named Magogites, but who are by the Greeks called Scythians." [21] (Antiquities 1:6:1)

Modern commentators claim that the ancient Roman Pliny said, "Heirapolis, taken by the Scythians, was afterward called Magog" and that Jerome (A.D.345-420) claimed the Jews in his time identified Magog with the Scythians. [22]

The identification of Magog with the Scythians and the phrase "remote parts of the north" give solid evidence that Ezekiel 38-39 refer to what we now call "Russia".

c. Rosh

Despite the temptation to identify "Rosh" with Russia, the word is a perfectly normal Hebrew word meaning "chief" or "first" as in "Rosh Hashanah," the first of the year. The phrase is probably best translated as in the KJV "the Chief prince of Meshech and Tubal." (Ezek. 38:3). Another support fo this more simple translation is that while Meshech and Tubal appear together many times (Gen. 10:2; 1 Chron. 1:5; Ezek. 27:13, 32:26), there would be no occurrence of three nations named, "Rosh, Meshech, and Tubal", unless it be in Ezekiel 38-39.

Feinberg traced an ancient Greek usage of "Rosh" for Russia in the Iliad, XIII. 5-6, and "Rosh" does appear as a proper name in Gen. 46:21. [23] He also cites later Byzantine and Arabic writers as mentioning a people called "Rus". [24] Gesenius' Hebrew dictionary agrees and defines "Rosh" as "undoubtedly Russians". [25] Yet, evidence as late as the 10th century AD and coming from Greece and not Israel is not sufficient to deny the normal meaning of "Rosh".

Ezek. 38:2 should probably be translated "chief (Hebrew "Rosh") prince of Meschech and Tubal." It is possible but not probable there is any reference to Russia even though the words sound the same. Ultimately, the view that Ezekiel 38-39 speaks of Russia does not depend on equating it with "rosh".

d. Meshech and Tubal

Pentecost and Lindsey identify "Meschech" as "Moscow". [26] However, similar sounds

---

[20] Hal Lindsey, *The Late Great Plant Earth*, reprint ed. (New York: Bantam Books, 1973), p. 54.

[21] Josephus, *Complete Works*, translated by William Whiston, reprint ed. (Grand Rapids: Kregal Publications, 1960), pp. 30-31.

[22] Hal Lindsey, *The Late Great Plant Earth*, p. 53; and Charles L. Feinburg, *The Prophecy of Ezekiel* (Chicago: Moody Press, 1969), p. 220.

[23] Ibid.

[24] Ibid.

[25] William Gesenius, *Hebrew and Chaldee Lexicon,* translated by Samuel Prideaux Tregelles, reprint ed. (Grand Rapids: Wm. B. Eerdmans Publishing Co., 1976), p. 752.

[26] Lindsey, *The Late Great Planet Earth*, p. 53; Dwight Pentecost, *Things to Come*, reprint ed. (Grand Rapids: Zondervan Publishing House, 1976), p. 328. Dr. Pentecost is quoting Louis

are not a sufficient basis for equating two words. Standard evangelical Bible encyclopedias cite impressive evidence from ancient inscriptions that Meshech and Tubal refer to places that are now in areas we call Turkey or maybe even Armenia. [27] Feinburg seems to accept this location and does not identify Meshech and Tubal with Moscow. [28] It is best to identify Meshech and Tubal with ancient Phrygia/Cappadocia, which is modern central to east Turkey and possibly Armenia. The area may be in Armenia and does feel Russian influence, but it is not likely that "Meshech" is Moscow.

e. Persia, Ethiopia, Put

These are three allies of Magog listed in Ezek. 38:5. Persia is modern Iran. The Hebrew word for Ethiopia is "Cush." Most Bible teachers identify "Cush" with Ethiopia or Sudan, both near Egypt.[29] The Septuagint translates Cush as "Ethiopia", and Ezek. 29:10 makes "Cush" border Egypt (see also Gen. 10:6; *Mizraim* is the Hebrew word for Egypt). Also, many Bible verses support the identification of Cush with Ethiopia (2 Chron. 21:16; Esther 1:1; 8:9; Psa. 68:31; Isa. 20:3,5; 45:14; Jer. 13:23 dark-skinned people; Ezek. 30:4).

Put can be identified with Libya. Josephus says (Antiquities 1:6:2), "Phut also was the founder of Libyia..." [30] The Septuagint translates "Put" as Libya and Pliny equates "Put" with "Mauritania" in Africa. [31] Russia will be Israel's main adversary, but it has some important allies in Iran, Ethiopia, and Libya.

f. Gomer

Gomer was the father of Ashkenaz and Togarmah (Gen. 10:3). The ancient Talmud and modern Jews identify "Ashkenaz" with Germany and East Europe. Most evangelical Christians conclude that Akkadian "gimirra" equals the Greek "Cimmerians" (a mobile group variously located in Eastern Europe, or the Caucasus Mountains, or Asia Minor).[32] Dyer identifies Gomer with Turkey probably on the strength of Gen. 10:3 compared with Jer. 51:27. [33]

g. Togarmah

Togarmah had already been mentioned in the book of Ezekiel and linked with Meshech and Tubal (Ezek. 27:13-14). Jer. 51:27 links Ashkenaz (the brother of Togarmah Gen. 10:3) with Ararat. This indicates an area in Eastern Turkey or what is now Armenia. Most authorities agree. [34] Pentecost quotes evidence from the ancient historian Tacitus and from the Assyrian Chronicles to support the idea that Togarmah equals Armenia. The Armenians claim they descend from the "House of Togarmah." [35]

h. Conclusions

Bauman who in turn quotes William Gesenius. The author was not able to find the original quote in Gesenius' lexicon (See p. 516 of lexicon under *Meschech*).

[27] Charles F. Pfeiffer, Howard F. Vos and John Rea, eds., *Wycliffe Bible Encyclopedia,* unabridged volume, (Chicago: Moody Press, 1983), pp. 1105-1106; Merrill Tenney, editor, *Zondervan Pictorial Encyclopedia of the Bible* (Grand Rapids: Zondervan Publishing House, 1975), 4:194-195 and 5:830.

[28] Feinberg, *The Prophecy of Ezekiel*, p. 220.

[29] See *Wycliffe Bible Encyclopedia*, p. 411; *Zondervan Pictorial Bible Encyclopedia*, 1:1047; and Feinburg, *The Prophecy of Ezekiel*, p. 221.

[30] Josephus, *Complete Works*, p. 31.

[31] William Gesenius, *Hebrew and Chaldee Lexicon*, p. 668.

[32] *Zondervan Pictorial Encyclopedia of the Bible*, 2:774-775; *Wycliffe Bible Encyclopedia*, p. 710; Lindsey, *The Late Great Planet Earth*, p. 58; Feinburg, *The Prophecy of Ezekiel*, p. 221; Pentecost, *Things To Come*, p. 330.

[33] Charles H. Dyer, *"Ezekiel,"* in *The Bible Knowledge Commentary* (Wheaton, Il: Victor Books, 1985), p. 1300.

[34] Feinburg, *The Prophecy of Ezekiel*, p. 221; *Zondervan Pictorial Encyclopedia of the Bible*, 5:766; *Wycliffe Bible Encyclopedia*, p. 1721.

[35] Pentecost, *Things to Come*, p. 330.

Although some identifications for the places in Ezekiel 38 are tenuous (e.g., Rosh with Russia and Meshech with Moscow), there is enough evidence from the phrase "remotest parts of the North" and from the identification of Magog with Scythia to support the view that Russia will invade Israel in the Tribulation. Her allies will include Iran, Ethiopia, Libya, Turkey, Armenia and likely (but not as certainly) the Eastern Europeans.

The existence of a strong Russia in the end times coupled with the absence of any Scriptural reference to the United States makes for interesting speculation. It is possible that the United States will be a second rate power in the end times. This may or may not signal its destruction as a nation for it is possible that America will be allied with or is under the protection of the other major end-time confederation in Western Europe.

The presence of all of these end-time powers will always make present world conditions interesting. Date setting is not proper, and one must remember that nothing needs to be fulfilled before the Rapture (prophetic fulfillment could all come together early in the Tribulation). Nevertheless it will continue to be reasonable to think that ongoing political, economic, and other conditions regarding Israel, western Europe, Russia, and lesser (in terms of prophetic emphasis) nations will be consistent with the Bible's picture of the world in the Tribulation.

4. Restored Babylon

Although many Bible teachers understand the "Babylon" of Rev. 17-18 to be figurative for a revived Rome, the view that Babylon in Rev. 17-18 refers to a literal Babylon has advocates. [36] This is not the place for a complete exegesis of Isaiah Chapters 13-14,

---

[36] See Allen, Kenneth W., "*Rebuilding and Destruction of Babylon*", *Bibliotheca Sacra* 133 (Jan.-March 1976): 19-27; and Tim LaHaye, *Revelation* (Grand Rapids: Zondervan Publishing House, 1975), pp. 224-244.

Jeremiah Chapters 50-51 and Revelation Chapters 17-18, but enough can be given to make the case for a revived Babylon credible.

a. Literal Interpretation

One of the main tenets of the dispensational/pretribulational camp is that of literal interpretation. We should interpret literally if possible.

> "And the woman whom you saw is **the great city**, which reigns over the kings of the earth" [Rev. 17:18].

> "And the kings of the earth, who committed acts of immorality and lived sensuously with her, will weep and lament over her when they see the smoke of her burning, standing at a distance because of the fear of her torment, saying, 'Woe, woe, **the great city**, Babylon, **the strong city**! For in one hour your judgment has come' " [Rev. 18:9-10].

b. Old Testament Prophecies about Babylon

Several Old Testament prophecies concern Babylon's destruction. Have they or have they not been fulfilled?

(1). Supernatural Destruction/Never to be Inhabited Again

Isaiah and Jeremiah depict a supernatural destruction upon Babylon from which the city is never rebuilt or inhabited.

> And Babylon, the beauty of kingdoms, the glory of the Chaldeans' pride, will be as when God overthrew Sodom and Gomorrah. It will **never be inhabited or lived in from generation to generation**; nor will the Arab pitch his tent there, nor will shepherds make their flocks lie down there. But desert creatures will lie down there, and their houses will be full of owls, ostriches also will live there, and shaggy goats will frolic

there. And hyenas will howl in their fortified towers and jackals in their luxurious palaces. Her fateful time also will soon come and her days will not be prolonged [Isa. 13:19-22].

"You will not be united with them in burial, because you have ruined your country, you have slain your people. May the offspring of evildoers not be mentioned forever....And I will rise up against them," declares the LORD of hosts, "and will cut off from Babylon name and survivors, offspring and posterity," declares the LORD. "I will also make it a possession for the hedgehog, and swamps of water, and I will sweep it with the broom of destruction," declares the LORD of hosts [Isaiah 14:20, 22-23].

"And they will not take from you even a stone for a corner nor a stone for foundations, but you will be **desolate forever**, declares the LORD....Her cities have become an object of horror, a parched land and a desert, and **a land in which no man lives**, and through which no son of man passes" [Jer. 51:26,43].

All must agree that the destruction of Babylon by the Medes and Persians (539 B.C.) is at least a partial fulfillment of these predictions and that the prophets included this historical destruction of Babylon in their predictions. Yet, Babylon was not overthrown by a directly supernatural manner at that time (i.e., fire and brimstone as in Sodom and Gomorrah), and it did not totally cease to be inhabited as proven by Allen and McDowell. [37]

---

[37] Kenneth W., Allen, *"Rebuilding and Destruction of Babylon,"* p. 21; Josh McDowell, *Evidence That Demands a Verdict*, Rev. Ed. (San Bernardino, CA: Here's Life Publishers, 1979), pp. 302-309.

If Babylon was still inhabited centuries after its destruction in 539 B.C., then it is possible to view a complete fulfillment occurring in the end times by another divine destruction of a rebuilt (and literal) city of Babylon.

(2). Contextual Indications of an End-time Event

Isaiah 13-14 is replete with indications that Isaiah also had in mind an eschatological destruction for the city of Babylon. This bolsters the view that the city of Babylon in Revelation 17-18 is literal and not a figure for Rome.

Isa. 13:6 refers to the Day of the LORD, and 2 Thess. 2:2-4 equates the Day of the LORD with end times.

Wail, for **the day of the LORD is near!** It will come as destruction from the Almighty [Isa. 13:6].

[T]hat you may not be quickly shaken from your composure or be disturbed either by a spirit or a message or a letter as if from us, to the effect that **the day of the LORD** has come. Let no one in any way deceive you, for **it** will not come unless the apostasy comes first, and the man of lawlessness is revealed, the son of destruction, who opposes and exalts himself above every so called god or object of worship, so that he takes his seat in the temple of God, displaying himself as being God [2 Thess. 2:2-4].

If Isa. 13:10-11 is literal, then the complete fulfillment of Babylon's destruction must be future. These things did not literally happen in 539 B.C. (i.e., cosmic changes, world punishment).

For the stars of heaven and their constellations will not flash forth their light; the sun will be dark when it rises, and the moon will not shed its light. Thus I will punish the world for its evil, and the wicked for their iniquity; I will also put an end to the arrogance of the proud, and abase the haughtiness of the ruthless [Isa. 13:10-11].

Isa. 14:7-8 predicts that after Babylon's destruction the whole world will be at "rest" and possess "joy". This fits a time of destruction followed by the Millennium.

"The whole earth is at rest and is quiet; they break forth into shouts of joy. Even the cypress trees rejoice over you, and the cedars of Lebanon, saying, 'Since you were laid low, no tree cutter comes up against us' " [Isa. 14:7-8].

If Isa. 14:10-17 refers to "Satan" as the power behind the king of Babylon, then complete fulfillment of Babylon's destruction occurs at the time Satan is cast into the pit, i.e., the end times (as shown in Rev. 20:1-3).

"Your pomp and the music of your harps have been brought down to Sheol; maggots are spread out as your bed beneath you, and worms are your covering.... But you said in your heart, 'I will ascend to heaven; I will raise my throne above the stars of God, And I will sit on the mount of assembly in the recesses of the north' ....**Nevertheless you will be thrust down to Sheol, to the recesses of the pit**. Those who will see you will gaze at you, They will ponder over you, saying, 'Is this the man who made the earth tremble, who shook kingdoms, who made the world like a wilderness and overthrew its cities...' " [Isa. 14:11,13, 15-16, 17].

And I saw an angel coming down from heaven, having the key of the abyss and a great chain in his hand. And he laid hold of the dragon, the serpent of old, who is the devil and Satan, and bound him for a thousand years, and **threw him into the abyss**, and shut it and sealed it over him, so that he should not deceive the nations any longer, until the thousand years were completed; after these things he must be released for a short time [Rev. 20:1-3].

c. Conclusions

The notion of a rebuilt city of Babylon deserves more attention than it has gotten in the past. (It is also interesting in the light of increasing Middle Eastern wealth.) Revelation 18 presents Babylon as a great economic power.

A possible role for rebuilt Babylon might be as follows: Babylon will be rebuilt primarily as an economic as opposed to a military power (through there may be some religious power as well). It is possible to view Babylon as an ally of Russia before the fiasco of its invasion of Israel. After Russian decline Babylon becomes supported (militarily) by the Beast (the Antichrist), but she is so wealthy that Babylon threatens to dominate him economically.

And he carried me away in the Spirit into a wilderness; and I saw a woman sitting on a scarlet beast, full of blasphemous names, having seven heads and ten horns...."And the ten horns which you saw are ten kings, who have not yet received a kingdom, but they receive authority as kings with the beast for one hour" [Rev. 17:3,12].

The Antichrist will grow jealous and feel so threatened by Babylon (perhaps through economic dependence) that he destroys it. In doing so he unknowingly does the will of God! God destroys Babylon for its greed, sensuality, and probably its apostate religion (which the antichrist has been using).

And he said to me, "The waters which you saw where the harlot sits, are peoples and multitudes and nations and tongues. And **the ten horns which you saw, and the beast, these will hate the harlot** and will make her desolate and naked, and will eat her flesh and will burn her up with fire. **For God has put it in their hearts to execute His purpose** by having a common purpose, and by giving their kingdom to the beast, until the words of God should be fulfilled. And **the woman whom you saw is the great city**, which reigns over the kings of the earth" [Rev. 17:15-18].

Admittedly, other interpretations can be developed; but all things being equal "Babylon" in Revelation 17-18 should be taken as a literal city. Babylon deserves to be listed among the gentile powers of the Tribulation period.

5. King of the North and King of the South

Dan. 11:36-45 mentions a tremendous end-time battle involving the king of the North and the king of the South. The description of this battle awaits a coming section. Our present goal is merely to identify the main nations in the tribulation period. While some believe the king of the North and the king of the South refer to additional powers in the Tribulation, it is preferable to link Dan. 11:36ff. with the invasion of Israel by Russia in Ezekiel 38-39. [38] This makes the king of the North to be the same as the ruler of the nation from the "remotest part of the North," i.e., likely Russia. The king of the South would probably be one of his prominent allies (Dan. 11:43 mentions Libya, Ethiopia, Egypt). [39]

---

[38] See Leon Wood, *A Commentary of Daniel* (Grand Rapids: Zondervan Publishing House, 1973), pp. 308-309.

[39] Unlike Libya and Ethiopia, Egypt is never specifically said to be an ally of Gog and Magog in Ezekiel 38-39; Dan. 11:42-43 teaches that the Antichrist will conquer Egypt.

In addition to the location "north", the timing for the battles favors the linking of Dan. 11:36-45 with Ezekiel 38-39. Evidence for this statement will come in a following section, "Battles in the Tribulation" (p. 441).

B. The Antichrist

1. The Origin of the Antichrist

a. Social Origin - Anarchy

The Antichrist will arise out of chaotic world conditions. This is obvious from general teachings about the Tribulation (Matt. 24:6 "wars and rumors of wars", and also Rev. 6:1ff.). The four horsemen of the apocalypse bring war, famine, and death. The first horseman (white) is probably the Antichrist. He will rise out of the sea, which stands for the turbulence of the nations (cf. Rev. 13:1, 17:15). No doubt the Antichrist will make great promises of hope as is customary for tyrannical movements (e.g., as in the French and Russian revolutions or the Nazis). People will look to him as a deliverer who can straighten out a world in a first rate mess.

b. Geographical or National Origin - Rome

Dan. 9:26 says that after Messiah's death "the people of the [evil] prince that shall come will destroy the city." The Romans destroyed Jerusalem in A.D. 70. It is likely that the Antichrist will rule over a revived Roman Empire. Luke 21:5ff. also intertwines the historical destruction of Jerusalem by Rome in A.D. 70 with end-time events.

Dan. 7:8-9 talks about a "little horn" rising out of the fourth beast or empire. The context of Daniel 7 is discussing end-time events (see vv. 13-14). Furthermore, Dan. 7:15ff. can be equated with the end-time evil empire. The description of the evil ruler as speaking blasphemy for 3 1/2 years and as waging war on the saints fits the end-time kingdom of the Antichrist (Rev. 13:1ff.). Also, both the fourth kingdom in Daniel and the beast in Revelation are described as having 10 horns (cf. Dan. 7:7-8, 19-20, 23-24;

Rev. 13:1; 17:11-14). The fourth kingdom in Daniel is the Antichrist's kingdom. Yet, historically the next great kingdom that followed Greece (definitely the third of Daniel's kingdoms, Dan. 8:21, 11:2) was Rome, and the fourth great kingdom from Daniel's time was Rome. Thus, it is likely that the Antichrist will rule over a revived Roman Empire.

c. Racial Origin

Ethnic derivation and citizenship are two different classifications. One can be American in citizenship and be Chinese in racial derivation. The conclusion that the Antichrist will rule over a revived Rome does not necessarily mean he will be Roman.

One idea is that he must be Jewish in order to pose as the false Christ. *Antichrist* means "in opposition" to Christ but also "in place of" Christ. It seems logical that being Jewish would assist the Antichrist in deceiving others about being the Messiah. Dan. 11:37 says that the Antichrist "will show no regard for the God of his fathers." Some take this to mean he must be an apostate Jew. There is even the theory that the Antichrist must rise from the tribe of Dan because Gen. 49:17 says "Dan shall be a serpent in the way" and because Dan is a tribe omitted from those sealed (protected) in Revelation 7 (implying a special judgment for Dan). Still another view as to the Antichrist's racial origin is that he is Syrian. Dan. 8:9-12,23-27 predict a coming ruler who arises from a crushed Greece and stops sacrifices in the temple. Historically, this would be Antiochus Epiphanes (a ruler from what now is Syria). He is a type of the Antichrist in Daniel 8 and more clearly in Daniel 11. Thus, some feel that the Antichrist will be Syrian (despite the difficulty in imagining a Syrian ruling the modern world).

The Antichrist will very likely be Roman in citizenship. He will come from some Western European nation. It is best to remain open as to his racial derivation. Of his spiritual origin there can be no doubt.

d. Spiritual Origin

The Antichrist comes from the Devil. It is logical to assume that the Devil always has a potential Antichrist waiting in the wings because he is ignorant about the time for the Rapture.

> And then that lawless one will be revealed whom the Lord will slay with the breath of His mouth and bring to an end by the appearance of His coming; that is, **the one whose coming is in accord with the activity of Satan**, with all power and signs and false wonders, and with all the deception of wickedness for those who perish, because they did not receive the love of the truth so as to be saved [2 Thess. 2: 8-10].

> And the beast which I saw was like a leopard, and his feet were like those of a bear, and his mouth like the mouth of a lion. And **the dragon** [Rev. 12:9] **gave him his power** and his throne and great authority....and they worshiped the dragon, [Rev. 12:9] because **he gave his authority to the beast**; and they worshiped the beast, saying, "Who is like the beast, and who is able to wage war with him?" [Rev. 13:2,4]

> And I saw coming out of the mouth of the **dragon** and out of the mouth of the **beast** and out of the mouth of the **false prophet**, three unclean spirits like frogs [Rev. 16:13] (The satanic trinity).

e. Providential Origin

God does not directly cause the rise of the Antichrist, but He will permit it and will use it. Thus, it is true to say that the Antichrist cannot rise to power without God allowing it. 2 Thessalonians 2 goes further by teaching that God will actually promote the advance of the Antichrist by reprobating the lost so that they fall for the Antichrist's propaganda. (The context has been quoted above).

> And you know what restrains him now, so that in his time he may be revealed [2 Thess. 2:6].

> And for this reason **God will send upon them a deluding influence** so that they might believe what is false, in order that they all may be judged who did not believe the truth, but took pleasure in wickedness [2 Thess. 2:11-12].

Notice that the "Lamb" is the one who has authority to begin the rise of the conqueror.

> And I saw when the Lamb broke one of the seven seals, and I heard one of the four living creatures saying as with a voice of thunder, "come". And I looked, and behold, a white horse, and he who sat on it had a bow; and a crown was given to him; and he went out conquering, and to conquer [Rev. 6:1-2].

2. Names for the Evil End-time Ruler

The Scriptures give various names and/or descriptions for an evil end-time ruler. Although the names are usually not equated by direct statement, common characteristics point to the same individual (e.g., blasphemy, war on the saints, sitting in the temple demanding worship).

a. Little Horn (Daniel 7:7-28)

The little horn arises from a beast with ten horns and destroys three of them (Dan. 7:7-8, 20, 24). Dan. 7:24 teaches that the horns refer to kingdoms. He is a braggart (Dan. 7:8,11,20,24-25), and a blasphemer (7:25) who attacks the saints (7:21,25) and subdues them for 3 1/2 years (i.e., time, times, and a half a time, 7:25).

> "After this I kept looking in the night visions, and behold a fourth beast, dreadful and terrifying and extremely strong; and it had large iron teeth. It devoured and crushed, and trampled down the remainder with its feet; and it was different from all the beasts that were before it, and it had ten horns. While I was contemplating the horns, behold, another **horn**, a **little** one, came up among them, and three of the first horns were pulled out by the roots before it; and behold, this horn possessed eyes like the eyes of a man, and a mouth uttering great boasts" [Dan. 7:7-8].

> "I kept looking, and that **horn** was waging war with the saints and overpowering them until the Ancient of Days came, and judgment was passed in favor of the saints of the Highest One, and the time arrived when the saints took possession of the kingdom. Thus, he said: 'The fourth beast will be a fourth kingdom on the earth, which will be different from all the other kingdoms, and it will devour the whole earth and tread it down and crush it. As for the ten horns, out of this kingdom ten kings will arise; and another will arise after them, and he will be different from the previous ones and will subdue three kings. And he will speak out against the Most High and wear down the saints of the Highest One, and he will intend to make alterations in times and in law; and they will be given into his hand for a time, times, and half a time.' " [Dan. 7:21-25].

b. The Coming Evil Prince

Daniel 9:26 mentions a coming prince who is in contrast to the Messiah. His people (apparently the Romans) will destroy the city (Jerusalem) and put a stop to the sacrifices in the temple. Verse 27 describes a period of seven years, which Christ associates with the Tribulation, (Matt. 24:15-21).

"Then after the sixty-two weeks the Messiah will be cut off and have nothing, and the people of the [evil] **prince who is to come** will destroy the city and the sanctuary. And its end will come with a flood; even to the end there will be war; desolations are determined. And he [the evil prince] will make a firm covenant with the many for one week, but in the middle of the week he will put a stop to sacrifice and grain offering; and on the wing of abominations will come one who makes desolate, even until a complete destruction, one that is decreed, is poured out on the one who makes desolate" [Dan. 9:26-27].

c. The Willful King

Dan. 11:35-12:3 concerns end-time events (see 11:35 and 12:1-3). The "king" who does as he pleases fits the blasphemous description given of the Antichrist in other places (especially Matt. 24:15; 2 Thess. 2:3-4; Rev. 13:15).

"Then **the king will do as he pleases** and he will exalt and magnify himself above every god, and will speak monstrous things against the God of gods; and he will prosper until the indignation is finished, for that which is decreed will be done. And he will show no regard for the gods (or God) of his fathers or for the desire of women, nor will he show regard for any other god; for he will magnify himself above them all. But instead he will honor a god of fortresses..."[Dan. 11:36-38a].

d. Man of Sin (or Lawlessness), Son of Perdition (or Destruction), Wicked One (or Lawless One)

It ought to be clear from the New Testament that the temple in Jerusalem has to be rebuilt during (or perhaps before) the tribulation period (Matt. 24:15; Mark 13:14; 2 Thess. 2:3-4, Rev. 11:1-2). The most common traits that link all of these names are persecution of the saints and unparalleled blasphemy to the point of demanding worship in the temple.

Let no one in any way deceive you, for it will not come unless the apostasy comes first, and the **man of lawlessness** is revealed, the **son of destruction**, who opposes and exalts himself above every so called god or object of worship, so that he takes his seat in the temple of God, displaying himself as being God....And then that **lawless one** will be revealed...[2 Thess. 2:3-4,8].

e. Abomination That Makes Desolate

There is a definite link between the "ABOMINATION OF DESOLATION" (Matt. 24:15) and the evil end-time ruler. It is possible that the "Abomination" has reference to a statue of the Antichrist, the familiar image of the beast from Rev. 13:14-15, standing in the temple. Yet, since the Antichrist himself will demand direct worship in the temple, it is just as likely that "Abomination" refers to the evil ruler himself.

"Therefore when you see the **ABOMINATION OF DESOLATION** which was spoken of through Daniel the prophet, standing in the holy place (let the reader understand), then let those who are in Judea flee to the mountains" [Matt. 24:15-16].

f. The Beast

The Book of Revelation has much material about the beast. "Beast" can refer to the entire evil empire. Yet, sometimes Revelation views "the beast" as an individual, the wicked ruler who represents the whole kingdom. There are many parallels between the description of Revelation's "beast" (Revelation 13 and 17) and the end-time ruler described by these other names (Little Horn, Evil Prince, Willful King, Man of Sin, Abomination). Practically all the names involve one who is blasphemous and persecutes believers. Parallels between "Beast" in Revelation 13 and 17 and "Little Horn" in Daniel 7 are especially close: (ten horns - Dan.7:7,20,24 cf. Rev. 13:1; 17:3,7,16-17, which are ten kingdoms - Dan. 7:24 cf. Rev. 17:12; demands worship and/or blasphemes God - Dan.7:8,11,20,24-25 cf. Rev. 13:3,6,8,12,15; war on the saints - Dan. 7:21,25 cf. Rev. 13:7; 3 1/2 years of total dominion - Dan. 7:25 cf. Rev. 13:5. Finally, both the Beast and the Man of Sin use false signs to evoke worship, cf. Rev. 13:13-15; 2 Thess. 2:9-10).

g. The Antichrist

Ironically the only name disputed in this list of names for the "Antichrist" is Antichrist. That name occurs five times in Scripture, all in John's epistles (1 John 2:18 twice, in 2:22, 4:3; 2 John 7). Regardless of whether the Scripture uses the name of "Antichrist" for the wicked end-time ruler, it is so entrenched in theology as to be irrevocably linked with him as a theological term. Nevertheless, "Antichrist" almost certainly ought to be taken to refer to the "Little Horn, The Coming Evil Prince, The Willful King, The Abomination, The Man of Sin, The Beast" (especially the first reference in 1 John 2:18). Even if John sometimes refers to more than an individual, the end-time tyrant is the ultimate example of the coming Antichrist among lesser antichrists.

Revelation 13 mentions a second beast called the "false prophet" (Rev. 13:11-17; 16:13). This second beast acts as a cheerleader to promote worship of the first beast. Some think that the second beast (false prophet) provides a better parallel to Christ than does the first beast and that the second beast is the "Antichrist." Christ is a prophet. The second beast is a prophet. Christ promotes worship of God the Father. The sec-

ond beast promotes the worship of the Man of Sin. Thus, it is reasoned that the term "Antichrist" fits the second beast not the first.

This is definitely a minority view and with good reason. The better parallel for the Satanic trinity (see Rev. 16:13) is Dragon (God the Father), Beast (God the Son), and False Prophet (God the Spirit). If the Beast parallels the Father and the False Prophet the Son, who corresponds to the Holy Spirit? The first beast seizes the world kingdom, which is rightfully Christ's Kingdom. Thus, the first beast best qualifies for the term "Antichrist" both in the sense that he tries to substitute for Christ, and he is the main opposition to Christ. It is true that Christ promotes worship of God the Father but just as true that He Himself is the object of worship and that the Holy Spirit promotes worship of Christ (John 16:14). If we must parallel the second beast to a member of the Trinity, then the Holy Spirit is a better candidate than the Son. The false prophet actually has the **role** and power of Elijah (Rev. 13:13, fire out of heaven, prophet, **forerunner**, see Mal. 4:5). It is far better to view the first beast as paralleling Christ. Thus, "Antichrist" is a fitting name for him.

3. The Antichrist's Rise to World Power

a. The Time for the Antichrist's Rise

The Antichrist cannot have dominion until God allows it (Rev. 6:1-2). The Restrainer of 2 Thessalonians 2 is the Holy Spirit. God the Holy Spirit prevents the rise of the Lawless One until such time as God wills. The idea of a removal of the Holy Spirit's restraining ministry is enough to favor (but alone not quite enough to prove absolutely) the removal of the church before the Antichrist comes to power. Other texts that more clearly teach the pretribulational Rapture make definite the implication from 2 Thessalonians 2 that the church will depart along with the removal of restraint by the Holy Spirit. With the Restrainer gone and the church raptured, evil will run rampant to unparalleled, unimaginable depths. The Antichrist can now rise through the chaos brought on by such deep evil. He will claim to be the answer to world anarchy.

> And you know what restrains him now, so that **in his time** he may be revealed. For the mystery of lawlessness is already at work; only he who now restrains will do so until he is taken out of the way. And then that lawless one will be revealed whom the Lord will slay with the breath of His mouth and bring to an end by the appearance of His coming [2 Thess. 2:6-8].

b. Inconspicuous Beginning

Ill-advised people make all kinds of sensational guesses as to the identity of the Antichrist. However, the title "Little Horn" (Dan. 7:7-8) implies that the Antichrist seems to come from nowhere to rise from relative obscurity. He will rise among the ten horns (10 kings) but not as one of them. The Antichrist will be what pundits call a "darkhorse" candidate for world dictator. It is a waste of time for those who live before the Rapture to try to identify him. Only after the Rapture can the "Little Horn" begin his meteoric rise to power.

> "While I was contemplating the horns, behold, another horn, a **little** one, came up among them, and three of the first horns were pulled out by the roots before it and behold, this horn possessed eyes like the eyes of a man, and a mouth uttering great boasts" [Dan. 7:8].

c. Treaty with Israel

The Antichrist will make a treaty with Israel at the beginning of the Tribulation. Although he does not yet rule the world, his support will be most welcome by the Jews. One may safely infer that the rebuilding of the temple will arouse great hostility toward tiny Israel who will need "friends" in the West.

> "And he will make a firm covenant with the many for one week..." [Dan. 9:27].

d. Rise to Power within the Empire

The Antichrist does not begin the Tribulation in control of the world. He must gradually conquer it (Rev. 6:2). His first move brings him control over the revived Roman Empire. The original New Rome will consist of a ten-nation confederation. The Antichrist will destroy three of these kings and gain control over the whole. The books of Daniel and Revelation refer to ten toes (Dan. 2:41) and ten horns (Dan. 7:7, 20,24; Rev. 12:3; 13:1; 17:3, 7,16). Dan. 7:24 and Rev. 17:12 make it clear that the ten horns stand for the kings and/or kingdoms.

> "As for the **ten horns**, out of this kingdom **ten kings** will arise..." [Dan. 7:24].

> "And the **ten horns** which you saw are **ten kings**..." [Rev. 17:12].

Daniel 7:8 and 7:24 give the basis for thinking the Antichrist destroys three kings in his conquest of New Rome.

> "While I was contemplating the horns, behold, another horn, a little one, came up among them, and **three of the first horns were pulled out** by the roots before it; and behold, this horn possessed eyes like the eyes of a man, and a mouth uttering great boasts....As for the ten horns, out of this kingdom ten kings will arise; and another will arise after them, and he will be different from the previous ones and will **subdue three kings**." [Dan. 7:8,24].

Apparently, the Antichrist replaces the three destroyed kings with puppet leaders, and then rules over the entire empire with ten kings subordinated to him (see Rev.

17:12-13). His power over New Rome must occur sometime in the first half of the Tribulation (or at least at the very beginning of the second half of the Tribulation). This inference follows from the fact that he will control the entire world for 3 1/2 years (see Dan. 7:25; Rev. 13:5).

e. The Antichrist and the Russian Invasion of Israel

Evidence for the equation of Dan. 11:36ff. with Ezekiel 38-39 will come in a following section, p. 441. If the king of the North at the close of Daniel 11 is identified as "Gog of the land of Magog" in Ezekiel 38-39, then the Antichrist plays some role in the invasion of Israel by the Northern federation (Russia and allies). Some speculate that it is the violation of the Antichrist's peace treaty with Israel at mid-tribulation that emboldens Russia to dare attack defenseless Israel. On the other hand, since Israel feels security before the Russian invasion (Ezek. 38:8,11,14), it is probably better to suppose Israel thinks the Antichrist is still her protector (through he may have told the Russians of a secret plan to turn on Israel). Regardless of the covenant status, the Antichrist plays some role in the fighting. Perhaps God destroys Magog before the Antichrist even has time to mobilize against Russia in Israel proper, but Daniel 11:42ff. pictures the Antichrist as invading northeast Africa either to confront Russia's allies as they invade or to mop up after God has sent them retreating by a more supernatural battle.

> "Then the king will do as he pleases, and he will exalt and magnify himself above every god, and will speak monstrous things against the God of gods; and he will prosper until the indignation is finished, for that which is decreed will be done....And at the end time the king of the South will collide with him, and the king of the North will storm against him with chariots, with horsemen, and with many ships; and he will enter countries, overflow them, and pass through. He will also enter the Beautiful Land, and many countries will fall....Then he will stretch out his hand against other countries and the land of Egypt will not escape. But he will gain control over the hidden treasures of gold and silver, and over all precious things of Egypt; and Libyans and Ethiopians will follow at his heels" [Dan. 11:36,40-41a, 42-43].

The Antichrist will definitely benefit from God's destruction of the Northern Confederation headed by Russia. As odd as it sounds, by destroying Russia God indirectly helps the Antichrist. Yet, it is time for God's plan to go forward including the world's first worldwide dictator. The Antichrist immediately occupies Israel, Egypt, Libya, and Ethiopia. It will not take long for everyone to realize that the defeated Northern powers had been the only human alliance strong enough to hinder the Antichrist from world domination. Now he can do as he pleases (including an occupation of Israel that signals the final demise of any treaty with the Jews).

f. Final World Dominion

During the last 3 1/2 years of the Tribulation, The Antichrist (and thus Satan) will exercise world dominion (see also Isa. 14:16-17; Matt. 4:8-9).

> And there was given to him a mouth speaking arrogant words and blasphemies; and authority to act for **forty-two months** was given to him....And it was given to him to make war with the saints and to overcome them; and authority over every tribe and people and tongue and nation was given to him. And all who dwell on the earth will worship him, everyone whose name has not been written from the foundation of the

world in the book of life of the Lamb who has been slain [Rev. 13:5,7-8].

Although the last half of the Tribulation will be worse in terms of God's judgment upon the world and the Antichrist's persecution of the saints, the first half will be the primary time for "wars and rumors of wars." The question, "who is like the beast, and who is able to wage war with him?" (Rev. 13:4) shows that human wars will tend to be reduced under the Antichrist's world dictatorship. No human power can fight him.

g. The Means of the Antichrist's Rise to World Power

The Antichrist will take advantage of chaotic world conditions (Matt. 24:6-8; Luke 21:25-26; Rev. 6:3-8) and use his demagoguery to its fullest potential (Dan. 7:8 "great boasts," etc.). He also deceives through Satanic signs and wonders (2 Thess. 2:9; Rev. 13:2,4,13-15, 16:13-14). There are indications that possibly Satan will give power to resurrect the Antichrist after a fatal wound (Rev. 13:3,12). However, "beast" in Revelation can also refer to the whole kingdom so that the coming to life may refer to the Roman Empire, which will be "resurrected" in the end time. In addition to miracles, the Antichrist definitely uses a false religion to consolidate power with commercial/penal sanctions to those who resist worshiping him (Rev. 13:8-18; 17:1-5). Finally, God assists in his rise to ascendancy in order to destroy him (2 Thess. 2:11-12).

4. The Antichrist's Personality Traits and Policies

a. He will make and break his treaty with Israel. He is capable of any treachery that will serve his ends (Dan. 9:27).

b. The Antichrist will deeply hate all Jews and all tribulational saints. It is clear that many, both Jews and gentiles, will trust in Christ after the Rapture (Rev. 6:9-11, 7:3,9,14).

After these things I looked, and behold, a great multitude, which no one could count, from every nation and all tribes and peoples and tongues, standing before the throne and before the Lamb, clothed in white robes, and palm branches were in their hands....And one of the elders answered, saying to me, "These who are clothed in the white robes, who are they, and from where have they come?" And I said to him, "My lord, you know." And he said to me, "These are the ones who come out of **the great tribulation**, and **they have washed their robes** and made them **white in the blood of the Lamb**" [Rev. 7:9, 13-14].

These saints, along with all Jews, whether believing or unbelieving Jews, will face great persecutions by the Antichrist (see also Rev. 11:7-8). Zech. 13:8-9 leads to a conclusion that two-thirds of all Jews will perish.

"I kept looking, and that horn was **waging war with the saints** and overpowering them....And he will speak out against the Most High and **wear down the saints** of the Highest One, and he will intend to make alterations in times and in law; and they will be given into his hand for a time, times, and half a time" [Dan. 7:21, 25].

"And it will come about in all the land," declares the LORD, "that **two parts in it will be cut off and perish**; but the **third will be left** in it. And I will bring the third part through the fire, refine them as silver is refined, and test them as gold is tested. They will call on My name, And I will answer them; I will say, 'they are My people, and they will say, the LORD is my God' "[Zech. 13:8-9].

"And unless those days had been cut short, **no life would have been saved**; but for the sake of the elect those days shall be cut short" [Matt. 24:22].

And leave out the court which is outside the temple and do not measure it, for it has been given to the nations; and they will **tread under foot the holy city** for forty-two months [Rev. 11:2].

And a great sign appeared in heaven: a woman clothed with the sun, and the moon under her feet, and on her head a crown of twelve stars; and she was with child; and she cried out, being in labor and in pain to give birth....And she gave birth to a son, a male child, who is to rule all the nations with a rod of iron; and her child was caught up to God and to His throne. And the woman fled into the wilderness where she had a place prepared by God, so that there she might be nourished for one thousand two hundred and sixty days....And when the **dragon** saw that he was thrown down to the earth, he **persecuted the woman who gave birth to the male child**. And the two wings of the great eagle were given to the woman, in order that she might fly into the wilderness to her place, where she was nourished for a time and times and half a time, from the presence of the serpent. [Rev. 12:1-2,5-6,13-14].

[A]nd it was given to him to make **war with the saints and to overcome them**; and authority over every tribe and people and tongue and nation was given to him [Rev. 13:7].

If anyone is destined for captivity, to captivity he goes; if anyone kills with the sword, with the sword he must be killed. Here is the perseverance and the faith of the saints [Rev. 13:10].

And there was given to him to give breath to the image of the beast, that the image of the beast might even speak and cause **as many as do not worship the image of the beast to be killed**. And he causes all, the small and the great, and the rich and the poor, and the free men and the slaves, to be given a mark on their right hand, or on their forehead, and he provides that no one should be able to buy or to sell, except the one who has the mark, either the name of the beast or the number of his name [Rev. 13:15-17].

c. As already mentioned under several other categories, the Antichrist will be a gifted orator who can sway people with smooth words. He will be extreme and arrogant in blasphemy.

"While I was contemplating the horns, behold, another horn, a little one, came up among them, and three of the first horns were pulled out by the roots before it; and behold, this horn possessed eyes like the eyes of a man, and **a mouth uttering great boasts**" [Dan. 7:8].

"Then I kept looking because of the sound of the **boastful words** which the horn was speaking..."[Dan. 7:11].

"[A]nd the meaning of the ten horns that were on its head, and the other horn which came up, and before which three of them fell, namely, that horn which had eyes and a **mouth uttering great boasts**, and which was larger in appearance than its associates" [Dan. 7:20].

"And he will **speak out against the Most High**..."[Dan. 7:25].

"Then the king will do as he pleases, and he will exalt and magnify himself above every god, and **will speak monstrous things** against the God of gods..."[Dan. 11:36].

...And I saw a beast coming up....on his heads were **blasphemous names**....his mouth like the mouth of a lion [Rev. 13:1-2].

And there was given to him a **mouth speaking arrogant words and blasphemies**; and authority to act for forty-two months was given to him. **And he opened his mouth in blasphemies** against God, to blaspheme His name and His tabernacle, that is, those who dwell in heaven [Rev. 13:5-6].

And he carried me away in the Spirit into a wilderness; and I saw a woman sitting on a scarlet **beast, full of blasphemous names**, having seven heads and ten horns [Rev. 17:3].

d. The Antichrist will claim to be deity. He will not stop at desiring worship. He will demand it (implied Dan. 9:27, 12:11).

"Then the king will do as he pleases, and **he will exalt and magnify himself above every god**, and will speak monstrous things against the God of gods; and he will prosper until the indignation is finished, for that which is decreed will be done" [Dan. 11:36].

"Therefore, when you see the ABOMINATION OF DESOLATION which was spoken of through Daniel the prophet, **standing in the holy place** (let the reader understand)" [Matt. 24:15] (see also Mark 13:14).

Let no one in any way deceive you, for it will not come unless the apostasy comes first, and the man of lawlessness is revealed, the son of destruction, who **opposes and exalts himself above every so-called god** or object of worship, so that he takes his seat **in the temple of God, displaying himself as being God** [2 Thess. 2:3-4].

[A]nd they worshiped the dragon, because he gave his authority to the beast; and they worshiped the beast, saying, "Who is like the beast, and who is able to wage war with him?"....And **all who dwell on the earth will worship him**, every one whose name has not been written from the foundation of the world in the book of life of the Lamb who has been slain....And he exercises all the authority of the first beast in his presence. And he makes the earth and those who dwell in it to **worship the first beast**, whose fatal wound was healed [Rev. 13:4,8,12].

The False Prophet (Rev. 13:11ff.; 16:13; 19:20) leads a propaganda program to create worship for the Beast. It may involve a restoration of the Beast from a fatal wound (Rev. 13:3,12,14) and will involve miracles (Rev. 13:13-14; 16:13-14; 19:20) such as causing an image of the Beast to speak (Rev. 13:15).

Those who refuse to worship the Beast will suffer economic penalties (Rev. 13:16-17) and death (Rev. 13:15), perhaps sometimes caused by miraculous fire from heaven (Rev. 13:13). The combination of propaganda and penalties will cause most of the world to worship the Antichrist (Rev. 13:8) and to receive his mark (666, Rev. 13:17-18).

e. The Antichrist and Babylon

Babylon in Revelation 17 may include a reference to a false religious system because "harlot" can connote spiritual harlotry and because Babylon has been historically associated with false religion. The Antichrist will definitely use a false religious system.

However, Babylon is primarily a city and primarily a center of commerce (Rev. 17:18, 18:3, 10ff.). Although Babylon seems allied with the Antichrist (at least after the destruction of Russia), the Antichrist will turn on Babylon and destroy it (in God's plan). This seems to take place just prior to the Second Coming.

> And the ten horns which you saw, and the beast, these will hate the harlot and will make her desolate and naked, and will eat her flesh and will burn her up with fire. For **God has put it in their hearts to execute His purpose by having a common purpose**, and by giving their kingdom to the beast, until the works of God should be fulfilled [Rev. 17:16-17].

f. Miscellaneous Facts about the Antichrist

During his rule the Antichrist will seek to change traditional customs. Daniel 7:25 teaches, "...he will intend to make alterations in times and law...". Perhaps the traditional calendar reminds the world of the real Christ and will need to be abolished.

The Antichrist will have no respect for morality. He will "do as he pleases" (Dan. 11:36) showing "no regard for the God (or gods) of his fathers" (Dan. 11:37). Paul's titles in 2 Thessalonians 2 aptly describe his character as the "Man of Sin" and "the Wicked or Lawless One." He will obviously be a military and political genius honoring "a god of fortresses" (Dan. 11:38). Both Daniel and Revelation stress that the Antichrist and his kingdom will be different from all previous rulers and kingdoms (Dan. 7:7,19,23,24, notice the word **different**; Rev. 13:4b).

5. The Doom and Destiny of the Antichrist

The demise of Satan's worldwide rule through the Antichrist will come about as described in the closing chapters of Revelation. The kings of the East proceed toward the Middle East (Rev. 16:12). They are probably included in the forces prompted by demons to resist Christ's Second Coming.

> And the sixth angel poured out his bowl upon the great river, the Euphrates; and its water was dried up, that the way might be prepared for the kings from the east. And I saw coming out of the mouth of the dragon and out of the mouth of the beast and out of the mouth of the false prophet, three unclean spirits like frogs; for they are spirits of demons, performing signs, which go out to the kings of the whole world, to gather them together for the war of the great day of God, the Almighty....And they gathered them together to the place which in Hebrew is called Har-Magedon [Rev. 16:12-14,16].

Around this time God destroys the city of Babylon as described in Revelation 18 (see Rev. 18:20-21). According to Rev. 17:17, God uses the Antichrist as an instrument of judgment upon Babylon (is there some bickering in the godless camp as the heathen await the inevitable doom?). The Antichrist and his armies will make war with the Lamb, but it will not be much of a "war" for the entire world's military forces do not amount to any resistance at all for Christ.

> "And he will pitch the tents of his royal pavilion between the seas and the beautiful Holy Mountain; yet **he will come to his end**, and **no one will help him**" [Dan. 11:45].

And then that lawless one will be revealed whom the **Lord will slay with the breath of His mouth** and bring to an end by the appearance of His coming [2 Thess. 2:8].

> "These will wage war against the Lamb, and **the Lamb will overcome them, because He is Lord of lords and King of kings**, and those who

are with Him are the called and chosen and faithful" [Rev. 17:14].

And I saw heaven opened; and behold, a white horse, and He who sat upon it is called Faithful and True; and in righteousness He judges and wages war. And His eyes are a flame of fire, and upon His head are many diadems; and He has a name written upon Him which no one knows except Himself. And He is clothed with a robe dipped in blood; and His name is called The Word of God. And the armies, which are in heaven, clothed in fine linen, white and clean, were following Him on white horses. And from His mouth comes a sharp sword, so that with it **He may smite the nations**; and **He will rule them** with a rod of iron; and **He treads the winepress of the fierce wrath of God**, the Almighty. And on His robe and on His thigh He has a name written, "KING OF KINGS, AND LORD OF LORDS." And I saw an angel standing in the sun; and he cried out with a loud voice, saying to all the birds which fly in midheaven, "Come, assemble for the great supper of God; in order that you may eat the flesh of kings and the flesh of commanders and the flesh of mighty men and the flesh of horses and of those who sit on them and the flesh of all men, both free men and slaves, and small and great." And I saw the beast and the kings of the earth and their armies, assembled to make war against Him who sat upon the horse, and against His army [Rev. 19:11-19].

After Armageddon the Beast and the False Prophet are cast into the Lake of Fire. An angel casts Satan into the abyss (Rev. 20:1-3). While Satan will experience a short release at the end of the Kingdom (Rev. 20:7-9), the Beast and False Prophet never have so much as a moment's release from eternal damnation. (The battle of Armageddon and its results are covered extensively on pp. 446-452). After the 1,000 year Kingdom Satan joins them in the Lake of Fire.

And the beast was seized, and with him the false prophet who performed the signs in his presence, by which he deceived those who had received the mark of the beast and those who worshiped his image; **these two were thrown alive into the lake of fire** which burns with brimstone. And the rest were killed with the sword which came from the mouth of Him who sat upon the horse, and all the birds were filled with their flesh [Rev. 19:20-21].

And the **devil** who deceived them was **thrown into the lake of fire** and brimstone, **where the beast and the false prophet are also**; and they will be tormented day and night forever and ever [Rev. 20:10].

C. Tribulational Battles

The Tribulation will be a time of unprecedented warfare (Matt. 24:6; Rev. 6:4 etc.). Scripture gives the details of two primary tribulational battles, Magog's invasion of Israel and Armageddon.

1. Magog's Invasion of Israel: the Participants

An earlier section identified the names in Ezekiel 38:1-6 (See pp. 423-26). The land of Magog is the area we now call Russia. Meshech and Tubal can be associated with Turkey and perhaps Armenia. Persia, Ethiopia and Put refers to Iran, Ethiopia, and Libya respectfully. Gomer may be either Eastern Europe or another part of Turkey. Togarmah is Armenia. This group may be called a Northern Confederation with Arab allies (some countries being culturally but not racially Arab). They will invade Israel.

2. Texts Concerning the Battle

Most premillennialists agree that Ezekiel 38-39 concerns this invasion. It is likely that Ezekiel 38-39 portrays the battle from God's perspective, and Dan. 11:36-45 describes the battle from a human perspective. There is no direct connection between Ezekiel 38-39 and Dan. 11:36ff., and they could be describing different battles. However, it is unlikely that there would be two battles of such intensity in the same area within the same time frame. Who else is the "king of the North" (Dan. 11:40) if he is not the leader of the nation from "the remote parts of the North" (Ezek. 38:6,15, 39:2)? The following ideas establish the probability that the battle in Dan. 11:36ff. should be equated with the battle in Ezekiel 38-39.

a. Since the Antichrist rules the entire world for the last 3 1/2 years of the Tribulation (Rev. 13:4-7), it is likely that both battles in Ezekiel 38-39 and Dan. 11:36ff. must occur in the first 3 1/2 years.

b. It is unlikely that the battle in Dan. 11:36ff. could occur before the one in Ezekiel 38-39 because then Israel would not be "dwelling securely" as Ezek. 38:8,11 and 14 requires. If Daniel 11 describes an invasion of the area before Ezekiel 38-39, then one would suppose Israel would feel great insecurity. Another consideration involves the African allies of Russia. Dan. 11:36ff. could not occur before Ezekiel 38-39 because it would mean that the Russian allies (Libya, Ethiopia) would have already been destroyed (Dan. 11:43). Dan. 11:36ff. cannot be easily placed before Ezekiel 38-39.

c. It is just as unlikely that Dan. 11:36ff. follows the Russian invasion of Israel. Presumably the destruction in Ezekiel 38-39 would mean that African allies such as Ethiopia and Libya would be too devastated to mount another serious invasion any time within the short time span of the tribulation period. The same weakness would be true of the nations to the north of Israel and especially true if "the King of the North" refers to any Russian leader.

d. Conclusions about the Equating of Daniel 11:36ff. with Gog's Invasion in Ezekiel

There may be possible scenarios to separate Dan. 11:36ff. from Ezekiel 38-39. However, based upon what we do know from Biblical details, it is best to view Daniel and Ezekiel as teaching about the same battle. It is unlikely there could be any invasion of the promised land before the Russian-Arab one that could still allow Israel to have a sense of security, unsuspecting of any attack from the North or from Africa, and that would still preserve any strength for Russian allies in northeast Africa. It is just as improbable that any "king of the North," especially Russian, and African states such as Libya and Ethiopia (Dan. 11:43) could mount another serious invasion a few years after the utter defeat described in Ezekiel 38-39. Thus, there are probably two texts describing Russia's invasion of Israel, Ezekiel 38-39 **and** Dan. 11:36ff. Ezekiel gives the battle from God's viewpoint. Daniel gives the battle from a human viewpoint.

3. The Time of the Battle

a. The Time in General

The prophets place the invasion of Israel by Magog in future contexts concerning end time events. It will occur after Israel has been restored to the Land (Ezek. 36:24ff.; 38:8,12; 39:25), near a time of resurrection (Ezek 37:12), near the future Kingdom (Ezek. 37:24-26). Both the contexts before (Chapters 36-37) and after (Chapters 40-48 on the millennial temple) the battle in Ezekiel 38-39 concern end time events. Ezekiel 38 places the battle in "the last days" (see also Dan. 11:35, "until the end time").

> "After many days you will be summoned; in the **latter years** you will come into the land that has been restored from the sword, whose inhabitants have been gathered from many

nations to the mountains of Israel...
[Ezek. 38:8].

"...It will come about in the **last days**
that I will bring you against my
land..." [Ezek. 38:16].

After this battle many, including Jews, will
turn to God. This fits a future period very
well (see Rev. 7:4-10, 14-17).

"And I shall magnify Myself, sanctify
Myself, and make Myself known in
the sight of **many nations**; and they
will know that I am the LORD"
[Ezek 38:23].

"And I shall set My glory among the
nations; and **all the nations will see**
My judgment which I have executed,
and My hand which I have laid on
them. And **the house of Israel will
know that I am the LORD their
God** from that day onward" [Ezek.
39:21-22].

b. The Specific Future Time for a Russian
Invasion of Israel

(1). Before the Rapture

One popular commentator on the book of
Revelation places the battle of Ezekiel 38-39
"before the Tribulation." [40] This supposedly
fits better with Israel dwelling in peace and
safety (Ezek. 38:8,11,14) and the fact that it
takes a full seven years to burn debris from
the battle (Ezek. 39:9-10). However, Israel
might also dwell in relative security any time
during the first 3 1/2 years of the Tribulation
because of her covenant of protection with
the Antichrist (Dan 9:27). Furthermore,
some battle debris may be burned during the

transition period from the Tribulation to the
Kingdom.

The greatest objection to placing this invasion before the Tribulation is that it also
likely places the invasion before the Rapture
and destroys the imminence of the Rapture.
Phrases such as "the latter days" (Ezek.
38:8,16) refer to a latter time for Israel not
the latter days of the Church Age.

(2). The Beginning of the Millennium

Another respected Bible teacher placed the
battle of Ezekiel 38-39 during the beginning
of the Millennium. [41] If anything this second
view has even less to commend it. Again, the
main argument is that the Millennium is a
better time in which to view Israel as dwelling securely in her land (Ezek. 38:8,11,14).
However, at the beginning of the Millennium, there will be no unsaved people on
planet earth that could generate an invasion
of Israel. At the Second Coming Christ separates and removes all the unsaved from the
earth (Matt. 25:31ff.; Rev. 19:15-18), wars
cease with plowshares being turned into
pruning hooks (Isa. 2:1-4, 9:6-7; Micah 4:3),
and Satan is bound (Rev. 20:1-3). It does not
make any sense to place an invasion by a
rebellious horde of unbelievers into such a
time period. In addition, the land of Israel
would then begin the millennial Kingdom in
a state of defilement for it will take seven
months to purify the land from dead bodies
(Ezek. 39:12-16).

(3). The End of the Millennium

Gog and Magog will definitely revolt against
Christ's rule at the very end of the 1,000-
year Kingdom. While the Millennium will
begin with a world devoid of unbelievers,
some of those born during the Millennium
will reject Christ and will start a revolution
under the lead of Satan during his short release from the abyss. The question remains
as to whether Rev. 20:7ff. concerns the same

---

[40] Tim LaHaye, *Revelation*, p. 268. LaHaye concludes the battle is before the Tribulation but may
not be before the Rapture. In theory there could
be a gap between the Rapture and the Tribulation. Yet, it is improbable that Satan will waste
any time in starting the rise of the Antichrist to
power once the church and the Restrainer are
removed.

[41] Arno C. Gaebelein quoted in J. Dwight Pentecost, *Things to Come*, p. 348.

or a different occasion than Ezekiel 38-39. The region is the same, but the time is not.

And **when the thousand years are completed**, Satan will be released from his prison, and will come out to deceive the nations which are in the four corners of the earth, Gog and Magog, to gather them together for the war; the number of them is like the sand of the seashore. And they came up on the broad plain of the earth and surrounded the camp of the saints and the beloved city, and fire came down from heaven and devoured them. And the devil who deceived them was thrown into the lake of fire and brimstone, where the beast and the false prophet are also; and they will be tormented day and night forever and ever [Rev. 20:7-10] (see also 20:1-3).

Ezek. 39:12,14 teaches it will take seven months to bury the dead after the battle. Yet, fire from heaven "devours" God's enemies in Rev. 20:9. If Dan. 11:36ff. concerns the invasion of Israel by Magog, then the Antichrist will be a participant. By contrast the battle of Rev. 20:7ff. concerns a time 1,000 years after (see Rev. 20:7) the "beast" has been permanently confined to the Lake of Fire (See Rev. 19:20 and 20:10). The invasion in Ezekiel 38-39 concerns an attack mainly from the North with a limited number of allies. The destruction occurs on the mountains of Israel (Ezek. 39:4). Rev. 20:7ff. involves an invasion by "the nations which are in the four corners of the earth" (Rev. 20:8) and its defeat occurs in the vicinity of "the beloved city" (i.e., Jerusalem, Rev. 20:9). The preceding context of the battle in Ezekiel 38-39 concerns events that transpire at the beginning of the Millennium, while Rev. 20:7ff. concerns only the very end of the Kingdom just before the new heavens and the new earth (Revelation 21). Although the places are the same, there are too many differences to equate Ezekiel 38-

39 with the battle at the end of the Millennium described in Rev. 20:7ff.

(4). In the Tribulation; Probably Sometime in the First Half

Although many prophetic students place the invasion of Israel by Magog near the end of the Tribulation, it is better to place the battle during the first half of the Tribulation or at the very beginning of the second half. [42]

Ezekiel says three times that Magog will invade Israel at a time when Israel feels secure (Ezek. 38:8,11,14). Israel cannot possibly be said to be a place of safety during the last half of the Tribulation (see Dan. 7:21,25; Zech. 14:2; Rev. 11:2; 12:3-6, 13-14; 13:5-7). The Antichrist breaks his covenant with Israel at the mid-point in the tribulation (Dan. 9:27) and persecutes her intensely for the last 3 1/2 years. While there will be many wars during the first half of the Tribulation, trouble for Israel will multiply during the second half. If one must find a time in the Tribulation for relative peace and security in Israel, it must be during the first half.

The burial period of seven months following the invasion (Ezek. 39:12,16) also creates a problem for viewing Magog's invasion of Israel at the very end of the Tribulation. Uncleanness would carry over into the Millennium. It is best not to view the land of Israel as in a state of defilement during the first months of the Kingdom. Therefore, it is best not to place Magog's invasion at the end of the Tribulation.

---

[42] Hal Lindsey, *The Late Great Planet Earth*, p. 60; Charles Feinberg, editor, *Prophecy in the Seventies*, (Chicago: Moody Press, 1971), p. 232; Merril F. Unger, *Ungers Bible Handbook*, (Chicago, Moody Press, 1966). p. 378; Charles Feinberg, *The Prophecy of Ezekiel*, p. 218; Leon Wood, *The Bible and Future Events*, (Grand Rapids: Zondervan Publishing House, 1973), p. 124. Only Wood places the battle earlier in the Tribulation.

The Antichrist completely dominates the world during the last half of the Tribulation (e.g., Rev. 13:4-8,12,14-17). No one is able to wage war on him or challenge his authority. Thus, the majority of strictly human wars between nations will occur during the first half of the Tribulation (Matt 24:6; Rev. 6:1ff.). It is best to view any strong confederation of nations, such as Ezekiel 38-39 describes, as having been destroyed before the second half of the Tribulation. Past the mid-point the Antichrist will consolidate power into a world dictatorship. Dan. 11:40 pictures the king of the South and the king of the North as attacking the willful end time king who considers himself a god (v. 36). Yet, the Antichrist will have no rivals during the last 3 1/2 years. It is far better to suppose that Russia and its allies meet doom sometime in the first half of the Tribulation. In fact, destruction of Russia at mid-tribulation would nicely explain how the Antichrist can dominate the rest of the world for the next 3 1/2 years and would also help explain a sudden breach of the covenant with Israel.

Finally, Ezekiel 38:23 and 39:21-22 teach that God's destruction of Magog becomes a sign to the nations and to Israel that God is the true God. If this sign brings many to the Lord, it must not occur at the very end of the Tribulation, as this would leave little time for conversion and refusal of the Beast's mark. Placing this battle earlier in the Tribulation better explains the conversions that result. By the end of the Tribulation virtually everyone will either have trusted Christ already or have accepted the mark of the Beast. Mass conversions at the very end of the Tribulation are harder to envision.

"And I shall magnify Myself, sanctify Myself, and make Myself known in the sight of many nations; and they will know that I am the LORD....And I shall set My glory among the nations; and all the nations will see My judgment which I have executed, and My

hand which I have laid on them. And the house of Israel will know that I am the LORD their God from that day onward" [Ezek. 38:23; 39:21-22]

Several lines of evidence indicate that the most likely time for a Russian invasion of Israel is during the first half of the Tribulation, perhaps at mid-tribulation. Neither the description of Israel dwelling in safety nor the presence of a Northern Confederation that is powerful enough to challenge the Antichrist fits well with known conditions for the last 3 1/2 years of the Tribulation. [43]

4. The Results of the Battle

"...and say, 'Thus, says the Lord God, "Behold, I am against you O Gog, prince of Rosh, Meshech, and Tubal. And I will turn you about and put hooks in your jaws, and I will bring you out, and all your army, horses and horsemen, all of them splendidly attired, a great company with buckler and shield, all of them wielding swords....And it will come about on that day, when Gog came against the land of Israel," declares the Lord God, "that My fury will mount up in My anger. And in My zeal and in My blazing wrath I declare that on that day there will surely be a great earthquake in the land of Israel. And the fish of the sea, the birds of the heavens, the beasts of the field, all the creeping things that creep on the earth, and all of the men who are on the face of the earth will shake at My presence; the mountains

---

[43] Ezek. 38:17 and 39:8 indicate this battle was predicted by other prophets prior to Ezekiel's time. This might favor an equation of Magog's invasion of Israel with the battle of Armageddon. Yet, perhaps these verses only mean that other prophets foresaw general end time wars and disasters. They need not mean that the invasion of Israel by Magog equals the battle of Armageddon.

also will be thrown down, the steep pathways will collapse, and every wall will fall to the ground. And I shall call for a sword against him on all My mountains," declares the Lord God. "Every man's sword will be against his brother. And with pestilence and with blood **I shall enter into judgment with him; and I shall rain on him,** and on his troops, and on the many peoples who are with him, a **torrential rain, with hailstones, fire, and brimstone.** And I shall magnify Myself, sanctify Myself, and make Myself known in the sight of many nations; and they will know that I am the LORD. And you, son of man, prophesy against Gog, and say, 'Thus says the Lord God, "Behold, I am against you, O Gog, prince of Rosh, Meshech, and Tubal; and I shall turn you around, drive you on, take you up from the remotest parts of the north, and bring you against the mountains of Israel. And I shall strike your bow from your left hand, and dash down your arrows from your right hand. **You shall fall on the mountains of Israel, you and all your troops,** and the peoples who are with you; **I shall give you as food to every kind of predatory bird** and beast of the field. You will fall on the open field; for it is I who have spoken" declares the Lord God. "And I **shall send fire upon Magog** and those who inhabit the coastlands in safety; and they will know that I am the LORD" [Ezek. 38:3-4,18; 39:6].

God Himself wills that Magog with her allies invade Israel (Ezek. 38:8, "will be summoned"; v. 16, "I shall bring you against My land"). He does so, however, in order to draw her to a supernatural destruction. Fire from heaven destroys the horde (Ezek. 38:22). The prophet uses personal language to convey God's hatred of Magog and His personal involvement in her downfall. "I am against you…I shall turn you around…I shall strike your bow…I will give you as food to every kind of predatory bird…I shall send fire upon Magog"(see Ezek. 39:1-6). It will take seven years to burn the weapons of battle (39:8-10) and seven months to bury the dead (39:11-16).

"Then those who inhabit the cities of Israel will go out, and make fires with the **weapons** and burn them, both shields and bucklers, bows and arrows, war clubs and spears and **for seven years they will make fires of them.** And they will not take wood from the field or gather firewood from the forests, for they will make fires with the weapons; and they will take the spoil of those who despoiled them, and seize the plunder of those who plundered them," declares the Lord God. "And it will come about on that day that I shall give Gog a burial ground there in Israel, the valley of those who pass by east of the sea, and it will block off the passers-by. So they will bury Gog there with all his multitude, and they will call it the valley of Hamon-gog. For **seven months** the house of **Israel will be burying them** in order to cleanse the land. Even all the people of the land will bury them; and it will be to their renown on the day that I glorify Myself," declares the Lord God. "And they will set apart men who will constantly pass through the land, burying those who were passing through, even those left on the surface of the ground, in order to cleanse it. At the end of seven months they will make a search. And as those who pass through the land pass through and anyone sees a man's bone, then he will set up a marker by it until the buriers have buried it in the valley of Hamon-gog. And even the name of the city will be Hamonah. So they will cleanse the land" [Ezek. 39:9-16]

If Dan. 11:36ff. describes the same battle as Ezekiel 38-39, then the Antichrist plays a role in it. Daniel never says that the Antichrist does any fighting in Israel proper although he will be able to occupy "The Beautiful Land" as a result of the battle (Dan. 11:41). Perhaps God has already destroyed Magog before the Antichrist can mobilize in Israel. The Antichrist either plays a secondary role in fighting Magog's African allies during the invasion, or else he finishes them off after a more supernatural destruction by God.

> "Then he (the "willful" end-times king) will stretch out his hand against other countries and the land of Egypt will not escape. But he will gain control over the hidden treasures of gold and silver, and over all the precious things of Egypt; and Libyans and Ethiopians will follow at his heels" [Dan. 11:42-43].

It seems that the Antichrist benefits greatly from Magog's (Russia's) destruction. He occupies the Promised Land, breaking any treaty with Israel. He also immediately occupies Russia's allies in northern Africa. Most important is that Russia's demise eliminates all challenge to world conquest. No one is left who can oppose the Antichrist.

If the idea of God giving indirect assistance to the Antichrist (by destroying Magog) seems troubling, remember that God wants the Antichrist to rise at this time in order that He may shortly destroy him.

5. A Question of Weapons

Ezekiel's prophecy contains references to ancient means of battle; horses (38:15), bows and arrows (39:3), shields, bucklers, war clubs, and spears (39:9). How could end time battles between armies that are now

technologically advanced be fought by such primitive means? It is hard to imagine any future Russian army using bows, arrows, spears, and war clubs. Some interpreters believe that Ezekiel used terms from his own times to describe weapons that were beyond his ability to comprehend or explain. They accept some elements of the battle as figurative. Others believe that the world will suffer such devastation in the early years of the Tribulation that there will be a reversion to primitive warfare. If wars, famines, earthquakes are severe enough, worldwide changes will result. Perhaps industry and transportation will break down to the point that nations cannot produce metals or secure oil. While it is silly to argue over such fine points, literal interpretation ought to be adopted as a primary method unless contextual evidence or parallel texts suggest figurative language. Ezekiel's statements sound very straightforward. "And you will come from your places, you and many peoples with you, all of them riding on horses" (Ezek. 38:15).

6. The Battle of Armageddon

The Greek word for battle, *polemos,* (cf. polemics) need not be limited to a single military encounter such as the English word "battle" may imply. [44] It might be clearer to refer to the "War of Armageddon" or the "Armageddon Campaign" which seems to involve a series of military encounters.

a. The Place

The Hebrew word "har" means "mountain or hill". Har-Megiddo means Mt. Megiddo and refers to a mountain and strategic mountain pass in Northern Israel. It stands at the entrance to a pass between the plain of Esdraelon (or Jezreel) and the Plain of Sharon. Armies that desire to move toward central Israel must come through this area. Like-

---

[44] Richard C. Trench, *Synonyms of the New Testament,* p. 322.

446

wise, armies that want to defend central Israel tend to make a stand here.

The plain gives adequate room for battle. Many Biblical battles (Deborah and Barak, Judges 4-5; Jehu, 2 Kings 9:27; Josiah, 2 Kings 23:29-30, 2 Chron 35:22) and non-Biblical battles (Crusaders, Napoleon, even World War 1) have occurred near Mt. Megiddo. The Greek transliteration of Har-Megiddo has come down into English as Armageddon (Rev. 16:16).

b. Texts Concerning the Armageddon Campaign

Many texts make a brief reference to Christ destroying His enemies upon His return (Dan. 2:35,44; 7:11-14, 21-22; 2 Thess. 2:8). Some texts give extended reference to an end time battle between all nations and God Himself.

"For behold, in those days and at that time when I restore the fortunes of Judah and Jerusalem, **I will gather all the nations**, and bring them down to the valley of Jehoshaphat. **Then I will enter into judgment with them** there on behalf of My people, and My inheritance, Israel, whom they have scattered among the nations; and they have divided up My land....proclaim this among the nations; prepare a war; rouse the mighty men! Let all the soldiers draw near, let them come up! Beat your plowshares into swords, and your pruning hooks into spears; let the weak say, I am a mighty man. Hasten and come all you surrounding nations, and gather yourselves there. Bring down, O LORD, thy mighty ones. Let the nations be aroused and come up to the valley of Jehoshaphat, for there **I will sit to judge all the surrounding nations. Put in the sickle, for the harvest is ripe. Come, tread, for the winepress is full**; the vats overflow, for their wickedness is great. **Multi-**

tudes, multitudes in the valley of decision! For the day of the LORD is near in the valley of decision**. The sun and moon grow dark, and the stars lose their brightness. And the LORD roars from Zion and utters His voice from Jerusalem, and the heavens and the earth tremble. But the LORD is a refuge for His people and a stronghold to the sons of Israel. Then you will know that I am the LORD your God, Dwelling in Zion My holy mountain, So Jerusalem will be holy and strangers will pass through it no more" [Joel 3:1-2, 9-17] (see preceding context for evidence that this battle refers to the end times.)

"Behold, I am going to make Jerusalem a cup that causes reeling to all the people around; and when the siege is against Jerusalem, it will also be against Judah, and it will come about in that day that I will make Jerusalem a heavy stone for all the peoples; all who lift it will be severely injured. **And all the nations of the earth will be gathered** against it" [Zech. 12:2-3].

"In that day the LORD will defend the inhabitants of Jerusalem, and the one who is feeble among them in that day will be like David, and the house of David will be like God, like the angel of the LORD before them. And it came about in that day that **I will set about to destroy all the nations that come against Jerusalem**. And I will pour out on the house of David and on the inhabitants of Jerusalem, the Spirit of grace and of supplication, so that they will look on Me whom they have pierced; and they will mourn for Him, as one mourns for an only son, and they will weep bitterly over Him, like the bitter weeping over a first-born. In that day there will be great mourning in Jerusalem, like the mourning of Hadadrimmon in the plain of Megiddo" [Zech. 12:8-11].

For I will gather all the nations against Jerusalem to battle, and the city will be captured, the houses plundered, the women ravished, and half of the city exiled, but the rest of the people will not be cut off from the city. **Then the LORD will go forth and fight against those nations, as when He fights on a day of battle. And in that day His feet will stand on the Mount of Olives**, which is in front of Jerusalem on the east; and the Mount of Olives will be split in its middle from east to west by a very large valley, so that half of the mountain will move toward the north and the other half toward the south. And you will flee by the valley of My mountains, for the valley of the mountains will reach to Azel; yes, you will flee just as you fled before the earthquake in the days of Uzziah king of Judah. **Then the LORD, my God, will come and all the holy ones with Him** [Zech. 14:2-5].

And I looked, and behold, a white cloud, and sitting on the cloud was one like a son of man, having a golden crown on His head, and a sharp sickle in His hand. And another angel came out of the temple, crying out with a loud voice to Him who sat on the cloud, "Put in your sickle and reap, because the hour to reap has come, because the harvest of the earth is ripe." And He who sat on the cloud swung His sickle over the earth; and the earth was reaped. And another angel came out of the temple which is in heaven, and he also had a sharp sickle. And another angel, the one who has power over fire, came out from the altar; and he called with a loud voice to him who had the

sharp sickle, saying, "Put in your sharp sickle and gather the clusters from the vine of the earth, because her grapes are ripe." And **the angel swung his sickle to the earth, and gathered the clusters from the vine of the earth, and threw them into the great wine press of the wrath of God. And the wine press was trodden outside the city, and blood came out from the wine press, up to the horses' bridles, for a distance of two hundred miles** [Rev. 14:14-20].

And the sixth angel poured out his bowl upon the great river, the Euphrates; and its water was dried up, that the way might be prepared for the kings from the east. And I saw coming out of the mouth of the dragon and out of the mouth of the beast and out of the mouth of the false prophet, three unclean spirits like frogs; for they are spirits of **demons**, performing signs, **which go out to the kings of the whole world, to gather them together for the war of the great day of God, the Almighty....And they gathered them together to the place which in Hebrew is called Har-Magedon** [Rev. 16:12-14, 16].

And I saw an angel standing in the sun; and he cried out with a loud voice, saying **to all the birds** which fly in mid-heaven, **"Come, assemble for the great supper of God; in order that you may eat the flesh of kings** and the flesh of commanders and the flesh of mighty men and the flesh of horses and of those who sit on them and the flesh of all men, both free men and slaves, and small and great." **And I saw the beast and the kings of the earth and their armies, assembled to make war against Him who sat upon the horse, and**

against His army. And the beast was seized, and with him the false prophet who performed the signs in his presence, by which he deceived those who had received the mark of the beast and those who worshiped his image; these two were thrown alive into the lake of fire which burns with brimstone. And the rest were killed with the sword which came from the mouth of Him who sat upon the horse, and all the birds were filled with their flesh [Rev. 19:17-21].

c. The Location of Battle[45]

Armageddon seems to be a campaign with a series of encounters. The location ranges in a north to south direction for a distance of approximately 200 miles.

(1). Mt. Megiddo

The Bible teaches that Mt. Megiddo is an end-time rendezvous spot for the world's armies. The Satanic trinity of Dragon, Beast, and False Prophet bring the "kings of the world" together to make war on Christ (Rev. 16:13-16). Zech. 12:11 also mentions the plain of Megiddo.

(2). The Valley of Jehoshaphat (The Valley of Decision)

Joel 3:2 and 3:12 place a final battle for the nations of the world in the "Valley of Jehoshaphat." Because Jehoshaphat means "God judges," Joel may intend for his readers to understand "Valley of Jehoshaphat" as a reference to an unspecified place where God judges the world. Emphasis would be upon ⌐od's judgment with the specific location less important than the decisions made there.

Perhaps the geographical place called the "Valley of Jehoshaphat" cannot be identified with any certainty. One idea is that it is the Valley of Beracah (2 Chron. 20:26) where

Judah's King Jehoshaphat assembled after a victory. Another guess is that the Valley of Jehoshaphat is the Kidron Valley just outside of Jerusalem. This fits the location given in Zech. 14:4. A final suggestion is a brand new valley created by Christ's coming to earth (Zech. 14:4). Although a location near Jerusalem is the most probable, none of these places can be proven to be "The Valley of Jehoshaphat."

(3). Jerusalem

Zechariah's prophecies give Jerusalem as the location of a great end time battle between God and the world's nations.

> "Behold, I am going to make Jerusalem a cup that causes reeling to all the peoples around; and when the siege is against Jerusalem, it will also be against Judah....In that day the LORD will defend the inhabitants of Jerusalem, and the one who is feeble among them in that day will be like David, and the house of David will be like God, like the angel of the LORD before them....In that day there will be great mourning in Jerusalem, like the mourning of Hadadrimmon in the plain of Megiddo [Zech. 12:2,8,11].

> For I will gather all the nations against Jerusalem to battle, and the city will be captured, the houses plundered, the women ravished, and half of the city exiled, but the rest of the people will not be cut off from the city [Zech. 14:2].

(4). Edom

In language similar to Revelation 14 and 19, Isaiah 63 seems to refer to God's final vengeance upon the nations (see also Isaiah 34). Isaiah pictures God as returning from a battle that had concluded in Edom.

> Who is this who comes from Edom with garments of glowing colors from

---

[45] Dwight Pentecost, *Things to Come*, p. 341; Tim LaHaye, *Revelation*, p. 266ff.

Bozrah, this One who is majestic in His apparel, marching in the greatness of His strength? "It is I who speak in righteousness, mighty to save." Why is Your apparel red, and Your garments like the one who treads in the winepress. "I have trodden the wine trough alone, and from the peoples there was no man with Me. I also trod them in My anger, and trampled them in My wrath; and their lifeblood is sprinkled on My garments, and I stained all My raiment. For the day of vengeance was in My heart, and My year of redemption has come" [Isa. 63:1-4].

(5). Conclusion

There is justification for viewing Armageddon as a campaign that ranges in the north near Mt. Megiddo to Edom, 200 miles to the south, with a major conflict around Jerusalem. This view corresponds to Rev. 14:20, which tells of blood splattered for a distance of 200 miles. It is difficult to know the precise geographical order of battle. While the Antichrist's armies initially gather at Megiddo, the Lord initially returns to the Mount of Olives near Jerusalem. Because an assault against Jerusalem is underway at Jesus' coming (Zechariah 14), it seems Jesus Christ will not fight elsewhere prior to the clash at Jerusalem.

> And the angel swung his sickle to the earth, and gathered the clusters from the vine of the earth, and threw them into the great wine press of the wrath of God. And the wine press was trodden outside the city, and blood came out from the wine press, up to the horses' bridles, **for a distance of two hundred miles** [Rev. 14:19-20].

d. Participants at Armageddon

(1). The World's Nations Led by the Antichrist

Unlike Magog's invasion of Israel, which involves a few nations, Biblical accounts of Armageddon picture a gathering of all the world's nations.

> "I will gather **all** the nations..." [Joel 3:2].

> "...I will make Jerusalem a heavy stone for **all** the peoples..." [Zech. 12:3].

> For I will gather **all** the nations against Jerusalem to battle...[Zech 14:2].

> ...the kings of the **whole world** to gather them together for the war... [Rev 16:14].

> And I saw the beast and the **kings of the earth** and their armies, assembled to make war against Him who sat upon the horse, and against His army [Rev 19:19].

(2). Israel

It is possible to view the early stages of the Armageddon campaign as a war between humans, the Antichrist and allies versus Israel. Zech. 14:2 pictures the nations engaged in an effort of genocide against Israel (cf. Matt. 24:22). Israel will not be able to withstand the onslaught and would be exterminated except for God's intervention (see also Dan. 11:45-12:1a).

> For I will gather **all the nations against Jerusalem** to battle, and the city will be captured, the houses plundered, the women ravished, and half of the city exiled, but the rest of the people will not be cut off from the city. Then the LORD will go forth and **fight against those nations**, as when He fights on a day of battle [Zech. 14:2-3].

> And the **dragon was enraged with the woman**, and went off to **make war with** the rest of **her offspring**,

who keep the commandments of God and hold to the testimony of Jesus [Rev. 12:17]. (See Rev. 12:5, where the woman gives birth to a male ruler. The woman is best understood as Israel.)

(3). Christ the Lamb of God

At a point where conditions could not be more hopeless from a human perspective, the Lamb, the rider on the white horse called Faithful and True, will come to rescue His people and destroy all opposition (see all of Rev. 19:11-20).

"These will wage war against the Lamb, and the Lamb will overcome them, because He is Lord of lords and King of kings and those who are with Him are the called and chosen and faithful" [Rev. 17:14].

And I saw the beast and the kings of the earth and their armies, assembled to make war against Him who sat upon the horse, and against His army [Rev. 19:19].

e. The Time

Revelation 19-20 presents the time for this great final battle at the time of transition from the end of the Tribulation to the beginning of the Kingdom.

f. The Outcome

From God's perspective the Battle of Armageddon is no battle at all. Christ slays the man of sin by a word from His mouth and by the brightness of His coming (2 Thess. 2:8). The Antichrist's world army becomes prey for birds to consume (Rev. 19:17-21). The Beast and False Prophet are thrown into an eternal lake of fire (Rev. 19:20). Satan is thrown into the abyss for the 1,000 years of Christ's earthly Kingdom (Rev. 20:1-3). From Satan's perspective, Armageddon results in total destruction. From Christ's perspective Armageddon is a complete victory (Rom. 8:37; 1 Cor. 15:57).

And then that lawless one will be revealed whom **the Lord will slay** with the breath of His mouth **and bring to an end** by the appearance of His coming [2 Thess. 2:8].

And I saw heaven opened; and behold, a white horse, and He who sat upon it is called Faithful and True; and **in righteousness He judges and wages war**. And His eyes are a flame of fire, and upon His head are many diadems; and He has a name written upon Him which no one knows except Himself. And He is clothed with a robe dipped in blood; and His name is called The Word of God. And the armies, which are in heaven, clothed in fine linen, white and clean, were following Him on white horses. **And from His mouth comes a sharp sword, so that with it He may smite the nations; and He will rule them with a rod of iron; and He treads the winepress of the fierce wrath of God, the Almighty**. And on His robe and on His thigh He has a name written, "KING OF KINGS, AND LORD OF LORDS." And I saw an angel standing in the sun; and he cried out with a loud voice, saying to all the birds which fly in mid-heaven, "Come, assemble for the great supper of God; in order that you may eat the flesh of kings and the flesh of commanders and the flesh of mighty men and of horses and of those who sit on them and the flesh of all men, both free men and slaves and small and great." And I saw the beast and the kings of the earth and their armies, assembled to make war against Him who sat upon the horse, and against His army. **And the beast was seized, and with him the false prophet** who performed the signs in his presence, by which he deceived those who had received the mark of the beast and those who had worshiped his image; **these two were thrown alive into the lake of fire** which burns with brimstone. And **the rest were killed with the sword**, which came from the mouth of Him who sat upon the horse, and **all the birds were filled with their flesh**. And I saw an angel coming down from heaven, having the key of the abyss and a great chain in his hand. And he laid hold of the dragon, the serpent of old, who is the devil and Satan, and bound him for a thousand years, and threw him into the abyss, and shut it and sealed it over him, so that he should not deceive the nations any longer, until the thousand years were completed; after these things he must be released for a short time [Rev. 19:11-20:3].

D. God and the Saints in the Tribulation

It would take an extensive study of the book of Revelation to give all the details of God's workings during the Tribulation. A survey is adequate for this more general study. God's work in the Tribulation will consist of judgment upon the world and evangelization of the world. Even in direct judgment God still offers grace.

1. God's Judgment in the Tribulation

The judgments of the "seals," "trumpets," and "bowls" in the book of The Revelation give many examples of God's wrath which He unleashes against the world during the Tribulation. Many have equated the four horsemen of the apocalypse (Revelation 6) with Christ's predictions in the Olivet Discourse of wars, famines, and pestilence (Matthew 24, Mark 13, Luke 21). Revelation 5 pictures a scroll that has been wound shut and sealed at seven different spots with seven seals. This scroll is similar to a "title deed" to the world and speaks of control over world history. The one who has the authority to open the seals also has the authority to allow events that bring calamity

upon the world and bring the history of a rebellious world to an end. No one has the authority to open the seals and reveal world events except the Lamb who had been slain. He takes the scroll from God the Father and begins to break the seals. By doing so He reveals and permits calamities that usher in the end of the world as a system in rebellion against God. The first seal unleashes the Antichrist on a white horse that he may destroy many in his effort to conquer the world. A second seal permits a rider on a red horse to bring war. The opening of a third seal gives permission for a third rider on a black horse to bring famine. The fourth horseman sits on a yellowish-green horse (NASB ashen, Greek *cloros*, as in chlorophyll), which probably speaks of sickness, the plagues of the Olivet Discourse (Luke 21:11). The fifth seal speaks of believers on earth being killed for their faith. The sixth seal brings an earthquake and changes in the heavenly bodies (see Joel 2:30ff.; Matt. 24:29). The judgment of the seventh seal contains seven trumpet judgments (see Rev. 6:8-9).

The first trumpet brings hail, fire, and blood raining down upon the earth. The second trumpet is a burning mountain that destroys one-third of the world's oceans. The third trumpet brings a burning star (meteor?) that pollutes one-third of the world's fresh water. The fourth trumpet causes darkness to be one-third longer each day. The fifth trumpet unleashes a horde of demonic creatures from the abyss that can torment but not kill humans for five months. Men will seek death rather than face the demonic peril. Yet, the sixth trumpet seems to unleash 200,000,000 more demons. This time they do kill.

The seventh trumpet announces that "the kingdom of this world is become the kingdom of our Lord and of His Christ, and He shall reign forever and ever" (Rev. 11:15). Because this final trumpet announces the end is near, it is safe to presume that the seven bowl judgments occur rapidly in the final days of the Tribulation (Revelation 16). The first bowl brings pitiful sores upon those who worship the Antichrist. The second bowl makes the sea like blood and kills all marine life. The third bowl destroys the world's drinking water. The fourth bowl increases the sun's heat in order to scorch humanity. The fifth bowl creates worldwide darkness. The sixth bowl dries up the already polluted Euphrates River to make it easier for the eastern armies to begin their trek to Armageddon. The final bowl brings earthquakes to destroy the world's major cities, to sink islands, and to topple mountains. As an extra measure of wrath, the seventh bowl also brings 100-pound hailstones. Numerical references in Revelation show that the majority of the world's population will die in the Tribulation.

> And authority was given to them [the four horsemen] over a **fourth of the earth, to kill** with sword and with famine and with pestilence and by the wild beasts of the earth [Rev. 6:8b].

> And the first sounded, and there came hail and fire, mixed with blood, and they were thrown to the earth; and **a third of the earth was burnt up...** [Rev. 8:7].

> And the four angels, who had been prepared for the hour and day and month and year, were released, so that they might kill a **third of mankind....A third of mankind** was killed by these three plagues, by the fire and the smoke and the brimstone, which proceeded out of their mouths[46] [Rev. 9:15,18].

---

[46] One can compute these fractions in two ways. One way is to subtract from the original total (100% minus 25%, minus 33 1/3%, minus another 33 1/3%). This means over 90% of the world's population would die in just three judgments, not even counting wars caused by humans. Another way would be to view the fractions as concerning the remaining population

Destruction on the scale described in Revelation 6-18 could indeed force the world back to primitive living standards where horses and ancient battle weapons are used in warfare. Only Christ's coming will save planet earth from total annihilation. The fact that God will offer salvation during this period of His wrath speaks of His deep grace.

2. God's Program of World Evangelization during the Tribulation

The Rapture will remove all believers from the world. Thus, the Tribulation begins with a world in total unbelief. However, God will still be active in a program of calling out people from darkness into His salvation. Many people will respond to God's grace even in the midst of a time of great judgment. There are many references to "saints" in tribulational contexts (see next section for additional references). The "Gospel of the Kingdom" will offer salvation through Christ's blood and also announce the soon arrival of the King. It must penetrate the entire world during the Tribulation.

> "And this **gospel** of the kingdom **shall be preached in the whole world** for a witness to all the nations, and then the end shall come" [Matt. 24:14].

> "And the **gospel** must first be **preached to all the nations**" [Mark 13:10].

God will send two special witnesses to earth during the Tribulation (probably during the

---

after the previous disasters. After the first disaster 75% of the original population would remain. The next judgment that comes with a fraction reduces those who survive by another one-third, leaving 50% of the original population. The final horror reduces those who survive by another one-third, leaving 33 1/3% of the original population. Again, this includes only the three judgments that give a fraction. Millions more will die in other judgments and wars. By either method the great majority of the world will perish in the Tribulation.

first half of the Tribulation). Revelation 11 does not identify these witnesses, but their actions parallel those of Elijah and Moses. They restrain rain, bring fire from heaven (1 Kings 17-18; 2 Kings 1; James 5:17), turn water into blood, and bring plagues (cf. Ex. 7-11). In addition, several verses predict that Elijah will come to earth before Christ comes in power (Mal. 4:5; Matt. 17:10-11).

No doubt the work of these prophets will serve to bring greater condemnation upon a rejecting world. Yet, some do trust in Christ. At one point in the Tribulation God even announces the gospel by means of an "angel flying in mid-heaven" (Rev. 14:6).

Rev. 7:3-8 teaches that God will seal 144,000 Jewish believers during the Tribulation. They will be especially protected from the perils of the Tribulation (cf. Ezek. 9:4-6). The text does not specifically teach that they will be involved in evangelism. Yet, it is safe to assume that 144,000 "bond-servants" will be doing much witnessing during a time in which the gospel must go to the ends of the earth within a few years. Although it is difficult to think of revival in the Tribulation and of the Tribulation as a time of blessings, many will find salvation despite intense pressure to side with the Antichrist.

> After these things I looked, and behold a great multitude, which no one could count, from every nation and all tribes and peoples and tongues, standing before the throne and before the Lamb, clothed in white robes, and palm branches were in their hands; and they cry out with a loud voice, saying, "Salvation to our God, who sits on the throne, and to the Lamb"....And He said to me, "These are the ones who come out of the great Tribulation, and they have washed their robes and made them white in the blood of the Lamb" [Rev. 7:9,10,14b].

3. The Saints in the Tribulation

The experiences of tribulational saints can be summed up by two contrasting words, "persecution" and "preservation." The topic of persecution for tribulational saints has already been covered as a part of the study of the Antichrist. Here are several examples (see also pp. 436-37 or Jer. 30:7; Dan. 12:1; Zech. 13:8-9; Matt. 24:16ff; Rev.11:2, 7-8; 12:1-2; 13:10; 14:13):

> "I kept looking, and that horn was **waging war with the saints and overpowering them** until the Ancient of Days came, and judgment was passed in favor of the saints of the Highest One, and the time arrived when the saints took possession of the kingdom....And he will speak out against the Most High and **wear down the saints** of the Highest One, and he will intend to make alterations in times and in law; and they will be given into his hand for a time, times, and half a time" [Dan 7:21-22,25].

> And it was given to him **to make war with the saints and to overcome them**; and authority over every tribe and people and tongue and nation was given to him....And there was given to him to give breath to the image of the beast, that the image of the beast might even speak and cause as many as do not worship the image of the beast to be killed. And he causes all, the small and the great, and the rich and the poor, and the free men and the slaves, to be given a mark on their right hand, or on their forehead, and he provides that **no one should be able to buy or to sell, except the one who has the mark**, either the name of the beast or the number of his name [Rev. 13:7,15-17].

Many believers will suffer martyrdom during the Tribulation. The aforementioned "sealing" does not pertain to all believers for God

454

does not choose to protect all from death (see Rev. 13:10). Their deaths bring about a greater judgment for the Antichrist and his followers.

> And when He broke the fifth seal, I saw underneath the altar **the souls of those who had been slain** because of the word of God, and because of the testimony which they had maintained; and they cried out with a loud voice, saying, "How long, O Lord, holy and true, wilt Thou refrain from judging and avenging our blood on those who dwell on the earth?" And there was given to each of them a white robe; and they were told that they should rest for a little while longer, until the number of their fellow servants and their brethren who were to be killed even as they had been, should be completed also [Rev. 6:9-11].

> After these things I heard, as it were, a loud voice of a great multitude in heaven, saying, "Hallelujah! Salvation and glory and power belong to our God; because his judgments are true and righteous; for He has judged the great harlot who was corrupting the earth with her immorality, and he has avenged the **blood of his bond-servants on her**" [Rev. 19:1-2].

Although not all tribulational saints will obtain God's protection, He definitely has a program to protect some of the tribulational saints from death. This is part of the purpose for sealing 144,000 Jewish believers (Rev. 7:3-8, cf. Ezek. 9:4-6). The refuge given to the "woman" in Revelation 12 teaches God will give some earthly protection to believing Israel during this terrible time.

> And she gave birth to a son, a male child, who is to rule all the nations with a rod of iron; and her child was caught up to God and to His throne. And the woman fled into the wilderness where **she had a place pre-**pared by God, so that there she **might be nourished** for one thousand two hundred and sixty days....And when the dragon saw that he was thrown down to the earth, he persecuted the woman who gave birth to the male child. And the two wings of the great eagle were given to the woman, in order that she might fly into the wilderness to her place, where **she was nourished** for a time and times and half a time, from the presence of the serpent. And the serpent poured water like a river out of his mouth after the woman, so that he might cause her to be swept away with the flood. And the earth helped the woman, and the earth opened its mouth and drank up the river which the dragon poured out of his mouth. And the dragon was enraged with the woman, and went off to make war with the rest of her offspring, who keep the commandments of God and hold to the testimony of Jesus [Rev. 12:5-6,13-17].

Along with the program of God's protection for tribulational saints, we must include the thought that God's intervention through the Second Coming of Christ protects believers from a total extermination which would otherwise take place.

> For, I will gather all the nations against Jerusalem to battle, and the city will be captured, the houses plundered, the women ravished, and half of the city exiled, but the rest of the people will not be cut off from the city. **Then the Lord will go forth and fight against those nations,** as when He fights on a day of battle. And in that day His feet will stand on the Mount of Olives, which is in front of Jerusalem on the east; and the Mount of Olives will be split in its middle from east to west by a very large valley, so that half of the

mountain will move toward the north and the other half toward the south. And you will flee by the valley of My mountains, for the valley of the mountains will reach to Azel; yes, you will flee just as you fled before the earthquake in the days of Uzziah king of Judah. Then the Lord, my God, will come, and all the holy ones with Him! And it will come about in that day that there will be no light; the luminaries will dwindle [Zech. 14:2-6].

"And unless those days had been cut short, no life would have been saved; but **for the sake of the elect those days shall be cut short**" [Matt. 24:22].

XII. The Transition from Tribulation to Kingdom

Many eschatological events happen as the Tribulation closes and the millennial Kingdom begins. The Second Coming results in the Battle of Armageddon, the destruction of the Antichrist, and the binding of Satan for 1,000 years. Also, the resurrection of Old Testament saints and martyred tribulational saints takes place at this time. Furthermore, Scriptures teach about two judgments that will result in the separation of believers from unbelievers. The Judgment of Israel and the Judgment of the Nations (gentiles) brings about the removal of all unsaved people from the world and the entrance into the Kingdom of all the saints who have survived the Tribulation.

A. The Second Coming or Revelation of Christ

Most eschatological details are not so important as to cause a division of fellowship. However, the Second Coming of Christ rightfully belongs among the fundamentals of orthodox Christianity. It is taught so thoroughly and clearly in Scripture that there can be no reason for denial, other than blatant

unbelief and heresy. In addition to the verses below see also: Job 19:25; Zech. 12:10; 14:4; Matt. 16:27; 24:42-44; Mark 13:26-27; Luke 12:40; 21:25-27; Rom. 11:26-27; 1 Thess. 3:13; 2 Thess. 2:8; 2 Peter 3:8-10; Jude 14-15; Rev.19:11-21.

"I kept looking in the night visions, and behold, with the clouds of heaven One like a **Son of Man was coming**, and He came up to the Ancient of Days and was presented before Him. and to Him was given dominion, Glory, and a kingdom, that all the peoples, nations, and men of every language might serve Him. His dominion is an everlasting dominion which will not pass away; and His kingdom is one which will not be destroyed" [Dan. 7:13-14].

"[A]nd then the sign of the **Son of Man will appear in the sky,** and then all the tribes of the earth will mourn, and they will see the Son of Man coming on the clouds of the sky with power and great glory. And He will send forth His angels with a great trumpet and they will gather together His elect from the four winds, from one end of the sky to the other" [Matt. 24:30-31].

"But when the **Son of Man comes** in His glory, and all the angels with Him, then He will sit on His glorious throne" [Matt. 25:31].

[A]nd they also said, "Men of Galilee, why do you stand looking into the sky? This **Jesus**, who has been taken up from you into heaven, **will come** in just the same way as you have watched Him go into heaven" [Acts 1:11].

[A]nd to give relief to you who are afflicted and to us as well when the **Lord Jesus shall be revealed** from heaven with His mighty angels in flaming fire, dealing out retribution to those who do not know God and to those who do not obey the gospel of our Lord Jesus [2 Thess.1:7-8].

Behold, he is coming with the clouds, and every eye will see Him, even those who pierced Him; and all the tribes of the earth will mourn over Him. Even so. Amen [Rev. 1:7].

1. The Time of Christ's Second Coming

The Old Testament portrays God's coming to cut short a time of terrible destruction. In Daniel 7 the Son of Man comes to earth and destroys the kingdom of the "little horn", the Antichrist. He establishes a worldwide Kingdom that is eternal in duration. Zechariah says that God Himself will come to Jerusalem to rescue it from an otherwise destructive conflict (Zech. 14:2ff.). Then Israel "will look on **Me** whom they have pierced" (see Zech. 12:2-3,10).

The New Testament clarifies that Messiah will come twice. His Second Coming will end a terrible period of tribulation (Matt. 24:21; 29-31; Mark 13:24-27; Luke 21:25-28; Rev. 19:11-21). Virtually all theological schools of thought that adhere to a tribulation period place the Second Coming of Christ at its end.

"[F]or then there will be a great tribulation, such as has not occurred since the beginning of the world until now, nor ever shall....But **immediately after the tribulation** of those days the sun will be darkened, and the moon will not give its light, and the stars will fall from the sky, and the powers of the heavens will be shaken, and **then the sign of the Son of Man will appear in the sky,** and then all the tribes of the earth will mourn, and they will see the Son of Man coming in the clouds of the sky with power and great glory. And He will send forth His angels with a great trumpet and they will gather together His elect from the four winds, from one end of the sky to the other" [Matt. 24:21,29-31].

2. The Place

Christ will return to the Mount of Olives outside Jerusalem.

And in that day **His feet will stand on the Mount of Olives**, which is in front of Jerusalem on the east; and the Mount of Olives will be split in its middle from east to west by a very large valley, so that half of the mountain will move toward the north and the other half toward the south [Zech.14:4].

[A]nd they also said, "Men of Galilee, why do you stand looking into the sky? This Jesus, who has been taken up from you into heaven, will come in just the same way as you have watched Him go into heaven". Then they returned to Jerusalem from the **mount called Olivet**, which is near Jerusalem, a Sabbath day's journey away [Acts 1:11-12].

3. Participants with Christ in the Second Coming

a. The holy angels (see also Matt. 13:41-42; 24:30-31; 25:31; 2 Thess. 1:7; also Rev. 14:14ff. if it describes Armageddon).

"And then they will see the SON OF MAN COMING IN CLOUDS with great power and glory. And then He will send forth the **angels,** and will gather together His elect from the four winds, from the farthest end of the earth, to the farthest end of heaven" [Mark 13:26-27].

b. The Saints (see p. 387 for a discussion of 1 Thess. 3:13)

And about these also Enoch, in the seventh generation from Adam, prophesied, saying, "Behold, the Lord came with many thousands of **His holy ones,** to execute judgment upon all, and to convict all the ungodly of all their ungodly deeds which they have done in an ungodly way, and of all the harsh things which ungodly sinners have spoken against Him" [Jude 14-15].

[S]o that He may establish your hearts unblamable in holiness before our God and Father at the coming of our Lord Jesus **with all His saints** [1 Thess. 3:13].

Perhaps the armies of heaven mentioned in Rev. 19:14 include both the elect angels and glorified saints (see also Zech. 14:5). Christ returns with myriads of followers and a display of unlimited power and glory.

And the armies which are in heaven clothed in fine linen, white and clean, were following Him on white horses [Rev. 19:14].

4. Circumstances Relative to Christ's Second Coming

a. Jerusalem in Ruins

The world's armies will have already been gathered at Armageddon (Rev. 16:13-16). Some of the force will sweep aside all initial Jewish resistance and will begin to destroy Jerusalem, the holy city (Zech. 14:1-4). It is possible that two-thirds of Israel has died (Zech. 13:8-9) with half of Jerusalem's population already captured (Zech. 14:2). Satanic forces are probably sitting in the Kidron Valley outside Jerusalem planning their final genocidal assault. This may be the Valley of Jehoshaphat where God meets the nations (see Joel 3:2,12,14). No doubt the heathen rage against God and His armies, confident of impending victory (Psalm 2).

b. Cosmic Wonders

Satan thought he had victory at the cross only to discover the cross was his doom.

Surely, at the Second Coming he knows the end is near despite outward evidences of victory (Rev. 12:12). At a time when the situation is utterly hopeless from a human perspective, the skies portend a dramatic and unstoppable reversal.

"But immediately after the tribulation of those days **the sun will be darkened, and the moon will not give its light, and the stars will fall** from the sky, and the powers of the heavens will be shaken, and then the sign of the Son of Man will appear in the sky..." [Matt. 24:29-30] (see also Mark 13:24-25, 28-29; Luke 21:25-28).

c. The Glorious Descent

The Son of Man (a messianic title from Daniel 7) will descend with the clouds with power, great splendor, and possibly with a flame of fire. Wearing bloody garments, He rides a white horse upon which are emblazoned: "King of kings and Lord of lords." (Rev. 19:16) Myriads of angels and saints follow in His train (see also: Matt. 24:30; Mark 13:26; Acts 1:9-11; 2 Thess. 2:8).

"And then they will see the Son of man coming in a cloud with power and great glory" [Luke 21:27].

Jesus said to him, "You have said it yourself; nevertheless I tell you, hereafter you shall see the **Son of Man sitting at the right hand of power, and coming on the clouds of heaven**" [Matt. 26:64 (see also Mark 14:62)].

[A]nd to give relief to you who are afflicted and to us as well when the Lord Jesus shall be revealed from heaven with His mighty angels **in flaming fire** [2 Thess.1:7]. (The phrase *in flaming fire* can also be taken with 1 Thess. 1:8)

458

And I saw heaven opened; and behold, a white horse, and He who sat upon it is called Faithful and True; and in righteousness He judges and wages war. And **His eyes are a flame of fire**, and upon His head are many diadems; and He has a name written upon Him which no one knows except Himself. And He is clothed with a robe dipped in blood; and His name is called The Word of God. And the armies which are in heaven, clothed in fine linen, white and clean, were following Him on white horses. And from His mouth comes a sharp sword, so that with it He may smite the nations; and He will rule them with a rod of iron; and He treads the winepress of the fierce wrath of God, the Almighty. And on His robe and on His thigh He has a name written, "**KING OF KINGS, AND LORD OF LORDS**" [Rev.19:11-16].

d. The World's Reaction: Tears

Christ's return will be as noticeable as a lightning bolt (Matt. 24:27). The entire world sees Him. As the defeated Jews in Jerusalem see the Lord coming to their rescue, they weep bitterly. Although many Jews are still unsaved and will not enter the Kingdom (Luke 13:28), it seems that some of this weeping involves tears of relief that the Antichrist's siege against the city will fail, and likely some will also shed tears of repentance. Perhaps many Jews now regret the fact that Christ had been rejected by His own at the first coming (John 1:11). The pouring out of the "Spirit of grace" must indicate some sort of spiritual response by the Jews at this time. Zech. 13:9 may teach that one third of the Jews will be believers.

"And I will pour out on the house of David and on the inhabitants of Jerusalem, the Spirit of grace and of supplication, so that they will look on Me whom they have pierced; and they will mourn for Him, as one mourns for an only son, and they will weep bitterly over Him, like the bitter weeping over a first-born" [Zech. 12:10].

Gentile nations will also see Christ and will weep. Obviously, those who have refused the mark of the beast will weep for joy, but the Bible stresses a weeping that has the nature of frustration at the turn of events and sheer terror.

"[A]nd then the sign of the Son of Man will appear in the sky, and then **all the tribes of the earth will mourn**, and they will see the Son of Man coming on the clouds of the sky with power and great glory" [Matt. 24:30].

Behold, He is coming with the clouds, and every eye will see Him, even those who pierced Him; and **all the tribes of the earth will mourn** over Him. Even so. Amen [Rev. 1:7].

e. Touchdown

As Christ's feet touch the Mt. of Olives, it will split into a great valley. Perhaps the rift creates room for the "armies of heaven." The believing remnant in the vicinity will flock to Christ for refuge.

And in that day His feet will stand on the Mount of Olives, which is in front of Jerusalem on the east; and the Mount of Olives **will be split in its middle from east to west by a very large valley,** so that half of the mountain will move toward the north and the other half toward the south. And you will flee by the valley of My mountains, for the valley of the mountains will reach to Azel; yes, you will flee just as you fled before the earthquake in the days of Uzziah king of Judah. Then the LORD, my God, will come, and all the holy ones with Him [Zech. 14:4-5].

If Joel's Valley of Jehoshaphat is near Jerusalem, then the armies of Christ and the armies of the Antichrist face each other, perhaps only for a moment.

Put in the sickle, for the harvest is ripe. Come, tread for the winepress is full; The vats overflow, for their wickedness is great. Multitudes, multitudes in the valley of decision! For the day of the LORD is near in the valley of decision [Joel 3:13-14].

f. Persistent Rebellion

The nations had gathered to oppose Christ's coming (Rev. 16:13-16). Although they mourn for fear, nothing stops their insane hatred. Incredibly, the Beast still has the audacity to engage in war. This can only be explained by Satan's blindness. God has decreed that those hardened nations will still believe the delusion (2 Thess. 2:11-12).

"And the ten horns which you saw are ten kings, who have not yet received a kingdom, but they receive authority as kings with the beast for one hour. These have one purpose and they give their power and authority to the beast. These will **wage war against the Lamb**... [Rev. 17:12-14a].

And I saw the beast and the kings of the earth and their armies, **assembled to make war** against Him who sat upon the horse, and against His army [Rev. 19:19].

g. Effortless Victory

History's fiercest battle is from Christ's perspective as easy as breathing or manifesting His unbearable glory (2 Thess. 2:8). Christ destroys the armies of the Antichrist from Megiddo to Edom (see pp. 446-452 for details on Armageddon). There is a 200-mile swath of blood. Isaiah 63 pictures Christ as ending His conquest in Edom.

Revelation 19 says that heaven's armies follow Christ to earth, but it does not teach that He actually employs His army in the battle. Christ Himself destroys the collected armies of the world, although one should leave room for some participation by a few angelic subordinates.

And the armies which are in heaven, clothed in fine linen, white and clean, were following Him on white horses. And from His mouth comes a sharp sword, so that with it He may smite the nations; and He will rule them with a rod of iron; and He treads the wine press of the fierce wrath of God, the Almighty [Rev. 19:14-15].

And I looked, and behold, a white cloud, and sitting on the cloud was one like a son of man, having a golden sickle in His hand. And another angel came out of the temple, crying out with a loud voice to Him who sat on the cloud, "Put in your sickle and reap, because the hour to reap has come, because the harvest of the earth is ripe." And He who sat on the cloud swung His sickle over the earth; and the earth was reaped. And another angel came out of the temple which is in heaven, and he also had a sharp sickle. And another angel, the one who has power over fire, came out from the altar; and he called with a loud voice to him who had the sharp sickle, saying, "Put in your sharp sickle, and gather the clusters from the vine of the earth, because her grapes are ripe". And the angel swung his sickle to the earth, and threw them into the great winepress of the wrath of God. And the wine press was trodden outside the city, and blood came out from the wine press, up to the horses' bridles, for a distance of two hundred miles [Rev. 14:14-20].

460

The Antichrist's army dies to the last man. It becomes food for birds (Rev. 19:17-18). Only the Beast and False Prophet remain alive from the forces in Israel. They are thrown alive into eternal damnation (Rev. 19:20).

> And the beast was seized, and with him the false prophet who performed the signs in his presence, by which he deceived those who had received the mark of the beast and those who worshiped his image; these two were thrown alive into the lake of fire which burns with brimstone. And the rest were killed with the sword which came from the mouth of Him who sat upon the horse, and all the birds were filled with their flesh[47] [Rev. 19:20-21].

h. Angelic Escorts, Satanic Imprisonment

The Beast and False Prophet face eternal punishment in the Lake of Fire. By contrast an angel places Satan in another place, the abyss. Unlike the Lake of Fire, the abyss is not a place of eternal punishment. It is a temporary place of punishment where confined fallen angels await a future transferal to permanent punishment in the Lake of Fire. Satan goes here because God will allow him a short release at the end of the Kingdom, in which he displays the incorrigible nature of his wickedness. Satan is bound for the entire Millennium.

> And I saw an angel coming down from heaven, having the key of the abyss and a great chain in his hand. And he laid hold of the dragon, the serpent of old, who is the devil and Satan, and bound him for a thousand

years, and threw him into the abyss, and shut it and sealed it over him, so that he should not deceive the nations any longer, until the thousand years were completed; after these things he must be released for a short time [Rev. 20:1-3 (see also vv. 7-10)].

Armageddon leaves the Antichrist's kingdom in ruins. Yet, there will be many people remaining alive, saved and unsaved, who were not in the vicinity of Jerusalem at the Second Coming. Christ sends His angels to gather the elect by means of sorting out believers from unbelievers at two major judgments that occur during the transition from Tribulation to Kingdom, the Judgment of Israel and the Judgment of the Nations. Angelic work in bringing the survivors of the Tribulation to and from judgment will cause these judgments to occur in a relatively short time. Each judgment will be studied in following sections.

> "The Son of Man will **send forth His angels, and they will gather out of His kingdom all stumbling blocks**, and those who commit lawlessness, and will cast them into the furnace of fire; in that place there shall be weeping and gnashing of teeth" [Matt. 13:41-42].

> "So it will be at the end of the age; **the angels shall come forth, and take out the wicked from among the righteous,** and will cast them into the furnace of fire; there shall be weeping and gnashing of teeth" [Matt. 13:49-50].

> "And he will send forth His **angels** with a great trumpet and they will **gather together His elect** from the four winds, from one end of the sky to the other" [Matt. 24:31 (also Mark 13:27)].

i. The Time Frame for the Transition from Tribulation to Kingdom

---

[47] The Beast and False Prophet presumably die physically after being thrown alive into the Lake of Fire. They seem to be its first inhabitants because prior to the Great White Throne judgment those who die in unbelief enter Hades to await judgment and transferal into the Lake of Fire.

The duration between the Antichrist's breaking his covenant with Israel and the end of the Tribulation is 1,260 days (see pp. 381-82). Although the Antichrist's rule is 1,260 days, Daniel 12:11 mentions 1,290 days as a special marking time. Daniel is even more excited about day 1,335.

> "How blessed is he who keeps waiting and attains to the 1,335 days" [Dan. 12:12].

The Bible does not say exactly what happens on day 1,290 and day 1,335. We do know that day 1,290 is a special day relative to sacrifices in the temple and that day 1,335 is a very special event. Dogmatism is most out of place, but one can hazard a reasonable attempt at interpretation. Presumably, the actual rule of the Antichrist ends at day 1,260, but it takes an additional 30 days to purify the earth from destruction and to judge and remove the lost from the Kingdom. Day 1,290 is likely the time for temple worship of the true God to begin or the day on which the last rebellious soul is taken away.

The most blessed day, 1,335, is perhaps "Inauguration Day" or "the 4th of July" for the Kingdom of Christ on earth. If these interpretations are valid, it takes 30 days to purify the earth through the Judgment of Israel and the Judgment of the Nations. Perhaps in the next 45 days the Old Testament and martyred tribulational saints (who are resurrected at the end of the Tribulation) receive their reward, and the Lord installs His followers to various positions of authority around the now submissive world (Matt. 19: 28; 2 Tim. 2:12; Rev. 1:6; 5:10; 20:4).

The world has never seen anything like the transformation that takes place in the transition between the Tribulation and the Kingdom, and it probably takes place in 75 days. The resurrection of Old Testament saints (and martyred tribulational saints), the Judgment of Israel, and the Judgment of the

Nations are topics that deserve separate attention.

B. The Resurrection of Old Testament and Tribulational Saints

Some theologians advocate a general resurrection of all, saved and unsaved, at the same time. Several verses such as Dan. 12:2 and John 5:28-29 could be understood to teach a general resurrection. However, other verses force another conclusion.

> "And many of those who sleep in the dust of the ground will awake, these to everlasting life, but the others to disgrace and everlasting contempt" [Dan. 12:2].

> "Do not marvel at this; for an hour is coming, in which all who are in the tombs shall hear His voice, and shall come forth; those who did the good deeds to a resurrection of life, those who committed the evil deeds to a resurrection of judgment" [John 5:28-29].

1. Time between Resurrection unto Life and Resurrection unto Judgment

Revelation 20 speaks of two kinds of resurrection, the first, and by implication, the second. By any premillennial scheme, whether pretribulational or posttribulational, there must be an interval of 1,000 years between the resurrection unto life and the resurrection unto condemnation. Church saints must be resurrected at the Rapture, that is, before the Millennium (by either view of the Rapture). The unsaved dead according to Revelation 20 are not resurrected until after the 1,000 years Kingdom. **The idea of a general one-time resurrection cannot be true.** Revelation 20 clearly places a 1,000 year interval between the resurrection of martyred tribulational saints and the resurrection of the unsaved dead.

> And I saw thrones, and they sat upon them, and judgment was given to

them. And I saw the souls of those who had been beheaded because of the testimony of Jesus and because of the word of God, and those who had not worshiped the beast or his image, and had not received the mark upon their forehead and upon their hand; and they came to life and reigned with Christ for a thousand years. **The rest of the dead did not come to life until the thousand years were completed**. This is the first resurrection....And **when the thousand years are completed**, Satan will be released from his prison.... And the devil who deceived them was thrown into the lake of fire and brimstone, where the beast and the false prophet are also; and they will be tormented day and night forever and ever....And I saw a great white throne and Him who sat upon it, from whose presence earth and heaven fled away, and no place was found for them. And I **saw the dead**, the great and the small, **standing before the throne**, and books were opened; and another book was opened, which is the book of life; and the dead were judged from the things which were written in the books, according to their deeds [Rev. 20:4-5,7,10-12].

2. Two Kinds of Resurrection

Daniel 12 and John 5 concern kinds of resurrections, not time of resurrection. If we were to assume passages like Dan. 12:2 and John 5:28-29 teach a general resurrection of all, saved and unsaved, at the same time, we would be mistaken. Apparently, these verses are not so much stressing the time of resurrection as they are two kinds of resurrection, i.e., one unto life and another unto punishment or the second death. Furthermore, if these texts do not teach a general resurrection of the saved and unsaved at the same time, one cannot assume they inherently prove that all the saints are resurrected to-

gether at the same time. Yet, all believers will experience resurrection unto life, and all unbelievers will experience a resurrection unto judgment. Daniel 12 and John 5 do not teach about the time of resurrection. They refer only to the two kinds of resurrection. Other passages, primarily Revelation 20, show that the saved and unsaved are **not resurrected at the same time;** and this opens the door to the possibility that those who experience the resurrection unto life are not resurrected at the same time. If other texts suggest various times for the resurrection of the just, Daniel 12 and John 5 cannot be used as objections.

3. Times for the Resurrection of the Saints

a. The Church

The "dead in Christ" rise at the Rapture (1 Thess. 4:16). Since the Rapture is pretribulational, **church saints rise before the Tribulation.**

b. Martyred Tribulational Saints

Tribulational saints who die in the Tribulation cannot be raised until after the Tribulation! Rev. 6:10-11 pictures the disembodied souls of martyred tribulational saints as crying out for vengeance during the Tribulation. According to Rev. 20:4-6 these souls were "beheaded because of the testimony of Jesus" and "come to life" just before the 1,000-year Kingdom, and share in Christ's rule. In the context, this resurrection occurs after the Second Coming and after Armageddon (Rev. 19:11ff.). Although the Bible does not specifically give a time for the rewarding of the tribulational saints, presumably they are rewarded in conjunction with the resurrection during the transition between Tribulation and Kingdom.

c. Old Testament Saints

There is evidence that places **the resurrection of the Old Testament saints after the Tribulation.** Dan. 12:1 mentions the Tribulation and Dan. 12:2 teaches about resurrection. Daniel 12 addresses Israel, "your people" (that is, Daniel's people). After the Tribulation "many" (but not all) Jews will rise. Unsaved Israelites who lived under the Law will not be raised to enjoy the Kingdom. They rise with the rest of the "dead" to stand before the Great White Throne, but saved Israel rises after the Tribulation to enter the Kingdom.

> "Now at that time Michael, the great prince who stands guard over the sons of **your people,** will arise. And there will be a **time of distress** such as never occurred since there was a nation until that time; and at that time **your people,** everyone who is found **written in the book,** will be rescued. And **many of those who sleep in the dust of the ground will awake,** these to everlasting life, but the others to disgrace and everlasting contempt" [Dan. 12:1-2].

Isaiah 26 also teaches about the resurrection of Old Testament saints. Although Isaiah 26 is not as clear as Daniel 12, it is interesting that the verse about resurrection is sandwiched between material about the Tribulation and references to the Second Coming.

> "We were pregnant, **we writhed in labor,** we gave birth, as it were only to wind. We could not accomplish deliverance for the earth nor were inhabitants of the world born. **Your dead will live; their corpses will rise.** You who lie in the dust, awake and shout for joy for your dew is as the dew of the dawn, and the earth will give birth to the departed spirits....For behold, **the LORD is about to come** out from His place to punish the inhabitants of the earth for their iniquity; and the earth will reveal her bloodshed, and will no longer cover her slain" [Isa. 26:18-19,21].

Ezek. 37:12 can be taken as a figurative reference to the restoration of Israel as a nation,

but it also can be understood as speaking of bodily resurrection. If the latter is correct, then the context places the resurrection of Old Testament saints after the Tribulation and just before the Millennium, the rule of David in Ezek. 37:24.

> "Therefore prophesy, and say to them, 'Thus says the Lord God, **Behold, I will open your graves** and cause you to come up out of your graves, My people; and I will bring you into the land of Israel. Then you will know that I am the LORD, when I have opened your graves and **caused you to come up out of your graves,** My people, And I will put My Spirit within you, and **you will come to life,** and I will place you on your own land. Then you will know that I, the LORD, have spoken and done it," declares the LORD...."And My **servant David will be king over them,** and they will all have one shepherd; and they will walk in My ordinances, and keep My statutes, and observe them" [Ezek. 37:12-14,24].

It is best to place the resurrection of the church at the Rapture, and the resurrection for martyred tribulation saints and Old Testament saints after the Tribulation. Presumably, these saints obtain rewards at this time (see Luke 14:14). They seem to be resurrected before the Judgment of the Israelites who have survived the Tribulation and the Judgment of the Nations, because the Lord warned that unbelieving Jews will weep when they see gentiles feasting with "Abraham, Isaac, Jacob, and all the prophets" while they are cast out of the Kingdom (Matt. 8:11-12; Luke 13:28-29). [48]

---

[48] The Lord's warning has more direct connection to entrance into the Kingdom if these unbelieving Jews are tribulational survivors who see gentiles about to enjoy a lengthy Kingdom with the Jewish patriarchs. However, one might also see a fulfillment for Jesus' prediction at the Great

d. Millennial Saints

Although effects from the curse of sin will be greatly minimized during the Millennium, they are not eradicated. Lifespans increase, but death is still a reality (see Isa. 65:20). It is safe to assume that saints will die during the Kingdom age, even if some do live many hundreds of years. Scripture says nothing about their resurrection and reward. Some adhere to the idea of instantaneous resurrection and reward for each saint who dies. Others believe that there will be group resurrection of all millennial saints at the end of the Kingdom.

C. Judgment for Israel

1. Texts

Ezekiel 20 and Malachi 3 warn of a future Judgment for Israel. In addition, several of Christ's parables concern a Lord who will return and cast unprofitable servants into outer darkness (see Luke 12:41ff., especially v. 46; Luke 19:14 and 27; Matt. 25:14ff., especially v. 30). The doctrine of Eternal Security compels one to adopt the view that these "servants" who end in torment are not part of the church, but rather they are unsaved Jews. Being Jewish, they are in a sense servants of God. Yet, when Christ returns some are excluded from Kingdom blessings. Details about a future judgment for Israel come primarily from the Old Testament.

> "As I live," declares the Lord God, "surely with a mighty hand and with an outstretched arm and with wrath poured out, I shall be king over you. And I shall bring you out from the peoples and gather you from the lands where you are scattered, with a mighty hand and with an outstretched arm and with wrath poured out; and I shall bring you into the wilderness of the peoples, and there I shall enter into judgment with you face to face. As I entered into judgment with your fathers in the wilderness of the land of Egypt, so **I will enter into judgment with you**," declares the Lord GOD. "**And I shall make you pass under the rod**, and I shall bring you into the bond of the covenant; and **I shall purge from you the rebels and those who transgress against Me**; I shall bring them out of the land where they sojourn, but they will not enter the land of Israel. Thus you will know that I am the LORD. As for you, O house of Israel," thus says the Lord GOD, "Go, serve everyone his idols; but later, you will surely listen to Me, and My holy name you will profane no longer with your gifts and with your idols. For on My holy mountain, on the high mountain of Israel," declares the Lord GOD, "there the whole house of Israel, all of them, will serve Me in the land; there I shall accept them, and there I shall seek your contributions and the choicest of your gifts, with all your holy things. As a soothing aroma I shall accept you, when I bring you out from the peoples and gather you from the lands where you are scattered; and I shall prove Myself holy among you in the sight of the nations. And you will know that I am the LORD when I bring you into the land of Israel, into the land which I swore to give to your forefathers. And there you will remember your ways and all your deeds, with which you have defiled yourselves; and you will loathe yourselves in your own sight for all the evil things that you have done. Then you will know that I am the LORD when I have dealt with you for My name's sake, not according to your evil ways or according to your

---

White Throne Judgment where unbelieving Jews may also see saved gentiles enjoying the company of Abraham, Isaac, and Jacob.

465

corrupt deeds, O house of Israel," declares the Lord God [Ezek.20:33-44].

"Behold, I am going to send My messenger, and he will clear the way before Me. And the **Lord,** whom you seek, **will suddenly come to His temple**; and the messenger of the covenant, in whom you delight, behold, He is coming," says the LORD of hosts. "But who can endure the day of His coming? And who can stand when He appears? For He is like a refiner's fire and like fullers' soap. And He will sit as a smelter and purifier of silver, and He will purify the sons of Levi and refine them like gold and silver, so that they may present to the LORD offerings in righteousness. Then the offering of Judah and Jerusalem will be pleasing to the LORD, as in the days of old and as in former years. **Then I will draw near to You for judgment** and I will be a swift witness against the sorcerers and against the adulterers and against those who swear falsely, and against those who oppress the wage earner in his wages, the widow and the orphan, and those who turn aside the alien, and do not fear Me," says the LORD of hosts. "For I, the LORD do not change; therefore, you, O sons of Jacob are not consumed" [Mal. 3:1-6].

2. The Subjects of the Judgment of Israel

Ezekiel 20 and Malachi 3 refer to a judgment for **Israel**, more specifically, **living as opposed to resurrected** Israel. Ezek. 20:39-40 addresses the "house of Israel." Verse 42 says the land of Israel is the land of the forefathers of those judged. Verse 36 speaks of these forefathers as being "in the wilderness in the land of Egypt," This means Israelites. Verse 34 says those who will be judged are brought "out from the peoples." Malachi 3 just as clearly speaks of a judg-

ment for the "sons of Levi" (v. 3), "Judah and Jerusalem" (v. 4), and the "sons of Jacob" (v. 6). Thus, Israel will be judged.

Neither chapter teaches about a resurrection from the dead. On the contrary, the people that Ezekiel has in mind come not from graves but out from the countries where they have been living (vv. 34 and 38). This judgment concerns **living** Israel and is not the same as a judgment for resurrected Old Testament saints.

3. The Time for Judgment on Living Israel

Ezek. 20:34-38 speaks of a time of restoration after dispersion. It is at a time of the direct rule of God, for this judgment is "face to face" (v. 35) with God Himself as king (v. 33). It is at a time when the New Covenant will be ratified with Israel (v. 37). After this judgment everyone left in Israel will be saved because v. 40 says "...**the whole house of Israel, all of them will serve Me** in the land; there I shall accept them" (see also v. 43). Rom. 11:26 says the time when all Israel is saved is at Christ's coming. All lines of evidence from Ezekiel 20 point to a judgment for living Israel, after the Second Coming but before the Kingdom.

Mal. 3:1-2a also places a judgment for living Israel at the time of the Lord's coming. "...And **the Lord**, whom you seek, **will suddenly come** to His temple ... behold He is coming ... who can endure the day of His coming..." (Mal. 3:1-2a).

By virtue of being a chosen people all Jews are in a sense the servants of God. Christ gave several parables in which a lord judges his servants after a return from a long journey. Some obtain rewards. Some obtain punishment with unbelievers (Matt. 24:50-51; 25:30 etc.).

When Christ returns He will judge all the Jews who have survived the tribulation period. The saved can enter the Kingdom. The unsaved cannot. [49]

4. The Place and Purpose for Judgment upon Living Israel

Angels assist in both gathering the elect (Matt. 24:31) and sorting out unbelievers (Matt. 13:41-42,49-50). Ezek. 20:35 teaches that Christ will judge living Israel "in the wilderness of the peoples," i.e., gentile territory outside of the entrance to the land of Israel. Verse 36 compares the future judgment to judgment with their forefathers in the wilderness wandering. Apparently, the Lord will set up "divine check points" along the borders of Israel. During the transition from Tribulation to Kingdom only saved Israelites may enter the land after Christ judges and gives clearance.

Ezek. 20:38 gives the purpose for judging living Israel as purging out the rebels and preventing them from entering the land of Israel. Mal. 3:2-3 teaches that the Lord will come to purify and refine Israel as fire refines precious metals and soap cleanses out filth.

"[A]nd **I shall purge from you the rebels** and those who transgress against Me; I shall bring them out of the land where they sojourn, but **they will not enter the land of Israel…**" [Ezek. 20:38].

"But who can endure the day of His coming? And who can stand when He appears? For He is like a **refiner's fire** and like fuller's soap. And He will sit as a smelter and **purify the sons of Levi** and refine them like gold and silver…"[Mal. 3:2-3].

God's purpose guarantees the results. The flock "passes under the rod" (Ezek. 20:37) so the shepherd can identify those who are His.

5. Results from the Judgment of Israel

a. Negative Results

All the unsaved Jews who have survived the Tribulation will be excluded from the Kingdom and cast into punishment. (See also Ezek. 20:38; probably Matt. 8:11-12; probably Luke 13:28-29, unless they refer exclusively to the Great White Throne).

"[T]he master of that slave will come on a day when he does not expect him and at an hour which he does not know, and shall cut him in pieces and assign him a place with the hypocrites; weeping shall be there and gnashing of teeth" [Matt. 24:50-51].

"And cast out the worthless slave into the outer darkness; in that place there shall be weeping and gnashing of teeth" [Matt. 25:30].

"[T]he master of that slave will come on a day when he does not expect him, and at an hour he does not know, and will cut him in pieces, and assign him a place with the unbelievers" [Luke 12:46].

b. Positive Results

The Judgment of Israel will be a blessing to the saved Jews who have survived the Tribulation. They can enter the Kingdom. Another result will be the fulfillment of those prophecies that predict a time when every

---

[49] One arrangement places the judgment of Jews who survive the Tribulation before the judgment of the gentile survivors. The thinking is that gentiles will be evaluated on how they treated Christ's Jewish brethren (Matt. 25:40,45). Thus, perhaps believing Jews must be first distinguished from unbelieving Jews so they can be used as examples for the judgment of gentiles that follows. That could be true. However, since unsaved Jews must see gentiles enjoying the Kingdom with the patriarchs (Matt. 8:11-12; Luke 13:28-29), we could easily argue the Judgment of the Nations comes before the Judgment of Israel.

Israelite on earth shall be saved (see also Ezek. 20:37-38).

"But this is the covenant which I will make with the house of Israel after those days," declares the LORD. "I will put My law within them, and on their heart I will write it; and I will be their God, and they shall be My people. And they shall not teach again, each man his neighbor and each man his brother, saying, know the LORD. For **they shall all know** Me, from the least of them to the greatest of them, declares the LORD, for I will forgive their iniquity, and their sin I will remember no more" [Jer. 31:33-34] (see also Heb. 8:11-12).

"For on My holy mountain, on the high mountain of Israel," declares the Lord God, "there **the whole house of Israel, all of them, will serve Me in the land;** there I shall accept them, and there I shall seek your contributions and the choicest of your gifts, with all your holy things" [Ezek. 20:40].

"For I will take you from the nations, gather you from all the lands, and bring you into your own land. Then I will sprinkle clean water on you, and **you will be clean,** I will cleanse you from all your filthiness and from all your idols" [Ezek. 36:24-25 (see also v. 26)].

"And I will bring the third part through the fire, refine them as silver is refined, and test them as gold is tested. They will call on My name, and I will answer them; I will say **'They are My people'**, and they will say, **'The LORD is my God' "** [Zech. 13:9].

And the LORD will be **king over all the earth**; in that day the LORD will be the only one, and His name the only one [Zech. 14:9].

[A]nd thus **all Israel will be saved**; just as it is written, "The Deliverer will come from Zion, He will remove ungodliness from Jacob" [Rom. 11:26].

D. The Judgment of the Nations

After the Second Coming, the Old Testament saints will be raised and living Israel will be judged. Christ will also judge all the gentiles who have survived the Tribulation to determine entrance into or exclusion from the Kingdom.

1. Texts Concerning the Judgment of the Nations

Two main texts cover the Judgment of the Nations that will take place after Christ's return (see also Matt. 13:41-43,49).

"For behold, in those days and at that time, when I restore the fortunes of Judah and Jerusalem, I will gather all the nations, and bring them down to the valley of Jehoshaphat. Then I will enter into judgment with them there on behalf of My people and My inheritance, Israel, whom they have scattered among the nations; and they have divided up My land....Let the nations be aroused and come up to the valley of Jehoshaphat, For there I will sit to judge all the surrounding nations....Multitudes, multitudes in the valley of decision! For the day of the LORD is near in the valley of decision" [Joel 3:1-2, 12,14]. (This text stresses Armageddon as God's judgment, but it might also include the Judgment of The Nations which follows the battle).

"But when the Son of Man comes in His glory, and all the angels with Him, then He will sit on His glorious throne. And all the nations will be gathered before Him; and will separate them from one another, as the shepherd separates the sheep from the goats; and He will put the sheep on His right, and the goats on the left. Then the King will say to those on His right, 'Come, you who are blessed of My Father, inherit the kingdom prepared for you from the foundation of the world. For I was hungry, and you gave Me something to eat; I was thirsty, and you gave Me drink; I was a stranger, and you invited Me in; naked, and you clothed Me; I was sick and you visited Me; I was in prison, and you came to Me.' Then the righteous will answer Him, saying 'Lord, when did we see You hungry, and feed You, or thirsty, and give You drink? And when did we see You a stranger, and invite You in, or naked, and clothe you? And when did we see You sick, or in prison, and come to You?' And the King will answer and say to them, 'Truly I say to you, to the extent that You did it to one of these brothers of Mine, even the least of them, you did it to Me.' Then He will also say to those on His left, 'Depart from Me accursed ones, into the eternal fire which has been prepared for the devil and his angels; for I was hungry, and you gave Me nothing to eat; I was thirsty, and you gave Me nothing to drink; I was a stranger, and you did not invite Me in; naked, and you did not clothe Me; sick, and in prison, and you did not visit Me.' Then He will answer them, saying, 'Truly I say to you, to the extent that you did not do it to one of the least of these, you did not do it to Me.' And these will go away into eternal punishment, but the righteous into eternal life" [Matt. 25:31-46].

2. The Time for the Judgment of the Nations

The section in Matthew 25 which teaches about a coming Judgment of the Nations begins with a reference to Christ's Second Coming (Matt. 25:31) and the formation of the Kingdom (v. 34). It also occurs in a context dealing with end-time events including the Second Coming (Matt. 24:30-31, 25:13). The Judgment of the Nations occurs after Christ's return to earth (see Matt. 8:11-12; Luke 13:28-29).

3. The Place for the Judgment of the Nations

Given that this judgment occurs after Christ's return, it follows that it takes place on earth. Joel 3 mentions a location that seems to be near Jerusalem, although the identity of the Valley of Jehoshaphat is not completely certain.

4. The Subjects of the Judgment of the Nations

There is **no mention of resurrection in Matthew 24-25**. Thus, the subjects for this judgment are those **who have lived through the Tribulation**. The word translated "nations" is *ethna* which could also be translated "gentiles." In the KJV, *ethna* was translated "nations" approximately 61 times, but translated "gentile" approximately 93 times. Upon His return Christ the King will judge all living **gentiles**. The word "nations" can be misunderstood if by it a reader thinks in terms of Christ's judgment upon Brazil, Germany, Egypt, or the United States. The judgment of the gentiles is a judgment of **individual gentiles who have survived the Tribulation**. By this judgment **Christ determines who can enter the Kingdom** (v. 34) and who has eternal life (v. 46). As the verses in other sections prove, salvation, including entrance into the Kingdom, is based upon a personal (not a national) decision. Therefore, the Judgment of the Nations concerns **individual gentiles who have lived through the Tribulation** on earth.

5. Purpose

No unsaved person may enter the Kingdom.

Jesus answered and said to him, "Truly, truly, I say to you, **unless one is born again, he cannot see the kingdom of God**" [John 3:3].

[A]nd said, "Truly I say to you, unless you are converted and become like children you shall not enter the kingdom of heaven" [Matt. 18:3].

By the Judgment of the Nations (gentiles), Christ determines who may enter and who may not enter His Kingdom. He uses angels to transport people to this judgment that sorts the "sheep" from the "goats", the "wheat" from the "tares", and the "good" fish from the "bad" (Matt. 25:32-34, 41, 46; 13:30, 36-43, 47-50).

6. The Basis for Judgment

The Bible teaches that salvation is by grace through faith (see pp. 130-32). The Lord specifically teaches that being "born again" is a qualification for entrance into the Kingdom (John 3:3; Matt. 18:3). Therefore, ultimately the issue at the Judgment of the Nations must be to separate those with faith from those without faith.

The King in Matt. 25:34-40 evaluates positively those who have fed, clothed, visited, and supported His "brethren" in their time of affliction. These can enter the Kingdom (v.34, 46b). In Matt. 25:41-45 the King evaluates negatively those who refused to feed, clothe, visit, and care for His "brethren" in their time of need. They end up in eternal fire (v.41, 46a). Unfortunately, it is not unusual for shallow Bible teachers to distort Matt. 25:31-46 in messages designed to promote humanitarian efforts to relieve physical suffering. By application, these verses do indeed show that God is pleased with good works to help the suffering. Nevertheless, **unless the passage is placed into its eschatological context and unless there is a firm commitment to salvation by faith, careless teaching of Matthew 25 can** leave the impression that eternal destiny is a matter of works.

On the contrary, Matt. 25:31ff. can be and indeed must be interpreted in a way that makes it compatible with justification by faith alone. It must not be taken to mean that people can earn salvation by their works of feeding, sheltering, or clothing the needy.

Christ's "brethren" are Jewish people. The setting as to time concerns a period in which the Antichrist has been slaughtering Jews. During the Tribulation only believing gentiles will refuse to worship the Beast and reject participating in his program of anti-Semitism. It is not that salvation can be earned because of kindness to Jews, but **salvation will definitely be exhibited by a person's kind treatment of Jews during the Tribulation.** The only friends Jewish people will have during this time of horrible persecution are going to be believers. Therefore, Christ can examine the matter of gentile deeds toward tribulational Jews as a **sure indication of whether a person has faith or not**. It is not that He grants salvation on the basis of works, rather He can examine attitudes and actions toward the Jews as a certain evidence of either the presence or absence of faith. Those who defy the Antichrist by protecting Jews demonstrate a heart of faith. Those who actively destroy or who are passively unconcerned about tribulational Jews demonstrate their unbelief.

7. Results of the Judgment of The Nations

The gentile "sheep" on the King's right have given a demonstration that they are believers through their willingness to befriend the Jews. They enter the Kingdom (Matt. 25:34), and have eternal life (v. 46b). Christ told the Jews of His day that many gentiles would enjoy the Kingdom (Matt. 8:11-12; Luke 13:28-29; see also Isa. 2:3, 55:5ff.; Dan. 7:14; Micah 4:2; Zech. 14:16-17 for gentiles in the Kingdom).

The gentile "goats" on the King's left have shown their lack of faith by helping the Antichrist persecute the Jews. They will enter eternal fire (Matt. 25:41,46a). [50]

The combined result of both the Judgment of Israel and the Judgment of the Nations will be that **the Kingdom begins with only saved people** (see also John 3:3, Matt. 13:41,49 18:3).

E. Appointments to Authority in the Kingdom

If the interpretation of Dan. 12:11-12 given earlier is adopted, then the judgment of all tribulational survivors, Jews and gentiles, takes about 30 days (p. 462).

It is possible that the next 45 days involve the appointment and installment of believers in various positions of authority around the world. Regardless of the exact time frame involved, the transition from Tribulation to Kingdom will involve a placement of saints in positions to share in Christ's reign (see also Rom. 4:13-15).

> And Jesus said to them, "Truly, I say to you, that you who have followed Me, in the regeneration when the Son of Man will sit on His glorious throne, you also shall sit upon twelve thrones, **judging the twelve tribes** of Israel" [Matt. 19:28].

> [O]r do you not know that the saints will judge the world... [1 Cor. 6:2a].

> If we endure, we shall also **reign** with Him...[2 Tim. 2:12].

---

[50] From the description in Matt. 25:41,46 it seems those unbelievers who survive the Tribulation are cast directly into the eternal Lake of Fire following the Judgment of the Nations. Perhaps they avoid Hades (the place of departed unsaved spirits prior to judgment at the Great White Throne). Perhaps these who have already been personally condemned by the Lord Jesus Christ need not face Him again at the Great White Throne Judgment following the Millennium.

> "And he who overcomes, and he who keeps My deeds until the end, **to him will I give authority over the nations; and he shall rule them with a rod of iron,** as the vessels of the potter are broken to pieces, as I also have received authority from My Father" [Rev. 2:26-27].

> "And Thou hast made them to be a kingdom and priests to our God; and they **will reign upon the earth**" [Rev. 5:10].

> Blessed and holy is the one who has a part in the first resurrection; on these the second death has no power, but they will be priests of God and of Christ and **will reign with Him for a thousand years** [Rev. 20:6] (see also v. 4).

F. Summary of Events in the Transition from Tribulation to Kingdom

At the close of the Tribulation, Christ returns to the Mount of Olives east of Jerusalem. He destroys the Antichrist's armies. Tribulation and Old Testament saints are resurrected to enjoy the Kingdom. Those who have survived the Tribulation will be judged to determine eligibility for entrance into the Millennium. Christ will separate believing Israel from unbelieving Israel at the Judgment of Israel and believing gentiles from unbelieving gentiles at the Judgment of the Nations. Then Christ's glorious reign on earth begins by placing glorified believers in leadership positions in His Kingdom.

XIII. Christ's Kingdom on Earth (Millennium)

The Bible uses the word *kingdom* with several nuances. It can refer to God's general rule over the entire universe at all times (Psa. 103:19). The church is also a form of God's *kingdom*. Those who trust in Christ are translated from the kingdom of darkness to the "*kingdom* of His beloved Son" (Col. 1:13). This portion of prophetic study will show that many texts, if interpreted in a literal (normal) manner, teach that Christ will come to earth to rule over the world from Jerusalem in a literal earthly Kingdom of God.

Many Biblical references to the Kingdom of God or to the Kingdom of heaven refer to this coming Messianic reign of our Lord Jesus Christ.[51]

Because large numbers of conservative Protestants do not adhere to premillennialism, it is necessary to prove that Christ will establish a Kingdom on earth before giving conditions that will exist during that Kingdom. It can be asserted without reservation that literal interpretation of the Old Testament will lead to premillennial theology. Furthermore, God's covenants with Abraham, David, and the nation of Israel guarantee that Israel will have a future Kingdom.

A. The Abrahamic Covenant and Premillennialism

1. Scriptural Texts

God made His initial promises to Abraham in Gen. 12:1-3, 7, and He also repeated and expanded upon them in Gen. 13:14-17; 15:1-7, 18; 22:15-18. God also repeated His promises to Isaac in Gen. 26:3-5 and to Jacob in Gen. 28:12-15 (see also. Gen. 35:9-12; 48:4).

2. Recipients of the Promises

The Abrahamic Covenant involves three main recipients: Abraham himself, Abraham's seed, and all the nations of the world.

a. Abraham Himself

God promised Abraham that he would be the father of a great nation, a great "seed", (Gen. 12:2; 13:15-16; 15:5). He would even father

kings and other nations beyond the main nation (Gen. 17:6). Abraham himself would be blessed, his name would be great, and he would be a blessing to others (Gen. 12:2).

b. Abraham's Seed

Abraham's seed would become a great nation (Gen. 12:2). It would possess the land of Israel forever (Gen. 13:14-15,17; 15:18; 17:8). This seed would be innumerable (Gen. 15:5). It is clear from Gen. 17:19 and other passages that Abraham understood "seed" to mean physical descendants.

c. All the Nations (Gentiles)

Genesis 12:3 promises that all the nations of the earth would be blessed through Abraham. The main, but not exclusive, blessing would be justification by faith through Abraham's seed, the Lord Jesus Christ (Gal. 3:8). Those who blessed Abraham would be blessed. Those who cursed him would be cursed (Gen. 12:3).

3. The Nature of the Abrahamic Covenant

It may seem odd that much of ones eschatological system comes from the interpretation of passages found in Genesis. Nevertheless, the nature of the Abrahamic Covenant is a major topic in eschatology.

If God's promises to Abraham were conditional and/or temporary, then one need not worry about a future for the Jewish people in a scheme of future events. On the other hand, if God's promises to Abraham are unconditional and eternal, then there must yet be an eternal possession of the land by the Jewish people by means of Christ's Kingdom on earth (the Millennium).

Premillennialists accept the point that faith is a requirement for individual enjoyment of Abrahamic blessings, but they would insist that unbelief and/or disobedience by many individual Israelites cannot cancel out full Abrahamic blessings for the remaining believers among Abraham's offspring. The Abrahamic Covenant provides a major sup-

---

[51] There need not be any great difference between the terms "Kingdom of God" and "Kingdom of heaven". Because Hebrews were hesitant to overuse the name "God", they would substitute "heaven" as the prodigal son does in Luke 15:21.

port for premillennialism if it can be defended as an unconditional covenant that is literal and eternal.

a. One Condition

The only condition in the Abrahamic Covenant is that Abraham leave his land and his family. The Hebrew sentence contains an indirect volitive chain, which means that all the following verbs after "go" have the nuance of purpose or result. Thus, Gen. 12:1ff. can be translated:

"Go... with the result that I will make of you a great nation ... with the result that I will bless you... with the result that I will make your name great ... with the result that you will be a blessing."

Abraham obeyed the stipulation of leaving his homeland, and God provided his descendants the land (Genesis 12). This was really not much more than an invitation to enter God's blessings. Additions to the Abrahamic Covenant in Gen. 13:14-17 and 15:5 occur without any conditions. Abraham himself met the only condition that God required to bring the covenant into force. When the covenant promises are repeated to Israel, they are based upon **Abraham's obedience** (see Gen. 26:5). Thus, the belief/disobedience of following generations of Abraham's offspring does not break the covenant. It is based upon Abraham's single act of **obeying** the call to leave his land and family and move to the Promised Land.[52]

---

[52] Abraham also obeyed in the matter of circumcision (Gen 17:11ff.) and the preparation to sacrifice Isaac (Gen 22:18). These seem to be examples of ongoing obedience that display the same character as Abraham's original obedience in leaving his homeland. Perhaps continued obedience confirmed God's wisdom in His choice of Abraham in the original covenant or deepened Abraham's own personal enjoyment of blessings under it. However, the Abrahamic Covenant was already operative before Genesis 17 and 22. Additional tests just proved Abraham to be as obedient as he had been in leaving his native

b. The Eternal Nature of the Abrahamic Covenant

The Bible stresses the eternal (and thus unchangeable and unbreakable) nature of the Abrahamic covenant. If "eternal" means "eternal", then Israel must yet obtain possession of the land to the borders promised in Gen. 15:18 and must retain **eternal possession** of it. Notice that many of these verses reaffirm the covenant to Abraham after literally centuries of failure by the bulk of the Jewish nation. Promises relative to other covenants are also repeated long after Israel's deepest failures.

[F]or all the land which you see, I will give it to you and to your descendants **forever** [Gen. 13:15].

"And I will establish My covenant between Me and you and your descendants after you throughout their generations for an **everlasting covenant,** to be God to you and to your descendants after you....A servant who is born in your house or who is bought with your money shall surely be circumcised; thus shall my covenant be in your flesh for an **everlasting covenant**...." But God said "No, but Sarah your wife shall bear you a son, and you shall call his name Isaac; and I will establish My covenant with him for an **everlasting covenant** for his descendants after him" [Gen. 17:7,13,19].

[A]nd He said to me, "Behold, I will make you fruitful and numerous, and I will make you a company of peoples, and will give this land to your

---

land. They can be viewed as extensions of Abraham's original obedience. Gen. 22:18 expresses God's delight in Abraham's recent obedience and a deeper emotional commitment to give His chosen servant what He had already promised. The fulfillment of the Covenant was not in doubt until Abraham prepared to sacrifice Isaac, but now God is even more pleased to bless Abraham.

descendants after you for an **everlasting possession**" [Gen. 48:4].

The covenant which He made with Abraham, and His oath to Isaac. He also confirmed it to Jacob for a statute, to Israel as an **everlasting** covenant [1 Chron. 16:16-17].

He has remembered His covenant **forever,** the word which He commanded to a thousand generations, the covenant which He made with Abraham, and His oath to Isaac. Then He confirmed it to Jacob for a statute, to Israel as an **everlasting covenant** [Psa. 105:8-10].

"Nevertheless, **I will remember My covenant with you in the days of your youth**, and I will establish an **everlasting covenant** with you. Then you will remember your ways and be ashamed when you receive your sisters, both your older and your younger; and I will give them to you as daughters, but not because of your covenant. Thus, I will establish My covenant with you and you shall know that I am the LORD" [Ezek. 16:60-62].

"**And they shall live on the land that I gave to Jacob My servant**, in which your fathers lived; and **they will live on it**, they, and their sons, and their sons' sons, **forever**; and David My servant shall be their prince forever. And I will make a covenant of peace with them; it will be an **everlasting covenant** with them. And I will place them and multiply them, and will set My sanctuary in their midst **forever**" [Ezek. 37:25-26].

c. The Failures of Abraham, Isaac, and Jacob

God promised blessing to Abraham conditioned upon his leaving his land and family.

Abraham complied. In the narratives about Abraham's subsequent life, God reiterates and enlarges His promises despite Abraham's disobedience. After Abraham sinned in Egypt (Gen. 12:10-20), God confirmed His promise (Gen. 13:14-17). Even after Abraham worked outside of God's will by fathering Ishmael (Gen. 16:1-16), God still restated His promise (Gen. 17:1-8).

The same chapter that describes Isaac's failure also confirms the covenant to him (Gen. 26:3-5). Likewise, after Jacob's treachery in Genesis 27, God still transfers the promise to him (Gen. 28:12; 35:9-12; 48:4). God did not place any conditions upon either Isaac or Jacob. [53] The Abrahamic Covenant is based upon a single act of Abraham's obedience. Subsequent failure by either Abraham or his seed cannot abrogate the promise of **everlasting possession of the land.**

d. One-Sided Contract

Gen. 15:8-17 discusses a ritual that confirms the Abrahamic Covenant. In ancient times parties to an agreement would walk between the carcasses of sacrificial victims to seal a treaty (see Jer. 34:18-19 for an example). The symbolism probably involves a curse that one who broke treaty stipulations would end up like the bloody and torn animals. In the ceremony relative to the Abrahamic Covenant, God put Abraham in a deep sleep and God alone passed between the parts of the sacrifice. This means that Abraham had no further obligation to meet in order for the covenant to be fulfilled. Relative to any further requirements for Abraham to meet, the covenant was totally unconditional. God alone incurred all the obligations to fulfill **His** promise.

---

[53] Gen. 26:3 does not condition the Abrahamic Covenant upon Isaac remaining in Canaan. Rather, the fact that God would give his descendants the land is the basis for staying. Though Isaac's level of personal blessing would increase by the obedience of remaining in the land, the overall covenant was already secure.

e. The New Testament on the Abrahamic Covenant

Two key New Testament passages teach that the Abrahamic Covenant is unchangeable. It is significant that texts coming after God had set aside Israel and started the church still say the covenant to Abraham can not be changed. Thus, Abraham's seed, Israel, must obtain eternal possession of the land to the borders mentioned in Gen. 15:18.

> What I am saying is this; the Law, which came four hundred and thirty years later, does not invalidate a covenant previously ratified by God, so as to nullify the promise [Gal. 3:17].

> For when God made the promise to Abraham, since He could swear by no one greater, He swore by **Himself**.... In the same way God, desiring even more to show to the heirs of the promise **the unchangeableness of His purpose**, interposed with an oath, in order that **by two unchangeable** things, in which is it impossible for God to lie, we may have strong encouragement, we who have fled for refuge in laying hold of the hope set before us [Heb. 6:13,17-18].

f. Expansion of the Abrahamic Covenant in other Old Testament Covenants for Israel

The Abrahamic Covenant is foundational to the other Old Testament covenants that follow it (Palestinian, Davidic, New). The following materials will argue that these other covenants are unconditional and must still be fulfilled. If these covenants are unconditional, then the foundational promises to Abraham must also be unconditional. Any verse that shows that God has a future work with the nation of Israel also proves the unconditional nature of the Abrahamic Covenant. Most of these verses will be used in following sections (see Jer. 31:35-37; Matt. 19:28; 20:20-23; Luke 1:32-33; 22:29-30;

Acts 3:17-26; Rom. 11:1,25-27: Rev. 7:3-8; 20:1-6).

g. Literal Fulfillment

Portions of the Abrahamic promise have already been fulfilled in a very literal sense. Therefore, we should anticipate that in the future all the remaining items in the covenant will be fulfilled in a literal, not symbolic, sense. Abraham did become great materially (Gen. 13:2,5-7; 24:34-35) and spiritually (Gen. 18:19ff.; 22:10ff.). He was called the "friend of God" (2 Chron. 20:7; Isa. 41:8; James 2:23). Abraham did gain a great name. To this day Jews, Christians, and Moslems revere him. Abraham did become the father of a great nation, Israel, and the ancestor of kings. He also became the progenitor of other peoples, Midianites, Edomites, Amalekites, and various Arab tribes. He has been a blessing to all the families of the earth in that the written Word of God has come through Israel and the Living Word of God was born an Israelite.

The many literal fulfillments of the Abrahamic Covenant provide a strong basis for expecting a literal fulfillment of the promise that the nation which arose from Abraham must yet possess the land to the extent promised in Gen. 15:18 and possess it eternally.

h. Summary of the Nature of the Abrahamic Covenant

God promised that Abraham's seed would possess the land of Canaan to the borders mentioned in Gen. 15:18 and would hold it in an eternal sense. This promise is eternal in duration and unconditional in nature (i.e., unconditional after Abraham's initial obedience in leaving his family and homeland). The many promises to Abraham that have already been fulfilled literally mean that unfulfilled aspects must also be fulfilled literally.

Abraham would have understood his seed to be his physical descendants, Israel. **Israel must yet possess the land eternally.**

Among the eschatological systems, **premillennialism makes room for a future Kingdom that is largely Jewish in nature**.

B. The Davidic Covenant and Premillenialism

1. Texts

God gave David a covenant in 2 Sam. 7:12-16 and in 1 Chron. 17:11-14. Notice that God does not make **any** requirements of David.

> "When your days are complete and you lie down with your fathers, I will raise up your descendant after you, who will come forth from you, and I will establish his kingdom. He shall build a house for My name, and I will establish the throne of his kingdom forever. I will be a father to him and he will be a son to Me; when he commits iniquity, I will correct him with the rod of men and the strokes of the sons of men, but My lovingkindness shall not depart from him, as I took it from Saul, whom I removed from before you. And your house and your kingdom shall endure before Me forever; your throne shall be established forever" [2 Sam. 7:12-16].

> "And it shall come about when your days are fulfilled that you must go to be with your fathers, that I will set up one of your descendants after you, who shall be of your sons; and I will establish his kingdom. He shall build for Me a house, and I will establish his throne forever. I will be his father, and he shall be My son; and I will not take My lovingkindness away from him, as I took it from him who was before you. But I will settle him in My house and in My kingdom forever, and his throne shall be established forever" [1 Chron. 17:11-14].

2. Promises in the Davidic Covenant

a. Temporal Promises

Through Nathan, God promised David that one of David's sons (Solomon) would succeed him and establish David's kingdom (2 Sam. 7:12; 1 Chron. 17:11). This son would build the temple instead of David (2 Sam. 7:13; 1 Chron. 17:12). Though God might chasten David's son, He would never remove his crown, as happened to Saul (2 Sam. 7:14-15; 1 Chron. 17:13). The covenant leaves open the possibility that those ruling after David's son might lose their power. All of these temporal provisions were fulfilled literally, which indicates that the eternal provisions of the Davidic Covenant must also be fulfilled literally.

b. Eternal Promises

The **throne** of Solomon's kingdom would be established **forever**.

> "...and I will establish the **throne** of his [Solomon's] kingdom **forever**" [2 Sam. 7:13b].

> "...and I will establish his [Solomon's] **throne forever**" [1 Chron. 17:12b].

> "...and his [Solomon's] **throne** shall be established **forever**" [1 Chron 17:14b].

God gave a very specific and carefully worded prediction concerning David's son, Solomon. **Nathan did not say that Solomon's seed would endure or rule forever**, only that the **throne** of his kingdom would endure forever. Actually, Solomon's direct line was cut off from the right to rule by Jeremiah.

> "Thus says the LORD, 'Write this man down childless, A man who will not prosper in his days; For no man of his descendants will prosper Sitting on the throne of David or ruling again in Judah' " ...."Therefore thus says the LORD concerning Jehoiakim king of Judah, 'he shall have no one to sit on

the throne of David, and his dead body shall be cast out to the heat of the day and the frost of the night' " [Jer. 22:30; 36:30].

Mary, the mother of our Lord, was indeed a descendant of David but not through Solomon (see Luke 3:31). Jesus Christ is a Son of David but not a son of Solomon (who was a remote great uncle).[55] God predicted that Solomon's throne would be eternal but did not specifically say a son from Solomon would rule on it. It is fascinating that the line of Israel's eternal monarchy that actually sits on the throne runs directly from David to his Son, Jesus Christ. The only one of Christ's physical ancestors to ever rule over Jerusalem was David himself. The observation that God promised Solomon's throne but not necessarily his seed would be eternal says something about the precise nature of Biblical prophecy. Every word has significance. Amillennialists who interpret prophecy in a non-literal fashion do not give the details of the prophetic word the careful attention that they deserve.

God promised that Solomon's throne (but not necessarily his seed) would reign forever, but to David God promised that his house, kingdom, and throne would be eternal. Each element of the promise deserves attention.

> "And your **house** and your **kingdom** shall endure before Me **forever**; your **throne** shall be established **forever**" [2 Sam. 7:16] (see also 1 Chron. 17:14).

When God promised David an eternal house, He was not referring to the eternality of the temple building. "House" in 2 Sam. 7:11,16 and 1 Chron. 17:10,14 refers to a dynasty or family. Historians speak of the "House of York" or the "House of Lancaster." The Bible uses the phrase "the House of Saul" or "the House of Ahab" to speak of royal families. The promise that David's "house" would be eternal is a guarantee that his family line would never end. Sometimes when a wicked king was overthrown his entire family would be massacred to end the dynasty. This happened to Ahab (see 2 Kings 10:10-11). God promised that there would be no end to David's line. His royal lineage would never be exterminated.

Next, God promised David an eternal Kingdom. This means that at some point in time David's descendants must come to power with such authority that the Israelite Kingdom would be eternal from that time forward.

Finally, God promised to David an eternal throne. This does not mean that one of David's descendants had to have actual political authority at all times. It means that the royal Davidic family would always have the divine right to legitimate power over the nation. The ultimate right of sovereignty would never be transferred to another family regardless of who may have temporarily occupied the throne. [56]

The covenant guaranteed that David's family would always exist and that it would always be the rightful royal dynasty with a moral right to the throne. Furthermore, there must at sometime be the establishment of a Davidic Kingdom and a Davidic throne that can never cease.

The fact that a Davidic king is not now ruling in Jerusalem is evidence that the eternal Kingdom and to some degree the eternal

---

[55] Joseph did arise from Solomon's line and was Jesus' legal father (Matt. 1:7ff.). However, since Jesus was not biologically related to Joseph, he avoided Jeremiah's curse. See J. Dwight Pentecost, *The Words and Works of Jesus Christ* (Grand Rapids: Zondervan Publishing House, 1981), pp. 33-39 for support on these remarks about the Lord's genealogy.

[56] This explains why King Herod (who was not racially Jewish) felt so threatened by one from David's line being born King of the Jews (Matt. 2:1ff.).

throne aspects to the Davidic Covenant are unfulfilled.

Premillennialists believe that the Davidic Covenant is still in force and must yet be fulfilled. A Davidic descendant must usher in a Kingdom and a throne that cannot end. Since no such Kingdom exists at the present time, it must be that Jesus Christ, the Son of David, will bring in this great and eternal Kingdom at His Second Coming.

c. The Davidic Covenant and the Broken Line of Rule

The fact that David's seed have not enjoyed unbroken rule and his kingdom has not lasted is no embarrassment to the promises made in the Davidic Covenant. The Davidic Covenant does not necessitate an unbroken succession of rule by David's descendants. It promised that David's family would endure, that it would always have the right to rule, and that eventually one of David's sons would indeed establish an eternal throne and Kingdom. However, the original covenant included the possibility that some of David's sons would lose actual rule before the establishment of this eternal Kingdom. David believed the promise that his family would endure and would at a certain point in time establish an eternal throne and Kingdom, but even he anticipated that in the meantime there need not be a completely unbroken succession of kings from his line (see Psa. 89:38-52 which stresses the eternal nature of the Davidic Covenant).

> Thou hast made his splendor to cease, and cast his throne to the ground [Psalm 89:44].

In fact, the "royal line" through which the ultimate Son of David, Christ Himself, comes **never** had actual control over the ancient kingdom of Israel. The lineage from David through Nathan, through Mary to Jesus, which will fulfill the promise of an eternal throne and Kingdom, has **never** actually ruled in Jerusalem. On the other hand, the

line of Davidic kings that did rule over Israel and Judah from Solomon to the Babylonian exile is **not** the lineage that brings in the eternal Davidic Kingdom. These facts ought to demonstrate that the Davidic Covenant never promised an unbroken line of kings who actually rule from David's own time into eternity. The covenant guarantees that David's family would endure and that royal prerogative and right to the throne would always belong to it. The right of David's line to the throne would never be lost even in sin, captivity, and dispersion. Eventually, one of David's descendants would establish an eternal Kingdom, but prior to that a continuous unbroken line of sons in control of government in Jerusalem is not necessary to the original stipulations of the covenant. In fact, while the house, right to the throne, and eventually the whole Kingdom must be eternal, the privilege of any given Davidic king ruling in Jerusalem was conditioned upon his obedience (1 Kings 8:25; 2 Chron. 6:16; Psa. 132:11-12).

In addition, every promise about the Davidic Kingdom written after the exile (586 B.C.) proves that God still considered the Davidic Covenant to be in force even though the Davidic line no longer actually ruled over Israel. By New Testament times David's descendants had not ruled over any part of Israel for between 500 and 600 years. Yet, the New Testament still teaches that a Son of David will bring in an eternal rule. God preserved David's "house" (family). It still had an eternal right to the throne. One of David's "sons", Christ, the Son of David, must still bring in an eternal throne and an eternal Kingdom in order to fulfill the Davidic Covenant. Nearly 600 years after the last Davidic king actually reigned in Jerusalem, God made this announcement about one who came from a branch of David's family that had never ruled:

> "He will be great, and will be called the Son of the Most High; and the Lord God will give Him **the throne**

of His father David; and He will reign over the house of Jacob forever; and His kingdom will have no end" [Luke 1:32-33].

3. Nature of the Davidic Covenant

There is little excuse for neglecting the truth that God's promises to David came without conditions and were eternal. The Davidic Covenant supports the premillennial system. Christ will return to bring in a literal/political dominion over the earth with Jerusalem as its capital.

a. The Davidic Covenant Stated to be Eternal

"He shall build a house for My name, and I will establish the throne of his kingdom **forever**....And your house and your kingdom shall endure before Me **forever**; your throne shall be established **forever**" [2 Sam. 7:13,16].

"Truly is not my house so with God? For He has made an **everlasting** covenant with me, ordered in all things, and secured; for all my salvation and all my desire, will he not indeed make it grow" [2 Sam. 23:5].

"He shall build for Me a house, and I will establish his throne **forever**....But I will settle him in My house and in My kingdom **forever**, and his throne shall be established **forever**" [1 Chron.17:12,14].

"Incline your ear and come to Me. Listen, that you may live; and I will make an **everlasting** covenant with you, according to the faithful mercies shown to **David**" [Isa. 55:3].

And the word of the LORD came to Jeremiah, saying, "Thus says the LORD, **if you can break My covenant for the day, and My covenant for the night**, so that day and night will not be at their appointed time,

then **My covenant may also be broken with David My servant that he shall not have a son to reign on his throne,** and with the Levitical priests, My ministers. **As the host of heaven cannot be counted,** and the sand of the sea cannot be measured, **so I will multiply the descendants of David** My servant and the Levites who minister to Me." And the word of the LORD came to Jeremiah saying, "Have you not observed what this people have spoken, saying, The two families which the LORD chose, He has rejected them? Thus they despise My people, no longer are they as a nation in their sight." Thus says the LORD, "if My covenant for day and night stand not, and the fixed patterns of heaven and earth I have not established, then I would reject the descendants of Jacob and **David** My servant, not taking from his descendants rulers over the descendants of Abraham, Isaac, and Jacob. But I will restore their fortunes and will have mercy on them" [Jer. 33: 19-26].

b. The Davidic Covenant Confirmed with an Unchanging Oath

"I have made a covenant with My chosen; **I have sworn to David My servant**, I will establish your seed **forever,** and build up your throne **to all generations**....My loving kindness I will keep for him **forever**, and My covenant shall be confirmed to him. So will I establish his descendants **forever**, and his throne as the days of heaven....But I will not break off My loving kindness from him, nor deal falsely in My faithfulness. **My covenant I will not violate,** nor will I alter the utterance of My lips. **Once I have sworn by My holiness; I will not lie to David.** His descendants shall endure forever, and **his throne** as the sun before Me. It shall be established **forever** like the moon, and the witness in the sky is faithful" [Psa. 89:3-4, 28-29, 33-37].

The Davidic Covenant is in reality an extension of the Abrahamic Covenant. Both are unconditional. Both are eternal. Just as God confirmed the Abrahamic Covenant with an oath (Heb. 6:17-18), so also He swore an unchangeable oath to David.

c. The Covenant Reaffirmed after Sin

Many of the following verses could be placed in previous categories. However, it is good to stress that God repeated His intention to keep His covenant with David even after generations of faithless apostasy. Reassurance that God considers the Davidic Covenant still operative was given when exile was certain, during the exile, and even in New Testament times.[57] The first ancestor associated with Christ is David in Matt. 1:1. The first quotation in the New Testament reads, "Joseph, son of David".... Throughout the New Testament (which is long after the exile and cessation of David's rule), there are still constant references to a Kingdom with Christ (David's son) being the King: Matt. 3:2; 4:17; 10:7; 19:28; 20:20ff.; 21:5,9,15; Luke 10:9; Acts 1:6-7; 3:19ff.; Rom. 11:25-27; Rev. 20:4).

> For a child will be born to us, a son will be given to us; and the government will rest on His shoulders; and His name will be called Wonderful Counselor, Mighty God, Eternal Father, Prince of Peace. There will be no end to the increase of His government or of peace, **on the throne of David** and over his kingdom, to establish it and to uphold it with jus-

tice and righteousness from then on and forevermore. The zeal of the LORD of hosts will accomplish this [Isa. 9:6-7].

"Behold, the days are coming, declares the LORD, when **I shall raise up for David a righteous Branch;** and He will reign as king and act wisely and do justice and righteousness in the land. In His days Judah will be saved, and Israel will dwell securely; and this is His name by which He will be called, 'The LORD our righteousness' " [Jer. 23:5-6].

"And it shall come about on that day", declares the LORD, of hosts, "that I will break his yoke from off their neck, and will tear off their bonds; and strangers shall no longer make them their slaves. But they shall serve the LORD their God, and **David their king,** whom I will raise up for them" [Jer. 30:8-9].

"Behold, days are coming, declares the LORD, "when I will fulfill the good word which I have spoken concerning the house of Israel and the house of Judah. In those days and at that time **I will cause a righteous Branch of David to spring forth;** and He shall execute justice and righteousness on the earth. In those days Judah shall be saved, and Jerusalem shall dwell in safety; and this is the name by which she shall be called; the LORD is our righteousness. For thus says the LORD, **David shall never lack a man to sit on the throne of the house of Israel....** Thus says the LORD, "**if you can break My covenant for the day, and My covenant for the night,** so that day and night will not be at their appointed time, then **My covenant may also be broken with David** My servant that he shall not have a son to

---

[57] Although the Davidic covenant is not mentioned directly in Romans 11, that chapter was written long after the exile and demise of the Davidic dynasty. Despite Israel's failures, Romans 11 clearly promises a future for Israel (see vv. 25-29).

reign on this throne, and with the Levitical priests, My ministers. As the host of heaven cannot be counted, and the sand of the sea cannot be measured, so I will multiply the descendants of **David My servant** and the Levites who minister to Me"....Thus says the LORD, "If My covenant for day and night stand not, and the fixed patterns of heaven and earth I have not established, then I would reject the descendants of Jacob and **David My servant**, not taking from his descendants rulers over the descendants of Abraham, Isaac, and Jacob. But I will restore their fortunes and will have mercy on them" [Jer. 33:14-17, 20-22, 25-26].

"And My servant **David will be king over them**, and they will all have one shepherd; and they will walk in My ordinances, and keep My statutes, and observe them. And they shall live on the land that I gave to Jacob My servant, in which your fathers lived; and they will live on it, they and their sons, and their sons' sons, forever; and **David My servant shall be their prince forever**" [Ezek. 37:24-25].

For the sons of Israel will remain for many days without king or prince, without sacrifice or sacred pillar, and without ephod or household idols. Afterward the sons of Israel will return and seek the LORD their God and **David their king**; and they will come trembling to the LORD and to His goodness in the last days [Hosea 3:4-5].

"In that day I **will raise up the fallen booth of David**, and wall up its breaches; and rebuild it as in the days of old" [Amos 9:11].

"And behold, you will conceive in your womb, and bear a son, and you shall name Him Jesus. He will be great, and will be called the Son of the Most High; **and the Lord God will give Him the throne of His father David**; and He will reign over the house of Jacob forever; and His kingdom will have no end" [Luke 1:31-33].

Both the force of the language and the timing of the restatement (after much sin by Israel) make the Davidic Covenant as certain as human words can. **If a Davidic Kingdom is still being promised after the exile and after six centuries without a descendant of David sitting on the throne, then what can possibly cancel the Covenant with David?** If Israel still has a future even after it had rejected the King at His first coming (Rom. 11:1,25-27), then what sin would possibly negate the promise of an eternal throne and an eternal Kingdom? **There must be a future Kingdom with David's Son on an eternal throne.** *Only* the premillennial position does justice to the Abrahamic and Davidic Covenants.

The third covenant that provides an important basis for premillennialism is the New Covenant.

C. The New Covenant and Premillennialism

The Bible predicts that God will make a New Covenant with Israel.

The New Covenant provides additional guarantees that Israel must yet enjoy a great Kingdom. Since the New Covenant has not yet been fulfilled relative to Israel, it must be that this Kingdom will come to pass after Christ's return (premillennialism).

1. Texts Concerning the New Covenant.

Many texts refer to a future covenant that God will make with Israel in contrast to the Old Covenant, which is the Law of Moses. Sometimes this future covenant is called the "New Covenant." Other designations that seem to be equivalent are "covenant of peace" and "everlasting covenant." [58] There are many texts which do not give any special name to the future covenant, but theologians usually prefer to call it the New Covenant because of the Lord's usage at the Last Supper. New Testament references to the New Covenant will be covered in a separate section as they raise some questions about whether the New Covenant is or is not currently in force (pp. 487-89).[59]

> "Behold, days are coming", declares the LORD, "when I will make a **new covenant** with the house of Israel and with the house of Judah, not like the covenant which I made with their fathers in the day I took them by the hand to bring them out of the land of Egypt, My covenant which they broke, although I was a husband to them", declares the LORD. "But this is the covenant which I will make with the house of Israel after those days", declares the LORD, "I will put My law within them, and on their heart I will write, it; and I will be their God, and they shall be My people. And they shall not teach again, each man his neighbor and each man his brother, saying, 'Know the LORD', for they shall all know Me, from the least of them to the greatest of them", declares the LORD, "for I will forgive their iniquity, and their sin I will remember no more." Thus says the LORD, who gives the sun for light by day, and the fixed order of

the moon and the stars for light by night, who stirs up the sea so that its waves roar; The LORD of hosts is His name, "If this fixed order departs from before Me", declares the LORD, "then the offspring of Israel also shall cease from being a nation before Me forever". Thus says the LORD, "if the heavens above can be measured, and the foundations of the earth searched out below, then I will also cast off all the offspring of Israel for all that they have done", declares the LORD...." And the whole valley of the dead bodies and of the ashes, and all the fields as far as the brook Kidron, to the corner of the Horse Gate toward the east, shall be holy to the LORD; it shall not be plucked up, or overthrown anymore **forever**" [Jer. 31:31-37, 40 (see also Ezek. 36:25ff. and 37:12-14ff. for predictions of similar spiritual conditions)

"And I will make an **everlasting covenant** with them that I will not turn away from them, to do them good; and I will put the fear of Me in their hearts so that they will not turn away from Me" [Jer. 32:40].

"And say to them, 'Thus says the Lord GOD, "Behold, I will take the sons of Israel from among the nations where they have gone, and I will gather them from every side and bring them into their own land; and I will make them one nation in the land, on the mountains of Israel; and one king will be king for all of them; and they will no longer be two nations, and they will no longer be divided into two kingdoms. And they will no longer defile themselves with their idols, or with their detestable things, or with any of their transgressions: but I will deliver them from all their dwelling places in which they have sinned, and will cleanse them.

---

[58] See Jer. 32:40 and Ezek. 37:26.

[59] See also Ezek. 16:60-62; Isa. 55:3; 61:8 and Jer. 50:5 for mention of a future everlasting covenant. Ezek. 34:25-27 gives a reference to the "covenant of peace". Several texts teach of an unspecified future covenant with Israel: Isa. 59:20-21 (cf. Rom. 11:25ff.), and Hosea 2:18-20. New Testament references to the New Covenant are Luke 22:20; 1 Cor. 11:25; 2 Cor. 3:6; Heb. 8:8, 10-13; 9:15; 12:24. Matt. 26:28, Mark 14:24, and Rom. 11:27 speaks of a covenant with Israel without using the word "new".

And they will be My people, and I will be their God. And My servant David will be king over them, and they will all have one shepherd; and they will walk in My ordinances, and keep My statutes, and observe them. And they shall live on the land that I gave to Jacob My servant, in which your fathers lived; and they will live on it, they, and their sons, and their sons' sons, forever; and David My servant shall be their prince forever. And I will make a **covenant of peace** with them, it will be an **everlasting covenant** with them. And I will place them and multiply them, and will set My sanctuary in their midst forever" ' " [Ezek. 37:21-28].

2. Promises in the New Covenant

a. Salvation for All Jews

How does amillennialism incorporate into its system the prediction that at a point in time all Jews on earth must be saved? Premillennialists find fulfillment early in the Kingdom after Christ judges Israel and allows only believing Israel to remain on earth. The New Covenant includes a promise of an Israel that is totally accepting of her Messiah.

"At that time, declares the LORD, "**I will be the God of all families of Israel**, and they shall be My people" [Jer. 31:1].

"But this is the covenant which I will make with the house of Israel after those days," declares the LORD, "I will put My law within them, and on their heart I will write it; and I will be their God, and they shall be My people. And they shall not teach again each man his neighbor and each man his brother, saying, know the LORD, for **they shall all know Me**, from the least of them to the greatest of them," declares the LORD, "for I will forgive their iniquity and their sin I will re-

member no more" [Jer. 31:33-34 (see also Ezek. 37:23)].

... [A]nd thus all Israel will be saved: just as it is written, "**The Deliverer will come from Zion, he will remove ungodliness from Jacob**" [Rom. 11:26-27] (see also Isa. 59:20).

b. The Return of a Deliverer

Regardless of the precise relationship of the church to the New Covenant, the church cannot be viewed as totally fulfilling the New Covenant. The New Covenant is not completely fulfilled until the return of the Deliverer (see Rom. 11:25ff.; Isa. 59:20). Also, whether one interprets "David" as resurrected David or a name for Christ as the greater "Son of David", it is evident the Old Testament predicts the ratification of a future covenant with Israel at a time when David rules (see Ezek. 36:23ff., 37:24ff.). Thus, the church cannot totally fulfill the New Covenant. Fulfillment must await Christ's return.

c. Eternal Restoration to the Land after a Time of Tribulation

The New Covenant will be fully operative at a time when the "Redeemer comes to Zion" (Isa. 59:20; Rom. 11:26-27), and all Israel is rightly related to God. While predictions of a restoration to the land could simply refer to a return after the Babylonian exile, it is not possible to conclude that an **eternal** restoration to the land has already taken place. An eternal restoration can only be a future promise that finds completion in a coming Kingdom of God on earth after the Second Coming. The New Covenant pertains to an eternal restoration to the land accompanied by peace from war and freedom from all threat of exile. This supports the premillennial view.

..."it shall **not be** plucked up, or **overthrown any more forever**" [Jer. 31:40].

"And they **will no longer be prey to the nations**, and the beasts of the earth will not devour them, but they will live securely, and no one will make them afraid" [Ezek. 34:28].

"And they shall live on the land that I gave to Jacob My servant, in which your fathers lived; and they will live on it, they, and their sons, and their sons' sons, **forever**; and David My servant shall be their prince **forever**. And I will make a covenant of **peace** with them; it will be an **everlasting** covenant with them, and I will place them and multiply them; and will set My sanctuary in their midst **forever**. My dwelling place also will be with them; and I will be their God, and they will be My people. And the nations will know that I am the LORD who sanctifies Israel, when My sanctuary is in their midst **forever**" [Ezek. 37:25-28].

"In that day I will also make a covenant for them with the beasts of the field, the birds of the sky, and the creeping things of the ground. And I will **abolish** the bow, the sword, and **war from the land**, and will make them lie down in safety" [Hosea 2:18].

The promise of an eternal return to the land was not fulfilled in the return after the Babylonian exile and certainly has not been fulfilled in the Church age. Attention to the contexts of promises concerning the New Covenant leads to the conclusion that its fulfillment comes in end times (see especially Jer. 30:8-9,24). Thus, Israel must yet have a glorious Kingdom at Christ's return (i.e., premillennialism).

The context of Jer. 31:31ff. contains references to the tribulation period, "the time of Jacob's Trouble" (30:7), the total destruction of Israel enemies (30:11, 16, 20), and a restoration of Israel to the land (30:3,18-20; 31:8,23-28). The context surrounding Ezek. 37:21ff. is entirely eschatological. Ezek. 36:8-15, 30 teaches that Israel will return and never again be subject to her enemies. Ezek. 37:12 gives a reference to a resurrection from the dead. Finally, all of Ezekiel 38-39 is eschatological in nature (Magog's invasion of Israel). The New Covenant concerns **Israel's future** (not just the church's present as amillennialism would assert).

d. Material Blessings

Passages which contain the promise of a New Covenant with Israel also speak of material prosperity. The temple will be built (Ezek. 37:26,28). There will be great agricultural production.

> Instead of your shame you will have a double portion, and instead of humiliation they will shout for joy over their portion. Therefore they will possess a double portion in their land, everlasting joy will be theirs. For I the LORD love justice, I hate robbery in the burnt offering; and I will faithfully give them their recompense, and I will make an everlasting covenant with them [Isa. 61:7-8].

"And I will make them and the places around My hill a blessing. And I will cause showers to come down in their season; they will be showers of blessing. Also the tree of the field will yield its fruit, and the earth will yield its increase, and they will be secure on their land. Then they will know that I am the LORD, when I have broken the bars of their yoke and have delivered them from the hand of those who enslaved them. And they will no longer be a prey to the nations, and the beasts of the earth will not devour them; but they will live securely, and no one will make them afraid" [Ezek. 34:26-28][60].

e. Spiritual Blessings

Section "a" developed the point that the New Covenant promises a time when all Israelites are saved. The New Covenant also promises the indwelling of the Holy Spirit (cf. Jer. 31:33 with Ezek. 36:27 and 37:14) and that all will be well taught in the things of God (Jer. 31:33-34). Israel will experience eternal forgiveness of sins (Jer. 31:34). The New Covenant does not just offer a return to the land (as after the Babylonian captivity) but an **eternal return** to the land accompanied by the **salvation of all Jews** and the indwelling ministry of the Holy Spirit in the hearts of all believing Jews. The indwelling ministry of the Holy Spirit in the hearts of all believing Jews did **not** occur at a past restoration to the land but rather refers to a **future regathering of Israel** after the Second Coming (i.e., premillennialism).

f. Summary of New Covenant Provisions

The New Covenant promises a time when the Redeemer comes to Zion and all Israel is saved. There will be an eternal restoration to the land without fear of enemies imposing another exile. This time also results in showers of blessings both spiritual and material. **By any literal sense the New Covenant promises a future for the nation of Israel.**

Jer. 30:24b says, "...**in the latter days** you will understand this." When all the information in contexts pertaining to a New Covenant with Israel is correlated, it is impossible to escape the conclusion that the New Covenant concerns Israel's future, and it cannot be totally fulfilled by the church in the present time.[61]

3. The Nature of the New Covenant as Unconditional and Eternal

Literal interpretation of the New Covenant supports premillennialism. Furthermore, it is virtually impossible to argue that the New Covenant was temporary and/or subject to conditions that would cause its cancellation.

> "Incline your ear and come to Me. Listen that you may live; and I will make an **everlasting covenant** with you, according to the faithful mercies shown to David" [Isa. 55:3].

> ... And I will make an **everlasting covenant** with them [Isa. 61:8].

> Thus says the LORD, who gives the **sun** for light by day and the fixed order of the **moon** and the **stars** for light by night, who stirs up the sea so that its waves roar: The LORD of hosts is His name: "**If this fixed order departs from before Me**".... "**Then the offspring of Israel also shall ease from being a nation** before Me forever." Thus says the LORD, "If the heavens above can be measured, and the foundations of the earth searched out below, then I will also cast off the offspring of Israel for all that they have done," declares the LORD [Jer. 31:35-37].

---

[60] Ezek. 34:25 and 28 may also link the New Covenant with the taming of wild animals as a reduction of the curse. Isa. 11:6-9 is even more clear on this. Certainly, wild animals are not now tame. Thus, the New Covenant has aspects that must be fulfilled in a future Kingdom with Israel.

[61] A Redeemer comes to Zion. All Israel is saved. There is a resurrection and eternal restoration of Israel to the land along with the complete and eternal destruction of Israel's enemies. The New Covenant is fulfilled after a time of "Jacob's trouble" (the Tribulation), and while King David rules over Israel. Other features surrounding a fulfillment of the New Covenant include a temple in Jerusalem, the reduction of the curse among wild animals, and the Holy Spirit's indwelling of Israel. How could we conclude these were fulfilled in the return of the exiles from Babylon or are being fulfilled in the present church dispensation?

"And I will make an **everlasting covenant** with them that I will not turn away from them, to do them good; and I will put the fear of Me in their hearts so that they will not turn away from Me" [Jer. 32:40].

"They will ask for the way to Zion, turning their faces in its direction; they will come that they may join themselves to the LORD in an **everlasting covenant** that will not be forgotten." [Jer. 50:5].

"Nevertheless, I will remember My covenant with you in the days of your youth, I will establish an **everlasting covenant** with you" [Ezek. 16:60].

"And I will make a covenant of peace with them; it will be an **everlasting covenant** with them..." [Ezek. 37:26].

The phrase "I will" occurs seven times within the four verses of Jer. 31:31-34. The New Covenant is a one-sided contract that depends upon God alone for its completion. No conditions for man are given (p. 494ff).

The Abrahamic Covenant is the foundation for the Palestinian, Davidic, and New Covenants. God's promises to Abraham concerned land, seed, and blessing. Each of the succeeding covenants seems to emphasize and enlarge a particular aspect of the Abrahamic covenant. The Palestinian covenant (Deut. 30:1-10) concerns the land, the Davidic concerns seed, and the New Covenant enlarges upon future blessings. Just as the Abrahamic Covenant was eternal and unconditional, so the New Covenant is unconditional and eternal. It guarantees a future for Israel and supports premillennialism.

4. The Church and the New Covenant

New Testament references to the New Covenant (New Testament means New Covenant) raise questions about the relationship of the church to the New Covenant. Is the New Covenant fulfilled presently in the church, or will it find completion with Israel in the future? Of course, the amillennialist position is that the church fulfills the New Covenant and that this means Israel has no future Kingdom on earth.

It is quite true that the church shares in some of the blessings of the New Covenant at the present time. Nevertheless, this is not the same as viewing the church as experiencing a complete fulfillment of the New Covenant. Complete fulfillment awaits a future time and must involve the nation of Israel.

Forgiveness of Israel's sin is a major blessing of the New Covenant (Jer. 31:34). In order to forgive Israel's sin, the true Lamb of God had to be slain. Of course, the same cross, which forms a basis for **future blessing** upon **Israel** in the New Covenant, is a means of blessing the **church** in the **present**. Thus, the church does indeed share in the benefits of the New Covenant. We share in the benefit of the broken body and shed blood, which will be the basis for Israel's eventual blessing under the New Covenant.

However, the fact that the church benefits from the New Covenant and shares "partially and presently" in its blessing does not mean that all aspects of the New Covenant are now in force or that Israel has lost its promises.

Regardless of present blessing for the church, the New Covenant must still be ratified with Israel and thereby fulfilled completely. The church without Israel cannot and will not totally fulfill the New Covenant even though the church does indeed presently enjoy some benefits arising from the New Covenant. There is a definite distinction between sharing with Israel and replacing Israel.

a. The Old Testament stresses that the New Covenant will be with Israel

The original recipients of promises concerning the New Covenant would have clearly felt it concerned Israel.

"...I will make a **new covenant** with **the house of Israel and with the house of Judah**" [Jer. 31:31] (see also Heb. 8:8).

"...I will make an everlasting, covenant **with them**..." (i.e., Israel, see also v. 36) [Jer. 32:40].

"In those days and at that time," declares the LORD, "the **sons of Israel** will come, both they and the **sons of Judah** as well; they will go along weeping as they go, and it will be the LORD their God they will seek. They will ask for the way to Zion, turning their faces in its direction; they will come that they may join themselves to the Lord in an **everlasting covenant** that will not be forgotten" [Jer. 50:4-5].

"Nevertheless, I will remember My covenant **with you** in the days of your youth, and I will establish an **everlasting covenant with you**" [Ezek. 16:60].

Previous covenants were made with Israel not the church. "You" in Ezek. 16:60 must refer to Israel.

"And say to them, 'Thus says the Lord GOD, "Behold, I will take the **sons of Israel** from among the nations where they have gone, and I will gather them from every side and bring them into their own land" ' " [Ezek. 37:21].

"And a Redeemer will come to Zion, and to those who turn from transgression in **Jacob**," declares the LORD. And as for Me, this is **My covenant with them**," says the LORD..." [Isa. 59:20-21].

[A]nd thus **all Israel** will be saved; just as it is written, "The Deliverer will come from Zion, He will remove ungodliness from **Jacob**. And this is

My **covenant** with them, When I take away their sins" [Rom. 11:26-27].

While the Old Testament might allow for the church sharing in blessings related to the New Covenant, the covenant primarily concerns Israel. If words mean anything and if promises mean anything, Israel, not the church, must be the recipients of complete New Covenant blessings. Many of the details surrounding the New Covenant are not and cannot be fulfilled in any literal sense in the present dispensation (e.g., all Israel saved, the Redeemer coming to Zion, no more war for Israel).

In addition, the fact that the New Covenant pertains to Israel is implied by its very name, for the Old Covenant was definitely a Jewish covenant (Rom. 2:14; 9:4; Eph. 2:12; Lev. 26:46; Deut. 4:8). If the New Covenant is not completely fulfilled by the church, then what is the relationship of the church to the New Covenant?

b. The New Testament on the New Covenant

Amillennialists claim that the church totally fulfills the New Covenant and that Israel has no future Kingdom. This cannot be true if Old Testament passages are interpreted at face value. Nevertheless, there are many important references to the New Covenant in the New Testament. It seems as though the New Covenant has been instituted but not completely fulfilled. The foundation for the New Covenant has been made in the Savior's blood and the church enjoys benefits arising from it, even though total fulfillment of the New Covenant awaits a future ratification with Israel.

And in the same way He took the cup after they had eaten, saying, "this cup which is poured out for you is the **new covenant** in My blood" [Luke 22:20].

In the same way He took the cup also, after supper, saying, "this cup is the **new covenant** in My blood; do this, as often as you drink it, in remembrance of Me" [1 Cor. 11:25].

[W]ho also made us adequate as servants of a **new covenant**, not of the letter, but of the Spirit; for the letter kills, but the Spirit gives life [2 Cor. 3:6].

"...Behold, days are coming," says the Lord, when I will effect a **new covenant** with the house of Israel and with the house of Judah....For this is the covenant that I will make with the house of Israel after those days, says the Lord: I will put my laws into their minds, and I will write them upon their hearts. And I will be their God, and they shall be my people. And they shall not teach everyone his fellow citizen, and everyone his brother, saying, 'know the Lord,' for all shall know Me, from the least to the greatest of them. For I will be merciful to their iniquities, and I will remember their sins no more." When He said, "A **new covenant**," He has made the first obsolete. But whatever is becoming obsolete and growing old is ready to disappear [Heb. 8:8,10-13].

And for this reason He is the mediator of a **new covenant**, in order that since a death has taken place for the redemption of the transgressions that were committed under the first covenant, those who have been called may receive the promise of the eternal inheritance [Heb. 9:15].

[A]nd to Jesus, the mediator of a **new covenant**, and to the sprinkled blood, which speaks better than the blood of Abel [Heb. 12:24].

Premillennialists include within their system room for the church sharing in blessings arising from the New Covenant but insist that Israel must also obtain all New Cove-

nant provisions in a coming Kingdom. There are three main positions among premillennialists concerning the relationship of the church to the New Covenant.[62]

(1). No Direct Relationship between Church and New Covenant

Darby's view was that the New Covenant does not relate to the church in any direct sense. The only relationship is that the blood of the cross that makes possible the provisions of the New Covenant with Israel also makes possible the blessings that the church enjoys.

(2). Two New Covenants

Chafer and Walvoord followed the idea that the Bible speaks of two New Covenants. There is one for Israel and one for the church. Only the context can determine which a Biblical author intends.

(3). Future Ratification with Israel

Scofield maintained that there is only one New Covenant. It is presently in force with the church in a partial sense, but it will also be totally fulfilled with Israel. There must be a future ratification with the nation Israel in order to complete New Covenant promises.

(4). Evaluation

All of the above Bible teachers are very credible, and the issue is not worth intense argument. The main concern of each is to preserve New Covenant blessings for Israel.

If preference is to be given, view three has the most to commend it. While Israel and the church are distinct, it seems that a rejection of any overlapping of the two is overzealous. Also, it would be hard to prove that the Bible clearly teaches two New Covenants. All the disciples were Jewish. When Christ said, "This is the New Covenant in My blood," we must presume a connection was made to

---

[62] The discussion here follows J. Dwight Pentecost, *Things to Come* (Grand Rapids: Zondervan Publishing House, 1976), pp. 121-127.

the New Covenant of Jeremiah 31 unless there is strong evidence to the contrary. Paul says in 2 Cor. 3:6, "we are ministers of the New Covenant." Unless there is specific language to identify another "New Covenant", we should presume that Paul, a Jew, expects his readers to equate "New Covenant" with the promises of Jeremiah. Although the author of Hebrews does not directly state that the New Covenant is in force, he does argue that a second covenant is in force and then proceeds to teach about the New Covenant (see Hebrews 8). Perhaps he is just using the promise of a New Covenant to establish that the Old Covenant (the Law) was temporal. However, Hebrews 8 can be taken to imply that the New Covenant of Jeremiah 31 is in some sense now in force. Because of passages like Luke 22:20, 1 Cor. 11:25, and 2 Cor. 3:6, that implication is best granted as valid.

Although zeal to keep Israel and the church distinct is commendable, premillennialism need not reject an overlapping between the two. The New Covenant with Israel will be based on the blood of Christ. The view that the church participates in the New Covenant in Christ's blood need not rule out a future and more complete ratification with Israel. To share with blessings for Israel is not the same as replacing Israel. There must yet be a complete enjoyment of the New Covenant by "the house of Israel and the house of Judah" (Jer. 31:31) in the millennial Kingdom.

D. Literal Interpretation and Premillennialism

There is strong support for premillennial theology in the Abrahamic, Davidic, and New Covenants. Yet, these still do not exhaust evidence for the concept of a future Kingdom for Israel. Virtually all conservatives agree that a literal (normal) interpretation of the Old Testament will lead to premillennial theology. The reader should keep in mind that a literal interpretation of verses

in the following sections also supports premillennialism. Passages which teach about Jerusalem being the world capital, or the absence of war, or complete justice in the courts, affirm a coming Kingdom of God on earth as much as the previous material on the covenants. Great emphasis should be placed upon how the original recipients would have understood such promises. To them "Israel" meant *Israel*, "Jerusalem" meant *Jerusalem*, "David" meant *David* and so forth. The reinterpretation of terms to cancel out a Kingdom for Israel is tantamount to making God untrue. How would a modern Christian react if 2,000 years from now someone said all the promises given to the church do not really apply to Christians because *church* does not really mean *church*?

God's unconditional covenants with Israel coupled with a literal interpretation of the Old Testament make as clear and emphatic a case for premillennialism as human language permits. While conservative amillennialists deserve respect for fidelity to the Bible in other areas of theology, the stark fact is that they cling to theological systems rather than build a theology from the Bible itself. The Reformation brought great improvements in correct understanding of the Bible, and the Reformers deserve high praise. However, they had too much of a background in the darkness of medieval Catholicism and were under too much pressure to reform all areas of theology. They reformed soteriology but never did thoroughly develop eschatology. Basically, they followed Augustine and the Catholic idea that the church is the fulfillment of the Kingdom of God on earth. Thus, major Protestant denominations have a heritage of state-churches. The Reformers did not reform all of the major sub-sections of theology. The early church was premillennial for its first three centuries. Thus, in reality premillennialists can claim both the Bible and church history for support. Amillennialism basically follows Reformation eschatology, whether it fits the Bible or not. It does not.

E. Amillennial Objections to Premillennialism

Amillennialists contradict each other as to why premillennialism cannot be true. They only agree that Israel has no future Kingdom on earth.

Conservative amillennialists are sound in other areas of theology, but they display a "have-your-cake-and-eat-it-too" mentality in their debate with premillennialists.

Amillennialists offer four or five main objections to premillennialism, but these contradict each other and cannot all be true at the same time. Some amillennialists claim that the promises to Abraham and David were fulfilled in the conquest of Joshua or in the glorious empire of Solomon's time. **This means the covenants were literal and unconditional but not eternal.** Others assert that Christ's place at the right hand of the Father in heaven fulfills the promise that a descendant of David would sit on David's throne forever. **This means the covenants were eternal and unconditional but not literal.** Another amillennial argument is that these covenants with Israel were conditional. Therefore, they have been cancelled because Israel failed to live up to the conditions. **This means that the covenants were literal and potentially eternal but were conditional.** It is, however, common for amillennialists to go a step further and teach that the church replaces Israel, i.e., the covenants to Israel are transferred to the church. **This means that the covenants were eternal but not literal** and **were conditional for Israel but are unconditional for the church.** Is anyone else confused by these amillennial "supports"?[63]

---

[63] See Charles Ryrie, *Basic Theology* (Wheaton, IL: Victor Books, 1986). pp. 455-56 for additional comments about amillennial arguments being a "self contradiction."

1. Fulfillment in Joshua's or Solomon's time

One common amillennial argument is that God has already totally fulfilled His promises to Abraham and David. Thus, there need be no future place for an Israelite Kingdom. Fulfillment supposedly came in the days of either Joshua or Solomon.

> "So the LORD gave Israel all the land which He had sworn to give to their fathers, and they possessed it and lived in it. And the LORD gave them rest on every side, according to all that He had sworn to their fathers, and no one of all their enemies stood before them; the LORD gave all their enemies into their hand. Not one of the good promises which the LORD had made to the house of Israel failed; all came to pass" [Joshua 21:43-45].

> Now Solomon ruled over all the kingdoms from the River to the land of the Philistines and to the border of Egypt; they brought tribute and served Solomon all the days of his life [1 Kings 4:21].

> [W]ho has kept with Thy servant David, my father, that which Thou hast promised him; indeed, Thou hast spoken with Thy mouth, and hast fulfilled it with Thy hand, as it is this day [2 Chron. 6:15].

Gen. 15:18 gives the boundaries of the Promised Land. Regardless of whether the "river of Egypt" is the Wadi-el-Arish in the Sinai or the Nile itself, neither Joshua nor Solomon occupied the **full** Promised Land **forever** as the covenants so repeatedly promise. In fact, other Scriptures teach that the conquest under Joshua was by no means complete.

> Now it came about after the death of Joshua that the sons of Israel inquired of the LORD saying, "Who shall go

up first for us against the Canaanites, to fight against them?" [Judg. 1:1].

But the sons of Benjamin did not drive out the Jebusites who lived in Jerusalem; so that the Jebusites have lived with the sons of Benjamin in Jerusalem to this day [Judg. 1:21].

But Manasseh did not take possession of... [Judg. 1:27].

And it came about when Israel became strong, that they put the Canaanites to forced labor, but they did not drive them out completely [Judg. 1:28].

Neither did Ephriam drive out the Canaanites... [Judg. 1:29].

Zebulun did not drive out the inhabitants...[Judg. 1:30].

Asher did not drive out the inhabitants...[Judg. 1:31].

Naphtali did not drive out the inhabitants...[Judg. 1:33].

Then the Amorites forced the sons of Dan into the hill country, for they did not allow them to come down to the valley...[Judg. 1:34].

I also will no longer drive out before them any of the nations which Joshua left when he died....whether they will keep the way of the LORD to walk in it as their fathers did, or not. So the LORD allowed those nations to remain, not driving them out quickly; and He did not give them into the hand of Joshua [Judg. 2:21-23].

It ought to be obvious that Israel did not fully possess the land in the days of Joshua and never **eternally** possessed the land whether in the days of Joshua or Solomon. Why are there so many promises about the covenants **after** the times of Joshua and Solomon? (Isa. 9:6ff., Luke 1:31-33, etc.) After direct and indirect references to main Old Testament characters,

including many after Joshua, the author of Hebrews says:

> And all these, having gained approval through their faith, **did not receive what was promised,** because God had provided something better for us, so that apart from us they should not be made perfect [Heb. 11:39-40].

Statements in Joshua 21 about the fulfillment of God's promises need to be balanced by other statements about the incompleteness of the conquest and God's statement that Israel would gradually conquer the land (Ex. 23:29-30; Deut. 7:22-24). There are options for an understanding of Josh. 21:43-45 that do not make it a complete fulfillment of the promises to the patriarchs, Abraham, Isaac and Jacob. There was under Joshua a comparative and incremental fulfillment to his point in time rather than a complete fulfillment of the promises to the patriarch. Joshua could claim **God had given the land He promised** within His unfolding plan for history **up to the time of the conquest.**

The conquest under Joshua did not completely fulfill promises to Abraham, but compared to the meager results that Abraham actually saw it could be called a fulfillment of the promises. Furthermore, it gave visible credibility that fulfillment of all promises would eventually come to pass. From the Israelite's perspective, God was actively working in the direction of a complete fulfillment of all His promises. There was now no doubt that the process was moving forward on all fronts. Thus, in a sense Israel could say, "God has done what He promised." It was not the case that all was actually accomplished but rather God had acted far enough towards completion that it was safe to assert His visible faithfulness in all respects. There could be no doubt of the direction of God's work for Israel. Since completion was only a matter of time, the author could assert, "Not one of the promises failed, all came to pass." Fulfillment of the promises was true comparatively (compared to what patriarchs actually saw of the promised fulfillment) and true relative to credibility (God had done so much that no one could doubt that the rest was as good as done). All God promised the patriarchs had been fulfilled when viewed incrementally up to the time of Joshua, but this was not all Israel would ever obtain.

God has promised salvation, resurrection, and heaven to believers. Has he failed or kept His promise? Would it not be true for a Christian to testify, "God has kept all His promises to me" even though some have not technically come to pass and await the future?

Likewise, Joshua asserts that God kept all His promises up to his generation even though not all that would ever be done to bless Israel had yet come to pass. To this day many promises to Israel still await a complete fulfillment.

2. Fulfillment by Christ's Presence on the Throne in Heaven

All Bible-believers agree that Christ is now seated in glory at the right hand of God the Father in heaven (Acts 7:56; Col. 3:1; Heb. 1:3; 8:1; 12:2). One branch of amillennialism/postmillennialism equates this with a fulfillment of the covenants with Israel.

The issue comes down to one of literal versus mystical interpretation. Those who advocate this position claim that the "throne of David" equals God's throne in heaven and that the "house of David" is the household of faith. Literal interpretation leads to premillennialism. Conservative amillennialists interpret the Bible literally in other areas but approach eschatology with a mystical or "spiritual" interpretation.

It is inconsistent to interpret by the literal method in all other areas but to reject this method in eschatology in order to force a conclusion that fits with amillennialism, i.e. traditional Reformed theology. One would think that if any material ought to be interpreted literally it would be promises, particularly promises concerning land. Title deeds to

land are carefully worded to avoid misunderstandings. Mystical interpretations to agreements about land would end up producing fraud.

Consideration should be given to how the original recipients of the covenants understood the promises. Obviously, God led Abraham to believe that his descendants would obtain a land on earth (Gen. 13:14-15; 15:18). David understood his "house" to refer to his posterity (2 Sam. 7:18-19,25,29; with parallels in 1 Chronicles 17) and interpreted the promises as referring to a literal throne and a literal Kingdom (see also Messianic Psalms 2, 45, 48, 72, 89, 110, and 132). Neither David nor Solomon would have understood the throne of David to refer to God's throne in heaven (likely a blasphemous thought) nor the house of David to refer to the household of faith. The rest of Biblical characters had the same understanding. To them the house of David referred to physical descendants. They believed that the throne of David was in Jerusalem, not heaven. (See also the following section that gives verses predicting Jerusalem as the world capital, and also previous sections on the provisions for the covenants).

> "And as for you, if you will before Me as your father David walked, in integrity of heart and uprightness, doing according to all that I have commanded you and will keep My statutes and My ordinances, then **I will establish the throne of your kingdom over Israel forever, just as I promised to your father David,** saying you shall not lack a man on the **throne of Israel**" [1 Kings 9:4-5].

> "Now therefore, O LORD, the God of Israel, keep with Thy servant David, my father, that **which Thou hast promised him**, saying, 'You shall not lack a man to sit **on the throne of Israel**, if only your sons take heed to their way, to walk in My law as you

have walked before Me' " [2 Chron. 6:16].

"I will establish your seed forever, and build up your throne to all generations....So **I will establish his descendants forever**, and **his throne** as the days of heaven. If his sons forsake My law, and do not walk in My judgments, if they violate My statutes, and do not keep My commandments, then I will visit their transgression with the rod, and their iniquity with stripes. But I will not break off my loving kindness from him, nor deal falsely in My faithfulness. My covenant I will not violate, nor will I alter the utterance of My lips....His descendants shall endure forever, and his throne as the sun before Me" [Psa. 89:4,29-34,36].

"[T]hen say to them, 'Thus says the LORD, Behold, I am about to fill all the inhabitants of this land - the **kings that sit for David on his throne**, the priests, the prophets and all the inhabitants of Jerusalem - with drunkenness!' " [Jer. 13:13].

[T]hen there will come in through the gates of **this city kings** and princes **sitting on the throne of David**, riding in chariots and on horses, they and their princes, the men of Judah, and the inhabitants of Jerusalem; and this city will be inhabited forever [Jer. 17:25].

For if you men will indeed perform this thing, then **kings** will enter the gates of this house, sitting in **David's place on his throne**, riding in chariots and on horses, even the king himself and his servants and his people....Thus says the LORD, write this man down childless, a man who will not prosper in his days; For no man of his descendants will prosper **sit-**

ting on the throne of David or ruling again in Judah [Jer. 22:4, 30].

"In those days and at that time I will cause a righteous Branch of David to spring forth; and He shall execute justice and righteousness on the earth. In those days Judah shall be saved, and Jerusalem shall dwell in safety; and this is the name by which she shall be called: the LORD is our righteousness. For thus says the LORD, '**David shall never lack a man to sit on the throne of the house of Israel**....' Thus says the LORD, "If you can break My covenant for the day, and My covenant for the night, so that day and night will not be at their appointed time, then My covenant may also be broken with David My servant that he shall not have a son to reign on his throne, and with the Levitical priests, My ministers...." Thus says the LORD, "If My covenant for day and night stand not, and the fixed patterns of heaven and earth I have not established, then I would reject the **descendants of Jacob and David** My servant, not taking **from his descendants rulers over the descendants of Abraham, Isaac, and Jacob**. But I will restore their fortunes and will have mercy on them" [Jer. 33:15-17, 20-21, 25-26] (See also: 2 Sam. 23:5; Isa. 9:6; Luke 1:31-32).

It ought to be obvious that Biblical characters understood the house of David to refer to David's physical descendants and the throne of David to refer to the throne in Jerusalem, not heaven. There are no directions in the Bible that tell its readers to substitute the "throne of David" with the throne of God in heaven. Acts 2:29-36 does not provide any clear example. "Raised up" in v. 32 refers to Christ's resurrection from the dead which Peter witnessed (See Acts 5:30). Witnesses in the Book of Acts primarily witnessed the risen Lord (Acts 1:8, 22; 2:32; 3:15; 4:33; 5:30; 10:39-41; 13:31). There should be no equation of this definition of "raising" (*from the dead*) to the reference of "raising" up Solomon from childhood to reign and build the temple in 2 Sam. 7:12. Peter's main point is Christ as the living Son of David qualifies to return and establish the throne of David in Jerusalem (Acts 3:20-21). Acts 2:34-35 finds parallels between David's throne on earth and the Messiah's throne in heaven (Psa. 110:1). Some might understand Christ's present rule in heaven as being a partial fulfillment or foreshadowing of Old Testament prophecy that a Son of David would rule (similar to John the Baptist foreshadowing Elijah). However, Peter's teaching may only mean that the Son of David eternally lives and presently has the authority and power to return and rule this earth. The Davidic throne in Jerusalem in the past and in the millennium may be viewed as an extension of heavenly rule. None of these semantic quibbles over details undermines the primary truth. **A full and satisfactory definition of David's eternal throne demands that Christ return and rule over a throne in Jerusalem.** Although David is mentioned approximately 59 times in the New Testament, no verse teaches a replacement of his house with the church or his throne with God's throne. If the throne of David equals Christ's position at the right hand of the Father in heaven, then how did Solomon sit on "David's throne"? If David's throne equals God's throne in heaven, then what need is there to establish it, for it has existed from eternity past?

Cults often use strange interpretations of prophetic Scripture to bolster their heretical systems. If one abandons literal interpretation, then prophecy can say whatever pleases an interpreter. Conservative amillennialists do not use prophetic portions to endorse heresy, but where does "mystical" interpretation of prophesy stop? If Jerusalem does not mean *Jerusalem*, then why must the church

mean the *church* when God promised to rapture it? If the house of David means the house of faith, then could one not born a Son of David be qualified as Messiah?

Portions of the covenants that have been fulfilled have been fulfilled literally. Thus, premillennialists are justified in anticipating literal fulfillment for all aspects of the covenants. Christ must yet come to rule on the throne of David in Jerusalem. He will come to bring a Kingdom on earth.

3. Cancelled Conditional Covenants

It is hard to believe that anyone could read all that the Bible says about the Abrahamic, Davidic, and New Covenants and conclude that they were conditional and/or temporal. Too many clear passages present them as unbreakable promises.

Perhaps some have a misunderstanding of what is specifically involved in an unconditional covenant. An unconditional covenant does not rule out the fact that individuals must meet certain conditions for personal participation in a covenant or enjoyment of covenant blessings. Premillennialists understand that Old Testament saints had to be believers in order to be brought into a full covenant relationship with God. Unbelievers will not enter the Kingdom of God (see John 3:3; Matt. 18:3). Just being born a descendant of Abraham is not enough for entrance into the Kingdom (Matt. 8:12). Furthermore, it is quite true that David's descendants had to be faithful to enjoy more fully the blessing of sitting on the Davidic throne. God promised He would not take the crown away from David's son, Solomon; but He warned that following descendants could indeed lose their position as rulers.

> "And as for you, if you will before Me as your father David walked, in integrity of heart and uprightness, doing according to all that I have commanded you and will keep My statutes and My ordinances, then I

will establish the throne of your kingdom over Israel forever, just as I promised to your father David, saying, 'You shall not lack a man on the throne of Israel.' But if you or your sons shall indeed turn away from following Me, and shall not keep My commandments and My statutes which I have set before you and shall go and serve other gods and worship them, then I will cut off Israel from the land which I have given them, and the house which I have consecrated for My name, I will cast out of My sight. So Israel will become a proverb and a byword among all peoples" [1 Kings 9:4-7].

"Now therefore, O LORD, the God of Israel, keep with Thy servant David, my father, that which Thou hast promised him, saying, 'You shall not lack a man to sit on the throne of Israel, if only your sons take heed to their way, to walk in My law as you have walked before Me' " [2 Chron. 6:16].

But Thou hast cast off and rejected, Thou hast been full of wrath against Thine anointed. Thou hast spurned the covenant of Thy servant; Thou hast profaned his crown in the dust [Psa. 89:38-39].

The LORD has sworn to David, a truth from which he will not turn back; "Of the fruit of your body I will set upon your throne. If your sons will keep My covenant, and My testimony which I will teach them, Their sons also shall sit upon your throne forever" [Psa. 132:11-12].

"For if you men will indeed perform this thing, then kings will enter the gates of this house, sitting in David's place on his throne, riding in chariots and on horses, even the king himself and his servants and his people. But if you will not obey these words, I swear by Myself, declares the LORD, that this house will become a desolation" [Jer. 22:4-5 (see also Jer. 17:24-25)].

Premillennialism accepts the fact that individual participation in and enjoyment of the covenants does have conditions. The individual must have faith, and obedience brings even more complete covenant blessings. However, this does not mean that the covenants were conditional. The real issue is this: can the unbelief and sin of individuals (even the majority) cancel the promises made to the whole nation (including godly ones)? Will the unbelief of many Israelites mean that people like Abraham, David, Elisha, Daniel, and even John the Baptist will not obtain the blessings of the covenants? Premillennialists agree that individual sharing in the covenants is conditional, but they insist that the overall covenant to the nation is unbreakable. No amount or degree of disbelief can abrogate God's promises to those who do believe. There is no question that a Son of David will establish an eternal throne over Israel, but in Old Testament times the right of each generation of David's descendants to rule was not guaranteed. There is no question that Israel will enjoy a future Kingdom. The only conditional issue is which individual Israelites will share in it.

Sometimes amillennialists will try to use passages like Gen. 17:7-10, the passage instituting circumcision, to argue that the Abrahamic Covenant was conditional. However, they confuse the conditional nature of an individual sharing in the blessing of the covenant with the unconditional nature of the promise to the whole nation. Circumcision was only fully valuable as a **sign of faith** (Rom. 4:11) and identified an individual Hebrew as sharing in the Abrahamic blessing. **However, the failure of many to believe would not cancel the blessings for those who did believe.** Amillennial arguments concerning the conditional nature of the covenants really confuse personal participation in covenants, which is conditional, with the overall nature of the covenants, which is unconditional. The covenants are **unconditional** and **eternal** once the individual is under the covenant blessing. There is no question the covenants to Israel will be fulfilled. The only question is whether an individual Jew will share in them.

4. Blessings Transferred from Israel to the Church

Perhaps the most common amillennial objection to premillennialism is that covenant blessings have been transferred from Israel to the church. Certain New Testament texts are used to show that the church equals Israel. These texts will be examined one by one.

Premillennialists can be overzealous in their efforts to keep Israel and the church so distinct as to deny all overlapping between these two main groupings of God's people. Often it is asserted that Israel enjoys only earthly blessings and the church enjoys only heavenly blessings. The author does not feel any threat in the admission that there are overlapping aspects between Israel and the church. The church will indeed share in many of Israel's blessings in the coming Kingdom. Believers are "sons of Abraham." Those with faith are the "true circumcision." However, the Scripture comes short of directly equating the church with Israel. Theologians might speak in loose terms of the church being a true Israel, but such language should be qualified, and it is not strictly Biblical terminology. All of the following Scriptures can be better interpreted by keeping Israel and the church distinct (although they do sometimes share in the same blessings).

Suppose for conjecture we consider that some verses do call the church "Israel". Would this prove amillennialism? No, for even if the church shares in all aspects of the covenant blessing, this still would not be the same as Israel losing her promises.[64] If I as a believer share in the future Kingdom, this still does not mean Israel will not. The New Testament still distinguishes between Israel and the church (e.g., 1 Cor. 10:32), and it still predicts a future for Israel (e.g., Rom. 11:25ff.). Usually interpreters give emphasis to the meaning of a passage to its original recipients. Abraham and David expected a future for Israel. It will come to pass regardless of the degree of the church's participation in it.

Verses that follow do not directly call the church "Israel." **Even if they did**, it would not be a sufficient basis for thinking that national Israel will have no future.

a. The Church as Israel

A literal translation of a key phrase in Rom. 9:6 says, "For not all they from Israel, these are Israel." Amillennialists interpret this verse to mean, "Not all of true Israel are Israelites." In other words, there is more to Israel than those who are ethnically Israelites, i.e., the church, is also Israel. While such an interpretation fits amillennial desire to equate the church with Israel and transfer all of Israel's blessings to the church, it is not the best interpretation of Rom. 9:6. Actually, one must first approach the text as an amillennialist to come away with this view.

Premillennialists understand that Rom. 9:6 refers to two kinds of Israelites within Abraham's physical descendants. There are physical Israelites who are not spiritual Israelites, and there are physical Israelites who are also spiritual Israelites. The verse does not include any references to the church at all. The NIV translation seems to follow the view that the distinctions of Rom. 9:6 concern only two types of Jews without reference to the church at all. "For not all who are descended from Israel are Israel" (Rom.

---

[64] Romans 11 teaches both that Israel has a future and that gentiles have been "grafted in" to share some of the covenant blessings with Israel.

9:6 NIV). In other words, being racially Jewish does not make one a true Jew unless a person also has faith.

There are several reasons for accepting the interpretation which does not equate the church with Israel. The context concerns racial Israel (Rom. 9:1-5) and the word "from" (Greek *ek*, out of) refers to Christ's descent from David in v. 5. Therefore, *ek* in v. 6 also ought to be understood as a reference to physical descent as the NIV translates. The phrase "not all from (*ek*) Israel" means "not all **descended** from Israel." It does not refer to a "spiritual" Israel (i.e., the church) as the amillennial view asserts.

A second consideration is that the following illustrations in Rom. 9:7-13 all concern the physical descendants of Abraham (Isaac, Ishmael by implication, Jacob and Esau). If **explanatory material concerns only** two categories of those **physically descended** from Abraham, then it stands to reason that **the verse being explained, v. 6, concerns** two categories of **those physically descended** from Israel without any reference to the church.

Thirdly, these illustrations in vv. 7-13 concern a large group of physical descendants that is distinguished from a smaller group of physical descendants who are also spiritual heirs. This pattern fits the premillennial understanding of Rom. 9:6. There is a larger group of physical descendants, but only a smaller section of them are true (spiritual) Israelites. [65]

The amillennialist says that Rom. 9:6 means that the spiritual heirs (the church as true Israel) extend far beyond physical descendants. Yet, the illustrations in the following context (vv. 7-13) concern only those physically descended from Abraham, and they do not argue that there is a larger spiritual group than the smaller physical group. The illustrations give the reverse pattern of a larger

group of physical descendants of whom only smaller groups are spiritual heirs.

One must first be an amillennialist to come up with an amillennial interpretation of Rom. 9:6.

Gal. 6:16 is another text that amillennialists use to assert that the church has replaced Israel.

> And those who will walk by this rule,
> peace and mercy be upon them, and
> upon the Israel of God [Gal. 6:16].

Amillennialists would teach that the last phrase of Gal. 6:16 identifies the church as the true "Israel of God." They would prefer that the word "and" be translated "even" or "as many as (are) the Israel of God." The NIV translation of Gal. 6:16 is more favorable to (but still does not prove) an amillennial view. "Peace and mercy to all who follow this rule, even to the Israel of God." The normal translation of the Greek word *kai* is "and". In Gal. 6:15-16 this would mean that Paul is referring to two groups, the New Creation (the church), the first group, with the second group being part of the whole, comprised of saved Jews whom he designated as "the Israel of God." Rather than identifying the whole church as Israel, Gal. 6:16 is more likely giving a blessing to saved Jews who are a part of the church. The primary meaning of a word (in this case "and") should be adopted unless the context clearly demonstrates that a secondary meaning must be preferred. In addition, the context favors a blessing upon saved Jews who have understood grace. After criticizing Jewish legalizers for an entire book, it is reasonable that Paul gives praise to Jewish people who have been justified by faith alone, "Peace and mercy... upon the Israel of God."

Suppose we do wish to adopt a more remote translation for *kai*. Still a secondary translation ("even" or "also") need not be taken as a equation of the church with Israel. To paraphrase, "God bless all who adhere to

---

[65] This is also the pattern in Rom. 2:28-29.

grace (including, also, even) believing Jews." This would be Paul's way of showing he was not critical of all Jews, only works-oriented legalistic Jews. Ryrie is correct in saying only a very narrow understanding of Gal. 6:16 leads to the amillennial position. Most options do not clearly identify the church as Israel. [66]

In no other undebatable case does Paul identify the church as Israel. Gal. 6:16 is a weak spot for finding a precedent. The duplication of the preposition "upon" (*epi*) also favors the view that Paul has two groups (the whole church and the Jewish portion of it) in mind rather than only one group designated by two names (the New Creation is the Israel of God). The identification of the church as Israel would have to be on other stronger grounds in order to find it in Gal. 6:15-16. Only pure theological preference, not linguistics or context, make Gal. 6:15-16 an amillennial proof-text.

b. The Church as "Sons of Abraham"

Galatians 3:7 calls believers "sons of Abraham."

> Therefore, be sure that it is those who are of faith who are sons of Abraham [Gal. 3:7].

The absence of the article seems important. Believers are not "the sons of Abraham" but rather "sons of Abraham." Paul stresses that believers have the quality of being Abraham's sons because they are people of faith like Abraham, but he does not technically make a complete identification of believers with the physical descendants of Abraham, Israel. Believers have the quality of Abraham's sons, but Paul does not teach that they have replaced Israel or that all promises to Israel have been transferred to the church. In his next statement (Gal. 3:8-9) Paul focuses on the point that believers share in the "all nations blessed" aspect of the Abrahamic

Covenant. As "sons of Abraham" believing gentiles primarily enjoy the blessing of being justified by faith. The blessing of justification by faith was a major fulfillment of God's promise to bless all families of the earth through Abraham (Gen. 12:3). This is the sense in which believers are blessed as "sons of Abraham."

> And the Scripture, foreseeing that God would **justify the Gentiles by faith** preached the gospel beforehand to Abraham, saying, **"all the nations shall be blessed in you."** So then those who are of faith are blessed with Abraham, the believer [Gal. 3:8-9].

Gal. 3:15-16 can be used as a proof text that the Abrahamic Covenant was unconditional and unchanging. While the church shares in the "all nations blessed" aspect of the Abrahamic Covenant (i.e., mainly spiritual blessings), Israel will yet obtain complete fulfillment of God's promises to Abraham, including eternal possession of the land (the full material blessings of the Abrahamic covenant).

Gal. 3:29 is similar to Gal. 3:7. Those who are a part of the church (believers) have the **quality** of Abraham's seed. Again the phrase, "seed of Abraham", lacks the definite article. Believers are not "the seed of Abraham" as though we are all Israelites. [67] We rather have the qualities of Abraham's

---

[67] The Bible uses the concept of Abraham's descendants (seed, children, sons) in at least four different senses. First, there are physical offspring from Abraham (see Gen. 15:4; 17:6,16; John 8:37). Another sense in which the idea of Abraham's children occurs is that of physical children who are also spiritual children (John 8:39; Rom. 2:28-29; 9:6; Rev. 2:9; 3:9). Thirdly, Christ is the primary seed of Abraham (Gal 3:16). Finally, all those with spiritual faith are the spiritual sons of Abraham (Matt. 3:9; Rom. 4:11-12, 16; Gal.3:7-9), and spiritual seed of Abraham (Gal. 3:29).

---

[66] Charles Ryrie, *Basic Theology*, p. 399.

seed by virtue of being like him in faith and by enjoying the promise of all nations being blessed through Abraham. Whatever participation the church has in the Abrahamic Covenant comes about through its relationship to Abraham's primary seed, i.e., the Lord Jesus Christ. Christ is Abraham's main "seed" (Gal. 3:16). While the church does enjoy blessings of the Abrahamic Covenant (certainly spiritual blessings, i.e., justification by faith, and likely also some material blessings of being co-heirs with Christ in His Kingdom), it does so by virtue of its relationship with Christ, not because it has replaced Israel as the beneficiary of the covenants. **The** sons of Abraham, i.e., Israel, must still obtain the land, throne, and eternal Kingdom blessings of the covenants.

Romans makes a similar point to Galatians Chapter 3. There Paul teaches that Abraham is the father of all who believe.

> [A]nd he received the sign of circumcision, a seal of the righteousness of the faith which he had while uncircumcised, that he might be **the father of all who believe** without being circumcised, that righteousness might be reckoned to them, and the father of circumcision to those who not only are of the circumcision, but who also follow in the steps of the faith of our father Abraham which he had while uncircumcised. For the promise to Abraham or to his descendants that he would be heir of the world was not through the Law, but through the righteousness of faith. For if those who are of the Law are heirs, faith is made void and the promise is nullified; for the Law brings about wrath, but where there is no law, neither is there violation. For this reason it is by faith, that it might be in accordance with grace, in order that **the promise may be certain to all the descendants**, not only to those who are of the Law, but also to those who

are of the faith of Abraham, **who is the father of us all,** (as it is written, "a father of many nations have I made you...") [Rom. 4:11-17].

The argument of this important section in Romans is that justification is by faith. The close of v. 11 shows that imputed (reckoned) righteousness, i.e., justification, is the main blessing that comes to believers through a sharing in the faith of their spiritual father, Abraham. Just as in Galatians 3, the primary blessing for the church that comes through Abraham is justification by faith. Through Abraham's seed, Christ, God blessed all the families of the earth by providing salvation for those with faith.

Verse 13 says that God promised Abraham that he would be "heir of the world." Verses 14 and 16 teach that those with faith share in this blessing. Does this mean that Israel's earthly blessings have been transferred to the church? At the most it means that the church will share in the spiritual and material blessings of the Kingdom by virtue of its relationship with Christ (co-heirs with Him, Rom. 8:17). We need not read into this passage a cancellation of the promises to national Israel. The idea of the church sharing in a coming world Kingdom does not mean Israel loses her promises.

Furthermore, the phrase "heir of the world" **may not even refer to land**. God did promise Canaan to Abraham but not specifically the whole world. Also, the context emphasizes spiritual blessings, not material. Maybe "world" means people, not land! Perhaps the sense in which Abraham became the heir of the world was that God gave him all the people of faith as his inheritance. Abraham lacked children for a long time, but God gave him the whole world of believers as an inheritance. Instead of no children, Abraham became the heir of a world full of spiritual children. These in turn were also the heirs of Abraham's blessings (Gal. 3:29; Rom. 4:14 and 16) primarily the "all-nations blessing"

(Cf. Gen 12:3 with Gal. 3:8). This inheritance involves spiritual blessings coming through Christ, especially justification by faith. Romans 4 can be interpreted as teaching that the church shares in only spiritual blessings of the Abrahamic Covenant. Even if one believes material blessings are also in view, this still need not destroy the concept of a future Kingdom for Israel. Yes, believers are sons of Abraham, but they are spiritual children whose main blessing under the Abrahamic covenant is justification by faith in Abraham's seed, the Lord Jesus Christ. Any future sharing in the Kingdom comes from a relationship to the King, not from replacing Israel.

c. The Church as the True Circumcision

Several passages contrast fleshly circumcision with a true circumcision, i.e., the cutting away of spiritual filth from the heart. The idea of a spiritual circumcision did not begin with the Apostle Paul. It was also an Old Testament concept (see Deut. 10:16; 30:6; Jer. 4:4; 9:25-26; Ezek. 44:7-9).

In Phil. 3:3 Paul says that believers have a true or better circumcision than do Jews who have only physical circumcision. Col. 2:11 also refers to a spiritual separation of the inevitable dominion of the flesh over a believer.

> [F]or we are the true circumcision, who worship in the Spirit of God and glory in Christ Jesus and put no confidence in the flesh [Phil. 3:3].

> [A]nd in Him you were also circumcised with a circumcision made without hands, in the removal of the body of the flesh by the circumcision of Christ [Col. 2: 11].

To say that believers have undergone a true circumcision is not the same as saying they are Israelites or that the church now replaces Israel in God's program. All it means is that believers have undergone a circumcision of the heart which cuts away sin's inevitable control. This true circumcision is better than the physical circumcision of racial Israel. Those who are Jewish need to have this spiritual circumcision in addition to fleshly circumcision. This is the point of Romans 2:28-29:

> For he is not a Jew who is one outwardly; neither is circumcision that which is outward in the flesh. But he is a Jew who is one inwardly; and circumcision is that which is of the heart, by the Spirit, not by the letter; and his praise is not from men, but from God [Rom. 2:28-29].

There is no special reason to think that Paul is identifying the church as true Israel in Romans 2. In vv. 25-27 he contrasts a hypothetical gentile who (though uncircumcised in the flesh) keeps God's commandments and is, therefore, spiritually circumcised; with a circumcised Jew who does not obey the Law and is, therefore, spiritually uncircumcised. This discussion is hypothetical, for in reality no one, Jew or gentile, actually keeps the Law. Nevertheless, Paul's point is that physical circumcision is of inferior value to spiritual circumcision (the cutting away of filth from the heart). The former without the latter is of little value. Thus, Jews are just as spiritually needy as gentiles. Both need justification by faith.

Some amillennialists view Rom. 2:28-29 as a contrast between racial Jews (v. 28) and Christians as "true Jews" (v. 29). While a contrast of Jews with gentiles is indeed in the context, Paul has not yet brought in any discussion of the church. There is no real reason to see the church in Romans 2. Verses 28-29 concern only national Israelites. Verse 28 refers to those who are racially Jewish but are not "Jewish" in the full sense of the term because they are unsaved and have not undergone circumcision of a more important kind. The true Jew in v. 29 is a physical Jew who also has a circumcised heart, i.e., he has been saved. These verses establish that being physically Jewish is not enough to please God or bring salvation. Jewish descent alone is insufficient without a heart that is right with God. Paul will explain in following chapters how gentiles may obtain salvation by faith and how Jews may become "true Jews" in the same way. While this passage does teach that gentiles may have a true circumcision (without yet specifically saying how), it does not equate saved gentiles with national Israel. It just says that it takes more for a Jew to be fully Jewish than just physical circumcision.

d. Transfer of the Kingdom to the Church

Amillennialists use Matt. 21:43ff. to assert that Israel will have no future Kingdom. It supposedly teaches that Israel has been set aside and the church obtains its place of blessings.

> "Therefore I say to you, the kingdom of God will be taken away from you, and be given to a nation producing the fruit of it....And when the chief priests and the Pharisees heard His parables, they understood that He was speaking about them" [Matt. 21:43,45].

This text is capable of several interpretations that do not support amillennialism. Matt. 21:45 clearly teaches that the "you" of v. 43 were the Chief Priests and Pharisees. They were not going to obtain the Kingdom. Another "nation" would.

The Lord may simply be saying that the present nation of Israel would not obtain any Messianic Kingdom, but a future nation of Israel would. In other words, the Israel of His generation would not obtain the Kingdom. The Kingdom had to await another generation when Israel would be a different nation. None of the first century Jewish nation would enjoy an earthly Kingdom, but a future Israelite nation would.

It is also possible to view "nation" as a reference to the church without drawing amil-

lennial conclusions. Although the church is not the millennial Kingdom, it is a form of God's Kingdom on earth (see Rom. 14:17; Col. 1:13; and Matthew Chapter 13 where the time period between the first and Second Coming is called the Kingdom). Furthermore, the Bible calls believers a nation in Rom. 10:19 and 1 Pet. 2:9-10 (the 1 Peter reference also quotes Psalm 118, as does Matthew 21). Perhaps the Lord is saying that the kingdom would be taken from those who led Israel in the first century and a form of the kingdom would be given to the church. This truth does not necessarily contradict the belief that Israel will in the future be returned to a primary place in God's work and will yet obtain a political Kingdom of God on earth. In fact, such an interpretation to Matt. 21:43ff. makes it parallel to Romans 11. In Romans 11 Paul argues that gentiles (including gentiles within the church) are in a place of blessing, but that same passage also teaches that Israel will yet return to God's favor and blessing. The identification of the "nation" in Matt. 21:43, whether the future generation of Israel or the church, is a secondary issue as to whether the removal of the kingdom from the leaders in Christ's day would be temporary or permanent. The millennial issue cannot be settled by Matthew 21 alone, but other texts make it clear that any removal of Israel from a position of blessings must be temporary and not eternal.

5. An Evaluation of Amillennial Arguments

The main arguments that amillennialists use to object to premillennialism contradict each other. Since these arguments cannot all be true at the same time, they do not have any cumulative strength. Individually, they are weak. Even if one adopts the amillennial interpretation of a given passage, that passage still does not disprove that Israel has a future. Even if some Bible texts do call the church a "true Israel," this still would not prove that God has cancelled His covenants with national Israel, only that the church has a share in them.

This may be a good point for the reader to go back and review the promises made to Israel discussed earlier in this chapter. Language could not state an unconditional and eternal promise more forcefully. Also, a review of the differences between Israel and the church might be helpful (see Chapter 11, The Doctrine of the Church, pp. 309ff.).

The New Testament still distinguishes between Israel and the church (e.g., 1 Cor. 10:32). While this alone does not prove that Israel has a future Kingdom, it does mean that God distinguishes between Israel and the church. This holds out the possibility of Israel having a future in God's program. The eternal nature of Israel's covenants coupled with the following texts makes that possibility a certainty. Long after Old Testament Israel had failed God and even after New Testament Israel had rejected her King, God still promises a glorious future for Israel (see also Rev. 1:6, 5:10, 20:4 and 6 for a future Kingdom on earth).

"And behold, you will conceive in your womb, and bear a son, and you shall name Him Jesus. He will be great, and will be called the Son of the Most High; **and the Lord God will give Him the throne of His father David; and He will reign over the house of Jacob forever; and His kingdom will have no end**" [Luke 1:31-33].

And Jesus said to them, "Truly I say to you, that you who have a followed Me, in the regeneration when the Son of Man will sit on His glorious throne, you also shall **sit upon twelve thrones, judging the twelve tribes** of Israel" [Matt. 19:28] (Note that this verse follows the prediction of a church in Matt. 16:18).

But when Peter saw this, he replied to the people, "Men of Israel, why do you marvel at this, or why do you gaze at us, as if by our own power or piety we had made him walk? The God of Abraham, Isaac, and Jacob, the God of our fathers, has glorified His servant Jesus, the one whom you delivered up, and disowned in the presence of Pilate, when he had decided to release Him. But you disowned the Holy and Righteous One, and asked for a murderer to be granted to you, but put to death the Prince of life, the one whom God raised from the dead, a fact to which we are witnesses....And now, brethren, I know that you acted in ignorance, just as your rulers did also. But the things which God announced beforehand by the mouth of all the prophets, that His Christ should suffer, He has thus fulfilled. Repent therefore and return, that your sins may be wiped away, **in order that times of refreshing may come from the presence of the Lord; and that He may send Jesus, the Christ appointed for you, whom heaven must receive until the period of restoration of all things** about which God spoke by the mouth of His holy prophets from ancient time [Acts 3:12-15, 17-21] (Even after the cross Peter still offers the Kingdom to the Jews).

I say then, God has not rejected His people, has He? May it never be! For I too am an Israelite, a descendant of Abraham, of the tribe of Benjamin....For I do not want you, brethren, to be uninformed of this mystery, lest you be wise in your own estimation, that a partial hardening has happened to Israel until the fullness of the Gentiles has come in; and **thus all Israel will be saved**; just as it is written, "The Deliverer will come from Zion, He will remove ungodliness from Jacob. And this is my covenant with them, When I take away their sins." From the standpoint of the gospel they are enemies for your sake, but from the standpoint of God's choice they are beloved for the sake of the fathers; for **the gifts and the calling of God are irrevocable** [Rom. 11:1,25-29].

And I heard the number of those who were sealed, one hundred and forty-four thousand sealed from **every tribe of the sons of Israel** [Rev. 7:4].

And he carried me away in the Spirit to a great and high mountain, and showed me the holy city, Jerusalem, coming down out of heaven from God....It had a great and high wall, with twelve gates, and at the gates twelve angels; and names were written on them, which are those of the **twelve tribes of the sons of Israel** [Rev. 21:10,12].

Premillennialism is unquestionably a Scriptural doctrine. We may now move from evidence proving the concept of a Kingdom on earth to the Bible's teachings about the nature of that Kingdom. Obviously, passages which concern the nature of the Kingdom also prove there will be a Kingdom!

F. The Nature of the Millennium

God will bring about a future Kingdom on earth in order to keep His covenants with Israel. This Kingdom will demonstrate the blessings that can come through recognition of God's authority by mankind.

1. The Duration of the Kingdom

Some verses give 1,000 years as the time period for God's Kingdom on earth. There are six references to 1,000 years within Rev. 20:1-7. The term *Millennium* comes from a Latin phrase meaning "one-thousand years."

Although Revelation 20 gives a 1,000 year reign, most Scriptures speak of an eternal aspect to Messiah's Kingdom on earth (see

sections dealing with the eternal aspects of the various covenants, pp. 473ff., or 2 Sam. 7:13,28-29; 1 Chron. 17:12,14,23; Psa. 72:5,17; 89:3-4, 34-37; Isa. 9:6-7; 55:3; 56:5; 60:19-21; 61:8; Jer. 32:40; 33:14-17, 20-21; Ezek. 16:60; 43:7-9; Dan. 9:24; Hosea 2:19; Amos 9:15; and Luke 1:30-33).

Blessed and holy is the one who has a part in the first resurrection; over these the second death has no power, but they will be priests of God and of Christ and will reign with Him for a **thousand years** [Rev. 20:6].

"And your house and your kingdom shall endure before Me **forever;** your throne shall be established **forever**" [2 Sam.7:16].

"I kept looking in the night visions, And behold, with the clouds of heaven One like a Son of Man was coming. And He came up to the Ancient of Days and was presented before Him. And to Him was given dominion, glory and a kingdom, that all the peoples, nations, and men of every language might serve Him. **His dominion is an everlasting dominion which will not pass away;** and His kingdom is one which will not be destroyed....."But the saints of the Highest One will receive the kingdom and possess the kingdom **forever, for all ages to come**....Then the sovereignty, the dominion, and the greatness of all the kingdoms under the whole heaven will be given to the people of the saints of the Highest one; His kingdom will be an **everlasting** kingdom, and all the dominions will serve and obey him" [Dan. 7:13-14,18,27].

But Judah will be inhabited **forever,** and Jerusalem for all generations [Joel 3:20].

And the seventh angel sounded; and there arose loud voices in heaven, saying, "The kingdom of the world has become the kingdom of our Lord, and of His Christ; and **He will reign forever and ever**" [Rev. 11: 15].

How is it possible for the Kingdom of God on earth to be 1,000 years in duration yet eternal at the same time? There need not be a contradiction. Such dramatic changes occur in Christ's rule at the end of the one thousand years that in a sense the Kingdom can be said to be ended. Yet, Christ's rule over the earth continues eternally. The Kingdom is actually eternal, but the end of 1,000 years brings in a new and different phase of that Kingdom. The reason the Kingdom can be viewed as both ending after 1,000 years and yet continuing eternally is that 1,000 years marks the earth's transformation into sinless resubmission to God and a total merger into the rest of God's universal Kingdom.

Christ will rule over the earth for 1,000 years with His capital at Jerusalem. While there is an overall righteousness and an overall blessing during this time, sin still exists, some people born during the Millennium will not trust in Christ, and there is still a measure, albeit greatly reduced, of the curse in effect. At the end of 1,000 years the old heavens and the old earth pass away. Either the present earth is renovated and restored to Edenic conditions, or God creates a completely new earth and transfers the earthly Kingdom to it. The throne of Christ as the Son of David continues forever, but at the end of the first 1,000 years the Kingdom changes greatly. Thus, in one sense the Kingdom ends after 1,000 years, but in another sense it is eternal.

At the end of the first 1,000 years the earthly Kingdom merges with the eternal Kingdom (1 Cor. 15:24-28). It might help to think of the earth as a rebellious province. Christ conquers it at His Second Coming and reoc-cupies it for 1,000 years. Then after Christ's rule over the earth has been established and the world has demonstrated its allegiance to God, this formerly rebellious province is annexed to God's universal Kingdom. The first 1,000 years marks the end of the "reconstruction" period. Thus, Christ's rule never ends. Yet, the earth changes greatly after 1,000 years. Sin is completely and eternally removed. The earth ceases to be viewed as a separate kingdom with a separate identity. A similar relationship exists in corporate mergers or political annexations. The old business or region still exists, but it is so transformed by merger and by change that it could also be said to have ended. Did the Buick Corporation cease to exist when Billy Durant bought it in 1904 and joined it to General Motors in 1907? In one sense it did cease. In another sense it did not. Has Wales ceased to exist because of its absorption into the United Kingdom or Texas because of its annexation into the United States?

2. General Conditions in the Millennium

a. Better Health Conditions

While there is some death and thus some sickness in the Millennium, the effects of sin's curse will be greatly diminished. [68] Total elimination of sickness awaits the Eternal State (Rev. 21:4), but Isaiah teaches that death at age 100 will be considered very premature in the coming Kingdom (Isa. 65:20). Christ greatly reduced sickness at His first coming in social circles where He was accepted as King. While He did not heal everyone, it is safe to assume He would have brought much more freedom from sickness had He been accepted as King. When He

---

[68] Church saints will have been glorified at the Rapture and are no longer subject to sickness or death. However, believers who survive the Tribulation will enter the millennial Kingdom. They and their offspring will have good health but will still be subject to physical sickness and even death.

finally does reign, lifespans will greatly increase, and misery due to sickness will greatly diminish. Some theologians believe that only "voluntary sickness" will exist in the Millennium, i.e., perhaps sickness comes only as a result of willful sin (See Jer. 31:30).

And on that day **the deaf shall hear** words of a book, and out of their gloom and darkness the eyes of **the blind shall see** [Isa. 29:18].

And **no resident will say, I am sick**..."[Isa. 33:24].

Then **the eyes of the blind will be opened**, and **the ears of the deaf will be unstopped**. Then **the lame will leap** like a deer, and the tongue of **the dumb will shout for joy** [Isa. 35:5-6].

"No longer will there be in it an infant who lives but a few days, or an old man who does not live out his days; for the youth will die at the age of one hundred and **the one who does not reach the age of one hundred shall be thought accursed**" [Isa. 65:20].

"For **I will restore you to health** and I will heal you of your wounds, declares the LORD..." [Jer. 30:17] (This could be spiritual healing).

"I will seek the lost, bring back the scattered, **bind up the broken, and strengthen the sick**..." [Ezek. 34:16].

"But for you who fear My name the **sun of righteousness will rise with healing in its wings**; and you will go forth and skip about like calves from the stall" [Mal. 4:2].

b. Increased Fertility

There will be both glorified and non-glorified people in the Kingdom. At the beginning, glorified saints (Old Testament saints, church saints, and martyred tribulational saints) will probably greatly outnumber the believing survivors of the Tribulation who still possess "normal" bodies. Over the 1,000 year period the number of glorified saints remains constant (Luke 20:35), but non-glorified people will multiply rapidly. Christ intends for the world to be filled after the destruction of the Tribulation. There will be little mortality, and given the better health conditions women may be fruitful for centuries with no danger of death in childbirth. The Millennium may start out with its glorified rulers outnumbering their subjects, but eventually glorified saints will be kept very busy administering a huge population.

"Then the **LORD your God will prosper you abundantly** in all the work of your hand, **in the offspring of your body** and in the offspring of your cattle and in the produce of your ground, for the LORD will again rejoice over you for good, just as He rejoiced over your fathers" [Deut. 30:9].

"**I will multiply them** and they shall not be diminished; I will also honor them, and they shall not be insignificant. Their children also shall be as formerly, and their congregation shall be established before Me" [Jer. 30:19b-20a].

"Behold, days are coming, declares the LORD, when I will **sow the house of Israel** and the house of Judah **with the seed of man** and with the seed of beast" [Jer. 31:27].

"No longer will there be in it an infant who lives but a few days..." [Isa. 65:20a].

"**And I will multiply men on you**, all the house of Israel, all of it; and the cities will be inhabited, and the waste places will be rebuilt. **And I** will **multiply on you man** and beast; and **they will increase and be fruitful**; and I will cause you to be inhabited as you were formerly and will treat you better than at the first. Thus you will know that I am the LORD" [Ezek. 36:10-11].

c. Labor and Productivity

The Millennium will not be a vacation period but a time when the earth is a "beehive" of activity. Christ will give an example of the blessings that result from obedience to His rule.

There will be increased rainfall in areas that are now agriculturally unproductive. It is possible that the sun will be modified to increase crop yield.

Then He will give you rain for the seed which you will sow in the ground, and bread from the yield of the ground, and it will be rich and plenteous; on that day your livestock will graze in a roomy pasture. Also the oxen and the donkeys which work the ground will eat salted fodder, which has been winnowed with shovel and fork. And on every lofty mountain and on every high hill there will be streams running with water on the day of the great slaughter, when the towers fall. **And the light of the moon will be as the light of the sun** and the light of the sun will be seven times **brighter**, like the light of seven days, on the day the LORD binds up the fracture of His people and heals the bruise He has inflicted [Isa. 30:23-26].

For **waters will break forth in the wilderness and streams in the Arabah**. And the scorched land will become a pool, and the thirsty ground springs of water; In the haunt of jackals, its resting place, grass becomes reeds and rushes [Isa. 35: 6b-7].

"And I will make them and the places around My hill a blessing. And I will cause **showers** to come down in their season and they will be **showers of blessing**" [Ezek. 34:26].

So rejoice, O sons of Zion, and be glad in the LORD your God; For He **has given you the early rain** for your vindication. And **He has poured down for you the rain,** the early and the latter rain as before [Joel 2:23].

The combination of God's grace and climatic changes will bring about unprecedented yields. The human race will forget famine and hunger.

Beat your breasts for the pleasant fields, for the fruitful vine, for the land of my people in which thorns and briars shall come up; yea, for all the joyful houses, and for the jubilant city. Because the palace has been abandoned, the populated city forsaken. Hill and watch-tower have become caves forever, a delight for wild donkeys, a pasture for flocks; until the Spirit is poured out upon us from on high, and the **wilderness becomes a fertile field and the fertile field is considered as a forest** [Isa. 32:12-15].

The wilderness and the desert will be glad, and **the Arabah will rejoice and blossom**; like the crocus it will blossom profusely...[Isa. 35:1-2a].

"And they shall come and shout for joy on the height of Zion, and they shall be radiant over the **bounty of the LORD** - over the grain, and the new wine, and the oil, and over the young of the flock and the herd; and their **life shall be like a watered garden**, and they shall never languish again" [Jer. 31:12].

"Also the tree of the field will yield its fruit, and the **earth will yield its increase,** and they will be secure on their land. Then they will know that I am the LORD, when I have broken the bars of their yoke and have delivered them from the hand of those who enslaved them" [Ezek. 34:27].

"But you, O **mountains of Israel, you will put forth your branches and bear your fruit for My people Israel,** for they will soon come. For behold, I am for you, and I will turn to you, and you shall be cultivated and sown. And I will multiply men on you, all the house of Israel, all of it; and the cities will be inhabited, and the waste places will be rebuilt. **And I will multiply on you** man and **beast**; and they will increase and be fruitful; and I will cause you to be inhabited as you were formerly and will treat you better than at the first. Thus you will know that I am the LORD" [Ezek. 36:8-11].

"Moreover, I will save you from all your uncleanness; and **I will call for the grain and multiply it,** and I will not bring a famine on you. And **I will multiply the fruit of the tree and the produce of the field,** that you may not receive again the disgrace of famine among the nations" [Ezek. 36:29-30].

Do not fear, O land, rejoice and be glad, for the LORD has done great things. Do not fear beasts of the field, for the pastures of the wilderness have turned green, for the tree has borne its fruit, the fig tree and the vine have yielded in full. So rejoice, O sons of Zion. And be glad in the LORD your God; for He has given you the early rain for your vindication. And He has poured down for you the rain, the early and the latter rain as before. And **the threshing floors will be full of grain,** and **the vats will overflow** with the new wine and oil. "Then I will make up to you for the years that the swarming locust has eaten, the creeping locust, the stripping locust, and the gnawing locust, My great army which I sent among you. **And you shall have plenty to eat and be satisfied,** and praise the name of the LORD your God, who has dealt wondrously with you; then My people will never be put to shame. Thus you will know, that I am in the midst of Israel, and that I am the LORD your God and there is no other; and My people will never be put to shame" [Joel 2:21-27].

And it will come about in that day that **the mountains will drip with sweet wine, and the hills will flow with milk,** and all the brooks of Judah will flow with water; and a spring will go out from the house of the LORD, to water the valley of Shittim [Joel 3:18].

"Behold, days are coming, declares the LORD, when **the plowman will overtake the reaper and the treader of grapes him who sows seed;** when the mountains will drip sweet wine, and all the hills will be dissolved. Also I will restore the captivity of My people Israel..." [Amos 9:13-14a].

"But now I will not treat the remnant of this people as in the former days, declares the LORD of hosts. For there will be peace for the seed; the vine will yield its fruit, **the land will yield its produce,** and the heavens will give their dew; and I will cause the remnant of this people to inherit all these things" [Zech. 8:11-12].

For what comeliness and beauty will be theirs! Grain will make the young men flourish, and new wine the virgins [Zech. 9:17].

The Millennium will not be the same as heaven with a complete absence of the curse. It is not even a restored Eden as sin and death will exist. Enough children will refuse to trust in Christ to allow for a final rebellion at the end of the 1,000 years (See Rev. 20:7-10). Although the curse will be diminished, it is not completely removed. Man still will have to work to survive. Many pursuits that occupy man's time and energy at present will continue on in the Millennium. Leon Wood surmises life in the Kingdom will be this way:

"Basic structures and institutions of society will probably continue. Lifestyles and patterns, with individuals manifesting their distinct personalities, will remain. People will eat, sleep, earn a living, marry, have children and finally die. There will be cities, farms, schools, industries, and stores. The difference will consist in the presence of proper, enjoyable relationships among people and especially toward God."[69]

Rather that being heaven or Eden, the Millennium will show what the earth could have been if Christ had been accepted as King at His first coming. The Millennium will prove that a sinful and fallen race still has a potential for great blessings if it will but subject itself to Christ's authority. Many verses give a picture of normal human work in the Kingdom such as planting and building (Deut 30:9; Isa. 62:8-9; 65:21-23; Jer. 31:5, 23-25). Many activities will be the same as now, but the resulting blessings from them will be much greater for many reasons. Satan will be bound. The curse will be diminished.

---

[69] Leon J. Wood, *The Bible and Future Events* (Grand Rapids: Zondervan Publishing House, (1973), p. 161

Rain will increase. There will be a perfect system of education, stable families, little crime, no war, few lazy and unproductive citizens to drain society, no medical or legal costs, access to God's wisdom, angelic presence, glorified rulers, etc. Although sin still exists and man must still work, there will be no lack of material blessings for a world that submits to Christ's authority and follows His wisdom. Production far exceeds need.

The Word of God especially emphasizes that the distribution of wealth will be completely fair. The only losers will be those who refuse to worship Christ (see Zech. 14:16ff.).

And each of them will sit under his vine and under his fig tree, with no one to make them afraid, for the mouth of the LORD of hosts has spoken [Micah 4:4].

The LORD has sworn by His right hand and by His strong arm, "I will never again give your grain as food for your enemies; nor will foreigners drink your new wine, for which you have labored. **But those who garner it will eat it,** and praise the LORD; and those who gather it will drink it in the courts of My sanctuary [Isa. 62:8-9].

"**They shall not build, and another inhabit, they shall not plant, and another eat;** for as the lifetime of a tree, so shall be the days of My people, and My chosen ones shall wear out the work of their hands. **They shall not labor in vain,** or bear children for calamity; for they are the offspring of those blessed by the LORD, and their descendants with them" [Isa. 65:22].

d. Partial Removal of the Curse

The partial removal of the curse during the Millennium has already been assumed in previous material. Here that idea is proven. Increase in lifespans, fertility, productivity, the reduction of sickness, and especially changes in animal behavior all indicate a lessening of sin's harmful affects. Since death still occurs in the Millennium, it is not correct to think the millennial Kingdom will be a total eradication of sin or a total removal of its curse, but the Millennium will bring in a great reduction in sorrow caused by sin. There was no death before the fall. Thus, we must assume that originally no animals consumed meat and that they were all tame and friendly to man. Millennial conditions for animals revert to the original pre-fall status (see also Isa. 35:9).

> And the **wolf** will dwell with the **lamb**, and the **leopard will lie down with the kid, and the calf and the young lion and the fatling together**; and a little boy will lead them. Also the cow and **the bear will graze**; their young will lie down together; and **the lion will eat straw** like the ox. And the nursing **child will play by the hole of the cobra**, and the weaned child will put his hand on the viper's den. They will not hurt or destroy in all My holy mountain, for the earth will be full of the knowledge of the LORD as the waters cover the sea" [Isa. 11:6-9].

> **"The wolf and the lamb shall graze together**, and **the lion shall eat straw** like the ox; and dust shall be the serpent's food. They shall do no evil or harm in all My holy mountain, says the LORD" [Isa. 65:25].[70]

> "And I will make a covenant of peace with them and **eliminate harmful beasts** from the land, so that they may live securely in the wilderness and sleep in the woods" [Ezek. 34:25].

---

[70] Note that snakes will still crawl in the dust during the Millennium. This supports the idea that the curse has not been fully removed (See Gen. 3:14).

> "In that day I will also make **a covenant for them with the beasts of the field**, the birds of the sky, and the creeping things of the ground. And I will abolish the bow, the sword, and war from the land, and will make them lie down in safety [Hosea 2:18].

e. Glory

Christ will return in a glorious manner and bring glory to the world. The Millennium will be a time of unimaginable splendor with visible displays of God's power, majesty, and wealth.

> [T]hen the LORD will create over the whole area of Mount Zion and over her assemblies a cloud by day even smoke, and the brightness of a flaming fire by night; for over all the **glory will be a canopy** [Isa. 4:5].

> Then the moon will be abashed and the sun ashamed, for the LORD of hosts will reign on Mount Zion and in Jerusalem, and His **glory** will be before His elders [Isa. 24:23].

> It will **blossom profusely** and rejoice with rejoicing and shout of joy. The glory of Lebanon will be given to it, the majesty of Carmel and Sharon. They will see the **glory** of the LORD, the **majesty** of our God [Isa. 35:2].

> "Then **the glory of the LORD will be revealed**, and all flesh will see it together; for the mouth of the LORD has spoken" [Isa. 40:5].

> "Arise, shine; for your light has come, and **the glory of the LORD has risen upon you**. For behold, darkness will cover the earth, and deep darkness the peoples; but the LORD will rise upon you, and **His glory will appear** upon you. And nations will come to your light, and kings to the **brightness** of your rising" [Isa. 60:1-3].

"For I know their works and their thoughts; the time is coming to gather all nations and tongues. And they shall come and see My **glory**" [Isa. 66:18].

f. Joy

The Kingdom period will be a time of happiness and joy.

Physical and emotional pain will be replaced by joy that comes from the personal presence of Christ the King.

The whole earth is at rest and quiet; they break forth into **shouts of joy**" [Isa. 14:7].

He will swallow up death for all time, and **the Lord God will wipe tears away from all faces,** and He will remove the reproach of His people from all the earth; for the LORD has spoken. And it will be said in that day, "Behold, **this is our God for whom we have waited** that He might save us, This is the LORD for whom we have waited; **let us rejoice and be glad** in His salvation" [Isa. 25:8-9].

You will have songs as in the night when you keep the festival; and **gladness of heart** as when one marches to the sound of the flute, to go to the mountain of the LORD, to the Rock of Israel [Isa. 30:29].

Sing to the LORD a new song, **sing His praise from the end of the earth!** You who go down to the sea, and all that is in it. You islands and those who dwell on them. Let the wilderness and its cities lift up their voices, the settlements where Kedar inhabits. Let the inhabitants of Sela sing aloud, let them shout for joy from the tops of the mountains. Let them give glory to the LORD, and de-

clare His praise in the coastlands [Isa. 42:10-12].

"Whereas you have been forsaken and hated with no one passing through, I will make you an everlasting pride, a **joy** from generation to generation" [Isa. 60:15].

Instead of your shame you will have a double portion, And instead of humiliation they will shout for joy over their portion. Therefore they will possess a double portion in their land, **everlasting joy** will be theirs [Isa. 61:7].

"But be glad and **rejoice forever** in what I create; for behold, I create Jerusalem for rejoicing, and her people for gladness. I will also rejoice in Jerusalem, and be glad in My people; and **there will no longer be heard in her the voice of weeping** and the sound of crying" [Isa. 65:18-19].

"Be joyful with Jerusalem and **rejoice** for her, all you who love her; be **exceedingly glad** with her, all you who mourn over her, That you may nurse and be satisfied with her comforting breasts, that you may suck and be delighted with her bountiful bosom." For thus says the LORD, "Behold, I extend the glory of the nations like an overflowing stream; and you shall be nursed, you shall be carried on the hip and fondled on the knees. As one whom his mother comforts, so I will comfort you; and you shall be comforted in Jerusalem. Then you shall see this, and **your heart shall be glad**, and your bones shall flourish like the new grass; and the hand of the LORD shall be made known to His servants, but He shall be indignant toward His enemies" [Isa. 66:10-14].

"Thus says the LORD, 'behold, I will restore the fortunes of the tents of Jacob and have compassion on his dwelling places; and the city shall be rebuilt on its ruin, and the palace shall stand on its rightful place. And from them shall proceed **thanksgiving and the voice of those who make merry**; and I will multiply them, and they shall not be diminished; I will also honor them, and they shall not be insignificant' " [Jer. 30:18-19].

"Then the virgin shall rejoice in the dance, and the young men and the old, together, for **I will turn their mourning into joy**, and will comfort them, and **give them joy** for their sorrow. And I will fill the soul of the priests with abundance, and My people shall be satisfied with My goodness," declares the LORD [Jer. 31:13-14].

Shout for joy, O daughter of Zion! Shout in triumph, O Israel! **Rejoice and exult with all your heart,** O daughter of Jerusalem! The LORD has taken away His judgments against you, He has cleared away your enemies. The King of Israel, the LORD, is in your midst; you will fear disaster no more. In that day it will be said to Jerusalem: "Do not be afraid, O Zion; Do not let your hands fall limp. The LORD your God is in your midst, a victorious warrior. He will exult over you with joy, He will be quiet in His love, He will rejoice over you with **shouts of joy**" [Zeph. 3:14-17].

g. Wealth

The wealth of the world will pour into Jerusalem and be given to Christ to whom it belongs. [71]

"And nations will come to your light, and kings to the brightness of your rising. Lift up your eyes round about, and see; They all gather together, they come to you. Your sons will come from afar, and your daughters will be carried in the arms. Then you will see and be radiant, and your heart will thrill and rejoice; because the abundance of the sea will be turned to you, **the wealth of the nations will come to you**. A multitude of camels will cover you, the young camels of Midian and Ephah; all those from Sheba will come; **they will bring gold and frankincense**, and will bear good news of the praises of the LORD. All the flocks of Kedar will be gathered together to you, the rams of Nebaioth will minister to you; they will go up with acceptance on My altar, and I shall glorify My glorious house. Who are these who fly like a cloud, and like the doves to their lattices? Surely the coastlands will wait for Me; and the ships of Tarshish will come first, to bring your sons from afar, **their silver and their gold with them**, and for the name of the Lord your God, and for the Holy One of Israel because He has glorified you. And foreigners will build up your walls, and their kings will minister to you; for in My wrath I struck you, and in My favor I have had compassion on you. And **your gates will be open continually; they will not be closed day or night, so that men may bring to you the wealth of the nations,** with their kings led in procession. For the nation and the kingdom which will not serve you will perish, and the nations will be utterly ruined. The glory

---

[71] It seems there will still be national distinctions in the Millennium (Isa. 19:21-23; Zech. 14:18).

Rev. 21:24 and 22:2 also refer to "nations" as existing either in the Millennium or in the Eternal State.

of Lebanon will come to you, the juniper, the box tree, and the cypress together, to beautify the place of My sanctuary; and I shall make the place of My feet glorious. And the sons of those who afflicted you will come bowing to you, and all those who despised you will bow themselves at the soles of your feet; and they will call you the city of the LORD, the Zion of the Holy One of Israel. Whereas you have been forsaken and hated with no one passing through, I will make you an everlasting pride, a joy from generation to generation. You will also suck the milk of nations, and will suck the breast of kings; then you will know that I, the LORD, am your Savior, and your Redeemer, the Mighty One of Jacob. **Instead of bronze I will bring gold, and instead of iron I will bring silver,** and instead of wood, bronze, and instead of stones, iron. And I will make peace your administrators, and righteousness your overseers" [Isa. 60:3-17].

"And I will shake all the nations; and **they will come with the wealth of all nations;** and I will fill this house with glory," says the LORD of hosts [Haggai 2:7].

And Judah also will fight at Jerusalem; and **the wealth of all the surrounding nations will be gathered,** gold and silver and garments in great abundance [Zech.14:14].

3. Political Conditions In the Millennial Kingdom

The world has been governed by fallen men for thousands of years. While Christians can applaud efforts to reduce bloodshed, it is quite unrealistic to expect that man can eliminate war. War is generated by man's selfishness (James 4:1-2). Without a change in man's sin nature, there can be no peace (Isa. 57:21). Christ Himself predicted an increase of wars in the end times (Matt. 24:6-7). Only after the "Prince of Peace" comes will there be world peace under a perfect government.

a. Perfect and Lasting Peace among the World's Nations

In his days may the righteous flourish, and **abundance of peace** till the moon is no more [Psa. 72:7].

And He will judge between the nations, and will render decisions for many peoples; and they will hammer their swords into plowshares, and their spears into pruning hooks. Nation will not lift up sword against nation, and **never again will they learn war** [Isa. 2:4].

...His name will be called...**Prince of Peace**. There will be no end to the increase of His government or of **peace**...[Isa. 9:6-7].

And the work of righteousness will be **peace**. Then my people will live in a **peaceful habitation**...Isa. 32:17-18].

"And all your sons will be taught of the LORD; and the **well-being** [Hebrew *Shalom*, i.e., peace] of your sons will be great. In righteousness you will be established; You will be far from oppression, for you will not fear; and from terror, for it will not come near you" [Isa. 54:13-14].

"**Violence will not be heard again** in your land, nor devastation or destruction within your borders..." [Isa. 60:18].

For thus says the LORD, "Behold, I extend **peace to her like a river**..." [Isa. 66:12].

"And they will live in it securely; and they will build houses, plant vine-

512

yards, and live **securely**..." [Ezek. 28:26].

"And I will make a **covenant of peace** with them.... they will be **secure** on their land....And they will no longer be a prey to the nations..." [Ezek. 34:25,27,28].

"...And I will **abolish the bow, the sword, and war** from the land..." [Hosea 2:18].

And He will judge between many peoples and render decisions for mighty, distant nations. They will hammer their swords into plowshares and their spears into pruning hooks; Nation will not lift up sword against nation, and **never again will they train for war** [Micah 4:3].

Rejoice greatly, O daughter of Zion! Shout in triumph, O daughter of Jerusalem! Behold, your king is coming to you; He is just and endowed with salvation, humble and mounted on a donkey, even on a colt, the foal of a donkey. And I will cut off the chariot from Ephraim, and the horse from Jerusalem; and the **bow of war will be cut off. And He will speak peace to the nations;** and His dominion will be from sea to sea, and from the River to the ends of the earth [Zech. 9:9-10].

World peace obviously brings with it security and protection for God's chosen nation, Israel. The prophets continually promised comfort for Israel (The following verses promise security, protection, comfort for Israel: Isa. 12:1-2; 29:22; 30:26; 40:1-2; 49:13; 51:3; 60:21; 61:4 and 7; 62:8a and 9; 65:21ff.; 66:13-14; Jer. 23:6; Ezek. 34:27; Joel 3:16-17; Amos 9:15; Zeph. 3:18-20; Zech. 8:14-15; 9:8; 14:11).

Then you will know that I am the LORD your God, dwelling in Zion My holy mountain. So Jerusalem will be holy, and **strangers will pass through it no more** [Joel 3:17].

"I will plant them on their land, and **they will not again be rooted out from their land** which I have given them, says the LORD your God" [Amos 9:15].

But I will camp around My house because of an army, because of him who passes by and returns; and **no oppressor will pass over them anymore**, for now I have seen with My eyes [Zech. 9:8].

And people will live in it, and there will be no more curse, for Jerusalem will **dwell in security** [Zech. 14:11].

b. The Kingdom's Judicial System

Christ will eliminate all perversion in the court system. The poor will be treated fairly, and those who oppress them unfairly will suffer punishment. Christ's administration of justice in the courts will ensure accurate verdicts and fair sentences. The prophets promise that each man will enjoy the fruits of his own labor without being defrauded by the criminal or the lazy (see Isa. 62:9, 65:22; Micah 4:4).

While millennial courts will not tolerate discrimination based on race or economic status, there will be discrimination based on "religion". Christ will chastise those who refuse to worship Him (see Zech. 14:16-19). There will be no "separation of church and state" in the Millennium for Christ has authority over both political and spiritual realms. Jerusalem will be the world's political capital **because** it will be the world's center for worship.

The very existence of a judicial system implies that people will still sin in the Millennium. Although Satan is bound, the sin nature will still produce a number who rebel against Christ and likely even some criminals. Christ rules with a "rod of iron," and perfect government will include capital punishment. (See Isa. 11:4; Jer. 31:30; possibly also Isa. 65:20; 66:24). Just as the present world system lacks peace so it also lacks a consistent system of justice. Wickedness goes unpunished. There is favoritism and oppression. Christ the perfect Judge will put an end to all injustice and usher in the ideal judicial system. (See also Psa. 45:6-7; 72:2, 4; 98:9; Isa. 32:1; 54:14; 62:8-9; 65:22-23; Jer. 31:29-30).

Before the LORD, for He is coming; for He is coming to judge the earth. He **will judge the world in righteousness,** and the peoples in His faithfulness [Psa. 96:13].

...For the law will go forth from Zion, and the word of the LORD from Jerusalem. And **He will judge between the nations,** and will render decisions for many peoples..." [Isa. 2:3b-4a].

There will be no end to the increase of His government or of peace, on the throne of David and over his Kingdom, to establish it and to uphold it with **justice and righteousness...** [Isa. 9:7].

...And He will not judge by what His eyes see, nor make a decision by what His ears hear; but **with righteousness He will judge the poor, and decide with fairness for the afflicted of the earth**; and He will strike the earth with the rod of His mouth, and with the breath of His lips He will slay the wicked. Also righteousness will be the belt about His loins, and faithfulness the belt about His waist [Isa. 11:3b-5].

Then **justice** will dwell in the wilderness, and righteousness will abide in the fertile field [Isa. 32:16].

The LORD is exalted, for He dwells on high; **He has filled Zion with justice and righteousness** [Isa. 33:5].

"Behold, My Servant, whom I uphold; My chosen one in whom My soul delights. I have put My Spirit upon Him; **He will bring forth justice to the nations.** He will not cry out or raise His voice, nor make His voice heard in the street. A bruised reed He will not break, and a dimly burning wick He will not extinguish; **He will faithfully bring forth justice.** He will not be disheartened or crushed, **until He has established justice in the earth;** and the coastlands will wait expectantly for His law" [Isa. 42:1-4].

"Behold, the days are coming," declares the LORD, "when I shall raise up for David a righteous Branch; and **He will reign as king and act wisely and do justice and righteousness in the land.** In His days Judah will be saved, and Israel will dwell securely; and this is His name by which He will be called, '**The LORD our righteousness**' " [Jer. 23:5-6].

"In those days and at that time I will cause a righteous Branch of David to spring forth; and He **shall execute justice and righteousness on the earth**" [Jer. 33:15].

...For **from Zion will go forth the law.** Even the word of the LORD from Jerusalem. And **He will judge between many** peoples and render decisions for mighty, distant nations... [Micah 4:2d-3].

c. Individual Welfare as a Priority

There is a difference between justice and goodness. Not only will Christ's millennial government be just, it will also be compassionate. Political repression will be long forgotten as Christ will make His subject's welfare and blessing a top priority. There will be a fair balance between justice and mercy, toughness and tenderness. Christ will be the only dictator who cares for the individual needs of His people.

Like a shepherd He will tend His flock, in His arm He will gather the lambs, and carry them in His bosom; He will gently lead the nursing ewes [Isa. 40:11].

d. The Millennial Government as Dictatorial in Form and World-wide in Extent

Christians should delight at the prospect of Christ's coming reign over the whole world. It will be a complete subjugation of the world both in terms of degree of control and geographical extent. Christ will rule with complete power and rule over the complete world.

"Ask of Me, and I will surely give the nations as Thine inheritance, and the **very ends of the earth as Thy possession.** Thou shalt break them with a rod of iron, Thou shalt shatter them like earthenware" [Psa. 2:8-9].

All the ends of the earth will remember and turn to the LORD, and all the families of the nations will worship before Thee. For the kingdom is the LORD'S and He rules over the nations [Psa. 22:27-28].

May he also rule from sea to sea, and from the River **to the ends of the earth** [Psa. 72:8].

And He will **judge between the nations**, and will render decisions for many peoples; and they will hammer their swords into plowshares, and their spears into pruning hooks. Nation will not lift up sword against nation, and never again will they learn war [Isa. 2:4].

...For **the earth will be full of the knowledge of the LORD** as the wa-

ters cover the sea. Then it will come about in that day that the nations will resort to the root of Jesse, who will stand as a signal for the peoples; and His resting place will be glorious [Isa. 11:9b-10].

"And your gates will be open continually; they will not be enclosed day or night, so that men may bring to you the wealth of the nations, with their kings led in procession. **For the nation and the kingdom which will not serve you will perish**, and the nations will be utterly ruined" [Isa. 60:11-12].

"Then the iron, the clay, the bronze, the silver and the gold were crushed all at the same time, and became like chaff from the summer threshing floors; and the wind carried them away so that not a trace of them was found. But the stone that struck the statue became a great mountain and **filled the whole earth**" [Dan. 2:35] (The great statue that is crushed refers to gentile kingdoms in the context. The smiting stone is the Messiah and His Kingdom).

"And to Him was given dominion, glory and a kingdom, that all the peoples, nations, and **men of every language might serve Him. His dominion is an everlasting dominion which will not pass away**; and His kingdom is one which will not be destroyed....Then the sovereignty, the dominion, and the greatness of **all the kingdoms under the whole heaven will be given to the people of the saints of the Highest One; His kingdom will be an everlasting kingdom, and all the dominions will serve and obey Him**" [Dan. 7:14,27].

And many nations will come and say, "Come and let us go up to the mountain of the LORD and to the house of the God of Jacob, that He may teach us about His ways and that we may walk in His paths." For from Zion will go forth the law, even the word of the LORD from Jerusalem. And **He will judge between many peoples and render decisions for mighty, distant nations.** Then they will hammer their swords into plowshares and their spears into pruning hooks; nation will not lift up sword against nation, and never again will they train for war [Micah 4:2-3].

"But as for you, Bethlehem Eph-rathah, too little to be among the clans of Judah, from you One will go forth for Me to be ruler in Israel. His goings forth are from long ago, from the days of eternity" [Micah 5:2].

"**For the earth will be filled with the knowledge of the glory of the LORD,** as the waters cover the sea" [Hab. 2:14].

"For then I will give to **the peoples** purified lips, that **all of them** may call on the name of the LORD, **to serve Him shoulder to shoulder**" [Zeph. 3:9].

"Thus says the LORD of hosts, 'It will yet be that peoples will come, even the inhabitants of many cities. And the inhabitants of one will go to an-other saying, "Let us go at once to entreat the favor of the LORD, and to seek the LORD of hosts, I will also go." '**So many peoples and mighty nations will come to seek the LORD** of hosts in Jerusalem and to entreat the favor of the LORD.' Thus says the LORD of hosts, 'In those days ten men from all the nations will grasp the garment of a Jew saying, "let us go with you, for we have heard that God is with you" ' " [Zech. 8:20-23].

And I will cut off the chariot from Ephraim, and the horse from Jerusa-lem; and the bow of war will be cut off. And He will speak peace to the nations; and **His dominion will be from sea to sea**, and from the River **to the ends of the earth** [Zech. 9:10].

And the LORD will be **king over all the earth**; in that day the LORD will be the only one, and His name the only one [Zech. 14:9].

"And he who overcomes, and he who keeps My deeds until the end, to him I will give **authority over the na-tions;** and he shall rule them with a rod of iron, as the vessels of the pot-ter are broken to pieces, as I also have received authority from My Fa-ther" [Rev. 2:26-27].

And the seventh angel sounded; and there arose loud voices in heaven, saying, "**The kingdom of the world has become the kingdom of our Lord, and of His Christ; and He will reign forever and ever**" [Rev. 11:15].

"These will wage war against the Lamb, and the Lamb will overcome them, because **He is Lord of lords and King of kings,** and those who are with Him are the called and cho-sen and faithful" [Rev. 17:14].

And from His mouth comes a sharp sword, so that with it **He may smite the nations; and He will rule them with a rod of iron;** and He treads the wine press of the fierce wrath of God, the Almighty. And on His robe and on His thigh He has a name written, "**KING OF KINGS, AND LORD OF LORDS**" [Rev. 19:15-16].

4. The Governors and the Governed in the Kingdom

a. Authorities in the Kingdom

(1). Obviously, the Messiah is the ultimate sovereign in the millennial Kingdom. Numerous verses have already established the fact of Christ's rule (Psa. 2:6; Isa. 9:6-7; Dan. 7:14; Luke 1:31-33; Matt. 19:28; 25:31; 1 Cor. 15:24, etc.). Various names for Christ also express His authority as the millennial King (Branch, The Lord Our Righteousness, Jehovah, Rod of Jesse, Son of Man, King, Judge, Lawgiver, Messiah which means "anointed one", King of kings and Lord of lords, Shepherd, The Light, Stone, Redeemer, Sun of Righteousness, Son of David). Isa. 33:22 is a good verse that summarizes Christ's eventual rule.

> For the LORD is our judge, the LORD is our lawgiver, the LORD is our king; He will save us [Isa. 33:22].

The three descriptions "judge, lawgiver, and king" remind us of the three branches of American government (executive, legislative, judicial). The Constitution of the United States created a system of checks and balances to prevent dictatorial rule. In the Millennium the Lord Jesus Christ will exercise ultimate control over all three areas of government. He will make law. He will administer the law. He will judge. The coming Kingdom will be a perfect dictatorship. It will not technically be a monarchy but a theocracy.

(2). King David as a Millennial Ruler

Many verses teach that "David" will rule in the Kingdom (in addition to verses below see: Isa. 55:3-4; Jer. 33:15-17; Amos 9:11).

> "But they shall serve the LORD their God, and **David their king, whom I will raise up** for them" [Jer. 30: 9].

> "Then **I will set over them one shepherd, My servant David,** and he will feed them; he will feed them himself and be their shepherd. And I, the LORD, will be their God, and **My servant David will be prince among them;** I, the LORD, have spoken" [Ezek. 34:23-24].

> **"And My servant David will be king over them,** and they will all have one shepherd; and they will walk in My ordinances, and keep My statutes, and observe them. And they shall live on the land that I gave to Jacob My servant, in which your fathers lived; and they will live on it, they and their sons, and their sons' sons, forever; and **David My servant shall be their prince forever"** [Ezek. 37:24-25].

> Afterward the sons of Israel will return and seek the LORD their God and **David their king;** and they will come trembling to the LORD and to His goodness in the last days [Hosea 3:5].

Some believe that "David" is a name for Christ Himself as the greater "Son of David." Others think that these "David" passages refer to the historical David of the Old Testament who will be resurrected to serve as a vice-regent under Christ.

Admittedly, these passages seem to refer to the supreme ruler during the Kingdom, and this makes interpreters think of "David" as a name for Christ. Yet, resurrected Bible saints will have positions in the Kingdom of God (see Matt. 8:11; 19:28; 20:23). Presumably, resurrected King David will have an extremely high position in the millennial reign from the throne of David. The name *David* should be taken as a literal reference unless there is strong evidence to the contrary. The Bible strongly associates Christ with David but comes short of calling Him "David" (*Branch* unto David Jer. 23:5; *Son* of David at least 15 times; *seed* of David John 7:42, Rom. 1:3, 2 Tim. 2:8; *root* of David Rev. 5:5; *root and offspring* of David Rev. 22:16). There can be no objection to the reasonable conclusion that David of old will become a "prime minister" in Christ's millennial government. Passages that seem to ascribe the highest rule to David may be speaking in terms of David as the highest authority over Israel (as opposed to a world sovereign) or of David as the highest millennial ruler from among those who had been part of the fallen race. Thus, while Jesus Christ will be the ultimate King, David will likely be a secondary king. The Scripture also teaches about tribal rulers.

(3). The Twelve Apostles

The twelve apostles will serve as judges for Israel's twelve tribes. The lost tribes of Israel may indeed be lost concerning human knowledge, but they are definitely known to God.

> And Jesus said to them, "Truly I say to you, that you who have followed Me, in the regeneration when the Son of Man will sit on His glorious throne, **You also shall sit upon twelve thrones, judging the twelve tribes of Israel**" [Matt. 19:28].

(4). Other Lesser Nobles and Judges over Israel

Several passages mention lesser millennial rulers in general terms. There will be princes, nobles, judges, and city officials. We do not know specific governmental structure, but the Bible gives enough information to conclude that there will be an elaborate system in place with **many** officials.

> Behold, a king will reign righteously, and **princes** will rule justly [Isa. 32:1].

> "This shall be his land for a possession in Israel; so **My princes** shall no longer oppress My people, but they shall give the rest of the land to the house of Israel according to their tribes" [Ezek. 45:8].

The **deliverers** will ascend Mount Zion to judge the mountain of Esau, and the **kingdom will be the LORD'S** [Obadiah v. 21].

> "And he said to him, 'Well done, good slave, because you have been faithful in a very little thing, **be in authority over ten cities**'....And he said to him also, 'And you are to be **over five cities**' " [Luke 19:17,19].

As Christ will be "King of **kings**," (establishing the existence of secondary kings) and will be a worldwide ruler, one can expect that the nations of the world will have officials under Christ. The Bible promises a role for glorified church saints in sharing in Christ's rule (see 1 Cor. 6:2; 2 Tim. 2:12; Rev. 2:26-27; 5:10; 20:4, 6).

b. Those Governed in the Kingdom

(1). Israel Restored

The restoration of Israel's people to the Promised Land is a major subject in Biblical prophecy (see Isa. 11:11ff.; 27:12; 43:5-7; Jer. 30:18, 31:8-9; 32:36-40; 33:11ff.; Ezek. 11:16ff.; 20:34,42; 28:25-26; 34:12ff.; 36:24ff.; all of Ezek. 37; Hosea 1:11; Joel 3:1; Amos 9:14-15; Obadiah v. 17; Micah 4:6-7; Zeph. 3:20; Zech. 8:8, 10:10). Complete fulfillment of these predictions did not take place in the return after the Babylonian exile. Often the promises of restoration mention **eternal restoration** and involve details of end-time events in the context.

> Then it will happen on that day that the **Lord will again recover the second time with His hand the remnant of His people** who will remain from Assyria, Egypt, Pathros, Cush, Elam, Shinar, Hamath, and from the islands of the sea. And He will lift up a standard for the nations, and will **assemble the banished ones of Israel, and will gather the dispersed of Judah from the four corners of the earth** [Isa. 11:11-12].

"Behold, **I will gather them out of all the lands** to which I have driven them in My anger, in My wrath, and in great indignation; and **I will bring them back** to this place and make them dwell in safety. And they shall be My people, and I will be their God" [Jer. 32:37-38].

"As a shepherd cares for his herd in the day when he is among his scattered sheep, so I will care for My sheep and will deliver them from all the places to which they were scattered on a cloudy and gloomy day. And **I will bring them out from the peoples and gather them from the countries and bring them to their own land;** and I will feed them on the mountains of Israel, by the streams, and in all the inhabited places of the land" [Ezek. 34:12-13].

"Also, **I will restore the captivity of My people Israel,** and they will rebuild the ruined cities and live in them, they will also plant vineyards and drink their wine, and make gardens and eat their fruit. **I will also plant them on their land, and they will not again be rooted out from their land** which I have given them, says the LORD your God" [Amos 9:14-15].

(2). Israel Reunited

Not only will Jews return to the land, they will also return as one united nation. After Solomon's death the country was split into the ten northern tribes called *Israel* and the two southern tribes called *Judah.* The prophets teach that when the Jews return to their land in the end times this division will be healed and long forgotten.

"In those days **the house of Judah will walk with the house of Israel,** and they will come together from the land of the north to the land that I gave your fathers as an inheritance" [Jer. 3:18] (see Jer. 33:14).

"And you, son of man, take for yourself one stick and write on it, 'For Judah and for the sons of Israel, his companions;' then take another stick and write on it, 'for Joseph, the stick of Ephraim and all the house of Israel, his companions.' Then join them for yourself one to another into one stick, that they may become one in your hand. And when the sons of your people speak to you saying, 'Will you not declare to us what you mean by these?'...."And say to them, 'Thus says the Lord GOD, behold, I will take the sons of Israel from among the nations where they have gone, and I will gather them from every side and bring them into their own land; and **I will make them one nation in the land,** on the mountains of Israel; and one king will be king for all of them; and **they will no longer be two nations, and they will no longer be divided into two kingdoms**" [Ezek. 37:16-18, 21-22].

Therefore thus says the Lord GOD, "Now **I shall restore the fortunes of Jacob,** and have mercy on **the whole house of Israel**; and I shall be jealous for My holy name" [Ezek. 39:25].

And the **sons of Judah** and the **sons of Israel** will be gathered **together,** and they will appoint for themselves one leader... [Hosea 1:11].

(3). Israel Regenerated

Israel will be reunited and restored to her land. The major difference between the prophetic restoration of Israel in the end times and the creation of the State of Israel in 1948 is that the Bible speaks of a return to Israel by **believing** peoples. In the Kingdom Israel will be dedicated to her Messiah.

[A]nd thus **all Israel will be saved**; just as it is written, "The Deliverer will come from Zion, He will remove ungodliness from Jacob. And this is my covenant with them, when I take away their sins" [Rom. 11:26-27].

"And they shall not teach again, each man his neighbor and each man his brother, saying, 'Know the LORD' for **they shall all know Me**, from the least of them to the greatest of them," declares the LORD, "for I will forgive their iniquity, and their sin I will remember no more" [Jer. 31:34].

[A]nd **I shall purge from you the rebels** and those who transgress against Me; I shall bring them out of the land where they sojourn, but **they will not enter the land of Israel**. Thus you will know that I am the LORD....For on My holy mountain, on the high mountain of Israel," declares the Lord GOD, **"there the whole house of Israel, all of them, will serve Me in the land**; there I shall accept them, and there I shall seek your contributions and the choicest of your gifts, with all your holy things" [Ezek. 20:38,40].

(4). Israel's Prominence

During the Millennium Israel will be the most powerful and prominent nation in the world. It will be the ultimate "superpower." Many verses specifically teach that all other nations will be subordinate to Israel. [72]

When the LORD will have compassion on Jacob, and again choose Israel, and settle them in their own land, then strangers will join them and attach themselves to the house of Jacob. And the peoples will take them along and bring them to their

place, and **the house of Israel will possess them as an inheritance in the land of the LORD as male servants and female servants; and they will take their captors captive, and will rule over their oppressors** [Isa. 14:1-2].

Thus says the Lord GOD, "Behold, I will lift up My hand to the nations, and set up My standard to the peoples; and they will bring your sons in their bosom, and your daughters will be carried on their shoulders. And **kings will be your guardians, and their princesses your nurses. They will bow down to you with their faces to the earth, and lick the dust of your feet:** and you will know that I am the LORD; those who hopefully wait for Me will not be put to shame" [Isa. 49:22-23].

"Surely the coastlands will wait for Me; and the ships of Tarshish will come first, to bring your sons from afar, their silver and their gold with them, for the name of the LORD your God, and for the Holy One of Israel because He has glorified you. And **foreigners** will build up your walls, and **their kings will minister to you;** for in My wrath I have struck you, and in My favor I have had compassion on you. And your gates will be open continually; they will not be closed day or night, so that men may bring to you the wealth of the nations, with their kings led in procession. **For the nation and the kingdom which will not serve you will perish**, and the nations will be utterly ruined. The glory of Lebanon will come to you the juniper, the box tree, and the cypress together, to beautify the place of my sanctuary; and I shall make the place of my feet glorious. **And the sons of those who afflicted you will come bowing to you, and**

---

[72] Egypt is mentioned by name in Isa. 19:21 and Zech. 14:18. Isa.19:22-25 mentions Assyria.

all those who despised you will bow themselves at the soles of your feet; and they will call you the city of the LORD, the Zion of the Holy One of Israel" [Isa. 60:9-14] (see also vv. 15-17).

And strangers will stand and pasture your flocks, and **foreigners will be your farmers and your vine-dressers**. But you will be called the priests of the LORD; you will be spoken of as ministers of our God. **You will eat the wealth of nations**, and in their riches you will boast [Isa. 61:5-6].

And **the nations will see your righteousness, and all kings your glory;** and you will be called by a new name, which the mouth of the LORD will designate. You will also be a crown of beauty in the hand of the LORD, and a royal diadem in the hand of your God. It will no longer be said to you, "Forsaken", nor your land will it any longer be said, "Desolate"; but you will be called, "my delight is in her", and your land, "Married"; for the LORD delights in you, and to Him your land will be married. For as a young man marries a virgin, so your sons will marry you; and as the bridegroom rejoices over the bride, so your God will rejoice over you [Isa. 62:2-5].

It will be a day when **they will come to you** from Assyria and the cities of Egypt, from Egypt even to the Euphrates, even **from sea to sea and mountain to mountain** [Micah 7:12].

"Thus says the LORD of hosts, 'In those days ten men **from all the nations of every language will grasp the garment of a Jew** saying, "Let us go with you, for we have heard

that God is with you" ' " [Zech. 8:23].

Glorified saints will be rulers in the Kingdom. Among non-glorified peoples those who are Jewish will be served by gentile peoples. Israel's prominence is largely due to the presence of God Himself in her midst.

(5). God's Presence in Israel

The prophets predict that God Himself will dwell in Israel during the coming Kingdom. All of these passages give indirect confirmation of Christ's deity. They also serve to explain Israel's domination of the rest of the world during the Millennium. God Himself will dwell in Israel. [73]

> Then you will know that **I am the LORD your God, dwelling in Zion** My holy mountain. So Jerusalem will be holy, and strangers will pass through it no more [Joel 3:17].

> The deliverers will ascend Mount Zion to judge the mountain of Esau, and **the kingdom will be the LORD'S** [Obadiah v. 21].

> And many nations will come and say, "Come and let us go up to the mountain of the LORD and to the house of the God of Jacob, that He may teach us about His ways and that we may walk in His paths." **For from Zion will go forth the law, even the word of the LORD from Jerusalem,** and He will judge between many peoples and render decisions for mighty, distant nations. Then they will hammer their swords into plowshares and their spears into pruning hooks; nation will not lift up sword against nation, and never again will they train

---

[73] Other verses that directly or indirectly establish the deity of the Messiah include: Psa. 2:7, 12; 45:6-7; 72:2-8, 17; 110:1; Isa. 7:14; 9:6; 40:3 and 10; Jer. 23:5-6; Dan. 7:13-14; Micah 5:2; Zech. 12:10; Mal. 3:1.

for war....and **the Lord will reign over them in Mount Zion**" [Micah 4:2-3, 7c] (see also Isa. 2:2-4).

Shout for joy, O daughter of Zion! Shout in triumph, O Israel! Rejoice and exult with all your heart, O daughter of Jerusalem! The LORD has taken away His judgments against you, He has cleared away your enemies. **The King of Israel, the LORD, is in your midst;** You will fear disaster no more. In that day it will be said to Jerusalem: "Do not be afraid, O Zion: do not let your hands fall limp. **The LORD your God is in your midst...**"[Zeph. 3:14-17a].

"Sing for joy and be glad, O daughter of Zion; for behold **I am coming and I will dwell in your midst, declares the LORD**....And the LORD will possess Judah as His portion in the holy land, and will again choose Jerusalem" [Zech. 2:10, 12].

"Thus says the LORD of hosts, 'I am exceedingly jealous for Zion, yes, with great wrath I am jealous for her.' "Thus says **the LORD, 'I will return to Zion and will dwell in the midst of Jerusalem.** Then Jerusalem will be called the City of Truth, and the mountain of the LORD of hosts will be called the Holy Mountain' " [Zech. 8:2-3].

Then **the LORD** will go forth and fight against those nations, as when He fights on a day of battle. And in that day **His feet will stand on the Mount of Olives,** which is in front of Jerusalem on the east; and the Mount of Olives will be split in its middle from east to west by a very large valley, so that half of the mountain will move toward the north and the other half toward the south....And **the LORD will be king over all the earth;** in that day the LORD will be the only one, and His name the only one [Zech. 14:3-4,9].

(6). Jerusalem as the World Capital

Jerusalem will be a world power center both politically and spiritually. The entire world will be governed from Jerusalem.

Now it will come about that in the last days, the mountain of the house of the LORD will be established as the chief of the mountains, and will be raised above the hills; and all the nations will stream to it. And many peoples will come and say, Come let us go up to the mountain of the LORD, to the house of the God of Jacob; that He may teach us concerning His ways, and that we may walk in His paths. **For the law will go forth from Zion, and the word of the LORD from Jerusalem.** And He will judge between the nations, and will render decisions for many peoples; and they will hammer their swords into plowshares, and their spears into pruning hooks. Nation will not lift up sword against nation, and never again will they learn war [Isa. 2:1-4] (see also Micah 4:1-3).

On your walls, O Jerusalem, I have appointed watchmen; all day and all night they will never keep silent. You who remind the LORD, take no rest for yourselves; and give Him no rest until **He establishes and makes Jerusalem a praise in the earth** [Isa. 62:6-7].

"At that time they shall call **Jerusalem 'The Throne of the LORD', and all the nations will be gathered to it, to Jerusalem...**" [Jer. 3:17].

"So many peoples and **mighty nations will come to seek the LORD of hosts in Jerusalem** and to entreat the favor of the LORD" [Zech. 8:22].

Then it will come about that any who are left of all the nations that went against Jerusalem will go up from year to year to worship the King, the LORD of hosts, and to celebrate the Feast of Booths. And it will be that whichever of the families of the earth does not go up **to Jerusalem to worship the King,** the LORD of hosts, there will be no rain on them[74] [Zech. 14:16-17].

5. Spiritual Conditions in the Millennium

a. Satan is bound for the entire 1,000 years (see Rev. 20:1-3). While the sin nature still exists, Satan's confinement in the abyss will definitely cause spiritual improvement in the Kingdom's people.

b. The curse will be partially lifted (see previous section, General Conditions in the Millennium, subsection, "Partial Removal of the Curse", pp. 508-509).

c. God the Son will reside on earth (see previous section, Political Conditions in the Millennium, subsection "God's Presence in Israel", p. 521-22).

d. All unsaved people will be excluded from the beginning of the Kingdom (see pp. 465-471, "The Judgment of Israel" and "The Judgment of the Nations" under the "Transition from Tribulation to Kingdom"). It is true that some who are born in the Millennium will not accept Christ as Savior. Nevertheless, the vast majority of people who live in the Kingdom will be saved in contrast to the present age where believers constitute only a small minority. The fact that an overwhelming majority of people will be believers contributes to the Millennium being the greatest time of spirituality in man's history.

e. There will be a Great Outpouring of the Holy Spirit

It would be interesting to know more about the Holy Spirit's work in the Millennium. His Kingdom ministry does not seem to be the same as it was under the Law administration or as it is now under the church administration. Isaiah clearly predicted that the Holy Spirit would guide the Messiah in His kingly rule.

Then a shoot will spring from the stem of Jesse, and a branch from his roots will bear fruit. And **the Spirit of the LORD will rest on Him...** [Isa. 11:1-2a].

In addition to enabling the Messiah to govern wisely and righteously, God will pour out the Holy Spirit upon virtually all Kingdom saints.

Until **the Spirit is poured out upon us** from on high... [Isa. 32:15].

"For I will pour out water on the thirsty land and streams on the dry ground; **I will pour out My Spirit on your offspring,** and My blessing on your descendants..." [Isa. 44:3].

"Moreover, I will give you a new heart and put a new spirit within you; and I will remove the heart of stone from your flesh and give you a heart of flesh. And **I will put My Spirit within you** and cause you to walk in My statutes, and you will be careful to observe My ordinances" [Ezek. 36:26-27].

"And I will not hide My face from them any longer for **I shall have poured out My Spirit** on the house of Israel," declares the LORD GOD [Ezek. 39:29].

Joel 2:28-29 is perhaps the most important text concerning the Holy Spirit's role in the Kingdom. Peter quotes it on Pentecost (see Acts 2:16ff.). It is important to note that the apostolic experiences on Pentecost illustrate Joel 2:28-29, but they do not specifically

---

[74] Again note references to saved in Egypt and Assyria (Isa. 19:21-25 and Zech. 14:18).

and totally fulfill Joel's predictions. There was no occurrence of cosmic signs, or blotting out of the sun, or judgment of the nations on Pentecost (see context of Joel 2:28-29 in Joel 2:30-3:2). Thus, Joel 2:28-29 does *not* **make a prediction about the church administration** but about Christ's future Kingdom on earth (see also Joel 2:30-3:2 to get the time frame on this prediction).

> "And it will come about after this that **I will pour out My Spirit on all mankind;** and your sons and daughters will prophesy, your old men will dream dreams, your young men will see visions. And even on the male and female servants **I will pour out My Spirit in those days**" [Joel 2:28-29].

Although one cannot be certain because of the paucity of references, it is likely that the Holy Spirit's millennial work will be similar to what would have happened at Christ's first coming had He been accepted as King. The miracles of the gospels gave a foretaste of the coming age (see Heb. 2:4, 6:5) The Lord's healing ministry was a partial fulfillment of what will be in the Kingdom (see Matt. 8:15ff.). There will be many prophets, many miracle workers, many healers in the Kingdom (in contrast to the present Rom. 8:22). We do not know whether there will be a Spirit-baptizing ministry into the body of Christ, but it is safe to think the Holy Spirit will indwell (see Ezek. 36:26 above) and regenerate (John 3:3,5). Imagine a world full of Joshuas, Gideons, Daniels, Elijahs and Elishas exhibiting the power of the Holy Spirit (see Matt. 11:11).

f. Unified Worship in Jerusalem

Many of the same verses which teach that Jerusalem will be a world political capital also teach that it will be a worldwide center for worship (see Isa. 2:2-4; Micah 4:1ff.; Zeph. 3:9-10; Zech. 8:20-23, 14:16-21). Both of the passages from Zechariah teach

that the world will celebrate the "Feast of Tabernacles" during the Millennium. Here is one of many indications that the spiritual system during the Kingdom will have many similarities to the dispensation of Law. Many practices from the Law of Moses will be reinstituted (see pp. 527-29 "The Millennial Temple/Millennial Worship"). The Millennium will definitely have a "Jewish flavor."

g. Abundant Spirituality

The existence of a court system and even the death penalty shows that sin still exists in the Millennium (Isa. 11:4; Jer. 31:30). While longevity increases, death still occurs; and this is another indication of sin in the millennial world (Isa. 65:20). Satan will be able to stir up elements of the millennial population against Christ during his short release from the abyss at the very close of the Kingdom period (see Rev. 20:3,7-10). This means that some of those born in the Millennium will reject Christ despite ideal conditions.

Nevertheless, the existence of sin and a small minority of unbelievers will be more than offset by an abundance of holiness, obedience, righteousness, and truth. The Kingdom will begin with all of its citizens having been saved. (See Matt. 13:41-43, 49-50; 25:34,41,46 and pp. 465-471 on "The Judgment of Israel" and "The Judgment of the Nations" under the "Transition from Tribulation to Kingdom".) These are either believing survivors of the Tribulation or resurrected and glorified believers. The majority of those born throughout the entire 1,000 years will trust and obey Christ. This effects all areas of civic life, e.g., economics, crime, education, etc.

> "Then I will restore your judges as at the first, and your counselors as at the beginning; after that **you will be called the city of righteousness, a faithful city.**" Zion will be redeemed

with justice, and her repentant ones with righteousness [Isa. 1:26-27].

And it will come about that he **who is left in Zion and remains in Jerusalem will be called holy** - everyone who is recorded for life in Jerusalem. When **the LORD has washed away the filth of the daughters of Zion,** and purged the bloodshed of Jerusalem from her midst, by the spirit of judgment and the spirit of burning [Isa. 4:3-4].

And a highway will be there, a roadway, and it will be called **the Highway of Holiness. The unclean will not travel on it,** but it will be for him who walks that way, and **fools will not wander on it.** No lion will be there, nor will any vicious beast go up on it; these will not be found there. But the redeemed will walk there [Isa. 35:8-9].

Awake, awake, clothe yourself in your strength, O Zion; clothe yourself in your beautiful garments, O Jerusalem, **the holy city. For the uncircumcised and the unclean will no more come into you** [Isa. 52:1].

"Violence will not be heard again in your land, nor devastation or destruction within your borders; but you will call your walls salvation, and your gates praise....**Then all your people will be righteous;** they will possess the land forever..." [Isa. 60:18,21].

For as the earth brings forth its sprouts, and as a garden causes the things sown in it to spring up, so **the LORD GOD will cause righteousness and praise to spring up** before all the nations [Isa. 61:11].

"'But this is the covenant which I will make with the house of Israel after those days," declares the LORD, "I will put My law within them, and on

their heart I will write it; and I will be their God, and they shall be My people. And they shall not teach again, each man his neighbor and each man his brother, saying, 'Know the LORD,' for **they shall all know Me,** from the least of them to the greatest of them," declares the LORD, "for I will forgive their iniquity, and their sin I will remember no more" [Jer. 31:33-34].

[A]nd **I shall purge from you the rebels** and those who transgress against Me; I shall bring them out of the land where they sojourn, but **they will not enter the land of Israel.** Thus you will know that I am the LORD....For on My holy mountain, on the high mountain of Israel, declares the Lord GOD, there **the whole house of Israel, all of them will serve Me in the land**; there I shall accept them, and there I shall seek your contributions and the choicest of your gifts, with all your holy, things....And there you will remember your ways and all your deeds, with which you have defiled yourselves; and you will loathe yourselves in your own sight for all the evil things that you have done" [Ezek. 20:38, 40, 43].

"For I will take you from the nations, gather you from all the lands, and bring you into your own land. Then I will sprinkle clean water on you and **you will be clean;** I will cleanse you from all your filthiness and from all your idols. Moreover, I will give you a new heart and put a new spirit within you; and I will remove the heart of stone from your flesh and give you a heart of flesh. And I will put My Spirit within you and cause you to walk in My statutes and **you will be careful to observe My ordinances**. And you will live in the land that I gave to your forefathers; so you will be My people, and I will be your God. Moreover, I will save you from all your uncleanness; and I will call for the grain and multiply it, and I will not bring a famine on you. And I will multiply the fruit of the tree and the produce of the field, that you may not receive again the disgrace of famine among the nations. Then you will remember your evil ways and your deeds that were not good, and you will loathe yourselves in your own sight, for your iniquities and your abominations" [Ezek. 36:24-31].

"And they will no longer defile themselves with their idols, or with their detestable things, or with any of their transgressions; but I will deliver them from all their dwelling places in which they have sinned, and will cleanse them. And they will be my people, and I will be their God. And My servant David will be king over them, and they will all have one shepherd; and **they will walk in My ordinances**, and keep my statutes, and observe them" [Ezek. 37:23-24].

And He said to me, "Son of man, this is the place of my throne and the place of the soles of My feet, where I will dwell among the sons of Israel forever. And **the house of Israel will not again defile My holy name**, neither they nor their kings, by their harlotry and by the corpses of their kings when they die....As for you, son of man, describe the temple to the house of Israel, that they may be ashamed of their iniquities; and let them measure the plan [Ezek. 43:7,10].

"In that day you will feel no shame because of all your deeds by which you have rebelled against Me; for **then I will remove from your midst your proud, exulting ones**. And you will never again be haughty on my

holy mountain....The remnant of **Israel will do no wrong** and tell no lies, nor will a deceitful tongue be found in their mouths; for they shall feed and lie down with no one to make them tremble" [Zeph. 3:11,13].

"Thus says the LORD, 'I will return to Zion and will dwell in the midst of Jerusalem. Then Jerusalem will be called **the City of Truth**, and the mountain of the LORD of hosts will be called **the Holy Mountain**' " [Zech. 8:3].

"In that day a **fountain** will be opened for the house of David and for the inhabitants of Jerusalem, **for sin and for impurity**....And I will bring the third part through the fire, refine them as silver is refined, and test them as gold is tested. **They will call on My name**, and I will answer them; I will say, '**They are My people**,' and they will say, 'The LORD is my God' " [Zech. 13:1,9].

In that day there will be inscribed on the bells of the horses, "HOLY TO THE LORD." And the cooking pots in the LORD'S house will be like the bowls before the altar. And every cooking pot in Jerusalem and in Judah will be holy to the LORD of hosts; and all who sacrifice will come and take of them and boil in them. And **there will no longer be a Canaanite in the house of the LORD of hosts in that day** [Zech. 14:20-21].

[A]nd thus **all Israel will be saved**; just as it is written, "the deliverer will come from Zion, **he will remove ungodliness from Jacob**" [Rom. 11:26].

It is possible that only saved people will be allowed to enter the land of Israel (Isa. 52:1; 60:21; Ezek. 20:40) and that there will be evangelistic efforts to the gentiles which are mostly successful (Isa. 42:6, 60:3).

h. Full Knowledge and Instruction in the Word of God

With Christ in residence in Jerusalem and with the Holy Spirit poured out upon God's people, there will be widespread knowledge of God's truth. Christ taught that John the Baptist's ministry would be insignificant compared to the Kingdom (Matt. 11:11). Satan will not be operative in his blinding work (Rev. 20:1-3), nor will Christ permit false prophets to deceive. Instead of social institutions suppressing the gospel, they will all promote it. Those who reject Christ at this time will be deeply foolish and deeply guilty (see also Isa. 2:2-4; Micah 4:1ff.).

For **the earth will be full of the knowledge of the LORD** as the waters cover the sea [Isa. 11:9b].

"And those who err in mind will **know the truth**, and those who criticize will **accept instruction**" [Isa. 29:24].

And each will be like a refuge from the wind, and a shelter from the storm, like streams of water in a dry country, like the shade of a huge rock in a parched land. Then the eyes of those who see will not be blinded, and the ears of those who hear will listen. And **the mind of the hasty will discern the truth**, and the tongue of the stammerers will hasten to speak clearly [Isa. 32:2-4].

"And **all your sons will be taught of the LORD;** and the well being of your sons will be great" [Isa. 54:13].

"Then I will give you shepherds after My own heart who will feed you on **knowledge and understanding**....At that time they shall call Jerusalem 'the Throne of the LORD.' And all the nations will **be gathered to it, to Je-**

rusalem, for the name of the LORD; **nor shall they walk anymore after the stubbornness of their evil heart** [Jer. 3:15, 17].

"I shall also raise up **shepherds over them** and they will tend them; and they will not be afraid any longer, nor be terrified, nor will any be missing," declares the LORD [Jer. 23:4].

"And they shall not teach again, each man his neighbor and each man his brother saying, 'Know the LORD, for **they shall all know Me,** from the least of them to the greatest of them,' declares the LORD, 'for I will forgive their iniquity, and their sin I will remember no more' " [Jer. 31:34] (see Heb. 8:8ff.).

"For the **earth will be filled with the knowledge of the glory of the LORD** as the waters cover the sea" [Hab. 2:14].

i. The Millennial Temple/Millennial Worship

The Scriptures clearly teach that the temple in Jerusalem will be rebuilt (see Matt. 24:15ff. and parallels, 2 Thess. 2:4; Rev. 11:1ff.). Apparently, this temple will be destroyed during the tribulational battles or judgments (perhaps at Armageddon, Zech. 14:2ff., but see also Rev. 11:2).

The millennial temple will possess architectural glory (Ezekiel 40-43), but of greater interest are the activities, objects, and participants associated with the millennial temple. Also, the glory of God which departed Solomon's temple before the exile (Ezek. 10:18-19; 11:23) returns to the millennial temple (Ezek. 43:5-7).

"I will also take some of them for **priests and for Levites,** says the LORD" [Isa. 66:21].

"[A]nd the Levitical **priests** shall never lack a man before Me to offer burnt **offerings**, to burn grain offerings, and to prepare **sacrifices** continually" [Jer. 33:18].

"For on My holy mountain, on the high mountain of Israel", declares the LORD GOD, "there the whole house of Israel, all of them, will serve Me in the land; there I shall accept them, and **there I shall seek your contributions and the choicest of your gifts,** with all your holy things. As a **soothing aroma** I shall accept you, when I bring you out from the peoples and gather you from the lands where you are scattered; and I shall prove Myself holy among you in the sight of the nations" [Ezek. 20:40-41].

Then it will come about that any who are left of all the nations that went against Jerusalem will go up from year to year to worship the King, the LORD of hosts, and **to celebrate the Feast of Booths.** And it will be that whichever of the families of the earth does not go up to Jerusalem to worship the King, the LORD of hosts, there will be no rain on them. And if the family of Egypt does not go up or enter, then no rain will fall on them; it will be the plague with which the LORD smites the nations who do not go up to **celebrate the Feast of Booths.** This will be the punishment of Egypt, and the punishment of all the nations who do not go up to celebrate **the Feast of Booths**....And every cooking pot in Jerusalem and in Judah will be holy the LORD of hosts; and all who **sacrifice** will come and take of them... [Zech. 14:16-19,21].

And in the porch of the gate were two tables on each side, on which to slaughter **the burnt offering, the sin**

offering, and the guilt offering [Ezek. 40:39].

Then he said to me, "The north chambers and the south chambers, which are opposite the separate area, they are the **holy chambers** where the **priests** who are near to the LORD shall eat the most holy things. There they shall lay the most holy things, **the grain offering, the sin offering, and the guilt offering for the place is holy** [Ezek. 42:13].

And He said to me, "Son of man, thus says the Lord GOD, 'These are the statues for the **altar** on the day it is built, to **offer burnt offerings** on it and to sprinkle blood on it. And you shall give to the **Levitical priests** who are from the offspring of Zadok, who draw near to Me to minister to Me,' declares the Lord GOD, 'a young bull for a **sin offering**' " [Ezek. 43:18-19] (see also v. 13).

"In the first month, on the fourteenth day of the month, you shall have the **Passover**, a feast of seven days; **unleavened bread** shall be eaten. And on that day the prince shall provide for himself and all the people of the land a bull for a **sin offering**. And during the seven days of the feast he shall provide as a **burnt offering** to the LORD seven bulls and seven rams without blemish on every day of the seven days, and a male goat daily for a **sin offering**. And he shall provide as a **grain offering** an ephah with a bull, an ephah with a ram, and a hin of oil with an ephah. In the seventh month, on the fifteenth day of the month, at the feast, he shall provide like this, seven days **for the sin offering, the burnt offering, the grain offering,** and the oil" [Ezek. 45:21-25].

Thus says the Lord GOD, "The gate of the inner court facing east shall be shut the six working days; but it shall be opened on the **Sabbath day,** and opened on the day of the **new moon**" [Ezek. 46:1].

"And you shall provide a **lamb** a year old without blemish **for a burnt offering** to the LORD daily; **morning by morning you shall provide it**" [Ezek. 46:13].

"But if he gives a gift from his inheritance to one of his servants, it shall be his until **the year of liberty...**" [Ezek. 46:17].

These verses teach that many millennial worship practices will be reinstitutions of Mosaic practices (priests, sacrifices, Jewish festivals, etc.). There is no direct mention of the Ark of the Covenant, or a golden lampstand, or the table of shewbread, or the Day of Atonement or Pentecost. Thus, Kingdom worship may not completely revert to Levitical practices; but it will be closer to the Law than to the church.

The idea of animal sacrifices in the Millennium is repulsive to some. They believe that it is inconsistent with the finality of Christ's sacrifice. The animal sacrifices of the Millennium will definitely not atone for sin. Christ's sacrifice was indeed perfectly sufficient. He rendered animal sacrifices obsolete. Animal sacrifices served as only a temporary covering for sin (Heb. 7:27; 9:12,26; 10:4,10,14,26).

However, premillennialists do not believe that millennial sacrifices are reinstituted as a means of covering sin or that such sacrifices will contribute anything to salvation. In fact, the Kingdom is based in the New Covenant founded on Christ's blood (see Jer. 31:31ff., cf. Luke 22:20). Although millennial sacrifices involve similar activities to the Old Testament sacrifices, **it must be the case that they function as memorials to**

Christ's sacrifice. Millennial animal sacrifices will probably play the same role as the communion ordinance does in the church dispensation. Communion is to "show the Lord's death **till He comes**" (1 Cor. 11:26 KJV). Perhaps after the Lord's return communion will be replaced by animal sacrifices as a more graphic memorial of the Lamb of God's perfect sacrifice. Also, the food generated by sacrifices becomes part of a long banquet celebration.

6. Summary on the Kingdom

The Kingdom will show what Christ can do through a fallen race that will trust and obey Him. For the first time in history, social, political, educational, and judicial systems will be permeated with godliness. While unbelievers think that submission to Christ would make life miserable, the truth is that when the world finally submits to Christ it will know its highest advancement and blessings.

7. Final Satanic Rebellion

God binds Satan in the abyss throughout the 1,000-year reign of Christ on earth. However, Revelation 20 teaches that God allows Satan a short release during the transition from the Kingdom to the Eternal State. The devil will find enough disgruntled people to initiate a rebellion against Christ the King. Here is another measure of sin's insanity. The devil and his allies have no hope of winning. Although they encircle Jerusalem, fire from heaven consumes them; and the devil finishes his "career" by an unwilling entrance into the eternal Lake of Fire. Perhaps God allows this final revolt to demonstrate Satan's incurable evil and to illustrate the righteousness in giving eternal punishment for the devil and his human followers. The unsaved choose the devil and hell over an ideal world with Christ as King! They too are incorrigible and deserve condemnation.

[A]nd threw him into the abyss, and shut it and sealed it over him, so that he should not deceive the nations any longer, until the thousand years were completed; after these things he must be released for a short time....And when the thousand years are completed, Satan will be released from his prison, and will come out to deceive the nations which are in the four corners of the earth, Gog and Magog, to gather them together for the war; the number of them is like the sand of the seashore. And they came up on the broad plain of the earth and surrounded the camp of the saints and the beloved city, and fire came down from heaven and devoured them. And the devil who deceived them was thrown into the lake of fire and brimstone, where the beast and the false prophet are also; and they will be tormented day and night forever and ever [Rev. 20:3,7-10]. [75]

XIV. Eternity

A study on the Eternal State must be divided into eternal punishment and eternal life in God's presence, that is, hell and heaven. Before detailed topical studies on hell and heaven, there are a few chronological matters concerning judgments unto damnation that must be treated.

A. The Judgment of angels

The Scripture definitely teaches that there will be an end time judgment for angels, specifically fallen angels.

Do you not know that we shall **judge angels**? [1 Cor. 6:3a].

For if God did not spare **angels** when they sinned, but cast them into hell

and committed them to pits of darkness, **reserved for judgment** [2 Pet. 2:4].

And **angels** who did not keep their own domain, but abandoned their proper abode, He has kept in eternal bonds under darkness for the **judgment** of the great day [Jude 6].

Although the Bible does not give a specific time for the judgment of fallen angels, it is sensible to believe that the punishment of fallen angels takes place along with (or at least by the time of) Satan's confinement into the Lake of Fire (Rev. 20:10). Also, time is literally running out as "time" ends and eternity begins. One cannot place angelic judgment past the transition from Millennium to eternity. The Lake of Fire was not made for humans but for "the devil and his angels" (see Matt. 25:41). Revelation 20 seems to be the point in time when God is emptying Hades (see v. 14) and the abyss (at least the devil vacates the abyss) and confining all wickedness, human and angelic, to the eternal Lake of Fire. It is the most logical point at which to place the judgment of fallen angels. 2 Peter 2:4 and Jude 6 mention the judgment of confined angels, but presumably the demons who have been loose and active also face judgment and definitely undergo eternal punishment.

Paul teaches that church saints will have a role in judging angels. This probably refers to fallen angels. Unless 1 Cor. 6:3 is interpreted to include the elect angels, there is no Biblical teaching about a judgment for the holy angels.

B. The Great White Throne Judgment

The Great White Throne Judgment is a major event in the transition from the Millennium to the Eternal State. Rev. 20:11 may indicate a time after the destruction of the present heaven and earth but before the creation or renovation of the new heavens and earth. God the Father has given all judgment

---

[75] In Rev. 20 "Gog and Magog" may refer to Russia as in Ezek. 38-39. Another option is to understand "God and Magog" figuratively as a battle cry ("Remember the Alamo") or a cliche meaning a disastrous and final defeat (as in "Waterloo").

to God the Son (John 5:22; Acts 17:31). Therefore, it is safe to assume that Christ presides over this final judgment of the lost. The dead, great and small, will be resurrected to face judgment. God has recorded all of their deeds in numerous books. However, the main concern is whether a person's name is or is not written in the book of life. Rejection of the Lord Jesus Christ is the ultimate basis for eternal condemnation (see John 3:18; 2 Thess. 1:8). Yet, there are several reasons for an interest in "deeds". The idea of degrees of punishment is addressed on pp. 541-42. While rejection of Christ is the basis for entrance into the Lake of Fire, works will be a factor in the degree of punishment. Also, perhaps Christ will examine a person's works to prove to the condemned that good works are insufficient for earning eternal life. Some will claim they have done great works in Christ's name, but the records establish the fact that they were really workers of iniquity and do not deserve entrance into heaven (see Matt. 7:22-23).

There is no question that the absence of ones name from the Book of Life by rejection of Christ is the basis for punishment at the Great White Throne. Another sure fact is that the majority (if not all) of those judged at the Great White Throne are sentenced to the second death, eternal punishment in the Lake of Fire. Essentially then, the Great White Throne is the judgment of the condemned. It is the resurrection unto condemnation mentioned in Dan. 12:2 and John 5:29. [76]

The Scripture does not say when the millennial saints are judged or glorified, nor does the Bible teach anything about any judgment or resurrection of those few who die during the Millennium. Perhaps they arise immediately, or perhaps they arise at the Great White Throne and a small minority at this

judgment does have their names in the Book of Life.

Many of the souls of those judged at the Great White Throne come from Hades (v. 13). They had died and now appear raised for judgment.

Presumably, those unsaved who survived the Tribulation and had previously been judged and confined to the Lake of Fire need not reappear for judgment at the Great White Throne (see Matt. 25:41,46). Technically, they were never a part of the dead who had been confined in Sheol/Hades (See Rev. 20:12) because they went directly from physical life to the Lake of Fire without a normal physical death on earth. [77]

C. Terms for Places of Punishment

Although speakers can be careless and use different terms interchangeably, the Bible differentiates several places of punishment. Any detailed study shows that these terms are not equivalent. They must be studied in order to give a thorough treatment of the topic of eternal punishment.

1. Hell

Hell is a general term that refers to any place of torment. It can be a useful word, but is not specific enough for a deep understanding.

2. Abyss

The Greek term *abyss* is often translated "pit" or "bottomless pit" in English. The abyss is the temporary place of imprisonment for some fallen angels (Luke 8:31; Rev. 9:1,2,11, 11:7, 17:8, 20:1-3). In Christ's day demons, free to roam actively,

---

[76] See also Acts 24:15; Heb. 9:27; and Rev. 20:5-6.

[77] Church saints raised at the Rapture and Old Testament/tribulational saints raised after the Tribulation do not appear at the Great White Throne judgment. They were raised and rewarded long before the end of the Millennium. Perhaps some millennial saints who had died are raised and rewarded at this time, but the Bible does not specifically teach when any millennial saints who die will be raised.

begged to enter swine rather than having to go to the abyss (see Luke 8:31). Some fallen angels are now in the abyss. The particular fallen angels in 2 Pet. 2:4 and Jude 6 are confined in the abyss (Peter calls the abyss "tartarus") until their final judgment and transfer to the Lake of Fire. The possibility that they participated in cohabitation with women has been discussed in Chapter 5, Demonology.[78] Apparently, some of the fallen angels in the abyss will be released from the abyss to bring torment to the earth during the Tribulation (see Rev. 9:1).

While the Beast and False Prophet go directly to the Lake of Fire at the end of the Tribulation, Satan spends 1,000 years of confinement in the abyss (see Rev. 20:1-3). After a short release from the abyss (and a short rebellion), Satan will be cast into the Lake of Fire. While the abyss is the temporary place of punishment for fallen angels, the Lake of Fire (made for the Devil and his angels, Matt. 25:41) is the eternal residence for fallen angels. Thus, after the angelic judgment the abyss is emptied, and all its fiends undergo a permanent transfer to the Lake of Fire.

3. Sheol or Hades[79]

Sheol is a Hebrew word. Its Greek equivalent is *Hades*. Both terms refer to the place of departed human spirits. The souls of the

unsaved go to Hades immediately upon death and remain there until the resurrection unto condemnation at the Great White Throne Judgment. Therefore, Hades is a temporary place of punishment for unsaved humans until their final resurrection, judgment, and transfer to the eternal Lake of Fire. It is to be contrasted with the abyss, which is a temporary place for fallen angels (not humans) and with the Lake of Fire (or Gehenna), which is an eternal place of punishment for both humans and angels after they have been judged. Specific characteristics of Hades will further highlight the contrast with other places of punishment.

a. Hades for Humans Only

The Bible does not teach that fallen angels ever enter Hades to await judgment. The temporary place of confinement for fallen angels who await final judgment is called the "abyss" or "tartarus." Hades is the temporary place of punishment for **unsaved humans** who await final judgment.

b. Hades for Human Spirits

Obviously, the bodies of the unsaved return to the dust at death. Only their souls enter Hades. Thus, Hades is a place for departed and **non-resurrected human spirits**. After they are raised to stand judgment, they will have a resurrection body perfectly suited to eternal flames (see Dan. 12:2; John 5:29; Rev. 20:12). Humans in the Lake of Fire will possess body and soul (see Matt. 10:28. Hell here is *Gehenna*), but those in Hades awaiting judgment **do not have a resurrection body** (see footnote 81).

c. The Location of Sheol/Hades

The location for the eternal Lake of Fire is unknown. The "heavens and earth" have fled before the Great White Throne Judgment (Rev. 20:11). This probably indicates the destruction of the present heavens and earth (see 2 Pet. 3:10-13). It follows that the Lake of Fire is not on this present earth. However, there are plenty of Scriptural phrases that

[78] See Chapter 5, Section II, "The Origin of Demons", p. 52.
[79] Discussion as to whether there were two compartments of Sheol/Hades before the cross is not within the domain of future events. Therefore, it is not included in this study. Many believe that Old Testament saints went to a righteous compartment of Hades at death. It is also believed that the Lord Jesus visited this section of Hades between His death and resurrection and brought the souls from there to heaven, perhaps at the ascension. The following texts might be explained by this theory although they can be given alternate interpretations (1 Sam. 28:13,15; Matt. 12:40; 27:51-53; Luke 16:19-31; John 20:17; Acts 2:27; Eph 4:8-9; 1 Pet. 3:18-20).

indicate that Sheol/Hades is in the center of the present earth.[80] This is another indication of the difference between Sheol/Hades as the **temporary** place of **human** punishment before the final judgment, and the Lake of Fire (or Gehenna) which is the **eternal** place of torment for **both fallen angels and unsaved humans**.

"They are high as the heavens, what can you do? **Deeper than Sheol,** what can you know?" [Job 11:8] (This verse contrasts heaven as up with Sheol which is down).

If I ascend to heaven, Thou art there; if I make my bed in Sheol, behold, Thou art there [Psa. 139:8]. (Again, Sheol is the opposite of ascent. Rather than going up to Sheol one goes **down**).

...her (i.e., the foolish woman) guests are in the **depths** of Sheol [Prov. 9:18b].

The path of life leads upward for the wise, that he may keep away from **Sheol below** [Prov.15:24].

Thus says the Lord GOD, "On the day when it **went down to Sheol** I caused lamentations; I closed the deep over it and held back its rivers. And its many waters were stopped up, and I made Lebanon mourn for it, and all the trees of the field wilted away on account of it. I made the nations quake at the sound of its fall when I made it go **down to Sheol** with those who go **down** to the pit; and all the well-watered trees of Eden, the choicest and best of Lebanon, were comforted in the **earth beneath.** They also went **down with it to Sheol** to those who were slain by the sword; and those who were its

strength lived under its shade among the nations" [Ezek. 31:15-17].

"Son of man, wail for the multitude of Egypt, and bring it **down,** her and the daughters of the powerful nations, **to the nether world,** with those who go **down** to the pit....The strong among the mighty ones shall speak of him and his helpers **from the midst of Sheol,** 'They have **gone down,** they lie still, the uncircumcised slain by the sword....' "Elam is there and all her multitude around her grave; all of them slain, fallen by the sword, who went **down** uncircumcised to the **lower parts of the earth,** who instilled their terror in the land of the living, and bore their disgrace with those who went **down to the pit**" [Ezek. 32:18,21,24].

"Though they **dig into Sheol,** from there shall My hand take them; and though they ascend to heaven, from there will I bring them down" [Amos 9:2].

"And you, Capernaum, will not be exalted to heaven, will you? You shall **descend to Hades;** for if the miracles had occurred in Sodom which occurred in you, it would have remained to this day" [Matt. 11:23].

"And you, Capernaum, will not be exalted to heaven, will you? You will be brought **down to Hades**" [Luke 10:15].

It is correct to think of the souls of the unsaved as going down to Hades upon death. While the body returns to dust, the soul still very much exists. Certain sects teach the heresy of soul-sleep, but the Scriptures teach that the departed lost are very much conscious.

d. Consciousness in Hades

---

[80] In addition to the verses in the text see also Isa. 14:9ff.

A following section will develop the truth that the saved continue in consciousness after death (pp. 546-48). This present material concerns the unsaved. The doctrine of "soul-sleep", which maintains that souls are unconscious after death, is totally without foundation and is inexcusable.

Regardless as to whether *Lucifer* in Isaiah is interpreted as a reference to Satan or to the King of Tyre (whom Satan supported), Isaiah 14 teaches that the lost are conscious in Sheol. They are aware and even communicate. Special attention should be paid to vv. 9, 10, and 16 where those in Sheol respond to Lucifer's entrance.

> "**Sheol from beneath is excited** over you to meet you when you come; it **arouses** for you **the spirits** of the dead, all the leaders of the earth; it raises all the kings of the nations from their thrones. **They will all respond and say** to you, even you have been made weak as we, you have become like us. Your pomp and the music of your harps have been brought down to Sheol; maggots are spread out as your bed beneath you, and worms are your covering. How you have fallen from heaven, O star of the morning, son of the dawn! You have been cut down to the earth, you who have weakened the nations! But you said in your heart, 'I will ascend to heaven; I will raise my throne above the stars of God, and I will sit on the mount of assembly in the recesses of the north. I will ascend above the heights of the clouds; I will make myself like the Most High.' "Nevertheless you will be thrust down to Sheol, to the recesses of the pit. Those who see you **will gaze at you, they will ponder over you, saying,** 'is this the man who made the earth tremble, who shook kingdoms, who made the world like a wilderness and overthrew its cities, who did not

allow his prisoners to go home?' " [Isa. 14:9-17].

Ezekiel Chapters 31 and 32 contain many references to Sheol. These also indicate that the lost in Sheol are very much conscious. Ezekiel 32:21 speaks of the inhabitants of Sheol reacting to Egypt's destruction. Verse 31 seems to be saying that Pharaoh will meet the leaders of the other destroyed kingdoms in Sheol.

> "Son of man, wail for the multitude of Egypt, and bring it down, her and the daughters of the powerful nations, to the nether world, with those who go down to the pit....**The strong among the mighty ones shall speak of him and his helpers from the midst of Sheol**..." [Ezek. 32:18,21].

> "**These Pharaoh will see,** and he will be comforted for all his multitude slain by the sword, even Pharaoh and all his army," declares the Lord GOD. "Though I instilled a terror of him in the land of the living, yet he will be made to lie down among the uncircumcised along with those slain by the sword, even Pharaoh and all his multitude," declares the LORD GOD [Ezek. 32:31-32].

Christ's teaching about the rich man and Lazarus in Luke 16:19-31 gives the most convincing argument that the lost are conscious in Hades. The rich man could see in Hades, he could feel, he could taste, he could think and respond.[81]

> "Now there was a certain rich man, and he habitually dressed in purple and fine linen, gaily living in splendor every day. And a certain poor man named Lazarus was laid at his gate, covered with sores, and longing to be fed with the crumbs which were

---

[81] It seems that even disembodied spirits have some kind of temporary body as Luke 16:19-31 tells of "eyes, fingers, and tongue".

falling from the rich man's table; besides, even the dogs were coming and licking his sores. Now it came about that the poor man died and he was carried away by the angels to Abraham's bosom; and the rich man also died and was buried. And in **Hades he lifted up his eyes**, being **in torment, and saw Abraham far** away, and Lazarus in his bosom. And **he cried out and said**, 'Father Abraham, have mercy on me, and send Lazarus, that he may dip **the tip of his finger** in water and cool off **my tongue**; for I am **in agony in this flame**.' But Abraham said, 'Child, remember that during your life you received your good things, and likewise Lazarus bad things; but now he is being comforted here, and **you are in agony**. And besides all this, between us and you there is a great chasm fixed, in order that those who wish to come over from here to you may not be able, and that none may cross over from there to us.' And he said, 'Then I beg you, Father, that you send him to my father's house for I have five brothers - that he may warn them, lest they also come to this place of **torment**.' But Abraham said, 'They have Moses and the Prophets; let them hear them.' But he said, 'No, Father Abraham, but if someone goes to them from the dead, they will repent!' But he said to him, 'If they do not listen to Moses and the Prophets, neither will they be persuaded if someone rises from the dead' " [Luke 16:19-31].

e. Hades and Torment

The Bible unquestionably presents Hades as a place of conscious torment. **Persons who reject Christ** are already condemned even as they live (John 3:18). **They are literally one heartbeat away from conscious, eternal torment.** Although Hades is a temporary

abode for the unsaved dead as they await judgment, a small time of release for judgment at the Great White Throne will be no comfort. The verdict and sentence are certain. Those in Hades will be resurrected unto certain condemnation and transferred to the eternal Lake of Fire (Gehenna). "Hell" is a broad enough term to cover both Hades (Sheol) and the Lake of Fire. Thus, it is true to assert that unbelievers enter Hell at death (see Luke 16:22-23). Hades is a place of misery and torment.

For a **fire** is kindled in My anger, and burns to the **lowest part of Sheol**... [Deut. 32:22a]

As sheep they are appointed for Sheol; Death shall be their shepherd; And the upright shall rule over them in the morning; And their form shall be for **Sheol to consume**, so that they have no habitation [Psa. 49:14].

The path of life leads upward for the wise, that he may **keep away from Sheol** below [Prov. 15:24] (Sheol is a place to be avoided!).

"And you Capernaum, will not be exalted to heaven, will you? You shall descend to **Hades**; for if the miracles had occurred in Sodom which occurred in you, it would have remained to this day. Nevertheless I say to you that it shall be **more tolerable for the land of Sodom** in the day of judgment, than for you" (Hades is worse than the fire and brimstone of Sodom.) [Matt. 11:23-24].

"I say to you, it will be **more tolerable in that day for Sodom,** than for that city....And you, Capernaum, will not be exalted to heaven will you? You will be brought down to **Hades!**" [Luke 10:12,15].

"And in Hades he lifted up his eyes, being in **torment**.... I am in **agony** in this **flame**.... you are in **agony**.... for

I have five brothers - that he may warn them, lest they also come to this **place of torment**" [Luke 16:23-25,28].

f. The Relationship of Hades to the Lake of Fire.

Hades (Sheol) is a temporary place where departed unsaved human spirits await the resurrection unto condemnation (John 5:29) to stand trial at the Great White Throne. Hades will give up its dead to face judgment and transferal to the eternal Lake of Fire. Presumably Hades, which is in the center of the earth, will then be destroyed with this old earth.

> And the sea gave up the dead which were in it, and death and **Hades gave up the dead** which were in them; and they were judged, every one of them according to their deeds. And death **and Hades were thrown into the lake of fire.** This is the second death, the lake of fire. And if anyone's name was not found written in the book of life, he was thrown into the lake of fire [Rev. 20:13-15].

There are ten references to Hades in the New Testament (Matt. 11:23; 16:18; Luke 10:15; 16:23; Acts 2:27,31; Rev. 1:18; 6:8; 20:13-14). **Anyone who does not approve of the concept of Hades will have to take issue with the teaching of the Lord Jesus Christ.** He taught about such a place as much as anyone. Upon death unbelievers go to Hades and are in confinement until the final judgment awaiting sentence and transferal to the Lake of Fire. Both places are hell with conscious torment.

4. Gehenna or the Lake of Fire

Unlike Hades (Sheol), the place *Gehenna*, also called the *Lake of Fire*, is the place of **eternal punishment** for the unsaved (see Mark 9:43-48 below) and not a place of temporary confinement while awaiting judgment. Also, unlike Hades, the Lake of Fire is a place for the punishment of **both unsaved humans and angels** (Matt. 25:41; Rev. 20:10,15). Those in the Lake of Fire will apparently have **resurrection bodies** that are perfectly suited to eternal torment without being consumed (see Matt. 10:28; Rev. 20:11-15, also Matt. 5:29-30; 18:9, which speak of bodies in Gehenna). While the unsaved enter Hades immediately upon death (Luke 16:22-27), they do not enter the Lake of Fire until after judgment (Matt. 25:41; Rev. 20:14-15). It appears that the Lake of Fire is empty at the present. Its first occupants will be the Beast and False Prophet, and soon thereafter the unsaved who have physically survived the tribulation period (see Matt. 25:41-46; Rev. 19:20).[82] Throughout the Millennium both Hades and the Lake of Fire will contain some of the unsaved. Hades will contain those who have died in previous dispensations and who have not faced God for judgment. The Lake of Fire will contain those who did not die in the Tribulation and, therefore, will face judgment shortly after the Second Coming. After the Judgment of Israel (Ezekiel 20) and the Judgment of the Nations (Matthew 25), the unsaved survivors of the Tribulation will be directly cast into the Lake of Fire without ever having experienced Hades. As has been discussed above, eventually Hades will be emptied and all the unsaved (with fallen angels) will spend eternity in the Lake of Fire (Rev. 20:14).

a. Origin of the Term "Gehenna"

Gehenna is a Greek word that comes from the original Hebrew meaning "Valley of Hinnom." Jeremiah condemned the human sacrifices that occurred in this valley during the reign of wicked kings Ahaz and Manasseh.

> "And they have built the high places of Topheth, which is in the valley of

---

[82] To enter Hades/Sheol one must first die physically. By contrast, the beast and the false prophet will be "thrown alive" into the Lake of Fire.

the sons of Hinnom, to burn their sons and their daughters in the fire, which I did not command and it did not come into My mind" [Jer. 7:31].

"[A]nd have built the high places of Baal to burn their sons in the fire as burnt offerings to Baal, a thing which I never commanded or spoke of, nor did it ever enter My mind; therefore, behold, days are coming," declares the LORD, "when this place will no longer he called Topheth or the valley of Ben-hinnom, but rather the valley of Slaughter" [Jer. 19:5-6].

Good King Josiah defiled the valley so that never again would human sacrifices be offered there.

He also defiled Topheth, which is in the valley of the son of Hinnom, that no man might make his son or his daughter pass through the fire for Molech [2 Kings 23:10].

In subsequent centuries Gai-Hinnom (the Valley of Hinnom) became the dumping grounds for Jerusalem. It was a place where the fires constantly burned dried sewage, trash, the corpses of dead animals, and executed criminals. Not only was it a trash heap whose fire never ended, it was a revolting place of maggots consuming rotting flesh. By 200 B.C. some Rabbis taught that the Valley of Hinnom (Gai-Hinnom) would be a place of eternal punishment.

The Lord Jesus Christ never taught that the location for eternal punishment was a dump outside Jerusalem, but by using the term "Gehenna" the Lord taught that the place of eternal punishment had similarities to the place "Gehenna" just outside of Jerusalem. Both are places of unending flames. Both are places of unending decay where the constant fire never consumes all the putrid flesh. The literal place of Gehenna outside of Jerusalem was a good way to describe the future destiny of the lost. They will be in a place of unending fire, but the unending fire will still never consume the flesh or end the putrefaction.

Gehenna is a name for a place of unending fire (Mark 9:43-48). Therefore, it must be the equivalent of the "Lake of Fire" which burns forever and ever (Rev. 14:11, 20:10,14). The similar description demands that the terms "Gehenna" and "Lake of Fire" be regarded as synonyms.

b. Uses of the Term *Gehenna*

The New Testament uses the word "Gehenna" 12 times. All but once (James 3:6) it comes from the lips of Christ Himself (Matt. 5:22,29,30; 10:28; 18:9; 23:15,33; Mark 9:43,45,47; Luke 12:5). It would be inconsistent to accept Christ's teachings on salvation or on ethics as authoritative but deny His assertions about eternal punishment. Those who respect Jesus Christ will believe in the existence of an eternal Lake of Fire.

c. General Descriptions of the Lake of Fire

The following concepts describe the condition of the unsaved in the Lake of Fire.

Cursed

"Then He will also say to these on His left, 'depart from Me, **accursed ones,** into the eternal fire which he has prepared for the devil and his angels' " [Matt 25:41].

If anyone does not love the Lord, let him be **accursed.** Maranatha [1 Cor.16:22].

But even though we, or an angel from heaven, should preach to you a gospel contrary to that which we have preached to you, let him be **accursed.** As we have said before, so I say again now, if any man is preaching to you a gospel contrary to that which you received, let him be **accursed** [Gal. 1:8-9].

Judged and condemned

"He who has believed and has been baptized shall be saved; but he who has disbelieved shall be **condemned**" [Mark 16:16].

"He who believes in Him is not judged; he who does not believe has been **judged already,** because he has not believed in the name of the only begotten Son of God" [John 3:18].

"Truly, truly, I say to you, he who hears My word, and believes Him who sent Me, has eternal life, and does not come into **judgment,** but has passed out of death into life" [John 5:24].

But when we are judged, we are disciplined by the Lord in order that we may not be **condemned** along with the world [1 Cor. 11:32].

Objects of God's vengeance

[D]ealing out **retribution** to those who do not know God and to those who do not obey the gospel of our Lord Jesus [2 Thess.1:8].

"For we know Him who said, **Vengeance** is Mine, I will repay..." [Heb. 10:30].

Objects of God's wrath

He therefore began saying to the multitudes who were going out to be baptized by him, "You brood of vipers, who warned you to flee from the **wrath** to come?" [Luke 3:7].

"He who believes in the Son has eternal life; but he who does not obey the Son shall not see life, but the **wrath** of God abides on him" [John 3:36].

Much more then, having now been justified by His blood, we shall be saved from the **wrath** of God through Him [Rom. 5:9].

[A]nd to wait for His Son from heaven, whom He raised from the dead, that is Jesus, who delivers us from the **wrath** to come [1 Thess. 1:10].

Destruction, perishing (see also Matt. 7:13; 18:14; John 10:28; Rom. 9:22; 2 Cor. 2:15; Phil. 1:28; 3:19; 2 Pet. 3:9).

"And do not fear those who kill the body, but are unable to kill the soul; but rather fear Him who is able to **destroy** both soul and body in hell" [Matt. 10:28].

"For God so loved the world, that He gave His only begotten Son, that whoever believes in Him should not **perish**, but have eternal life" [John 3:16].

For the word of the cross is to those who are **perishing** foolishness, but to us who are being saved it is the power of God [1 Cor. 1:18].

And these will pay the penalty of **eternal destruction**, away from the presence of the Lord and from the glory of His power [2 Thess. 1:9].

d. Specific Descriptions of the Lake of Fire

Separation from God (see also Matt. 25:30, "cast out").

"And then I will declare to them, 'I never knew you; **depart from Me**, you who practice lawlessness' " [Matt. 7:23].

And these will pay the penalty of eternal destruction, **away from the presence of the Lord** and from the glory of His power [2 Thess. 1:9].

Denial, shame (see 2 Tim. 2:12b)

"And many of those who sleep in the dust of the ground, will awake, these to everlasting life, but the others to disgrace and everlasting contempt" Dan. 12:2].

"And then I will declare to them, '**I never knew you**; depart from Me, you who practice lawlessness' " [Matt 7:23] (Luke 13:25).

"But whoever shall deny Me before men, **I will also deny** before My Father who is in heaven" [Matt. 10:33].[83]

"For whoever is ashamed of Me and My words in this adulterous and sinful generation, the Son of Man will also be **ashamed** of him when He comes in the glory of His Father with the holy angels" [Mark 8:38].

Exclusion from heaven

"Once the head of the house gets up and shuts the door, and you begin to stand outside and knock on the door, saying, 'Lord, **open up to us!**' then He will answer and say to you, '**I do not know where you are from**' " [Luke 13:25].

...and nothing unclean and no one who practices abomination and lying, **shall ever come into it**, but only those whose names are written in the Lamb's book of life [Rev. 21:27].

Outside are the dogs and the sorcerers and the immoral persons and the murderers and the idolaters, and everyone who loves and practices lying [Rev. 22:15].

Unending "worms"

As the worms continually fed on the rotting flesh in Gehenna, the garbage dump outside Jerusalem, so there will be an unending condition of rottenness and pain in the Lake of Fire. The fire will never consume the flesh

but it will produce rottenness (corruption) and pain in the bodies of the lost. One would probably not be too far off in imagining maggots causing both rottenness and pain by gnawing on a living body. It may be doubtful whether there are real worms in the Lake of Fire, but the ugliness, deep horrors, pain, and putrefaction produced by parasitical worms on living flesh is as close as language can come to describing hell.

"Then they shall go forth and look on the corpses of the men who have transgressed against Me. For **their worm shall not die**, and their fire shall not be quenched; and they shall be an abhorrence to all mankind" [Isa. 66:24].

"[W]here **their worm does not die**, and the fire is not quenched" [Mark 9:48]

Darkness

"Hell" will not be a place of drinking, parties, and camaraderie. Perhaps only God knows how a place of fire can also be a place of "outer darkness." Maybe those in the Lake of Fire are blind! Darkness speaks of terror, panic, and isolation. There will be great fear, great confusion, and great loneliness.

"[B]ut the sons of the kingdom shall be cast out into the outer **darkness**, in that place there shall be weeping and gnashing of teeth" [Matt. 8:12].

"Then the king said to the servants, 'bind him hand and foot, and cast him into the outer **darkness**; in that place there shall be weeping and gnashing of teeth' " [Matt. 22:13].

"And cast out the worthless slave into the outer **darkness**; in that place there shall be weeping and gnashing of teeth" [Matt. 25:30].

These are springs without water, and mists driven by a storm, for whom

---

[83] For further discussion of this verse relative to this denial see Chapter 9, pp. 152-156.

the **black darkness** has been re-served. [2 Pet. 2:17].

[W]ild waves of the sea, casting up their own shame like foam; wandering stars, for whom the **black darkness** has been reserved forever [Jude 13].

Weeping, gnashing of teeth

There will be a definite consciousness in the Lake of Fire, but it will be anything but pleasant. The many references to teeth are interesting. The lost will be resurrected but with a body suited to eternal damnation. This kind of body will suffer but never be consumed.

[B]ut the sons of the kingdom shall be cast out into the outer darkness; in that place there shall he **weeping and gnashing of teeth** [Matt. 8:12].

"[A]nd will cast them into the furnace of fire; in that place there shall be **weeping and gnashing of teeth**....and will cast them into the furnace of fire; there shall be **weeping and gnashing of teeth**" [Matt. 13:42,50].

"Then the king said to the servants, 'bind him hand and foot, and cast him into the outer darkness; in that place there shall be **weeping and gnashing of teeth**' "[Matt. 22:13].

"And cast out the worthless slave into the outer darkness; in that place there shall be **weeping and gnashing of teeth**" [Matt. 25:30].

There will be **weeping and gnashing of teeth** there when you see Abraham and Isaac and Jacob and all the prophets in the kingdom of God, but yourselves being cast out [Luke 13:28].

Torment

Just as the rich man found Hades to be a place of torment (Luke 16:22-28), so the Lake of Fire is a place of deep torment.

"And the smoke of their **torment** goes up forever and ever; and they have no rest day and night..." [Rev. 14:11].

And the devil who deceived them was thrown into the lake of fire and brimstone, where the beast and the false prophet are also; and they will be **tormented** day and night forever and ever [Rev. 20:10].

Brimstone

When it is burned, sulphur produces a terrible odor and noxious fumes. Perhaps those in hell will experience gagging, choking, and terrible smells that bring suffocation.

...and he will be tormented with **fire and brimstone** in the presence of the holy angels and in the presence of the Lamb [Rev. 14:10].

...these two were thrown alive into the lake of fire which burns with **brimstone** [Rev. 19:20].

And the devil who deceived them was thrown into the lake of **fire and brimstone**... [Rev. 20:10].

"But for the cowardly and unbelieving and abominable and murders and immoral persons and sorcerers and idolaters and all liars, their part will be in the lake that burns with **fire and brimstone,** which is the second death" [Rev. 21:8].

Death, specifically the second death

The Lake of Fire is death in the sense of **eternal separation** from God. The phrase "second death" refers to the fact that for unbelievers "hell" is a second death that takes place after physical death. There is nothing more fearful than death. The Lake of Fire is unending death.

> Blessed and holy is the one who has a part in the first resurrection; over these the **second death** has no power... [Rev. 20:6].

> And death and Hades were thrown into the lake of fire. This is the **second death**, the lake of fire [Rev. 20:14].

> "But for the cowardly and unbelieving and abominable and murderers and immoral persons and sorcerers and idolaters and all liars, their part will be in the lake that burns with fire and brimstone, which is the **second death**" [Rev. 21:8].

Fire

The most common description for the eternal place of punishment for the lost is *fire*. This is probably literal fire. At the very least fire is the closest object known to man that describes the pain of the punishment that awaits those who reject Christ as Savior. All the verses which use the word "Gehenna" speak of fire.[84] Likewise, the following verses contain the phrase "Lake of Fire"; (Rev. 19:20; 20:10,14,15; 21:8). Other descriptive phrases include "furnace of fire" (Matt. 13:42), "unquenchable fire" (Matt. 3:12; Mark 9:43,48), "everlasting fire" (Matt. 18:8; 25:41; Jude v. 7), "fury of fire" (Heb. 10:27), and "fire" used without any further description (Matt. 13:40; Luke 3:9).

> "[A]nd will cast them into the **furnace of fire**; in that place there shall be weeping and gnashing of teeth....
> And will cast them into the **furnace of fire**; in that place there shall be weeping and gnashing of teeth" [Matt. 13:42,50].

> ...Where their worm does not die, and the **fire** is not quenched [Mark 9:48].

e. Degrees of Punishment

While all sin is reprehensible, the Scripture does teach that some sins are worse than others. In John 19:11 Christ told Pilate, "...he who delivered me up to you has the **greater** sin." In other passages the Lord ranked commandments as to lesser or greater importance (see Matt. 5:19; 22:37-40). While the basis for entrance into eternal condemnation is rejection of Christ, it is possible that deeds play a role in determining the degree of punishment (with all of it being unimaginably bad). This may be one of the reasons for books containing deeds being examined at the Great White Throne Judgment (Rev. 20:12).[85]

Eternal hell will be great pain and misery for all, but several verses indicate there will be degrees of punishment. Those who rejected Christ in person, and those today who reject Him despite a great knowledge of the truth will be especially accountable. Imagine the guilt of those who rejected despite being eyewitnesses to Christ's actions on earth. No doubt God will also inflict special judgment upon those who have martyred His children.

> "Truly, I say to you, 'it will be **more tolerable** for the land of Sodom and Gomorrah **in the day of judgment, than for that city'** " [Matt. 10:15].

> Then He began to reproach the cities in which most of His miracles were done, because they did not repent. "Woe to you, Chorazin! Woe to you, Bethsaida! For if the miracles had occurred in Tyre and Sidon which occurred in you, they would have repented long ago in sackcloth and ashes. Nevertheless I say to you, it shall be **more tolerable** for Tyre and

---

[84] See the beginning of this sub-section on "Gehenna or the Lake of Fire," p. 537.

[85] God might also use books that record works to prove to unbelievers their good works were not sufficient to earn salvation (Matt. 7:21-23).

Sidon **in the day of judgment, than for you**....Nevertheless I say to you that it shall be **more tolerable** for the land of Sodom **in the day of judgment, than for you**" [Matt. 11:20-22,24].

"And that slave who **knew his master's will** and did not get ready or act in accord with his will, shall receive **many lashes**, but the one who **did not know** it and committed deeds worthy of a flogging, will receive but **few**. And from everyone who has been given much shall much be required; and to whom they entrusted much, of him they will ask all the more" [Luke 12:47-48].

[A]nd they cried out with a loud voice, saying, "How long, O Lord, holy and true, wilt Thou refrain from **judging and avenging our blood** on those who dwell on the earth?" [Rev. 6:10].

"Pay her back even as she has paid, and give back to her double according to her deeds; in the cup which she has mixed, mix twice as much for her....Rejoice over her, O heaven, and you saints and apostles and prophets, because **God has pronounced judgment for you against her**....And in her was found **the blood of prophets and of saints** and of all who have been slain on the earth" [Rev. 18:6,20,24].

f. The Location for the Lake of Fire

While Hades seems to be "below," the location for the Lake of Fire is unknown. Rev. 20:11 may be teaching that the present heavens and earth are destroyed before the Great White Throne Judgment. [86] The new heavens

and earth do not appear until after the lost are cast into the Lake of Fire (Rev. 20:11, 21:1-5). Therefore, the Lake of Fire does not seem to be in the center of this earth. Its location is a mystery.

g. Glimpse into Hell

Will the saints ever be able to see what goes on in hell? There will certainly be a barrier between heaven and hell for there will be no escape or transfer out of eternal punishment, but possibly saints will be able to see what horrors they have missed by the Lord's grace (perhaps temporarily in the immediate aftermath of Armageddon).

"Then **they shall go forth and look** on the corpses of the men who have transgressed against Me. **For their worm shall not die, and their fire shall not be quenched;** and they shall be an abhorrence to all mankind [Isa. 66:24].

[He] also will drink of the wine of the wrath of God, which is mixed in full strength in the cup of His anger; and he will be tormented with fire and brimstone in the **presence of the holy angels and in the presence of the Lamb** [Rev. 14:10].

It is best not to hold any dogmatism on this point. Isaiah may be only referring to viewing the corpses after Armageddon. We can be certain that if the saints do see a glimpse of hell their response will not be one of sorrow but of gratitude towards God for His great salvation. [87]

5. The Duration of Punishment

---

[86] Other texts on the destruction of this earth include: Matt. 24:35; Luke 21:33; 2 Pet. 3:10-13; 1 John 2:17.

[87] Those in hell are separated from God's presence in the sense that they are unaware of His presence and will not experience any divine action on their behalf. **From the human perspective,** hell is away from God's presence as in 2 Thess. 1:9 and a **separation** from God. From **God's perspective**, the condemned will be eternally present before Him as in Rev. 14:10.

Because the idea of unending punishment in the Lake of Fire is so horrible, people often reject it. Some who believe in the existence of such a place might skirt its unpleasant aspects by teaching that there can be a second chance for salvation after one has entered the flames. Others think unbelievers are totally annihilated, suffering for only a brief duration. Still others have developed the unscriptural notion of purgatory. This makes the Lake of Fire into a place of temporal punishment from which people can escape after a limited amount of suffering for sin.

It is quite fair to admit that the subject of eternal punishment is terrifying and repulsive. Nevertheless, it is very much Scriptural.

a. The Issue of Hell's Eternality

Will people in the Lake of Fire obtain a second chance for salvation? Will they be annihilated, suffering only briefly? Do the Greek words translated into English as "eternal" and "everlasting" actually mean "unending"? If they do, then there is no means of a lost soul ever leaving hell or ever escaping pain through annihilation.

b. The Word *Eon*

One of the Greek words translated "eternal" or "everlasting" is *eon.* To many people the English word *eon* refers to a very long period of time but to a span that does have limits. Consider the sentence, "It was eons before the bus from St. Louis arrived." *Eon* in this sentence refers to an especially long period but one that was limited. It does not mean eternal. Indeed, in at least 37 of 95 New Testament occurrences *eon* refers to a limited time span.

"[A]nd the enemy who sowed them is the devil, and the harvest is the end of the age [*eon*]; and the reapers are angels. Therefore just as the tares are gathered up and burned with fire, so

shall it be at the end of the age" [*eon*] [Matt. 13:39-40].

"Tell us, when will these things be, and what will be the sign of Your coming, and of the end of the age" [*eon*] [Matt. 24:3b].

And do not be conformed to this world [*eon*]... [Rom. 12:2].

Now these things happened to them as an example, and they were written for our instruction, upon whom the ends of the ages [*eons*] have come [1 Cor. 10:11].

In these verses the word "*eon*" refers to a long but limited period of time. Why then have conservative theologians interpreted the same word to mean "everlasting" when used in contexts about the punishment of the lost (e.g., Jude 13; Rev. 14:1; 19:3; 20:10)? The first step in resolving this issue involves evidence that "eon" can mean eternal time. Just as the word *may* mean "a long but limited age", it is also **capable of meaning eternal** in some contexts and with some subjects. This is easy to prove.

c. The Word "*Eon*" Meaning Eternal

While in some contexts "*eon*" may refer to a limited time span, it also means "unending, eternal, everlasting" in other contexts. *Eon* **definitely means eternal when** used with:

God

Now to the King **eternal**... [*eon*] [1 Tim. 1:17].

Jesus Christ is the same yesterday, today, yes and **forever** [unto the *eons* or ages] [Heb. 13:8]. [88]

---

[88] See also Heb. 1:12 for Christ's eternality. The author of Hebrews intends the same in Heb. 13:8.

God's Word [89]

"...The Word of the Lord abides **forever**..." [unto the *eons*] [1 Pet. 1:25].

God's Kingdom

"[A]nd He will reign over the house of Jacob **forever;** [unto the *eons*] and His kingdom will have no end" [Luke 1:33].

"...For thine is the kingdom, and the power, and the glory, **forever** [unto the *eons*]. Amen." [Matt. 6:13].[90]

The Believer's Life

"...if any man eats of this bread, he shall live **forever**..." [for the *eon*] [John 6:51].

"...if anyone keeps my word he shall *never* [literally, not for the *eon*] see death" [John 8:51] (see also v. 53).

"[A]nd everyone who lives and believes in Me shall *never* [not for the *eon*] die" [John 11:26] (see also John 10:28).

These are enough examples to show that the Greek word *eon* does have a capacity to mean "eternal or everlasting." This opens the door very widely to the possibility that the word means *everlasting* in contexts concerning punishment. In fact, because of a **special construction and because of other descriptive phrases, this word must mean everlasting in contexts that concern punishment for the lost.**

d. The Phrase "unto e*ons* of e*ons*"

Thus far we have concluded that the word translated age (*eon*) can mean eternal in certain contexts even when it is used only once. Furthermore, it is vital to realize that in 3 out

---

[89] See Matt. 24:35 for different phraseology showing the Word of God is eternal.

[90] This portion of Matt. 6:13 may not be a part of the original text. However, it would still illustrate the definition of the word *eon*.

---

of 4 verses cited as using *eon* in reference to punishment the apostle John uses a special construction. Rev. 14:11; 19:3; 20:10 all repeat some form of the word *eon* in a phrase that can be roughly translated "unto *eons* of *eons*." A further study of the approximately 22 uses of this phrase leads to the conclusion that it **always means everlasting.** It is used of the length for God's existence, rule, or glory in Rom. 16:27; Gal. 1:5; Eph. 3:21; Phil. 4:20; 1 Tim. 1:17; 2 Tim. 4:18; Heb. 13:21; 1 Pet. 4:11, 5:11; Rev. 1:6,18; 4:9,10; 5:13; 7:12; 10:6; 15:7 and of the duration of God's Kingdom in Rev. 11:15. These total 18 times. The phrase is used of the duration for the believer's life in Rev. 22:5. The three remaining times refer to the length of punishment (Rev. 14:11; 19:3; 20:10). The word "*eon*" by itself can mean eternal. The phrase "unto *eons* of *eons*" **always means eternal,** even when speaking of the duration of hell. Here are some clear examples of this definition:

> Now to God and Father be the glory **forever and ever**. Amen [Phil. 4:20].

> ...I am the first and the last, and the living One; and I was dead, and behold, I am alive **forevermore**... [Rev. 1:17-18].

> ...and thanks to Him who sits on the throne, to Him who **lives forever and ever** [Rev. 4:9].

> "...and they [God's servants] shall reign **forever and ever** [Rev. 22:5].

e. Conclusion on *Eon*

It is true that the particular Greek word translated "*eon*" can mean a long, but limited time in certain contexts (and does so at least 37 out of 95 times). Nevertheless, that word can also mean "eternal" because it is used of the length for God's existence, His Word, His rule, and the duration of a believer's life. Even more important is the fact that **the phrase "unto the *eons* of *eons*" always means eternity because it refers to**

God in 18 out of 22 usages. Three of the remaining references concern punishment. The only objective conclusion from the Biblical data is that unbelievers will suffer eternal punishment.

> "And the smoke of their torment goes up **forever and ever;** and they have no rest day and night, those who worship the beast and his image, and whoever receives the mark of his name" [Rev. 14:11].

The word *eon* was discussed first because it provides the only possible angle for objections by those who deny the eternality of hell. The extensive discussion given to a refutation of this false notion should not cause the reader to think that the doctrine of eternal punishment rests on the meaning of this one word. In reality, there are at least two supports for the doctrine of eternal punishment that are even more persuasive.

f. Descriptions which Establish Eternal Punishment

The concept of unending time can be expressed without using a specific word for "everlasting." The idea of "unquenchable fire" (Matt. 3:12 and Mark 9:43,48) coupled with an "undying worm" (Mark 9:48) speaks of everlasting fire without cessation of existence.

> "And if your hand causes you to stumble, cut it off; it is better for you to enter life crippled, than having your two hands, to go into hell, into the **unquenchable fire**....and if your eye causes you to stumble, cast it out; it is better for you to enter the kingdom of God with one eye, than having two eyes, to be cast into hell, where their **worm does not die**, and the **fire is not quenched**" [Mark 9:43,47-48] [91]

g. A Second Greek Word Meaning Eternal

In addition to the word *"eon"* discussed above, there is a second Greek word that teaches **even more conclusively** the doctrine of everlasting punishment (*eonios* or *aionios*). In the **64 uses when it is used without reference to punishment, it always means eternal.** There are 42 associations with the length of a believer's life. (Three times this term speaks of eternity past, three times of future glory, twice of the length of God's life, twice of the length of the Holy Spirit's life, once of Christians' eternal inheritance, once of eternal salvation, once of eternal redemption, once of the eternal covenant, once of the duration of heaven, once of the eternal gospel, once of the immortal nature or endurance of the glorified body, once of an eternal commandment, and four miscellaneous references.) One does not have the option of changing the meaning for the six remaining usages that speak of the duration of punishment. They unquestionably teach that the Lake of Fire will be eternal. **Punishment in hell will be as long as God's life. Torment will be as everlasting as is the life given to believers.**

> "And if your hand or your foot causes you to stumble, cut it off and throw it from you; it is better for you to enter life crippled or lame, than having two hands or two feet, to be cast into the **eternal fire**" [Matt. 18:8].

> "Then He will also say to those on His left, 'Depart from Me, accursed ones, into the **eternal fire** which has been prepared for the devil and his angels'....And these shall go away into **eternal punishment**, but the righteous into eternal life" [Matt. 25:41,46] (the duration of life for the saved and the duration of punishment for the unsaved is the same).

And these will pay the penalty of **eternal destruction** away from the presence of the Lord and from the glory of His power [2 Thess. 1:9].

---

[91] Note again descriptions of the body in hell.

Just as Sodom and Gomorrah and the cities around them, since they in the same way as these indulged in gross immorality and went after strange flesh, are exhibited as an example in undergoing the **punishment of eternal fire** [Jude 7].

[O]f instruction about washings, and laying on of hands, and the resurrection of the dead, and **eternal judgment** [Heb. 6:2].

Bible doctrine is not determined by its popularity or comfort level. Man does not have the freedom to accept or reject a Biblical teaching based on his own fallen sense of justice or depraved sense of reason. It seems "reasonable" to many that salvation comes through works, but the Bible teaches otherwise. To some it seems "reasonable" that a Christian can lose salvation, but the Scriptures teach eternal security. The Scripture is our authority for doctrine and ethics. Regardless of whether eternal punishment seems reasonable to a given individual, unending punishment for those who reject Christ is a Biblical fact. Rejection of God's Son is a far more serious sin than many people realize. **God will in no way tolerate those who regard His Son as a worthless waste of time.** *Let the reader be warned.* **Trust in Christ as Savior or face God's wrath.**

D. The Future of the Saved

The "intermediate state" concerns the time after death but before resurrection and judgment. Although the intermediate state is not an end time event, it is obviously something that lies in an individual's future should death occur before the Rapture. Therefore, it is often classified under Eschatology. Furthermore, eternity for believers involves the heavenly city upon a new earth. Both subjects belong in the category "the future of the saved."

1. The Intermediate State of the Saved

a. Present with Christ

At death a believer's soul goes to be with Christ. Christ dwells in heaven (Acts 7:56; Col. 3:1; Heb. 1:3; 8:1; 12:2). Sometimes it is important to note what the Bible does not teach. It does not teach about the existence of any place between Hades and Paradise. At death unbelievers enter Hades, and believers enter Christ's presence.[92] There is no third place such as purgatory where a soul may undergo a time of reform/punishment and then attain heaven.

And He said to him, "Truly I say to you, today, **you shall be with Me** in Paradise" [Luke 23:43].

And they went on stoning Stephen as he called upon the Lord and said, "Lord Jesus, **receive my spirit**" [Acts 7:59].

[W]e are of good courage, I say, and prefer rather to be **absent from the body and to be at home with the Lord** [2 Cor. 5:8].

But I am hard-pressed from both directions, having the **desire to depart and be with Christ**... [Phil. 1:23].

b. Departed Saints are Alive and Conscious

Several verses teach that believers never die. Of course, Christians die physically, but it is impossible for a Christian either to die spiritually or to cease to exist. The Bible defines death as the separation of the soul from the body (James 2:26). It is not the end of existence for a soul but rather a change in residence for the soul.

"I am the God of Abraham, and the God of Isaac, and the God of Jacob? God is not the God of the dead but of the **living**" [Matt. 22:32].

---

[92] Perhaps angels escort the soul to Christ's presence as in the pre-cross parallel in Luke 16:22.

The Lord's point is that Abraham, Isaac, and Jacob still existed in Moses' day even though they had died centuries before Moses' time.

> "And he cried out and said, 'Father Abraham, have mercy on me, and send Lazarus, that he may dip the tip of his finger in water and cool off my tongue; for I am in agony in this flame' "....And he said, "Then I beg you, Father, that you send him [Lazarus] to my father's house" [Luke 16:24,27].

Lazarus certainly was conscious after death.

> "Truly, truly, I say to you, if anyone keeps My word he **shall never see death**" [John 8:51].

> "[A]nd everyone who lives and believes in Me **shall never die**. Do you believe this?" [John 11:26].

> And if Christ is in you, though the body is dead because of sin, yet **the spirit is alive** because of righteousness [Rom. 8:10].

The body may die, but a Christian's spirit can never cease to exist.

> And when He broke the fifth seal, I saw underneath the altar the souls of those who had been slain because of the word of God, and because of the testimony which they had maintained; and **they cried out with a loud voice**, saying, "How long, O Lord, holy and true, wilt Thou refrain from judging and avenging our blood on those who dwell on the earth?" And there was given to each of them a white robe; and they were told that they should rest for a little while longer, until the number of their fellow servants and their brethren who were to be killed even as they had been, should be completed also [Rev. 6:9-11].

The tribulational saints who die are very much conscious after death.

The Bible does not say whether departed saints can observe events on earth. Angels do observe the church (Eph. 3:10). Heb. 12:1 might indicate some heroes of the faith observe us some of the time. Presumably, departed saints are not totally ignorant of life on earth, but we simply do not know any details. No doubt the departed saints gather news from believers who have recently died. God would not allow Lazarus to come back to earth with any communication for the rich man's brothers (Luke 16:26-31). Scripturally, the area of communication with the dead falls under the topic of necromancy. Seances do not result in actual communication with the dead. (Note the witch's total surprise at actually hearing Samuel, 1 Sam. 28:12). In reality demonic spirits mimic the dead person's voice to ensnare the gullible. Christians need to entrust their departed loved ones to God's care and strictly avoid Satanic games. We can be satisfied that departed believers are consciously enjoying Christ's presence and would not want to return to this evil world.

c. Conditions in the Intermediate State of the Saved

The Bible gives few specifics about the nature of the intermediate state of the saved. We do not know all the facts, but we do know important facts. Departed Christians are with Christ. They are in a better place. They experience unspeakable wonders and are in a place that can be called Paradise.

Obviously, Christian bodies return to dust at death to await the resurrection. Yet, souls in the intermediate state seem to have some sort of "temporary spirit-body." Lazarus had a "finger" that could have brought water (Luke 16:24). The souls of tribulational saints are clothed in "white robes" (Rev. 6:11).

But I am hard-pressed from both directions, having the desire to depart and be with Christ, for that is **very much better** [Phil. 1:23].

I know a man in Christ who fourteen years ago - whether in the body I do not know, or out of the body I do not know, God knows - such a man was caught up to the third heaven. And I know how such a man - whether in the body or apart from the body I do not know, God knows - was caught up into **Paradise**, and heard inexpressible words, which a man is not permitted to speak [2 Cor. 12:2-4].

2. Heaven

a. The Destruction of the Present Universe

After the Millennium, but probably before the Great White Throne Judgment, God will destroy this present earth and with it the entire universe as we know it (see also Luke 16:17).

"**Heaven and earth will pass away,** but My Words shall not pass away" [Matt. 24:35].

"**Heaven and earth will pass away,** but My words will not pass away" [Luke 21:33].

And, "Thou, Lord, in the beginning didst lay the foundation of the **earth**, and the **heavens** are the works of Thy hands; **they will perish**, but Thou remainest; and they all will become old as a garment, and as a mantle Thou wilt roll them up; as a garment they will also be changed. But Thou art the same, and Thy years will not come to an end" [Heb. 1:10-12].

But the day of the Lord will come like a thief, in which **the heavens will pass away** with a roar and the elements will be destroyed with intense heat, and **the earth and its**

works will be burned up [2 Pet. 3:10].

And **the world is passing away**, and also its lusts; but the one who does the will of God abides forever [1 John 2:17].

And I saw a great white throne and Him who sat upon it, from whose presence **earth and heaven fled away,** and no place was found for them [Rev. 20:11].

b. New Heavens and Earth

The Bible predicts new heavens and a new earth. We know very little about them. Rev. 21:1 teaches that there will be no sea on this new earth. Some Bible teachers believe that God will create a completely new planet. An earth without a sea would indeed be a drastic change. Others view the new earth as a renovation of the old earth rather than an entirely new planet. God will burn and purge this earth and then will reform it into a "new earth." It is not possible to be dogmatic, but the idea of a renovation has the advantage of explaining how Abraham's offspring can possess the land of Israel forever.

"For behold, **I create new heavens and a new earth**; and the former things shall not be remembered or come to mind" [Isa. 65:17].

"For just as **the new heavens and the new earth which I make** will endure before Me," declares the LORD [Isa. 66:22].

But according to His promise we are looking for **new heavens and a new earth,** in which righteousness dwells [2 Pet. 3:13].

And I saw **a new heaven and a new earth**; for the first heaven and the first earth passed away, and there is no longer any sea [Rev. 21:1].

c. The Heavenly City, New Jerusalem

There is more complete revelation about New Jerusalem than on any other subject pertaining to the Eternal State (see Rev. 21:2 - 22:5). Most theologians agree that Rev. 21:1-8 concerns a heavenly city as it exists in the Eternal State. Yet, another view takes Rev. 21:9 as a retrogression that pictures the heavenly city as it functions in the Millennium. Before studying a description of the heavenly city, we must study the time setting of the account in Rev. 21:2ff. **Sections (1) and (2) below give the strongest arguments possible for each position** with other possibilities following.

> And I saw a new heaven and a new earth; for the first heaven and the first earth passed away, and there is no longer any sea. And I saw the holy city, new Jerusalem, coming down out of heaven from God, made ready as a bride adorned for her husband. And I heard a loud voice from the throne, saying, "Behold, the tabernacle of God is among men, and He shall dwell among them, and they shall be His people, and God Himself shall be among them, and He shall wipe away every tear from their eyes; and there shall no longer be any death; there shall no longer be any mourning, or crying, or pain; the first things have passed away". And He who sits on the throne said, "Behold, I am making all things new." And He said, "Write, for these words are faithful and true." And He said to me, "It is done. I am the Alpha and the Omega, the beginning and the end. I will give to the one who thirsts from the spring of the water of life without cost. He who overcomes shall inherit these things, and I will be his God and he will be My son. But for the cowardly and unbelieving and abominable and murders and immoral persons and sorcerers and idolaters and all liars, their part will be in the lake that burns with fire and brimstone, which is the second death" [Rev. 21:1-8].

(1). New Jerusalem as a Millennial City

New Jerusalem exists right now (see John 14:1-6; Gal. 4:26; Heb. 11:16; 12:22ff.). Therefore, one cannot automatically rule out that it will play a role in the Millennium. Although the New Jerusalem described in Rev. 21:1-8 is the eternal city, perhaps it descends upon the earth during the Millennium. Some believe that certain indications in Rev. 21:9ff. point to a millennial setting.

Rev. 21:24-26 speaks of kings and nations. Reasoning that there can be no king in heaven but God alone and that the existence of governmental structures implies the existence of evil, some think that Rev. 21:9ff. cannot refer to heaven but to the Millennium as the Kingdom of God on earth.

> And the **nations** shall walk by its light, and the kings of the earth shall bring their glory into it....and they shall bring the glory and the honor of the **nations** into it... [Rev. 21:24,26].

Another supposed indication for a millennial setting comes in the phrase "the leaves of the trees were for the **healing** of the nations" (see Rev. 22:2). Since there will be no need for "healing" in the Eternal State, some believe the city in Rev. 21:9ff. should be placed in a millennial setting.

(2). The New Jerusalem in the Eternal State

It is possible to view Rev. 21:2ff. as restricted to the Eternal State. The Garden of Eden contained neither sin nor sickness, but it still had a tree of life to maintain health. The presence of the tree of life need not prove that John describes the heavenly city as being on earth during the Millennium. It is just as likely that the tree of life preserves the life of those in eternal heaven.

Likewise, the term "nations" simply means ethnic groups. It need not refer to full governmental structure designed to curtail wickedness. There will be ethnic groups in eternity. Apparently, some will have higher positions than others in heaven and may be called "kings".

There are many descriptions in Revelation 21-22 that rule out a millennial context for New Jerusalem. Virtually everyone takes Rev. 21:1-8 as referring to the city in the Eternal State. Therefore, one must demand the strongest and clearest of evidence to make Rev. 21:9ff. a retrogression to the Millennium.

Rev. 21:1 speaks of a new earth in which there is no sea (see Rev. 20:11). Yet, several verses teach that in the Millennium Christ will rule from "sea to sea" (see Psa. 72:8; Zech. 9:10). Rev. 21:4 describes a city in which there is no pain, no sorrow, and no death. Although lifespans increase during the Kingdom age, death still exists (see Isa. 11:4; 65:20; Jer. 31:29-30) It is no wonder that all take Rev. 21:1-8 to refer to the heavenly city in the Eternal State. As the text proceeds, there is little reason to change.

The descriptions in vv. 2 and 10 are similar and show that v. 9 has not regressed to a millennial setting. The dimensions of New Jerusalem make it difficult to place it in the Millennium. The city is approximately 1,906,300 square miles (see Rev. 21:16). This single city is between seven and eight times the size of Texas. It is very difficult to picture it as descending upon the present Jerusalem.

Rev. 21:22 says that there will be no temple in the New Jerusalem. Yet, the Millennium will clearly have a temple (see Ezekiel 40-48).

While the heavenly city has no sun or moon (Rev. 21:23), those in the millennial Kingdom will praise Christ from the rising to the setting of the sun (see Mal. 1:11). No unbeliever may enter the heavenly city (see Rev. 21:27), but some born in the millennial pe-

riod will not accept Christ (Rev. 20:7-9). While we might be able to view a city that is off limits to unbelieving millennial citizens, it is better to place all of Revelation 21 in the Eternal State.

(3). Conclusion

If one must chose between the Millennium and the Eternal State as the time setting for John's description of the New Jerusalem, then the evidence favors the Eternal State. Many of the descriptions in Revelation 21 **must** be the Eternal State. All statements are compatible with an eternal setting including the presence of the nations and the tree of life that brings "healing." A third view sees the heavenly city as playing a role in both the Millennium and the Eternal State. It is grounded in logic and speculation as opposed to exegesis of Revelation 21-22, but it should be included.

(4). The Satellite View

If one feels that a tree for healing and the existence of kings/nations demands that New Jerusalem be given a millennial setting, one might want to consider the satellite view. However, the main reason for this view is that it allows the church to remain in its "heavenly mansions" during the Millennium.

The Lord promised to prepare a place for believers (John 14:2-3). Since the New Jerusalem is the church's dwelling place for eternity (see Rev. 21:9; 22:5), it has to be the place Christ prepares for the church. After the Rapture, Christ takes the church to her heavenly city. Will church saints be forced to vacate their eternal home to go back to earth for 1,000 years? Will believers leave heaven to live on the earth again? While this may not be impossible, such a transferal would seem to be a diminished blessing. The satellite view of the city cannot be proven, but it would allow for the church to have permanent residence in its eternal home.

Adherents believe that the city of Revelation 21-22 is indeed the eternal city. While Revelation 21-22 describes its descent onto the new earth and not the millennial city, it is possible that the heavenly city will also play a role in the Millennium. The "satellite" theory envisions that the heavenly city will descend toward (but not upon) the earth at the beginning of the Kingdom. It will hover as a satellite (2/3 the size of the moon) in earth's orbit to serve as the residence for glorified saints. Thus, Christians will not need to abandon their heavenly abode to live on earth. They can simply commute to their assigned tasks on earth by the speed of thought.

By this view the nations of the Millennium can literally walk in the light of the New Jerusalem (Rev. 21:24,26) and obtain healing from its tree of life (Rev. 22:2) Then the city will be raised for the destruction of the present earth and afterward descend to settle on the new earth (a descent described in Rev. 21:1-8).

The satellite view of New Jerusalem is just a theory with no direct and clear Biblical support. However, it explains how the church saints can enjoy their heavenly abode and still serve in the millennial Kingdom. It allows the "healing" of Rev. 22:2 to be taken in a therapeutic (the exact Greek word in Rev. 22:2) and not just preventative sense.

Regardless of the role (or lack thereof) for the New Jerusalem in the Millennium, it is the eternal city. The rest of this study focuses on New Jerusalem as a description of what Christians call "heaven."

(5). Other Texts on the Heavenly City

We need to appreciate the fact that Revelation 21-22 describes the **relocation but not the creation** of the eternal city. This glorious city already exists. Many other verses teach of the city's existence.

> "In My Father's house are many dwelling places; if it were not so, I would have told you; for I go to prepare a place for you. And if I go and

prepare a place for you, I will come again, and receive you to Myself; that where I am, there you may be also" [John 14:2-3].

> But the Jerusalem above is free; she is our mother [Gal. 4:26].

> [F]or he [Abraham] was looking for the city which has foundations, whose architect and builder is God....But as it is, they desire a better country, that is a heavenly one. Therefore God is not ashamed to be called their God; for He has prepared a city for them [Heb. 11:10,16]. [93]

(6). Descriptions of New Jerusalem

Misinterpretation of Rev. 21:9b has caused some to view Revelation 21 as a figure that describes the church's glory.

> "... Come here, I shall show you the bride the wife of the Lamb" [Rev. 21:9b].

Language could hardly make a more clear presentation of a literal city. John gives precise dimensions (v. 16). He discusses the walls, gates, foundations, streets, etc. (see v. 11ff.). To see this literal city is to see the church's future through the place of the church's eternal residence and eternal glory. A view of the heavenly city is a view of the church, specifically its final destiny. Rev. 21:9b is not incompatible with taking Revelation 21 as a literal city. In essence the angel tells John, "Come, I will show you the church's eternal future." His method of revealing the church's destiny involves giving John a glimpse of the church's eternal abode. By seeing this **real city** John learns of the church's future because New Jerusalem will be the everlasting residence for the church.

(a). Size

---

[93] See also Heb.13:14 and Rev. 3:12.

Rev. 21:16 gives the "city limit" boundaries to the New Jerusalem.

> The city was laid out like a square, as long as it was wide. He measured the city with the rod and found it to be 12,000 stadia in length, and as wide and high as it is long [Rev. 21:16 (NIV)].

The Greek phrase is "12,000 stadia." A major Bible encyclopedia gives the length for a stadia as 607 1/2 feet. [94] Thus, the city is approximately 1,380 miles long, wide, and high. It is possible to view the city as either a cube or a pyramid.[95] Does the extension of the city upward imply levels in its dwelling places?

(b). Composition

The walls of New Jerusalem are composed of jasper that seems to be diamond-like in appearance (see v. 11, crystal clear). These walls are 144 cubits (i.e., approx. 216 feet) high (or thick) (see Rev. 21:17-18). The "city was pure gold like clear glass" (Rev. 21:18). This probably means the buildings in the city are composed of a material that is like golden crystal (including believers' dwelling places). It is golden-toned but transparent. Verse 21 teaches that the city's street also has the same material. "And the street of the city was pure gold like transparent glass." The singular reference to street may be a singular with a plural meaning. Likely, there is more than one street in this large city.

John devotes much attention to the city's gates and foundations. New Jerusalem has 12 gates within its walls (v. 12). There is an angel guarding each gate (v. 12), and they are equally divided at 3 gates for the east, 3 for the north, 3 for the south and 3 for the west (v. 13). In v. 21 we learn that each gate is a single pearl! It is significant that the twelve tribes of Israel are written on the gates (v. 12). The heavenly city may be the eternal residence of the church (v. 9), but Israel is also welcome there. Israel's tribes are not lost to God. Heb. 11:10 and 16 teach that God has prepared this city for Abel, Enoch, Noah, and Abraham just as much as Christ prepared it for the church (John 14:2-3). These gates are always open (v. 25). Open gates speak of constant traffic and constant involvement in God's work. This city is not a vacation spot but a beehive of activity for God's servants (see Rev. 22:3).

There are 12 foundation stones below the jasper wall (see Rev. 21:14). This could mean 12 massive stones (with perhaps one under each gate as John returns to the subject of the pearly gates almost in conjunction with the material on the foundation stones, vv. 19-21). Yet, it is better to think of 12 layers of foundation stones extending all around the city wall (see v. 19). Each layer contains the name of an apostle. The apostles were the foundation for the church (Eph. 2:20). Their association with the heavenly city's foundations shows that the city is the eternal abode of the church. It is the church's eternal glory. Technically, the Book of The Revelation does not say that the 12 foundational layers are made of solid gemstones. Verse 19 says that these foundation stones were adorned (Greek *kosmeo*, cf. cosmetic) with 12 kinds of precious stones. We are safe in imagining liberal use of these beautiful stones. Complete evidence for possible identifications for each stone cannot be given here, but the following list gives reasonable conclusions as to their colors (see Rev. 21:19-20):[96]

---

[94] F.B. Huey, Jr., Weights and Measures, *The Zondervan Pictorial Encyclopedia of the Bible*, 5 vols. (Grand Rapids: The Zondervan Corporation, 1976), 5:915. This entry gives 202 1/2 yards as a stadia, which equals 607 1/2 feet.
[95] If a cube, this is about 2,628,000,000 cubic miles!

[96] This chart was developed from research from many sources including Mulholland, John, *Advanced Eschatology*, unpublished lecture notes, Capital Bible Seminary, 1982.

Name	Probable Color
Jasper	Clear – Diamond color see v. 11
Sapphire	Blue
Chalcedony	Sky Blue with stripes
Emerald	Bright Green
Sardonyx	Red and White
Sardius	Red or "honey color"
Chrysolite	Clear Golden
Beryl	Sea Green
Topaz	Clear yellowish-green
Chrysoprase	Green
Jacinth	Violet
Amethyst	Purple

(c). New Jerusalem's Appearance

New Jerusalem is no doubt more stunning than words can describe. Rev. 21:2 employs the most beautiful imagery on earth, a bride on her wedding day. Yet, Rev. 21:11 actually goes further **"having the glory of God."**

This city radiates God's own glory (v. 23). Imagine a pyramid or cube nearly 1,400 miles on each side. Its over all appearance is "as a stone of crystal clear jasper" (v. 11). It dazzles as a diamond with 1,400-mile dimensions as it reflects God's own glory! No wonder Paul could not describe Paradise in 2 Cor. 12:4.

While the city's overall splendor is as a huge clear crystal, there must also be some measure of a golden tint because of its buildings and street of golden crystal (v. 18b. and v. 21). Finally, the combination of light from God's glory and the countless varied gemstones in its foundation must mean that to some extent it magnifies and radiates the full spectrum of colors. Perhaps the city gives off a clear glow from a distance but gives more rich and complex colors when viewed

at a close range. There are no words to adequately describe it. The city is better than imagination allows, but we must insist that the Lamb of God surpasses all attractions.

Now to Him who is able to do exceeding abundantly beyond all that we ask or think according to the power that works within us, to Him be the glory in the church and in Christ Jesus to all generations forever and ever. Amen [Eph. 3:20-21].

d. The River and the Tree of Life

And he showed me a river of the water of life, clear as crystal, coming from the throne of God and of the Lamb, in the middle of its street. And on either side of the river was the tree of life, bearing twelve kinds of fruit, yielding its fruit every month; and the leaves of the tree were for the healing of the nations. And there shall no longer be any curse; and the throne of God and of the Lamb shall be in it, and His bond-servants shall serve Him; and they shall see His face, and His name shall be on their foreheads. And there shall no longer be any night; and they shall not have need of the light of a lamp nor the light of the sun, because the Lord God shall illumine them; and they shall reign forever and ever [Rev. 22:1-5].

The river of the water of life flows from God's throne and from the Lamb. While there is a real river of crystal clear water, this phrase also teaches the lesson that eternal life springs forth from Christ. God's invitation to drink in Rev. 22:17 is in reality an invitation to salvation, but presumably the inhabitants of New Jerusalem will drink of the river of life. It probably maintains and/or enhances life in some unrevealed way.

Bible students are familiar with the tree of life from Gen. 2:9 and 3:22-24. The Scriptures close with a return to the beginning. In this heavenly city Paradise lost is more than regained.

Rev. 22:2 gives a description that is hard to imagine. A broad golden (Rev. 21:21) thoroughfare extends from God's throne. Instead of a median, the river of life that also extends from God's throne bisects this wide street. John says, "and on either side of the river was the tree of life." How can a tree extend on both sides of a river?

Some view the river as relatively narrow or the tree as astronomical in size. They view the tree of life as on an island in the middle of the river with roots and limbs that are wide enough to extend across the river in both directions. Another alternative is to view the tree of life as a banyan tree with multiple trunks (through this seems perhaps bizarre and grotesque). A third option that appeals to the writer's sense of beauty takes "tree of life" as a phrase denoting a kind of tree rather than a single tree. In the sentence "The river banks are lined with maple," maple meaning a *kind* of tree. Perhaps a great river bisects the golden street that comes from God's throne. Both sides of this crystal street are lined with rows of beautiful "tree of life" trees. Whatever the exact appearance, we can be sure heaven will surpass any national forest or park for the beauty of its river and tree(s).

Previous studies on the resurrection body discussed its ability to consume food. The inhabitants of New Jerusalem enjoy the tree of life. Rev. 22:19 speaks of having a "part from the tree of life." Rev. 22:2 mentions fruit on the tree of life. Rev. 2:7 promises the privilege of feasting on it to those who overcome. John had written in 1 John 5:4 that those with faith are the overcomers.

> "He who has an ear, let him hear what the Spirit says to the churches. To him who overcomes, I will grant to eat of the tree of life, which is in the Paradise of God" [Rev. 2:7].

The tree of life produces 12 kinds of fruit and does so on a monthly cycle (Rev. 22:2). Those in heaven enjoy both variety and freshness. It may be a sort of fruit-of-the-month with a different fruit each month, or there may be 12 kinds of fruit on the same tree with a new crop each month. A third possibility occurs if "tree of life" refers to a kind of tree and not just a single tree. Perhaps the "tree of life" orchard yields 12 various fruits among its many trees. One tree produces one kind of fruit each month. Another tree produces another fruit. Regardless of the details, we can be certain the food in heaven will be glorious. (The existence of monthly cycles in "eternity" is also interesting.)

John does not say how the leaves function for the healing of the nations. Is it the shade from the leaves? Tea from the leaves? Do people eat the leaves with the fruit? We do not know.

There can be no sickness in the New Jerusalem (Rev. 21:4; 22:3, no curse). What need is there for "healing" (the Greek word form from which English derives therapeutic)? Those who prefer the satellite view of the heavenly city think that the tree of life actually heals sick people from the millennial Kingdom down on earth. Whatever role the tree of life plays in the Millennium, it also seems to maintain health or extend life eternally for those in heaven. At the very least fruit and leaves from the tree of life somehow enrich the quality of life in heaven.

(7). Conditions in New Jerusalem

(a). No Curse/No Suffering

There will be no trace of sin or its harmful affects in the eternal city. Thus, there can be no sickness, pain, or death. While there might be some shame at the Judgment Seat of Christ over failures on earth, there can be no tears in New Jerusalem. All sufferings associated with the present earth will be long forgotten in eternity.

"[A]nd **He shall wipe away every tear from their eyes**; and there shall no longer be any death; there shall no longer be any mourning, or crying, or pain; the first things have passed away" [Rev. 21:4].

And there shall **no longer by any curse...** [Rev. 22:3].

(b). Enjoyment and Possession of All Things

The Bible promises that Christians are co-heirs with Christ (Rom. 8:17) who is the heir of all things (Heb. 1:2). Through Christ, believers are the ultimate possessors of all things (1 Cor. 3:22; 1 Tim. 6:17). This inheritance in heaven is reserved (Eph. 1:11; 1 Pet. 1:3-4) for believers.

[I]n order that in the ages to come He might show the **surpassing riches of His grace** in kindness toward us in Christ Jesus [Eph. 2:7].

He who overcomes **shall inherit these things**, and I will be his God and he will be My son [Rev. 21:7] (note that 1 John 5:4 teaches that "overcomers" are those with faith).

(c). No Marriage

Marriage is an earthly relationship while we live. We will love each other even more in heaven. There will be only one family in heaven.

"For in the resurrection **they neither marry, nor are given in marriage**, but are like angels in heaven" [Matt. 22:30].

"[B]ut those who are considered worthy to attain to that age and the resurrection from the dead, **neither marry, nor are given in marriage**; for neither can they die anymore, for they are like angels, and are sons of God, being sons of the resurrection" [Luke 20:35-36].

(d). Service

God had ordained work for man even before the fall (Gen. 2:15). Of course, work in heaven will not involve any of the unpleasant aspects of the curse (Rev. 22:3). The fact that the eternal city's gates never close speaks of continual work. Believers will serve Christ in tasks that are now unspecified.

...its gates shall never be closed [Rev. 21:25b].

And there shall no longer be any curse; and the throne of God and of the Lamb shall be in it, and **His bond-servants shall serve him** [Rev. 22:3].

(e). Direct Worship

Heaven has no temple. It does not need one as we will be able to worship directly. There will be a "face to face" involvement with God.

And I saw no temple in it, for the Lord God, the Almighty, and the Lamb, are its temple [Rev. 21:22].

[A]nd **they shall see His face**, and His name shall be on their foreheads [Rev. 22:4].

In Revelation Chapters 4 and 5 those in heaven worship before God's throne. It is likely Ezekiel's descriptions of the cherubim with wheels beneath are the Bible's description of God's throne (Ezekiel 1 and 10). The cherubim form four wheels upon which rides the chariot of God. Above the cherubim is a crystal (like ice) expanse (Ezek. 1:22). Does Ezek. 1:26 mean God's throne looks blue (lapis lazuli)? Ezek. 1:28 and Rev. 4:3 also mention the colors of the rainbow surrounding the throne.

(f). No Sun or Moon

The light of God's glory will be more than adequate for illumination. The absence of darkness suggests that the resurrection body will never need rest.

And the city **has no need of the sun
or of the moon** to shine upon it, for
the glory of God has illumined it, and
its lamp is the Lamb [Rev. 21:23].

...there shall be **no night** there...
[Rev. 21:25].

And there shall no longer be any
night; and **they shall not have need
of the light of a lamp nor the light
of the sun**, because the Lord God
shall illumine them... [Rev. 22:5].

(g). Eternal Reign

Saints will enjoy an eternal reign with
Christ. If we will be rulers, who will be our
subjects? Believers will be higher than angels (implied Heb. 2:9-16; 1 Cor. 6:3). Are
there other creatures of which we are presently ignorant?

...they shall reign **forever and ever**
[Rev. 22:5].

(8). Inhabitants in New Jerusalem

(a). Unsaved Excluded

Contrary to liberal theology, not everyone
will enter heaven. God will exclude those
not written in the Lamb's book of life. The
key word in Rev. 21:8 is "**unbelieving**."
Unbelievers may not enter New Jerusalem.
The vices listed in Rev. 21:8 describe the
habitual characteristics displayed by unbelievers. It is not that an isolated sin such as
an act of lying can exclude one from heaven,
rather those whose lifestyle can be described
as being murderers, liars, etc. show that they
are unbelievers (1 Cor. 6:9-10; Gal. 5:19-21;
Eph. 5:5 are similar). These texts do not say
that an act of sin condemns but that a full life
of certain sins gives evidence of unbelief.
Only those written in the Book of Life may
enter heaven.

"But for the cowardly and **unbelieving** and abominable and murderers
and immoral persons and sorcerers
and idolaters and all liars, their part

will be in the lake that burns with fire
and brimstone, which is the second
death" [Rev. 21:8].

[A]nd nothing unclean and no one
who practices abomination and lying,
shall ever come into it, but only those
whose names are written in the
Lamb's book of life [Rev. 21:27].

Outside are the dogs and the sorcerers and the immoral persons and the
murderers and the idolaters, and everyone who loves and practices lying
[Rev. 22:15].

(b). God Himself

The greatest blessing in heaven will be God
Himself. He will live among His children.
Believers will see Christ and partial manifes-
tations of the other Persons of the Trinity.[97]
(See Matt. 5:8, 1 Cor. 13:12)

And I heard a loud voice from the
throne, saying, "Behold, the tabernacle of God is among men, and He
shall dwell among them, and they
shall be His people, and **God Himself shall be among them**" [Rev.
21:3].

"He who overcomes shall inherit
these things, and **I will be his God**
and he will be My son" [Rev. 21:7].

And he showed me a river of the water of life, clear as crystal, coming
from **the throne of God and of the
Lamb** [Rev. 22:1].

...the throne of God and of the Lamb
shall be in it [Rev. 22 :3].

[A]nd **they shall see His face**...
[Rev. 22: 4].

(c). Angels

---

[97] God may be seen "fully" (1 Cor. 13:12) as
compared to the present level, but God's invisible
nature means He can never be totally visible (see
p. 23).

God has stationed angels at New Jerusalem's gates (Rev. 21:12). Although Heb. 12:22-23 concerns heaven's present inhabitants, it no doubt reflects its eternal inhabitants. Heb. 12:22 mentions "myriads of angels."

(d). The Saved of All Dispensations

John emphasizes the fact that the heavenly city is for those who have salvation in Christ (Rev. 21:27b; 22:17 and 19). The cumulative evidence indicates that believers of all dispensations will enjoy the heavenly city.

Believing Israel

Israel's tribal names appear on the pearly gates (Rev. 21:12). The patriarchs looked for a heavenly city (Heb. 11:10), and God will not disappoint them (Heb. 11:16). Israel will be most welcome in New Jerusalem.

> It had a great and high wall, with twelve gates, and at the gates twelve angels; and names were written on them, which are those of **the twelve tribes of the sons of Israel** [Rev. 21:12].

> [F]or he was looking for the city which has foundations whose architect and builder is God....But as it is, they desire a better country, that is a heavenly one. Therefore God is not ashamed to be called their God; for He has prepared a city for them [Heb. 11:10,16].

Other Saints

John's account of the heavenly city mentions blessings for the earth's "nations" (Rev. 21:24, 26). All saved peoples can enjoy heaven even if they are not a part of believing Israel or the church. Actually, Hebrews 11:16 includes such pre-Law believers as Abel, Enoch, and Noah. Believers from the dispensations prior to the Law, as well as, tribulational saints and millennial saints, all will enjoy heaven. Hebrews 12:23 is very inclusive, "the spirits of just men made perfect."

And the **nations** shall walk by its light, and the kings of the earth shall bring their glory into it [Rev. 21:24].

Church Saints

Christ has promised to prepare dwelling places for believers (John 14:2-3). Peter glories in our "inheritance reserved in heaven" (1 Pet. 1:4). The heavenly city belongs to the church in a special sense. The apostles who are the church's foundation (Eph. 2:20) have their names on heaven's foundations (Rev. 21:14) The church's future is so intertwined with the eternal city that a view of that city is the same as a view of the church's eternal condition.

> "...Come here, I shall show you the bride the wife of the Lamb." And he carried me away in the Spirit to a great and high mountain, and showed me the holy city, Jerusalem, coming down out of heaven from God [Rev. 21:9b].

(e). Summary

Although Hebrews 12 lists the present inhabitants of the eternal city, it surely also lists those who will enjoy it for eternity. Regardless of how it is interpreted, Heb. 12:22-24 gives an inclusive enrollment in heaven for all believers. The means of entrance is, by "Jesus the mediator" and by His "sprinkled blood." **Those with faith in the Lord Jesus Christ and His shed blood as an atonement for sin will be welcome in heaven.**

> But you have come to Mount Zion and to the city of the living God, the heavenly Jerusalem, and to myriads of angels, to the general assembly and church of the first-born who are enrolled in heaven, and to God, the Judge of all, and to the spirits of righteous men made perfect, and to Jesus, the mediator of a new covenant, and to the sprinkled blood,

which speaks better than the blood of | Abel [Heb. 12:22-24].

Select Bibliography

Berkhof, L. *Systematic Theology.* 4th ed. Grand Rapids: Wm. B. Eerdmans Publishing Co., 1977.

Boice, James Montgomery, ed. *The Foundation of Biblical Inerrancy.* Grand Rapids: Zondervan Publishing House, 1978.

Chafer, Lewis Sperry. *Systematic Theology.* 7 vols. Dallas: Dallas Theological Seminary Press, 1948.

DeHaan, Richard W. *Satan, Satanism, and Witchcraft.* Grand Rapids: Zondervan Publishing House, 1972.

Dickason, C. Fred. *Angels Elect and Evil.* Chicago: Moody Press, 1975.

Edgar, Thomas R. *Miraculous Gifts.* Neptune, NJ: Loizeaux Brothers, 1983.

Hodge, A.A. *Outlines of Theology.* reprint ed. Grand Rapids: Zondervan Publishing House, 1973.

Hodges, Zane C. *Absolutely Free: A Biblical Reply to Lordship Salvation.* Grand Rapids and Dallas: Zondervan Publishing House and Redencion Viva, 1989.

Lindsell, Harold. *The Battle for the Bible.* Grand Rapids: Zondervan Publishing House, 1976.

Lindsell, Harold. *The Bible in the Balance.* Grand Rapids: Zondervan Publishing Co., 1979.

Morris, Leon. *The Apostolic Preaching of the Cross,* 3rd ed. Grand Rapids: Wm. B. Eerdmans Publishing Co., 1980.

Pentecost, Dwight J. *Things to Come*. Reprint ed. Grand Rapids: Zondervan Publishing House, 1976.

Ryrie, Charles C. *Basic Theology*. Wheaton, IL: Victor Books, 1988.

Ryrie, Charles C. *So Great Salvation*. Wheaton, IL: Victor Books, 1989.

Strong, Augustus H. *Systematic Theology*. Rev. ed. Old Tappan, NJ: Fleming H. Revell Co., 1976.

Thiessen, Henry C. *Lectures in Systematic Theology*. Grand Rapids: Wm. B. Eerdmans Publishing Co., 1975.

Walvoord, John F. *Jesus Christ Our Lord*. Chicago: Moody Press, 1969.

Walvoord, John F. *The Blessed Hope and the Tribulation*. Grand Rapids: Zondervan Publishing House, 1976.

Walvoord, John F. *The Millennial Kingdom*. Rev. ed. Grand Rapids: Zondervan Publishing House, 1979.

Walvoord, John F. *The Rapture Question*. Rev. ed. Grand Rapids: Zondervan Publishing House, 1979.

Warfield, Benjamin B. *Biblical and Theological Studies*. Philadelphia: Presbyterian and Reformed Publishing Co., 1968.

Wood, Leon J. *The Bible and Future Events*. Grand Rapids: Zondervan Publishing Co., 1973.

Scripture Index

Scripture Index

Selected Topical Index

Selected Topical Index

Note: Each Chapter begins with an extensive Outline